European Labour Law

Brian Bercusson

Professor of Law
University of Manchester

Butterworths
London, Charlottesville, Dublin, Durban, Edinburgh,
Kuala Lumpur, Singapore, Sydney, Toronto, Wellington
1996

United Kingdom	Butterworths, a Division of Reed Elsevier (UK) Ltd, Halsbury House, 35 Chancery Lane, LONDON WC2A 1EL and 4 Hill Street, EDINBURGH EH2 3JZ
Australia	Butterworths, SYDNEY, MELBOURNE, BRISBANE, ADELAIDE, PERTH, CANBERRA and HOBART
Canada	Butterworths Canada Ltd, TORONTO and VANCOUVER
Ireland	Butterworth (Ireland) Ltd, DUBLIN
Malaysia	Malayan Law Journal Sdn Bhd, KUALA LUMPUR
New Zealand	Butterworths of New Zealand Ltd, WELLINGTON and AUCKLAND
Singapore	Reed Elsevier (Singapore) Pte Ltd, SINGAPORE
South Africa	Butterworths Publishers (Pty) Ltd, DURBAN
USA	Northwestern University Press, 625 Colfax Street, EVANSTON, Illinois 60208-4210

Reprinted 1997

A CIP Catalogue record for this book is available from the British Library.

ISBN 0 406 04595 X

Set in Baskerville by B & J Whitcombe, Nr Diss, Norfolk, IP22 2LP
Printed and bound in Great Britain by Mackays of Chatham PLC, Chatham, Kent

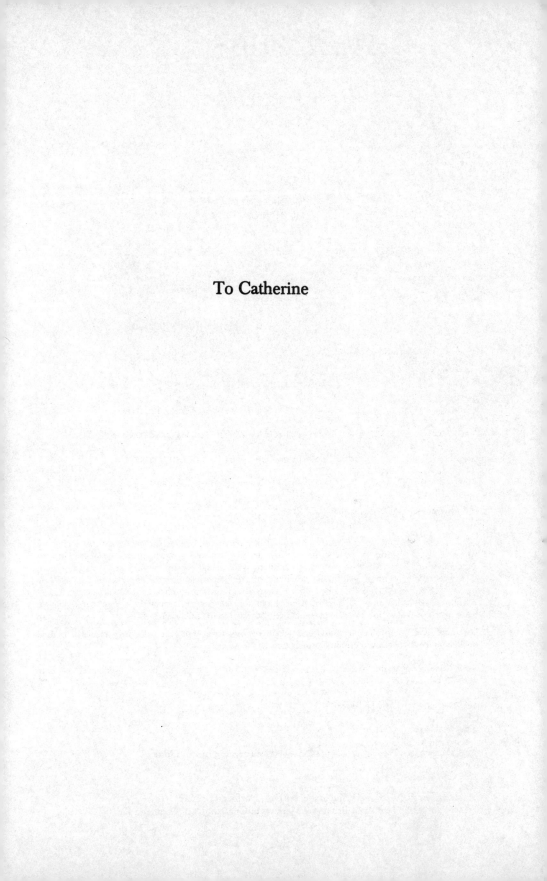

To Catherine

Preface

The aim of this book is to build on the vision of European labour law passed on by comparativists. Their perspective of different national labour law systems focused on comparison, mutual influences, transplantation, and so on. But national, not a transnational, European labour law was the centre of their attention.

The argument of the book is that European labour law now has come into its own, as a complex distillation of national labour laws into something original and distinct – and genuinely European in character. This is illustrated throughout the book in the form of distinctive models of regulation on issues ranging from working time to safety representatives.

It has been my good fortune to have become engaged in European labour law during the past ten years, which were probably the most exciting in the history of the labour and social law of the European Union, reflected in the sudden outpouring of texts on the subject in many countries and languages.

The structure of European labour law presented here is not set in stone. My thinking on European labour law has evolved over the past decade, reflecting changes in the labour law environment at national and EU levels. Major developments – the launching of the European social dialogue in 1985, the Single European Act 1986, the Charter of Fundamental Social Rights of Workers of 1989, the Maastricht Protocol and Agreement on Social Policy of 1991, the Commission's Action Programme and the Directives of the early 1990s, adhesion of new Member States in 1995 – all had an influence on the shape of underlying structures, and make any definitive framework seem all too contingent.

The whole should still be seen in the context of evolutionary change. But there can be little doubt that European labour law is a force to be reckoned with. The fascinating question is what shape it will take. This book adopts a relatively long-term perspective. Not perhaps the *longue durée*, but going beyond the next decision of the European Court, proposal of the Commission, or meeting of the Council of Social Affairs Ministers.

At the end of 1995, the *long-term* perspective is dominated by two features. First, the accession of three new Member States and the implications of this for voting in the Council and its general stance on social affairs (for example, the Swedish government's views on social convergence criteria for monetary union). Secondly, the implementation of the Social Protocol following the Commission's Communication of December 1993 and the prospects for further operationalisation of the European social dialogue.

In the *medium-term* perspective (two to three years) the Commission's Green and White Papers on Social Policy indicated the general direction in terms of substance. But the Member States seem reluctant to embark on a comprehensive legislative programme. It seems likely that there will be single issue initiatives to establish minimum social standards. The 'spill-over effect' teaches us not to underestimate the unexpected potential of apparently circumscribed measures, as a European law on worker representation belatedly emerges in 1994 from Directives of 1975 and 1977.

In the *short-term*, there is plenty of unfinished business, with outstanding proposals on posted workers, part-timers, revision of the Acquired Rights Directive, burden of proof in sex discrimination, and so on. There is also the major challenge of implementation of the first European Social Dialogue Framework Agreement on Parental Leave, raising many fascinating legal questions which will set out markers for the future development of European labour law.

At the end of 1995, the short-term also includes the 1996 Intergovernmental Conference, with potentially fundamental long-term consequences if the strategy proposed in the final chapter of this book is adopted.

For the UK, European labour law has rarely been more potentially explosive. The Working Time Directive, if it survives the UK government's challenge, is likely to have a major impact once it comes into effect in November 1996 (the 48 hour maximum working week potentially affects 16% of the workforce, 25% of male workers). The European Works Councils Directive, despite the UK opt-out, will affect many hundreds of UK enterprises and thousands of workers. The European Court judgment in Cases 382/92 and 383/92: *EC Commission v UK*[1] has led to the UK government proposing legislation on worker representation, which itself faces the imminent challenge of judicial review on grounds of non-compliance with European law.

The ramifications for UK domestic labour law and policy, therefore, reach far beyond the area of sex equality which has heretofore dominated. It requires a radical rethinking of the concept of national labour law, not only in the UK but in other Member States. This book aims also to assist in this reassessment of the priorities and contours of UK labour law.

I would like to thank the many friends, students, researchers and colleagues who have helped me to arrive at a better understanding of national and European labour laws through participation in seminars and conferences at the European University Institute, the University of Siena and other universities across Europe. I am grateful to officials and others at the European Commission, the European Parliament, the Economic and Social Committee, and other EC institutions, who gave of their time to enable me to gain insight into the workings of the European Union. The European Trade Union Confederation and its associated organisations, and many national trade unions, in particular in Italy and the UK, the Labour Research Department, and Thompsons, Solicitors, in London pinpointed issues of particular importance in the evolution of European labour law.

Ulrich Mückenberger and Alain Supiot, with their profound understanding of the German and French systems of labour law, provided me with an essential background for the writing of this book. Our intense and enlightening discussions were the intellectual sustenance for a collaboration which continues.

---

1   [1994] ECR I-2435, decided 8 June 1994.

Finally, I would like to thank my wife, Catherine, for her paradoxical help: her discouragement of cosmic ambitions, her impatience with easy formulas, and her constant interruptions of a serenely workaholic routine made writing a less pompous and, perhaps, less pretentious exercise. The book was made better by our living as a family for a long period in another European country, with the pains and pleasures of intimate knowledge of two cultures.

Brian Bercusson
January 1996

Contents

Acknowledgments

I wish to express my appreciation to the following for allowing me to use contributions of mine which originally appeared in their publications, but which have been rewritten, often substantially, for the purposes of this book:

Blackwell, publishers of the *Modern Law Review* (1990), the *Industrial Relations Journal* (1992), (1993) and the *European Law Journal* (1995);
The Industrial Law Society, for the *Industrial Law Journal* (1994), (1995);
Kluwer, Deventer, publisher of the *International Journal of Comparative Labour Law and Industrial Relations* (1995);
C H Beck, Munich, publisher of R Dehousse (ed) *Europe After Maastricht: An Ever Closer Union?*, 1994;
Sweet and Maxwell, publisher of R Benedictus and B Bercusson *Labour Law: Cases and Materials*, 1987;
Mansell Publishing Limited, publisher of K D Ewing, C A Gearty and B A Hepple (eds) *Human Rights and Labour Law: Essays for Paul O'Higgins*, 1994;
Thompsons, Solicitors, for the *European Law Bulletin* (1994), (1995);
Institute of Employment Rights, publisher of *Working Time in Britain: Towards a European Model*, Parts 1 and 2, 1994.

I am also grateful to the following for contributions I have written for conferences and projects which they have sponsored:

Commission of the European Communities, Conference on Social Protection for Self-Employed Persons, 1993;
European Foundation for the Improvement of Living and Working Conditions, Background and Concept Reports for the Project on Equal Opportunities and Collective Bargaining in Europe, 1994, 1995;
Trades Union Congress, Project on Safety Representatives in EC Law and UK Law, 1995;
FIDE, XVI Conference, UK National Report, 1994.

Table of Statutes

References in this Table to *Statutes* are to Halsbury's Statutes of England (Fourth Edition) showing the volume and page number at which the annotated text of the Act may be found.

List of Cases

PAGE

Decisions of the European Court of Justice are listed below numerically

THESE DECISIONS ARE ALSO INCLUDED IN THE PRECEDING ALPHABETICAL LIST

Title I

Labour Law and Europe

Part I

European Labour Law and the UK

Chapter 1

European Labour Law

INTRODUCTION

European labour law, when it has exceptionally appeared in texts on British labour law, has been a vehicle for traditional comparative law insights,[1] or the manifestation of specific European Community (EC) law requirements on domestic legal development. It is ironic that British labour law is perceived as European only in these ways. For the dominant conceptualisation of British labour law is the intellectual product of Otto Kahn-Freund, a labour lawyer who analysed the British system using the tools of the German labour law tradition founded by Sinzheimer – an intellectual legacy with a specific set of normative assumptions.[2]

Although the vision of British labour law has been filtered through this continental lens, the focus of the discipline is still on the domestic context. The orthodox analysis is that of a fundamentally voluntarist-abstentionist tradition reflecting domestic historical origins, followed by corporatist legal interventions from the mid-1960s to the late 1970s, and decollectivisation and deregulation beginning with the election of the Conservative government in 1979.[3]

European legal developments, however, are intruding upon this national perspective.[4] UK labour law, like that of the other Member States, is increasingly influenced by EC labour law. The dynamic of national labour laws is no longer determined solely or even mainly by domestic developments. It is not merely that UK labour law is required to incorporate EC norms. EC norms are themselves the reflection of the national labour laws of Member States. In this indirect way, other national labour laws are influential in the development of UK labour law.

This will be particularly so for UK labour law following ratification of the Maastricht Treaty and its Social Policy Protocol and Agreement. EC labour law

---

1   The most dedicated comparativist in this sense was Otto Kahn-Freund in his *Labour and the Law* (1972) 3rd edition, edited and with an introduction by P L Davies and M R Freedland, Stevens, London 1983.

2   See R Lewis 'Kahn-Freund and Labour Law: An Outline Critique' (1979) 8 *Industrial Law Journal* 202.

3   Lord Wedderburn, R Lewis and J Clark (eds) *Labour Law and Industrial Relations: Building on Kahn-Freund*, Clarendon Press, Oxford 1983.

4   This was recognised in particular by Bob Hepple: see B A Hepple 'The Crisis in EEC Labour Law' (1987) 16 *Industrial Law Journal* 129; B A Hepple and A Byre 'EEC Labour Law in the United Kingdom – A New Approach' (1989) 18 *Industrial Law Journal* 129; and B A Hepple 'Social Rights in the European Economic Community: A British Perspective' (1990) 11 *Comparative Labor Law Journal* 425.

will reflect ever more the experience of the labour laws of the other fourteen Member States, which the UK will have to incorporate when eventually a government is elected with a commitment to join the process of social policy formation in the European Union.[5]

The labour law of the UK, and of other Member States, is, and will become, more truly European than appears from the formal imprint of EC labour law. It is European rather as reflecting the cumulative experience of national labour laws, filtered through the prism of the EC institutions and refined in the crucible of the developing European polity. The tendency towards convergence of UK labour law with the labour laws of other Member States of the EC is driven in the main by the institutional pressures of EC membership, and, to a lesser extent, is the consequence of the workings of an international economy and, though less significant, a single European labour market. The dynamic of this convergence process is complex and its results are far from complete. But European labour lawyers must come to terms with this new dynamic of labour law evolution and its results.

AN ANALYTICAL FRAMEWORK FOR EC LABOUR LAW

The European Community was created by the Treaty of Rome of 1957. Its history includes that of the European Coal and Steel Community (ECSC) founded by the Treaty of Paris in 1951. The law of the EC was famously declared by the European Court of Justice in *Van Gend en Loos* to be:[6]

'a new legal order of international law for the benefit of which the states have limited their sovereign rights, albeit within limited fields, and the subjects of which comprise not only Member States but also their nationals.'

This new legal order may also be said to have a labour law.

Since its beginnings, a fundamental debate has been conducted on whether the framework of analysis of the law of the EC should be inspired by the law of international organisations (international law) or by the law of an emerging confederation of states ((supra)national constitutional law).[7] A third, more recent, approach is inspired by the sociology of law and analyses EC law looking beyond the interaction of Member States and EC institutions.[8]

This debate is of fundamental importance for the understanding also specifically of the labour law of the EC. International labour law, national labour laws and sociology of labour law provide different frameworks for the analysis of both the content and the anticipated evolution of EC labour law. Just as the debate over EC law in general has benefited by the potential use of concepts adopted from the different analytical frameworks of international and constitutional law and, more recently, sociology of law, similarly EC labour law may benefit from these different approaches.

---

5   B Bercusson 'Maastricht: a fundamental change in European labour law' (1992) 23 *Industrial Relations Journal* 177. Also 'The dynamic of European labour law after Maastricht' (1994) 23 *Industrial Law Journal* 1.
6   Case 26/62: *Algemene Transport-en Expeditie Onderneming van Gend & Loos NV v Nederlandse administratie der belastingen (Netherlands Inland Revenue Administration)* [1963] ECR 1 at 12.
7   J H H Weiler 'The Transformation of Europe' (1991) 100 *Yale Law Journal* 2403.
8   F Snyder *New Directions in European Community Law*, Weidenfeld & Nicolson, London 1990.

Contrasting international and EC labour law

International labour law has its most important source in the norms promulgated by the International Labour Organisation (ILO), established in 1919, which declared as one of its principles that 'labour should not be regarded merely as a commodity or article of commerce'.[9] The analytical framework for such norms addresses their content, the procedures of their adoption and mechanisms of their enforcement.

In terms of their content, ILO norms have slowly but surely increased in number and scope and are now numerous and cover a huge range of topics. However, the standard of the norms adopted has often been minimal: the lowest common denominator. In terms of their adoption and enforcement, the tripartite principle of participation of representatives of employers and workers alongside governments has increased the likelihood of approval of norms by ILO institutions and enhanced their legitimacy. However, the mechanisms of enforcement of norms adopted have been acknowledged as often inadequate.[10]

EC labour and social law does not strictly conform to this framework of analysis. Labour, and even more so social matters, are relatively marginal to the original objectives of the European Economic Community, founded in 1957 to establish a common market for goods, services, capital and labour. In terms of their content, the development of norms regarding labour during almost four decades of existence of the EC has been spasmodic, episodic and unsystematic. They have ranged unsystematically from norms in which the principle of freedom of movement in a Community-wide labour market overrides social considerations of protection of workers (as when technical standards for products are stipulated which are lower than national labour law standards) to norms which have provided rights and protection far beyond existing Member State provisions (as in equality between men and women). In terms of their adoption and enforcement, tripartism has been limited, until recently, and there has been frequent institutional blockage of approval of norms proposed. However, the mechanisms of enforcement extend far beyond the possibilities available to the ILO machinery.

These qualities of content and procedures of adoption and enforcement of norms are important to understanding the specificity of EC labour law. Its content is much less comprehensive and systematic than the ILO norms. Given the quite different objectives of the EC, the influence of ILO norms has been relatively insignificant. The absence of tripartism has adversely affected both the approval and the effective enforcement of norms, despite the fact that EC enforcement procedures are formally more constricting than those of the ILO. The role of Member States and their national labour laws has been greater than that in international labour law and organisations.

9 Article 427 of the Treaty of Versailles 1919, which contained the first ILO Constitution. The Constitution was revised in 1944, and Article 1 declared its aims and purposes to be those of the Declaration annexed to the Constitution, which 'reaffirms the fundamental principles on which the Organisation is based and, in particular, that – (a) labour is not a commodity'.

10 See the essays by B Creighton 'The ILO and Protection of Freedom of Association in the United Kingdom', and G S Morris 'Freedom of Association and the Interests of the State', in K D Ewing, C A Gearty and B A Hepple (eds) *Human Rights and Labour Law: Essays for Paul O'Higgins*, Mansell, London 1994, at pp 1 and 29; also P O'Higgins 'Britain and international labour standards', in R Lewis (ed) *Labour Law in Britain*, Blackwell, Oxford 1986, Chapter 20.

National labour laws

National labour legislation emerged much earlier than international and EC labour law. But it is important to emphasise that the conceptualisation of these legislative and other norms into national labour laws with coherent intellectual frameworks was much more recent. This can be demonstrated in a number of Member States.[11]

In *Britain*, for practitioners and most scholars in universities, labour law scarcely existed before 1960. In 1959, only four of about 20 law faculties taught labour law and of these only one could go back to before World War I: the London School of Economics. A major stimulus was the arrival in 1933 of Otto Kahn-Freund, who wrote seminal papers in 1954 and 1959. As labour relations gradually became a focus of economic and political debate, the first books on modern labour law were published in the 1960s. By 1966, 13 of 24 law faculties had a modern labour law course option.

In contrast, *Germany* has one of the longest established traditions of legal education in labour and social law, though it was only in the years between 1918 and 1933 that it took shape in recognisably modern form. The tradition was revived after the Second World War, and in 1986 all 31 (West) German law faculties and departments of legal studies had one or more professorships in labour law. In the *Netherlands*, although a separate labour law chair was established at the University of Amsterdam in 1926, it has been asserted that those appointed before 1954 were generalists with interests in labour law, whereas specialists in the subject only came afterwards.

In *France*, until World War II labour law was not really considered to be a separate discipline, not having yet emerged from the confines of civil law. After 1945 the subject was increasingly included in faculty syllabuses until in 1955 it became a compulsory subject: there were two student books in 1950, but eight in 1986. In *Belgium* also labour law became a subject for teaching at the law schools only after World War II, though only in the late 1950s did it become mandatory.

In *Italy*, labour law was long perceived either as a branch of private or company law or ideologically linked to trade union autonomy until the subject was renewed by Giugni and Mancini in the 1950s, the former elaborating the theory of *ordinamento intersindacale* in 1960. The first professorial chair in labour law was only established in *Sweden* at the University of Stockholm in 1966, and the first chair of labour law in *Denmark* was only recently occupied.

In general, therefore, the formation of the intellectual framework for national labour laws, in the case of the original six Member States, took its modern form only in the years following the end of World War II, that is to say, almost contemporaneously with or not far from the founding of the ECSC and EEC and the first developments of its labour and social law.

European labour law: a symbiosis of EC and national labour laws

National labour laws in the original six Member States were not conceived of in terms of the EC and its labour law. But the evolution and conceptualisation

---

11   For an account, see B Bercusson 'Law, legal education and practice and labour and social law', in B De Witte and C Forder (eds) *The Common Law of Europe and the Future of Legal Education*, Kluwer, Deventer 1992, p 423.

of the labour and social law of the EC was inevitably influenced by the mature and maturing conceptualisations of the national labour laws of the original Member States and of later adherents. Conversely, as EC labour and social law norms developed, they began to influence the formulation and conceptualisation of national labour laws. The two processes are thus linked in a specific symbiosis.[12]

A major premise in understanding EC labour law is, therefore, the need to avoid thinking about it *exclusively* in terms of EC institutions and legal provisions. Many accounts of EC labour law begin with a description outlining these institutions and the basic legal framework of the EC. This is necessary, of course. But equally, if not more necessary, is an appreciation of the relationship of EC labour law with national labour law systems.

It is easy to demonstrate that national labour law systems were subjected to mutual influences. One can cite the influences of Germany on Denmark,[13] France on Belgium,[14] various foreign influences on French labour law,[15] the revolution wrought by the German-trained Otto Kahn-Freund on British labour law,[16] and, more recently, that of the Italian Workers' Statute of 1970 on Spanish labour law.

It would seem likely, therefore, that EC labour law also is not wholly autonomous and independent. It is easy to point to many developments due to the influence of highly developed and technically sophisticated national labour law systems. Not surprisingly, in formulating EC labour law, the law- and policy-making institutions of the EC had to come to terms with these systems and were influenced by them.

A number of examples from different periods illustrate the historical continuity of this influence. The insertion of Article 119 into the Treaty of Rome was due to the insistence of France, concerned to extend its own legislation on equal treatment for men and women. The Commission's proposals beginning in the 1970s on workers' participation in company structures owe their inspiration to the German labour law on co-determination. The Thatcher government's declared policy of labour law deregulation in Britain during the 1980s led to the blockage of new EC social regulations during that decade. The Danish tradition of basing labour law primarily on collective agreements between the social partners (trade unions and employers' associations) rather than legislation, and Italian emphasis on the autonomy of the social partners, led to pressures allowing for EC labour law Directives to be implemented through collective agreements. Finally, the experience of the constitutionalisation of social and economic rights in the new or revised constitutions of Spain, Portugal, Greece

---

12 The EC influence is most obvious in the case of the later adherents to the EC, especially those emerging from dictatorships in the 1970s, Spain, Portugal and Greece. EC labour law was an established body of norms to which the new Member States were required to conform. This also occurred in countries of the European Economic Area and may be expected to occur in those countries of central and eastern Europe professing their intention to join the EC.

13 O Hasselbach 'Denmark', in S Edlund (ed) *Labour Law Research in Twelve Countries*, Stockholm 1986, p 12.

14 R Blanpain 'Belgium' in Edlund, ibid, p 139.

15 G Lyon-Caen 'Les apports du droit comparé au droit du travail', *Livre du centenaire de la société de législation comparée*, 1969, pp 315–28.

16 Lord Wedderburn, R Lewis and J Clark (eds) *Labour Law and Industrial Relations: Building on Kahn-Freund*, Clarendon Press, Oxford 1983.

and the Netherlands contributed to the formulation of the Community Charter of Fundamental Social Rights of Workers of December 1989.

A different rhythm of interaction is evident in the dynamics of national labour law systems in relation to EC labour law. It is illuminating to look at developments in national labour laws *during* the evolution of EC labour law. What were the main concerns of national labour laws of the Member States during the period in question, and did the focus on certain issues in collective and individual labour law in Western Europe during this period change over time?

I have argued that certain issues were the focus of attention in the national labour laws of Member States over the last twenty years which can be distinguished from other issues predominating at earlier times or during this period.[17] Certain substantive issues absorbed the attention of national labour lawyers, in legislatures, academe and practice. For example, in the sphere of individual employment law, regulation of new forms of work and protection against termination of employment. In collective labour law, the framework of attention shifted between regulation of outcomes of collective bargaining, of the processes of reaching agreements, and of the organisations of workers and employers themselves. Different periods can be identified by their concentration on different substantive issues.

Whatever the mutual influences of national labour laws and EC labour law, these dynamics within national labour law systems were not necessarily synchronised with developments in EC labour law. Looking at the same period, clear divergences are apparent between labour policies pursued at national level and at EC level. A number of contrasts may be presented between developments at national level and developments at EC level during the same period. Often what emerges is not a parallel development at all, but rather something completely different.

Three examples will illustrate this. First, the Treaty of Paris in 1951 provided the ECSC authorities with powers to enable them to restructure the coal and steel industries. This included measures to deal with the social consequences for workers of this process, including retraining, relocation and housing. The policies adopted are recognisable as a form of active labour market policy which was at the time only beginning to develop in Sweden, and was relatively unknown in Member States of the then future EC. The Treaty of Rome, much closer in spirit to the labour market policies of Member States during the 1950s, did not follow the precedent of the ECSC. The earliest EC labour law, the ECSC's provisions on social policy, was quite different from the national labour law and policy of Member States.

Secondly, the first fifteen years of the EC, 1957–1972, are usually identified as its neo-liberal phase,[18] with the emphasis on free movement of workers and labour mobility within the common market, to the exclusion of other social policy initiatives. This was the period of economic boom in Western Europe, the consolidation of the welfare state, of managed capitalism, workers' rights and industrial democracy initiatives. This was to have its impact on EC labour

---

17   B Bercusson 'Europäisches und nationales Arbeitsrecht – Die gegenwärtige Situation', [1991] *Zeitschrift für ausländisches und internationales Arbeits- und Sozialrecht* 1–40.
18   B Hepple 'European Labour Law: The European Communities', in R Blanpain (ed) *Comparative Labour Law and Industrial Relations in Industrialised Market Economies,* 3rd ed, 1992, p 300.

law only later in the 1970s, after the Paris Summit of 1972 and the Action Programme of 1974.

Finally, the social dialogue at European level as an instrument of EC social policy only emerged after 1985, when periods of neo-corporatist concertation were all but finished in Member States. Its late institutionalisation in the Protocol and Agreement on Social Policy of the Maastricht Treaty on European Union negotiated in 1991 stands out in contrast to national labour law tendencies.

In sum: the symbiosis of national labour law systems and EC labour law is of major importance in understanding both EC law and national labour laws. The nature of their relationship, however, is complex, with major dissonances between them at certain periods, and variation between Member States in terms of their interaction with EC labour law.

Sociology of labour law

The sociological approach to EC labour law looks beyond the interaction between Member States and EC institutions. It looks also at the role of sub- and supra-national actors, processes and outcomes as being of equal importance to those on the State level: a shift from the dominant focus on the Member State–Community axis to other levels where non-State actors are involved. This includes how interest groups *within* Member States influence national law and politics as they interact with Community law, and how the organisation of interests at *European* level (employers, trade unions, the poor, farmers, women's groups, and so on) interacts with both Community and national law and politics. In this approach, EC labour law focuses not only on Community or national institutions, but also on EC law as influenced (eg as regards formulation) by other supra-national actors and (eg as regards implementation) by sub-national actors.

One illustration of the implications of this approach is the question of the legitimacy of EC law. It follows that issues of legitimacy incorporate a wider range of polities, with institutional arrangements for representation of interests going beyond State and Community structures. The interaction of legitimacy arrangements within interest groups with those of Community law-making institutions produces a wider and more complex politics than is normally admitted by constitutional or supra-national architects. Legitimacy as an issue implies this wider politicisation of the process of European law-making.

The sociological approach is particularly significant for EC labour law in view of the potential significance of the European social dialogue, including as major protagonists the organisations of workers and employers at European level, in the formulation and implementation of EC social and labour law.

CHRONOLOGY AND CONTEXT: THE DYNAMICS OF EC LABOUR LAW

The meaning of 'labour law' derives from a specific context. In the case of the ILO norms, for example, the historical context following World War I dictated that the norms promoted have as their objective the protection of workers and their organisations, and that workers' and employers' organisations take part in

their formulation. The EC context is quite different. Indeed, contrast between
the EC and the ECSC demonstrates just how significant the context is in determining the meaning of 'labour law'. As described above, the active labour
market policy of the ECSC, with labour representation in its major organs, was
in stark contrast with the neo-liberal labour market policy which prevailed in
the EC between 1957–1972.

Free movement of workers in a common market

The EC was founded to create a common market in services, goods, capital
and labour. Freedom of movement for labour in a common market as a founding objective is quite different from the objectives associated with national
labour laws and also those of international labour standards. This primary
association of EC labour law with free movement provides the initial context of
labour and social law of the Community in its earlier stages. Certain qualities
emerged from this experience which are worth exploring.

Free movement of labour is often perceived as *the* social dimension of the
EC. The project of creating a common market implies free movement of workers in a neo-liberal labour market. Prima facie, then, free movement is an
economic, not a social concept. But free movement creates many problems
said to be of a purely social nature: transfer of pensions and social benefits,
entitlements of migrant workers to unemployment, social security and other
benefits, family issues of education, housing, and so on. So many social issues
may come to be dealt with under the rubric of economic free movement of
labour.

The balance between the economic and the social perceptions of free movement as an area of EC labour law is always in question. Legislative provisions
and court decisions may be concerned with economic and not social consequences – that is, restraints on free movement and not the social consequences
of these restraints. 'Anti-social' restrictions and penalties *are* allowed up to the
point where they interfere with freedom of movement. The derogations
allowed for public policy, security and health reasons emphasise how 'unsocial'
this part of EC law is.

The EC law prohibition on discrimination illustrates this. The ban emerges
primarily from the 'equality' principle prohibiting discrimination against non-
nationals. If the same 'anti-social' treatment is meted out to nationals,[19] it is
lawful. The curtailment of social vision by economic ideology is clear where
the Court refuses to protect nationals against their own State where EC
migrants would be protected.[20]

On the other hand, this overlap of EC economic and social policy in the area
of free movement has been the source of major developments in EC social policy with potentially far-reaching implications. For example, the definition of
'worker' by the European Court under the Treaty provisions dealing with free
movement developed independently of national legal definitions.[1] Albeit sharing

---

19   For example, the case of identity cards in Case 321/87: EC *Commission v Belgium* [1989] ECR 997.
20   So-called 'reverse discrimination': see Case 175/78: *R v Saunders* [1979] ECR 1129.
1   Case 75/63: *Hoekstra (née Unger) v Bestuur* [1964] ECR 177.

certain core elements, it has asserted its claim to override national legal definitions.[2] This has important implications for national labour laws, and not only in the regulation of free movement.[3]

From free movement to labour and social law and policy

How did EC labour and social law develop beyond the confines of free movement of workers? This is a fundamental issue of much more than historical interest. It concerns an explanation of the dynamics of EC social policy development. What factors operate to develop, either progressively through new initiatives, or regressively through repeal of previous initiatives, the social dimension of the EC? There are at least two approaches to explaining the substance and development of EC labour law and social policy.

The first takes as its starting point the Treaties and other legal measures and EC institutions. The law contained in these instruments is the substantive basis for social policy; its development is a function of the dynamic operation of the EC institutions. But the law operates to limit the potential creativity of the EC institutions within the confines of the competences allowed for by the Treaties.

An example of this approach would be the dispute over the legal status of the Maastricht Protocol and Agreement on Social Policy. Vogel-Polsky denies these instruments any status in EC law since, according to her reading, they do not fall within the possibilities offered by the Treaty of Rome.[4] Their adoption is portrayed as the exploitation of ambivalent Treaty provisions by Member States who have no power to create a new social order, though the Member States may mislead the public into thinking there is such power.

Of course this legalistic approach does not exclude social policy development, provided it falls within the legal prospect of the Treaty. This leaves much room for creativity. Vogel-Polsky herself made such a contribution when she argued for the direct effect of Treaty provisions, later approved by the European Court in *Defrenne*.[5] It also allows for unilateral initiatives to be taken by EC institutions, again within the constraints of EC law. Examples would be the development by interpretations of the Court of Justice of principles such as that of non-discrimination, or the initiative of the Commission in the form of the European social dialogue launched by its President, Jacques Delors, in 1985.

This approach, which focuses on internal dynamics within the EC – its law and institutions – to explain social policy development may be contrasted with a second approach which incorporates and emphasises a dynamic between EC law and institutions and the external environment, comprising also non-EC law

2   Case 53/81: *Levin v Secretary of State for Justice* [1982] ECR 1035. The Court has so far refused to adopt this approach in other areas of EC labour law: Case 105/84: *Mikkelsen* [1986] 1 CMLR 316.
3   For a critical view, see the discussion in A Supiot *Critique du Droit du Travail*, Presses Universitaires de France, 1994, chapitre preliminaire, 'Entre contrat et statut: une vue européenne de la relation de travail', p 13 at pp 22–7.
4   E Vogel-Polsky 'Evaluation of the social provisions of the Treaty on European Union agreed by the European Summit at Maastricht on 9 and 10 December 1991', Committee on Social Affairs , Employment and the Working Environment of the European Parliament, 7 February 1992, DOC EC/CM/202155, PE 155.405.I.
5   Case 43/75: [1976] ECR 455.

and non-Member State actors.

A major force in the development of EC labour and social law and policy is the interaction of Member States, both individually and collectively, with EC institutions. This is not simply to look to the role of the Council of Ministers, as an EC institution, and its activities in the EC law and policy-making process. It is a political perspective which looks to the policies of individual Member States, or some of them, and regards their pressures upon EC institutions, including the Council of Ministers, but also, and, in particular, the Commission and even other EC institutions, as a major determinant of EC social law and policy. These pressures as a factor in the development of EC labour law may be illustrated by the cases mentioned earlier of influences of national labour law on EC labour law.

The difference between the two approaches lies in whether the emphasis is put on law or politics as an explanation for the development of EC labour law and social policy. It is a question of emphasis because those who take the legalistic approach do not exclude political pressures, and those who emphasise politics do not exclude legal constraints and possibilities. The question is whether one starts with a view of the law as setting the limits to EC labour law and social policy, or whether one starts with the view that the political will and ability of the actors involved determines its development. As put by a former Commissioner for Social Affairs, commenting on the adoption of the path-breaking Social Action Programme of 1974:[6]

'(it) reflected a political judgment of what was thought to be both desirable and possible, rather than a juridical judgment of what were thought to be the social policy implications of the Rome Treaty.'

AN INTELLECTUAL CHALLENGE: CONCEPTUALISING EUROPEAN LABOUR LAW

The conceptualisation of European labour law is influenced by the symbiosis of national labour law systems and EC labour law, and the interaction of law and context. This can be illustrated by looking at a number of textbooks which have recently appeared proposing frameworks for EC labour law. Different structures of EC labour and social law emerged depending on the approach adopted. Since all seek to expound the law on the basis of the same legal measures, it is all the more remarkable that the picture of EC labour law which emerges from them is so very different.

The intellectual challenge of competing conceptualisations is a hallmark of EC law, and EC labour law is no exception. Students of the subject are confronted with very different perspectives on the same material – a highly stimulating prospect allowing for debate over the merits of different analytical frameworks. It is to provide this stimulus that the following examination of competing conceptualisations is presented.

It has the additional advantage of highlighting how EC law (and EC labour law) is an intellectual discipline which is in the process of being developed by academics (and practitioners and judges) from all over Europe. The shape of EC labour law is not determined by those steeped in the UK or any other

6   M Shanks *European Social Policy, Today and Tomorrow* (1977), p 13.

national labour law tradition. Among others, Belgian, Danish, French and Italian, as well as British labour lawyers are engaged in proposing conceptual frameworks for the EC labour law that applies in their jurisdictions. A number of the attempts that have emerged in the European legal literature so far reveal certain trends which illuminate the characteristic intellectual constructs available. These will be reviewed prior to presenting the proposed structure for the new discipline of European labour law offered in this book.

In the texts on EC labour law which have appeared in different Member States so far, four models may be identified:

1. EC labour law as equal treatment and health and safety at work;
2. EC labour law in the traditional model of national labour law;
3. EC labour law as a new model of national labour law focusing on labour markets; and
4. EC labour law as common market law.

EC labour law as equal treatment and health and safety at work

In two complementary volumes,[7] Angela Byre collected laws, cases and materials on the social policy of the EC: *Leading Cases and Materials on the Social Policy of the EEC*, and *EC Social Policy and 1992: Law, Cases and Materials*.

The 1989 volume brought together nearly 20 Directives and 50 judgments of the European Court, mostly dating from the 1980s. The structure was relatively simple. The text of 532 pages was divided, after a brief section of general Treaty extracts and the Social Action Programme (11 pages) into 3 Parts. The longest of these was Part I on 'Equal Treatment' (294 pages: 55.26% of the text). The next longest was Part II on 'Health and Safety at Work' (126 pages: 23.68% of the text). The shortest section was Part III on 'Employment Protection' (88 pages: 16.54%).[8]

The outstanding features of this structure are, first, the division into only three main elements: sex equality, safety and employment protection; and secondly, that more than half of EC labour law and social policy is concerned with equality between the sexes, and almost a quarter with health and safety, leaving less than a quarter to other matters.

The 1989 volume took account of developments up to the end of 1988. The volume published in 1992 was intended to update this, and in this way it charts relative changes in the importance of topics in EC labour law. However, while the second volume differed in its structure, it did not differ with respect to the outstanding feature noted above: the proportion of the text dedicated to the topics of sex equality and health and safety at work.

The text of 393 pages (plus a 3-page introduction), after a brief introductory Part I on 'EC Social Policy and 1992' (11 pages), consists of a Part II divided into 13 different 'Action Areas'. The longest of these is Section 10 on 'Health protection and safety at the workplace' (137 pages: 35.03% of the text). The next longest is Section 8 on 'Equal treatment for men and women' (101 pages: 25.83%). The third substantial Section is on 'Improvement of living and working

---

7 Published by Kluwer, Deventer, in 1989 and 1992.
8 Each section includes extracts from the Treaty and Commission Action Programmes, Directives and judgments of the European Court of Justice.

conditions' (63 pages: 16.11%). Again in the second volume, therefore, the two subjects of sex equality and health and safety at work account for over 60% of the text, though the balance in the second volume emphasises safety over equality.[9]

Taking the two volumes together as a collection of primary materials on EC labour law and social policy (with only some minor duplication of primary legislation), the combined text of 925 pages (532+393) includes 395 pages (42.65%) on equality issues, 263 pages (29.25%) on health and safety, and 151 pages (16.30%) on employment protection.

A vision of EC labour law which concentrates on these specific topics is completely at variance with the structure and proportions of national labour law texts. While national labour law texts often deal with equality and safety, these matters are relegated to a much inferior position both in terms of their place in the overall structure of national labour law, and in the amount of space allocated to them.

EC labour law as it emerges from this text is primarily about equal treatment of men and women and protection of health and safety in the working environment.[10] Is this concentration of legal materials on certain subject matters convincing as a framework of EC labour law and social policy?[11]

The traditional model of national labour law

The text entitled *Droit du Travail Communautaire* is by Roger Blanpain, a Belgian, and Jean-Claude Javillier, a Frenchman, both professors of labour and social law.[12] Their text of 222 pages is divided into three parts.

Part I, 'Generalities', is 64 pages long, comprising 28.8% of the text, of which almost half is on the institutions and instruments of EC law in general.[13] This introduction of the text by an account of the law and institutions of the Community is a common feature of those texts which have so far emerged. It is

9 The proportion allocated to the matters regarded as employment protection, found under Section 3 on improvement of living and working conditions, accounts, as in the first volume, for about one-sixth of the text. The remaining roughly 20% of the text is divided among ten other sections: information, consultation and participation (19 pages), employment and remuneration (16 pages), freedom of movement (11 pages), the elderly, and the disabled (6 pages each), vocational training, and the labour market (5 pages each), social protection, and association and collective bargaining (3 pages each) and protection of children (2 pages).

10 Article 118A of the EC Treaty: 'the Member States shall pay particular attention to encouraging improvements, especially of the working environment, as regards the safety and health of workers, and shall set as their objective the harmonisation of conditions in this area'. It is worth noting the potential of this provision. In the Explanatory Memorandum (p 17, para 33) to the Working Time Directive 89/391/EEC, the Commission emphasised the World Health Organisation's definition that: 'health is a state of complete psychic, mental and social well-being and does not merely consist of an absence of disease or infirmity'. The Commission appears to have moved towards the Nordic countries' concept of physical, psychological and social aspects such as monotony, lack of social contacts at work or a rapid work pace.

11 Byre does not explain this concentration of legal materials on certain subject matters. One may note that she was the first co-ordinator of the Community's network of experts on equality law.

12 Litec, Paris 1991.

13 Chapter 1, the constitutional framework, 28 pages. The specific labour law competences of the EC are dealt with in 6 pages (Chapter 3), followed by a brief account of the development of Community labour law (Chapter 4: 17 pages).

presumably justified by the assumption that the labour law reader is relatively ignorant of the rudimentary elements of Community law.[14] A comparable introduction to a text on national labour law would be highly unlikely. In part, knowledge of the elements of national law and institutions may be presumed. More importantly, however, its omission implies the recognition that labour law in many countries is not perceived as deriving solely, or even mainly, from the normal law-making institutions and procedures. Rather, the evolution of labour law has been towards autonomy from civil law. The role of the social partners in the formulation and implementation of labour law norms means that an introduction to national labour law by way of 'normal' law-making procedures and institutions would be seriously misleading.

The question is whether the inclusion of this material in EC labour law texts proceeds from the assumption that EC labour law, unlike national labour law, *does* derive from the same institutional sources as other EC law, and that its nature and origins are not autonomous and different. This assumption is questionable at least. To start a text with such an account, without questioning this assumption, may be to lay the foundations for a misapprehension of EC labour law. This misapprehension is mitigated in the Blanpain–Javillier text by the inclusion in this first part of a section on 'The Social Partners' at European level, UNICE and the ETUC,[15] explaining their composition and constitution and their roles within the Community.[16] In contrast with national labour law, however, collective bargaining or social dialogue does not appear in an important role.

Part II, entitled 'Individual Labour Law', is the longest, 118 pages and comprises 53.2% of the total text. About one-third of it is concerned with free movement of workers.[17] Two other chapters each comprise about one-fifth: equal treatment between men and women, and re-structuring enterprises.[18] The EC law on equality thus comprises only 11.26% of the total text.[19] Chapter 8 on restructuring enterprises covers the Directives on collective dismissals, transfers of undertakings and employer insolvency. These provide for protection of the rights of individual employees affected by such events. However, the first two Directives also include important provisions concerning the provision of information to, and consultation of, employee representatives. Nonetheless, these instruments are classified under 'Individual Labour Law'.

Part III, entitled 'Collective Labour Law', is only 30 pages long (13.5% of the text), a proportion abnormally low when compared with texts on national labour law. Moreover, only 2 pages are on collective bargaining. In contrast, 28 pages are on worker participation (Chapter 2).

The overall impression that emerges from the Blanpain–Javillier text is that EC labour law is structured using the traditional categories of individual and

14 It is obviously otiose for those readers coming from an EC law background – an interesting assumption that EC law specialists will be less interested in the subject of EC labour law than labour law specialists.
15 UNICE: Union des Confédérations de l'Industrie et des Employeurs d'Europe; ETUC: European Trade Union Confederation.
16 Chapter 2: 9 pages.
17 Chapter 1: 37 pages.
18 Respectively, Chapter 4: 25 pages; and Chapter 8: 24 pages.
19 It is given shorter treatment not only than freedom of movement, but also than either the constitutional framework (Chapter 1 of Part I: 28 pages) or workers' participation (Chapter 2 of Part III: 26 pages).

collective labour law. However, there are a number of unusual features which render these categories suspect. Individual labour law is dominated by free movement of workers. It also includes instruments with a strong collective dimension (collective dismissals, transfer of undertakings). There is relatively little space for collective labour law, and what there is is almost exclusively to do with workers' participation, not collective bargaining. Finally, despite the relatively large amount of EC legislation and case law on equality between men and women and on health and safety, neither of these is given a proportionate amount of attention: equality gets 25 pages (11% of the total) and health and safety less than half that.[20]

EC labour law as it emerges from this text is premised on the traditional dichotomy between individual and collective labour law. But, in contrast with traditional texts on national labour law, EC individual labour law is dominated by rights to free movement of workers, with less attention to sex equality and workers' rights in a context of enterprise restructuring. EC collective labour law is about worker participation in the enterprise.

The new model of national labour law

The text on *Diritto del Lavoro della Comunità Europea* by Massimo Roccella and Tiziano Treu, both Italian labour law professors, comprises 386 pages of text.[1] Part I, entitled 'Principles and Sources',[2] deals with the social policy principles and provisions of the Treaties and their historical development,[3] and institutions, sources and legal consequences of EC law in general.[4] Part II is entitled 'Employment Policies' and at 110 pages comprises 28.5% of the text. Almost half of it is the chapter on free movement of workers.[5] In addition, the third chapter in this Part, entitled 'Social Security' begins by explaining that social security under the Treaty is functionally associated with free movement and hence focuses on migrant workers only.[6]

The book is on EC *labour* law, not social security law, and the importance of social security entitlements and their mobility to the free movement of workers in the EC is undeniable. But social security has an autonomous set of objectives and doctrines which goes far beyond assisting free movement. The impression given is that social security is subordinated in EC labour law to the exigencies of assisting free movement. This distorts both the broader scope of social security, and also those potential links between labour and social security law which go beyond labour mobility.

Together, these two chapters concerned with free movement of workers

---

20 Chapter 7: 12 pages.
1 Cedam, Padova 1992; 73% longer than that by Blanpain–Javillier.
2 At 63 pages long, it is almost the same as the equivalent section in Blanpain–Javillier, but in this text it comprises only 16.3% of the total (compared to 64 pages and 28.8% of the text in Blanpain–Javillier).
3 Chapter 1: 34 pages.
4 Chapters 2 and 3: 29 pages.
5 Chapter 4: 53 pages. This probably fits better under the rubric of employment policy than under that of individual labour law in Blanpain–Javillier. The chapter on promotion of employment and vocational training is similarly well placed under this heading (Chapter 6: 32 pages).
6 Chapter 5: 33 pages.

comprise 86 pages or 22.27% of the text.[7] The emphasis on employment and labour market policy is consistent with a trend in academic treatment of national labour law systems. The large quantity of legal material (regulations and case-law) on free movement of workers in EC labour law is a further influence in this direction. The question remains whether free movement is a social policy objective or an economic policy objective. It sits uneasily with traditional formulations of labour law in terms of rights and protection of individual workers and collective labour relations.

The predominance given to free movement of workers[8] is evident when contrasted with other topics treated in the text. Part III entitled 'Individual Relations' is only marginally longer than Part II on 'Employment Policies'.[9] It comprises six chapters on different topics, none of which is accorded treatment as long as any of the three chapters in Part II. The first and longest chapter is on 'Atypical Work' (Chapter 7: 31 pages) – another new trend in labour law studies related to employment policy.[10]

The chapter on 'Equality and Non-Discrimination' is 25 pages long,[11] and that on 'Safety and the Working Environment' is 17 pages.[12]

Part IV on 'Collective Relations'[13] is far shorter than either of the two preceding parts on 'Employment Policies' and 'Individual Relations'. It includes brief chapters on 'The Europeanisation of Collective Relations',[14] 'European Trade Unions and Representation in the Enterprise',[15] and a longer chapter on 'European Collective Bargaining'.[16] In clear contrast to Blanpain–Javillier, collective bargaining is given overall treatment more extensive than that allocated to the subject of workers' participation through information and consultation, dealt with in the final chapter.[17]

The overall impression of the Roccella–Treu volume is that EC labour law is distinguished from national labour law, and largely characterised, by the element of regulation of freedom of movement by workers through the common market. The insertion of a substantial Part II on 'Employment Policy',

7　Compared to 37 pages and 16.66% of Blanpain–Javillier.
8　86 pages.
9　117 v 110 pages: 30.3% v 28.5%.
10　The chapter is mainly concerned with proposals for Directives not yet approved (only one approved Directive is discussed) and, despite the lengthy treatment, concludes with a section entitled 'Absence of a European model of regulation of atypical work and defects in EC proposals'.
11　Chapter 10. It seems questionable that the importance of this subject in EC labour law – covering equal pay, equal treatment in employment and in social security – merits only 6.47% of the entire text, being shorter than seven other chapters.
12　Again, this seems extremely short given the volume of regulation and importance of the subject; a similar amount of space is allocated to 'Working Time' (Chapter 10: 13 pages), though when the book was written there was little regulation at EC level. The remaining chapter in this Part is entitled 'Proof of an Employment Contract', a misnomer referring to the title of the original proposed Directive, not that eventually approved (Chapter 8: 4 pages). In contrast, a chapter on 'Restructuring and Enterprises in Difficulty' (Chapter 12: 23 pages) includes the three Directives on collective dismissals, transfers of undertakings (with their collective elements) and employer insolvency. As in Blanpain–Javillier, this chapter appears in the Part on Individual Relations.
13　76 pages: 19.7% of the text.
14　Chapter 13: 10 pages.
15　Chapter 14: 13 pages.
16　Chapter 15: 26 pages.
17　Chapter 16: 26 pages.

separated from individual employment rights or protection of employees, proceeds from a conceptualisation of the subject in terms of labour market regulation. This is reflected in the chapter on social security, part of the 'Employment Policy' section in this text. It is also evident in the treatment of 'Atypical Work', the longest chapter in the Part on 'Individual Relations'. In contrast, traditional topics – equality between men and women and health and safety, despite substantial EC regulation, are allocated much less space. On the collective side, however, in contrast with Blanpain–Javillier, the authors choose to emphasise collective bargaining at European level, rather than workers' participation within enterprises, or within Community institutions.

Labour law as common market law

The authors of the text entitled *Droit Social Européen* are Nicole Catala, a French professor of labour law, and René Bonnet, editor of a French legal journal on social security.[18] The text of 400 pages is divided into three parts. Unlike the two previous texts, EC labour law is regarded as only one part of European Social Law. Book I, the 'General Presentation of European Social Law' (54 pages) covers the Council of Europe, the ILO and bilateral and multilateral Treaties, as well as a brief account of the institutions and social objectives of the Rome and Paris Treaties. Book III, 'European Social Security Law' (160 pages) is autonomous and granted almost equal status (in terms of detailed coverage) to EC labour law, which is covered in Book II (180 pages).

Book II on 'Community Labour Law' adopts a structure which follows neither the traditional national labour law framework of individual and collective labour law of Blanpain–Javillier, nor the more recent trend in national labour law studies towards conceptualising the subject as labour market regulation, a tendency evident in Roccella–Treu. Rather, it adopts a framework familiar from texts on EC law in other fields: the emphasis is on free movement, as with goods, services and capital, in this case of labour,[19] and harmonisation of different national regulations within a common market[20] – together constituting 90% of the text.

Such a perspective, however, finds it difficult to accommodate the concept of an EC social policy independent of the creation of a common market. As a result, other policies such as employment policy (the European Social Fund) and vocational training are relegated to summary treatment at the end.[1] Significant developments at odds with this purely common market oriented perspective, such as the Community Charter of Fundamental Social Rights of Workers, are marginalised in a separate chapter comprising three pages. Given the trend indicated by the Maastricht Social Protocol and Agreement, this conceptualisation seems unlikely to be sustainable.

In Title II on 'Harmonisation of National Laws', Chapter 5 on 'Collective Labour Relations and Workers' Association with the Enterprise' (38 pages), is concerned almost exclusively with workers' representation, primarily within

18   Paris, Litec 1991.
19   'Free Movement of Persons': 49 pages (27.22%).
20   'Harmonisation of National Laws': 114 pages (63.33%).
1   'Employment and Vocational Training': 10 pages (5.55%).

company structures. Collective bargaining is only mentioned as regards the difficulties in elaborating EC law regarding collective agreements with an international character (Section III, 5 pages).[2]

Of the five chapters in Title II, 'Harmonisation of National Laws', the longest is Chapter 3: 'Conditions of Employment and Work' (40 pages), of which 19 pages are on the 'Principle of Equal Treatment of Men and Women'. This comprises 10.55% of Book II on EC Labour Law and 4.75% of the whole text on European Social Law. 'Health and Safety' is covered in 6 pages.[3] Other sections are on 'Pay' (Section II, mainly protection against employer insolvency: 7 pages) and 'Working Time' (Section III: 11 pages).[4]

The overall impression of the Catala–Bonnet text is that EC labour law is placed in a European social law context which includes non-EC law, and which attributes to social security an equal importance to labour law. Within EC labour law, the structure is influenced more by general EC law than traditional labour law. The pillars are free movement of labour and harmonisation of national laws. In sum, the Catala–Bonnet text sees EC labour law more as EC law than labour law. Emerging issues in labour law – atypical work, employment and labour market policy – are not as evident as the traditional EC themes of freedom of movement and harmonisation within a common market, lacking a social policy dimension. There is scant treatment of health and safety, and little more on equality issues. EC collective labour law emphasises workers' participation to the virtual exclusion of collective bargaining. It is not clear how the Maastricht Protocol and Agreement (which are attached as an Addendum to the text) could be accommodated within this framework.

Conceptualising EC labour law: comparative models

The book entitled *The Social Dimension of the European Community* by Ruth Nielsen and Erika Szyszczak, respectively labour law academics in Denmark and the UK, comprises 258 pages of text divided into seven chapters.[5] The text begins with a chapter on 'The Historical and Legal Basis of EC Social Policy Law' (40 pages) and concludes with a chapter on 'The Future Direction of EC Social Policy Law' (9 pages). There are five substantive chapters. The longest of

2   The Directives on collective dismissals and transfers of undertakings, although they have a collective dimension, are treated in a separate Chapter 2 entitled 'Protection of Employment'. This focus on workers' participation in company structures, and hiving off of the Directives on dismissals and transfers, is also to be found in the Blanpain–Javillier volume. In one way, this perspective on collective labour law in the EC reflects the French labour law emphasis on worker representation within the enterprise. In fact, the inspiration for the EC law on worker participation in company structures derives more from the German labour law experience.
3   3.33% of EC Labour Law, 1.5% of European Social Law.
4   A separate Chapter 4 in Title II on 'Harmonisation of National Laws' is on 'Provisions for Specific Categories of Workers' (10 pages covering commercial agents, long distance drivers, young workers, migrant workers and disabled workers). These issues do not appear in the other texts on EC labour law. On the other hand, there is nothing in this chapter on the proposals regarding atypical workers (though Chapter 2 on 'Protection of Employment' has a section on 'Temporary Work', number IV: 6 pages). The topic of atypical work was the subject of separate chapters in Roccella–Treu (the longest chapter, 31 pages, in the section on Individual Relations) and in Blanpain–Javillier (Chapter 3 in Part II on Individual Labour Law: 7 pages).
5   2nd ed, Handelshojskolens Forlag, Copenhagen 1993.

these is Chapter 3 on 'Equal Treatment between Men and Women' (70 pages: 27.14% of the text). Chapter 2 on 'Free Movement of Persons' is next with 64 pages (24.80% of the text), followed by Chapter 6 on 'The Working Environment' with 34 pages, 'The Protection of Employment Rights' (Chapter 4: 32 pages) and 'Information, Consultation and Worker Participation' (Chapter 5: 30 pages).

The striking characteristic of this text recalls that of the Byre volumes of materials on EC labour law and social policy: the prominent place attributed to two aspects of EC labour law, sex equality and the working environment (health and safety). Sex equality covers 70 pages (27.14%) in Nielsen–Szyszczak, compared to 25 (11.26%) in Blanpain–Javillier, 25 (6.47%) in Roccella–Treu and 19 (10.55%) in Catala–Bonnet. Similarly, the treatment of health and safety covers 30 pages in Nielsen–Szyszczak (13.18%), compared to 12 (5.40%) in Blanpain–Javillier, 17 (4.40%) in Roccella–Treu, and 6 (3.33% of Book II on EC labour law) in Catala–Bonnet. This is not necessarily at the expense of the treatment of free movement of workers, which receives 64 pages (24.8%).[6]

Nielsen–Szyszczak use substantive fields to structure EC labour law. Within those substantive fields, the traditional framework of employee protection and employee rights prevails. Their text may be compared with another book in which a group of Scandinavian labour law academics argue that the labour law systems of Sweden, Norway, Denmark and Finland constitute *The Nordic Labour Relations Model*.[7] This text is divided into 6 sections, five of which are on different substantive areas. Interestingly, 4 of the 5 substantive areas which form the framework of the Nordic model parallel chapters in the Nielsen–Szyszczak text on the social dimension of the EC: equality, protection of employment rights, worker participation and working environment.

Where they differ is that the Nordic model does not have a section on free movement of workers. This is effectively the case also among the Nordic countries. More important, the book on the social dimension of the EC does not have a chapter on trade union activity – a crucial difference between the Nordic model and the EC model. The role of trade unions in labour law cannot be overestimated. This difference is visible in the levels of union membership in the Nordic countries and the EC, and its implications for labour law are fundamental.[8] The role of unions and their activities in the Nordic countries, and in the Member States of the EC, transforms the labour law applicable in virtually all substantive areas. A formal structure based on substantive topics must address the trade union impact on the labour law being analysed.

Conclusions

A number of conclusions can be drawn from this review of recent texts on EC labour law. First, there is the major discrepancy among them regarding the relatively substantial amount of primary legal materials, legislation and judicial

---

6   Compared to 37 (16.66%) in Blanpain–Javillier, 53 (13.73%) in Roccella–Treu and 49 (27.22% of Book II on EC labour law) in Catala–Bonnet.
7   Dartmouth, London 1992. The authors are a group of Scandinavian labour law academics: Niklas Bruun, Boal Flodgren, Marit Halvorsen, Hakan Hyden and Ruth Nielsen.
8   As Jelle Visser points out, the difference in trade union density is the most significant social-political indicator in comparing industrial societies. 'In Search of Inclusive Unionism' (1990) 18 *Bulletin of Comparative Labour Relations*, Kluwer, Deventer, at p 239.

decisions, on the topics of sex equality and health and safety. These are highlighted in the Byre volumes, compared to the relatively meagre treatment of these topics in most of the texts. The exception to this, Nielsen–Szyszczak, only confirms the point.

Secondly, there is the different approach to treatment of the collective dimension of EC labour law. In Roccella–Treu, the emphasis is on collective bargaining and the autonomous organisations of workers and employers at European level. In Blanpain–Javillier, Nielsen–Szyszczak and, even more so, in Catala–Bonnet, the emphasis is on worker participation, information and consultation, mainly through integration into company structures or at enterprise level. This uncertainty about the collective dimension is manifest also in the classification of the Directives on collective dismissals and transfers of undertakings. In Blanpain–Javillier and Roccella–Treu, these are dealt with under the general rubric of individual employment relations. The sub-heading is that of restructuring enterprises, which allows for recognition of the collective dimension, but the framework is that of protection of individual rights. This is made explicit in the Catala–Bonnet text, and is also indicated in Nielsen–Szyszczak.

Thirdly, the texts vary greatly in their treatment of social security in the framework of EC labour law. The traditional distinction between labour law and social security law is maintained even where European social security law receives the most extensive treatment, in Catala–Bonnet. In Roccella–Treu, social security is treated in the chapter following free movement, within the general section on employment policies. In Blanpain–Javillier it receives only marginal attention, and in Nielsen–Szyszczak, only a mention.

In sum, the structures of EC labour law adopted by these texts reflect different points along a spectrum ranging from pure EC law to traditional labour law. At one end of the spectrum, the Catala–Bonnet text classifies the subject along strictly EC law lines: freedom of movement and harmonisation are the organising categories. At the other end, Blanpain–Javillier classify the subject along the traditional labour law lines of individual employment protection and rights and collective labour law, albeit the latter is given relatively scant treatment and collective bargaining is marginalised.

Between these, Roccella–Treu opt broadly for the individual–collective dichotomy of traditional national labour laws, but add a substantial new section on employment policies. It is not clear whether this reflects EC law imperatives, since much of it is concerned with freedom of movement, or whether it reflects a new trend in conceptualising labour law as labour market regulation. However, their treatment of the collective dimension of EC labour law places the emphasis firmly on the traditional sphere of collective bargaining.

Nielsen–Szyszczak do not explicitly opt for the individual–collective division of national labour laws. Their chapters appear to be framed more in terms of substantive issues which contain a mixture of collective and individual. The substantive issues are, however, conceptualised in the traditional terms of employment protection and collective rights, and not the new trend of labour market regulation.

The two ends of the spectrum: EC law–national labour law interact. On the one hand, the emphasis on free movement of workers within a common market in EC law finds an echo in the trend in national labour laws towards conceptualisation of the subject in terms of labour market regulation. On the other hand, the traditional national labour law objectives of individual employment protection and collective labour rights are increasingly reflected in many EC labour law provisions. The result is a significant dynamic: the older conceptions of EC labour law in terms of free movement find vindication in new developments in national labour law in the form of labour market regulation. The older national labour law conceptions of employment protection and collective labour rights find an echo in the new developments in EC labour law.

A PROPOSED STRUCTURE FOR EUROPEAN LABOUR LAW

The structures of EC labour law found in existing texts demonstrate the influence of prototypical models of EC law and national labour laws. The EC law model dictates an emphasis on individual employment and free markets in labour, with an emphasis on the internal dynamics of EC institutions. The model derived from national labour laws adopts the traditional dichotomy of individual employment protection and collective labour rights, with occasional recognition of labour market policy and the role of the social partners.

This legalistic approach to EC labour law has the merit of a clear structure. The legal institutions of the Community: Council, Commission, Court and so on, and its legal provisions: Treaties, Regulations, Directives and other legal measures determine the structure. The account comprises the description of the institutions, and groups together the legal provisions in various combinations or categories more or less familiar from national labour law traditions. The outcome constitutes the structure of EC labour law.

A contextual approach to EC labour law does not offer such a clear structure. One possibility is to adopt a chronological account as a substitute for an analytical framework. Understanding the historical evolution of EC labour law is necessary. But a chronological account is not sufficient.[9] Nor can an account of EC labour law be purely a political narrative of its evolution. There is a need to put the history and politics into a legal context. What is required is a structure which takes both features into account: the historical and political context, but also the importance of legal technique, the constraints imposed by legal provisions and processes of law-making and law-interpreting.

Hence, the evolution of EC labour law will be analysed in terms of a number of different legal strategies which have been adopted. These strategies are the consequence of the political context involving dynamics both internal to the Community, between the EC institutions, and external to the Community, between the Community and external actors including Member States and organisations of interest groups at national, supra- and sub-national levels.

A proposed structure for *European* labour law must also take into account the national labour laws of Member States and their very different labour law traditions. EC labour law is only partly an instrument of the EC institutions. It is also, even primarily, an instrument regulating employment and labour relations in Member States. As such it is an instrument of the Member State governments,

---

9   The result can resemble a list of dates and facts. EC labour law becomes a chronological recital of what are held to be significant pieces of legislation (Regulations on free movement, harmonising Directives), or European Court decisions (on equality), or provisions of and amendments to the Treaty of Rome (Article 119, the Single European Act, the Maastricht Treaty on European Union). Again, the structure divides the materials listed chronologically into categories more or less familiar from national labour law traditions.

and of organisations of interests, mainly employers and workers, within the Member States. The legal measures which result from EC legal strategies interact with national labour law traditions. The interaction occurs at the point of formulation, when national labour laws influence the form and content of EC labour law, and also at the point of implementation, when these national labour law systems determine the impact of EC labour law within Member States. A structure of *European* labour law has to reflect the different traditions of national labour law systems of Member States.

The proposed structure that emerges should reflect the law and context of both the EC and of Member States' labour law traditions, both the various legal strategies adopted as a consequence of the political conjuncture of the EC at different moments of its history, and the interaction of these strategies with national labour laws.

Finally, the proposed structure poses the question of whether *European* labour law is merely the passive reflection of EC law and national labour laws. Is there discernible a specific identity which, taking account of both these sources of inspiration, begins to constitute a structure of European labour law?

Title I begins with Part I, comprising this introduction (Chapter 1), and an account of the relationship between the UK and EC labour law (Chapter 2). Thereafter, the book proposes a structure which seeks to reflect three specific qualities of European labour law.

The first specific quality of European labour law is the variety of legal strategies which have been utilised in the formulation and enforcement of EC labour law – a consequence of its search for an appropriate framework of instruments and measures in the political context of the general development of EC law.

Part II of the book begins with an account of the historical development of EC labour law through an analysis of these different legal strategies (Chapters 3–6). Part III continues with an account of the variety of legal mechanisms available to implement and enforce EC labour law (Chapters 7–11).

The second specific quality of European labour law is that certain substantive areas of EC law have had a significant impact on the labour law of the Member States. Detailed exposition of both its substance and the context of its implementation in different national labour law systems reveals a body of labour law of a distinctly *European* character.

This exposition is provided in Title II of the book. This comprises Part IV, an account of the European law on equality between men and women (Chapters 12–15), followed by Part V on the European norms governing labour in the enterprise (Chapters 16–20) and Part VI, an account of the European labour law on health and safety in the working environment (Chapters 21–24) and concludes with Part VII, the new European labour law on migrant workers (Chapters 25–27).

The third specific quality of European labour law derives from the emergence of two structural pillars: first, a typology of individual employment relationships regulated by European labour law, and, secondly, the role of social dialogue and collective agreements as definitive features in the European regulation of labour.[10]

---

10 Tendencies mooted in B Bercusson 'Maastricht: a fundamental change in European labour law', (1992) 23 *Industrial Relations Journal* 177–90.

These are called structural pillars because they constitute the poles of attraction around which the future European labour law will crystallise. Formulation of this law will involve techniques increasingly linked to collective bargaining and social dialogue. Substantive content will reflect the exigencies of protection of a fragmented workforce requiring a regulatory framework appropriate to its particular circumstances. The challenge for European labour law will be to find a structure which reconciles general collective regulation with diversified categories of individual employment.[11]

The elaboration of these structural pillars is the subject of **Title III**. The first pillar is covered in **Part VIII**, an account of the emerging typology of individual employment relationships (such as part-time workers, temporary workers, workers without a contract but with an 'employment relationship', workers with very long hours and so on (**Chapters 28–32**). The second pillar is dealt with in **Part IX**, a description of the principles and autonomous development of collective labour law in the European Union (**Chapters 33–36**).

In conclusion, **Title IV** is concerned with the future development of European labour law. This is examined through a detailed analysis in **Part X** of the Community Charter of Fundamental Social Rights of Workers of 1989 (**Chapters 37–38**). It is argued that the 1996 Intergovernmental Conference presents an opportunity for the strategic integration of the Charter and the Protocol and Agreement on Social Policy of the Maastricht Treaty into a social constitution for the European Union (**Chapter 39**).

This book is intended as a contribution to understanding European labour law through the developing labour law of the European Union. The combination of a variety of legal strategies, areas of significant substantive regulation, and two structural pillars constitutes the proposed structure of European labour law.

---

11   See the discussion in U Mückenberger and S Deakin 'From deregulation to a European floor of rights: Labour law, flexibilisation and the European single market', in [1989] 3 *Zeitschrift für ausländisches und internationales Arbeits- und Sozialrecht* 153.

Chapter 2
EC Labour Law and the UK

INTRODUCTION

The UK is singular in that for the last sixteen of the twenty-three years of its membership of the EC, 1973–1995, a single government has been in power. The Conservative government elected in May 1979, first under the leadership of Margaret Thatcher and then under John Major, pursued a specific social and labour policy with remarkable consistency and determination throughout that period.

The consequences for the UK's relationship to European labour law – both the impact of EC law on domestic labour law, and also the impact of the social and labour policies of UK governments on the development of EC labour law – have been unmistakable. The mutual impact can be described in terms of a reversal of policy flow: up to 1979, UK domestic labour law policy was influenced in important ways by EC labour law; since 1979, it is EC labour and social policy which has been heavily influenced by domestic UK social and labour policies.

The accession to the EC of the UK in 1973 coincided with the beginning of a period of legislative activity in the EC which has been so far unique. The equality Directives (equal pay,[1] equal treatment,[2] social security[3]) and the Directives on collective dismissals,[4] acquired rights upon transfers of undertakings[5] and protection of workers in insolvency[6] were mostly approved by the Council of Ministers during the period of the Labour governments of 1974–1979. Their impact on domestic labour and social law has been profound. Since 1979, and mainly during the 1980s, the principal EC legislative activity on labour policy has been confined to the sphere of health and safety at work. Otherwise, since 1979, EC legislative activity in the labour field has largely halted in the face of the UK government's rejection of almost all proposals from the Commission, and their consequent failure to achieve the necessary unanimous approval in the Council of Ministers.

This UK veto was one of the reasons which led Jacques Delors, the newly

---

1   Directive 75/117/EEC of 10 February 1975, OJ L45/19 of 19.2.1975.
2   Directive 76/207/EEC of 9 February 1976, OJ L39/40 of 14.2.1976.
3   Directive 79/7/EEC of 19 December 1978, OJ L6/24 of 10.1.1979; Directive 86/378/EEC of 24 July 1986, OJ L225/40 of 12.8.1986; Directive 86/613/EEC of 11 December 1986, OJ L359/56 of 19.12.1986.
4   Directive 75/129, OJ L48/29 of 22.2.1975.
5   Directive 77/187, OJ L61/26 of 5.3.1977.
6   Directive 80/987, OJ L283/23.

elected President of the Commission, to initiate the policy in 1985 of stimulating the European social dialogue as an alternative path to a social dimension for the EC. The development of the social dialogue, its gradual emergence as a pillar of EC social policy, formalised in the Maastricht Protocol and Agreement, is the unintended and unforeseen consequence of UK domestic policy. It is ironic that the Conservative government's policy of reducing the influence of trade unions and de-collectivising industrial relations domestically should have been a prime cause of the emergence of the trade unions and of collective bargaining as a major instrument of social and labour policy at European level.

The account of the dynamic tension between EC and UK labour law and policy begins with an analysis of the effects of EC intervention on the UK labour law and labour relations system. This mainly reflects the legislation of the 1970s, as developed by decisions of the European Court of Justice. Account will also be taken of the health and safety legislation of the 1980s, and of the few pieces of legislation which survived the UK veto in the aftermath of the new impetus generated by the Community Charter of Fundamental Social Rights of Workers of 1989.

The 1980s witnessed a dramatic transformation of the attitudes, contributions and reactions of the national actors in the UK to European social integration. The government became hostile to the social dimension of the integration process, while trade unions reversed their previous hostility. At the same time, the UK courts became more familiar with the techniques and potential of EC law. These changes were reflected in the willingness of various national actors to allow for delegation upward to supranational bodies of competences and actions in the social field.

The reactions and adaptations of domestic labour law to the unified European market reflected the tension between, on the one side, a UK government which promoted unrestrained competition on labour standards and sought to restrict collective determination of such standards by the social partners, and, on the other side, other Member State governments which insisted on some supranational minima below which labour standards should not descend. This tension was reflected in the attitudes and behaviour of the social partners in the the UK, as well as those of the various Member States and at EC level.

The end result of this tension was manifest in the Community Charter of Fundamental Social Rights of Workers of 1989, signed by all the Member States with the exception of the UK. The contradiction between Member State policies has now formally been incorporated into EC law by the Maastricht Protocol and Agreement on Social Policy. The UK government has opted out of this 'Social Chapter' of the Treaty on European Union, but the UK social partners remain within the organisations of labour and management at EC level, the European Trade Union Confederation (ETUC) and the European Employers' Confederation (UNICE), which are empowered under the Maastricht Agreement to develop the labour and social law and policy of the European Union.

The future of this dynamic tension depends, in part, upon the electoral prospects of the UK Conservative government. However, the momentum of the European social dialogue, generated by the UK's blockage of the institutional legislative process of the EC, may have become unstoppable. In this way, the UK government's policy of the 1980s may have succeeded, despite itself, in projecting at European level the model of collective bargaining autonomy which was the distinguishing characteristic of UK labour law up to the 1980s.

THE EFFECTS OF EC INTERVENTION ON UK LABOUR LAW

EC social and labour law has been incorporated into UK labour law in various ways. First, by the passing of legislation: an example is the Social Security Act 1989 which implemented the requirements of EC Directive 86/378 on equal treatment for men and women in occupational social security schemes.[7] Secondly, EC law may be implemented through secondary legislation. Section 2(2) of the European Communities Act 1972 gives power to Ministers to make regulations; for example, the Equal Pay (Amendment) Regulations 1983 amended the Equal Pay Act 1970 to incorporate the possibility of claims based on equal value in accordance with Directive 75/117.[8] Thirdly, the UK courts have come to accept the EC law doctrines of vertical direct effect (*Defrenne,*[9] *Marshall,*[10] *Foster*[11]) and, more gradually, that UK legislation is to be interpreted in accordance with the requirements of Community law (*Garland,*[12] *Duke,*[13] *Litster*[14]).[15] Where such means have not sufficed to secure the incorporation of EC labour legislation, the Commission has pursued infringement proceedings under Article 169 of the Treaty of Rome.[16]

The impact of EC labour law on UK labour law has been greatest in the field of equality between the sexes. The Equal Pay Act 1970 preceded the UK joining the EC, and, following infringement proceedings, had to be amended by the Equal Pay (Amendment) Regulations 1983. Similarly, the UK Sex Discrimination Act 1975 was passed before the Equal Treatment Directive, but again, following infringement proceedings, the legislation was amended, beginning with the Sex Discrimination Act 1986. Subsequent legislation has been required to take account of decisions of the Court of Justice.[17] The hours thresholds which exclude many part-timers from statutory rights have been reviewed following the decision of the House of Lords in *R v Secretary of State for Employment, ex p Equal Opportunities Commission.*[18] The annulment of the compensation limits for discrimination require further legislation.[19] Similarly, the 1986 Directive on equality in social security required enactment of s 23 and Schedule 5 of the Social Security Act 1989, which outlawed discrimination in occupational benefit schemes. More recently, Directive 92/85/EEC which sets out minimum employment rights for pregnant workers has required extensive amendments introduced through legislation in 1993.[20]

---

7   Directive 86/378/EEC of 24 July 1986, OJ L225/40 of 12.8.1986.
8   Directive 75/117/EEC of 10 February 1975, OJ L45/19 of 19.2.1975.
9   Case 80/70: [1971] ECR 445.
10 Case 152/84: [1986] ECR 723.
11 Case C-188/89: [1991] 1 QB 405.
12 Case 12/81: [1982] ECR 359.
13 [1988] AC 618, HL.
14 [1989] ICR 341, HL.
15 For further details, see Chapter 10.
16 As in the case of equality legislation: Case 61/81: EC *Commission v UK* [1982] ECR 2601; Case 165/82: [1984] ICR 192.
17 Case 222/84: *Johnston v RUC* [1986] ECR 1651.
18 [1995] 1 AC 1.
19 Case 271/91: *Marshall v Southampton and South West Hampshire Area Health Authority (No 2)* [1993] ECR I-4367.
20 Directive 92/85/EEC of 19 October 1992, OJ L348/1 of 28.11.92. E Ellis concludes: 'The directive will require little or no change to the law in any Member State apart from the UK'; (1993) 22 *Industrial Law Journal* 63 at 67.

The UK government does claim a better than average record of compliance.[1] Nonetheless, there was dissatisfaction with the then Labour government's legislative implementation of EC law requirements during the 1970s. In the 1980s, the tension between the Conservative government's EC obligations and its avowed commitment to non-intervention in labour standard fixing led to an approach of minimum compliance. This in turn bred litigation strategies whereby individuals and groups (such as the Equal Opportunities Commission) pursued claims, invoking the Treaty's Article 177 reference procedure to the European Court of Justice. The strategy of seeking to compensate for the UK government's resistance through interpretations of the European Court has sometimes paid off spectacularly. But the tension has some overall negative effects. This can be illustrated by two other Directives of the 1970s.

Perhaps the clearest example of the UK government's minimalist approach to EC labour law combining with its overall market philosophy to produce inadequate implementation of EC law has been the case of the Acquired Rights Directive 77/187/EEC.[2] The UK Transfer of Undertakings (Protection of Employment) Regulations 1981 excluded non-commercial ventures. This gave a clear passage to the privatisation policies of the government during the 1980s, largely premised on the ability of the private contractors for formerly public services to compete by reducing existing pay and labour standards. The guarantees of the Directive were deemed inapplicable by the implementing legislation which deemed public services to be 'non-commercial'. However, later decisions of the European Court called this into question.[3] The consequence is not only a belated amendment of the implementing legislation, but also mass litigation to compensate those who suffered loss of pay and worsened conditions when their jobs were transferred to private contractors without the EC law guarantees.[4]

A second example of the tension between UK government policy and EC labour law is the requirement of the Collective Dismissals Directive 75/129/EEC that representatives of the workforce be consulted.[5] At the time of the Directive's passage, there had been a procedure in UK law by which workers could require employers to recognise their representatives.[6] In line with the policy of de-collectivisation of industrial relations, the Conservative government repealed this legislation.[7] Hence, the UK implementing legislation does not allow for the case where the requirement of consultation is frustrated by the inability of workers to require employers to recognise their representatives.[8]

---

1   For example, the Secretary of State for Employment, G Shepherd claimed in a speech just prior to the UK taking up the Presidency of the Council in July 1992, that the UK was the first Member State to have implemented all 18 Directives in the social field which were then due for implementation, a record matched only by Germany. *Industrial Relations Legal Information Bulletin* No 450, June 1992, p 15.

2   OJ L61/26 of 5.3.1977.

3   Case C-29/91: *Dr Sophie Redmond Stichting v Bartol* [1992] IRLR 366.

4   Five public sector trade unions have now issued 128 writs against the UK government, on the basis of the *Francovich* principle (see Chapter 10), relating to a large number of employees affected in the past by compulsory competitive tendering as a result of which the employees lost their jobs or were re-employed by contractors at lower rates of pay or on less favourable terms and conditions. *Industrial Relations Law Bulletin* No 488, January 1994, p 16.

5   OJ L48/29 of 22.2.1975.

6   Employment Protection Act 1975, section 11.

7   Employment Act 1980.

8   B A Hepple and A Byre 'EEC law in the UK – A new approach' (1989) 18 *Industrial Law Journal* 129. See the comment by L Dolding in (1992) 21 *Industrial Law Journal* 310 at 314.

The infringement proceedings brought by the Commission resulted in the European Court condemning the UK government for failure adequately to implement the Directive[9] and the government has now had to produce legislative proposals for mandatory worker representation.[10]

Reliance on litigation strategies to balance the UK government's minimalist approach depends on vigilance and resources. Where these are lacking, the government's failure to adequately implement EC law can produce long periods during which EC labour law fails to operate as it should in the UK.

THE UK AND EUROPEAN SOCIAL INTEGRATION

There was a dramatic transformation of the attitudes of the national actors in the UK to European social integration in the 1980s. The change of government in 1979 transformed the official attitude to one of fundamental hostility to the social dimension of the integration process. On the other hand, the trade union and labour movement reversed their previous hostility. In the face of government hostility at the national level, they began to espouse the cause of social and labour policy at EC level.

An example of the potential conflict between the ambitions of EC social and labour policy and the radically different approach of the Conservative government elected in 1979 is the field of health and safety at work. The Commission's Third Action Programme on health and safety of 1987 was inspired by the enactment of Article 118A, inserted into the Treaty of Rome by the Single European Act 1986. In its programme, the Commission proposed an extensive list of new health and safety Directives. Framework Directive 89/391/EEC[11] included provision for a series of individual Directives ('daughter' Directives) to cover specific risks, of which several have so far been adopted.

In the UK, the Workplace (Health, Safety and Welfare) Regulations 1992 implement the EC Framework Directive and six of its 'daughters', and came into force on 1 January 1993. This new legislation repealed much of the preceding industry-specific legislation: large sections of the Factories Act 1961 and the Offices, Shops and Railway Premises Act 1963 were repealed. In support of the new legislation, it is said that 'they simplify much of the outdated industry-specific legislation . . . by making many requirements universal to all worksites'.[12]

However, the aim of the Health and Safety Commission in implementing the Directives was not to go beyond their strict requirements, to minimise the impact of any changes in the law. In a number of areas, the wording of the Regulations is different to the wording of the Directive. Also, in some cases, previously more detailed duties in the old legislation have been replaced with more general duties in the new Regulations. It has been argued that in some respects, therefore, the Regulations fail to meet the standards required by the Directives, though this apparent lacuna may be met through judicial interpretation.

9   Cases C-382/92 and C-383/92: *EC Commission v UK*, decided 8 June 1994, [1994] ECR I-2435 and [1994] ECR I-2479.
10   Collective Redundancies and Transfer of Undertakings (Protection of Employment) (Amendment) Regulations 1995, SI 2587, coming into force on 26 October 1995.
11   Of 12 June 1989, OJ L183/1.
12   (1993) *Occupational Health Review* (January/February), p 3.

What emerges is that the EC attempt to achieve European standards of health and safety has been seized upon as the excuse by the UK government for an effort at deregulation. The tendency was repeated with the publication on 18 January 1994 of the Deregulation and Contracting Out Bill. Clause 27 of the Bill provided the Secretary of State for Employment with potentially sweeping powers of repeal and revocation applicable to all safety legislation. It has been said that, with these powers, it will be necessary to ensure that the new Bill is not used to repeal any legislation that would bring it into conflict with the Framework Directive, the preamble of which states that it 'does not justify any reduction in levels of protection already achieved in Member States'.[13]

The UK government's attitude towards EC health and safety legislation is not one which aims at harmonising its standards with a view to improvement up to those of other Member States; rather it has been turned to the ends of a domestic political objective of deregulation, which, with respect to existing standards in some cases, has been argued to be regressive.

SUBSIDIARITY

The UK's willingness to allow for delegation upward to supranational bodies of competences and actions in the social field is encapsulated in one word: subsidiarity. Its view was manifest in an often isolated role in blocking social policy proposals during the 1980s. For example, the provisions in paragraph 2 of Article 100A, added to the Treaty of Rome by the Single European Act 1986, excluded from qualified majority voting proposals 'relating to the rights and interests of employed persons'. This addition was the result of pressures from the UK government.

This perspective was and is manifest in respect of a number of proposals. The UK government criticised the legal basis chosen for the maternity rights Directive, arguing that they were concerned with employment and pay, hence requiring unanimity in the Council of Ministers. It argues that neither of the legal bases chosen for the European Company Statute proposals is appropriate.[14]

An example illustrating the contrasting attitudes of the UK government and those of the other Member States towards delegation upward is that of the Council Directive on working time. On 25 July 1990, the Commission of the European Communities adopted a proposal for a Council Directive concerning certain aspects of the organisation of working time.[15] Following a lengthy legislative itinerary, at a meeting of the Ministers of Social and Labour Affairs on 1 June 1993, all the other Member States voted in favour. The UK abstained and announced its intention to challenge the legal basis of the proposed Directive in the European Court.[16] The Directive was adopted by the Council at

---

13   *Health and Safety Information Bulletin* No 219, March 1994, pp 8–9.
14   M Hall 'The Social Charter Action Programme: Progress and Prospects' (1991) 20 *Industrial Law Journal* 147, at 148–9.
15   COM (90) 317 final – SYN 295, Brussels, 20 September 1990; OJ C254 of 9 October 1990, p 4.
16   *European Industrial Relations Review* No 233, June 1993, p 2; *Industrial Relations Law Bulletin* No 475, June 1993, p 12.

a meeting on 23 November 1993 and has become the law of the EU.[17]

The legal basis of the Directive is Article 118A of the EC Treaty which stipulates that:

'the Member States shall pay particular attention to encouraging improvements, especially of the working environment, as regards the safety and health of workers, and shall set as their objective the harmonisation of conditions in this area.'

The Commission's Explanatory Memorandum emphasised the World Health Organisation's definition that:[18]

'health is a state of complete psychic, mental and social wellbeing and does not merely consist of an absence of disease or infirmity.'

The Commission takes the view that it is not necessary for working time to create serious health hazards to fall within Article 118A. EC legislation on working time is justified as regards psychological and social aspects of the working environment, such as monotony, lack of social contacts at work or a rapid work pace.[19]

The UK government insisted that the proposal related to working conditions, not health and safety. Hence, the correct legal basis required a unanimous vote. The UK government lodged an appeal with the European Court of Justice to challenge the legal basis selected and has asserted that it will not introduce implementing legislation until the Court has reached its decision.[20]

Its abstention is a further indication of the UK government's unwillingness to delegate competence in the social field. This is further evidenced in Article 18 of the Directive, which contains 'Final provisions' and prescribes the standard obligation of Member States to comply (as envisaged in Article 189 of the EC Treaty): 3 years after adoption of the Directive.[1] Exceptionally, Article 18(1)(b)(i) begins: 'However, a Member State shall have the option not to apply Article 6 ...' (48-hour maximum weekly working), and ends:

'Before the expiry of a period of seven years counted from the expiry of the period of three years referred to in (a), the Council shall, on the basis of a Commission proposal accompanied by an appraisal report, re-examine the provisions of this point (i) and decide on what action to take.'

The possible delay in the implementation of Article 6 of the Directive for up to ten years, and possibly longer, was much vaunted by the UK government as a major success in its negotiations over EC social policy. It both reflects a grave weakness in the application of EC standards, and demonstrates vividly the lengths to which delegation of national competence in the social field will be resisted by the UK government.

---

17 Council Directive 93/104/EC of 23 November 1993 concerning certain aspects of the organisation of working time, OJ L307/18 of 13.12.93. *Europe* No 6113, 24 November 1993, p 10.

18 Op cit.

19 For an acute and detailed analysis by a Danish labour lawyer of the scope of Article 118A in light of various Community labour law initiatives, see the LL.M dissertation by Jacob Sand 'The Social Dimension of the Internal Market: Health and Safety at Work', 1993, on file at the European University Institute, Florence.

20 See the accounts in *Industrial Relations Law Bulletin* No 475, June 1993, p 12; *Europe* No 5991 of 2 June 1993, p 7.

1 Article 18(1)(a).

THE ATTITUDE OF THE UK GOVERNMENT TO INTERNATIONAL COMPETITION AND ITS IMPLICATIONS FOR LABOUR STANDARDS

One possible method of mitigating international competition over labour standards is through the stipulation of common compulsory labour standards: eg in the form of collective agreements. The extent to which the UK government has been willing to acknowledge this labour law tradition of a number of Member States as a potential inspiration for EC labour law proposals on common labour standards is revealing of its views on international competition and its implications for labour standards. An example will illustrate the UK government's attitude.

The introduction of Portuguese workers into France by a Portuguese construction firm led to a complaint by the French authorities. The invocation of the principle of freedom to provide services, albeit through employees, brought the case before the European Court, which declared:[2]

> 'in response to the concern expressed in this connection by the French government, that Community law does not preclude Member States from extending their legislation, or collective labour agreements entered into by both sides of industry, to any person who is employed, even temporarily, within their territory, no matter in which country the employer is established; nor does Community law prohibit Member States from enforcing those rules by appropriate means.'

The principle of compulsory adherence to collective agreements by all employers was familiar to the French labour law tradition, and inspired the Court. It was adopted by the Commission in the proposal for a Council Directive on the posting of workers in the framework of the provision of services.[3] Article 3(1) of the proposed Directive provided that:

> 'Member States *shall see to it* that, whatever the law applicable to the employment relationship, the undertaking . . . does not deprive the worker of the terms and conditions of employment which apply for work of the same character at the place where the work is carried out, provided that (a) they are laid down by laws, regulations and administrative provisions or by collective agreements . . .'

In this way, EC legislation would establish a mandatory level of labour standards in an attempt to preclude competition over working conditions between firms engaged in transnational economic activities.

However, the UK government's position on this Directive was negative: it 'believes that the Directive should only be adopted if it is necessary to deal with real problems at Community level and is workable in practice. At present, the Government sees little evidence that legal uncertainty or differences in legislation among Member States are significant obstacles to the posting of workers'.[4]

---

2 Case C-113/89: *Rush Portuguesa Lda v Office National d'Immigration* [1990] ECR I-1417 at 1445, paragraph 18.
3 COM (91) 230 final, SYN 346, Brussels, 1 August 1991. Subsequent amendments introduced changes designed to accommodate the different traditions of other Member States; for details, see Chapter 27.
4 *Industrial Relations Legal Information Bulletin* No 444, March 1992, at p 9.

THE UK AND THE MAASTRICHT PROTOCOL AND AGREEMENT

The Treaty on European Union signed by the Member States of the European Community on 7 February 1992 includes a 'social chapter' in the form of the Protocol on Social Policy (No 14) and an Agreement, annexed to the Protocol, between 11 (now 14) Member States, with the exception of the UK, also on Social Policy. The Protocol notes that 14 Member States 'wish to continue along the path laid down in the 1989 Social Charter [and] have adopted among themselves an Agreement to this end'; accordingly, all 15 Member States:

'1. Agree to authorise those 14 Member States [excluding the UK] to have recourse to the institutions, procedures and mechanisms of the Treaty for the purposes of taking among themselves and applying as far as they are concerned the acts and decisions required for giving effect to the abovementioned Agreement.'

The Protocol on Social Policy forms an integral part of the EC Treaty.[5] The Agreement is stated in the Protocol to be annexed to the Protocol. The presumption is that both Protocol and Agreement are, therefore, part of Community law. Similarly, any measures adopted using the institutions, procedures and mechanisms of the Treaty will have effects in Community law as far as the 14 Member States are concerned.

The Protocol further provides that:[6]

'The United Kingdom of Great Britain and Northern Ireland shall not take part in the deliberations and the adoption by the Council of Commission proposals made on the basis of this Protocol and the abovementioned Agreement.'

This paragraph goes on to outline the voting procedures in the absence of the UK, and paragraph 3 provides that the:

'Acts adopted by the Council and any financial consequences other than administrative costs entailed for the institutions shall not be applicable to the United Kingdom of Great Britain and Northern Ireland.'

By virtue of these provisions, the UK 'opted-out' of the 'social chapter' of the TEU.

However, it is unthinkable that the Maastricht Treaty provisions on social policy precluded forever the opting in by the UK and were intended *permanently* to exclude the UK. According to the Social Policy Protocol, the UK does not take part in the procedures when the new social policy is invoked, and the outcomes of those procedures do not apply to it. If it is assumed that this exclusion was *not* intended to be permanent, three alternative strategies would enable the UK to join the new social policy.

Treaty amendment/revision

Opting-in could be achieved by an amendment to Protocol 14, in other words, to the Treaty. This amendment could take two forms. First, the deletion of the entire Protocol and Agreement *and* the substitution of the existing EC Treaty

5 Article 239: 'The Protocols annexed to this Treaty by common accord of the Member States shall form an integral part thereof'.
6 Article 2, paragraph 1.

provisions with the new formulation of Articles 118 et seq now in the Agreement. Alternatively, by changing the text of the first line of the preamble to the Protocol from '14' to '15' Member States, and including the UK in the following list; also in paragraph 1 of the Protocol and similarly in the Agreement; and deleting paragraph 2 of the Protocol entirely.

Interpretation of the Protocol

Rather than amend the Protocol, the question can be posed as one of interpretation of the Protocol. Can it be read to allow for the UK to opt in or not? It is submitted that the Protocol can be read as implying that when the UK does take part in the deliberations of and the adoption by the Council of Commission proposals,[7] the acts adopted shall be applicable to the UK.

Adhesion to the Agreement

The Protocol applies so long as the UK does not adhere to the Agreement. This is the precondition for participation in decision-making by the Council. All 15 Member States authorise recourse to EC machinery to give effect to the Agreement. The preamble to the Protocol notes that only 14 Member States have adopted the Agreement. It follows that the UK is excluded and is not bound. *What is necessary is that the UK adheres to the Agreement, not to the Protocol.* This does not require amendment of the Protocol at all. Following adhesion, it is obvious that all 15 Member States authorise use of EC machinery to give effect to the Agreement through procedures involving also the participation of the UK.

In conclusion: as between (1) amendment of the Protocol, (2) interpretation of the Protocol, and (3) adhesion to the Agreement, the latter two strategies obviously involve much lighter procedures. The other Member States clearly wished the UK to join the new social policy initiatives. Under any of the three procedures, the UK retains the right to refuse to take part until it wishes to join.

The Protocol on Social Policy and UK domestic law

These alternative strategies throw some light on the debates over the legal consequences of the itinerary of the Maastricht Bill in the UK Parliament. The European Communities (Amendment) Act 1993, which received the Royal Assent on 20 July 1993, includes two provisions which, combined, have already produced a legal challenge and could in the future have unforeseen consequences. Section 1(1) of the 1993 Act excludes the Protocol on Social Policy from the instruments which are given legal effect in domestic law by the European Communities Act 1972, section 2(1). Section 1(2) approves the Treaty on European Union for the purpose of section 6 of the European Parliamentary Elections Act 1978.

---

7   Assuming also adhesion to the Agreement – see next paragraph.

The challenge, in *R v Secretary of State for Foreign and Commonwealth Affairs, ex p Rees-Mogg,* argued that section 1(2):[8]

'does not approve the Protocols, and in particular does not approve the Protocol on Social Policy, which is specifically excluded from the operation of section 1(1) of the Act.'

The Court rejected the argument, distinguishing between the purposes of section 1(1) and section 1(2):[9]

'What could have been the point of incorporating all the Protocols, in English domestic law, save only Protocol 14 (on Social Policy), unless it was intended by Parliament that the Protocols should be approved for ratification?'

This highlights the horns of the dilemma. All Protocols are ratified, but one of them, on Social Policy, is excluded from having domestic legal effects. Three interpretations are possible of the resulting situation.

First, this is an apparently clumsy and illogical double negative. The Protocol itself provides that the acts adopted by the Council shall not be applicable to the United Kingdom. The 1993 Act declares in effect that any non-applicable acts adopted shall have no effect in domestic law. Logically, it is tempting to argue that this implies that applicable acts shall have effect in domestic law![10]

Secondly, also clumsy, the Protocol on Social Policy is ratified, but the door is left open to the UK opting in by a declaration of adhesion to the Agreement and participation in the procedures. However, an amendment of section 1(1) of the 1993 Act deleting the exclusion of the Protocol would then still be necessary.

Thirdly, as in the first legal challenge, there is a question of the relationship of the social policy opt out to ratification. All Member States ratifying the Treaty approved the opt out in the Protocol. For the UK to further deny legal effect in domestic law to the Protocol is unnecessary and inconsistent with ratification.

The issue could come before both the UK courts and the European Court. In another challenge to the 1993 Act's exclusion of the Social Policy Protocol from having domestic legal effect, the UK courts might hold that this does not affect ratification and uphold the deletion of the Social Policy Protocol from EC Treaties having legal effect. The issue could still come before the European Court under an Article 177 reference.

The European Court might hold that the 1993 Act does not affect ratification. All the Member States ratified the Treaty, including the Protocol, and thereby granted it the requisite legal effect in domestic law. The problem then is that the Protocol is unnecessarily denied legal effect in UK law by the 1993 Act.

There are at least two options available to the European Court, more or less dramatic, and both annoying to the UK government. Less dramatically, the Court might hold that the UK ratified the Protocol and Agreement on Social Policy, but simply avoids its effects by not participating as provided for in the

8 Queen's Bench Division, 30 July 1993 (Lloyd, Mann LJJ, Auld J) [1994] 2 WLR 115 at 120.
9 Lloyd LJ, ibid, at 122.
10 The exclusion might perhaps make sense if there were other potential instruments which might otherwise be applicable under the Protocol – such as EC-level agreements.

Protocol. When it does choose to participate, it will be required to amend the 1993 Act so as to include the Protocol and Agreement among those instruments having legal effects in domestic law.

The more dramatic option would have the Court holding that the UK cannot single out the Protocol and deny it legal effect despite its ratification. The provision in the 1993 Act is inconsistent with ratification. The UK must recognise the new social competences of the EC.[11] The Protocol still allows for the UK to opt out by not participating in the procedures for the adoption of acts of the Council under those new competences.[12] By such a decision of the Court, the formal division of the Community into two on social policy issues is avoided. Sooner or later a UK government is bound to adhere to the social policy of the rest of the Community. The Court will simply anticipate the inevitable. The choice of which option it chooses will determine whether a legislative amendment to the 1993 Act is necessary in order for the UK to opt in.[13]

CONCLUSION

The Maastricht Protocol and Agreement represent the formal recognition of the fundamental divide between the present UK government and the governments of the other Member States regarding the social dimension of the European Union. The division lasted for well over a decade and a half, and seemed likely to remain as long as the institutional procedures for developing the social dimension remained those of the Treaty of Rome.

However, the institutional arrangements for the production of European labour law were changed dramatically by the Protocol and Agreement on Social Policy attached to the Maastricht Treaty on European Union.[14] Collective bargaining agreements reached through the social dialogue at EC level were given the potential to be transposed into the sphere of EC labour law.

The social dialogue was prescribed as a mandatory step in the formulation of EC labour and social law and policy. The Commission, when envisaging and actually proposing labour and social policy initiatives, is obliged to consult the social partners at EC level.[15] When the social partners are consulted, they may assume the responsibility for making an agreement at EC level which shall be implemented in a number of prescribed ways in the Member States.[16]

The significance of this change in the institutional procedures for the formulation and implementation of EC labour law is that it may enable the 14 other Member States to develop the social dimension despite the opposition of the

11 More fancifully, to the same end, the Court might hold that the exclusion of any legal effects for the Protocol is a double negative; hence, the UK impliedly adopts the Protocol and Agreement on Social Policy!

12 This leaves open the question of the effect of EC-level agreements adopted under the Agreement on Social Policy.

13 It also may have implications for the effect of EC-level agreements.

14 B Bercusson 'Maastricht: a fundamental change in European labour law' (1992) 23 *Industrial Relations Journal* 177. Also 'The dynamic of European labour law after Maastricht' (1994) 23 *Industrial Law Journal* (March) 1.

15 Agreement on Social Policy (annexed to the Protocol on Social Policy of the Treaty on European Union) concluded between the Member States of the European Community with the exception of the United Kingdom of Great Britain and Northern Ireland, Article 3(1–3).

16 Ibid, Articles 3(4) and 4.

UK government. Moreover, the opting out of the UK government will not preclude the participation of the social partners from the UK – the TUC and the CBI – in the European social dialogue. In this way, EC labour law may continue to affect the UK.

The potential was dramatically illustrated by the experience of the Commission proposal of January 1991 on European Works Councils. Following the UK government's rejection of this proposal, and the subsequent coming into force of the Treaty on European Union on 1 November 1993, the proposal became, on 18 November 1993, the first to engage the procedure under the Maastricht Agreement. Consultations with and negotiations among the social partners at EC level (including their UK representatives) came very close to reaching an agreement, which would have been implemented under Article 4(2) of the Agreement. However, the last minute withdrawal of the CBI from the negotiations led to their collapse, and the Commission resumed the legislative track, though with a text inspired by the European social dialogue. This then became the European Works Council Directive, the first to be adopted under the procedure of the Maastricht Protocol and Agreement on Social Policy.[17]

The future relationship of EU labour law to UK domestic labour law depends largely on the eventual opting in of the UK, and, until then, participation of the UK social partners in the development of EU labour law through the European social dialogue.

---

17   Directive 94/45/EC of 22 September 1994, OJ L254/64 of 30.9.1994.

Part II

History and Strategies of European Labour Law

Chapter 3

Two Contrasting Strategies: the ECSC and the EEC

INTRODUCTION

The history of labour law in the European Union is best understood in the context of the evolution of the European Communities in general since their foundation with the European Coal and Steel Community in 1951. Throughout this almost half century, the Community has experimented with a variety of different legal strategies for the formulation and implementation of labour law and social policy. These strategies responded to different economic and political conjunctures. Whatever may have been the original vision of a particular cohort of national and Community leaders when the Communities were founded, this long period has witnessed dramatic changes in the economic and political context. It is not surprising, therefore, that the labour law and social policy of the Community have reflected these changes.

The striking feature of this history is precisely the great variety of legal strategies which have characterised attempts by the European Communities to achieve a coherent social policy and labour law. To some extent this reflects the dialectic between the common problems facing the labour markets of the Member States and the variety of national contexts and traditions in which these problems are confronted.

A key moment was the period following the oil and energy crises beginning in 1973. Various national labour law systems were confronted with common problems of high unemployment and recession in industry. These combined the inadequacy and unsatisfactoriness of participative structures and processes at enterprise level between workers' organisations and employers, and the negative consequences for individual workers, who lost jobs or skills without satisfactory compensation, and for employers who were subject to delay, prevented from achieving desired flexibility, or exposed to additional labour costs at times of crisis. Writing at this time, Gérard Lyon-Caen stated that:[1]

> 'Labour law, as elaborated and applied in European States since the middle of the last century, was a response to a certain economic organisation resulting from the "industrial revolution".'

He referred to the abandonment of the 'human relations' philosophy of personnel management at enterprise level, with the coming of the economic crisis, in

---

1 G Lyon-Caen 'La crise du droit du travail', in *In Memoriam: Sir Otto Kahn-Freund,* München, 1980, p 517 (my translation).

favour of a purely 'financial' management (or 'monetarisation' one might say).[2] He pointed out the need to resort to a vocabulary of economics or sociology to describe what was new in the approach to labour. The 'translation' of the new situation into juridical terms had not yet been done.

Since this period, there have been elements of the crisis of labour in the enterprise which are common to all the Member States – the inexorable rise in unemployment to heights unheard of in almost half a century, the increasing economic concentration of capital and diversification of the legal forms of capital, the changes in the international division of labour affecting in similar ways the industrial economies of Western Europe. But these major changes have as yet not been wholly integrated into concepts of labour law. For example, lawyers in the UK, France and Italy all pointed out the inability of labour law to incorporate manpower policy, which in many cases vitally affected the then crucial legal problems of re-structuring labour in the enterprise.[3]

The difficulty is compounded at the European level. Despite any assertions of fundamental traits of European labour law and of common economic and social developments, the reality is one of great differences in State structures and national labour movements. It seems less than likely that similarities can be found in the labour law of the early 1980s of Italy – with a weak and unfriendly State and a strong and politicised though united labour movement – and of France – with a strong and friendly State, but a weak and politicised but divided trade union movement. Could workers' rights in the UK – with a strong and very hostile government, massive unemployment and a weakened labour movement – be similar to those in Sweden – with a powerful labour movement, relatively low open unemployment and a friendly government? And would any of these find parallels in the Federal Republic of Germany – with a federal system of government, in unfriendly hands, and a united trade union movement facing a rising level of unemployment?

The underlying question is whether the *differences* among national labour laws are more important than the *common* elements of a 'European' labour law, looked at over a longer historical period in different countries.[4] The answer suggested is that the 'European labour law' which evolved over the almost half century since the foundation of the European Communities is characterised by a variety of common strategies adopted at different moments. The evolution of European labour law is explored through an account of these different legal strategies. More detail will be provided of two strategies particularly relevant to contemporary developments: harmonisation and the European social dialogue.

The earliest strategy is that which characterised the founding of the European Coal and Steel Community in 1951: active labour market policy and labour involvement in regulation. In complete contrast, the following period was

---

2   'Rentabilité, rationalisation, restructuration sont les mots du jour', ibid, p 519. He insists that this is not a complete volte-face for a labour law always at the service of capitalist enterprise, and states: 'The absolute power of management by the head of the enterprise, as sole judge of the measures necessary for its progress, has always been the corner-stone of labour law'.

3   Lyon-Caen, ibid, at p 517; G Giugni, in *Prospettive del Diritto di Lavoro per gli Anni '80*, AID-LESS No 10, Bari 1982, at pp 34ff; Lord Wedderburn of Charlton 'Labour Law Now – a Hold and a Nudge', (1984) 13 *Industrial Law Journal* 73, at p 82.

4   See B Bercusson 'Workers' Rights in the Recession', in N Bruun (ed) *New Technology – A New Labour Law*, Congress papers presented at a symposium in Helsinki, November 1984, published by SAK (Finnish Trades Union Confederation), Helsinki 1985, pp 110–43.

characterised by a strategy of neo-liberal laissez-faire, reflected in the almost total absence of social policy and labour law provisions in the Treaty of Rome of 1957. This strategy was in turn replaced by an ambitious Social Action Programme adopted in 1974 which sought to harmonise labour legislation in the common market. The abrupt halt to this strategy caused by the election of a Conservative government in the UK in 1979 led to a search for a non-legislative strategy in the form of indirect financial instruments and the launching of the European social dialogue in 1985. The 1992 objective of the European Single Market led to pressures for a strategy to achieve a social dimension through fundamental social and economic rights. Most recently, the social dialogue strategy has been institutionalised in the Maastricht Protocol and Agreement on Social Policy.

What this history shows is the extraordinary range of legal strategies which have characterised attempts to construct a European labour law, and the struggles that have taken place among the Member States, the Community institutions and organised interest groups, primarily the social partners, in the course of developing these strategies.

THE EUROPEAN COAL AND STEEL COMMUNITY: ACTIVE LABOUR MARKET STRATEGY

The predecessor of the Treaty of Rome was the Treaty of Paris setting up the European Coal and Steel Community (ECSC) with the six Member State founder-members in 1951. This was designed to create a common market in coal and steel, essentially an economic, not a social policy objective. However, Article 2 of the Treaty of Paris made it one objective to contribute to the development of employment and improvement of the standard of living of the Member States. Article 3 stated that the purposes of the institutions of the new Community were 'to promote improved working conditions and an improved standard of living for the workers in each of the industries for which it is responsible'. Comparison may be made with Article 117 of the Treaty of Rome: 'Member States agree upon the need to promote improved working conditions and improved standards of living for workers . . .'

The objective of the 'employment policy' of the ECSC was *not* stability of employment but, on the contrary, the *adaptation* of workers to economic change. The creation of a common market in coal and steel meant closure of some plants and reconversion of others. The ECSC provided help to support the reconversion of enterprises and the redeployment of workers who lost their jobs. The idea was that workers ought not to have to bear the consequences of economic change which technical progress makes inevitable. Enterprises which are being transformed can be given temporary assistance to avoid the need to lay off their employees. And if they close down, wholly or partly, assistance can be given directly to the workers, to enable them to search for work elsewhere, or to retrain for other jobs.

The policy was not to protect jobs in the sense of offering stable employment: rather it was to accept technological change with all the implications for restructuring labour in the enterprise, including loss of employment, but without the workers suffering *financial* detriment. They must be helped to find other work or a different occupation: 'For stability of employment there was substituted a necessary *continuity* of employment, along with changes in work'.[5]

The Paris Treaty gave the ECSC High Authority powers to finance substantial resettlement schemes, including free vocational training. From 1954 to the end of 1971, some $333m had been spent, 50% by the High Authority and 50% by Member States to help 44,000 displaced coal and steel workers to find new jobs. The High Authority had a specific remit to help mobility by assisting in the finance of housing for coal and steel workers. By the end of 1974, more than 130,000 such houses had been financed by low-interest ECSC loans.

The decisions of management in restructuring the workforce must have been considerably influenced by the existence of the ECSC, all the more so when such industries became publicly owned, as in the UK. The 'labour law' component is to be found not only in the financial provisions relating to labour mobility, but also in two other aspects.

First, the attempt by France to insert into the Treaty of Paris a commitment to harmonise wages and social charges, arguing that higher wages and conditions and better social provision in France placed French industry in a disadvantageous competitive position. This was rejected by the other Member States, but Article 68 did authorise the High Authority to intervene if wage levels and social provisions led to a distortion of competition within the market. It has never been used.

Secondly, there was labour representation on the High Authority, the ECSC executive composed of nine members, which included a trade union representative. In addition, the High Authority was flanked by a Consultative Committee composed of employers' and workers' representatives, chosen from lists put forward by representative organisations. The High Authority was later dissolved into the EC Commission and Council, and the Consultative Committee into the Economic and Social Committee.

The remarkable quality of this European labour law and policy, combining active labour market policy with labour involvement in the mechanisms of adjustment, is highlighted by the contrast with what succeeded it in the Treaty of Rome.

THE EUROPEAN ECONOMIC COMMUNITY: A STRATEGY OF NON-INTERVENTION IN THE COMMON MARKET

The foundation of the European Economic Community by the same six Member States signing the Treaty of Rome in 1957 did not appear to represent an immediate and total break with the experience of the ECSC. The ECSC High Authority in the 1950s had set up two sector committees in coal and steel, involving the social partners, to do groundwork for harmonising working conditions. Their work was considered a success, so that the Commission of the European Economic Community during the 1960s established similar committees for other economic sectors.[6] Their purpose was to 'keep watch on economic and social developments in their sectors, seek to conclude model col-

---

5   G and A Lyon-Caen *Droit Social International et Européen*, 7ème ed, 1991, p 153
6   Between 1955 and 1982 eight had been set up, in coal, steel, agriculture, road transport, footwear, railways, sea fishing and inland navigation. C Brewster and P Teague *European Community Social Policy: Its Impact on the UK*, Institute of Personnel Management, 1989, pp 40–2.

lective agreements and submit programmes for Community action to institutions'.[7] This legacy was not to bear fruit for a considerable time.

In 1958, the Commission had begun to plan the implementation of Article 118 of the Treaty of Rome, which provided:

'Without prejudice to the other provisions of this Treaty and in conformity with its general objectives, the Commission shall have the task of promoting close cooperation between Member States in the social field, particularly in matters relating to:

- employment;
- labour law and working conditions;
- basic and advanced vocational training;
- social security;
- prevention of occupational accidents and diseases;
- occupational hygiene;
- the right of association, and collective bargaining between employers and workers.

To this end, the Commission shall act in close contact with Member States by making studies, delivering opinions and arranging consultations both on problems arising at national level and on those of concern to international organisations.

Before delivering the opinions provided for in this Article, the Commission shall consult the Economic and Social Committee.'

To this end, the Commission sought the opinions of representatives of the social partners in the six Member States and agreement was reached on a series of issues which would be the subject of detailed investigation by the Commission, to be followed by the social partners who would discuss the action to be taken. It is claimed that although consultations were time-consuming, 'they took place in an excellent atmosphere'. What happened next was described as follows:[8]

'Suddenly, several governments questioned the consultations with employers' and employees' organisations. This was the beginning of the most difficult period for the Commission in relation to social policy, a period which lasted for some years ... A solution was found on 18 December 1966, when, at a meeting in Brussels, the Council opted for a very modest form of ad hoc cooperation based on studies.'

What had happened was simply that the founding Member State governments had taken a clear position on social policy and were not going to allow the Commission to gainsay it.

Title III of the Treaty of Rome, 'Social Policy', contained only two chapters with only 12 articles. In the first Chapter on Social Provisions, this was expressed in the first of the six articles comprising the Chapter, Article 117, as follows:

'Member States agree upon the need to promote improved working conditions and an improved standard of living for workers, so as to make possible their harmonisation while the improvement is being maintained.

They believe that such a development will ensue not only from the functioning of the common market, which will favour the harmonisation of social systems, but also from the procedures provided for in this Treaty and from the approximation of provisions laid down by law, regulation or administrative action.'

---

7   Ibid, p 42. Only the Agricultural Workers Committee succeeded in concluding a 'Community Agreement'. This agreement stipulated that the hours worked by agricultural workers across the Community should be set at 44 hours. As agreements at the national level went much further than this stipulation, the general verdict is that it was not that important.

8   L H J Crijns 'The social policy of the European Community', *Social Europe* 1/88, p 51 at 53.

The Member States' decision, embodied in the Rome Treaty, was taken follow-ing two reports in 1956, one of a committee set up by the Member States (the Spaak Report) and another by a committee of experts from the International Labour Organisation (the Ohlin Report). Both reports recommended that there was no need for an interventionist social dimension for the proposed common market, save for certain measures against 'unfair competition'. The Member States' decision was:[9]

'. . . not because the drafters did not expect the Common Market to produce social benefits for the workers and citizens of the Member States. On the contrary. But these benefits were to be delivered through market mechanisms, not legislation. Legislation could be justified only where necessary to remove obstacles to the proper functioning of the market, and it was anticipated that such occasions for legis-lating would be few.'

The Community institutions were not to be permitted by the Member States in the Council of Ministers to use their initiative to counter this strategy. As put laconically by another author:[10]

'As early as 1959, the EEC Commission stressed that it could not conceive of a Community without social objectives and that it did not intend to place a narrow interpretation on the social provisions of the Treaty (in particular Article 117).

Moreover, by means of this declaration the Commission closes ranks with the European Parliament which, at its January 1959 part-session, invited the Governments of the Member States and the Commission to ensure the greatest possible improve-ment of social provisions and in particular of working conditions, whilst maintaining improvements already made.

However, it was not until 1971 that proposals began to emerge for a more system-atic approach to European social policy . . .'

What was left of social policy was that consistent with the common market: the free movement of labour. The first EC Regulation on free movement was Regulation 15 in 1961.[11] To oversee its implementation and advise the EC a Consultative Committee was established comprising two government officials from each Member State and two representatives from each of the social partners.

The other Chapter of Title III of the Treaty of Rome was Chapter 2 on 'The European Social Fund', the main function of which was 'to improve employ-ment opportunities for workers in the common market'.[12] The Social Fund was regarded as a weaker version of the training and retraining schemes established by the ECSC.[13] But, up to 1968, many interventions of the Social Fund were used to reskill redundant workers and encourage emigration to other parts of the EC. By the end of 1968, 543,000 Italian workers had been retrained, and 340,000 resettled in France and Germany. One evaluation concludes that the Social Fund had 'played a positive role in reducing the labour surplus problem inside one part of the Community'. But this was action always in the perspec-tive of easing free movement within a common market, an economic, not a social policy.[14]

9　P L Davies 'The Emergence of European Labour Law', in W McCarthy (ed) *Legal Intervention in Industrial Relations: Gains and Losses*, Blackwell, Oxford 1992, p 313 at 324–5.
10　L Wallyn *Social Europe*, 1/87, pp 13–14.
11　15 August 1961, JO p 1073/61.
12　Article 123; this chapter also had six articles, Articles 123–128.
13　Brewster and Teague, op cit, at p 51.
14　Ibid, pp 59–60.

Chapter 4

Harmonisation Strategy: the Social Action Programme 1974

INTRODUCTION: DISPUTED ORIGINS, INSPIRATION AND OBJECTIVES

The policy of non-intervention adopted by the founding Member States in 1957 was gradually being worn down by developments during the 1960s. The Commission was laying the foundations for a resurgent social policy by the accumulation of statistical information and comparative studies. It systematically maintained the link with social policy in forums dealing with other areas of policy.

New structures of the social partners emerged at European level, in particular, a European liaison body was established between the two strongest union federations in France and Italy, the CGT and the CGIL, which had not been active in the Community until then. This development was actively assisted by the Commission insisting on the involvement of the social partners as much as possible in the integration process in general and in social and economic policy in particular:[1]

> 'They were not only involved in the policy informally; formal structures were also created providing them with opportunities such as tripartite committees for the European Social Fund, for the free movement of employees, for vocational training, for the social security of migrant workers, the Standing Committee on Employment (established 14 December 1970) and a number of joint consultative committees on which the two sides were equally represented, to deal with social problems in specific sectors . . .'

The breakthrough came at the summit of the Heads of the Member States in Paris in October 1972, which concluded with the final communiqué that the Member States:

> 'attached as much importance to vigorous action in the social field as to the achievement of economic union . . . (and considered) it essential to ensure the increasing involvement of labour and management in the economic and social decisions of the Community.'

Accordingly, the Commission was instructed to draw up a Social Action Programme. By a Resolution adopted on 21 January 1974, the Council of Ministers approved the Social Action Programme involving over 30 measures over an initial period of 3–4 years.

1 *Social Europe* 1/88, p 54.

The explanation often put forward for the reversal of the policy of non-intervention is that presented by Michael Shanks, who became the Commissioner for Social Affairs responsible for the implementation of the Social Action Programme:[2]

> 'the major threat . . . was a political backlash . . . The Community has to be seen to be more than a device to enable capitalists to exploit the common market; otherwise it might not be possible to persuade the peoples of the Community to continue to accept the disciplines of the market.'

Another account stresses a variety of factors, worth quoting at length to illustrate the complexities of the evolution of social policy in the Community. The highlighting of the role of interest groups, particularly trade unions and employers' associations, and internal political changes *within* Member States, as well as the relations *between* the EC and Member State governments can shed light on the prospects for future shifts of policy:[3]

> 'First, there was a growing sense of urgency over the severe social strains in the Community. The Italians and French were particularly concerned about the growing social divide. The wave of student protests and worker strikes that swept through the industrialised West in 1968 and 1969 were especially acute in Italy and France. Germany and the Benelux countries were similarly, if less urgently, concerned with solving the underlying social problems . . .
>
> A second major factor . . . was the planned expansion of the Community. The decisions to include Norway, Denmark, the United Kingdom and Ireland meant that the EEC would henceforth include a more diverse set of social systems with a broad range of commercial and employment practices. Thus, future efforts to harmonise competition would need to increasingly focus on social aspects of the production process.
>
> A third incentive . . . evolved out of the political campaigns over EEC membership in the prospective Member States. The British public voted to join the Community by a very narrow margin, and the opposition Labour Party was committed to reversing this decision if elected. The Norwegian public voted in a referendum not to enter the EEC . . . It was therefore apparent that (the EEC) needed to put a human face on its role in European affairs.
>
> Finally, the shift in the EEC's agenda reflected political change within the Community's most influential nations. In Germany, Chancellor Willy Brandt was determined to reverse post-war German reluctance to exercise political power commensurate with its economic strength. Brandt had several reasons for making the development of an EEC social agenda an early goal of the new German political philosophy. He and his party, the Social Democrats, were committed to social progress, particularly in the employment field. In addition, the introduction of Community worker protection and worker rights legislation compatible with German legislation would undercut the argument of German employers that the proposed domestic legislation would reduce the competitiveness of German industry. Community employment legislation would also eliminate the incentive for employers to shift investment from Germany to other European countries. The retirement of French President Charles de Gaulle changed that country's whole attitude toward the Community. De Gaulle's successors proved to be less preoccupied with French autonomy and more committed to European integration.'

2   M Shanks 'The Social Policy of the European Communities' (1977) 14 *Common Market Law Review* 373 at 377; quoted in P L Davies, op cit, p 326; also Brewster and Teague, op cit, p 68. Nielsen and Szyszczak, op cit, p 41 concede 'there is some academic debate as to the motivation for the changes in social policy emphasis in the early 1970s'.

3   A L Sandler 'Players and Process: The Evolution of Employment Law in the EEC' (1985) 7 *Comparative Labor Law* 1 at pp 3–4.

To repeat the earlier judgment of the political inspiration of the Social Action Programme adopted by the Council of Ministers in 1974, the Commissioner charged with its implementation asserted that it:[4]

'. . . reflected a political judgment of what was thought to be both desirable and possible, rather than a juridical judgment of what were thought to be the social policy implications of the Rome Treaty.'

The three main objectives were, first, attainment of full and better employment in the Community, secondly, improvement of living and working conditions, and, thirdly, increased involvement of management and labour in the economic and social decisions of the Community and of workers in the life of undertakings.

The link between European labour *law* and social *policy* was unavoidable. Social policy had to be expressed through the law governing the common market, including a common market in labour. 'Harmonisation' was the magic word to achieve the desired synthesis. It was at once recognised, and yet resisted in a early review of the progress of harmonisation of labour law in the Community. This publication covered:[5]

'those aspects of the Community's social policy that would help bring about the alignment of various national rules and regulations. What it does not cover are the structural aspects of social policy that are implemented with the help of such resources as the Social Fund or the Regional Development Fund, eg, employment policy. We are trying to give the reader information about an important area of Community Social policy that is governed by legal instruments (Regulations, Directives or Recommendations).'

A similar dilemma was evident in an early discussion of a draft of the Directive on Collective Dismissals. The different viewpoints demonstrate the continuity of debates, as they reflect the national delegations' perspectives on the proposal then being formulated. As put by the UK delegation:

'the Commission proposal was not concerned with individual rights, but was an attempt to resolve problems arising in the employment market by a series of procedures aimed at reducing or eliminating the negative effects on the employment market caused by collective redundancies.'

The German delegation pointed out that the aim of the Community rules was less to afford increased protection for workers affected by mass dismissals than to establish criteria to ensure that the labour market worked properly. In contrast, the French delegation:[6]

'considered that the aim of the Directive should be to protect workers against collective dismissals. But the text proposed by the Commission . . . was more concerned with the interests of the undertakings.'

The strategy of harmonisation brought into sharp focus a number of central issues of EC labour law and social policy. Not least, the relation between them. But also, and perhaps most important, the inevitability of incorporating the

---

4   M Shanks *European Social Policy Today and Tomorrow* (1977) at p 13.
5   *The Stage Reached in Aligning Labour Legislation in the European Community*, Economic and Social Committee of the EC, Brussels 1978, p iv.
6   See *European Industrial Relations Review* No 2 (February 1974), p 2 at pp 3 and 5; No 4 (April 1974), p 18 at p 19.

industrial relations, and, in particular, the collective bargaining context into a policy of harmonisation.

These issues will be explored in this chapter through a general discussion of the problem of harmonisation of labour law in different industrial relations contexts regarding the problem of restructuring the labour force in the enterprise. Linked to this is a specific case study of formal labour law harmonisation: the Collective Dismissals Directive.

HARMONISATION OF LABOUR LAW

The starting point of a policy of harmonisation is the identification of a problem *common* to various European countries and the attempt to harmonise the law and practice relating to the problem. It emerges, however, that the identification of *common* problems, when related to the *varying* labour laws of selected national systems, does not produce a harmonised view of law and practice. This is the result of a combination of two factors.

First, where similar labour laws are invoked, their effects on different industrial relations systems give rise to variable results. This is mirrored in the *formal* successes of harmonisation policy (eg Directives), but in the variable consequences in practice of this formal success.

Secondly, different industrial relations systems mean that the national labour laws invoked to deal with the problem are different.[7] This has been a major obstacle at which progress towards harmonisation as a legal policy of the EC has been halted. For example, the minority statement from the employers' group (Group 1) on the Economic and Social Committee concerning the Vredeling proposals on worker participation concluded: 'The difficulty and inappropriateness of bringing all industrial relations within the Community into one framework given the existing differences between Member States is Group 1's fundamental objection to the proposed Directive'.[8]

Attempts to overcome this obstacle were made. The European Parliament's Social Affairs and Employment Committee revised the Vredeling proposals to provide for harmonising rules on employee workplace representation. This revised version required Member States to adopt uniform rules on the election of employee representatives in each Community subsidiary of a transnational/multi-plant undertaking with at least 50 employees and granted these representatives special rights to information and consultation. However, this proposal was rejected by the then Social Affairs Commissioner, Mr Ivor Richard, who was said to believe 'that the task of the "Vredeling" Directive is to ensure that workers are informed, not to reform national industrial relations systems'.[9]

---

7   The impact on national labour laws of not only differing industrial relations systems, but also of other differences in the environment affecting labour problems, leads to difficulties for harmonisation. For example, the comparative analysis by the Commission of the laws of the Member States relating to employees' claims in the event of the employers' insolvency distinguished three main systems of *commercial* practice relevant to the problem. See *European Industrial Relations Review* No 47 (November 1977), p 21.
8   See *European Industrial Relations Review* No 98 (March 1982), p 24 at p 25.
9   See *European Industrial Relations Review* No 100 (May 1982), p 6; No 107 (December 1982), p 2; and no 109 (February 1983), p 21.

Each of the two problem areas for harmonisation policy will now be examined: that arising from differing industrial relations contexts, and that arising from differing formal labour laws.

The issue to illustrate these two problems will be that which was at the centre of attention in the European Community during the 1970s' strategy of harmonisation: restructuring the labour force in the enterprise. The context existing during that period will be described to illustrate the challenges facing the European Community's attempts to harmonise labour law on this issue.

Harmonisation and industrial relations context: the case of restructuring labour in the enterprise

The general problem of restructuring the labour force in the enterprise in practice is composed of a multitude of component problems: redundancy and alternatives to dismissal, redeployment and job and income security (deskilling and downgrading). Different industrial relations systems have radically different effects on a national approach to these problems through labour law.

Redundancy and alternatives to dismissal

The ability of employers to declare redundancies will be affected by the nature and level of *trade union organisation and collective bargaining* in different industries or different countries. A policy on plant closures will vary in its form and impact depending on the strength and unity of trade union organisation – regardless of legal provisions.

For example, in 1978 an international survey of short-time, lay-off and redundancy provisions in the textile industry of eight countries (Belgium, Denmark, France, Germany, Italy, Netherlands, UK and Sweden) found that, with the exception of Germany and the UK, there were single industry collective agreements covering all the various sectors of the textile industry. In Germany, negotiations took place on the regional rather than the national level, whereas in the UK there were numerous separate negotiating groups or sectors.[10]

Similarly, *State policy in the manpower and industrial field* (particularly the politically acceptable level of unemployment) will affect redundancy policy, apart from labour law: for example, a policy of public subsidies to employers who lay off employees during times of recession – as an alternative to redundancies and in order to enable employers to retain trained labour.[11] The differences between French solidarity contracts (State–company agreements providing subsidies) and Italian solidarity contracts (trade union–company agreements subsidised by State funds) have attracted comment.[12]

In particular, provisions as to lay-offs and short-time working. An OECD study examined the position in eleven countries and concluded that three

---

10 See *European Industrial Relations Review* No 51 (March 1978), p 7.
11 See the ten country survey in *European Industrial Relations Review* No 111 (April 1983), p 15; also the four country study (Belgium, France, UK and Germany) of the effects of early retirement schemes, which highlighted how some publicly financed schemes make manpower restructuring easier; *European Industrial Relations Review* No 143 (December 1985), p 20.
12 See eg *European Industrial Relations Review* No 116 (September 1983), p 7.

groups of countries could be distinguished. Those in the first group, including the UK, 'tend to discourage the use of partial unemployment, severely restricting compensation for a reduction in daily or weekly hours of work'. The second group, including Germany, is characterised as 'being neutral from the point of view of the choice which may be made between redundancy, reduction in daily hours of work and the use of temporary lay-offs, when economic activity is reduced'. The third group, including France and Italy, are placed in an 'intermediate position'. In these countries, either lay-offs (Italy) or reduction in daily working hours (France) may be encouraged.[13]

Not least, if among the most difficult to establish, there is the difference between *managerial styles* which determines responses to similar labour restructuring problems. For example, with respect to those arising from the introduction of new technology, a report on developments in Germany concluded:[14]

'Technical innovations do not result directly in personnel changes. Rather, such changes depend on a company's personnel policy – its prerequisites, objectives and the instruments applied ... (if flexibility is a principle of personnel policy), technical and organisational changes in a company do not become directly evident as the reason for changes in the workforce (reduction of the workforce, selection of personnel).'

Conversely, the dismissal of employees for 'individual' reasons by introducing stricter standards, closer supervision and severe discipline is not unknown in the UK as a prelude to major changes with personnel implications.

The *composition of the labour force* may affect selection, along the lines identified by dual labour market theory: secondary workers go first. This has already given rise to legal problems with respect to the selection of part-timers (mostly women) for redundancy, and the restrictions imposed by rules on equal treatment.[15] Again, the *structure of trade unions or workers' organisations at plant level*, whether divided along craft, political, or manual/non-manual lines can affect selection procedures.

Redeployment

The *structure of employing organisations* will be critical in policies of redeployment.[16] For example, the problems of non-EC employers with undertakings in

---

13   B Grais *Lay-Offs and Short-Time Working in Selected OECD Countries*, OECD, 1983, p 11.
14   F Bohl and K Dull *Changes in Organisation, Employment and Worker Representation*, Commission Doc V/507-83-EN, Brussels, July 1982, p 1. In the FRG, therefore, the authors found that: 'Although comprehensive technical and organisational changes by all means take place, they hardly become evident as the cause for a reduction of the workforce. Rather, such reductions in the number of employees are generally justified by economic factors (decrease in the number of orders received, etc) and the termination of employees for personal and behavioural reasons and "voluntary" fluctuation). In principle, this situation is the result of company strategies intended to divorce a company's personnel policy from its technical and organisational changes' (p 3).
15   In the UK, contrast the decisions in *Clarke and Powell v Eley (IMI) Kynoch Ltd* [1982] IRLR 482, EAT, and *Kidd v DRG (UK) Ltd* [1985] IRLR 190, EAT. Cf the selection of older workers in redundancy situations, which has been the subject of attention in the Netherlands and Germany.
16   For discussion of how flexibility of labour is affected by the structure of firms at different levels in an industry, see J Rubery, F Wilkinson and R Tarling 'Flexibility in the use of labour and fixed wage-costs', in *EEC Labour Market Studies*, by the University of Cambridge for the EC Commission, Doc V/621-83-EN, at pp 16–20 and 34–38.

the Community and of EC-based companies with employees in non-Member States raise conflicts of laws issues in labour law. The Commission made an early attempt to tackle these issues in the proposals for the Directive on protection of workers in the event of their employers' insolvency.[17]

The problems were clearly recognised with respect to the Vredeling proposals on workers' participation. The Economic and Social Committee's Opinion on the proposed Directive acknowledged that:[18]

'The principles on which information and consultation are based do not change as the structure becomes more complex; but the procedures become more complicated, and determining which information is relevant and which decisions affect which employees becomes more difficult as the number of establishments – or countries in which a firm operates – grows.'

The controversy over the identification of a 'decision-making centre' for the purpose of imposing obligations on employers to disclose information and consult with employee representatives illustrates the problems presented by complex employer legal structures.[19]

Restructuring of labour, in light of the (average) *size of enterprises* might be so concentrated in its impact that the focus of policy ought not, perhaps, to be the enterprise, but the community. This emerged from an OECD conference which looked to the effects of import penetration on employment: 'in view of the stark effects of trade displacements on communities in declining regions, a community-based approach, embodying the best elements of several different programmes, is vital for such areas.'[20]

Deskilling and downgrading

The *structure of the union movement* and particularly the divisions between skilled and unskilled, manual and non-manual workers has attracted much comment with respect to the problems of restructuring which affect the skills of workers. This will be more difficult when unions are organised on craft lines with strict demarcation than where general or industrial unions predominate. For example, in the UK, manual workers' unions tended not to negotiate 'new technology' agreements, and rather relied on traditional collective bargaining. New technology agreements were overwhelmingly the province of unions representing non-manual staff.[1]

An Anglo-German study concluded 'that the German trade unions ought organisationally to be better equipped to handle technological change than their British counterparts; it is less clear that they are'; the study focused rather

17 See *European Industrial Relations Review* No 53 (May 1978), p 21.

18 See text in *European Industrial Relations Review* No 53 (May 1978), p 21.

19 See the definition in the original draft Vredeling Directive, *European Industrial Relations Review* No 82 (November 1980), p 22: 'The place where the management of an undertaking actually performs its functions' [Article 2(c)]. A policy oriented definition is indicated, eg in the area of accident prevention by Directive 82/501/EEC on major accident hazards from certain industrial activities, which focuses on the 'manufacturer', defined as 'any person in charge of an industrial activity' [Article 1(2) (b)]; *European Industrial Relations Review* No 96 (January 1982), p 23.

20 J B Bolger 'The employment and adjustment implications of international trade', in *Employment Growth and Structural Change*, OECD, 1985, p 18 at p 20.

1 See *European Industrial Relations Review* No 102 (July 1982), p 25 at p 26.

on the inadequacy of existing bargaining structures in both countries.[2]

A report of the European Trade Union Institute on new technology noted that 'the tendency is for the introduction of microelectronics to lead to a polarisation in employment between semi-skilled operatives on the one hand and highly skilled technical staff on the other, with a disappearance of employment for skilled manual workers'.[3] An Italian trade union official is quoted as saying that new technology strikes at the heart of Italy's union movement, because shop-floor representatives are elected by and from workers employed on similar tasks. Fragmentation of tasks with new technology breaks up the solidarity of the Italian system, and is used by management to undermine collective bargaining and union authority.[4] A similar conclusion was reported in Britain by a survey of the literature on the impact of information technology on workers' bargaining power: 'the problem with any new technology or rationalisation is that it breaks up existing shop floor work groups. In Britain, workers' bargaining strength has traditionally been concentrated at this level'.[5]

The extent of downgrading would vary with the rigidity and complexity of job or wage structures (eg the frequency of the use of job evaluation), the scope of union protection and the degree of government intervention. One comparison of the employment effects of the restructuring of the steel industry in France and Germany highlighted various differences in the national industrial relations systems.

For instance, the German steel industry is mainly privately owned, whereas the two French steel companies (USINOR and SACILOR) are both State-owned. IG Metall and other trade unions organise about 90% of the workforce, negotiating a sector-level agreement supplemented by many regional agreements, whereas the five nationally recognised trade unions in France (CGT, CFDT, FO, CGC and CFTC) have organised only about 20% of the workforce. The German government believed in non-interference, whereas the French government had wide-ranging interventionist plans for the industry.

So, for example, in the German industry, IG Metall negotiated for redeployment, and for arrangements to guarantee the earnings of redeployed workers at the same level as that of their former jobs. In France, workers made redundant could receive temporary wage guarantees should they accept a job elsewhere which pays a wage lower than their former wage; these guarantees being financed 25% by the industry and 75% by the government.[6]

Conclusion

National labour laws may all address a common set of problems, but when refracted through different industrial relations systems, two alternatives tend to result.

2 Jim Conway Memorial Foundation, Cleveland, report for the EC Commission on *New Technology and Changes in Industrial Relations,* Commission Doc V/509-83-EN, Brussels, paragraph 4.4.7, pp 60–1 and Chapter 4 generally (pp 43–62).
3 Quoted in *European Industrial Relations Review* No 72 (January 1980), p 25 at p 26.
4 Matteo Rollier, in *European Industrial Relations Review* No 73 (February 1980), p 6 at p 7.
5 A Friedman *Managerial, Organisational and Industrial Relations Implications of Advances in Data Processing and Information Technology: Survey of Research,* unpublished report for the Social Science Research Council, UK (ref HG 1314/11), March 1983, at pp 26–7.
6 See *European Industrial Relations Review* No 132 (January 1985), p 17.

One is that *formally similar* laws emerge as very different in their practical operation.[7] Alternatively, the different industrial relations systems dictate *different labour law* approaches to the common problem.[8]

The fragmentation of the general problem of restructuring labour into a multitude of component problems exacerbates the difficulties of an EC strategy of harmonisation. Different countries may choose to focus on different subsets of problems, and a single country may change the focus of its attention over time.

For example, a review in January 1979 of rationalisation agreements in Germany highlighted a shift from the 'classical' approach (which emphasised consultation, transfers to similar jobs, retraining and income protection) to a new approach which focused on protection from downgrading and a fear of technological deskilling.[9] Whereas 'social plans' in the 1960s dealt primarily with severance payments, by the end of the 1970s the emphasis had shifted to transfer provisions, wage guarantees and early retirement options as well.[10]

Efforts at harmonisation might well balk at the daunting task of choosing, from among the multiplicity of problems (redundancy, redeployment and so on) and the different legal responses to them in various national industrial relations contexts, a single strand of labour law which could be uniformly drafted. The attempts – via Directives on Collective Redundancies, etc – appear daring to so boldly select at least one major issue, while catering only incidentally, or not at all, for important associated issues.

For example, the amended proposal for a Directive 'on the harmonisation of the legislation of the Member States relating to collective redundancies' presented to the Council by the Commission on 1 November 1973 provided that consultation of workers' representatives:[11]

'should cover in particular:

- the possibilities of avoiding or reducing the proposed dismissals,
- what criteria to apply when deciding which workers to dismiss,
- the possibility of giving other jobs in the same enterprise to workers threatened with dismissals, whether by retraining, by transfer to another part of the enterprise or by amending their conditions of employment,
- possibly, compensation for reductions in salary and other benefits,

---

7   This should not be exaggerated, of course. For instance, consider the discussion of the problems arising from the various definitions of the phrase 'pressing business reasons' justifying dismissal under a draft of the Acquired Rights Directive. The Commission recognised the 'elastic definition of this concept' and refused to define it, leaving it to the courts of the Member States, an approach criticised by the European Parliament (see *European Industrial Relations Review* No 5 (May 1974), p 9 at p 13 and No 13 (January 1975), p 6). In contrast, in a report to the Council on legislation concerning individual dismissals, the Commission concluded that 'all Member States would appear to accept that a reduction in the volume of business or the introduction of rationalisation measures, that is, economic grounds, are sufficient justification for dismissal' (see *European Industrial Relations Review* No 30 (June 1976), p 21.

8   For example, an Anglo-German comparative study which highlighted the contrast between the 'voluntaristic' (yet 'adversarial') industrial relations system of the UK with the 'legalistic' (yet 'cooperative') system of the FRG. See the report on *New Technology and Changes in Industrial Relations* by the Jim Conway Memorial Foundation, Cleveland, for the EC Commission, Doc V/509-83-EN, pp 7–10.

9   See *European Industrial Relations Review* No 60 (January 1979), p 14.

10   See *European Industrial Relations Review* No 83 (December 1980), p 6.

11   Article 4(2).

- measures to be taken in favour of workers to be dismissed, in particular with regard to the possibility of severance grants and priority for re-employment,
- procedural details, in particular the staggering of dismissals.'

This list was later dropped.[12] The great gaps left in workers' protection despite this initiative on redundancy dismissals were adverted to in a report by the Commission to the Council in 1976 which stated:[13]

'. . . the Commission considers it necessary to work towards an improvement of Member States' legislation in favour of the workers affected by individual dismissals and towards the approximation of such legislation while the improvement is being maintained within the meaning of Article 117 of the Treaty in order to provide a logical and meaningful supplement to the measures for the protection of workers contained in the Council Directive of 17.2.75 on the approximation of the laws of the Member States relating to collective redundancies.'

Harmonisation and formal labour law provisions: a case study of the Collective Redundancies Directive 1975

As a case study of attempts at harmonisation of labour law and their consequences in different industrial relations contexts, this section examines the Directive on Collective Redundancies.[14] The questions addressed include: does experience of this Directive point to successful harmonisation only of the *form* of law, or also of its *substance*, as manifested in industrial relations practice? To what extent was the Directive implemented in different forms, reflecting different industrial relations systems, in order to achieve *substantive* harmonisation, and to what extent was this successful?

At an early stage of its formulation, an Explanatory Statement accompanying the amended proposal for a Council Directive on the harmonisation of the legislation of the Member States relating to mass dismissals stated that comparison of national provision on dismissals showed notable *differences* as regards conditions and procedures and the measures taken to lessen the negative consequences of dismissal for workers. Reflecting the imperatives of the Rome Treaty, this was said to have:[15]

'. . . a direct effect on the functioning of the Common Market in so far as they create disparities in conditions of competition which are likely to influence the decisions by enterprises, whether national or multinational, on the distribution of the posts they have to be filled. It must for example be expected that any firm intending to reorganise itself by a plan including the partial or total closedown of certain departments, will decide which departments to close down on the basis, at least in part, of the level of protection offered to the workers.'

The statement went on to maintain the necessity of eliminating known disparities by harmonising the relevant national provisions.

It is interesting to note that the statement was careful to insist that the initiative to harmonise legislation did not imply that the autonomy of management

12   See *European Industrial Relations Review* No 2 (February 1974), p 2 at p 3; No 7 (July 1974), p 2 at p 3
13   See *European Industrial Relations Review* No 30 (June 1976), p 21 at p 25.
14   Directive No 75/129 of 17 February 1975, OJ L48/29 of 22.2.1975.
15   See text in *European Industrial Relations Review* No 1 (January 1974), p 18.

and labour would be called in question. Harmonisation was not the only consideration. Social policy considerations applied also. Hence:[16]

> '... systematic joint action by management, the authorities and workers' representatives is the best method of obtaining Community regulations of mass dismissals which will best serve their dual purpose – of providing social protection and acting as an economic regulator.'

Before and after the 1975 Directive

National legal provision *prior* to the 1975 Directive was extremely varied. This can be shown by a brief review of the legal position *prior* to the Directive in five Member States: Italy, France, the UK, Germany and Belgium.

In *Italy* it was said that the main procedures were very much in line with the Directive's provisions, albeit taking a very different legal form.[17] At that stage, the employees' position with regard to collective dismissals was safeguarded by criteria established in a General Agreement of 1966 between the main union and employers' confederations. Collective dismissals 'in a redundancy situation' were first regulated by an Ordinance of 14 July 1960, which itself incorporated the terms of a general agreement between employers and unions made on 20 December 1950. But in February 1966, the Constitutional Court had declared that the Ordinance contravened the Italian Constitution. To clarify the position, a new general agreement was drawn up on 5 May 1966, initially intended to run for some two years, but in the event it ran on unamended.

Under the 1966 Agreement, companies with 10 or more employees were required to inform district unions of decisions to reduce the workforce and provide certain other information. On receipt of such information, union officials could, within 7 days, invite management to a meeting for discussions, limited to 25 days' duration (15 for firms of under 100 employees), during which period no dismissals could be put into effect. If dismissals were to take place, selection operated in accordance with certain criteria.

In practice, companies either used this procedure or simply notified the factory council. In the latter case, the union representatives would usually seek a legal ruling under the Workers' Statute 1970 to the effect that the individual dismissals would be without 'just cause'. If successful, the workers would be reinstated and management would then follow the correct procedure under the 1966 Agreement. The position in practice as it then stood was summarised as follows:[18]

> '... one of the most notable and recurring problems for workers and their representatives in these redundancy situations, is the difficulty of counteracting a management decision that staff reductions are necessary. The company is able to demonstrate that a critical situation has arisen on the basis of its own knowledge of the situation, whereas the unions may be unaware of all the facts.'

In *Germany* at the time of the enactment of the Directive, it was said that the protection afforded to employees in a redundancy situation was even stronger than that provided by the Directive.[19] The relevant German legislation was the

16   Ibid, at p 19.
17   See the account in *European Industrial Relations Review* No 16 (April 1975), p 14.
18   Ibid, at p 16.
19   See *European Industrial Relations Review* No 18 (June 1975), p 12.

Protection Against Dismissals Act of 1969 and the Works Council Act of 1972 (amending the 1951 Act). The 1969 Act protected individual workers against 'socially unjustified dismissals' and specified methods of objecting to such dismissals. The law obliged the employer to inform the Regional Department of Labour in the event of mass redundancies, providing reasons for the dismissals and including the opinion of the Works Council. The Department could delay the dismissals up to two months. The actual decision to defer particular dismissals is taken by a tripartite committee of the Labour Department.

The 1972 Act, while very much in line with the Directive in providing for pre-redundancy consultation procedures, went one stage further by providing for the formulation of redundancy schemes or 'social plans', to be drawn up in negotiations between the Works Council and the employer. The social plan (covering who is to be made redundant, when the dismissals are to take effect, the level of redundancy payments) has the status of a plant agreement. If no agreement is reached, provisions exist for mediation and eventually a social plan can be imposed by a Conciliation Board.

In practice, however, it was said at the time that many employers chose to avoid the extensive consultations with the Works Council by offering instead large lump sum payments to workers who voluntarily accepted redundancies:[20]

'... although a programme of voluntary redundancies may still be costly to the employers, it has generally been found to be a speedier and less hazardous alternative to notified collective redundancies ... With higher levels of unemployment, however, the financial burden which is incurred with collective dismissals has made it necessary for firms to rethink their policies and introduce voluntary redundancy, or reduce their work-force at a slower pace by means of natural wastage.'

In *France*, it was only a new law of 3 January 1975 which brought French legislation into line with the Directive.[1] Since 1945 there had been a requirement on employers in the commercial and industrial sectors to obtain prior authorisation for redundancies from the Regional Department of Labour. It was acknowledged, however, that the requirement had rarely been observed in practice. The new legislation strengthened the provisions and provided penal sanctions for non-compliance.

In addition, a law of 13 July 1973 imposed on firms employing more than 10 people obligations with respect to individual redundancies, including a meeting with the employee and Labour Inspector. Moreover, the French Employers' Confederation (CNPF) agreed with the trade unions in November 1974 that the Works Council should be informed of proposed individual redundancies. Where more than 10 redundancies within 30 days are proposed, the 1974 agreement provided for information to be disclosed for the purposes of consultation with the Works Council, which can then delay the final decision. The 1975 legislation implemented many of the collectively agreed requirements, though at the time it was stated: 'It is too early to say whether the penal sanctions introduced by the 1975 Act will be effective'.[2]

In the *UK* the only legislation on redundancy prior to 1975 was the Redundancy Payments Act 1965, which provided some compensation to workers losing their jobs in a redundancy situation. The gap was not filled by collective

20   Ibid, at pp 12–13.
1   *European Industrial Relations Review* No 19 (July 1975), p 10.
2   Ibid, at p 9.

bargaining. A 1968 survey found that only a quarter of establishments with 500 or more employees had a formal written agreement with trade unions over redundancy; a further quarter had a more informal understanding.[3] A Code of Practice accompanying the Industrial Relations Act 1971 laid down certain points of guidance including: 'Responsibility for deciding the size of the work force rests with management. But before taking the final decision to make any substantial reduction, management should consult employees or their representatives, unless exceptional circumstances make this impossible'; it also recommended notification of the Department of Employment about impending redundancies.[4]

The non-legally binding provisions of the Code of Practice were given statutory backing by the Employment Protection Act 1975, s 99, which, in compliance with the Directive, made consultation and notification mandatory when redundancies are proposed. In 1977, a survey found that half of all establishments having 50–5,000 employees had a formal agreement with trade unions over redundancy, and a further quarter had a less formal understanding. There appeared to have been a very substantial increase in the extent of redundancy agreements over the ten-year period between 1968–77.[5] How much of this preceded, or is attributable to the Directive is unclear.

In *Belgium* the legal position prior to the Directive was governed by two principal sets of legal provisions. First, an Act of 28 June 1966[6] included the requirement that those responsible for undertakings disclose information to the public authorities, to the chairmen of joint industrial committees of union and employer representatives, as well as to the workers affected by any closure decision. The joint industry committees under the Act had the responsibility, inter alia, for 'determining the methods whereby prior notice is to be given to the authorities and bodies concerned and to the workers affected, in the event of the closure of an undertaking' (Article 3). Secondly, on 8 May 1973, Belgium's major union and employers' confederations reached a national agreement on collective redundancies within the framework of the National Labour Council. This agreement was subsequently extended to non-signatories and given legal force by its conversion into a Royal Decree on 6 August 1973. The Decree provided, inter alia, that Works Councils (or in their absence, union shop stewards) must be informed in advance of any collective redundancy. This information must 'give rise to an exchange of views during which the workers' representatives will make known their observations and suggestions'.

Shortly following the Directive, on 2 October 1975, two new national agreements were reached within the framework of the National Labour Council. The second of these replaced and extended the provisions relating to disclosure of information in the Agreement of 8 May 1973 by requiring that where an employer decides to carry out a collective redundancy, he has to inform the workers' representatives of his decision and follow this up with consultations: 'the

3 S R Parker et al *Effects of the Redundancy Payments Act*, Office of Population Censuses and Surveys (OPCS), HMSO, London 1971.

4 The Industrial Relations Code of Practice 1972, paragraphs 44 and 46(i).

5 W W Daniel and E Stilgoe *The Impact of Employment Protection Laws* (1978) pp 21–3. See generally, B Bercusson, Chapter 2 ('Employment Protection'), in C D Drake and B Bercusson *The Employment Acts 1974–1980* (1981) pp 22–7.

6 This Act was extended and modified by Acts of 30 June 1967 and 28 July 1971. See *European Industrial Relations Review* No 23 (November 1975), p 8, from which the following account is derived.

consultations shall deal with the possibility of avoiding and reducing the collective redundancy as well as alleviating its consequences' (Article 6). To this end, the employer is obliged to provide any useful information.

The interesting fact about the changes in Belgian law following the Directive is that the review which set out the information above concluded by commenting:[7]

'Despite the variety of these changes they are not, in general, expected to have a great impact on those involved with collective redundancies in Belgium . . .

Belgian unions . . . do not foresee any great change in the procedures governing collective redundancies as a consequence of bringing the country into line with EC rules. For example, Mr Grynberg, an official of the FGTB – the country's major socialist-orientated union federation – [said] that as far as disclosure of information was concerned, only smaller firms where there is a low level of unionisation (and consequently little pressure of improving provisions beyond nationally agreed or statutory minima) are likely to be affected.'

The legal position after the Directive

The legal position in the various Member States in the period after the date when they were required to implement the Directive through national legislation (10 February 1977) does not indicate complete harmony. A review in March 1978 of redundancy provisions in the textile industry in the five countries reviewed above showed the following:[8]

BELGIUM	FRANCE	GERMANY	ITALY	UK
There will generally be prior consultations with the Works Council, but no set procedures as regards the order of redundancies.	There will generally be prior discussions with the worker(s) but no set procedures as regards the order of redundancies.	No set procedures as regards the order of redundancies.	Established selection criteria take account of various factors.	No set procedures as regards the order of redundancies but LIFO[9] is usual.

The differences evident here with respect to consultation and selection procedures are found also in the provisions on financial compensation for those selected for dismissal in a redundancy situation.[10]

---

7   Ibid, at p 10. This despite the official's pointing out that the number of collective redundancies had increased dramatically during the previous few months. For an account of how redundancies were handled in the Belgian textile industry some two years later, see *European Industrial Relations Review* No 46 (October 1977), p 18, which highlights the importance of laws on short-time working and work-sharing, as well as the law on unemployment benefit.

8   Extracted from the survey in *European Industrial Relations Review* No 51 (March 1978), p 7.

9   LIFO = last in – first out.

10   A ten country survey in 1980 found that, in most countries, special redundancy payments only become available in a 'collective redundancy' situation, where significant numbers of workers are to be made redundant. However, in France and the UK (as well as Ireland) workers are entitled to special payments in an individual redundancy situation; *European Industrial Relations Review* No 75 (April 1980), p 14.

Another survey of provisions on collective dismissals in 1980, three years after the compliance date, revealed the following differences at the level of *formal* law, let alone at the level of practice:[11]

BELGIUM	FRANCE	GERMANY	ITALY	UK
1. Definition of 'collective dismissal'				
Dismissal for 'economic and technical' reasons.	Dismissal on 'one or more grounds not attributable to the workers themselves'.	Dismissal for 'urgent operating requirements'.	No statutory definition; but collective agreement refers to changes in organisation and production.	Where employers' requirement for employees has ceased or diminished.
2. Procedures prior to dismissal				
Consultation and discussions; representatives to be given information; notify regional labour office. Note: special provisions on closures.	(10 or more workers): consult and give 'all useful information'; inform Labour Inspectorate; wait for a 'reflection period'; request Labour Inspectorate authorisation.	Consult and ascertain works council opinion; and notify local labour office.	Unions can call meeting for discussions; union regional office to be given information. Note: regional labour office may intervene.	Consultation; employer must consider union views and provide information; notify Department of Employment.
3. Payments				
Special payment as of right in collective dismissals.	No special statutory payments but individual dismissal payments.	Special negotiable payments if collective dismissal.	No special statutory payments, but recourse to *cassa integrazione guadagni.*	No special statutory payments for collective dismissals but individual redundancy payments.

A similar survey three years later indicated that only France had instituted changes in the procedures applicable, and that in Italy there was a legally

11   Extracted from the survey in *European Industrial Relations Review* No 76 (May 1980), p 19.

enforceable collective agreement for the industrial sector defining the circumstances of a collective dismissal.[12] As to compliance with the requirements of the Directive, only Italy has been subject to a finding by the European Court of Justice (in June 1982) that it failed to comply with the Directive's requirements.[13]

Conclusion

Prior to the Directive, there was some law concerning collective dismissals, and there was considerable established industrial practice, depending on union strength and circumstances. But there was considerable variation, both among the laws of different countries, and within countries, between law and practice.

After the Directive had been promulgated, there was considerably more law on collective dismissals, but again there were considerable divergences between the laws in terms of their detailed requirements and wording. Similarly, whatever the legal changes that may have occurred consequent upon the Directive, there is some doubt as to its effect upon established industrial custom and practice concerning collective redundancies. Where this was less well established (as in the UK), there may have been changes. Where the law and practice were already well established (as in Germany), there was little. In conclusion, it is difficult to describe this process as, or ascribe it to, a wholly effective policy of harmonisation of labour law in the European Community.

---

12   *European Industrial Relations Review* No 109 (February 1983), p 12.
13   Case 91/81: *EC Commission v Italian Republic* [1982] ECR 2133. See the account in *European Industrial Relations Review* No 104 (September 1982), p 19.

Chapter 5

Strategies to Outflank the UK Veto: Financial Instruments and Qualified Majority Voting Procedures

INTRODUCTION

The Commission's strategy of harmonising legislation was premised on the assumption that the Member States would approve the measures proposed unanimously. This was a prerequisite of the legal basis proposed for these measures: Articles 100[1] and/or Article 235[2] of the Treaty of Rome. The election of a Conservative government in the UK in 1979 put an end to the Commission's strategy. In line with its domestic policy on labour law, ostensibly deregulation, the UK would not agree to further initiatives on labour law at Community level.

Two strategies were developed to maintain and continue Community social policy and labour law. The first was the use of indirect financial instruments to promote social policy initiatives and to further labour law objectives. The principal instrument was the European Social Fund, which took on a new dynamism in the 1980s. The second strategy involved amending the Treaty of Rome to allow for qualified majority voting on social policy issues. This culminated in the Single European Act 1986.

INDIRECT FINANCIAL INSTRUMENTS: THE EUROPEAN SOCIAL FUND

A principal instrument of the new social policy was the European Social Fund (ESF). The Fund goes back to the very origins of the Community.[3] The 1951 Treaty setting up the ECSC envisaged cash aids to workers whose firms were

---

1 Article 100 (first paragraph):
    'The Council shall, acting unanimously on a proposal from the Commission, issue directives for the approximation of such provisions laid down by law, regulation or administrative action in Member States as directly affect the establishment or functioning of the common market.'
2 Article 235 (first paragraph):
    'If action by the Community should prove necessary to attain, in the course of the operation of the common market, one of the objectives of the Community and this Treaty has not provided the necessary powers, the Council shall, acting unanimously on a proposal from the Commission and after consulting the European Parliament, take the appropriate measures.'
3 European File 2/84, January 1984.

closed or restructured. Since the 1960s the ECSC has supported projects which aim to maintain the income of such workers at a reasonable level and assist them to retrain and find new jobs, if necessary, in different areas.

The scale of Community cash aid increased sharply in 1981 when it took part in emergency measures – such as early retirement schemes – designed to soften the impact of the massive restructuring of the steel industry. In 1983 113 m ECU was spent on emergency action of this kind, benefiting about 110,000 people. In the same year, the traditional ECSC retraining aids totalled 115 m ECU and assisted about 33,500 coal and steel workers.

The Treaty of Rome copied and extended the activities of the ECSC in this area. The Treaty provided for the creation of a Social Fund 'to improve employment opportunities for workers in the common market and to contribute thereby to raising the standard of living'.[4] The aim was to compensate certain groups of people for the difficulties caused by the economic changes resulting from the creation of a common market. Between 1960 and 1973 more than 1.5 million workers were helped in this way.

But for a variety of reasons (its weighty procedures and limited aims especially) the European Social Fund was not wholly successful in this first stage. The Fund was revised in 1971 and began activities in its new form on 1 May 1972. The types of activities funded increased considerably. Instead of continuing, as at first, simply to refund Member States for their own efforts, the Social Fund has increasingly supported policies identified as priorities at Community level.

Significantly, major change in the Social Fund came with the massive increase in its budget in the early 1980s. In 1983, the Social Fund budget was 1.76 billion ECU. In 1982 it had already reached 1.58 billion ECU, or 5.8% of the total Community budget. This represented a 42.4% increase on 1981 and a 270% increase on 1978.

Nevertheless, because of the recession, the gap between demand and available funds is still large. In 1982 only 55% of eligible requests were met. On 17 October 1983, Employment and Social Affairs Ministers of the Ten Member States adopted new regulations to guide Social Fund policy from 1984 onwards. Whilst safeguarding the interests of priority regions, the revised Fund was to concentrate principally on job promotion for young people. Special efforts were also to be made to develop small and medium-sized businesses. The share of the Fund devoted to pilot projects and experimental programmes in the battle against unemployment was also to increase sharply to 5% of the total.

The Social Fund concentrated on eight areas: problem regions, the young, the handicapped, migrants, women, adaptation of industry to technical progress, textiles and agriculture. The Social Fund aids technical progress and the modernisation of firms in all branches of the economy. Projects have included the training and retraining of car, telecommunications and newspaper workers. The Fund also helps to pay for the technical updating of the production and management methods of small and medium-sized businesses, as well as protection of jobs threatened by the introduction of new technologies. In expanding sectors, such as information technology, the Fund pays for the training of workers for

4   Article 123.

genuinely new jobs. In 1982, the Fund gave 58.5 m ECU to programmes of this kind, assisting 35,400 people.

In the textile and clothing industries, and others where restructuring has meant large-scale redundancies (shipbuilding, for instance), assistance is also provided by the Fund. In 1982, the Fund gave 43.2 m ECU towards the training or retraining of 25,850 workers, including more than 16,000 in the textile and clothing industries. The aim of the projects is to retrain workers for viable jobs in their original industry or some other sector of the economy. In agriculture, the flight from the land has been slowed by the lack of job opportunities in industry. Nevertheless, the Social Fund spent 9.6 m ECU in 1982 to retrain 7,558 farmers, to support farm workers and families wishing to quit their land or to promote activities complementary to agriculture, such as farm holidays and rural crafts.

From 1984, all the eight categories concentrated on were to be rearranged under two principal types of Social Fund aid. The first, and largest, was to be reserved for young people aged less than 25. Projects to promote the employment of young people were in future to take up 75% of the cash available. Social Fund grants were, however, to continue to be available to the unemployed (especially the long-term unemployed), workers threatened with redundancy or part-time employment, and workers (especially in small or medium-sized businesses) who needed retraining to keep abreast of new technologies and new methods of production and management.

However, a recital of funding and programmes does not suffice to indicate the significance of the Social Fund. One study, critical of the procedures adopted and the marginal impact of the Fund on the policies and programmes of Member States, concluded by underlining the responsibility of the Member States:[5]

'A major weakness of the nineteen seventies was the inability of the EC to establish the larger policies in which the work of the ESF could be integrated. Thus the hope that the fund would play a larger part in the strengthening of the EC has been tarnished. The continual hesitations of the members which have inhibited the transfer of effective power in regional policies, in industrial development and employment policies have prevented the development of the fund as an effective instrument in integration. At best a sharing of the decision-taking has occurred. The Commission may have looked forward to a function defined as "helping to achieve a qualitative improvement in employment policies in the context of community solidarity", (3rd ESF Report, p 6) but the refusal of national governments to change anything very much, and the British experience shows how strong national inertia can be, suggests that only minor achievements are in practice likely. Even on a smaller scale the dream of the co-ordination of Community instruments, so often trumpeted at the beginning of the guidelines, is more conspicuous by its absence than its operation. The general marking time in the Community has meant that the ESF has not been able to fulfil the hopes underlying the reform of ten years ago.'

The Social Fund was reformed again after the Single European Act 1986. The number of people affected by its activities was more than 2.7 million per annum. Aid for vocational training accounts for about 90% of its annual budget.[6] It constitutes a major social policy resource.

5   D Collins *The Operation of the European Social Fund*, Croom Helm, London 1983, at p 104.
6   *Social Europe*, 2/91, p 10.

QUALIFIED MAJORITY VOTING: THE SINGLE EUROPEAN ACT

Article 100A(2)

The Commission's proposal of the Single European Market Programme in 1985 implied the approval of a large number of Directives aimed at eliminating the many obstacles identified. To achieve the approval of these Directives, the Single European Act 1986 derogated from the requirement of unanimity laid down in Article 100 by adding to the Treaty of Rome a new Article 100A allowing for qualified majority voting:[7]

> '1. ... The Council shall, acting by a qualified majority on a proposal from the Commission in cooperation with the European Parliament and after consulting the Economic and Social Committee, adopt the measures for the approximation of the provisions laid down by law, regulation or administrative action in Member States which have as their object the establishment and functioning of the internal market.'

However, at the insistence of the British government, fearful of its opposition to social policy initiatives being diluted, there was inserted into the new Article 100A paragraph 2:

> '2. Paragraph 1 shall not apply to fiscal provisions, to those relating to the free movement of persons nor to those relating to the rights and interests of employed persons.'

It has been argued that, as a consequence of this addition, Article 100A is 'of little significance in the employment field, for Article 100A(2) provides that it shall not apply, inter alia, to provisions relating to the rights and interests of employed persons'.[8] However, there is an argument to the contrary. Three possible interpretations can be offered of the restriction imposed by Article 100A(2).

A first interpretation would argue that any proposal which touches, *however indirectly and partially*, the rights and interests of employees, is excluded from majority voting. For example, the proposal for a European company statute, though primarily aimed at the commercial field, will undoubtedly affect the interests of employees, and certain provisions in the proposal explicitly give employees rights to participation.[9] Does this render the entire proposal subject to unanimous approval in the Council of Ministers? Again, most proposals affecting competition will affect the labour market interests of employees; does this mean they fall within the wording of Article 100A(2)?

A second possible interpretation of Article 100A(2) points out that most proposals put forward by the Commission will have multiple concerns, the weight of each varying with the perspective of those affected by it. Past initiatives of the

---

7   Added by Article 18 of the Single European Act 1986, which came into force on 1 July 1987.
8   D Wyatt 'Enforcing EEC social rights in the United Kingdom', (1989) 18 *Industrial Law Journal* 197, 199.
9   In July 1989 the Commission presented the final draft of the European Company Statute, including a choice among three systems of worker involvement. The Commission argued that only a majority vote was required in Council as the statute was part of the programme to remove the remaining internal barriers to the Single European Market. The United Kingdom, however, argued that the measure was a tax and social law, and thus needed a unanimous vote in the Council.

Commission may be perceived in this light. Equal pay for women was notoriously included in the Treaty of Rome for reasons of competition over labour costs, though it undoubtedly affected the rights and interests of employees. The Directive regarding collective dismissals combats the harmful effects of sudden disequilibria in the labour market caused by mass dismissals as much as they affect employees. The provisions of the Directive on Transfers of Undertakings affect potential union opposition to such transfers as much as they benefit employees. Does Article 100A(2) exclude from majority voting only those proposals the *predominant* aim or effect of which concerns the rights and interests of employees? Is a proposal on a minimum wage concerned with unfair competition in labour costs or employee rights and interests? Do proposals on health and safety require enterprises to bear equal burdens in reducing the costs of accidents, or do they concern the rights and interests of employees?

A third interpretation of Article 100A(2) highlights the fact, though rare, that certain proposals may be *solely* concerned with the rights and interests of employees, and be concerned with nothing else.

In sum, *unanimity* in the Council of Ministers may be required for:

–   *any* proposal, however partially and indirectly concerned with employees' rights and interests; or
–   only those proposals concerning *solely* the rights and interests of employees alone; or
–   those proposals which *predominantly* (though not exclusively) are concerned with employees' rights and interests.

To the extent that labour is a factor of production in the establishment of a unified market, *most* proposals affecting that market will relate to the rights and interests of employees in some way or other. Which of these interpretations of Article 100A(2) is adopted depends upon the vision of the Community held by its author.

This issue is as old as labour and social law itself, and is a well known problem in many Member States. Judges are frequently called upon to adjudicate when the rights and interests of employees concerned outweigh other considerations. Does a requirement of consultation on matters of employees' health and safety include the introduction of new technology?[10] Is certain industrial action by employees 'wholly or mainly' related to their terms and conditions of employment?[11] Is the exclusion of enterprises employing fewer than 15 employees concerned with employees' interests or those of small employers?[12] The European Court of Justice could be confronted with similar questions.

In practice, Article 100A has not been invoked as a basis for social policy

10   A judgment of the Federal Labour Court in Germany held that works councils have no general right of co-determination on how visual display units (VDUs) are to be designed or installed. Under the Works Council Act 1972, s 87(1)(vii), works councils have co-determination rights on 'arrangements for the prevention of industrial accidents and occupational diseases, and for the protection of health on the basis of legislation or safety regulations'. The Court concluded, however, that if the works council's demand went beyond underpinning existing legislation or safety regulations, there was no right to co-determination: *European Industrial Relations Review* No 124, May 1984, p 9 at p 10.

11   In the UK, TULRECA, s 244(1), formerly the Trade Union and Labour Relations Act 1974, s 29(1), as amended by the Employment Act 1982, s 18. See R Benedictus and B Bercusson *Labour Law: Cases and Materials,* 1987, pp 560–1.

12   An issue decided by the Italian Constitutional Court in 1989.

initiatives, and its usefulness has probably been overtaken by the Maastricht Protocol and Agreement on Social Policy which allocated the requisite social competences to the Member States (the UK opting out).

Article 118A

A second avenue outflanking the UK veto on social policy initiatives was the new Article 118A of the Treaty of Rome, also inserted by the Single European Act:[13]

'1. Member States shall pay particular attention to encouraging improvements, especially in the working environment, as regards the health and safety of workers, and shall set as their objective the harmonisation of conditions in this area, while maintaining the improvements made.
2. In order to achieve the objective laid down in the first paragraph, the Council, acting by a qualified majority on a proposal from the Commission, in cooperation with the European Parliament and after consulting the Economic and Social Committee, shall adopt, by means of directives, minimum requirements for gradual implementation, having regard to the conditions and technical rules obtaining in each of the Member States.'

Once again, this provision can be interpreted in at least three ways:

(i) as limited to the protection of working activity in the strictest sense;
(ii) as including all conditions of work which have or could have effects on the safety and health of workers, including duration of work, its organisation and its content (so as to cover, for example, night work and various forms of 'atypical' work);
(iii) as including the working environment in the widest sense of the term, workers' welfare and wellbeing, as well as occupational accidents and illness and protection of health at the workplace.

Whatever interpretation is adopted, there are also the clauses restricting the Article to minimum provisions, gradual implementation and protection of small and medium enterprises, each of which is itself open to interpretation.

To illustrate the problem, the Commission's 1989 Social Action Programme referred to the significance for competitiveness of flexibility of working time. It was argued that this implies a need for harmonisation of standards regulating such flexibility across the Community to avoid distortions in the labour market which would affect competition between firms. This is to raise the well-known issue of 'social dumping', where regulatory controls on working time in one country could be undermined by competition from countries where absence of such regulatory controls gives a competitive advantage to firms.

The legal basis of a proposal on working time could have looked to its effects on competition in the internal market (the 'social dumping' argument), and invoked Article 100A. This would have allowed for approval by qualified majority voting, outflanking a UK veto. The question would then have been raised whether the proposed Directive was excluded from the qualified majority voting regime by virtue of paragraph 2 of Article 100A – raising the issues of interpretation discussed earlier.

---

13   Single European Act 1986, Article 21.

In the event, the Commission opted to argue that the diversity of regulatory practices regarding flexibility of working time posed a potential threat to the wellbeing and health of workers. This hazard allowed for potential recourse to article 118A, which also allows for qualified majority voting in the Council in matters concerning the 'working environment, as regards the health and safety of workers'. The UK challenged before the Court of Justice this legal basis for the Working Time Directive subsequently adopted by the Council.

The prospects for the social policy of the Member States depend on how the institutions of the European Community exercise their discretion in interpreting the provisions of these articles and how they act on their interpretations.[14]

---

14 Constitutional history demonstrates that, as Kahn-Freund commented on the Australian federal experience in unifying labour law: 'The courts may yield to the vital needs of society, whatever intellectual processes they use in order to satisfy them'. O Kahn-Freund 'The impact of constitutions on labour law', (1976) 35 *Cambridge Law Journal* 240, at p 255.

Chapter 6

The Strategy of European Social Dialogue

INTRODUCTION

The UK government's stance from 1979 in preventing the adoption at Community level of legislation on labour policy was dictated by its domestic policy. This stance coupled similar 'deregulation' at domestic level with an equally wholesale policy of exclusion of trade unions. This included both exclusion of trade unions from areas of policy where they had previously been part of tripartite policy-making machinery (such as industrial training and manpower policy) and, more crucially, the reduction and weakening wherever possible of collective bargaining.

It is, therefore, ironic that it was this UK blockage of labour legislation at EU level which provided the critical impetus to a transformation in legal strategy for social policy and labour law at EU level: the emergence of dialogue between the social partners at European level. The doubtless unintended consequence of the UK government policy of decollectivisation of industrial relations at domestic level was the huge advance in collectivisation of industrial relations at EU level.

Since the ECSC, there had been a long-standing range of formal machinery incorporating representatives of the trade union movements and employer organisations in EC policy-making. The explanation for their involvement is part of a general theory which perceives the Community as not just a bilateral arrangement between Community institutions and Member States, but a complex polity which engages a wide range of other actors in social (and other) policy formation and implementation.

At a general level, the dependence of the Community on Member State co-operation in pursuing its policies means it is important to engage powerful national interest groups, such as trade union confederations and employers' organisations, in the policy process. At the stage of policy formation also, the need for consensus in achieving passage of legislative proposals means that if trade unions and employers' organisations can be mobilised to support the Community proposals, national opposition may be at least neutralised. The resources of the social partner organisations can also be a useful supplement to the strained information gathering capacity of the EC institutions.

The involvement of the social partners reflected, in part, the internal dynamics of the Community institutional machinery. The Commission is most involved and was most active in establishing consultation bodies at EC level.

72

Writing in the mid-1980s, one observer stated:[1]

'The Commission has adopted a unique approach to further its employment law agenda. It has not only maintained regular contact with the representatives of workers and employers, but has actively encouraged the development of Community level worker and employer organisations. It has done so by offering such groups the opportunity to engage in extensive negotiations on all Community employment proposals.'

The European Parliament too was very open to relations with the social partners, partly because these organised interests were important to the electability of the Members of Parliament, who could also benefit from their resources for collecting information needed by MEPs, but also because the social partners could be mobilised in support of the Parliament's campaign for a greater role in EC policy-making.

This Commission–social partners–Parliament coalition emerged as a powerful force for social policy development during the 1980s. It served to offset the power of national veto in the Council of Ministers, which had a less active relationship with the social partners and did not encourage interest group involvement.

The development of the European social dialogue was supported by experience, but also by principle and pragmatic expediency. The democratic principle favours the maximum involvement of employers and workers in the formulation of the rules governing their relationship. Participation by the social partners in the formulation and definition of international standards has been a key element in the success of the International Labour Organisation. The concept of social dialogue incorporates a principle critical in the EC context. It stipulates a relationship between collective bargaining and law which assumes a multiplicity of forms within Member States and is extremely flexible in its application within the context of Community social policy.

Social dialogue does not simply equate with collective bargaining. It implies a flexible relationship between social dialogue at all levels and Community and national institutions. Writing in 1989, I argued that 'it could take the form of a dialogue between the social partners at European level leading to proposals in the form of Directives, and/or lead directly to collective bargaining and agreements within Member States'.[2] The relationship is contingent upon national traditions of social dialogue within Member States. Collective bargaining in the UK is not the same as that in France, Italy or Germany. Besides bilateral bargaining, the social dialogue may adopt the form of tripartite structures, assume roles for public authorities and/or establish mechanisms for representation of the unorganised.

The emergence of the European social dialogue in the mid-1980s was dictated by the conjuncture of the 1985 Single European Market programme being threatened by the UK veto on the development of a parallel social dimension. The crucial initiative was taken by Jacques Delors, the incoming President of the Commission in January 1985. Presenting the Commission's

---

1   A L Sandler 'Players and process: The evolution of employment law in the EEC', (1985) 7 *Comparative Labor Law* 1, at 16.
2   B Bercusson, in Cassese et al (eds), op cit (1991) at p 208.

programme to Parliament, he:[3]

> 'stressed that the creation of a large market had to go hand in hand with the creation and organisation of a European social area; one of its cornerstones should be the social dialogue, the negotiations between employers' and workers' organisations at Community level.
>
> With a view to relaunching the Community social dialogue, the Commission President urged the various economic and social groups to mobilise and play their part in this new stage in the building of Europe, inviting to a meeting at Val Duchesse the chairmen and general secretaries of all the national organisations affiliated to UNICE, CEEP and ETUC.'[4]

The social partners met at the castle of Val Duchesse outside Brussels on 31 January 1985 and agreed to engage in furthering the social dialogue. At a second meeting on 12 November 1985, they set up two joint working parties: one to examine macroeconomic problems and the other to study problems raised by the introduction of new technologies. The Macroeconomic Working Group adopted two 'joint opinions' on 6 November 1986 and 26 November 1987. The Working Party on New Technologies and the Social Dialogue adopted a joint opinion on training and motivation, and information and consultation on 6 March 1987.

The social dialogue received crucial formal recognition through the insertion into the Treaty of Rome, by the Single European Act 1986, of a new Article 118B:[5]

> 'The Commission shall endeavour to develop the dialogue between management and labour at European level which could, if the two sides consider it desirable, lead to relations based on agreement.'

The social dialogue moved to a second phase with a meeting held at the Palais d'Egmont on 12 January 1989, which set up a political steering group. Further working parties were set up and further joint opinions were produced in the years that followed.

As the term 'joint opinions' may indicate, the social partners engaged in the dialogue, and in particular the employers' organisations, were ambivalent about the formal outcomes of the process they were involved in. The employers' organisations could hardly resist the pressures coming from the Commission to participate, and they supported the Single European Market programme on the whole, but that did not imply a commitment to what Article 118B characterised as 'relations based on agreement'.

'SOCIAL DUMPING' AND 'SOCIAL REGIME COMPETITION'

The attitudes of the social partners have to be seen in the context of the 1992 Single European Market programme as a whole. The creation of the single European market allows for enterprises heretofore operating in the context of a

---

3   *Joint Opinions*, European Social Dialogue Documentary Series, Commission of the European Communities, p 19, (n.d).
4   ETUC: the European Trade Union Confederation, founded in 1973; UNICE, the Union of Industrial and Employers' Confederations of the European Communities, formed in 1958; CEEP: the European Centre of Public Enterprises.
5   Single European Act, Article 22.

national market to be exposed to competition with others in other Member States. This means that pressure will be exerted on enterprises with high *direct* wage costs to secure the productivity that will enable them to compete with enterprises elsewhere in the Community with lower wage costs. This aspect of competition, aimed at rewarding productivity, was one of the objectives of the Single European Market programme.

However, national systems of labour law and social protection impose *indirect* labour costs on enterprises, such as the costs of compliance with labour standards and the costs of contributing to social protection schemes. Lower labour and social standards in some Member States may entail lower indirect labour costs for enterprises in those Member States. The result is to give enterprises in those countries with lower indirect labour costs a competitive advantage compared with enterprises in Member States with higher labour and social standards. This advantage may be offset by other factors which favour enterprises in countries with higher labour and social standards, such as better transport infrastructures or a more highly trained and skilled workforce. Nonetheless, differences in direct and indirect labour costs may constitute a significant competitive edge.

One consequence of such differences has been argued to raise the threat of 'social dumping'. As a result of what has been called 'social policy regime competition'[6] between Member States, Member States will be under pressure to reduce their labour and social standards in order to ease the burden of high indirect wage costs on enterprises. Enterprises, particularly multinational enterprises, will be tempted to locate new investments or even relocate existing establishments to countries where lower labour and social standards entail lower indirect labour costs.[7] Two tables graphically illustrate this:[8]

HOURLY LABOUR COSTS IN INDUSTRY IN THE EC, 1990 IN ECUS[9]	
Germany	20.08
Belgium	19.30
Netherlands	17.47
Denmark	17.19
France (1988)	15.27
Luxembourg (1989)	14.48
Italy (1988)	14.24
UK	12.20
Ireland	11.64
Spain	11.30
Greece (1988)	5.24
Portugal	3.57

6 W Streeck 'La dimensione sociale del mercato unico europeo: verso un'economia non regolato?', (1990) 28 *Stato e Mercato* 29 at p 48.

7 A notorious case was that of the relocation by Hoover of a manufacturing plant in Dijon in France to Cambuslang in Scotland. 'The Hoover affair and social dumping', *European Industrial Relations Review* No 230, (March 1993) p 14.

8 Ibid, pp 18–19.

9 Source: Eurostat (1992) 'Labour costs: updating 1989–90', Luxembourg.

THE STRUCTURE OF LABOUR COSTS IN INDUSTRY IN THE EC, 1990[10]				
Country	*Direct cost*	*Of which, direct remuneration*	*Indirect cost*	*Of which, social security*
Denmark	96.2%	83.1%	3.8%	3.0%
UK	86.8%	84.2%	13.2%	11.5%
Luxembourg (1988)	82.8%	67.4%	17.4%	16.3%
Ireland	82.2%	70.5%	17.8%	14.9%
Greece (1989)	80.0%	61.0%	19.0%	19.0%
Germany (1989)	76.3%	56.0%	23.7%	21.5%
Spain	74.9%	55.3%	25.1%	24.5%
Portugal	74.2%	56.0%	25.8%	21.7%
Netherlands	73.3%	54.3%	26.7%	23.2%
Italy (1989)	70.0%	50.3%	30.0%	26.7%
Belgium	69.5%	49.1%	30.5%	28.9%
France (1989)	68.0%	51.4%	32.0%	28.6%

Social dumping posited two alternative scenarios for the institutional arrangements of formulation and implementation of EU labour law and social policy. One scenario envisaged the *transfer* of social policy jurisdiction to the EU level. Harmonised or uniform social and labour standards throughout the Community, established through EU legal measures, would secure the objective of greater equalisation of indirect labour costs for all enterprises, and reduce, if not eliminate, the threat of unequal standards distorting competition in favour of Member States with lower standards. The second scenario favoured the opposite: *retention* of national competence over social and labour standards, accepting the consequence of direct competition between different Member State social regimes.

These two scenarios were obviously linked with wider political strategies concerned with the pace and direction of European integration in general. In that general context of European integration, however, the interesting feature of the two apparently opposing scenarios regarding EU social policy and labour law is that *both* lead to a *loss* of Member State *autonomy* in these fields of policy.

The first scenario is explicit about this result: Member States relinquish their competence over social policy and labour law in favour of regulation of these areas by harmonised and uniform EU standards. Future developments in these policy areas are thereby left to EU initiatives.

But the second scenario also, though not so explicitly, entails the reduction or elimination of national autonomy in social policy and labour law making. This is because Member States considering initiatives in the field of social policy or labour law will be highly conscious of the implications of undertaking such initiatives for enterprises on their national territory. Any initiative which involves compliance costs with labour regulations or social protection measures will impose higher indirect labour costs compared with enterprises in the other

10   Ibid.

Member States. This is bound to make it more difficult to obtain internal political consensus for such social legislation. Moreover, the pressure will continue on Member States to reduce their social and labour standards to the levels prevailing in countries with competing enterprises.

What both scenarios have in common, therefore, is a policy of 'deregulation' at national level; either because this is the result of social policy regime competition, or because regulation at national level is replaced by exercise of regulatory competence in social and labour matters at EU level.

The dangers posed by 'social dumping' and 'social regime competition' as a result of the 1992 Single European Market programme led to a fierce and protracted political battle between the social partners – a kind of class struggle at European level.

The strategy of the trade unions at European level has been characterised as dictated by a 'political-distributive' logic.[11] This recognised the dangers posed by social dumping in the single market, but also acknowledged the advantages to be reaped by enterprises free to compete without national hindrance. The aim was to achieve a balance between the costs of the social protection necessary to offset the risk of social dumping, and the losses to enterprises entailed by this necessary degree of regulation. The strategy, therefore, was one of political *regulation* at European level to secure the fair distribution of the benefits of the single market, requiring attention to questions of labour and social standards and implementation mechanisms.

The strategy of employers' organisations has been characterised as dictated by an 'economic-productive' logic.[12] The social dimension of the single market was to aim at achieving the maximum productive and competitive efficiency. For firms in the European Community, the principal competitive challenge came from outside the EC – mainly the USA and Japan. Enterprises in those countries benefited from significantly lower social and labour standards, a competitive advantage which hindered enterprises in Europe. The social policy of the EC in the new single European market should, therefore, aim at reducing this competitive advantage by eliminating that social and labour regulation which was such a burden on European enterprises. Freed of such a burden, the productive and competitive efficiency of European enterprise would achieve the requisite growth generating the economic benefits for living and working standards. European employers, therefore, had a positive social policy: that of *deregulation* to allow for the necessary flexibility and competitiveness.

Each of these social policy strategies for the single European market had an accompanying *legal* strategy. The deregulation strategy put forward by the employers' organisations was based on the assumption that there were to be no common social and labour standards imposed through EC measures. This had the advantage that it would reduce the need for a central regulatory bureaucracy, not required, given the non-interventionist policy. It had the corollary benefits of operating to inhibit social regulation initiatives at national level, for fear of burdening Member State enterprises. Finally, it allowed for regulatory social regime competition, in which Member States would compete against each other to lower indirect social and labour costs.

The consequences for labour of such a strategy would have been negative.

11   W Streeck, op cit.
12   Ibid.

The benefits of the single European market were, at that stage, purely speculative and highly uncertain. The exclusion of any attempt at social regulation meant the widely anticipated restructuring of enterprises would be unrestrained. There would be no EC political regulatory regime capable of supporting social protection or labour rights, collective or individual. And the prospect of social dumping would become a reality, with particular threats to social security regimes imposing employer contributions.

The struggle that ensued between these protagonists and their strategies involved not only the social partners but also the Community institutions which also had a stake in the outcome. Its outcome to date is marked by two major developments: the Community Charter of Fundamental Social Rights of Workers of December 1989, and the Protocol and Agreement on Social Policy of the Treaty on European Union agreed at Maastricht in December 1991, which came into effect in November 1993. It is too early in the life of these landmarks to know whether they signalled victory or defeat for either strategy. The struggle goes on into the Intergovernmental Conference planned for 1996.

EUROPEAN LABOUR LAW AND SECTORAL BARGAINING IN THE MEMBER STATES OF THE EC

What both the Charter of 1989 and the Protocol and Agreement of 1991 did push into prominence, however, was the consensus between the two sides that the social dialogue should become a, if not the, primary instrument for social and labour regulation in the EU. The prospects of a strategy of European social dialogue for European labour law may be better assessed in the light of a more detailed analysis of the potential of social dialogue at *sectoral* level, both in the Member States and at EU level.

The question is whether European labour law will develop towards recognition of labour law standards established through the European social dialogue. In particular, whether the level of the sector is adapted to assume the role proposed by the Maastricht Agreement for the formulation of EC social policy, and the embodiment of EC labour standards.

Recent trends in sectoral bargaining

The importance of the sectoral level of bargaining is increasing in Europe, with the exception of the UK. This was one of three trends in collective bargaining identified by a study carried out for the Commission by Vaughan-Whitehead.[13] His analysis suggests that within the majority of Member States sectoral bargaining has moved into the position once occupied by multi-sector national level bargaining, while at the same time company bargaining has taken up some of the issues which might previously have been resolved at sectoral level. Issues such as flexibility, early retirement and training, previously the subject of national bargaining, are moving down to the sectoral bargaining level, whilst

---

13   D Vaughan-Whitehead 'Wage Bargaining in Europe: continuity and change', *Social Europe*, Supplement 2/90. The three trends were decentralisation to company level, diversification of remuneration and extension of sectoral bargaining.

wage bargaining, previously an area determined by sectoral bargaining, is moving down to enterprise bargaining.

This shift is particularly important when considering an EC-wide framework for social dialogue. For although it has been well recognised that wage bargaining is unlikely to be the subject of Europe-wide agreement, it is precisely those areas which are now identified within Member States as being within the competence of sectoral bargaining that could most easily be translated into European agreements.

With the exception of Luxembourg, where practically no sectoral bargaining occurs, and Greece and Portugal, where bargaining has not yet developed extensively at this level, in every Member State the range of new topics covered by sectoral bargaining has opened up. Until the early 1980s, sectoral bargaining covered a very limited range of issues, usually wages and working conditions (mainly holidays) and hours. In only one Member State, Italy, did sectoral negotiations include items such as health and safety and information rights; in only three Member States, Germany, France and Luxembourg (and in the case of the latter this was the only sectoral bargaining which took place) was job classification a subject for bargaining; and in three Member States only, Germany, Italy and France, was the duration or content of the employment contract a subject for bargaining at this level. By contrast with this earlier period, Vaughan-Whitehead found fifteen new areas of bargaining since 1986, covering a whole range of diverse issues, from pensions to new technology.[14]

Vaughan-Whitehead suggested that sectoral bargaining has become important precisely because enterprise bargaining had emerged as a dominant form of bargaining in the 1980s. Sectoral bargaining, he argued, fulfils a number of functions. 'Far from ignoring sectoral discussion of the same topics, company agreements adapt the procedures agreed at that level in line with company requirements'.[15] However, 'this flexibility is selective since it does not affect what are regarded as fundamental guarantees of social welfare, including protection against unfair dismissal'. 'In addition, the numerous company agreements on the reduction and adjustment of working hours ... have merely led to the adaptation to local conditions of the rules agreed at sectoral level pursuant to the relevant national legislation'. 'Lastly, sectoral bargaining appears to guarantee company compliance with rules'. In other words, it ensures that company bargaining occurs on a level playing field for all in the sector, by denying the right to compete unfairly to companies who would otherwise ignore guarantees of basic working conditions, whilst at the same time leaving them relatively free to set pay levels.[16]

The current position within Member States

Among Member States, the importance of sectoral bargaining is variable. The following is a brief summary of the position in the private sector. It also aims to

14 This information is derived from the survey by Vaughan-Whitehead, ibid.
15 Ibid. He gives the example of flexibility agreements in Italy. The broad guidelines are drawn up at national level (eg organisation of working hours) or sectoral level, despite being applied with a certain freedom by companies. This and the following quotations are to be found on p 14 of the Report.
16 In some circumstances this relationship between enterprise and sectoral bargaining can be even more specific as, for example, in Italy, where company bargainers are precluded from covering topics the subject of sectoral agreement.

indicate the possible articulation of EC-level sectoral agreements with sectoral bargaining within Member States.[17]

In *Belgium*, sectoral agreements are dominant in the textile, printing, building, paper, wood and oil refinery sectors. In *Denmark*, there is centralised bargaining establishing a framework, but it is the sectoral agreements covering pay and working conditions negotiated by industry unions and employers which are most significant. In *France*, there are 65 major industrial sectors and each year agreements are concluded in about half and cover about 21 million employees.[18] In *Germany*, collective bargaining is conducted by industry federations at regional level. However, the fact that most agreements are concluded at this level does not in itself indicate a wide area of divergence.[19] By and large regional sectoral agreements mirror one another.[20]

In *Great Britain*, a large number of agreements have been concluded at sectoral level, usually through the format of a National Joint Council (NJC) or National Joint Industrial Council (NJIC), for example in chemicals, print and footwear. But in recent years the trend has been to move away from this level of bargaining. The latest workplace industrial relations survey[1] shows a decline in the numbers covered from 65% of manual workers in 1984 to 54%. Non-manuals register a similar decline.

In *Greece*, of the three levels of bargaining, national, sectoral and undertaking, it is sectoral agreements at the national level, applicable to a single industry, which are the subject of the most important bargaining. In *Ireland*, collective bargaining tends to be localised at company level, though a 1987 Tripartite Programme for National Recovery fixed central pay guidelines. However, industry-wide bargaining is conducted through Joint Industrial Councils (construction, electrical contracting, banking, baking) or Joint Labour Committees in areas of low pay and weak unionisation (tailoring, hairdressing, hotels and contract cleaning). In *Italy*, in all there have been about 100 sectoral agreements, although some have recently lapsed. Four major agreements dominate, those for construction, chemicals, textiles and metalworking. In *Luxembourg*, collective bargaining is at the level of the undertaking or group of undertakings.

In the *Netherlands*, the centralised form of bargaining which prevailed until 1970 has become decentralised towards sectors and undertakings. In 1990 2.7 million (out of 3.3 million) workers were covered by 199 separate sectoral agreements. Sectoral bargaining is the most significant form of bargaining. In *Portugal*, the tripartite Permanent Council for Social Coordination is playing an increasing role, but the level at which bargaining takes place depends on, among other factors, the level of organisation among employers. Enterprise

---

17   Three sources provide expanded summaries: (1) European Trade Union Institute *Workers' Representation and Rights in the Workplace in Western Europe*, 1990 (and see the extracts in the Working Documents compiled by the ETUI for the ETUC conference of June 1992, 'The European Dimensions of Collective Bargaining After Maastricht', Brussels 1992, pp 15–29); (2) Labour Research Department *Across the Table: Collective Bargaining in Europe* – a trade union negotiator's guide, 1992; (3) 'The Regulation of Working Conditions in the Member States of the European Community', *Social Europe*, Supplement 4/92.

18   'Collective Bargaining in France', *European Industrial Relations Review* No 225 (October 1992).

19   There are a few agreements with individual employers, like that at Volkswagen, but these are the exception to the general rule of sectoral bargaining.

20   'Collective Bargaining in the West in 1991', *European Industrial Relations Review* No 221 (June 1992), p 14.

1   N Millward et al *Workplace Industrial Relations in Transition*, Dartmouth 1992.

agreements represent only 20% to 25% of all collective agreements. In *Spain*, unions are anxious to develop sectoral bargaining to provide a base for company bargaining. However, to date it is provincial bargaining which dominates. According to the UGT trade union confederation, the 1992 bargaining round reinforced sectoral bargaining, with 90% of the agreements concluded in the first seven months of 1992 being at that level.[2]

Articulation with EC level social dialogue

This brief survey provides some indication that sectoral bargaining is alive and well in most Member States. It would therefore have some potential for articulation with sectoral bargaining at EC level.[3]

Nonetheless, Member State collective bargaining systems throw up numerous obstacles to articulation aimed at giving effect to EC-level sectoral agreements. Examples include conditions on representativeness of workers' organisations (Belgium, Spain, France), requirements of ratification by vote of the membership (Denmark), non-legally enforceable agreements (UK, Ireland) and regionalisation of sectoral bargaining (Germany, Spain).

On the other hand, a number of Member State systems have features which could reinforce the effect of EC-level sectoral agreements: in particular, the many procedures, of varying scope and complexity, for extending collective agreements to the whole of a sector (Belgium, France, Germany, Greece, Luxembourg, Netherlands, Portugal, Spain) or even enlargement to other sectors as in France.[4] In contrast, a number of Member States have no provision for formal extension procedures (Denmark, Ireland, Italy, UK). Attention needs to be directed, both at national and European levels, to the formulation of a set of conditions which would promote the articulation of EC-level sectoral labour standards negotiated in the European sectoral social dialogue with collective bargaining in Member States. Specifically, the reinforcement of sectoral bargaining, legally enforceable agreements, and erga omnes extension procedures.[5]

An historical reminder

Understanding the development of sectoral social dialogue at EC level may benefit from a brief historical reminder of the evolution of sectoral bargaining

2   *European Industrial Relations Review* No 224 (September 1992).
3   One of the methods envisaged by Article 4(2) of the Maastricht Agreement for implementing EC level agreements. See Chapter 35.
4   These reinforce myriad doctrines aimed at supporting the effect of collective agreements; see Lord Wedderburn 'Inderogability, Collective Agreements and Community Law', (1992) 24 *Industrial Law Journal* 245.
5   A survey produced by Bob Hepple outlined some of the legal and practical difficulties in the 12 Member States. He concluded: 'There is a great variation between these countries in the nature and extent of decentralisation of collective bargaining, in the degree of legal support for bargaining and for the extension erga omnes of agreements. While the new institutional arrangements may provide a stimulus, the implementation of European standards will eventually turn on the strength and determination of the social partners in each country'. B A Hepple 'The interaction between collective bargaining at European and national levels', paper for the ETUC Athens Conference, 'From Maastricht to the EMU: role and responsibilities of the social partners', 9–11 November 1992 (mimeo), p 11.

in some Member States.[6]

In the *UK*, industry level bargaining at local or regional level to replace unilateral employer or trade union determination of conditions of employment was obstructed by trade union structures of a predominantly craft and general nature, and a lack of congruence with employers' organisations. The massive State intervention in industry during the first World War and the development of the Whitley Joint Industrial Councils following the peace laid the basis for potential sectoral organisation. But regulation at sectoral level remained weak, for reasons attributed to the lack of legal support and fragmented industrial structure, making adherence to agreements difficult to sustain and, particularly in engineering, a readiness to locate at enterprise level the focus of bargaining. In the post-war period, however, sectoral-level regulation was strong in the public/nationalised sector – up to the decentralisation and privatisation of the 1980s.

In *Germany*, at the end of the last century, sectoral organisation was adopted by employers to compete with British industry and also more effectively to blacklist trade union activists. On the trade union side it was a question of a compromise between socialist and craft (liberal) tendencies. After World War I, employers accepted reformist trade unionism; enterprise councils established in 1920 reinforced trade union sectoral tendencies away from craft traditions. After the Nazi period, since the legislation of 1949, collective bargaining has been based on sectoral organisation, national and regional. Sectoral organisation has a legal basis, but its strength comes from the organisation of the social partners. The unions are organised on strictly sectoral lines. Employers' associations are more decentralised and diverse, but demonstrate unity in collective bargaining.

In *Italy*, the sectoral level is always present, but in a dialectic with either the inter-professional (multi-sector) or enterprise levels; it is not always the dominant element. In the period 1945–1954, the inter-professional level dominated. Changes began in the 1950s and the period 1954–1968 saw the sectoral role affirmed. Sectors became central beginning in the 1960s. Decentralisation was the hallmark of the period 1968–1975. The enterprise level became decisive as from 1968 with the explosion of trade union strength at enterprise level and the revolt against Taylorist methods. The 1970 Workers' Statute protected trade unions in the enterprise; it did not regulate collective bargaining. The sectoral level assumed the role of generalising successes achieved by collective bargaining in large enterprises. The onset of the economic crisis beginning in 1975 saw a return to centralised regulation. The inter-professional level regained importance; again it was the turn of the dynamic of sectoral/inter-professional levels, with the latter dominating and taking on a political character with tripartite pacts involving the State through subsidies for lay-offs (*cassa integrazione guadagni*) and fiscal policy. But during the latter 1980s, the inter-professional

6   Reports on the development of sectoral bargaining in a number of Member States were prepared for the project on 'La Régulation de Branche dans l'Europe Communautaire', directed by A Lyon-Caen. They may be found in the following two publications of the Ministère du Travail, de l'Emploi et de la Formation Professionnelle, Service des Etudes et de la Statistique, Paris: *Les Relations Sociales en Europe*, 2ème séminaire, 31 mai et 1 juin 1990, pp 78–111: reports on Italy by T Treu, Spain by F Valdes Dal Re, the UK by P Davies, Germany by J Weyand, France by J Saglio; *Convergence des Modèles Sociaux Européens*, 4ème séminaire, 8–9 octobre 1992, pp 340–67, General Report by A Jobert, A Lyon-Caen, J Saglio, M Tallard; national reports by F Valdes, S Negrelli, A Pollert.

level again lost importance to sector and enterprise levels.

Two conclusions can be drawn from this brief comparative exercise, with implications for the sectoral social dialogue in the EC. First, sectoral bargaining is a highly contingent phenomenon. There is no inevitable evolution towards sectoral level regulation; it is historically variable. Sectoral regulation interacts with inter-sectoral regulation above and enterprise regulation below. The nature of the articulation, and the dominant level is variable. Secondly, the contingency is subject to strategic decision-making. Preference for sectoral level regulation is a strategic choice on the part of the actors involved, the social partners and State authorities. The definition of sectors is also a strategic choice; specifically, they need not be tied to a geographical territory, national, regional or administrative.

The implications for EC social dialogue are that evolution towards sectoral regulation at EC level is not inevitable but is possible; that it implies articulation with supra- and sub-sectoral levels; that it is a strategic choice of the actors involved; and that the geographical spread may exceed national boundaries, but need not include the whole territory of the EC.

THE SECTORAL SOCIAL DIALOGUE AT EC LEVEL

Joint committees in sectors most affected by activities of the EC and ECSC were set up in the early days with Commission assistance: the first in coal and steel as early as 1955, others in agriculture (1963), road transport (1965), inland water transport (1967), sea fishing (1968) and rail transport (1971). The extent of their activity was said to reflect:[7]

> 'one of the preconditions for the successful operation of a joint committee ... the existence of an integrated Community policy for a sector (hence) it is the committees for agriculture and sea fishing which have the longest records of continuous activity.'

Others became dormant, or revived after collapse of the initial impulse.

The membership of the sectoral committees is drawn from European level representatives of national employers' associations and trade unions in the sector concerned. On the union side, unions in particular sectors in ETUC-affiliated national confederations are grouped in 15 European Industry Committees, which provide the union representation on the sector joint committees.[8] However, European employers are not so organised by UNICE, with consequent problems of employer representation on the committees.

The joint sectoral committees' statutes aim to contribute to Community social policy regarding working conditions in their sectors. Despite the Commission's ambitions as regards the development of sectoral collective bargaining, these joint committees produced only opinions and recommendations, save in one instance where the committee for agriculture produced more substantial texts on working time in 1968, 1971 and 1981. The European Federation of Agricultural Workers' Unions stated that the purpose of these 'European Recommendations'

---

7 'The sectoral social dialogue', *European Industrial Relations Review* No 224 (September 1992), p 14: a review describing the actors, processes and outcomes of the social dialogue at the European sectoral level as it has developed over the past 30 years.

8 There is a list of these Committees in *European Industrial Relations Review* No 211 (June 1992).

is in the nature of framework agreements: to set out the objectives for collective bargaining at the national level.

The absence of effective employer organisation and lack of interest in going beyond diffuse joint opinions continue to hamper the efforts of the European Commission to develop the sectoral social dialogue at European level. Further efforts at stimulation in the early 1980s did lead to the creation of informal working groups to carry out studies of employment in their sector. These have had occasional results, such as the memorandum on vocational training in the retail trade, signed on 19 October 1988,[9] and the ETUC/CEEP framework agreement on vocational training and other issues in rail transport and energy distribution.[10] But a major obstacle continues to be:[11]

> 'the perennial problem of the lack of employers' organisations willing or able to rep-resent sectoral employers on social matters, and in some sectors the lack of any employers' bodies at all . . . the dialogue is often hamstrung by the lack of represen-tative employers' bodies, in contrast to the relatively well-organised sectoral union organisations.'[12]

In order to explore the potential of EC-level sectoral social dialogue, two sec-tors, construction and woodworking, and metalworking, will be discussed where steps have been taken to develop the social dialogue. One objective of this discussion is to indicate the different directions which this development may take: towards sectoral collective agreements at EC-level (construction and woodwork), and/or towards EC-level coordination of sectoral bargaining at Member State level (metalworking).

The construction sector

The trade unions

At European level, labour is represented by the European Federation of Building and Woodworkers (EFBWW), established in 1958 as a consultative committee representing construction workers in the original six Member States of the EEC. Its purpose was limited to collation of information. In 1974 it formally separated itself from the International Federation of Building and Wood Workers (IFBWW) and by 1979 had decided to expand its role 'to actively co-ordinate the interests of building workers in Europe'.[13] In 1983 the Federation decided to seek formal entry into the ETUC.

Today, the EFBWW has 50 affiliated member unions,[14] including unions from all EC Member States, except Greece. In some Member States more than one union is affiliated; in France and Italy there are three affiliated unions

---

9   For the text, see *European Industrial Relations Review* No 182 (March 1989), p 31.
10 Text in *European Industrial Relations Review* No 205 (February 1991), p 30.
11 *European Industrial Relations Review* No 224 (September 1992), pp 16, 17.
12 W Streeck says this 'desired organisational weakness' of European management is translated into a 'political strength' as regards the objective of avoiding EC-level bargaining. 'La dimen-sione sociale del mercato unico europeo: verso un'economia non regolato?', (1990) 28 *Stato e Mercato* 29 at p 48.
13 European Federation of Building and Woodworkers *What is the EFBWW? – origins, history, functions* (1992), at p 5.
14 As of 1 January 1992.

which organise within the construction industry, in the UK four, and in Denmark, nine. The EFBWW reflects the range of national unions. However, the level of union membership within the industry varies greatly between countries, as is indicated in the following Table.

UNIONS AND UNIONISATION RATE[15]		
Country	*Unions*	*Unionisation rate*
Belgium	CCTBB; CG	95%
France	FNTC; FCNB; FO; BATI-MAT; CGC	3–5%
Germany	IGBSE	48%
Italy	FILLEA; FILCA; FENEAL	38%
Spain	FICOMA; FEMCA; FCM	n/a
UK	UCATT; TGWU; GMBATU; FTAT	30%

Supreme authority within the EFBWW rests with its General Assembly which meets every four years[16] – the next meeting is to take place in November 1995. Voting at General Assembly meetings is in relationship to affiliated union size measured by the amount of affiliation fee paid. The General Assembly elects the Federation's Executive Committee, its president, vice president and general secretary.

Between General Assemblies it is the Executive Committee which assumes authority within the Federation. This committee meets at least twice a year and endeavours to 'achieve the widest possible measure of agreement' (Article 7). The Secretariat, operating with a full-time general secretary since 1988, is responsible for influencing policy and political lobbying, developing a European trade union policy for the sectors represented by the EFBWW, representation and co-operation with sister and other organisations and research.[17] A Management Committee, consisting of the elected officials and a maximum of four Executive Committee appointees, is the administrative body of the Federation responsible for executing the decisions of the Executive Committee and giving effect to General Assembly mandates. It is the Management Committee members who attend the social dialogue meetings.

The gathering and dissemination of information, not collective bargaining, was the role envisaged for the EFBWW at its inception. Negotiations with employers were the responsibility of national unions. Under its constitution, its responsibilities were defined as the creation of close co-operation between national unions in EC States and furthering the interests of building and woodworkers on all social and economic problems. This has now changed, most notably with the adoption, by its General Assembly, of a new constitution in December 1991.

The new constitution states that the activities of the EFBWW are to be

---

15 The information for this Table was compiled from a research study undertaken between 1987–89, published by the EC Commission, C Pellegrini *Collective Bargaining in the Construction Industry*: wages, hours and vocational training in Belgium, the Federal Republic of Germany, France, Italy, Spain and the United Kingdom, Document EC-MD-99, pp 44–131.
16 Constitution of the EFBWW, Article 6.
17 EFBWW *What is the EFBWW?* (1992) p 7.

directed 'towards achieving the necessary social reforms with a view to creating the conditions for a sound social policy, strengthening democracy, promoting equal rights and equal treatment of all workers, improving conditions of employment . . .'[18]

The constitution appears specifically to empower the Federation to act to improve conditions of employment. Although it states that affiliated organisations 'have autonomy in all matters concerning their national and international activities', it also obliges the same national organisations 'to jointly support and develop European and national decisions and positions adopted', and to 'undertake to strengthen the coordinating role of the EFBWW and to further develop European co-operation through the EFBWW' (Article 3). Article 3 further states that the tasks of the Federation shall include:

'to perform all necessary representation activities connected with the above aims and tasks, and to represent the affiliated organisations at European level. In this representative capacity, the policy for the industries represented by the EFBWW, as jointly agreed in the General Assembly and Executive Committee, shall be actively promoted in contacts with all relevant institutions and organisations.'

These paragraphs appear to envisage a role for the Federation in collective bargaining at European level on behalf of affiliated unions. Article 4 of the Constitution goes on to elaborate further on this role, stating that in its relations with other trade union organisations it 'shall seek to promote the coordinated representation of workers' interests at European level'. A decision at the 1987 General Assembly to enlarge the Federation's Management Committee, which now includes representatives of unions from the UK, Germany, Denmark, the Netherlands, Italy and France, has allowed that body better to reflect the overall membership within Member States.

The employers

The European Construction Industry Federation (FIEC), founded in 1905 as the International Federation of Building and Public Works, is the organisation of employers involved in the social dialogue with the EFBWW. There are 28 affiliated employers' organisations, including those from all 12 Member States (before 1995) as well as 9 from non-Member States. It is recognised as representative by the Commission though it does not represent small and medium firms in every Member State: it does so in Germany (ZDB), Belgium (CNC) and France, but in Italy, Spain and the UK only larger employers are represented. In terms of the proportion of employees employed within Member States this means that a significant number are not represented due to the dominance of small firms within the sector as a whole. There are a multiplicity of organisations covering the public or private sectors, and small, medium or large firms.

Only in Belgium and Spain does a single employers' organisation represent all sections of the industry and in every Member State there are employers who are not members of any of the national bodies. The proportion of employers they represent is in general higher than the proportion of workers represented by the national unions. In Germany, at least 80% of all firms are in membership of one of the two bodies and similar high levels of affiliation appeared in all the other EC Member States surveyed by Pellegrini.

---

18   Article 3.

EMPLOYERS' BODIES AND COVERAGE [19]				
Country	*Body*	*Cover*	*Number of firms*	*Number of employees*
Belgium	CNC	general	13,000	n/a
Germany	HDB	medium/large	n/a	300,000
	ZDB	small	47,000	700,000
France	FNTP	large	5,500	260,000
	FNB	small/medium	50,000	870,000 (estimate)
Italy	ANCE	large (private)	19,000	700,000
	ANIEM	small/med (private)	n/a	n/a
	INTER-SIND	(public)	n/a	n/a
	artisans	4 organisations	n/a	n/a
Spain	CNC	general	n/a	n/a
UK	BEC	general	9,000	660,000 (estimate)
	FCEC	civil engineering	400	n/a
	FMB	small	n/a	n/a

The Statutes of FIEC, approved on 18 June 1992, provide for a General Assembly comprising delegates from each full member Federation or Association, which meets at least once a year (Article 8). The General Assembly elects the President and members of a Steering Committee. It votes by majority, although voting is weighted in favour of larger states. Between Assemblies, the Steering Committee, which comprises the President, Vice Presidents and Treasurer and other members elected to ensure geographical representation, has full power concerning the management of FIEC, respecting decisions taken by the General Assembly (Article 9). FIEC also has a Council, meeting in principle twice a year, made up of Presidents of each affiliate and past Presidents of FIEC itself. Its role includes advising FIEC on strategy and putting forward proposals to go to the General Assembly (Article 11). The 1992 Statutes also provide for the appointment of Permanent Commissions and other ad hoc bodies to deal with specific issues (Article 12). A Director General, a permanent officer of FIEC, is responsible to the Steering Committee for implementation of decisions taken (Article 17).

The 1992 FIEC Statutes give as its principal objectives the promotion and defence of the specific interests of its members, to bring together its members at international level with a view to promoting and defending the interests of the industry, to ensure adequate representation for the European Construction Industry, exchange of experiences and information, and to study and deal with all international problems relating to the construction industry (Article 6.I). To this end FIEC especially shall collect and distribute information, draw up collective policies, carry out actions connected with FIEC objectives, give support to similar bodies, and organise seminars and conferences (Article 6.II).

Thus the FIEC Statutes do not explicitly give FIEC the power to enter into collective bargaining on behalf of its members. However, Article 6 does allow

19   The source of this information is Pellegrini, op cit.

it to 'carry out actions that are connected directly or indirectly, wholly or in part, with its objectives' and this could provide it with the authority to enter into negotiations.

The strategy in the construction sector: EC-level agreements

The strategic objective of the EFBWW is that the social dialogue at EC level serves as 'a basis for future negotiations on conditions of employment at European level whereby we must seek to obtain collective agreements and press for a European social policy'.[20] There are addressed the problems of the legal effect of such agreements and the extent to which they can be made binding on affiliated organisations, an issue 'closely linked to the degree of internal discipline within the employers' organisations but also within the workers' organisations', which raises the issue of the lack of representativeness of employers' organisations at European level.[1] If clear agreement on delegation of bargaining powers to the EC-level organisations can be achieved, and collective agreements can be reached between them, 'then these agreements will filter through into national trade union policy'.[2] As to its content, many topics are said to suggest themselves: health and safety, environmental questions, vocational training, future outlook of the industry, and so on. The ultimate aim is EC-level collective agreements binding on sectoral organisations within the Member States.

The potential of the European social dialogue in the construction industry is evidenced from the Commission's proposals for a Council Directive concerning the posting of workers in the framework of the provision of services.[3] This has particular relevance as construction workers are increasingly posted abroad, following employers with interests throughout Europe.

The EFBWW had already been engaged in an intensive lobbying process on an earlier Directive on public procurement in the construction industry. Although a final text of a Directive was adopted by the Council of Ministers in mid-1989, its social clauses had been much diluted. The EFBWW, together with the ETUC, thus continued to press for a specific Community instrument on posted workers. By early 1991 the Federation was deeply in consultation with the Commission, Members of the European Parliament and permanent representatives of Member States on various alternative drafts for a potential Directive. The role played by the Federation grew until by mid-1992 it was in charge of coordinating the ETUC's contribution to the debate. It worked with MEPs to draft amendments to the Commission's original proposals and by February 1993 could point to a measure of success when the European Parliament adopted some of its proposals. Its influence is apparent throughout the amended text presented by the Commission on 10 May 1993.[4]

20   'The social dialogue and the consequences of Maastricht', Working Paper for the EFBWW Thematic Meeting, Luxembourg, 20 November 1992, Discussion memo on 'Social dialogue in the industries represented by the EFBWW', p 4.
1   Ibid, p 5.
2   Ibid.
3   COM (91) 230 final, SYN 346, Brussels, 1 August 1991.
4   Amended proposal for a Council Directive concerning the posting of workers in the framework of the provision of services (presented by the Commission pursuant to Article 149(3) of the EEC Treaty, dated 10 May 1993. OJ C187 of 9 July 1993, p 5.

Whatever the outcome on the Directive itself, the EFBWW and its constituent unions are now committed to its main principles to the extent that they have adopted it as one of the central issues over which the Federation is anxious to reach formal agreement with FIEC. Here there has been some progress. A first meeting between the social partners took place in June 1993 and a draft framework agreement was being prepared for adoption.

The latest draft of the Directive prepared for the meeting of the Council of Ministers of Social Affairs at the end of 1994 contained further radical amendments.[5] Most significant was the proposal that wages and conditions contained in collective agreements should apply only in specific sectors listed in Annex A to the Directive. This Annex contains only a long list of activities in the construction industry.

The metalworking sector

The trade unions

The European metalworkers' unions were for long the dominant element in the International Metalworkers' Federation (IMF),[6] founded in 1893 when metalworkers in six European countries took joint action for the eight hour day. The European Metalworkers' Federation (EMF) was created as a separate body to coordinate IMF work in Europe and held its first European conference in 1969. The EMF has affiliates from unions based in EC Member States and others, with a total affiliated membership of 6 million workers, most of which is from EC Member States.

Within the EC Member States (12) there are 26 trade unions affiliated to the EMF; in only half of the Member States does a single organisation represent the interests of all metalworkers. The EMF membership of 6 million means that its affiliates directly represent about half of the EC Member State workforce in engineering. Union density figures, where they are available, are shown in the following Table, based on union membership calculated as a proportion of employees in the industry.[7]

---

5   Document SN 4755/1/94 REV 1 (SOC), Brussels, 7 November 1994. For detailed discussion of this proposed Directive, see Chapter 27.

6   MacShane, Denis 'Reflexions sur l'histoire de la Fédération Internationale des Ouvriers de la Métallurgie (FIOM)', in *Syndicalisme - Dimensions Internationales*, ed G Devin (1990) Editions Européennes Erasme, Chapter 13.

7   Data reflect the situation pre-dating the new accessions to the EC of 1995. But, as Marsh et al found, it is difficult to calculate union density in engineering. IG Metall, for example, normally calculates its union density rate from figures from establishments with a works council. This tends to over-emphasise its membership base. But this too is likely to give an overestimate since, first, union membership figures themselves can be notoriously unreliable, and, secondly, they may include among members those who have left the industry or who are out of work for some other reason but maintain membership. With this proviso, the figures presented do at least give a general picture of the rate of unionisation and do allow comparisons to be made between Member States. The unionisation rate of 48% for the Netherlands is probably a slight over-estimate since it is derived from statistics which include a minority of workers employed in other sectors. A Marsh et al *Workplace Relations in the Engineering Industry in the UK and the Federal Republic of Germany*, Anglo-German Foundation for the Study of Industrial Society (1981). In the UK, the latest workplace industrial relations survey suggests a union density rate of 30–32%, but of 56% within the vehicle sector. N Millward, et al *Workplace Industrial Relations in Transition*, Dartmouth 1992.

TRADE UNIONS IN EC MEMBER STATES AFFILIATED TO THE EMF			
Member State	*Unions*	*Union Membership*	*%*
Belgium	CMB; CEMB		
Denmark	CO Metal		
France	FGMM; FOM; FO Defense; FEAE; FM		
Germany	IGMetall	2,727,000	61.5%
Greece	POEM		
Ireland	SIPTU		
Italy	FLM	758,304	52.4%
Luxembourg	OGB-L; LCGB		
Netherlands	FNV; CNV	282,611[8]	48%
Portugal	SIMA		
Spain	UGT Metal; ELA-STV; FM/CCOO		
UK	AEEU; GMB; ISTC; MSF; TGWU		30-32%, but in vehicles 56% rising to 68% for manual workers[9]

IG Metall not only dominates bargaining within Germany but is capable of playing a significant role in Europe. With 2.7 million members in engineering it dwarfs all other Member State engineering unions. Thus any coordinated European bargaining strategy must likely fit its agenda.

Supreme authority within the EMF rests with the General Assembly, which determines the general policy direction, meeting at least every four years. The Assembly is composed of delegates from national unions on the basis of union membership size, by country and by union. The Statutes emphasise that it should do 'its utmost to bring about agreement'; a two thirds majority is needed for votes.[10]

The General Assembly elects members of the Executive Committee, again composed of national representatives, weighted by size of membership, which meets at least three times a year. The Executive Committee 'endeavours to the best of its ability to reach unanimity. Decisions require a two-thirds majority of the vote'.[11] A Secretariat headed by a General Secretary and Assistant General Secretary (elected by the General Assembly on the recommendation of the Executive Committee) direct the day-to-day work of the Federation.[12]

---

8   This figure includes workers in some other sectors, like chemicals.
9   Department of Employment *Gazette*, May 1993.
10   Statutes of the European Metalworkers' Federation (EMF) in the Community, Chapter II, Article 1.
11   Ibid, Chapter II, Article 2.
12   Ibid, Chapter II, Article 3.

Organisations affiliated to the EMF retain their autonomy 'as far as their own trade union activities are concerned'. However, the EMF endeavours 'to achieve common action by all metalworkers' unions in the Community'. Members 'pledge themselves to respect and support, as far as possible, the decisions and principles of the competent EMF organs. At their ordinary union conventions, they shall report on EMF policy and activities and submit these reports for discussion'. The Statutes oblige national affiliates 'in addition ... to examine more advanced forms of trade union co-operation within the framework of the EMF'.[13] This obligation on members to report on EMF business to all national union fora could lend itself to a prospective of coordinated bargaining.

The concern with coordinated activity is expressed through the focus of EMF aims on three areas: 'co-operation between affiliates and coordination of joint demands, protection of metalworkers' interests with regard to European Community policy, and creation of a trade union counterweight to European employers' organisations and top multinational company management within the EC'.[14] A series of committees and working parties have been set up to carry out EMF activities. On sectoral policy, there are working parties in a number of major industrial sectors. A Collective Bargaining Committee meets at regular intervals to discuss common collective bargaining policy aims and ways and means of achieving these. On multinational companies, a number of EMF coordinating committees exist, often in co-operation with the IMF.

The employers

The Western European Metal Trades Employers' Organisation (WEM) was founded on an ad hoc basis in 1962 and formalised in 1970. It represents engineering employers' organisations in nine of the (12) Member States (there is no representation from Greece, Ireland and Portugal), and others outside the EC. Its federated members are recognised as 'being responsible for the conclusion of the collective agreements in the metal industry of the countries concerned'.[15]

From the EC Member States there are 11 national metal trade employers' organisations affiliated to WEM, one for each of eight Member States and three from Italy:

MEMBER STATE ORGANISATIONS AFFILIATED TO WEM	
Belgium	Fabrimétal
Denmark	DI
France	UIMM
Germany	Gesamtmetall
Italy	Federmeccanica; AIL; AMMA
Luxembourg	GISL
Netherlands	Vereniging FME
Spain	Confemetal
UK	EEF

13   Ibid, Chapter I.
14   Sheet published by the EMF entitled: 'The EMF – 6 Million European Metalworkers', February 1993.
15   This, and the following, information is taken from the WEM publication, *Key Data on WEM*, June 1992.

According to WEM its membership represents about 50,000 member companies employing 10 million workers. Since some 12.7 million workers in Member States work in engineering, and given that WEM's membership includes some non-Member States, it can be assumed that within the 12 Member States it represents some 75% of the sector. In the UK, for example, the EEF claims to have about 5,000 firms as affiliates.

The supreme policy-making body within WEM, responsible for determining the principles and objectives of co-operation, is its Plenary Meeting composed of the Presidents of national member-organisations and the Directors of the Federations.[16] This meets every two years. At that meeting the President and one or more Vice Presidents are elected. In between the Plenary Meetings, a Conference of the Directors takes place at least once a year, which decides upon 'the tasks and activities to be deployed in accordance with the principal goals of WEM'. It can set up permanent or ad hoc groups to carry out these tasks.[17]

A Steering and Finance Committee, appointed from among members of the Directors' Conference, carries out the administrative work towards organisation of the Plenary Meeting and the meetings of Directors. This committee also represents WEM in its dealings with third parties. A Secretary General, who works to the direction of the Chairman of the Committee and who is bound to decisions of the Plenary Meetings and Directors' Conferences, is responsible for the execution of the current activities of WEM. Article 5 provides that 'Decisions can be taken on behalf of all Members by a simple majority of the votes polled . . .'

According to the Statutes:[18]

> 'WEM's primary purpose is to promote the exchange of information and views among its members on all social issues which affect engineering interest. It is also to facilitate concerted views and the formulation of statements on matters of common interest. In achieving the primary purpose WEM may make such representation to international organisations as is required.'

To carry out its primary purpose WEM compiles documentation on the political and economic background, employment, legislation, union claims, negotiations, strikes, agreements, statistics on earnings and other working conditions, unit labour costs and productivity, as well as various specific subjects.[19]

The Statutes provide that affiliated members 'retain their full national autonomy and independence' (Article 2). In 1989, however, two special Sub-Committees were created, one to deal with 'collective bargaining' matters, and the other to deal with 'EC' matters.[20] Given its intensive information gathering and exchange functions, WEM is an organisation well placed to coordinate its members' activities in the field of collective bargaining.

The strategy in the metalworking sector: EC-level coordination

The EMF's strategy is premised on the view that 'a prerequisite for a coordinated bargaining policy in Europe is the strengthening and revival of regional and

16   Western European Metal Trades Employers' Organisation, Statutes adopted by the 13th Plenary Meeting, 8 June 1984, Article 4(1).
17   Ibid, Article 4(2).
18   Ibid, Article 3.
19   *Key Data on WEM*, op cit, pp 2–3.
20   Ibid, p 2.

national trade union bargaining policies in the countries of the Community'.[1]
The 'starting point is the grass roots workers' movement':[2]

> 'bargaining policy in Europe must be constituted at grass roots level and must be
> properly organised at company, regional and national levels, as well as being coordi-
> nated in a politically effective manner across the whole of Europe. Branches and
> sectors shall retain their sovereignty with regard to collective bargaining ... The
> European metalworkers' unions shall endeavour to coordinate their national collec-
> tive bargaining structures, institutions and procedures in the interests of an ability to
> take joint action at European level ... The EMF will step up its efforts to coordinate
> national bargaining policies and implement common goals.'

Despite mention of agreements between the European social partners at various
points,[3] the emphasis of the strategy is on *coordination* of national collective bargaining efforts through the EMF. It is possible that this could be accomplished
through agreements with the employers' associations, but the emphasis is on
guidelines to national bargainers, not EC-level agreed standards imposed on them.

This approach is reflected in the history of the campaign for the reduction of
working time. Between 1967 and 1972, hours reductions were won in all the
then Member States. In a 1969 paper the EMF identified the reduction of working time as one of the common points of bargaining policy in Member States
having the potential to 'serve as starting points or basis for the coordination of
the collective bargaining policy in the metal trade unions in the EEC'.[4]

However, the campaign for reduced working hours in the late 1960s was *not*
the result of some strategic plan drawn up by the EMF, whose Member State
unions would be under instruction to commence bargaining according to a pre-
arranged timetable. What did take place was that unions drew upon the
experiences of the earliest winners (most notably the German unions) to then
pursue their own bargaining agenda. The most recent round of reductions in
the working week appears to have had a similar history. Again, it was not the
case that the EMF decided that a campaign should commence and then set its
members the task of negotiating. What happened was that negotiations commenced in one or two Member States and their successes led unions in other
Member States to make similar demands. The results have been that in recent
years hours reductions have been won in Denmark, Germany, Ireland, Italy
and the UK. If these are the results of an uncoordinated campaign, they may
be seen as an indication of the potential of an active strategy of coordination,
which has yet, however, to be implemented in practice.

CONCLUSION

Sectoral bargaining is well established in all Member States of the EC and, with
the exception of the UK, its scope is expanding to cover topics which lend

1 'Collective Bargaining Policy in a Changing Europe', statement of principle on collective bargaining policy by the EMF, for the EMF Collective Bargaining Policy Conference,
   Luxembourg, 11–12 March 1993, p 14.
2 Ibid, p 15.
3 Ibid, pp 11, 15 and 16: The last states that 'The EMF shall seek to secure collective agreements covering all the qualitative issues which are of importance for the European industrial
   culture as a whole ...'
4 'Structure and Development of Collective Bargaining. Negotiations in the Metal Industries of
   the EEC', Information Bulletin of the European Committee for the Metalworkers' Unions, No
   4/69 (September–December), at p 12.

themselves to regulation by sectoral agreements at EC level. Mechanisms exist, and may be developed, to assist in the articulation of sectoral agreements at Member State and EC levels.

The success of EC-level bargaining is premised on the effective presence of EC-level organisations representing sectoral associations of employers and trade unions. Two sectors, construction and woodwork, and metalworking, have been described as possessing the potential for EC-level sectoral regulation. The strategies adopted by the trade union organisations in these two sectors – the EMF and the EFBWW – have been contrasted. The EMF tends towards coordination of collective bargaining by its national affiliates. There is potential for such coordination in the campaigns for reduction of working time. The EFBWW aims at negotiation of EC-level sectoral agreements with binding effect on affiliated organisations.

Both strategies are capable of exploiting the interaction of EC-level sectoral social dialogue with the potential of the Maastricht Agreement. That Agreement's new procedures for involvement of the social partners at EC level in the process of EC law-making in the social policy area have been described as 'bargaining in the shadow of the law'.[5] The case of the proposed Directive on the posting of workers was presented as an illustration of EC-level bargaining in the construction sector 'in the shadow of proposed EC legislation'.

The tradition in national labour laws to support labour standards in collective agreements is reflected in the trend in EC labour law towards recognition of collectively bargained standards in a number of recent legislative initiatives. If this trend can be linked with, and reinforced by, sectoral bargaining at EC-level, the emergence of a European labour law incorporating collective agreements as well as legislation and judicial decisions will come nearer to realisation.

---

5   See for details Chapter 35.

Part III

Enforcement of European Labour Law

Chapter 7

Enforcement of EU and National Labour Law

INTRODUCTION

European labour law, as the law of the EU, has specific qualities of enforceability which distinguish it from *domestic* labour laws. However, European *labour* law also has specific qualities which distinguish it from *other branches* of EC law.

In domestic law, it is recognised that different branches of law have adapted specialised enforcement mechanisms to their specific exigencies. As the various branches of EU law develop, it becomes apparent that to talk in general terms of enforcement of EU law risks overlooking the specific enforcement mechanisms adopted in different branches.

Comparative analysis of national systems of labour law reveals differences between the enforcement mechanisms used in labour laws of different countries. The enforcement of EU law will have its own characteristics, but it will bear the imprint of the national system in which it operates.[1]

The specific quality of EU labour law, in terms of the combination of different enforcement mechanisms to be adopted, is still open to debate. Everything that has been said about the nature of European labour law, its synthesis of national experience in the form of EU level regulation, applies also to the issue of enforcement of EU labour law. Enforcement mechanisms of European labour law cannot be a wholly autonomous product. National traditions of labour law enforcement will not easily give way to purely EU legal technique. Rather, the EU has experimented with a number of traditional techniques, some of which have had more success than others.

The enforcement of EU labour law is relatively straightforward where it grants clear rights to individuals and national law has implemented these rights through legal measures capable of enforcement through the domestic courts. Enforcement is not so straightforward where EU law confers rights on individuals, but their implementation in national law is subject to dispute. In such cases, enforcement may proceed through the domestic courts using doctrines of direct and indirect effect, or invoking *Francovich* remedies. Such situations make it necessary to rethink the way in which domestic legal frameworks of enforcement are conceptualised.

---

1 For a comparative exercise outlining the different roles for social partners, the administration and the judiciary in the application of labour law in France, Germany, Italy, Spain and the UK, see A Supiot et al 'L'Application de droit du travail dans les pays membres de la CE', Documentation de Ministère de Travail, 1989.

PUBLIC/PRIVATE SECTOR EMPLOYEES

For example, in many continental jurisdictions, the special position of public sector employees, in particular civil servants, has been recognised by the specific legal status attributed to them, their exclusion from the normal judicial procedures and enforcement of labour law, and the availability of alternative, often public law, administrative procedures for the vindication of their rights. In the UK, public sector employees are usually placed in the same position as private sector employees as regards the enforcement of domestic labour law.

EU labour law cuts across these differences. The supra-national nature of EU law has placed States under special obligations. This has required domestic courts to interpret national law in light of EU law, and also to allow for claims against the State even by private sector employees (*Francovich* remedies).

In particular, however, the doctrine of direct effect has potentially dramatic consequences for the enforcement of EU labour law in the public sector. The scope of the potential defendants – emanations of the State – and the already extensive and increasing use of Directives as the form of EU labour law, mean that employees of these emanations may be able to claim rights before domestic courts which are not available to private sector employees. The continental dichotomy of public/private sector employees may come to be replicated in the UK as a consequence. On the other hand, the specificity of the public/private employee distinction may be eroded through the development of remedies of private employees against the State for failures to adequately implement Directives guaranteeing employment rights (*Francovich* claims).

The outcome may be the emergence of a code of public sector employment rights which can be derived from already determined directly effective provisions of Directives and Treaty Articles; this may be supplemented by close scrutiny of other Directives not yet declared directly effective, but having that potential and promoting litigation to secure direct effect.[2]

The recognition of public sector/service employees as a distinct category of employment in European labour law is an unintended consequence of the doctrine of vertical direct effect. Such employees may accumulate an arsenal of labour law rights enforceable before domestic tribunals based on directly effective provisions of Directives. The growth of a distinctive set of directly enforceable rights may have long-term consequences for the special treatment of this category of employees. It is consistent with a trend to be explored later in this book whereby EU labour law develops special regimes for specific categories of workers.

A similar trawl among EU labour law measures might produce a list of potential *Francovich* actions based on inadequate implementation by the State. This could allow for claims against a widely defined range of employers constituting emanations of the State, in particular, as the concept of the State in EC law develops away from ownership criteria or legal form, and focuses on public service, public control and/or special powers. These are some of the potential

2   Examples would be recent Directives on working time, provision of information to employees, health and safety measures and the older Directives on collective dismissals and acquired rights.

consequences for enforcement of national labour law which arise from the interaction of domestic and supra-national jurisdictions.[3]

ADEQUACY OF REMEDIES AND SANCTIONS

The domestic provision of remedies in the enforcement of labour law is subject to scrutiny where it is EU labour law which is being enforced. A number of cases have already found domestic procedures and sanctions wanting, particularly, but not exclusively, in sex discrimination cases. The limitations on awards of compensation and the rules on the burden of proof have both had to be revised.

More generally, national enforcement of labour law has been criticised in a number of areas: from the adequacy of industrial tribunal procedures to the sanctions available for breaches, including the compensation awarded for damage suffered. In a number of cases, the compensation awarded has been reduced by complex provisions for set-off. Such provisions have been condemned by the European Court of Justice already in the case of 'protective awards' for failure to consult workers' representatives as required by EU law.[4]

Set-off provisions exist in other parts of domestic labour law, some of which have been criticised in similar terms to the arguments advanced in *EC Commission v UK*. To bring the battery of EU labour law to bear on such provisions, it is necessary to have a basis in EU law for the right being claimed. Once this is available, the domestic provisions for compensation may be attacked as falling below the EU standard.

By far the most important area of workers' compensation is for personal injury at work. Coincidentally, it is also the area where a great deal of EU legislation is to be found. Compensation for injury at work is subject to a highly sophisticated set of rules, some of which provide for set-off. These range from doctrines of employees' contributory negligence to claw-back provisions whereby the State seeks to re-coup social security benefits paid to workers off work due to injury. It may be that such provisions are vulnerable to the charge that they infringe the principle that violations of EU law be effectively compensated and deterred.

EU labour law on health and safety has been regarded mainly in terms of its impact on substantive law. But the implications for the domestic remedies available for violations of EU health and safety law – from the role of the Health and Safety Executive to the availability of monetary compensation – could be substantial.

---

3 There are wider constitutional implications going beyond labour law. It changes the terms of the debate away from the issue of public ownership and towards more general issues of what constitutes public service, State responsibility towards its own employees and for implementation of social policy in general. It even has implications for the convergence criteria for economic and monetary union, which might have to consider the consequences for threatened public services and public sector employment – said to be one of the reasons Norway rejected EU membership. Changes along these lines have been put to the Reflection Group preparing the 1996 Intergovernmental Conference by the Swedish government. *Financial Times*, 6 September 1995, p 2.

4 Cases C-382/92 and C-383/92: *EC Commission v UK* [1994] ECR I-2435 and [1994] ECR I-2479, decided 8 June 1994.

STRUCTURE OF PART III

The success of enforcement of EU labour law has perhaps been greatest where the EU legal technique meshes with the national tradition. This will be explored through a number of examples in which national experience will be placed in the European context. The examples are those of administrative enforcement, implementation through the social partners, the potential of judicial liability mechanisms, and a strategy of 'euro-litigation'.

The problems of *administrative* enforcement at EU level are evident. The question is how to co-opt national administrative enforcement mechanisms. An illustration will be provided in the form of a national enforcement mechanism which has been taken up in part at EU level: contract compliance.

Where the *social partners* are the instruments of implementation and enforcement of national labour law, the use of this mechanism as a channel for EU labour law implementation is promising. The evolution of the EU law allowing for the social partners to take upon themselves the role of implementing and enforcing EU labour law will be analysed.

The development of *judicial liability* for breaches of EU law is particularly important in systems where litigation plays an important role in labour law enforcement. The European Court has made a sustained effort to scrutinise the remedies, sanctions and procedures available at national level for the enforcement of EU law. The many illustrations of this effort in the field of labour law will be examined.

Finally, EU law offers new possibilities in the form of strategies aimed at countering national law perceived as contrary to EU policy. A classic example of this in the UK was the use of EU law to undermine attempts to prevent large retail outlets from opening on Sundays – the so-called 'Sunday trading' cases. The potential of such '*euro-litigation*' strategies in the labour law context will be explored through the case of using EU law to counter 'de-recognition' of trade unions.

Chapter 8

Administrative Enforcement of European Labour Law

INTRODUCTION

The EU institutions do not possess the resources which can even begin to equate to the resources of national Ministries of Labour or labour inspectorates. The original vision might have been that the EU itself should police observance by the Member States of their obligations. To this end, Article 169 of the Treaty of Rome provides:

'If the Commission considers that a Member State has failed to fulfil an obligation under this Treaty, it shall deliver a reasoned opinion on the matter after giving the State concerned the opportunity to submit its observations.

   If the State concerned does not comply with the opinion within the period laid down by the Commission the latter may bring the matter before the Court of Justice.'

Complaints by the Commission of non-compliance by Member States have had important consequences. A number of cases involving the UK demonstrate the impact: from the complaint leading to the decision in 1982 which forced the UK to introduce the Equal Value Regulations 1983 to implement Article 119 of the Treaty of Rome allowing women to claim their work was of equal value to that of a man,[1] to the complaint leading to the decision on 8 June 1994 which requires the UK to introduce legislation on worker representation in order to comply with the Directives on information and consultation of worker representatives of 1975 and 1977.[2]

As these examples demonstrate, however, the procedure of administrative enforcement through Commission complaint is extremely slow: failure to comply with EU legislation is condemned more than a decade later. An illustration from another country of the inefficacy of the procedure is the case of Italy, using an example of administrative enforcement of labour law which culminated in the European Court condemning Italy in 1989. First, the context of the judgment.

By the end of 1988 the number of EC Directives in effect was 622, and Italy had up to then failed to implement 278, for 196 of which the date for implementation had already passed, and for 48 of these last the expiry date for implementation was over 5 years previously. Italy was one of the countries

---

1   Case 61/81: EC *Commission v United Kingdom of Great Britain and Northern Ireland* [1982] ECR 2601; similarly Case 165/82: [1983] ECR 3431.
2   Cases C-382/92 and C-383/92: *EC Commission v UK* [1994] ECR I-2435 and [1994] ECR I-2479.

most frequently condemned by the European Court for violating its EU obligations. Up to the end of 1988 there were 34 judgments condemning Italy which had not been complied with, and another 28 proceedings pending; moreover, there were 5 cases where Italy had been condemned twice for the same failure to comply, including failure to implement Directive 75/129 of 17 February 1975 on collective dismissals.[3]

In this context, a case of administrative enforcement of EU labour law is that of the condemnation of Italy on 2 February 1989 for failure to implement Council Directive 80/987 of 20 September 1980 on the protection of workers in the event of the insolvency of their employer.[4] The 23 October 1983 was the date by which the transposition of Council Directive 80/987 of 20 September 1980 was to be completed and the Member States were to have notified to the Commission the text of the provisions adopted.

On 3 November 1983 the Commission sent to the Italian government a request to this effect and the Italian government sent a list of provisions which it considered should be taken into account regarding transposition. Over 17 months later, on 24 April 1985, the Commission, having examined these provisions, conveyed to the Italian government its view that these provisions were not sufficient to constitute adequate transposition, and requested the Italian government to reply within two months.

The Italian government did not reply. Almost 11 months later, on 19 March 1986, the Commission gave a formal reasoned opinion under Article 169 of the Treaty to the effect that Italian law did not conform to the requirements of the Directive and formally invited the Italian government to adopt the requisite provisions within one month. In reply to this opinion, the Italian permanent representative to the Community sent a note on 25 April 1986 pointing out the problems confronting Italy in the current situation which precluded complete transposition, and, to show its good will, established a special committee to prepare the necessary proposals, asking in the meanwhile for an extension of time to find the most appropriate solution.

The Commission refused to grant the extension and, 9 months later, on 28 January 1987 commenced proceedings before the European Court of Justice for non-fulfilment by Italy of its Treaty obligations. Over 2 years later, the Court gave judgment against Italy on 2 February 1989, some 9 years and 4 months after the Directive had been adopted unanimously by all the Member States, including Italy.

The enforcement of EU labour law by a central Brussels administration is not presently on the cards. However, administrative enforcement of EU labour law may be improved if national authorities undertake this task. The co-option

---

3   Cases 91/81: [1982] ECR 2133 and 131/84: [1985] ECR 3531. To complete the picture, Italy had also been condemned by the Court for failing to implement Directive 77/187 of 14 February 1977 on transfers of undertakings and protection of employees; Case 235/84: [1986] ECR 2291; A Zambelli, comment on the judgment of the European Court in Case 22/87: *EC Commission v Italian Republic* [1989] ECR 143, decided 2 February 1989; 'Diritto comunitario e tutela contro l'insolvenza dell'imprenditore: l'ennesima inadempienze dell'Italia', (1991) *Rivista Italiana di Diritto del Lavoro* 269, at pp 275–89.

4   Ibid. Of particular importance as it was this failure which was held subsequently to justify a claim against the Italian State for damage caused to workers who were thus unable to benefit from this EC Directive: Cases C-6/90 and 9/90: *Francovich and Bonifaci v Italian Republic* [1991] ECR I-5357.

of national administrative authorities by the EU administration is a complex process, the workings of which are only beginning to be explored.[5] The Commission's most recent Medium Term Social Action Programme 1995–1997 has a separate section entitled 'Towards a more effective application of European Law'.[6] This provides for more information on transposition and implementation to be reported. It formalises the established Committee of Senior Labour Inspectors which had been operating in the area of health and safety at work, and intends to reflect on how to extend labour inspectors' networks to other fields.[7] But progress is likely to be slow.

AN ILLUSTRATION: CONTRACT COMPLIANCE

The enforcement of labour standards through contract compliance – the imposition of prescribed conditions for their employees on contractors with public authorities – is a long-established mechanism of enforcement of labour law. Such clauses may be found in the ILO Labour Clauses (Public Contracts) Convention No 94 of 1949 and Recommendation No 84 of the same name and date. There are similar provisions in the labour laws of Member States of the EU, including, up to 1983, in the UK – the Fair Wages Resolutions 1891– 1946,[8] which inspired the ILO provisions. There have been calls for the inclusion of a social clause in the GATT Uruguay Round.[9]

At EU level, contract compliance emerged in the context of the regulation of public procurement in a single market. A number of Directives on Public Procurement have been approved, and the Commission has indicated that labour standards are among the conditions which will be regulated for contractors. The potential of public procurement as an administrative technique of enforcing EU labour standards will be examined with a view to exploring how it could be developed as an instrument for the enforcement of EU labour law.

Public authorities at national and sub-national levels may insert labour clauses in public contracts. These may come into conflict with the law of the EU. The legal position was stated in a Commission Communication of 22 September 1989 on regional and social aspects of public procurement:[10]

'(in) a broad range of social matters including, for example, professional training, health and safety, labour relations and the suppression of racial, religious discrimination or discrimination on the grounds of sex . . . the procurement Directives neither forbid nor expressly authorise Member States to regulate the matter. Accordingly, they and procuring entities are free under Community law to pursue such objectives, provided they respect the Directives' provisions and the constraints

---

5   F Snyder 'The Effectiveness of European Community Law: Institutions, Processes, Tools and Techniques', (1993) 56 *Modern Law Review* 19, at 27–40.
6   Communication from the Commission, COM (95) 134 final of 12 April 1995, Brussels, Chapter 11, pp 31–4.
7   Ibid, paragraphs 11.1.6–11.1.7.
8   For an exhaustive account, B Bercusson *Fair Wages Resolutions*, Mansell, London 1978.
9   Commission syndicale consultative auprès de l'Organisation de coopération et de développement économiques, *La lutte contre le chomage: une stratégie internationale* – contribution du TUAC à l'étude de L'OCDE sur l'emploi et le chomage, Paris 1993, p 35.
10   OJ C311/7 of 12 December 1989, p 12, para 46. This relied on the decision of the European Court of Justice in Case 31/87: *Gebroeders Beentjes BV v Netherlands* [1988] ECR 4365.

of the Treaty. It also follows that Member States are free under Community law to restrict the capacity of procuring entities to pursue objectives of this kind.'

The issue is whether the EU could and should pursue a policy of enforcing labour law standards by requiring the insertion of labour clauses in public contracts. The Action Programme relating to the implementation of the Community Charter of Fundamental Social Rights for Workers declared that 'the Commission could formulate a proposal aiming at the introduction of a "social clause" into public contracts'.[11]

This has not yet been done. EC public procurement Directives themselves have a variety of clauses which are of interest in formulating a social clause. A labour clause was originally attached to the EC Directive on public works and other EC legal instruments contain provisions of interest. Drawing mainly on the experience at EC level in formulating social clauses, three issues will be addressed: the standards prescribed in a labour clause, the scope of a labour clause, and the enforcement of a labour clause.

The standards prescribed in a labour clause

EU legal instruments prescribe labour standards which could be sources of inspiration for a labour clause. These include EU public procurement Directives and EU labour standards legislation.

Social clauses in EC public procurement Directives

There are four principal public procurement Directives:

1. *Council Directive 93/37/EEC* of 14 June 1993 concerning the coordination of procedures for the award of public works contracts[12] (hereafter referred to as the *works* Directive).
2. *Council Directive 93/36/EEC* of 14 June 1993 coordinating procedures for the award of public supply contracts[13] (hereafter referred to as the *supplies* Directive).
3. *Council Directive 93/38/EEC* of 14 June 1993 on the procurement procedures of entities operating in the water, energy, transport and telecommunications sectors[14] (hereafter referred to as the *entities* Directive).
4. *Council Directive 92/50/EEC* of 18 June 1992 relating to the coordination of procedures for the award of public service contracts[15] (hereafter referred to as the *services* Directive).

---

11   COM (89) 568 final, Brussels, 29 November 1989, p 24.
12   OJ L199/54 of 9.8.93, consolidating Council Directive 71/305/EEC of 26 July 1971 concerning the coordination of procedures for the award of public works contracts, OJ L185/5 of 16.8.71, as amended by Council Directive 89/440/EEC of 18 July 1989, OJ L210/1 of 21.7.89.
13   OJ L199/1 of 9.8.93, consolidating Council Directive 77/62/EEC of 21 December 1976 coordinating procedures for the award of public supply contracts, OJ L13/1 of 15.1.77, as amended by Council Directive 88/295/EEC of 22 March 1988, OJ L127/1 of 20.5.88.
14   OJ L199/84 of 9.8.93, replacing Council Directive 90/531/EEC of 17 September 1990 on the procurement procedures of entities operating in the water, energy, transport and telecommunications sectors, OJ L297/1 of 29.10.90.
15   OJ L209/1 of 24.7.92.

These Directives include various provisions relevant to labour standards.

PROVISION OF INFORMATION ON OBLIGATORY EMPLOYMENT
PROTECTION PROVISIONS AND WORKING CONDITIONS

The *works* Directive provides in Article 23(1):[16]

'The contracting authority may state in the contract documents, or be obliged by a Member State to do so, the authority or authorities from which a tenderer may obtain the appropriate information on the obligations relating to the employment protection provisions and the working conditions which are in force in the Member State, region or locality in which the works are to be executed and which shall be applicable to the works carried out on site during the performance of the contract.'

This makes it *optional* for the contracting authority and the Member State to provide the information on employment protection provisions and working conditions. But as regards the tenderer these are *obligatory*: they 'shall be applicable to the works carried out on site during the performance of the contract'.

OBLIGATORY EMPLOYMENT PROTECTION PROVISIONS AND WORKING
CONDITIONS FOR TENDERERS

The *works* Directive provides in Article 23(2):[17]

'The contracting authority which supplies the information referred to in paragraph 1 shall request the tenderers or those participating in the contract procedure to indicate that they have taken account, when drawing up their tender, of the obligations relating to employment protection provisions and the working conditions which are in force in the place where the work is to be carried out.'

If the information required by Article 23(1) is provided, paragraph 2 reinforces this obligation by requiring tenderers to indicate their compliance with employment protection provisions and working conditions in advance. The relevant applicable provisions which tenderers are required to take into account are those 'in force in the Member State'. It would be possible to specify:

'employment protection obligations towards workers, labour law obligations towards their representatives and working conditions in accordance with the legal provisions applicable, including those in legislation, collective agreements and contracts.'

EXCLUSION OF CONTRACTORS WHO HAVE NOT FULFILLED LEGAL OBLIGATIONS

The *supplies* Directive provides in Article 20(1)[18] that any supplier may be excluded from participation in the contract who:

'(e) has not fulfilled obligations relating to the payment of social security contributions in accordance with the statutory provisions of the country in which he is established or with those of the country of the contracting authority;
(f) has not fulfilled obligations relating to the payment of taxes in accordance with the legal provisions of the country in which he is established or those of the country of the contracting authority.'

16 Substantially similar, though not quite identical provisions are to be found in the *entities* Directive, Article 29 and the *services* Directive, Article 28.
17 Substantially similar, though not quite identical provisions are to be found in the *entities* Directive, Article 29 and the *services* Directive, Article 28.
18 See such clauses also in the *services* Directive, Article 29 and the *works* Directive, Article 24.

It would be possible to add a 'labour law clause' excluding from participation any supplier who:

> 'has not fulfilled employment protection obligations towards workers and labour law obligations towards their representatives in accordance with the legal provisions applicable, including those in legislation, collective agreements and contracts.'

SPECIFIED STANDARDS

Prior to amendment, the *supplies* Directive included in Article 7(1) the following requirement:[19]

> 'The technical specifications defined in Annex II and the description of testing, checking and acceptance methods shall figure in the general or the contractual documents relating to each contract. Such technical specifications may be defined by reference to appropriate standards.
>   In this case it is appropriate to make reference, in order of preference, to:
> 1. Community standards which are binding by virtue of an act of the Communities;
> 2. other Community standards (in particular ECSC standards) or European standards (in particular ESC and CENELAC standards) accepted by the country of the contracting authority;
> 3. international standards accepted by the country of the contracting authority (in particular ISO and IEC standards);
> 4. the national standards of the country of the contracting authority;
> 5. any other standard.'

The original Article 7 was replaced by a new Article 7 by Council Directive 88/295/EEC of 22 March 1988,[20] and is now, with slight modification in the *supplies* Directive:[1]

> '1. The technical specifications defined in Annex III shall be given in the general documents or the contractual documents relating to each contract.
> 2. Without prejudice to the legally binding national technical rules in so far as these are compatible with Community law, the technical specifications mentioned in paragraph 1 shall be defined by the contracting authorities by reference to national standards implementing European standards, or by reference to European technical approvals or by reference to common technical specifications.
>   . . .
> 5. In the absence of European standards or common technical specifications, the technical specifications may be defined, without prejudice to the principles of equivalence and mutual recognition of national technical specifications, by reference to other documents. In this case it is appropriate to make reference in order of preference to:
>   (a) national standards implementing international standards accepted in the country of the contracting authority;
>   (b) other national standards of the country of the contracting authority;
>   (c) any other standard.'

These provisions could include the requirement, for the purpose of defining labour specifications, that reference should be made to EU, ILO and/or other labour standards.

---

19 Directive 77/62 of 21 December 1976, OJ L.13/1 of 15.1.77.
20 OJ L.127/1 of 10.5.88.
1 Article 8. See the identical clauses in Article 10 in the *works* Directive and the *services* Directive, Article 14, and the shorter formulation in the *entities* Directive, Article 18.

CRITERIA FOR AWARD OF CONTRACT

The *supplies* Directive provides in Article 26(1):[2]

'The criteria on which the contracting authority shall base the award of contracts shall be:
(a) either the lowest price only;
(b) or, when the award is made to the most economically advantageous tender, various criteria according to the contract in question: eg price, delivery date, running costs, cost-effectiveness, quality, aesthetic and functional characteristics, technical merit, after-sales service and technical assistance.'

It would be possible to add to the list in (b):

'. . . respect for employment protection obligations towards workers and labour law obligations towards their representatives in accordance with the legal provisions applicable, including those in legislation, collective agreements and contracts.'

EU labour standards legislation

A long-standing EU policy has been to protect labour standards at times when these are threatened by changes affecting employment. Examples are the three Directives on *Collective Dismissals*,[3] on *Acquired Rights*[4] and on protection in the event of employer's *Insolvency*.[5] These Directives are one aspect of an EC social policy to protect workers' employment rights and working conditions. This policy forms part of a social dimension of the EC beyond the pure common market ethic.

The three Directives established a series of protective labour standards. The *Collective Dismissals* Directive requires notification of information to and consultation of workers' representatives. The *Acquired Rights* Directive requires information and consultation of workers' representatives, but also protects employment conditions embodied in individual contracts, prohibits dismissals due to transfer alone and maintains union recognition and collective agreements. The *Insolvency* Directive protects employment rights embodied in individual contracts, but also requires the public authorities to guarantee the rights protected.

In particular, the Acquired Rights Directive is concerned with transfers of undertakings. It applies both to transfers between private individuals, and also, it is now acknowledged, to privatisation – the transfer of public undertakings to the private sphere.[6] It prescribes the maintenance of labour standards in the

---

2   Similar provisions are to be found in the *works* Directive, Article 30(1); criteria listed include: 'eg price, period for completion, running costs, profitability, technical merit'; also in the *entities* Directive, Article 34(1), and in the *services* Directive, Article 36(1).

3   Council Directive 75/129/EEC of 17 February 1975 on the approximation of the laws of the Member States relating to collective redundancies, OJ L48/29 of 22.2.1975; as amended by Council Directive 92/56/EEC of 24 June 1992, OJ L245/3 of 26.8.92.

4   Council Directive 77/187/EEC of 14 February 1977 on the approximation of the laws of the Member States relating to the safeguarding of employees' rights in the event of transfers of undertakings, businesses or parts of businesses, OJ L61/26 of 5.2.1977.

5   Council Directive 80/987/EEC of 20 October 1980 on the approximation of the laws of the Member States relating to the protection of employees in the event of the insolvency of their employer; OJ L283/23.

6   Case C-382/92: *EC Commission v UK* [1994] ECR I-2435, decided 8 June 1994. See generally Brian Napier, *CCT, Market Testing and Employment Rights. The Effects of TUPE and The Acquired Rights Directive*, Institute of Employment Rights, 1993.

form both of individual contracts and collective agreements, and also protects job security and union recognition.

Labour clauses in public contracts are a logical continuation of this policy. Formerly, public authorities provided for themselves much of the goods, services and works they required. Privatisation means public authorities transfer these activities to private contractors. A consistent policy of maintaining labour standards and protecting employment and union recognition should cover all public procurement contracts, not only those which are being privatised.

Another aspect of EU social policy to protect workers' employment rights and working conditions looks to collective agreements as sources of EU labour standards. This is manifest in the Directive requiring employers to provide information about their working conditions to workers.[7] This Directive reinforces employment rights embodied in individual contracts, designates collective agreements as essential conditions of employment and regards collective agreements as a reference source for information about conditions of work.

The Directive on Working Time includes a large number of new provisions which give collective bargaining a role in the setting of EU labour standards on working time.[8] In the past, collective bargaining was largely confined to derogations from prescribed standards. The Directive also allows for collective agreements to define labour standards.

An instrument on a labour clause could enforce the labour standards achieved by the existing EU legislation. This could comprise the following elements:

(a)   requiring information and consultation of workers' representatives;
(b)   protecting employment conditions embodied in individual contracts;
(c)   prohibiting dismissals save in prescribed circumstances;
(d)   maintaining union recognition and collective agreements;
(e)   designating collective agreements as essential conditions of employment;
(f)   recognising as EC labour standards on, eg night working, rest breaks, maximum hours of work, and working time arrangements in general those negotiated in collective agreements;
(g)   requiring public authorities to guarantee the rights protected.

A comparison: the original labour clause attached to the Public Works Directive

The European Parliament attempted to attach a labour clause to the Public Works Directive in 1988. Paragraph 1 of the amendments accepted by the Parliament is as follows:

> 'Without prejudice to the provisions of the Treaties and to measures adopted in accordance with them, the contracting authority shall set out, in the contract documents, the obligations relating to employment conditions which exist in the Member State, region or locality where the work is to be carried out and which will, in consequence, be applicable for work executed on site during the execution of the contract.'

---

7   Council Directive 91/533 of 14 October 1991 on an employer's obligation to inform employees of the conditions applicable to the contract or employment relationship, OJ L288/32 of 18.10.91.
8   Council Directive 93/104/EC of 23 November 1993 concerning certain aspects of the organisation of working time, OJ L307/18 of 13.12.1993.

This clause is similar to that included in the 1989 amendment to the *works* Directive, which inserted a new Article 22a.[9] A critical comparison of the two clauses shows up the points to be borne in mind in drafting a labour clause.

The '*obligations relating to employment conditions*' are not specified. Article 23 amplified this to read 'obligations relating to the employment protection provisions and the working conditions'. It is not clear whether this includes obligations arising from labour legislation, judicial decisions, doctrine, collective agreements at different levels and/or individual contracts. Does it include collective as well as individual rights, rights of workers only or also of their representatives?

The obligations relate to employment conditions '*which exist*'. Article 23 changed this to read 'in force'. It is not clear whether this means that the conditions must be in force legally, be effective, whether legally binding or not, or merely exist, whether effective or not.

The conditions are those in force '*in the Member State, region or locality*'. It is clear that the obligation extends beyond national provisions, but the position is not clear with regard to conflict between provisions at different levels.

The conditions which exist '*will, in consequence, be applicable*'. It is unclear if one or two conditions apply: either two conditions: they must exist and must also be applicable; or one condition: they exist, and in consequence they are applicable by virtue of this clause. Article 22a clarified this by providing simply that the conditions 'shall be applicable'.

Conclusions

An instrument on a labour clause could maintain at least the labour standards achieved by the existing EU legislation. A starting point could be the existing provision in Article 23 of the *works* Directive.[10] Article 23(1) would be improved by making it obligatory for the contracting authority and the Member State to provide information on the employment protection provisions and working conditions which are obligatory as regards the tenderer.

The obligations in Article 23(2) would be improved by requiring the contracting authority to establish (not merely request) that tenderers demonstrate (not merely indicate) that they have respected (not merely taken account of) employment obligations and working conditions in force, which should be more clearly specified.

Provisions in the *supplies, services* and *works* Directives exclude contractors who have not fulfilled tax or social security obligations. A similar labour law clause would exclude contractors who have not fulfilled labour law obligations.

All four procurement Directives (*works, supplies, services, entities*) make provision for the inclusion in the general or contractual documents relating to contracts of technical specifications defined by reference to national or European standards. The labour clause which the European Parliament attempted to attach to the public *works* Directive in 1988 would have required the specification of the labour standards applicable. The Working Time Directive includes a large number of provisions which give collective bargaining a role in the setting of EU

9 Now Article 23 in the consolidated *works* Directive of 1993. The text of Article 23 is quoted above.
10 Substantially similar, though not quite identical provisions are to be found in the *entities* Directive, Article 23 and the *services* Directive, Article 28.

labour standards. This emphasis on collective agreements as sources of EU labour standards could be transposed to a labour clause. The *supplies* Directive provides in Article 26(1) for various criteria for the award of a contract: either the lowest price only, or, when the award is made to the most economically advantageous tender, various criteria. It would be possible to *qualify* the lowest price criteria by reference to labour standards. The references to labour standards in the labour clause could specify *at least* the obligations to be found in existing EU legislation.

The scope of the labour clause: persons and works covered

The scope of the labour clause determines which persons – public authorities, private employers and workers – are covered. The scope of the clause is defined mainly in terms of the types of legal instruments (contracts, subsidies, etc) and the type of goods obtained (works, supplies, services, etc).

Contracts

TYPES OF CONTRACTS COVERED

The *supplies* Directive provides a definition of 'public supply contracts' falling within the scope of the Directive. The definition *before* the 1988 amendment provided in Article 1[11] (my italics):

> '(a) "public supply contracts" shall be contracts for pecuniary consideration concluded in writing between a supplier (a natural or legal person) and one of the contracting authorities defined in (b) below *for the delivery of the products.* Such delivery may in addition include siting and installation operations.'

The amended provision followed the GATT Government Procurement Agreement and is arguably narrower. As reproduced in the consolidated *supplies* Directive of 1993 it reads (my italics):

> '(a) "public supply contracts" are contracts for pecuniary interest concluded in writing *involving the purchase, lease, rental or hire purchase, with or without option to buy,* of products between a supplier (a natural or legal person) and one of the contracting authorities defined in (b) below. The delivery of such products may in addition include siting and installation operations.'

Contracts for the delivery of products which do not involve one of the italicised legal forms fall outside the scope of the Directive, providing an incentive for the development of forms evading the Directive.

The equivalent provision in the *works* Directive is (Article 1) (my italics):

> '(a) "public works contracts" are contracts for pecuniary interest concluded in writing between a contractor and a contracting authority as defined in (b), which have as their object either the *execution or both the execution and design, of works* related to one of the activities referred to in Annex II or a work defined in (c) below, or the execution by whatever means of a work corresponding to the requirements specified by the contracting authority.'

---

11 Council Directive 77/62/EEC of 21 December 1976 coordinating procedures for the award of public supply contracts, OJ L13/1 of 15.1.77. This was amended by Council Directive 88/295/EEC of 22 March 1988, OJ L127/1 of 20.5.88.

That in the *services* Directive is (Article 1) (my italics):

'(a) "public service contracts" shall mean contracts for pecuniary interest concluded in writing between a *service provider* and a contracting authority, to the exclusion of . . .' (There follows a long list.)

The scope of the Directives is execution/design of works, provision of services and delivery of products – though the last is limited to certain types of contracts.

TYPES OF CONTRACTING AUTHORITIES COVERED

The *works, supplies* and *services* Directives specify in more or less similar terms which contracting authorities fall under the scope of the Directives. In the terms of the *works* Directive: [12]

'(b) "contracting authorities" shall be the State, regional or local authorities, bodies governed by public law, associations formed by one or several of such authorities or bodies governed by public law.
A body governed by public law means any body:
– established for the specific purpose of meeting needs in the general interest, not having an industrial or commercial character, and
– having legal personality, and
– financed, for the most part, by the State, or regional or local authorities, or other bodies governed by public law; or subject to management supervision by those bodies; or having an administrative, managerial or supervisory board, more than half of whose members are appointed by the State, regional or local authorities or by other bodies governed by public law.
The lists of bodies and categories of bodies governed by public law which fulfil the criteria referred to in the second subparagraph are set out in Annex I. These lists shall be as exhaustive as possible and may be reviewed in accordance with the procedure laid down in Article 35. To this end, Member States shall periodically notify the Commission of any changes of their lists of bodies and categories of bodies.'

The equivalent provisions in the *entities* Directive extend the scope of the Directive beyond public authorities as defined in the other Directives. The Preamble explains that the main reason for special provisions in these sectors (Recital 8):

'was that entities governing such services are in some cases governed by public law, in others by private law'

and opening up of the market and fair balance require that (Recital 9):

'entities to be covered must be identified on a different basis than by reference to their legal status.'

Article 2 of the *entities* Directive therefore provides:

'1. This Directive shall apply to contracting entities which:
(a) are public authorities or public undertakings and exercise one of the activities referred to in paragraph 2 . . .'

Article 1 provides that 'For the purposes of this Directive':

'2. "public undertaking" shall mean any undertaking over which the public authorities may exercise directly or indirectly a dominant influence by virtue of their ownership of it, their financial participation therein, or the rules which govern it.

12 Article 1. The provisions in the *services* Directive, Article 1(b), and in the *supplies* Directive, Article 1(b) are virtually identical.

A dominant influence on the part of the public authorities shall be presumed when these authorities, directly or indirectly, in relation to an undertaking:
- hold the majority of the undertaking's subscribed capital, or
- control the majority of the votes attaching to shares issued by the undertaking, or
- can appoint more than half of the members of the undertaking's administrative, managerial or supervisory body.'

The labour clause policy extends now beyond the formal category of State or public bodies. Private undertakings under some dominant public influence are bound.

Subsidies

The 1989 amendment of the *works* Directive[13] inserted a new Article 1a, now Article 2(1) of the 1993 consolidated *works* Directive:

'1. Member States shall take the necessary measures to ensure that the contracting authorities comply or ensure compliance with this Directive where they subsidise directly by more than 50% a works contract awarded by an entity other than themselves.'

The *services* Directive included an identical provision regarding (Article 3(3)):

'a service contract awarded by an entity other than themselves in connection with a works contract within the meaning of Article 12(2) of Directive 71/305/EEC' (the *works* Directive).

The category of private undertakings falling under the labour clause is extended beyond those under dominant public influence. Private entities undertaking works contracts which are directly subsidised by more than 50% are bound by the policy.[14]

Concessions and licences

The 1989 amendment of the *works* Directive[15] included in the definitions section a provision on concession contracts:[16]

'(d) "public works concession" is a contract of the same type as that indicated in (a) except for the fact that the consideration for the works to be carried out consists either solely in the right to exploit the construction or in this right together with payment.'

The original *works* Directive had provided that:[17]

'the provisions of this Directive shall not apply to this so called "concession" contract.'

13   Council Directive 89/440/EEC of 18 July 1989, OJ L210/1 of 21.7.89, amending Council Directive 71/305/EEC of 26 July 1971 concerning the coordination of procedures for the award of public works contracts, OJ L185/5 of 25.8.71.
14   This is in line with the ILO Recommendation No 84, which provides in Article 1: 'In cases where private employers are granted subsidies . . . provisions substantially similar to those of the labour clauses in public contracts should be applied'.
15   Council Directive 89/440/EEC of 18 July 1989, OJ L210/1 of 21.7.89, amending Council Directive 71/305/EEC of 26 July 1971 concerning the coordination of procedures for the award of public works contracts, OJ L185/5 of 25.8.71.
16   Article 1(d), now Article 1(d) of the consolidated *works* Directive of 1993.
17   Council Directive 71/305/EEC of 26 July 1971 concerning the coordination of procedures for the award of public works contracts, OJ L185/5 of 25.8.71, Article 3(1).

This provision was repealed by the amending Directive (Article 1(4)). It seems, therefore (though this is not explicit), that the provision in Article 1(d), which characterises concession contracts as of the same type as public works contracts in (a), renders concession contracts also subject to the Directive.

This does not seem to be the case in the *supplies* Directive. The definition (Article 1(a)) of 'public supply contracts' as those for 'pecuniary interest' appears to exclude them, at least where the sole interest is the concession. The only reference to such contracts is in Article 2(2), which merely stipulates that 'the body in question must observe the principle of non-discrimination by nationality when awarding public supply contracts to third parties'.

The *services* Directive provides (Article 6):

'This Directive shall not apply to public service contracts awarded to an entity which is itself a contracting authority within the meaning of Article 1(b) on the basis of an exclusive right which it enjoys pursuant to a published law, regulation or administrative provision which is compatible with the Treaty.'

However, the *entities* Directive provides (Article 2):

'1. This Directive shall apply to contracting entities which:
   (a) are public authorities or public undertakings and exercise one of the activities referred to in paragraph 2;
   (b) or, when they are not public authorities or public undertakings, have as one of their activities any of those referred to in paragraph 2 or any combination thereof and operate on the basis of special or exclusive rights granted by a competent authority of a Member State.
   . . .

3. For the purpose of applying paragraph 1(b), special or exclusive rights shall mean rights deriving from authorisations granted by a competent authority of the Member State concerned, by law, regulation or administrative action, having as their result the reservation for one or more entities of the exploitation of an activity defined in paragraph 2 . . .' (There follow various exceptions regarding, eg bus transport, etc.)

In sum, the application of the procurement Directives to concession contracts is far from uniform: it applies to entities, it appears to have been amended so as to apply to works, there is a narrow application to supplies, but it does not apply to services.

There is nothing in the procurement Directives which explicitly refers to licensing arrangements – though these may overlap with concessions.[18]

Sub-contractors

The 1989 amendment of the *works* Directive,[19] Article 1.16 inserted a new Article 20b:[20]

'In the contract documents, the contracting authority may ask the tenderer to indicate in his tender any share of the contract he may intend to subcontract to third parties.

18 ILO Recommendation No 84 provides in Article 1: 'In cases where private employers are . . . licensed to operate a public utility, provisions substantially similar to those of the labour clauses in public contracts should be applied'.
19 Council Directive 89/440/EEC of 18 July 1989, OJ L210/1 of 21.7.89, amending Council Directive 71/305/EEC of 26 July 1971 concerning the coordination of procedures for the award of public works contracts, OJ L185/5 of 25.8.71.
20 My italics; now Article 20 of the consolidated *works* Directive of 1993. The consolidated *works* Directive introduced one change: the last word 'liability' was substituted for the word 'responsibility' in the 1989 amendment.

> This indication shall be without prejudice to the question of the principal contractor's *liability*.'[1]

The liability referred to is not explicitly stated. It could be towards workers, the public authorities and/or others. The responsibility could regard completion of work and/or, following the sense of the policy, regard compliance with labour standards by sub-contractors.

The 'Labour' Clause amendments accepted by the European Parliament included the following (my italics):

> 'III. In the contract documents, the contracting authority shall ask the tenderer to indicate in his tender any share of the contract he may intend to sub-contract to third parties. For each sub-contract the principal contractor shall retain full *responsibility*.'

Again, the question is: what responsibility? It is worth noting that there is nothing specific about labour-only sub-contracting; there is nothing about further sub-contracting down; there are no express obligations on the sub-contractor; and there is no obligation on the principal contractor to impose obligations on sub-contractors.[2]

Works/workplaces/persons covered

The *works* Directive provides in Article 23(1) that contracting authorities may set out:[3]

> '. . . information on the obligations relating to the employment protection provisions and the working conditions . . . which shall be applicable to the works carried out *on site during* the performance of the contract.'

The scope is limited in space and time. In *space*: it extends only to *on site* work; it is not clearly applicable to materials produced for the contract off site. It is

---

1   The 1989 amending Directive inserted a more specific provision regarding concession contracts: (new Article 1b, now Article 3(2) of the consolidated *works* Directive) –

   '2.   The contracting authority may:
   - either require the concessionaire to award contracts representing a minimum of 30% of the total value of the work for which the concession contract is to be awarded, to third parties, at the same time providing the option for candidates to increase this percentage. This minimum percentage shall be specified in the concession contract,
   - or request the candidates for concession contracts to specify in their tenders the percentage, if any, of the total value of the work for which the concession contract is to be awarded which they intend to assign to third parties.'

   No mention is made of the concessionnaire's responsibility for the sub-contractors.

2   ILO Convention No 94 provides in Article 1(3): 'This Convention applies to work carried out by subcontractors or assignees of contracts; appropriate measures shall be taken by the competent authority to ensure such application'. This imposes the obligations directly on sub-contractors, but does not explicitly render the main contractor responsible. The Fair Wages Resolution 1946 provided in clause 6: 'The contractor shall be responsible for the observance of this Resolution by sub-contractors employed in the execution of the contract, and shall if required notify the department of the names and addresses of all such sub-contractors'.

3   My italics. Substantially similar, though not quite identical provisions are to be found in the *entities* Directive, Article 29(1): '. . . works carried out or the services performed on site during the performance of the contract', and the *services* Directive, Article 28(1)· 'services provided on site during the performance of the contract'. A similar formulation was contained in the labour clause amendments accepted by the European Parliament (para 1): 'applicable for work executed on site during the execution of the contract'.

also unclear if it covers only work on the *contract* on site or *all* work executed on site, whether on the contract or not.

In *time*: it covers the works *during* the performance not of the work, but of the contract. The duration of the contract is not always clear. Also, only works during, not before or after, the performance of the contract are covered. So follow-up, controls and maintenance will be excluded unless the contract clearly provides for these works.[4]

The enforcement of a labour clause

The enforcement of a European labour clause in public contracts has two levels.

– At *Member State* level, to ensure that employers observe the standards prescribed by EC and national law. Various mechanisms exist which are specific to different national legal traditions. A number of techniques have already been prescribed by EC Directives: information/publicity in advertising contracts and in the contracts themselves; maintaining lists of eligible contractors; requiring qualifications and references for those tendering; and examining tenders to ensure compliance with standards. These techniques could also be applied to secure labour standards.
– At *EC* level, to ensure that the standards prescribed are adequately incorporated into national law and observed by Member States and contracting authorities. This was the objective of Council Directive 89/665/EEC of 21 December 1989 on the coordination of the laws, regulations and administrative provisions relating to the application of review procedures to the award of public supply, public works and public service contracts.[5]

Information/publicity

IN THE NOTICE ADVERTISING THE CONTRACT

Information on labour standards could be specified in the notice advertising the contract. For example, the *works* Directive provides that the notice advertising the contract (Article 11(6)):

'shall be drawn up in accordance with the models given in Annexes IV, V and VI and shall specify the information requested in those Annexes.'

Annex IV: 'Model Contract Notices' includes different requirements for open and restricted procedures. For open procedures (B), the following is required:

'11. Minimum economic and technical standards required of the contractor to whom the contract is awarded.
13. Criteria for the award of the contract. Criteria other than that of the lowest price shall be mentioned where they do not appear in the contract documents.'

---

4 The Fair Wages Resolution 1946 provided in clause 2: 'The contractor shall in respect of *all persons employed by him (whether in execution of the contract or otherwise)* in every factory, workshop or place occupied or used by him for the execution of the contract comply with the general conditions required by this Resolution'.
5 OJ L395/33 of 30.12.89, as amended by the *services* Directive, Council Directive 92/50/EEC of 18 June 1992 relating to the coordination of procedures for the award of public service contracts, OJ L209/1 of 24.7.92, Article 41.

For restricted procedures (C):

> '8. Information concerning the contractor's personal position, and minimum economic and technical standards required of the contractor to whom the contract is awarded.
>
> 9. The criteria for the award of the contract where they are not mentioned in the invitation to tender.'[6]

An obligation to provide information on labour standards in the notice advertising the tender could have potentially serious consequences for Member States following the decision of the European Court in *Francovich.*[7] That decision imposed liability on Member States to compensate workers who suffer damage due to failure to implement Directives. Member States could face potential liability if they fail to publish the information, undertakings are consequently not bound, and workers lose their entitlements to the relevant EC labour standards.

IN THE CONTRACT ITSELF

There are provisions for the insertion into the contract of specified standards in the form of technical specifications.[8] These could include labour standards.

The *works* Directive, Article 23(1),[9] currently provides for a tenderer to obtain 'information on the obligations relating to the employment protection provisions and the working conditions which are in force'. The information in question could be inserted directly by the contracting authority into the contractual conditions.[10]

Lists of eligible contractors

Tenderers, to qualify for a contract, may be required to be listed in a register of qualified persons. The *works* Directive provides that:[11]

> 'Any contractor wishing to take part in a public works contract may be requested to

---

6   There is similarly in Annex VI a 'Model notice of works contracts awarded by the concessionaire'.

7   Cases 6/90 and 9/90: *Francovich and Bonifaci v Italian Republic* [1992] ECR I-5357, decided 19 November 1991.

8   In the *works, supplies, entities* and *services* Directives.

9   Substantially similar, though not quite identical provisions are to be found in the *entities* Directive, Article 29(1) and the *services* Directive, Article 28(1).

10 For example, ILO Recommendation No 84 of 1949 concerning Labour Clauses in Public Contracts provides (Article 2):

   'Labour clauses in public contracts should prescribe, either directly or by reference to appropriate provisions contained in laws or regulations, collective agreements, arbitration awards or other recognised arrangements –
   (a) the normal and overtime rate of wages (including allowances) to be paid to the various categories of workers concerned;
   (b) the manner in which hours of work are to be regulated, including wherever appropriate –
      (i) the number of hours that may be worked in any day, week or other specified period in respect of which normal rates of wages are to be paid;
      (ii) the average number of hours that may be worked by persons working in successive shifts on continuous processes; and
      (iii) where hours of work are calculated as an average, the period of time over which this average may be calculated and the normal maximum number of hours that may be worked in any specified period;
   (c) holiday and sick leave provisions.'

11 Article 25. There is a similar provision in the *supplies* Directive, Article 21(1), and in the *services* Directive, Article 30(2).

prove his enrolment in the professional or trade register under the conditions laid down by the laws of the Member State in which he is established . . .'

The *works* Directive refers to: [12]

'Member States who have official lists of recognised contractors . . .'

The *entities* Directive provides (Article 30):

'1. Contracting entities which so wish may establish and operate a system of qualification of suppliers, contractors or service providers.
2. The system, which may involve different qualification stages, shall operate on the basis of objective criteria and rules to be established by the contracting entity. The contracting entity shall use European standards as a reference where they are appropriate . . .'

Qualifications and references

The contractor may be required to establish qualifications and provide references to prove his capacity. The *works* Directive provides –[13]

Article 26:

'1. Evidence of the contractor's financial and economic standing may, as a general rule, be furnished by one or more of the following references . . .'

Article 27:

'1. Proof of the contractor's technical capability may be furnished by:
    (a) the contractor's educational and professional qualifications and/or those of the firm's managerial staff, and, in particular, those of the person or persons responsible for carrying out the works;
    . . .

    (d) a statement of the firm's average annual manpower and the number of managerial staff for the last three years;
    (e) a statement of the technicians or technical bodies which the contractor can call upon for carrying out the work, whether or not they belong to the firm.'

These qualifications and references do not clearly refer to labour standards. But Article 27 has implications for personnel management's capacity and competence.

The original labour clause attached to the public works Directive accepted by the European Parliament included the following:

'Contractors when submitting tenders shall submit "a statement concerning compliance with the wage agreements and other provisions of labour law applicable to the undertaking".'

The precise content and legal status of this 'statement' contained in the tender is unclear. 'Wage agreements' may include other conditions of work, and the scope of the applicable 'provisions of labour law' is very wide. It may refer to past compliance, in which case it may be necessary for records and other evidence of compliance to be produced. It may also be considered a future provision of the contract so as to constitute part of the contractor's future obligations.

---

12 Article 29(1). A similar provision is in the *services* Directive, Article 35.
13 Articles 26–27. Similar provisions are to be found in the *supplies* Directive, Articles 22–23, and in the *services* Directive, Articles 31–32.

Examining tenders

The Directives include provisions which envisage examining tenders to ensure they comply with criteria, which could include compliance with labour standards. The *works* Directive provided in the 1971 version:[14]

'(5) If, for a given contract, tenders are obviously abnormally low in relation to the transaction, the authority awarding contracts shall examine the details of the tenders before deciding to whom it will award the contract. The result of this examination shall be taken into account.

For this purpose it shall request the tenderer to furnish the necessary explanations and, where appropriate, it shall indicate which parts it finds unacceptable.'

This was replaced by amending Council Directive 89/440/EEC of 18 July 1989, and is now in Article 30 of the consolidated *works* Directive of 1993:[15]

'(4) If, for a given contract, tenders appear to be abnormally low in relation to the works, the contracting authority shall, before it may reject those tenders, request, in writing, details of the constituent elements of the tender which it considers relevant and shall verify those constituent elements taking account of the explanations received.

The contracting authority may take into consideration explanations which are justified on objective grounds including the economy of the construction method, or the technical solution chosen, or the exceptionally favourable conditions available to the tenderer for the execution of the work, or the originality of the work proposed by the tenderer.'

In the proposal for a Council Directive on *posted workers*,[16] there were specific provisions anticipating the need to examine labour standards (Article 4(1) and (2)):

'(1) Member States shall provide for cooperation between public authorities in matters relating to the application of this Directive. To this end they shall designate liaison offices. The relevant details shall be notified to the other Member States and to the Commission.
(2) The assistance referred to in paragraph 1 shall consist in particular in replying to any request for information concerning the working conditions applicable to posted workers . . . Mutual administrative assistance shall be provided free of charge.'

Member States could be expected to provide the same facilities regarding labour standards applicable to public contractors.

Review procedures and remedies

Remedies for those harmed by an infringement of labour standards may be adapted from those techniques prescribed in Council Directive 89/665/EEC of 21 December 1989 on the coordination of the laws, regulations and administrative provisions relating to the application of *review procedures* to the award of

---

14   Article 29. Council Directive 71/305/EEC of 26 July 1971 concerning the coordination of procedures for the award of public works contracts, OJ L185/5 of 16.8.71.
15   There are similar provisions in the *services* Directive, Article 37, the *supplies* Directive, Article 27 and the *entities* Directive, Article 34(5).
16   COM (91) 230 final – SYN 346, Brussels, 1 August 1991.

public supply and public works contracts: [17]

> '1. The Member States shall take the measures necessary to ensure that ... decisions taken by the contracting authorities may be reviewed effectively and, in particular, as rapidly as possible ... on the grounds that such decisions have infringed Community law in the field of public procurement or national rules implementing that law.
>
> ...
>
> 3. The Member States shall ensure that the review procedures are available ... at least to any person having or having had an interest *in obtaining* a particular public supply or public works contract *and* who has been or risks being harmed by an alleged infringement ...'

The provision is aimed at potential *contractors*. It could be adapted to enable workers or others harmed by an infringement of labour standards to use the review procedure. A possible model is the provision in the proposed Directive on *posted workers* (Article 5):

> 'Member States shall provide appropriate remedies in the event of failure to comply with this Directive and in particular shall ensure that adequate procedures exist at the suit of workers and/or their representatives for the enforcement of obligations under this Directive.'

This provision could itself benefit from the further elaborations in the *review procedures* Directive (Article 2):

> '1. The Member States shall ensure that the measures taken concerning the review procedures specified in Article 1 include provision for the powers to:
> (a) take, at the earliest opportunity and by way of interlocutory procedures, interim measures with the aim of correcting the alleged infringement or preventing further damage to the interests concerned ...
> (b) either set aside or ensure the setting aside of decisions taken unlawfully, including the removal of discriminatory technical, economic or financial specifications in the invitation to tender, the contract documents or in any other document relating to the contract award procedure;
> (c) award damages to persons harmed by an infringement ...
>
> ...
>
> 7. The Member States shall ensure that decisions taken by bodies responsible for review procedures can be effectively enforced.'

Beyond these remedies before national courts or tribunals, there is provision for enforcement by Community organs in the *review procedures* Directive (Article 3):

> '1. The Commission may invoke the procedure for which this Article provides when, prior to a contract being concluded, it considers that a clear and manifest infringement of Community provisions in the field of public procurement has been committed during a contract award procedure ...
> 2. The Commission shall notify the Member State and its contracting authority ... and request its correction ...
> 3. Within 21 days of receipt of the notification ... the Member State shall communicate to the Commission:
> (a) its confirmation that the infringement has been corrected; or
> (b) a reasoned submission as to why no correction has been made; or
> (c) a notice to the effect that the contract award procedure has been suspended ...'

---

17   Article 1 (my italics). OJ L395/33 of 30.12.89, as amended by the *services* Directive, Article 41.

Conclusion

The EU law on public procurement has developed few provisions for the protection of labour standards. The general social and labour policy of the EU has developed far beyond this stage. There are various instruments which could inspire a European instrument on labour clauses in public contracts. An instrument of this kind would be a powerful force towards the effective administrative enforcement of EU labour law.

Chapter 9

Implementation and Enforcement of European Labour Law through the Social Partners

INTRODUCTION

Compared with administrative officials or judges, the social partners are much less remote from the site of enforcement of labour law. Their proximity means that they have the potential to be effective guarantors of the application of the rules. This function is reinforced by EU law's recognition of the role of collective agreements in implementing Directives – a recognition that emerged slowly from the case law of the European Court of Justice.

THE EVOLUTION OF THE CASE LAW

Article 189 of the Treaty of Rome stipulates that:

> 'A directive shall be binding, as to the result to be achieved, upon each Member State to which it is addressed, but shall leave to the national authorities the choice of *form* and *methods*.'

Non-compliance with this obligation allows the Commission eventually to make a complaint to the European Court. Directives habitually referred to the obligation of Member States to implement their provisions through 'laws, regulations and administrative provisions'.[1]

In *EC Commission v Italian Republic*,[2] the Italian government argued 'in substance' that legislation, regulatory provisions and collective agreements combined to achieve adequate implementation of Directive 75/129 on collective dismissals. The Italian government argued that to take the contrary view was formalist:[3]

> 'In its opinion, the Commission set out from the formalistic stand-point that the directive can be complied with only by the adoption of implementing measures, irrespective of where the provisions of directives are already complied with in the legal order of a Member State. It contends that the Commission inferred purely from the fact that the implementing measures were not put into effect that the Italian

---

1   For example, Council Directive 77/187 of 14 February 1977 on the approximation of the laws of Member States relating to the safeguarding of employees' rights in the event of transfers of undertakings, businesses or parts of businesses, OJ 1977, L61/26, Article 8: '1. Member States shall bring into force the laws, regulations and administrative provisions needed to comply with this Directive'.
2   Case 91/81: [1982] ECR 2133.
3   Ibid, at 2142.

Government had not complied with the obligations arising out of the directive, without ascertaining whether the aims of the directive were already ensured in the Italian legal order.'

Responding to this argument, Advocate-General Verloren Van Themaat came to a specific conclusion regarding the role of collective agreements in implementing Directives:[4]

> 'with regard to Article 100 of the EEC Treaty and Article 6 of the directive, they cannot be regarded as "methods" within the meaning of Article 189 of the Treaty or as "laws, regulations or administrative provisions" within the meaning of Article 6 of the directive.'

To the contrary, the Court seemed to respond in some degree to the substantive argument of the Italian government. Upholding the Commission's complaint, the European Court pointed out that certain sectors were not covered by agreements, and that the agreements did not include all the provisions required by Community law.[5] The conclusions of Advocate-General Verloren Van Themaat had also pointed out the defects of the Italian agreements regarding their coverage and scope. But, significantly, there was no reference in the Court's judgment to his conclusion regarding the formal role of collective agreements. It appeared that the Court was unwilling to hold collective agreements formally inadequate when there was no need to, as they were, on the facts of the case, in any event substantively inadequate.

This preference for substantive over formal logic was again manifested in *EC Commission v United Kingdom of Great Britain and Northern Ireland.*[6] The European Court held that the failure of the UK government to enact legislation providing for the nullification of collective agreements violating the provisions of Directive 76/207 on equal treatment of men and women constituted non-fulfilment of its obligations under Article 189. Although collective agreements in the UK lacked legal effect, the European Court stated:[7]

> 'The directive thus covers all collective agreements without distinction as to the nature of the legal effects which they do or do not produce. The reason for that generality lies in the fact that, even if they are not legally binding as between the parties who sign them or with regard to the employment relationships which they govern, collective agreements nevertheless have important de facto consequences for the employment relationships to which they refer, particularly in so far as they determine the rights of the workers and, in the interests of industrial harmony, give undertakings satisfy or need not satisfy *(sic).* The need to ensure that the directive is completely effective therefore requires that any clauses in such agreements which are incompatible with the obligations imposed by the directive upon the Member States may be rendered inoperative, eliminated or amended by appropriate means.'

In this the Court reflected the realist view of Advocate-General Rozès, who stated:[8]

> '. . . a situation in which possibly discriminatory provisions continue to exist in documents such as collective agreements . . . is just as ambiguous – above all for workers who in most cases have no legal training . . . workers have easier access to collective

4   Ibid, at 2145.
5   Ibid, at 2140, paragraphs 8–9.
6   Case 165/82: [1983] ECR 3431.
7   Ibid, at 3447, paragraph 11.
8   Ibid, at 3454.

agreements ... than to Directive 76/207 or to the United Kingdom laws depriving those documents, in general, of legally binding force. Thus, workers may believe that because their contracts of employment reproduce possibly discriminatory provisions from the types of document referred to they are legal and may not be challenged at law and the workers may therefore be deprived of the advantages of a directive which was in fact adopted for their benefit. In order to avoid such risks of confusion, the best course is to make it possible for such discriminatory provision to be removed from those documents, as required by the directive.'

A definitive step towards formal recognition of collective agreements was taken in *EC Commission v Kingdom of Denmark.*[9] In that case, the Danish government's position was explicitly that collective agreements were its choice of form and method for implementation of the obligations of Council Directive 75/117 on equal pay. It was argued that the Danish legislation was but a secondary guarantee of the equality principle in the event that this principle was not guaranteed by collective agreements. An agreement of 1971 made such provision and covered most employment relations in Denmark.[10]

Significantly, in this case Advocate-General Verloren Van Themaat did not refer to his earlier conclusion excluding collective agreements as measures implementing Council Directives. He merely noted that:[11]

'From the point of view of legal certainty it would undoubtedly have been preferable had Denmark simply incorporated in its legislation the interpretation of the principle of equal pay laid down in Article 1 of the directive, in accordance with the view of the Commission.'

The Court held:[12]

'that Member States may leave the implementation of the principle of equal pay in the first instance to representatives of management and labour. That possibility does not, however, discharge them from the obligation of ensuring, by appropriate legislative and administrative provisions, that all workers in the Community are afforded the full protection provided for in the directive. That State guarantee must cover all cases where effective protection is not ensured by other means, for whatever reason, and in particular cases where the workers in question are not union members, where the sector in question is not covered by a collective agreement or where such an agreement does not fully guarantee the principle of equal pay.'

However, in a second case involving Italy, *EC Commission v Italian Republic,*[13] Advocate-General Sir Gordon Slynn returned to the attack. He invoked the conclusion of Advocate-General Verloren Van Themaat in the earlier case involving Italy: 'a collective bargaining agreement is not a "method" for implementing a directive under Article 189 of the Treaty'.[14] He also cited the text of the Directive in question (Directive 77/187), which, following the language normally used in Directives, specified implementation through laws, regulations or administrative provisions – not mentioning collective agreements.[15] Despite this, the Court cited its own judgment in *EC Commission v*

 9   Case 143/83: [1985] ECR 427.
10   Ibid, at 434, paragraph 7.
11   Ibid, at 430.
12   Ibid, at 434–5, paragraph 8.
13   Case 235/84: [1986] ECR 2291.
14   Ibid, at 2295.
15   Ibid.

Kingdom of Denmark and reiterated that:[16]

> 'it must be remembered that, as the Court held in its judgment of 30 January 1985 in Case 143/83 (*EC Commission v Denmark* [1985] ECR 427), it is true that the Member States may leave the implementation of the social policy objectives pursued by a directive in this area in the first instance to management and labour. That possibility does not, however, discharge them from the obligation of ensuring that all workers in the Community are afforded the full protection provided for in the directive. The State guarantee must cover all cases where effective protection is not ensured by other means.'

The substantive logic received a further impulse in *EC Commission v French Republic*.[17] The Commission challenged the French government's delegation to the social partners of the task of amending agreements violating the provisions of Directive 76/207 on equal treatment. This time Advocate-General Sir Gordon Slynn argued that 'it was not sufficient to leave it to labour and management without specific requirements as to the time or methods of enforcement'.[18] Moreover, he pointed out, 'There is no State guarantee of effective enforcement of the principle of equality should the negotiation process between the two sides of industry fail'.[19] To support this he added:[20]

> 'The results of the legislation in practice demonstrate the absence of any effective State guarantee of compliance, notwithstanding the existence of a procedure for government approval of collective agreements. It appears that in 1983 in France 1,050 collective agreements were concluded in branches of working activity and 2,400 in individual undertakings. In 1984 the figures were 927 and 6,000 respectively. By contrast, only 16 collective agreements were renegotiated on a non-discriminatory basis.'

Citing these figures, the Court concluded:[1]

> 'Such figures are extremely modest when compared with the number of collective agreements entered into each year in France ... The requirement that collective agreements must be approved and the possibility that they may be extended by the public authorities have therefore not led to a rapid process of renegotiation.
>
>   The French Government's argument that collective negotiation is the only appropriate method of abolishing the special rights in question must be considered in the light of that conclusion.
>
>   In that regard, it is enough to observe that, even if that argument were to be accepted, it could not be used to justify national legislation which, several years after the expiry of the period prescribed for the implementation of the directive, makes the two sides of industry responsible for removing certain instances of inequality without laying down any time-limit for compliance with that obligation.
>
>   It follows from those considerations that the French Government's argument that the task of removing special rights for women should be left to the two sides of industry working through collective negotiation cannot be accepted.'

This case also illustrates the limitations of the litigation procedure. The figures cited do not indicate what proportion of agreements contained discriminatory clauses. The figure of sixteen agreements amended has to be assessed not

16   Ibid, at 2302, paragraph 20.
17   Case 312/86: [1988] ECR 6315.
18   Ibid, at 6329.
19   Ibid.
20   Ibid.
 1   Ibid, at 6637–8, paragraphs 20–23.

against the total number of agreements, but against those containing clauses requiring amendment. Research by the French Commission Nationale de la Négociation Collective has produced reports on the number of agreements containing such clauses.[2] These indicate that relatively few contain clauses pertaining to equality. This puts the evaluation by the Court and the Advocate-General in a different light.

Subsequently, there has been a series of other decisions of the European Court reinforcing the substantive approach to collective agreements in the area of equal pay and equal treatment. Collective agreements are condemned if they make unequal provision for men and women,[3] provide for discriminatory criteria for pay calculations and lack transparency as regards pay determination.[4] Each case involved the Court making a close examination of the practical workings of a collective agreement. In each case it was the substance of the agreement that was condemned. But it was already clear by 1989 that collective agreements were formally acceptable as instruments for the implementation of Community law obligations.

THE ACKNOWLEDGMENT BY COUNCIL AND COMMISSION

This was evident in the Preamble to the Community Charter of Fundamental Social Rights of Workers of 1989:[5]

'Whereas such implementation may take the form of laws, collective agreements or existing practices at the various appropriate levels and whereas it requires in many spheres the active involvement of the two sides of industry.'

The Charter further declared in Article 27:

'It is more particularly the responsibility of the Member States, in accordance with national practices, notably through legislative measures or collective agreements, to guarantee the fundamental social rights in this Charter.'

The Commission followed suit. In proposals under the Action Programme to give effect to the Charter, it began to insert an implementation provision, which accords a role to collective bargaining.[6] More than one such proposal has already been approved by the Council of Ministers. For example:[7]

'Member States shall adopt the laws, regulations and administrative provisions necessary to comply with this Directive no later than 30 June 1993, or shall ensure by that

---

2 Commission Nationale de la Négociation Collective, *Bilan Annuel de la Négociation Collective 1984, L'Egalité professionnelle entre les femmes et les hommes* (Ministère des Affaires Sociales et de l'Emploi, June 1985, mimeo), and similar reports published in following years.

3 Case 170/84: *Bilka-Kaufhaus GmbH v Weber von Hartz* [1986] ECR 1607. Case C-33/89: *Kowalska v Freie und Hansestadt Hamburg* [1990] ECR I-2591.

4 Case 109/88: *Handels- og Kontorfunktionaerernes Forbund i Danmark v Dansk Arbejdsgiverforening* [1989] ECR 3199.

5 The text of the Charter is published in *Social Europe*, 1/90.

6 Proposal for a Council Directive on certain employment relationships with regard to distortions of competition, Article 6; COM (90) 228 final–SYN 280, Brussels, 13 August 1990. Proposal for a Council Directive concerning certain aspects of the organisation of working time, Article 14; COM (90) 317 final–SYN 295, Brussels, 20 September 1990.

7 Council Directive 91/533 of 14 October 1991 on an employer's obligation to inform employees of the conditions applicable to the contract or employment relationship, OJ 1991 L288/32, Article 9(1).

date that the employers' and workers' representatives introduce the required provisions by way of agreement, the Member States being obliged to take the necessary steps at all times to guarantee the results imposed by this Directive.'

Article 2(4) of the Agreement annexed to the Protocol on Social Policy of the Treaty on European Union, signed at Maastricht on 7 February 1992, stipulates:[8]

'A Member State may entrust management and labour, at their joint request, with the implementation of directives ... In that case, it shall ensure that, no later than the date on which a directive must be transposed in accordance with Article 189, management and labour have introduced the necessary measures by agreements, the Member State concerned being required to take any necessary measure enabling it at any time to be in a position to guarantee the results imposed by that directive.'

It provides the latest point[9] of a long process whereby first individual Member States, then the European Court, then eleven Member States in Article 27 of the Community Charter, and finally the Council have formally recognised the role of collective bargaining in the implementation of EC labour law.

The importance of this method of enforcement of European labour law is likely to increase in the future. The Commission's Medium Term Social Action Programme 1995–1997 provides:[10]

'11.1.9   –implementation of Directives by collective agreements: in light of the European Court of Justice case law and the Agreement on Social Policy, and taking into account diverse national practices, the Commission will present a Communication addressing the entire area of implementation of Community directives by collective agreements. The Communication will also consider and reflect on ways and procedures to involve the social partners in the process of control of transposition and enforcement of Community law (1996).

11.1.10 A clause concerning implementation by collective agreements will be inserted in all future directives, where the issues may fall under the bargaining power of the social partners.'

---

8   This version was derived from the ETUC/UNICE/CEEP Accord of 31 October 1991, and differs from that initially proposed by the Dutch Presidency: 'A Member State may entrust management and labour with the implementation of all or part of the measures which it has laid down in order to implement the directives adopted in accordance with paragraphs 2 and 3'. *Europe Documents* No 1734, 3 October 1991, proposal for new Article 118(4).

9   The background to Article 2(4) of the Maastricht Agreement is discussed in Chapters 34 and 35 concerned with the Protocol and Agreement on Social Policy of the Treaty on European Union.

10   COM (95) 134 final, Brussels, 12 April 1995, paragraphs 11.1.9–11.1.10.

Chapter 10

Judicial Liability

INTRODUCTION

The development of a model whereby EC labour law could be enforced by individuals seeking redress before national tribunals and courts – a judicial liability model – could have followed one of at least two tracks. Enforcement of EC law could have been left entirely to national law. The national system of remedies, procedures and sanctions could have been exploited to maximise the enforcement of substantive EU labour law rights. Building on the foundation of these purely national remedies, procedures and sanctions, an effort might be made to develop certain minimum standards of enforcement.

Alternatively, the attempt might be made to create an entirely original form of judicial liability system, developing a new EC law on remedies, procedures and sanctions, to which national law must conform. This solution would require the EU institutions to prescribe a system of harmonised rules on enforcement covering remedies, procedures and sanctions. The legislative organs of the EU have refused to do so; there is lacking a consensus among Member States that this is either necessary or desirable.

The consequence of the failure to develop a harmonised system of enforcement of EU labour law is, however, that there may be considerable diversity among Member States with regard to the efficacy of enforcement of generally applicable EC labour law norms. Those Member States with less efficacious remedies, more procedural restrictions and weaker sanctions may better be able to avoid compliance with EC labour law by effectively reducing the likelihood of judicial redress for those benefiting from it, or the likelihood of liability of those subject to it.

The failure of the legislative organs of the EU to develop a judicial liability model has in some measure been compensated for by the efforts of the European Court of Justice to develop a role for the national judiciaries in securing enforcement of EC law, including labour law. Member State obligations regarding compliance with EC law are set out in Article 5 of the Treaty of Rome:

'Member States shall take all appropriate measures, whether general or particular, to ensure fulfilment of the obligations arising out of this Treaty or resulting from action taken by the institutions of the Community. They shall facilitate the achievement of the Community's tasks.

They shall abstain from any measure which could jeopardise the attainment of the objectives of this Treaty.'

One avenue for the enforcement of this obligation was through measures adopted by national governments in the Council of Ministers. Another could be through the EU's administration, the Commission, creating links with national administrations responsible for law enforcement. However, national judiciaries are also organs of the Member States, and, as such, incur responsibility for ensuring fulfilment of the Article 5 obligation. A third possibility, therefore, was the chain linking the European Court with national judiciaries through the Article 177 preliminary reference procedure. This could be used as a separate channel for developing rules concerning the enforcement of EU law.

The constitutional novelty of recasting national courts as part of a supranational judicial hierarchy, with the European Court at its apex, was a major enterprise. Article 177 contained the seeds of such an enterprise by providing that, on questions of EC law, *any* court or tribunal may:

> 'if it considers that a decision on the question is necessary to enable it to give judgment, require the Court of Justice to give a ruling thereon.'

The undermining of national hierarchies by allowing lower courts to leapfrog higher levels was thus encouraged. The European Court was also situated within national hierarchies by virtue of the last paragraph of Article 177:

> 'Where any such question is raised in a case pending before a court or tribunal of a Member State, against whose decisions there is no judicial remedy under national law, that court or tribunal shall bring the matter before the Court of Justice.'

These provisions were the constitutional basis allowing the European Court to adapt and develop remedies for EC labour law violations. The supremacy of EC law would allow for rules so developed to prevail over national rules which might restrict the enforcement of EC labour law, even where this meant that national legislation was to be ignored or supplemented, or new remedies created.

The disintegrative effects of such doctrines on national state structures – disrupting judicial hierarchies and constitutional linkages between the judicial, executive and legislative branches of Member States – may be seen as part of the catalytic effect of the emergence of a supranational entity.

A preliminary point to be emphasised is that the effort to develop a judicial liability model for enforcement of EC labour law is contingent on the existence of substantive labour law rights. Liability only arises where there are substantive EC law rights to be violated. There has to be an EC law right before there can be an attempt to exploit EC law to expand domestic remedies, procedures and sanctions to protect that right.

The multiplier effect is evident in so far as EC law infiltrates UK domestic law through various doctrines: for example, the doctrine requiring domestic law to be interpreted consistently with EC law. So where such domestic law, permeated by EC law, is not adequately enforced, EC law on remedies, procedures and sanctions may be invoked to achieve the effectiveness required by EC law. The issue may be perceived as the engagement by the European Court of domestic courts in the enforcement of EC law; a subtle strategy of co-operation or co-optation or even seduction.

Naturally, this process has not been uncontroversial: in particular, where the judicial liability model for enforcing EC law has impinged directly on Member States. The prospect of empowering national courts to uphold liability of

Member States for violations of EC law, perhaps in conditions where national law explicitly prohibits such liability, has created anxiety among Member States.

There are many other dimensions which require closer attention. The technique adopted by the European Court of laying down EC law principles, but leaving the application of these principles to national courts is fraught with difficulty. EC labour law is no exception. For example, the European Court has laid down the principle that indirect discrimination is justifiable on objective grounds, which must, however, comply with the general principle of proportionality – but both objective grounds and proportionality are to be left for national courts to decide; or that the doctrine of the direct effect of Directives is limited to emanations of the State, as defined by certain criteria, but that it is for national courts to apply these criteria in deciding whether a particular entity is an emanation of the State.

This chapter is concerned with the European Court's principles regarding the effective enforcement of EC labour law, where it has prescribed such principles regarding remedies, procedures and sanctions.

A SUPRANATIONAL JUDICIAL LIABILITY SYSTEM

The starting point for enforcement of European labour law is the recognition of the supranational quality of EC labour law. This is a labour law which is not determined or confined by national jurisdictions. National rules on law enforcement continue to play a, perhaps the, major role. But the nature and quality of these national rules have been transformed by the infusion of rules having supranational origin: EC law.

This is something both fundamental and difficult to grasp. It requires a mental shift: from seeing UK labour law as a *national* and autonomous system of rules and institutions, to seeing UK labour law as *part* of a transnational system of rule-making and enforcement machinery comprising the institutions of the EC established by the Member States, including the UK.

The distinctive quality of the EC Treaty was defined by the European Court of Justice in *Van Gend en Loos*:[1]

'The objective of the EEC Treaty, which is to establish a Common Market, the functioning of which is of direct concern to interested parties in the Community, implies that this Treaty is *more* than an agreement which merely creates mutual obligations between the contracting States. This view is confirmed by the preamble to the Treaty which refers not only to governments but to peoples. It is also confirmed more specifically by the establishment of institutions endowed with sovereign rights, the exercise of which affects Member States and also their citizens. Furthermore, it must be noted that the nationals of the States brought together in the Community are called upon to cooperate in the functioning of this Community through the intermediary of the European Parliament and the Economic and Social Committee.

---

1 Case 26/62: *Algemene Transport- en Expeditie Onderneming van Gend & Loos NV v Nederlandse administratie der belastingen (Netherlands Inland Revenue Administration)* [1963] ECR 1, 12 (italics added).

In addition the task assigned to the Court of Justice under Article 177,[2] the object of which is to secure uniform interpretation of the Treaty by national courts and tribunals, confirms that the States have acknowledged that *Community law has an authority which can be invoked by their nationals before those courts and tribunals.*

The conclusion to be drawn from this is that *the Community constitutes a new legal order of international law for the benefit of which the States have limited their sovereign rights,* albeit within limited fields, *and the subjects of which comprise not only Member States but also their nationals.* Independently of the legislation of Member States, *Community law therefore not only imposes legislation on individuals but is also intended to confer on them rights* which become part of their legal heritage. These rights arise not only where they are expressly granted by the Treaty, but also by reason of obligations which the Treaty imposes in a clearly defined way upon individuals as well as upon the Member States and upon the institutions of the Community.'

This principle of supranational law was reaffirmed by the European Court in *Costa v ENEL*:[3]

'By contrast with ordinary international treaties, the Treaty has created its own legal system which, on the entry into force of the Treaty, became an integral part of the legal systems of the Member States and which their courts are bound to apply.'

But the significance of the ruling that EC law could create enforceable legal rights for individuals in national courts was greatly magnified by the European Court ruling that precedence was to be accorded to EC law over domestic law. The Court not only characterised EC law as part of domestic law, it declared the *supremacy* of EC law over other domestic law:[4]

'The precedence of Community law is confirmed by Article 189,[5] whereby a regulation "shall be binding" and "directly applicable in all Member States". This provision, which is subject to no reservation, would be quite meaningless if a State could unilaterally nullify its effects by means of a legislative measure which could prevail over Community law.'

---

2 'Article 177. The Court of Justice shall have jurisdiction to give preliminary rulings concerning:
   (a) the interpretation of this Treaty;
   (b) the validity and interpretation of acts of the institutions of the Community;
   (c) the interpretation of the statutes of bodies established by an act of the Council, where those statutes so provide.
   Where such a question is raised before any court or tribunal of a Member State, that court or tribunal may, if it considers that a decision on the question is necessary to enable it to give judgment, request the Court of Justice to give a ruling thereon.
   Where any such question is raised in a case pending before a court or tribunal of a Member State, against whose decisions there is no judicial remedy under national law, that court or tribunal shall bring the matter before the Court of Justice.'
3 Case 6/64: *Costa v Ente Nazionale per l'Energia Elettrica (ENEL)* [1964] ECR 585.
4 Ibid.
5 'Article 189. In order to carry out their task and in accordance with the provisions of this Treaty, the European Parliament acting jointly with the Council, the Council and the Commission shall make regulations and issue directives, take decisions, make recommendations or deliver opinions.
   A regulation shall have general application. It shall be binding in its entirety and directly applicable in all Member States.
   A directive shall be binding, as to the result to be achieved, upon each Member State to which it is addressed, but shall leave to the national authorities the choice of form and methods.
   A decision shall be binding in its entirety upon those to whom it is addressed.
   Recommendations and opinions shall have no binding force.'

This goes beyond the incorporation into domestic law of certain rules. It means that rules may be created by EC institutions even where the UK opposes such rules in those EC institutions. These rules must be enforced in UK courts even where this involves overriding rules produced by domestic law-making institutions.

EC labour law rules take precedence over domestic labour law rules. This is well known in certain areas of substantive law, such as the law on sex discrimination, where UK domestic law has been shaped, and, in cases of conflict, has been repeatedly overridden by EC law. Probably the best known example of the impact of these rulings in labour law is the *Defrenne* case, where the European Court decided that:[6]

> 'The principle that men and women should receive equal pay, which is laid down by Article 119, may be relied on before the national courts. These courts have a duty to ensure the protection of the rights which that provision vests in individuals, in particular in the case of those forms of discrimination which have their origin in legislative provisions . . .'

The wider the range of competences of the EC institutions, the more the EC law they create will come to replace increasingly wide areas of UK labour law. Indeed, the 'spill-over' effect makes it difficult to insulate most areas of UK labour law from the influence of EC labour law.[7]

Given that it may be applied in national courts, the doctrine of supremacy also applies to rules on enforcement of labour law, including remedies and procedures. EC law has developed special techniques and principles by which EC labour law may be enforced in national courts. Where EC enforcement requirements come into conflict with national procedures and remedies, again, they take precedence and must be applied by national courts overriding domestic rules. Some spectacular instances have included the *Factortame* decision allowing interim remedies against the Crown contrary to domestic rules, and the decision in *Marshall (No 2)* abolishing the limits on compensation for sex discrimination in the UK legislation.[8]

These techniques of enforcement of EC labour law in national courts include doctrines of 'direct' and 'indirect' effect and State liability. EC law has also developed principles concerning procedures and remedies available for violations of EC labour law which must be applied by national courts.

DIRECT EFFECT

Decisions of the European Court have attributed to Treaty articles and Regulations the legal quality of 'direct effect', their provisions being enforceable by individuals in national courts and taking precedence over domestic law. However, there was little labour law to be found in the Treaty, and that in Regulations was primarily concerned with free movement of workers. Most EC

---

6   Case 43/75: *Defrenne v Sabena* [1976] ECR 455.
7   On the spill-over effect in the collective labour law of the EU, see Chapter 33.
8   Case C-213/89: *R v Secretary of State for Transport, ex p Factortame Ltd* [1990] ECR 1-2433. Case C-271/91: *Marshall v Southampton and South West Hampshire Area Health Authority (Teaching) (No 2)* [1993] ECR I-4367.

labour legislation takes the form of Directives. The decision of the European Court to extend the principle of direct effect to Directives was of crucial importance:[9]

> 'If, however, by virtue of the provisions of Article 189 regulations are directly applicable and, consequently, may by their very nature have direct effects, it does not follow from this that other categories of acts mentioned in that article can never have similar effects. It would be incompatible with the binding effect attributed to a directive by Article 189 to exclude, in principle, the possibility that the obligation which it imposes may be invoked by those concerned. In particular, where the Community authorities have, by directive, imposed on Member States the obligation to pursue a particular course of conduct, the *useful effect* of such an act would be weakened if individuals were prevented from relying on it before their national courts and if the latter were prevented from taking it into consideration as an element of Community law . . .
>
> Accordingly . . . (the provision in the Directive in question) confers on individuals rights which are enforceable by them in the courts of a Member State and which the national courts must protect.'

The rationale for attributing direct effect to Directives was to secure the 'useful effect' (*effet utile*) of EC legislation. The preceding doctrines, that EC law was a new transnational legal order capable of conferring rights on individuals, produced an interpretation of Article 189 which emphasised the binding result to be achieved by the Directive, rather than leaving 'to the national authorities the choice of form and methods'.

However, given that Directives were drafted with a view to prescribing 'the result to be achieved' rather than individual rights, the Court was cautious in treating them as always straightforwardly applicable law to be implemented by national courts:[10]

> 'It is necessary to examine, in every case, whether the nature, general scheme and wording of the provision in question are capable of having direct effects on the relations between Member States and individuals.'

In the case of the Directive in question the Court emphasised that:[11]

> 'the provision lays down an obligation which is not subject to any exception or condition and which, by its very nature, does not require the intervention of any act on the part either of the institutions of the Community or of Member States.'

The impulse to secure the effectiveness of EC law was the initial rationale for direct effect. But a different rationale soon emerged which, while upholding the applicability of the doctrine to Directives, had implications for its potential scope. The Court emphasised again, as regards a Directive as an act of EC law, that:[12]

> 'the effectiveness of such an act would be weakened if persons were prevented from relying on it in legal proceedings and national courts prevented from taking it into consideration as an element of Community law.
>
> Consequently a Member State which has not adopted the implementing measures required by the directive in the prescribed periods *may not rely*, as against individuals, *on its own failure* to perform the obligations which the directive entails.

---

9   Case 41/74: *Van Duyn v Home Office (No 2)* [1974] ECR 1337, paragraph 12 (italics added).
10   Ibid.
11   Ibid, paragraph 23.
12   Case 148/78: *Pubblico Ministero v Ratti* [1979] ECR 1629, paragraphs 21–23 (italics added).

It follows that a national court requested by a person who has complied with the provisions of a directive not to apply a national provision incompatible with the directive not incorporated into the internal legal order of a defaulting Member State, must uphold that request if the obligation in question is unconditional and sufficiently precise.'

In terms of justifying direct effect of Directives, the 'effectiveness' (*effet utile*) rationale implied a general prospect of enforcement in national courts by individuals of rights granted by Directives. In contrast, the 'estoppel' (reliance on own failure) rationale appeared to imply a number of restrictions on this general prospect. It presupposes that the defendant in the action is the State, that this defendant is a part of the State responsible for implementation of the Directive, and that the defendant has failed to perform its obligations in such a manner as to preclude it from denying the plaintiff's action.

These restrictions on the doctrine of direct effect as applied to Directives would confine its application to legal actions by citizens against the State – so-called 'vertical' direct effect. Enforcement of rights contained in Directives would not be allowed against private individuals ('horizontal' direct effect). This was finally made explicit in *Marshall (No 1)*:[13]

'With regard to the argument that a directive may not be relied upon against an individual, it must be emphasised that according to Article 189 of the EEC Treaty the binding nature of a directive, which constitutes the basis for the possibility of relying on the directive before a national court, exists only in relation to "each Member State to which it is addressed". It follows that a directive may not of itself impose obligations on an individual and that a provision of a directive may not be relied upon as such against such a person.'

On the other hand, the State as respondent could appear in a number of guises:[14]

'. . . it must be pointed out that where a person involved in legal proceedings is able to rely on a directive as against the State he may do so regardless of the capacity in which the latter is acting, whether employer or public authority. In either case it is necessary to prevent the State from taking advantage of its own failure to comply with Community law.'

The scope of the different guises of the State depends on the criteria developed by the Court to define the State. These were laid down in *Foster v British Gas*:[15]

'It follows from the foregoing that a body, whatever its legal form, which has been made responsible, pursuant to a measure adopted by the State, for providing a public service under the control of the State and has for that purpose special powers beyond those which result from the normal rules applicable in relations between individuals is included in any event among the bodies against which the provision of a directive capable of having direct effect may be relied upon.'

Directives may confer directly enforceable rights on employees of the State. Such employees in EC labour law have the considerable advantage of being able to rely directly on provisions in EC Directives as well as on national legislation. The scope of the definition of the State has the result that a considerable proportion of the national workforce is in this fortunate position.

13   Case 152/84: *Marshall v Southampton and South West Hampshire Area Health Authority (Teaching)* [1986] ECR 723, paragraph 48.
14   Ibid, paragraph 49.
15   Case C-188/89: [1990] ECR I-3313, paragraph 20.

The potential scope of the definition of the State in EU law might not exclude privatised industries or services: for example, a private company in the now privatised water industry.[16] The legal form of the body is irrelevant, so long as it is responsible for providing a public service under the control of the State and has for that purpose special powers.

INDIRECT EFFECT

The discrepancy between employees of the State and employees of private employers in terms of their ability to claim rights under Directives under the doctrine of direct effect has been partly remedied by the doctrine of 'indirect effect'.[17] This achieves indirectly, through the technique of judicial interpretation of domestic law, the result obtainable through the doctrine of direct effect:[18]

> '. . . the Member States' obligation arising from a directive to achieve the result envisaged by the directive and their duty under Article 5 of the Treaty to take all appropriate measures, whether general or particular, to ensure the fulfilment of that obligation, is binding on all the authorities of Member States including, for matters within their jurisdiction, the courts. It follows that, in applying the national law and in particular the provisions of a national law specifically introduced in order to implement Directive No 76/207, national courts are required to interpret their national law in the light of the wording and the purpose of the directive in order to achieve the result referred to in the third paragraph of Article 189.'

The logic which dictated this result has been taken beyond the case of interpreting domestic legislation introduced to implement EC law:[19]

> 'It follows that, in applying national law, where the provisions in question were adopted *before or after* the directive, the national court called upon to interpret it is required to do so, *as far as possible*, in the light of the wording and the purpose of the directive in order to achieve the result pursued by the latter and thereby comply with the third paragraph of Article 189 of the Treaty.'

The UK courts have demonstrated varying degrees of willingness to follow this injunction where this would challenge traditional canons of statutory interpretation, such as the strict literal meaning of statutory language.[20] Seizing upon the discretion apparently granted to them, the House of Lords declared:[1]

> 'a national court must construe a domestic law to accord with the terms of a directive in the same field only if it is possible to do so. That means that the domestic law must be open to an interpretation consistent with the Directive whether or not it is also open to an interpretation inconsistent with it.'

---

16   *Griffin v South West Water Services Ltd* [1995] IRLR 15.
17   C Docksey and B Fitzpatrick 'The Duty of National Courts to Interpret Provisions of National Law in Accordance with Community Law' (1991) 20 *Industrial Law Journal* 113.
18   Case 14/83: *Von Colson and Kamann v Land Nordrhein-Westfalen* [1984] ECR 1891, paragraph 26.
19   Case C-106/89: *Marleasing Ltd v La Comercial Internacional de Alimentacion* [1990] ECR I-4135, paragraph 8 (italics added).
20   Contrast *Pickstone v Freemans plc* [1989] AC 66, HL, and *Litster v Forth Dry Dock and Engineering Co Ltd* [1990] 1 AC 546, HL, with *Duke v GEC Reliance Ltd* [1988] ICR 339, HL.
1   *Webb v EMO Air Cargo Ltd* [1993] ICR 175, per Lord Keith.

It seems that the European Court means the doctrine of indirect effect to go beyond a mere interpretative aid to domestic legislation. This emerged in *Coloroll Pension Trustees Ltd v Russell*:[2]

'. . . national courts are bound to provide the legal protection which individuals derive from the direct effect of provisions of the Treaty . . . They are therefore bound, particularly in the context of Article 119, to the full extent of their discretion under national law, to interpret and apply the relevant domestic provisions in conformity with the requirements of Community law and, where this is not possible, to disapply any incompatible domestic provisions.'

Indirect effect can thus be seen both as an addition to and as the corollary of the doctrine of direct effect. In the case of EC laws having direct effect, as in the case of Article 119, but presumably also where provisions of Directives have direct effect, and even where they do not, the doctrine of indirect effect allows for national courts to disregard domestic law where interpretation cannot resolve a conflict between the Directive and domestic law. This will be of vital importance to the enforcement of EC rights against private persons (horizontal direct effect), where domestic law is the only legal basis. In the case of provisions lacking direct effect, the interpretative effort must be made, but it is not certain how far the UK courts will go, nor how energetically the European Court will encourage them, in disregarding national legislation inconsistent with EC law.

STATE LIABILITY

Enforcement of rights granted by EC law is constantly under the pressure to reflect a logic which looks to the Treaty of Rome as an international law instrument, and hence engaging exclusively mutual responsibility among the Member States, or their responsibility vis-à-vis the institutions of the EU. However, the supranational jurisdiction of the European Court has had a disaggregating effect upon concepts of State liability. The nation state as the traditional subject of international law is not treated as a monolithic entity, but broken up into elements which can be separately subjected to different pressures of EC law enforcement.

Above all, the European Court singled out national courts as independent organs of the State responsible for enforcement of EC law rights through doctrines of direct and indirect effect. This has forced national courts to confront the other organs of the State, the legislature and executive, in case of the latter's failure to implement or apply EC law. Further disaggregation is manifest in the European Court's holding different emanations of the Member States responsible under the doctrine of direct effect.

The doctrine of direct effect itself, however, can be seen still as hamstrung by the insistence of the European Court on the exclusively *vertical* responsibility of the State for implementation of EC Directives, even where EC law imposes responsibilities on private individuals. The *effet utile* rationale for direct effect would incline towards holding even private individuals responsible for directly

---

2 Case C-200/91: [1994] ECR I-4389.

enforceable provisions of EC law which should be effective. The 'estoppel' rationale for direct effect is an uneasy compromise: emanations of the State are liable even where the responsibility for the non-implementation of the EC Directive lies with *other* organs of the State.

The European Court made a succinct statement of the existence of State liability as a matter of principle in the *Francovich* case.[3] Workers who suffer damage when their employer becomes insolvent were the subject of an EC Directive which required Member States to secure their protection.[4] Italy failed to implement the Directive. The individual workers brought a claim before their national courts for compensation for the damage they had suffered due to this failure. In a preliminary reference under Article 177, the European Court appears to have greatly reinforced the rights of individuals to claim a remedy which results from breaches of Community law for which the State can be held responsible:[5]

'The full effectiveness of Community rules would be impaired and the protection of the rights which they grant would be weakened if individuals were unable to obtain redress when their rights are infringed by a breach of Community law for which a Member State can be held responsible.

The possibility of obtaining redress from the Member State is particularly indispensable where, as in this case, the full effectiveness of Community rules is subject to prior action on the part of the State and where, consequently, in the absence of such action, individuals cannot enforce before the national courts the rights conferred upon them by Community law.

It follows that the principle whereby a State must be liable for loss and damage caused to individuals as a result of breaches of Community law for which the State can be held responsible is inherent in the system of the Treaty . . .

It follows from all the foregoing that it is a principle of Community law that the Member States are obliged to make good loss and damage caused to individuals by breaches of Community law for which they can be held responsible.'

The principle of State liability was said to be also explicit in Article 5 of the Treaty. It relies on a basic principle of the new legal order: that national courts must protect the rights conferred by EC law on individuals, including enforcement of these rights where the State is responsible.

The principle of State liability thus established was not unconditional:[6]

'Although State liability is thus required by Community law, the conditions under which that liability gives rise to a right to reparation depend on the nature of the breach of Community law giving rise to the loss and damage.

Where, as in this case, a Member State fails to fulfil its obligation under the third paragraph of Article 189 of the Treaty to take all the measures necessary to achieve the result prescribed by a directive, the full effectiveness of that rule of Community law requires that there should be a right to reparation provided that three conditions are fulfilled.

The first of those conditions is that the result prescribed by the directive should entail the grant of rights to individuals. The second condition is that it should be

---

3   Joined Cases C-6/90 and C-9/90: *Francovich and Bonifaci v Italian Republic* [1991] ECR I-5357.
4   Directive 80/987/EEC, OJ L283/23.
5   *Francovich v Italian Republic*, paragraphs 33–35, 37.
6   Ibid, paragraphs 38–41.

possible to identify the content of those rights on the basis of the provisions of the directive. Finally, the third condition is the existence of a causal link between the breach of the State's obligation and the loss and damage suffered by the injured parties.

Those conditions are sufficient to give rise to a right on the part of individuals to obtain reparation, a right founded directly on Community law.'

The conditions for *Francovich* liability are the subject of further preliminary references.[7]

The elements of liability which emerge from the *Francovich* decision include (i) a breach of EC law; (ii) attributable to the Member State; (iii) which causes damage to an individual.

The breach of EC law in the *Francovich* case itself was a violation of the EC Directive by reason of the national legislator failing to act to implement it. But total failure to implement a Directive is only one type of violation of EC law. Implementation of a Directive by a Member State may be partial or incorrect or inadequate. There are numerous decisions of the European Court upholding complaints against the UK government for faulty implementation of a Directive. Breaches may also occur of EU laws other than Directives, as when a Member State fails to adapt its national law to the requirements of other EC laws.

Advocate-General Léger in *Hedley Lomas* has taken the view that the principle of State responsibility is not limited to claims for a remedy against EC measures lacking 'direct effect', as was the position in the *Francovich* case. It is a principle of judicial protection of the individual's EC rights:[8]

'My conclusion from this is that an action for damages against a State is not only a remedy for imperfect direct effect. It is not limited to the situation in *Francovich*. It is a vital component of the judicial protection of individuals relying on Community law, from the moment when the provision or decision occasioning the damage is capable of giving rise to rights on the part of individuals.'

Hence, while a decision of the European Court condemning a Member State for violation of Community law (as was the case in *Francovich*) may be sufficient, it is not necessary.[9]

The breach in the *Francovich* case was attributable to the national legislature, for failure to implement the Directive. It is evident that violations of EC law may also be committed by other emanations of the State, as established in the doctrine of the direct effect of Directives. Advocate-General Léger in *Hedley Lomas* argued that the principle applies regardless of which organ of the State is responsible for the violation of EC law – even the legislature or the courts:[10]

'The State as a whole incurs liability for a breach of Community law, irrespective of whether the damage is attributable to the legislature or to administrative action – or even to a court judgment incompatible with the Treaty.'

---

7   Joined Cases C-46/93 and C-48/93: *Firma Brasserie du Pecheur SA v Federal Republic of Germany, R v Secretary of State for Transport, ex p Factortame Ltd*, Report for the Hearing on 25 October 1994. Case C-5/94: *R v Ministry of Agriculture, Fisheries and Food, ex p Hedley Lomas (Ireland) Ltd*, Opinion of Advocate-General M Phillipe Léger, 20 June 1995.
8   Ibid, paragraph 94.
9   Ibid, paragraph 177.
10 Ibid, paragraph 114.

One of the questions currently before the European Court is whether the entitlement to compensation is conditional on fault (intent or negligence) on the part of the State officials responsible for the failure to adapt national law.

The argument has been advanced that State responsibility should parallel that of the non-contractual liability of the Community institutions. As developed by the Court in its case law on Article 215 of the Treaty, this imposes a heavy burden on the plaintiff to prove fault by the defendant institutions. Advocate-General Léger in *Hedley Lomas* rejected this parallel; instead, he asserted that the degree of fault required for State responsibility was variable depending on the nature of the Community obligation violated and the nature of the violation committed:[11]

'... the nature of the wrongful act or omission required in order for the State to incur liability depends on the nature of the Community obligation incumbent on it and on the nature of the breach committed.'

There are a number of questions which arise from comparing State responsibility under *Francovich* and the doctrine of direct effect. Both require the claimant to demonstrate that the Directive confers rights. But, for the purposes of *Francovich* liability, the right granted by the Directive need not be so clearly and precisely defined as is required for it to have direct effect. The European Court held that the rights in the 1980 insolvency Directive at issue in *Francovich* were insufficiently defined for the purposes of direct effect, but *were* adequately defined for the purposes of State liability.

The principle of State responsibility has potentially enormous implications for the enforcement of EC labour law. If an individual has a definable interest protected by the Directive, failure by the State to act to protect that interest may lead to State liability where the individual suffers damage, provided causation can be demonstrated. The Directives on health and safety at work, on equal treatment of men and women, and an increasing number of Directives regulating individual and collective interests of workers are a fertile field for exploration of the scope of State liability.

REMEDIES IN NATIONAL COURTS

The European Court cannot itself adjudicate on complaints by individuals that rights under EC law, deriving from the doctrines of direct effect and *Francovich* liability, have been violated. These doctrines have been developed through the requests by national courts for preliminary rulings under Article 177 of the Treaty of Rome. The substantive claim based on EC law will be initiated before a national court. The role of national courts in the enforcement of EU law was described as follows by the European Court:[12]

'... in the absence of any relevant Community rules, it is for the national legal order of each Member State to designate the competent courts and to lay down the procedural rules for proceedings designed to ensure the protection of the rights which individuals acquire through the direct effect of Community law, provided that such

11   Ibid, paragraph 169.
12   Case 45/76: *Comet v Produktschap* [1976] ECR 2043, paragraphs 13, 16.

rules are not less favourable than those governing the same right of action on an internal matter ... The position would be different only if those rules and time-limits made it impossible in practice to exercise rights which the national courts have a duty to protect.'

Given the variety of national court structures, procedures and sanctions available in different national systems, it is likely that the efficacy of enforcement of EC law will reflect this variety. The European Court has recognised the necessity for enforcement of EC law in national courts, insisting that national courts exert themselves to enforce EC law:[13]

'... although the Treaty has made it possible in a number of instances for private persons to bring a direct action, where appropriate, before the Court of Justice, it was not intended to create new remedies in national courts to ensure the observance of Community law other than those already laid down by national law. On the other hand the system of legal protection established by the Treaty, as set out in Article 177 in particular, implies that it must be possible for every type of action provided for by national law to be available for the purpose of ensuring observance of Community provisions having direct effect, on the same conditions concerning the admissibility and procedure as would apply were it a question of ensuring observance of national law.'

The European Court has attempted to maintain an equilibrium between the autonomy of national systems to enforce EC law and the imperative of effective and uniform enforcement of EC law across all Member States. Referring to the third paragraph of Article 189 of the Rome Treaty, the Court held:[14]

'Although that provision leaves Member States to choose the ways and means of ensuring that the directive is implemented, that freedom does not affect the obligation imposed on all the Member States to which the directive is addressed, to adopt, in their national legal systems, all the measures necessary to ensure that the directive is fully effective, in accordance with the objective which it pursues.'

The European Court has moved in the direction of scrutinising national systems of judicial protection of EC law rights by laying down some general principles regarding the adequacy of national laws on remedies. In the context of an EC Directive on sex discrimination, it stated:[15]

'... full implementation of the directive does not require any specific form of sanction for unlawful discrimination, it does entail that that sanction be such as to guarantee real and effective judicial protection. Moreover it must also have a real deterrent effect on the employer. It follows that where a Member State chooses to penalise the breach of the prohibition of discrimination by the award of compensation, that compensation must in any event be adequate in relation to the damage sustained.'

The principle of equivalence of EC law remedies to national remedies, and the requirement that remedies for breach of EC law be effective were reiterated by Advocate-General Léger in *Hedley Lomas*.[16] National autonomy as regards enforcement of EC law is subject to these principles.

---

13 Case 158/80: *Rewe v Hauptzollamt Kiel* [1981] ECR 1805, paragraph 44.
14 Case 14/83: *Von Colson and Kamann v Land Nordrhein-Westfalen* [1984] ECR 1891, paragraph 15.
15 Ibid, paragraph 23.
16 *Hedley Lomas*, paragraph 149.

SANCTIONS

The *Von Colson* case illustrates the approach by the Court of critical scrutiny of the remedies for sex discrimination provided under German law by way of compensation:[17]

'... national provisions limiting the right to compensation of persons who have been discriminated against as regards access to employment to a purely nominal amount, such as, for example, the reimbursement of expenses incurred by them in submitting their application, would not satisfy the requirements of an effective transposition of the directive.'

However, the European Court has put limits on its intervention:[18]

'Article 6 (of the Equal Treatment Directive) requires Member States to introduce into their national legal systems such measures as are necessary to enable all persons who consider themselves wronged by discrimination "to pursue their claims by judicial process".'

The Court regarded this as requiring Member States:[19]

'to adopt measures which are sufficiently effective to achieve the objective of the directive and to ensure that those measures may in fact be relied on before the national courts by the persons concerned.'

As regards specific sanctions, however, the Court was cautious:[20]

'Such measures may include, for example, provision requiring the employer to offer a post to the candidate discriminated against or giving candidate adequate financial compensation, backed up where necessary by a system of fines. However, the directive does not prescribe a specific sanction; it leaves Member States free to choose between the different solutions suitable for achieving its objective.'

The equilibrium is nicely illustrated by the Court's decision regarding UK law remedies for sex discrimination in *Marshall (No 2)*:[1]

'24. ... the objective is to arrive at real equality of opportunity and (this) cannot therefore be attained in the absence of measures appropriate to restore such equality when it has not been observed...

25. Such requirements necessarily entail that the particular circumstances of each breach of the principle of equal treatment should be taken into account. In the event of discriminatory dismissal contrary to Article 5(1) of the Directive, a situation of equality could not be restored without either reinstating the victim of discrimination or, in the alternative, granting financial compensation for the loss and damage sustained.

26. Where financial compensation is the measure adopted in order to achieve the objective indicated above, it must be adequate, in that it must enable the loss and damage actually sustained as a result of the discriminatory dismissal to be made good in full in accordance with the applicable national rules.'[2]

---

17   Case 14/83: *Von Colson*, paragraph 24.
18   Ibid, paragraph 18.
19   Ibid.
20   Ibid.
1   Case C-271/91: *Marshall v Southampton and South West Hampshire Area Health Authority (Teaching) (No 2)* [1993] ECR I-4367, paragraphs 24–6.
2   In his Opinion in *Hedley Lomas*, Advocate-General Léger cited *Marshall (No 2)* and emphasised: 'In the case of State liability for breach of Community law, the damage suffered must be compensated *in full*. The restitutio in integrum principle will only allow the injured person to be placed in the position in which he would have been had it not been for the breach of Community law'. Op cit, paragraph 186.

The adequacy of sanctions provided by national law for the enforcement of individual rights in EC law has been challenged in other labour law contexts. The Directives on Collective Dismissals of 1975[3] and Acquired Rights of 1977[4] both require employers to inform and consult employee representatives. The 1981 Regulations which implemented the latter Directive in UK law provided that an employer who fails to consult employee representatives may be ordered to pay appropriate compensation to employees affected by the transfer. The compensation payable (called a 'protective award') was subject to a maximum of two weeks' pay (increased to four weeks' pay by the Trade Union Reform and Employment Rights Act 1993). In addition, the Regulations allowed for compensation awarded to be set off against other compensation which might be awarded to the employee. On the Commission's complaint that these sanctions were inadequate, the European Court agreed that:[5]

'The financial penalty is accordingly weakened; if not entirely removed . . . It follows that if an employer is also found to be at fault on the basis of the (Employment Protection Act), the penalty is not truly deterrent. Accordingly, the United Kingdom legislation does not comply on this point with the requirements of Article 5 of the Treaty.'

On the complaint regarding the Collective Dismissals Directive, the Court held similarly:[6]

'By providing that a "protective award" may be set off in full or in part against any amounts otherwise payable by an employer to an employee under the latter's contract of employment or in respect of breach of that contract, the United Kingdom legislation largely deprives that sanction of its practical effect and its deterrent value. Moreover, an employer will not be penalised even moderately or lightly by the sanction except and only to the extent to which the amount of the "protective award" which he is ordered to make exceeds the sums which he is otherwise required to pay to the person concerned.'

The adequacy of financial *compensation* as a remedy in labour law may be questioned. Particularly in the case of the exercise of collective rights, such as information and consultation, it is arguable that the award of compensation to employees affected by the employer's failure to inform or consult employee representatives is insufficient to achieve 'real and effective judicial protection and have a real deterrent effect on the employer'.[7]

The question whether national rules restricting remedies available for violations of EU law could be ignored was answered in the affirmative in *Factortame*. The plaintiff had asked for interim relief against the Crown. The request was initially denied by the UK courts on the grounds that UK law did not allow ·for such a remedy against the Crown. On a reference for a preliminary ruling under Article 177:[8]

'The Court has also held that any provision of a national legal system and any legislative, administrative or judicial practice which might impair the effectiveness of

3 Council Directive 75/129/EEC, OJ L4829 of 22.2.75.
4 Council Directive 77/187/EEC, OJ L6126 of 5.3.77.
5 Case C-382/92: *EC Commission v UK* [1994] ECR I-2435, paragraphs 57–58, decided 8 June 1994.
6 Case C-383/92: *EC Commission v UK*, ibid, paragraph 42.
7 Case C-271/91: *Marshall v Southampton and South West Hampshire Area Health Authority (Teaching) (No 2)* [1993] ECR I-4367, paragraph 24.
8 Case C-213/89: *R v Secretary of State for Transport, ex p Factortame Ltd (No 2)* [1990] ECR I-2433, paragraphs 20–21.

Community law by withholding from the national court having jurisdiction to apply such law the power to do everything necessary at the moment of its application to set aside national legislative provisions which might prevent, even temporarily, Community rules from having full force and effect are incompatible with those requirements, which are the very essence of Community law . . .

It must be added that the full effectiveness of Community law would be just as much impaired if a rule of national law could prevent a court seised of a dispute governed by Community law from granting interim relief in order to ensure the full effectiveness of the judgment to be given on the existence of the rights claimed under Community law. It follows that a court which in those circumstances would grant interim relief, if it were not for a rule of national law, is obliged to set aside that rule.'

An illustration from labour law of the application of these EC law rules challenging the adequacy of compensation and claiming the alternative remedy of injunctive relief is a complaint alleging failure to inform and consult employee representatives. The response of the UK court illustrates the difficulties of persuading UK judges to exploit the potential of EC law to scrutinise the adequacy of remedies under UK law:[9]

'. . . where, as here, the Directive leaves to the Member State the choice of remedy for breach of the Directive, the Directive cannot be interpreted so as to require the Member States to select one mode of sanction for breach of the Directive in preference to another, at any rate where the sanction selected is capable of guaranteeing real and effective judicial protection and real deterrent effect.

. . . the sanction selected by Parliament for breach of s 188 is . . . a protective award . . . Whilst, therefore, there may be a question, as there was in case C-383/92, as to the adequacy of the award which the industrial tribunal is empowered to make having regard to some feature of the legislation which provides for the sanction, I do not consider that it is open to me to disregard the exclusive sanction which Parliament has selected for giving effect to the duty to consult, where it arises, and to grant to the plaintiffs a form of relief for which the 1992 Act makes no provision.

Even if it were open to me in appropriate circumstances to disregard the exclusive sanction which Parliament has provided and grant injunctive relief of the kind sought, I am not persuaded that I would have any sufficient grounds for doing so. It seems to me that an order restraining an employer from effecting any redundancies unless he has "consulted with" his employees' representatives "with a view to reaching an agreement", which is what the plaintiffs seek, is one which is fraught with practical difficulties, not the least of which would be the difficulty faced by the employer in knowing just what he would be obliged to do and over what period in order to achieve compliance with the order and avoid proceedings for contempt.

The vagueness and uncertainty inherent in an order of the kind sought was, as it seems to me, well illustrated by Mr Hendy's description of the process which an injunction would require . . . :

"All that is required is for representatives of SWW (the employer) to sit down with representatives of Unison (the trade union) having given them the chance to absorb the material disclosed in this case, and say, 'This is what we propose: what do you say, can we reach an agreement?' They must listen, take on board what is said, see what can be the subject of agreement and what not, and then carry out what they, SWW, have decided in the light of those consultations to do."

I can well see, therefore, why Parliament has chosen to provide for breaches of the duty to consult and inform under s 188 by leaving it to an industrial tribunal which is particularly well equipped to consider such matters and, where a breach is established, by providing for the breach to be penalised by an award of compensation.'

---

9   *Griffin v South West Water Services Ltd* [1995] IRLR 15, ChD, Blackburne J, paragraphs 162–166.

The choice of remedy for breach of the Directive may be left to national law, but EC law requires this choice to be scrutinised closely. That the UK Parliament does not allow a remedy by way of injunctive relief does not preclude consideration of this remedy if it is capable of guaranteeing real and effective judicial protection and a real deterrent effect.

PROCEDURES

The adequacy of sanctions is only one aspect of the enforcement of EC law. National procedures for obtaining redress can also obstruct the real and effective judicial protection guaranteed by EC law. *Access* to the judicial process has been held to be a general principle of law which must be taken into consideration in Community law. 'The right to an effective judicial remedy' was elaborated in *Johnston v RUC*, which asked the European Court: [10]

> '13.   . . . whether Community law, and more particularly Directive No 76/207, requires the Member States to ensure that their national courts and tribunals exercise effective control over compliance with the provisions of the directive and with the national legislation intended to put it into effect . . .
> 17. As far as this issue is concerned, it must be borne in mind first of all that Article 6 of the directive requires Member States to introduce into their internal legal systems such measures as are needed to enable all persons who consider themselves wronged by discrimination "to pursue their claims by judicial process". It follows from that provision that the Member States must take measures which are sufficiently effective to achieve the aim of the directive and that they must ensure that the rights thus conferred may be effectively relied upon before the national courts by the persons concerned.'

Johnston v RUC concerned the provision in UK law which allowed a government minister, by issuing a certificate on grounds of national security or public safety or order, to exclude from the courts a complaint based on a Directive. The European Court condemned the issuing of such a certificate on the grounds that it: [11]

> '. . . allows the competent authority to deprive an individual of the possibility of asserting by judicial process the rights conferred by the directive. Such a provision is therefore contrary to the principle of effective judicial control laid down in Article 6 of the directive.'

This provision of the Directive guaranteeing access to justice was held to be directly effective: [12]

> 'As regards Article 6 of the directive . . . in so far as it follows from that article, construed in the light of a general principle which it expresses, that all persons who consider themselves wronged by sex discrimination must have an effective judicial remedy, that provision is sufficiently precise and unconditional to be capable of being relied upon as against a Member State which has not ensured that it is fully implemented in its internal legal order.'

The EC law right to an effective judicial remedy raises a number of questions about access to justice for complainants. Particular procedures for obtaining access to industrial tribunals might be demonstrated to have a deterrent effect on

10   Case 222/84: [1986] ECR 1651, paragraphs 13, 17.
11   Ibid, paragraph 20.
12   Ibid, paragraph 58.

claimants wishing to invoke EC labour law rights. Failure to provide adequate avenues of redress is a breach by the Member State of its obligations.

An example of the extent to which national procedures providing redress for breaches of EC law can be questioned is where a Member State applies its normal procedure of establishing liability to labour law. In European civil law procedure, the burden of proving the claim is normally imposed on the plaintiff. In Dutch law, a legal action in damages based on breach of the principle of equal treatment embodied in a Directive could succeed only if the plaintiff proved the employer to be at fault. This was challenged as violating the Directive on the basis that infringement of the equal treatment principle, once established, is sufficient to make the employer liable without proof of fault. The European Court held: [13]

'It must be observed that, if the employer's liability for infringement of the principle of equal treatment were made subject to proof of a fault attributable to him and also to there being no ground of exemption recognised by the applicable national law, the practical effect of those principles would be weakened considerably.

It follows that when the sanction chosen by the Member State is contained within the rules governing an employer's civil liability, a breach of the prohibition of discrimination must, in itself, be sufficient to make the employer liable, without there being any possibility of invoking the grounds of exemption provided by national law.'

Similarly, the Court was prepared to shift the burden of proof in an equal pay claim concerned with a system of individual pay supplements completely lacking in transparency. The Court held that female employees seeking to prove their claim: [14]

'would be deprived of any effective means of enforcing the principle of equal pay before the national courts if the effect of adducing such evidence was not to impose upon the employer the burden of proving that his practice in the matter of wages is not in fact discriminatory . . .

. . . under Article 6 of the Equal Pay Directive Member States must, in accordance with their national circumstances and legal systems, take the measures necessary to ensure that the principle of equal pay is applied and that effective means are available to ensure that it is observed. The concern for effectiveness which thus underlies the directive means that it must be interpreted as implying adjustments to national rules on the burden of proof in special cases where such adjustments are necessary for the effective implementation of the principle of equality.'

These cases demonstrate that the remedies available under national law are open to challenge. The effectiveness of EC law is too important to be left to national enforcement procedures. That this is increasingly felt is manifest in the Commission's Medium Term Social Action Programme 1995–1997, which provides: [15]

'– sanctions: Member State authorities must ensure that Union legislation is fully enforced through inter alia appropriate systems of control or sanctions, which are effective in practice and have a deterrent value. The Commission will insert in all future legislation a standard clause establishing an obligation for Member States to impose sanctions which are effective, proportionate and dissuasive.'

---

13   Case C-177/88: *Dekker v Stichting Vormingscentrum voor Jong Volwassenen (VJV Centrum) Plus* [1990] ECR I-3941, paragraphs 24–5.
14   Case 109/88: *Handels- og Kontorfunktionaerernes Forbund i Danmark v Dansk Arbejdsgiverforening (Danfoss)* [1989] ECR 3199, paragraphs 13–14.
15   COM (95) 134 final, Brussels, 12 April 1995, paragraph 11.1.8.

Chapter 11

Euro-litigation: an Enforcement Strategy for European Labour Law

INTRODUCTION

The enforcement of EU labour law goes beyond the tactics of identifying new categories of plaintiff or defendant, or criticising the adequacy of domestic remedies. It has strategic potential in the form of what has come to be known as 'Euro-litigation'.[1]

EU law is mostly used in two ways. First, as a source of *substantive* rules.[2] Secondly, to provide *remedies* against the State[3] or just better remedies.[4] But EU law can also be used in a litigation strategy. This was shown by the strategic use of EU law against the UK legislation prohibiting Sunday trading.

The strategy of the big stores which wanted to stay open on Sunday was twofold. In the short term, they sought to attack, in pre-emptive fashion, local authority attempts, based on the UK legislation, to stop Sunday trading. They claimed that the UK legislation violated Article 30 of the Treaty of Rome on free movement of goods, as it precluded the stores from selling imports. The stores' use of EU law demonstrated to the local authorities that attempts to stop Sunday trading could be costly, as the local authorities would be liable to compensate the stores for any losses suffered by unlawful closure. Moreover, in the interim, the local authorities could be required to give financial undertakings to provide such compensation if the stores' claim was ultimately successful. The strategy was helped by the Attorney-General's refusal to support the local authorities.

In the long term, by preventing enforcement of the UK law against Sunday trading, the stores aimed to legitimise the practice of Sunday trading in public opinion, with the aim of preparing the way for UK legislation. The strategy was

---

1 R Rawlings 'The Eurolaw Game: Some Deductions from a Saga' (1993) 20 *Journal of Law and Society*, p 309, from which the following material on the Sunday trading litigation is drawn.
2 For example, to override restrictive national law which fails to implement EC law adequately – as when the UK Transfer of Undertakings (Protection of Employment) Regulations 1981 were both interpreted in light of the Acquired Rights Directive of 1977 (*Lister v Forth Dry Dock and Engineering Co Ltd* [1990] 1 AC 546, HL) and condemned as not complying with the Directive (Case 382/92: *EC Commission v UK* [1994] ECR I-2435).
3 Cases C-6/90 and 9/90: *Francovich and Bonifaci v Italian Republic* [1991] ECR I-5357: State responsibility to compensate workers suffering damage by reason of failure to implement Directive granting employment rights.
4 Case 271/91: *Marshall v Southampton and South West Hampshire Area Health Authority (Teaching) (No 2)* [1993] ECR I-4367: statutory limitation on compensation for sex discrimination overruled.

vindicated when, even though their claim based on EU law was rejected by the courts, the government introduced legislation permitting trading on Sunday.

The question is whether EU law has potential use in a litigation strategy in the field of labour law. What follows is an illustration of the potential use of this strategy against employer attempts to derecognise trade unions. The objective in the short term would be to make attempts at derecognition costly for employers; in the long term, to delegitimise derecognition and prepare the way for a legal right to recognition.

A CASE STUDY IN EURO-LITIGATION IN CONTEXT: TRADE UNION DERECOGNITION

The most notorious case of derecognition in recent history has been the GCHQ case, where the Conservative government banned union membership in one of its intelligence establishments. The failure of law to protect individual trade unionists or the unions was very discouraging. An attempt was made to use international labour law in the form of ILO Conventions, but again, the result has heretofore been one of disillusion.[5] Is EU law any more use as a strategy against derecognition?

The context: the derecognition problem

A recent survey found that more than half of the 79 unions responding said they had no experience of an employer attempting to derecognise; findings in the period 1988–94 included:[6]

- 379 cases of derecognition: 330 of actual derecognition, 17 threatened but not carried out, 32 successfully resisted;
- there was an absolute increase in number of cases since 1988; the annual rate increased from c 35 to c 70 per year;
- during the period investigated, between 135–150,000 workers had recognition rights withdrawn;
- 192 cases involved non-manual workers/staff. Of those identifiable, 68 involved managerial and professional staffs, 10 clerical and technical and 19 both groups. There were 143 cases involving manual workers;
- in 101 of the cases, personal contracts were introduced to replace collective bargaining: 69 of these were in the newspaper and magazine industry; and all but 10 in professional/managerial staffs.

Derecognition takes different forms. While partial derecognition, most commonly, occurs where unions were derecognised for bargaining over pay, complete derecognition applies to all bargaining issues. Derecognition may be general, for all workers employed, or grade specific or plant specific, or both grade and plant specific. In practice, grade specific and partial derecognition

---

5   K Ewing *Britain and the ILO*, Institute of Employment Rights, London 1989.
6   G Gall and S McKay 'Trade Union Derecognition in Britain 1988–1994' (1994) 32 *British Journal of Industrial Relations* 433, on which the following account is based.

predominate. Only in a minority of cases does derecognition affect all workers and involve complete derecognition over all bargaining issues.

The industrial/sectoral distribution of derecognition is very distinctive. Of 379 cases in the period 1988–94:

–   121 (c one third) were in media and communications (57 in provincial newspapers);
–   56 (c one sixth) were in manufacturing (26 in metal goods, engineering and vehicles, and 30 in other manufacturing);
–   37 were in public administration (c 10%, of which 23 were in hospitals and ambulance services);
–   30 were in energy (18) and water supply (12).

Derecognition is primarily located in a small number of sectors. There has been relatively little change in this respect despite the large increase in derecognition. Those most affected are newspapers/magazines/books, ports/shipping, the public sector, electricity/water supply and the onshore oil industry. One change worth noting is the rise in cases in the public sector, such as local authorities or NHS Trusts breaking away from national agreements. This sectoral breakdown means that the specific unions targeted are:[7]

NUJ	89 (c 18%)
TGWU	77 (c 15%)
GPMU	71 (c 14%)
AEEU	46 (c 9%)
NALGO	32 + NUPE 28 + COHSE 16 + UNISON 1 = 77 (c 15%)
MSF	30
GMB	29
UCATT	18
BIFU	14

NUJ and GPMU, both in the newspaper industry, account for 160: c one third.

The reasons given by employers for derecognition included low trade union membership, move to performance related pay, changes in working conditions, job cuts, move to single union/fewer unions, part of a wider dispute on pay, jobs, conditions, privatisation/deregulation, reorganisation, takeover and economic competition.

Employer tactics are frequently through offering personal contracts, or 'salami' tactics – derecognising different groups, one at a time. Union responses include pressure, up to the threat of industrial action (where sometimes the employer has backed down) and strikes (though in many cases these fail even to get through the compulsory ballot stage). There have been a few cases where legal remedies have been tried.

Gall and McKay conclude that the ideological importance of derecognition outweighs its actual importance. In practice, the employer's objective is not derecognition of the union, but to push through changes – either negotiated or, if necessary, unilateral. The prominence of derecognition in the printed media gives it disproportionate exposure.

---

7   The total of 504 is more than the 379 cases as more than one union may be derecognised in one place.

UK law[8]

UK law has two fundamental flaws regarding derecognition: unions have no right to be recognised, and employers are not compelled to honour collective agreements. Legal defences to derecognition fall back on the law of individual employment contracts and unilateral changes in terms and conditions, redundancies and unfair dismissal.

Against derecognition of the union, the law of contract at best might provide to employees deprived of their union a limited implied term requiring the employer to behave reasonably. It might be that incorporation of collective agreements could obstruct derecognition by implying 'appropriate' terms as to rights of former lay officials to time off and facilities and rights of members to be represented by the union. Again, unilateral changes by the employer might be countered by the employee's express dissent, though continuing to work might imply subsequent consent. Unilateral changes might allow for an injunction.[9]

In the case of derecognition through offering personal contracts, dismissing and rehiring employees, the law on dismissals might at best provide an obligation to consult, or allow for complaints that the employer was buying out union representation to discourage or deter union membership. This argument was ultimately unsuccessful in *Associated British Ports v Palmer* and *Associated Newspapers v Wilson*.[10] It is now also subject to the TURER amendment holding that an employer's purpose to change the relationship with a class of employees overrides any other (unlawful) purpose.[11] A further option might be judicial review in the case of certain employers with a public law character.

EC law

All this shows is that UK law is a very fragile foundation for a litigation strategy combating derecognition. Such a strategy aims to hinder or stop derecognition by relying on legal rules which obstruct or prohibit it, and invoking remedies which effectively stop the employer carrying out derecognition. What is needed is some *remedy* based on violation of a legal rule which occurs when an employer tries to derecognise a union.

EC law norms could be invoked if they have direct effect, or have not been, or have been inadequately, implemented into UK law, or require the reinterpretation of UK law in light of the EC norm. The big stores trading on Sunday stopped local authority enforcement by invoking Article 30 of the Treaty of Rome – that the ban on Sunday trading was a measure of equivalent effect to quantitative restrictions on imports, and, hence, an unlawful violation of the free movement of goods in the EC.

Are there EC law provisions which can be used to combat derecognition? A number of possibilities will be explored:

–   the Acquired Rights Directive;
–   the Collective Dismissals Directive;

---

8   For a detailed account, S Auerbach *Derecognition and Personal Contracts*, Institute of Employment Rights, London 1993.
9   The fast track under RSC Order 14A.
10   [1995] IRLR 258, HL, on 16 March 1995, overturning the decision of the Court of Appeal [1993] IRLR 336.
11   Section 13, amending TULRCA, s 148(3).

- the Directive requiring written information on (collectively agreed) working conditions;
- the Directives on health and safety;
- the EC law on equality between women and men; and
- the Working Time Directive.

The Acquired Rights Directive

The only EC law which explicitly covers the problem of derecognition is the Acquired Rights Directive.[12] Article 5 provides (my italics):

'1. If the business preserves its autonomy, the *status and function*, as laid down by the laws, regulations or administrative provisions of the Member States, of the *representatives* or of the *representation* of the *employees affected by the transfer* within the meaning of Article 1(1) *shall be preserved.*

   The first subparagraph shall not apply if, under the laws, regulations, administrative provisions or practice of the Member States, the conditions necessary for the reappointment of the representatives of the employees or for the reconstitution of the representation of the employees are fulfilled.

2. If the term of office of the representatives of the employees affected by a transfer within the meaning of Article 1(1) *expires as a result of the transfer*, the representatives shall continue to enjoy the protection provided by the laws, regulations, administrative provisions or *practice* of the Member States.'

This was translated into Regulation 9 of the Transfer of Undertakings (Protection of Employment) Regulations 1981 (TUPE), which provide (my italics):

'(1) This Regulation applies where after a relevant transfer the undertaking or part of the undertaking transferred maintains an identity distinct from the remainder of the transferee's undertaking.

(2) *Where* before such a transfer an independent trade *union is recognised* to any extent *by the transferor* in respect of employees of any description who in consequence of the transfer become employees of the transferee, then, after the transfer –

   (a) the *union shall be deemed to have been recognised by the transferee* to the same extent in respect of employees of that description so employed; and

   (b) any agreement for recognition may be varied or rescinded accordingly.'

EC law reflects a clear policy *against* derecognition, here limited to the circumstances of transfer of undertakings, businesses or parts of businesses. Recognition includes status and function – both are to be preserved: representation activities, not only the representatives themselves. There are no exceptions to this: recognition 'shall be preserved'.[13]

There is no time limit in the Directive. The implication is that reappointment may substitute for preserving the status and function of existing representatives,

---

12 Council Directive 77/187/EEC of 14 February 1977 on the approximation of the laws of the Member States relating to the safeguarding of employees' rights in the event of transfers of undertakings, businesses or parts of businesses, OJ L61/26 of 5.3.1977.

13 This contrasts with dismissals resulting from a transfer: both the Directive (Article 4(1)) and Regulations (Reg 8(2)) allow dismissals for (Article 4(1)): 'economic, technical or organisational reasons entailing changes in the workforce.' Note that Reg 8(2) uses 'a reason' in the singular, raising a question whether this is a correct transposition of EC law, which seems to exclude only one reason being sufficient for a dismissal.

and if their term of office expires, they shall retain protection. Guidance as to the Directive's objective may be derived from Article 3(2). This provides that:

> 'Following the transfer ... the transferee shall continue to observe the terms and conditions agreed in any collective agreement ... until the date of termination or expiry of the collective agreement or the entry into force or application of another collective agreement.
>
> Member States may limit the period for observing such terms and conditions, with the proviso that it shall not be less than one year.'

Both this provision and that requiring that recognition be preserved fall under the rubric 'Safeguarding of employees' rights'. These clearly include *collective* rights of employees. This raises questions as to whether Reg 9(2)(b) of the UK law, which implies that recognition may be withdrawn, is a correct transposition of the Directive's objective. It may be unlawful to withdraw recognition at all, or at least for one year after the transfer.

Article 5(2) guarantees protection to representatives whose term of office 'expires as a result of the transfer'. The concept of 'expiry upon transfer' is not easy to translate into UK experience. It could be argued that an employer de-recognising trade unions after a transfer is bringing about the expiry of the term of office of representatives of the employees. However, the representatives might wish to continue to carry out their functions. If expiry upon transfer is construed in the UK context as 'derecognition', EC law guarantees employee representatives protection. Article 5(1) states that their status and function 'as laid down by the laws, regulations or administrative provisions of the Member States' shall be preserved. This is the necessary protection in the absence of any attempt to derecognise. In the event of a derecognition attempt, Article 5(2) applies to safeguard their position. Article 5(2), moreover, adds that these representatives 'shall continue to enjoy the protection', not only of laws, regulations and administrative provisions, but also of 'practice'. This could be argued to include time off and facilities agreements: these must continue to be respected.

There is nothing in the UK Regulations about this. This is arguably a violation of the duty of the UK government to transpose the Directive into domestic law.

Not surprisingly, most attention on TUPE has been focussed on the employees transferred, to ensure that their representatives are not denied recognition by the transferee employer. However, the employees affected by the transfer include also those who remain with the transferor.

The Directive is very precise. Article 3(1) on the safeguarding of employees' contractual rights applies explicitly to the obligations of the transferee and the rights of the employees transferred. Similarly, Article 3(2) provides for the collective agreement to apply to the transferee. Article 4 on dismissals, however, explicitly applies to both transferor and transferee employers. Article 5, preserving recognition, refers to neither transferor nor transferee, but only to 'employees affected by the transfer'. The clear implication is that employee representatives of *all* employees – those transferred and those remaining with the transferor employer – are protected.

The UK Regulations have not been so careful. Only Regs 10 and 11, on the duty to inform and consult trade union representatives, extend the definition of 'an affected employee' to include 'employees of the transferor or the transferee'. The provisions on contractual rights and obligations correctly refer to employees transferred and their rights as regards the transferee employer

(Reg 5). Similarly, the provisions on transfer of collective agreements correctly refer to the agreement having been made by or on behalf of the transferee employer (Reg 6). The provisions on dismissals also correctly refer to employees of both transferor and transferee employers (Reg 8(1)).

However, Reg 9(2) confines the Directive's guarantee that recognition be preserved to the employees who become employees of the transferee and to the transferee employer. This is arguably insufficient. Transferor employers must preserve recognition of the representatives of employees who are not transferred, but who are nonetheless affected by the transfer. This is most clearly the case when the transfer is the occasion for an attempt by the transferor employer to derecognise the union. All the points made above concerning Article 5 apply to 'employees affected by a transfer'.

In sum, EC law in the form of the 1977 Acquired Rights Directive requires that in the event of a transfer:

1. Derecognition is unlawful: recognition shall be preserved (Article 5).
2. Not only employees' representatives, but also their activities are to be preserved (Article 5(1)).
3. Arguably, derecognition is unlawful before at least one year has passed: perhaps more (Article 3(2)).
4. Arguably, derecognition constitutes 'expiry' of the term of office of representatives, whose position continues to be safeguarded: perhaps even including time off and facilities where this is the practice (Article 5(2)).
5. Transferor employers must also continue recognition and cannot use the transfer as the occasion for derecognising unions representing employees not transferred (Article 5).

The conditions for all this are that, first, there has been a transfer within the meaning of Article 1(1), which reads:

> 'This Directive shall apply to the transfer of an undertaking, business or part of a business to another employer as a result of a legal transfer or merger.'

Secondly, that the business preserves its autonomy (Article 5(1)).[14] A large number of derecognition cases identified by Gall and McKay probably satisfy these conditions: deregulation/privatisation (30 cases), reorganisation (25 cases), and takeovers (22 cases). Attempts at derecognition in these cases can be obstructed or stopped using EC law.

The question is how far can the scope of these conditions be stretched so as to include attempts at derecognition in other circumstances. Experience with the Acquired Rights Directive has shown that its scope, as interpreted by the European Court[15] is much wider than the UK legislation and courts have been prepared to acknowledge.[16]

14 Though this condition does not qualify protection of representatives whose term of office has expired as a result of the transfer.
15 In cases such as Case C-29/91: *Dr Sophie Redmond Stichting v Bartol* [1992] ECR I-3189; Case C-209/91: *Rask and Christensen v ISS Kantineservice AS* [1992] ECR I-5755; Case C-392/92: *Schmidt v Spar- und Leihkasse der früheren Ämter Bordesholm, Kiel und Cromshagen* [1994] ECR I-1311; but see most recently Case C-48/94: *Ledernes Hovedorganisation, acting on behalf of Ole Rygaard v Dansk Arbejdsgiverforening, acting on behalf of Strø Mølle Akustik A/S* [1996] IRLR 51, decided on 19 September 1995.
16 But see the judgment of the Court of Appeal overturning the EAT in *Dines v Initial Health Care Services Ltd* [1994] IRLR 336, decided 19 May 1994.

One obstacle to wider application of the Directive to derecognition cases is that the EC law refers to a 'transfer ... to *another employer* as a result of a legal transfer or merger'. The case law of the European Court has demonstrated that the legal nature of this transfer may assume many different forms: more than one transaction may be involved; there may be no direct link between transferor and transferee as a third party may interpose. The substantive essence of the transfer is less the *legal* quality of the transaction than the fact that a *change* has occurred regarding the employer, and 'the *business* preserves its autonomy' (Article 5(1)) or 'maintains an identity distinct' (Reg 9(1)).

As to the *latter*, UK law only refers to an undertaking or part of an undertaking. The Directive also covers a business or part of a business. For the Directive, *legal* separateness is not necessary for an undertaking to exist. An undertaking, business or part of a business may be a bundle of premises, equipment, services and employees without a separate legal identity. What is transferred is an autonomous function.

As to the *former*, what change must occur regarding the employer before the Directive applies? Both UK law and the EC Directive refer to 'another employer'. The question is: who is another employer? Formally, this seems to mean another legal person in the relationship of employment. The undertaking or business is now subject to another employer. However, the undertaking itself need not formally be a separate legal entity. The logical thrust of the European Court's judgments on the Directive is towards holding that the Directive applies when an autonomous *function* is transferred. The question is whether this same logic can be applied to the requirement that there be a transfer to another employer.

An employer is defined *not* in terms of separate legal existence, but rather in terms of contractual relationship to the employee. A change of employer occurs, arguably, when the relationship with the employee *changes*. The argument is that the Directive applies not only when there is a transfer to a separate legal person, but when there is a change in the employer's relationship with the employee. There is a *functional* transfer in the position of the employer, even though formally the employment relationship with the employee has not changed. The policy of the Directive is that a major *change* in the employer's relationship with employees should not change arrangements regarding union recognition. 'If the business preserves its autonomy', so should recognition.

The significance of this for derecognition disputes in the UK is clear. Research shows that frequently derecognition attempts occur with moves to performance related pay, changes in working conditions, or job cuts. None of these involve changes in the legal identity of the employer. But all involve major changes in the functional relationship between employer and employees. The whole nature of the employment relationship is transformed. In these circumstances, can the changes be deemed a 'transfer' so as to prohibit derecognition attempts by requiring that union recognition be preserved?

Perhaps the clearest example is the common derecognition tactic of terminating the contracts of unionised employees which incorporate collective agreements and offering them personal contracts. This case is legally analogous to the case of transfer to another legal person – the transferee. Only here, the transferee is also the transferor. The transferor employer has transferred the autonomous business, consisting of the employees, to the transferee, who happens also to be the transferor.

It was argued above that, as regards recognition, the Directive also protects employees not transferred, though affected by the transfer. Also, Article 5 (unlike Articles 3, 4 and 6) does not use the word transferor or transferee. The key term is 'business preser(ving) its autonomy'. The change in the identity of the employer is secondary when preserving recognition is in question. It seems entirely consistent with the policy of the EC Directive that EC law should protect the employees' representatives and union recognition where the employer introduces major changes in the functional relationship with employees.

In conclusion, in the Sunday trading cases, EC law was used by the big stores to frustrate, temporarily, enforcement of closure by local authorities. The stores achieved this by seeking a temporary injunction against the local authority's action, pending a reference to the European Court to clarify a point of EC law. On the balance of convenience, the UK courts held that the local authority's action was sustainable, but only if it gave a financial undertaking to compensate any losses suffered by the stores through forced closing. This requirement of an onerous financial undertaking proved sufficient to deter the local authorities' attempts to stop Sunday trading.

Can the Acquired Rights Directive prohibiting derecognition be used to frustrate derecognition? Can a temporary injunction stopping derecognition be sought pending a reference to the European Court to clarify a point of EC law? Does the balance of convenience favour such an injunction? What undertakings could be required of the employer who resisted an injunction?

It can be argued that a number of points of interpretation of the Directive could be referred to the European Court. In the short term, a strategy of battering the courts and tribunals with requests for references to the European Court to clarify points of EC law in the Directive, with appropriate interim remedies, could set back derecognition attempts. In the long term, this would be part of a political strategy. In the UK, the aim would be to transform the climate against derecognition attempts as violating the European law rights of workers.

The Collective Dismissals Directive

Workers resisting derecognition can suffer detriment, or even be dismissed. If there was EC law protecting this resistance, it might be possible to stop derecognition, or at least delay it and organise resistance while the European Court considered the matter.

Council Directive 75/129 of 17 February 1975 on the approximation of the laws of the Member States relating to collective redundancies[17] contains the potential for legal tactics defending resistance to derecognition. This is by requiring that procedures be followed when dismissals may be contemplated following derecognition.

PROCEDURES REQUIRED WHEN DISMISSALS MAY BE CONTEMPLATED
FOLLOWING DERECOGNITION

Directive 75/129, as translated into UK law, has been understood to require the employer to inform and consult workers' representatives when he contemplates redundancy dismissals. However, it followed the earlier definition of redundancy

---

17   OJ L45/19 of 19.2.1975, as amended by Council Directive 92/56 of 24 June 1992, OJ L245/3 of 26.8.92.

used for unfair dismissal and redundancy payments: cessation or diminution of the employer's requirements for work.[18]

This was an inaccurate transposition of the Directive. The Directive defines 'collective redundancies' as meaning:[19]

'dismissals effected by an employer for one or more reasons not related to the individual workers concerned.'

The amendment of the Directive in 1992 reinforced this by adding a new paragraph that 'terminations of an employment contract which occur to the individual workers concerned shall be assimilated to redundancies'.

The UK law was finally changed to correctly implement the Directive's requirements by TURER s 34(5), which substituted a new s 195 of TULRCA to reflect the EC law definition of redundancy:

'references to dismissal as redundant are references to dismissal for a reason not related to the individual concerned or for a number of reasons all of which are not so related.'

An employer attempting derecognition may (and should) contemplate employee resistance which could lead to a dismissal. Dismissals for refusal to accept derecognition are dismissals by reason of 'one or more reasons not related to the individual workers concerned'. The Directive (and the UK law) applies.

Comparison may be made with the Court of Appeal decision that detriment due to refusal to accept personal contracts, was for the purpose of deterring trade union membership or activity.[1] The legislative amendment which followed tried to overturn this by providing:[2]

'In determining what was the purpose for which action was taken by the employer against the complainant in a case where –
(a) there is evidence that the employer's purpose was to further a change in his relationship with all or any class of his employees, and
(b) there is also evidence that his purpose was one falling within s 146 (anti-trade union)
the tribunal shall regard the purpose mentioned in paragraph (a) (and not the purpose mentioned in paragraph (b)) as the purpose for which the employer took the action . . .'

Ironically, as far as the government is concerned, this implies that in offering personal contracts with the objective of derecognising the union: 'the employer's purpose was to further a change in his relationship with all or any class of his employees' – ie in the words of the new s 195 of TULRCA, reflecting the EC law definition of redundancy: 'one or more reasons not related to the individual workers concerned'!

If the Directive and UK law applies, what protection do workers and unions resisting derecognition have? The Directive (as amended in 1992) requires that when an employer (considering derecognition) contemplates that dismissals

---

18   TULRCA, s 195, formerly EPCA, s 81(2).
19   Article 1(1)(a).
1   *Associated British Ports v Palmer; Associated Newspapers v Wilson* [1993] IRLR 336; later overturned by the House of Lords [1995] IRLR 258.
2   TURER, s 13, inserting new TULRCA, s 148(3), the so-called '*Wilson/Palmer* amendments'.

may result (certainly a possible, if not probable consequence due to employee and union resistance):[3]

> 'he shall begin consultations with workers' representatives in good time with a view to reaching an agreement.'

As it now stands, the employer considering derecognition who contemplates that dismissals may result must observe the following:

– 'consult representatives of the union about the dismissal' (TULRCA, s 188(1)).
– 'The consultation must begin at the earliest opportunity ...' (TULRCA, s 188(2)).
– 'disclose in writing to the trade union representatives –
   (a) the reasons for his proposals ...
   ...
   (d) the proposed method of selecting the employees who may be dismissed ...' (TULRCA, s 188(4)).
– 'The consultation required by this section shall include consultation about ways of –
   (a) avoiding the dismissals,
   (b) reducing the numbers of employees to be dismissed, and
   (c) mitigating the consequences of the dismissals,
   and shall be undertaken by the employer with a view to reaching agreement with the trade union representatives' (new TULRCA s 188(6)).

In the context of an attempt at derecognition, the argument is that the employer must consult with the union about derecognising the union, give in writing his reasons for derecognising the union and why certain employees are being selected for dismissal, and consult about ways of avoiding dismissals.

Can the employer be genuinely concerned to avoid dismissals when these follow from resistance to derecognition? If he must examine possibilities to avoid or reduce dismissals, what could be easier than continuing recognition to avoid the dismissals, or adopting some compromise? The final and tantalising paradox is that these consultations 'shall be undertaken by the employer with a view to reaching agreement with the trade union representatives'. Can an employer be said to genuinely consult 'with a view to reaching agreement' with a union about that union's demise?

The argument is that underlying the Collective Dismissals Directive is an EC policy which requires recognition of employee representatives. Derecognition is therefore contrary to EC law. It is a contradiction in terms to require consultation with a view to agreement with employee representatives to eliminate those representatives. Employee representatives must be recognised to be consulted under EC law. At worst, consultations with a view to an agreement could aim to continue recognition, but on different terms: eg representational rights over certain topics.[4]

---

3 New Article 2(1) replacing the 1975 Directive's provision; the 1992 Directive's amendments were incorporated by TURER s 34 (2).
4 New provisions following the 1992 amendment to the Directive should also be noted. New Article 2(4) on controlling enterprises provided: 'The obligations ... shall apply irrespective of whether the decision regarding collective redundancies is being taken by the employer or by an undertaking controlling the employer'. This may be particularly relevant for derecognition through 'salami' tactics, where a large enterprise seeks to derecognise one of its establishments.

Attempts at derecognition without following the procedures of information and consultation of the union are arguably a violation of the EC Directive. If there is doubt, there should be a reference to the European Court. To prevent violations of EC law, an interim remedy stopping dismissals and derecognition is in order. The strategic use of EC law is, as always, not only to win cases. Its function is to, in the short term, delay employer attempts at derecognition, and in the long term, affect the political climate.[5]

DIRECT EFFECT OF THE 1975 DIRECTIVE AND MANDATORY RECOGNITION

Another tactic involving the Collective Dismissals Directive would be to argue that it entailed mandatory recognition of employee representatives through the EC law giving Directives direct effect, or by interpretation of UK law in light of the European Court decision in *EC Commission v UK* of 8 June 1994.[6]

Direct effect   The rights of information and consultation conferred by Article 2 of the 1975 Directive are granted to 'the workers' representatives'. They arguably satisfy the conditions of being unconditional and sufficiently precise to have direct effect under EC law.[7]

The possible enforcement of these rights by workers' representatives was foreseen by the 1992 amending Directive inserting a new Article 5a:

> 'Member States shall ensure that judicial and/or administrative procedures for the enforcement of obligations under this Directive are available to the workers' representatives and/or workers.'

Up to now, Directives have had direct effect only against public employers – the State or an emanation of the State ('vertical' direct effect).[8] It would be sensible in initiating litigation claiming direct effect of the 1975 Directive to carefully select such an employer. For example, a government agency or local authority seeking to derecognise a union, in a context where dismissals are contemplated.

Careful attention will be needed to formulating the remedy. But an application for an interim injunction stopping derecognition, pending a decision of the European Court, would be a powerful disincentive to a hesitant employer.

Mandatory recognition   UK law in TULRCA s 190 provides for an 'appropriate trade union', to present a complaint for failure to inform or consult, but limits this right to a 'recognised' union. The UK courts should interpret national law to ensure that the objectives of a Directive are achieved.[9]

Cases C-382/92 and C-383/92: *EC Commission v UK* concerned complaints

---

5   This can be seen in light of the *Wilson/Palmer* amendments. Originally, the UK law on action short of dismissal for anti-union reasons was added to an existing provision on dismissal for anti-union reasons. The *Wilson/Palmer* amendments are a reversal of policy, allowing for discriminatory action following derecognition. However, if *dismissal* for refusal to accept personal contracts is protected by EC law, the anomalous nature of the legislative amendment is clearer. EC law success in fighting dismissals resulting from derecognition would create pressure to repeal the *Wilson/Palmer* amendments, reinstate the Court of Appeal's judgment, and bring UK policy back into line with EC law requirements.

6   Case C-383/92: [1994] ECR I-2435.

7   Case 9/70: *Grad v Finanzamt Traunstein* [1970] ECR 825.

8   Case 152/84: *Marshall v Southampton and South-West Hampshire Area Health Authority (Teaching) (Marshall No 1)* [1986] ECR 723.

9   As was done by the House of Lords in *Litster v Forth Dry Dock* [1990] 1 AC 546.

by the Commission about allegedly defective implementation by the UK of the Acquired Rights and Collective Dismissals Directives with respect to the duty to designate workers' representatives. Both Directives require workers' representatives to be informed and consulted. The UK legislation implementing the Directives provides for information and consultation only where there are 'recognised' trade unions.[10] The Commission complained that the UK had not provided rules for the designation of workers' representatives where this does not take place on a voluntary basis.

The complaints were upheld by the European Court of Justice. In his Opinion which also supported the complaint, Advocate-General Van Gerven emphasised, the 'essential point . . . is that the designation of workers' representatives must not depend exclusively on the free choice or recognition of the employer'.[11] The UK legislation is clearly in conflict with the Directive and should be interpreted to exclude the requirement of employer recognition. As with direct effect, a case of derecognition involving dismissals would be the opportunity to test this argument. The implications of the Court's decision for an EC law strategy on derecognition are that derecognition attempts are met with the warning that this is contrary to EC law; if necessary, litigation challenging the derecognition is initiated and interim injunctions should be made to stop derecognition. If the UK court still has doubts, a reference under Article 177 of the Rome Treaty should be sought for clarification by the European Court, with interim orders stopping derecognition.

Directive 91/533 requiring written information on (collectively agreed) conditions of employment

One tactic used by employers with the objective of derecognition is to offer personal contracts to employees to induce them to abandon the union. Council Directive 91/533 of 14 October 1991 on an employer's obligation to inform employees of the conditions applicable to the contract or employment relationship[12] makes it more difficult for the tactic of personal contracts to achieve this objective.

The Directive obliges an employer to notify employees 'of the essential aspects of the contract or employment relationship'.[13] The information must be in written form and may be given to the employee 'in the form of . . . a written contract of employment'.[14] Where the employee already has a contract, any change in the details of the information given 'must be the subject of a written document'.[15]

The Directive presents a lengthy list of the information to be provided in writing. It includes, in particular, information on:[16]

'where appropriate:
  (i) the collective agreements governing the employee's conditions of work; or
 (ii) in the case of collective agreements concluded outside the business by special joint bodies or institutions, the name of the competent body or joint institution within which the agreements were concluded.'

10 TULRCA, s 188(1); TUPE, Reg 10(2).
11 In an Opinion delivered on 2 March 1994, paragraph 14.
12 OJ L288/32 of 18.10.1991.
13 Article 2(1).
14 Article 3(1)(a).
15 Article 5(1).
16 Article 2(2)(j).

The UK legislation implementing the Directive[17] requires the written statement to include particulars of:[18]

'any collective agreements which directly affect the terms and conditions of the employment including, where the employer is not a party, the persons by whom they were made.'

It is arguable that the EC Directive's provision has direct effect. Further, that the UK law must be interpreted consistently with the objectives of the Directive.

There is much that requires clarification in these provisions of the Directive and the UK law; for example, which collective agreements must be covered, and what information about the agreement needs to be provided: parties, date, establishments and/or categories of employees covered, etc.[19] These issues await testing. There is scope for litigation where personal contracts fail to include information on collective agreements, or include information contradicting collectively agreed provisions.

If there is no reference in the personal contract to agreements which arguably govern conditions of work, this is a violation of the EC and UK law. An adequate and effective remedy is required. There is an arguable case that the sanctions envisaged by UK law[20] are not adequate. Complaints to tribunals could require a reference to the European Court to clarify these ambiguities. The issuance of personal contracts should be halted by interim injunction.

In sum: one objective of derecognition is to get rid of collective agreements. If employers are forced to withdraw personal contracts in the face of arguments that these must include detailed information on collective agreements, they may be deterred from attempting derecognition.

The Directives on health and safety

EC law regards workers' health and safety as having a collective dimension. Derecognition may conflict with this view. EC Directives include specific provisions giving employee representatives responsibility for health and safety and protecting them from the employer. Where these representatives are union representatives, EC law may stop the employer derecognising them.

Council Directive 89/391 of 12 June 1989 on the introduction of measures to encourage improvements in the safety and health of workers at work (the Framework Directive) provides for workers' representatives with specific responsibility for health and safety:[1]

'workers' representative with specific responsibility for the safety and health of workers: any person elected, chosen or designated in accordance with national laws and/or practices to represent workers where problems arise relating to the safety and health protection of workers at work.'

This highlights the importance of union members choosing or electing, or unions designating representatives. These representatives have rights and protections under the Directive which can be used to obstruct attempts at derecognition.

17   TURER, s 26 and Schedule 4, which substitutes ss 1–6 of the EPCA on written particulars of employment.
18   Ibid, section 1(3)(j).
19   Some of the ambiguities of this Directive are analysed in more detail in Chapter 33.
20   EPCA, s 11.
1   OJ L183/1. Article 3(c) (definitions).

For example, Article 11 provides for a number of issues on which workers' safety representatives must be 'consulted in advance and in good time': in Article 11(2)(a): 'any measure which may substantially affect safety and health'. Article 11(4) then provides:

> 'workers' representatives ... may not be placed at a disadvantage because of their ... activities.'

To implement this EC law, TURER 1993 s 28 and Schedule 5 inserted new provisions into the EPCA providing:[2]

> '(1) An employee has the right not to be subjected to any detriment by any act, or any deliberate failure to act, by his employer on the ground that –
> ...
> (b) being a representative of workers on matters of health and safety at work, or a member of a safety committee –
>> (i) in accordance with arrangements established under or by virtue of any enactment, or
>> (ii) by reason of being acknowledged as such by the employer,
> he performed, or proposed to perform, any functions as such a representative or a member of such a committee.'

New s 57A declares a dismissal for such reasons an inadmissible reason.

Under the UK law, safety representatives have the right to complain to an industrial tribunal if they are dismissed, or 'subjected to any detriment' for carrying out, or proposing to carry out, their health and safety duties. Under the EC Directive, they 'may not be placed at a disadvantage'.

The provisions apply to all health and safety representatives or safety committee members appointed under the Safety Representatives and Safety Committees Regulations 1977, as well as to any representatives designated, or acknowledged as such, by the employer. This latter point raises the question of whether 'acknowledge' means recognise. Can it be revoked unilaterally, or is this a form of detriment for a representative taking too active a role?

The central question, however, is whether derecognition constitutes a detriment or disadvantage. Here the difference between the UK law and the EC Directive is important. It is arguable that the concept of 'being placed at a disadvantage' is much wider than being 'subjected to any detriment'. Being subjected to a detriment implies some personal loss to the individual; being placed at a disadvantage refers to the consequences for the representational activities carried out by the individual. The UK law does not adequately transpose the EC Directive.

The trade union link is arguably an enormous advantage in carrying out the activities of safety representatives. The trade union is a major source of information, advice, and solidarity. It will have resources of experience and expertise which the individual representative lacks. Derecognition deprives the representative of this inestimable advantage.

The *collective* dimension of health and safety is apparent in various provisions of the EC Framework Directive. Directive 89/391 requires the employer to implement measures on the basis of the following general principles of prevention:[3]

> 'giving collective protective measures priority over individual protective measures.'

2 New s 22A.
3 Article 6(2)(h).

According to Article 6(3)(c), the employer shall:

'ensure that the planning and introduction of new technologies are the subject of consultation with the workers and/or their representatives, as regards the consequences of the choice of equipment, the working conditions and the working environment for the safety and health of workers.'

Article 11 deals generally with the consultation and participation of workers. Workers' representatives with specific responsibility for safety and health:[4]

'shall take part in a balanced way, in accordance with national laws and/or practices, or shall be consulted in advance and in good time by the employer with regard to:
(a) any measures which may substantially affect safety and health . . .'

This collective dimension is threatened and undermined by derecognition. Apart from the disadvantage caused to workers' representatives, derecognition fundamentally unbalances the participation of the workers in measures which may affect their safety and health.

Derecognition is, therefore, arguably a violation of Articles 11(2) and 11(4) of the Directive. These provisions may have direct effect, or EPCA s 22A must be interpreted consistently with them. The effect of an attempt at derecognition on safety representatives should allow for immediate challenge:

–   to request a UK court to refer to the European Court the question as to whether UK law is an adequate implementation of the Directive;
–   to ask whether Article 11(4) (and perhaps also Article 11(2)) of the Directive has direct effect;
–   to request appropriate interim remedies stopping derecognition.

The EC law on equality between men and women

The EC law on equality between men and women has achieved some recent successes in the UK. The exclusion of part-timers from many employment rights has been condemned;[5] the remedies in the UK law on discrimination have been declared inadequate.[6] Derecognition may constitute indirect discrimination under EC law. Its negative impact may be greater for women than men. This may be evident in specific cases.[7] Derecognition in the form of an offer of personal contracts to workers often focuses on changes in pay determination. The *Danfoss* decision scrutinised individualised pay arrangements and required that, as a matter of EC law, these had to be transparent, and that the burden of proof was on the employer to demonstrate that women were not less favourably treated.[8] Personal contracts require such transparency to prove that discrimination is avoided.

---

4   Article 11(2).
5   *R v Secretary of State for Employment, ex p Equal Opportunities Commission* [1995] 1 AC 1, HL.
6   Case C-271/91: *Marshall v Southampton and South West Hampshire Area Health Authority (Teaching) (No 2)* [1993] ECR I-4367.
7   A report by the Equal Opportunities Commission demonstrated that contracting-out of public services had a disproportionately negative effect on women employees. K Escott and D Whitfield *The Gender Impact of CCT in Local Government* (1995). See the summary in *IRS Employment Trends* No 585, June 1995, p 14.
8   Case 109/88: *Handels- og Kontorfunktionaererernes Forbund i Danmark v Dansk Arbejdsgiverforening (Danfoss)* [1989] ECR 3199.

Derecognition is often partial, category or plant specific. If the category or establishment derecognised is predominantly male (eg management), the effects may be arguably indirectly discriminatory: for example, as a result of personal contracts being offered to that category, their remuneration increases proportionately more than other (female) categories. Conversely, if the category or establishment derecognised is predominantly female (clerical), the effects may be lower remuneration, similarly a discriminatory effect. If derecognition affects one sex disproportionately, it will require justification.

Derecognition in general, apart from specific cases, means denying workers the potential benefits of union representation. This may impact disproportionately on one sex. For example, a union may be particularly active in pursuing equal pay. Derecognition of a group of women workers who are members of that union is likely to prejudice them disproportionately.

Derecognition is likely to be detrimental to one sex. Unionisation of women being lower, it is more hard-won and its loss is more difficult to recoup. Men are more likely to be unionised. A derecognition campaign is likely to be detrimental to men more than women. An example of such a disparate impact is where there is derecognition in a predominantly female industry. The withdrawal by the Conservative government of collective bargaining in education disproportionately affected women, arguably negatively.

Such cases have not heretofore been perceived as justiciable. It would not be easy to find a good test case. But it may be useful to consider the uses of EC law and the procedures and remedies under it in a context of derecognition.

The Working Time Directive 93/104

Derecognition aims to exclude collective bargaining. This may create problems for employers due to Council Directive 93/104 of 23 November 1993 concerning certain aspects of the organisation of working time.[9]

The Directive includes provisions which make collective bargaining an element in the setting of EC standards on working time. It does so in two ways. First, collective agreements may derogate from prescribed standards. Secondly, collective agreements may fix or define relevant standards.

This is less immediately a ground for a legal challenge to a specific derecognition attempt. But the Directive does provide important disincentives to employers to abandon collective bargaining. For example, collective agreements can define night workers.[10] Article 8 prescribes for night workers normal hours not exceeding an average of 8 hours in any 24-hour period. However, the reference period over which the average is calculated is not specified and Member States may provide for the *reference period* to be *defined* by collective bargaining.[11] Collective bargaining may also *define* the *kind of work* which prohibits averaging out the maximum 8 hours work in any 24-hour period.[12]

During working hours, the Directive gives *priority* to collective agreements over legislation in *determining* the EC standard.[13] The standard is to be determined by

---

9 Council Directive 93/104/EC of 23 November 1993 concerning certain aspects of the organisation of working time, OJ L307/18 of 13.12.93.
10 Article 2(4)(b).
11 Article 16(3).
12 Article 8(2).
13 Article 4.

collective bargaining (though without specifying the appropriate level), and only in its absence by legislation.

Article 13 focuses on the employer who envisages organising work according to a certain rhythm. He is to be required to take account of the general principle of adaptation of work to human beings. This could be read as implying a requirement of consultation and participation of workers and their representatives.

Article 6 prescribes maximum weekly working time of 48 hours. The reference period over which the average 48 hour weekly working time is to be calculated is not to exceed four months. Certain extensions of the reference period can only be accomplished by collective agreement.[14]

Article 17(3) permits derogation by national or regional agreements, or lower level agreements in conformity with rules laid down by national or regional agreements. It strictly confines enterprise level agreements to the framework established by national or regional agreements. This has implications for derecognition attempts at industry level.

In sum, if employers derecognise trade unions, they lose the opportunity offered by the Directive's provisions to flexibilise their working time arrangements. In some cases, it may be extremely difficult to avoid relatively rigid parameters set down in the Directive except through the mechanism of collective bargaining. Derecognition is deterred by the provisions of EU law which, to be operative, demand the presence of trade unions.

Conclusion

Euro-litigation is one strategy for the enforcement of EC labour law. This was illustrated by the case of trade union recognition. The current domestic political context in the UK promotes derecognition. It comes into conflict with EC law in various forms.

There are EC law *defences* to derecognition. To exploit these defences, trade unions have some potential advantages (like the big stores in the Sunday trading cases). They can be repeat players: combining their resources to maintain a legal team with the continuity and expertise to undertake repeat battles. The objective is *not* one big European Court test case. The Court's judgments are usually ambiguous and leave the door open for further testing of EC law defences. Rather the objective is to combat derecognition attempts by relying on the uncertainty of EC law; to stave off derecognition by invoking the ambiguities of EC law to obtain interim remedies halting derecognition; alternatively, to seek financial undertakings if derecognition is held unlawful.

The strategy is to exploit these EC law ambiguities in lower courts all over the UK, relying on the tactics of delay, uncertainty, hesitation and referrals to the European Court.

The objective is, in the short term, to stop the trend towards trade union derecognition by a firm challenge to it, using the resources of the trade union movement to fight it. In the long term, the political strategy is to change the climate against derecognition.

International union resources could also be exploited. There are emerging

14   Article 17(2)–(4).

European networks involving unions' legal experts. There is often greater protection against derecognition in other countries. It might be easier to obtain a favourable European Court decision from a derecognition attempt in another Member State, and then attempt to apply the more favourable language of the European Court to the UK context.

In sum: Euro-litigation is, in this case, essentially a spoiling action against a government-encouraged policy of derecognition. The trade unions have the advantage of being able to sponsor a lengthy litigation campaign through creative advocacy. The objective is not to win a battle – it is the long war that counts: to create a social context unfavourable to derecognition, using EC law to outflank domestic law.

Enforcement of EU law is important not only because of its supremacy over UK law and potentially direct effect. Enforcement can proceed through innovative legal strategies. A Euro-litigation strategy relies on delay, uncertainty and remedies to encourage the courts to use the Article 177 procedure to make references to the European Court and provide interim remedies. The case study of derecognition is an exemplar of this strategic enforcement of EU law.

Title II

European Labour Law in Context

Part IV

Sex Equality in European Labour Law

Chapter 12

Origins and Development of EC Labour Law on Sex Equality

INTRODUCTION

There is an interesting paradox at the origins of the EU labour law on sex equality. The quantitative and qualitative significance of the EU law on equality between men and women is undisputed. The amount of legislation and the number and importance of decisions by the European Court exceed any other area of social policy. The fundamental principles created in the context of this evolution have had an impact on EU law going far beyond the area of policy concerned. It has probably had greater influence on the domestic law of the Member States than any other area of social law and policy.

Equal opportunities between women and men has been in the forefront of the social policy of the European Community since its beginnings. Article 119 of the Rome Treaty, Directives on equal pay,[1] equal treatment[2] and social security,[3] the extensive case law of the European Court of Justice (beginning with *Defrenne v Belgium*[4]), and a quantity of 'soft law' (such as the Recommendation on the Promotion of Positive Action[5]) have contributed to the prominence of this social policy. It has been argued that equal treatment of men and women has achieved the status of a 'fundamental right'.[6]

The concept of equal opportunities in the EC has undergone an impressive theoretical development following debates in the women's movement. The

---

1 Council Directive 75/117/EEC of 10 February 1975, on the approximation of the laws of the Member States relating to the application of the principle of equal pay for men and women, OJ L45/19 of 19.2.1975.
2 Council Directive 76/207/EEC of 9 February 1976, on the implementation of the principle of equal treatment for men and women as regards access to employment, vocational training and promotion and working conditions, OJ L39/40 of 14.2.1976.
3 Council Directive 79/7/EEC of 19 December 1978, on the progressive implementation of the principle of equal treatment for men and women in matters of social security, OJ L6/24 of 10.1.1979; Council Directive 86/378/EEC of 24 July 1986, on the implementation of the principle of equal treatment for men and women in occupational social security schemes, OJ L225/40 of 12.8.1986; Council Directive 86/613/EEC of 11 December 1986, on the application of the principle of equal treatment between men and women engaged in an activity, including agriculture, in a self-employed capacity, and on the protection of self-employed women during pregnancy and motherhood, OJ L359/56 of 19.12.1986.
4 Case 80/70: *Defrenne v Belgian State* [1971] ECR 445, 25 May 1971.
5 Council Recommendation 84/635/EEC of 13 December 1984, on the promotion of positive action for women, OJ L331/84.
6 C Docksey 'The principle of equality between men and women as a fundamental right under Community law' (1991) 20 *Industrial Law Journal* 258.

original concept of direct and intentional discrimination in the form of less favourable treatment of women by reason of their sex expanded to include, among others, indirect discrimination, positive action, critical review of protective legislation, pregnancy, maternity and childcare and sexual harassment. The scope of the concept expanded beyond pay to include discrimination in access to work, conditions of work, vocational training, pensions, both public and private, and social welfare.

Yet these major EU initiatives towards the achievement of equality between men and women were undertaken despite the fact that women as a pressure group were relatively unorganised. During the period when these legal foundations were being laid, it was argued that the women's movement had little impact on political institutions and on the political arena in general. Hoskyns concludes that:[7]

> 'the scope and form of the European policy is such that it does not connect easily with either the thinking or the practice of the women's movement as this has developed since the early 1970's. Nor is the European Community set up in such a way that makes it easy for grassroots movements to become involved in its activities.'

The impressive expansion of the EU law on equality was decidedly top-down in its origins. The French government negotiating the Treaty of Rome of 1957 was sufficiently anxious about competition with its domestic textile industry from the Belgians to insist on the inclusion of Article 119 on equal pay, to preclude under-cutting by lower-paid Belgian women workers. The Council of Ministers, in its path-breaking Resolution concerning a social action programme of 21 January 1974, famously reaffirmed the conclusions of the Paris Conference of October 1972 and declared:[8]

> 'that they attach as much importance to vigorous action in the social field as to the achievement of Economic and Monetary Union and invited the Community institutions to draw up a social action programme providing for concrete measures and the corresponding resources . . .'

Specifically:

> '– to undertake action for the purpose of achieving equality between men and women as regards access to employment and vocational training and advancement and as regards working conditions, including pay, taking into account the important role of management and labour in this field,
> – to ensure that the family responsibilities of all concerned may be reconciled with their job aspirations.'

The inspiration of Article 119 and the initiatives that followed received the benediction of the Court of Justice in its judgment in *Defrenne v SABENA*:[9]

> '8. Article 119 pursues a double aim.
> 9. First, in the light of the different stages of the development of social legislation in the various Member States, the aim of Article 119 is to avoid a situation in

---

7   C Hoskyns 'Women, European Law and Transnational Politics' (1986) 14 *International Journal of the Sociology of Law* 299, at 300.
8   (1974) OJ C13/01.
9   Case 43/75: *Defrenne v Societe Anonyme Belge de Navigation Arienne (SABENA)* [1976] ECR 455, 8 April 1976, paragraphs 8–12.

which undertakings established in States which have actually implemented the principle of equal pay suffer a competitive disadvantage in intra-Community competition as compared with undertakings established in States which have not yet eliminated discrimination against women workers as regards pay.

10. Secondly, this provision forms part of the social objectives of the Community, which is not merely an economic union, but is at the same time intended, by common action, to ensure social progress and seek the constant improvement of the living and working conditions of their peoples, as is emphasised by the Preamble to the Treaty.

11. This aim is accentuated by the insertion of Article 119 into the body of a chapter devoted to social policy whose preliminary provision, Article 117, marks "the need to promote improved working conditions and an improved standard of living for workers, so as to make possible their harmonisation while the improvement is being maintained".

12. This double aim, which is at once economic and social, shows that the principle of equal pay forms part of the foundations of the Community.'

It is important to appreciate, therefore, that the specific nature of the EU law on equality may be explicable in terms of its development *apart* from the women's movement. However, the feminist critique which has gathered apace with the evolution of the body of European law on equality is beginning, and continues to have a major formative influence on its future development.

FUTURE DEVELOPMENTS

In contrast, the labour and trade union movement in the Member States and at EU level has been formidably organised. Yet, measured in terms of the development of EU labour law, it has to be conceded that, during the period when equality law was in the forefront of developments of EU social and labour law, the successes of the European trade union movement were few and far between. The failures with respect to the proposed 'Vredeling' Directive on information and consultation were particularly evident.

This situation is now changing. EU social and labour law is currently receiving a powerful impulse from organised labour. The institutionalisation of the European social dialogue and the new competences acquired by the Community under the Maastricht Treaty's Protocol and Agreement on Social Policy are the concrete evidence of organised labour's new influence. On the other hand, it seems that the original inspiration for the EU law on sex equality is diminishing. This is in part due to the critique of the legal concept of equality embedded in the legislation and case law, which has led to efforts being directed elsewhere than the law.

One of these directions, perhaps the most promising, is an attempt to build on the presence of women in the trade union and labour movement to further the interests of women workers. If the European social dialogue is to assume an ever greater role in the formulation and implementation of EU social and labour law, it is seen as important that equal opportunities for women in collective bargaining be one of the priorities.

The EC's equal opportunities policy has looked primarily to formal legal means of implementation: legislation and enforcement through the courts or administrative agencies. However, doubts have been expressed as to whether reliance on these legal mechanisms is sufficient to achieve the policy objectives.[10] There is no detailed system of Community required procedures and remedies laid down as minimum requirements for the enforcement of European gender equality law.[11] However, national approaches may encompass social regulation through collective bargaining as well as the enactment of legislation or other means.[12] In some countries, social regulation is prioritised over legal regulation.[13] The increased importance of collective bargaining in equal opportunities policy has been emphasised by the European Commission: 'The social partners will also be encouraged to make equal opportunities an issue in the collective bargaining process'.[14]

At EC level, the growing awareness of the role of collective bargaining in implementing equal opportunities policy coincides with developments which recognise and promote the role of social dialogue in EC social policy. As noted, these developments were formalised in the Protocol and Agreement on Social Policy of the Treaty on European Union, which came into effect 1 November 1993.

The Agreement on Social Policy attached to the Protocol explicitly recognises the implementation of Community social policy and labour law through collective bargaining within Member States.[15] The agreement provides a role for the social partners at EC level in formulating Community social policy and labour law.[16] Finally, if the social partners at EC level reach agreements, it appears that Member States are obliged to implement these agreements within their national legal orders.[17]

Conversely, the evolution of the EU social and labour law on sex equality has provided valuable lessons to the trade union and labour movement in its

10   See the Report on the 1992 Louvain-la-Neuve Conference on procedures and remedies: access to equality between women and men in the EC, C McCrudden (1993) 22 *Industrial Law Journal* 77 (March). Also 'The effectiveness of European equality law: national mechanisms for enforcing gender equality law in the light of European requirements' (1993) 13 *Oxford Journal of Legal Studies* 320.
11   But see K Banks 'Equal pay and equal treatment for men and women in Community law', and D Kontizas 'Equal treatment in social security', in *Equal Opportunities for Women and Men, Social Europe*, 3/91, 1991, Chapter 2, pp 61–84.
12   See the national reports vol 2 of *Equality in Law between Men and Women in the European Community*, M Verwilghen (ed), Louvain-La-Neuve, 1986.
13   In the case of equal pay, for example, the Danish government argued, and the European Court accepted, that the main implementation mechanism was collective agreements (Case 143/83: *EC Commission v Denmark* [1985] ECR 427). In Italy, the Positive Action Act 1991 empowers various agents to promote positive action and considers collective agreements as the ideal means to control and promote positive action. Priority for reimbursement of expenses is given to positive action programmes agreed upon by employers and representative unions. M V Ballestrero 'New Legislation in Italian Equality Law' (1992) 21 *Industrial Law Journal* 152. See generally, L Gaeta and L Zoppoli (eds) *Il Diritto Diseguale: La legge sulle Azioni Positive* Giappichelli, Torino 1992.
14   European Commission, Third Action Programme on Equal Opportunities, 1991. In response, in a meeting of the Social Dialogue Committee on 11 February 1994, the social partners at EC level (ETUC, UNICE, CEEP) proposed to undertake a joint project on equal opportunities. *ETUC Report* – Press Department 5–94.
15   Article 2(4).
16   Articles 3 and 4(1).
17   Article 4(2). B Bercusson 'Maastricht: a fundamental change in European labour law' (1992) 23 *Industrial Relations Journal* 177; 'The dynamic of European labour law after Maastricht' (1994) 23 *Industrial Law Journal* (March) 1.

attempts to assume a greater role in determining EU labour law through social dialogue. The critique of equality law by the women's movement has contributed to radical rethinking of the shape of the future EU social and labour law. It is women's influx into the labour force that has produced many of the new ideas on organisation of working time, new forms of employment, and reconciliation of work and private/family life. Some of these aspects are explored in other chapters in this book: the gender implications of the EU labour law on working time, and the regulation of new forms of employment, in particular, part-time workers, most of whom are women. The critical analysis of equality law by the women's movement, therefore, has had important consequences for the general direction of EU labour law.

The substantive law on sex equality: equal pay, equal treatment, social security, has been the subject of several monographs.[18] The purpose of the following chapters is to put this law in its context. Specifically, the contribution which the feminist critique emerging from the women's movement has made in shaping the debates over EU labour law on equality, and, beyond, the emerging alternative means of implementation, and the latest proposals from the Commission. This will be undertaken in three separate chapters. First, the critique of equality law as it has developed will be presented. Then, the implications of using social dialogue and collective bargaining as the instrument for equality law will be explored. Finally, the impact of the critique of equality law on the developing EU social law and policy on reconciliation of work and family life will be examined.[19]

---

18 B Creighton *Working Women and the Law* Mansell 1979; S Prechal and N Burrows *Gender Discrimination Law of the European Community* Dartmouth 1990; E Ellis *European Community Sex Equality Law* OUP 1992; T Hervey *Justifications for Indirect Discrimination* Sweet & Maxwell 1993.

19 The writing of these chapters has benefited considerably from my participation in the International Research Group on Equal Opportunities and Collective Bargaining, supported by the European Foundation for the Improvement of Living and Working Conditions, Dublin. Parts of the chapters are inspired by drafts of the Concept Report prepared for this Group, which was written by Professor Linda Dickens of Warwick University, and myself.

Chapter 13

The Critique of the EC Labour Law on Sex Equality

FORMAL AND SUBSTANTIVE EQUALITY

The most familiar criticism of the concept of equality employed in EU law is that it is limited to formal equality, involving a conceptual distinction between equality of treatment and equality of outcomes.[1]

Formal equality embodies liberal notions of equality of opportunity with an emphasis on formal, procedural equality where everyone is to be helped to compete equally on the basis of their individual talents (requiring removal of discrimination and limited positive action to compensate for disadvantage). The concept of formal equality presupposes autonomous individuals making choices. It fails to recognise the 'private' sphere and the construction of women there which defines their 'public' life. It is criticised as inadequate to a world where distribution of goods is structured along gender lines.[2] On this basis, people treated differently in the past will be in dissimilar positions when compared now. A clear indication of this is the persistent occupational sex segregation of the labour force.[3]

In contrast, equality of outcomes focuses on substantive equality rather than formal equality, on 'equal shares' rather than 'equal treatment'; it is concerned with the outcomes of the game rather than the rules of play, with the finishing line, not the starting line. This distinction is echoed by that between the individual justice model and group justice model, posed as alternative models of the objectives of anti-discrimination legislation.[4] Such an approach tends to call for direct intervention in workplace practices to achieve a fair (representative/

---

1   For example, N Jewson and D Mason 'The theory and practice of equal opportunities policies: liberal and radical approaches' (1986) 34 *Sociological Review* (No 2) 307; J Gregory *Sex, Race and the Law* (1989).

2   N Lacey 'Legislation against sex discrimination: Questions from a feminist perspective' (1987) 14 *Journal of Law and Society* 411 at 413, 415.

3   See J Rubery and C Fagan *Occupational Segregation amongst Women and Men in the European Community* Manchester School of Management, UMIST, October 1992: a synthesis report of the network of experts on the situation of women in the labour market.

4   C McCrudden 'The Effectiveness of European Equality Law' (1993) 13 *Oxford Journal of Legal Studies* 320. McCrudden argues that European equality law adopts modified versions of both. But see also S Fredman 'European Community Discrimination Law: A Critique' (1992) 21 *Industrial Law Journal* (No 2) 119. In the UK context, the national application of European law has been characterised as adopting an individualised, liberal conceptualisation; L Dickens 'Anti-discrimination Legislation: Exploring and Explaining the Impact on Women's Employment', in W McCarthy (ed) *Legal Intervention in Industrial Relations*, Blackwell 1992.

proportional) distribution of outcomes; it adopts a group perspective and is associated with such measures as quotas, preferential hiring, etc.

The concern with ensuring equality of opportunity at the outset ignores the *process* of arriving at the outcome. The presupposition is that open and free competition guarantees the fairness of the outcome. The existing distribution of goods structured on gender lines is already an obstacle to such a conclusion. But the process of *competition* itself is not necessarily neutral; it can be and often is *legally structured* to secure results which are far from conducive to equality of outcomes and serve to perpetuate discrimination.[5]

The solution of substantive equality to formal equality's defects is for redistributive mechanisms to compensate. This confronts the challenge of structuring market mechanisms to achieve this result – not an approach instinctively favoured by the liberal capitalist inspiration of the European Economic Community in its early decades. But as competing concepts of competition itself have come under close scrutiny, interventions of this nature have become acceptable.[6] Collectivisation of individualistic processes in the labour market is one such mechanism to structure the process so as to achieve the desired substantive equality.[7]

EQUALITY AND DIFFERENCE

More contentious among feminist theorists is the question of difference (special treatment) v equality. Even within 'equal treatment' there is room for divergence, as the debate around the question of sameness or difference (as between men and women) reveals.[8]

The case for 'difference' argues from biological differences, and also alleged strengths and attributes specific to women. The counter-argument points to the danger that insisting on biological differences implies protection and special treatment which can lead to restrictions on women's activity – the disputes over night work for women being a prime example. It is argued that these restrictive conditions contribute to the alleged strengths and attributes (forced parenting, lack of physical autonomy, dependency on mediation skills); and it is questioned whether it is desirable to maintain conditions which give rise to these qualities.[9]

Special treatment is thus a double-edged sword. If there are objectively real differences, then special treatment would seem warranted. But if these differences are socially constructed, it is equal treatment which is required. Otherwise, the notion that difference equals disadvantage is reinforced. Socially constructed stereotypes, which may be rejected by legislation insisting on

---

5   On the use of legal instruments to structure competition against actors whose objectives contradict specific economic policies, and shield from competition those whose objectives are consistent with public policy, see B Bercusson 'Economic Policy: State and Private Ordering', in T C Daintith (ed) *Law as an Instrument of Economic Policy: Comparative and Critical Approaches* (1988) Walter de Gruyter: Berlin and New York, pp 359–420.

6   F Snyder 'Ideologies of Competition in European Community Law' (1989) 52 *Modern Law Review* 149.

7   But see A Lester and D Rose 'Equal value claims and sex bias in collective bargaining' (1992) 21 *Industrial Law Journal* 163.

8   C Bacchi *Same Difference: Feminism and Sexual Difference* (1990).

9   L Alcoff 'Cultural feminism versus post-structuralism: The identity crisis in feminist theory' (1988) 13 *Signs*, No 3, 405 at 414.

equality, are reintroduced through ideas of 'what counts as less favourable or detrimental treatment, or justifiable requirements or conditions'.[10] Reproductive differences may mean worse treatment rather than being valued, if the solution is to treat pregnancy like illness. It treats women as victims and devalues them.[11] A concept such as indirect discrimination allows for justification for unequal treatment. It leaves a vacuum to be filled by objectives provided by politicians or judges.[12]

But the demand for *equal* treatment is also problematic. The prevailing assumption is that the male norm is the standard for deciding what constitutes 'equal' or 'special' treatment. If equal opportunity is seen as requiring men and women to be treated the same, this may lead to women being offered equality only on male terms. The *same* treatment means conforming to male-centred norms and requirements. Equality as a concept is gendered. The objective of *equal* treatment becomes the *same* standard as men. It is the maleness of the equal treatment standard which is challenged by feminist theorists:

> '. . . equal rights can be no more than a demand for access to the structure. If it is the structure which is the problem, equal rights to it are not an exciting prospect.'[13]

It is the gendered constructions, not the concept of equality which should be at issue.[14]

Related to this issue is the extent to which *equality* is perceived as calling for *changes* in male gendered (but often taken as neutral) organisational and occupational structures, practices, cultures, norms, value systems, etc. Equal opportunities may be conceptualised as requiring 'women-friendly' provisions to help women adapt to, and get on within, structures as they currently are, or, alternatively, as calling for changes in those structures, cultures etc to accommodate women. The first approach is part of what has been termed a 'short' agenda for equal opportunities, while the second approach belongs to a 'long' agenda, which Cockburn sees as a project of transformation for organisations.[15]

Illustrations from the EC law on equality

The issues of equality and the male norm, equality and difference, and equality as neutrality have been confronted on various occasions in the EC law on equality.[16]

---

10 N Lacey, op cit, p 415.
11 Lacey, op cit, p 417.
12 C Hoskyns and L Luckhaus 'The European Community Directive on Equal Treatment in Social Security' (1989) 17 *Policy and Politics* 321, at p 334.
13 S Gibson 'The structure of the veil' [1989] 52 *Modern Law Review* 420 at 439.
14 An alternative approach, therefore, is to conceptualise equal treatment as requiring parity of treatment as between men and women (recognising differences), rather than the same treatment, a call for equivalence rather than equality – an argument made by C Cockburn *In the Way of Women* (1991).
15 Ibid, also 'Equal opportunities: the short and long agenda' (1989) 20 *Industrial Relations Journal* (Autumn), No 3, 213.
16 The article by S Fredman 'European Community Discrimination Law: A Critique' (1992) 21 *Industrial Law Journal* 119–34, cogently rehearses the well-known critique of equality as an instrument to combat discrimination and disadvantage and describes the case-law of the European Court of Justice.

On the issue of *equality and the male norm* as the standard of comparison, the case of dismissal by reason of pregnancy in the decision in *Dekker* is put forward.[17] In the European Court's judgment, pregnancy is not to be judged on the basis of a male norm of absence from work. Rather, absence due to pregnancy was held to be special and unique to women, *not* comparable to men's disability. This may be contrasted with the judgment in *Hertz*, where the male norm of absence from work was applied in the case of long-term consequences of pregnancy and maternity leave.[18]

Another example, the case of *Rummler*, concerned the criteria for job evaluation in a pay structure.[1] The job evaluation scheme applied physical effort as a neutral criterion, on the assumption that the male norm of physical strength is the objective standard. This was upheld by the Court; however, it did stipulate that equality for women should be attained by balancing this male norm with other criteria in the job evaluation scheme favourable to women.

The problem of the dominance of the male norm is illustrated by the extent to which occupational segregation based on sex is effective in preventing women claiming equal pay. One example is by the law's limiting the scope of comparisons. A minor breach in this obstacle is *Macarthys Ltd v Smith*, which allowed comparison between *successive* female and male employees in the same post, obviating the requirement that the comparator be in contemporaneous employment.[2] The recent decision in *Enderby* also overrode occupational segregation, reflected in separate collective bargaining arrangements for male and female dominated categories of workers, to allow a claim for equal pay.[3] The concept of indirect discrimination developed by the Court has been a powerful weapon in the hands of part-time workers, predominantly women.[4] But again, their entitlement is limited pro rata to the norms established for male full-timers.

On the issue of *equality and difference*, the danger that, by protecting differences, the law may be perpetuating stereotypes has been recognised in the literature. On occasion, the Court has been less attentive to this dimension. Directive 76/207 on equal treatment includes in Article 2(3) a derogation for reasons of pregnancy and maternity. In *Hofmann*, the Court simply refused to consider questions of family organisation or division of parental responsibility.[5] The Court was more forthcoming in a case of French collective agreements granting parental leave and other benefits exclusively to women, rejecting the defence of the agreements as reflecting cultural norms.[6] In a case affected by the Directive's Article 2(2), excluding from coverage occupations where sex is a determining factor, the Court rejected the argument as applied to the protection of policewomen from carrying fire-arms, but left open the possibility of occupational specificity – subject to the principle of proportionality.[7]

---

17 Case C-177/88: *Dekker v Stichting Vormingscentrum voor Jong Volwassenen Plus* [1990] ECR I-3941.
18 Case C-179/88: *Handels- og Kontorfunktionaerernes Forbund i Danmark (acting for Hertz) v Dansk Arbejdsgiverforening (acting for Aldi Marked A/S)* [1990] ECR I-3979.
1 Case 237/85: *Rummler v Dato-Druck GmbH* [1986] ECR 2101.
2 Case 129/79: [1980] ECR 1275.
3 Case C-127/92: *Enderby v Frenchay Area Health Authority* [1993] ECR I-5535.
4 Case 170/84: *Bilka-Kaufhaus GmbH v Weber von Hartz* [1986] ECR 1607.
5 Case 184/83: *Hofmann v Barmer Ersatzkasse* [1984] ECR 3047.
6 Case 312/86: *EC Commission v French Republic* [1988] ECR 6315.
7 Case 222/84: *Johnston v Chief Constable of the RUC* [1986] ECR 1651.

The perspective of *equality as neutrality* is criticised as assuming a symmetry of position between men and women, ignoring disadvantages of the latter in the labour market. An illustration is the *Integrity* case.[8] A claim by married men self-employed workers to the same social security rights as married women was upheld. Advocate-General Jacobs argued there was no need for a gender perspective. Policy-makers could look at each case for relevant factors of income, dependence and so on for decisions on social security, ignoring structural disadvantages of women. This prospect of individualised assessment, too costly in practice, militates against provision for the structurally disadvantaged. Provision for the latter might be justified even if not neutral, but discriminatory in favour of the disadvantaged.

THE CONCEPT OF GENDER

Much feminist theory of the concept of equality starts from the concept's negation of a specific gender dimension, with the consequence, as described above, that it is male definitions that are adopted of norms, of the normal, of the neutral. The substantive content of the standards to which all are to have equal access is defined in male terms; in particular, the standard employment relationship of the full-time, permanent, continuous, paid worker.

One strand of feminist theory argues that there is a specifically female perspective which is required to correct the dominant male perspective. Providing this correction allows for definition of standards which accommodate women as well as men. This is the approach, for example, of the late Tove Stang Dahl, in the field of law.[9] Her analysis seeks to change the categories classifying different fields of law to reflect women's reality.

A different approach is that of cultural or standpoint feminism, as argued by Catherine MacKinnon, which holds that the law is inextricably bound up with male domination.[10] The problem is to identify the forms this domination takes, and identify the specifically female standpoint. Thereafter, the two strategies described earlier emerge: equal or special treatment. Exponents of women's difference would argue that special provisions are required to recognise and protect these differences. Exponents of equality argue that men and women are equal in all respects, and that the law must recognise this sameness. The first strategy would demand special treatment related to maternity; the second would stress equal provision to that of men with equivalent biological needs – short-term physical indisposition or vulnerability.

Each of these strands rejects law's claim to be gender-neutral. The argument of the first is that law needs a new equilibrium reflecting women's reality. The argument of the second is that law cannot be constructed using men's reality; the dominant sex's partial perception can only be replaced by the correct perception of the oppressed sex.

A different strand of feminist theory objects that to define law as masculine implies that there is a definable reality attaching to each of the categories 'man' and 'woman'. This is challenged by Carol Smart, with respect to 'woman' as a

---

8   Case 373/89: *Integrity v Rouvroy* [1990] ECR I-4243.
9   *Women's Law: An Introduction to Feminist Jurisprudence*, Norwegian University Press (1987).
10   *Feminism Unmodified: Discourses on Life and Law*, Harvard University Press (1987).

category of feminist thought, by referring to the fragmented experience of women of difference races, classes, and so on.[11] There is no epistemologically defensible concept of femaleness (or maleness) outside a specific cultural context. Different cultural contexts and histories produce different definitions of women and men.

The problem is how to define the concept/category 'woman' in the absence of any 'natural' core. Smart argues that feminist theory can challenge the claim of law to 'truth' as a form of knowledge, but is precluded from asserting its own perspective as 'true'. Moreover, there is the trap of 'relying on a biological signifier and thereby becoming eternally wedded to a binary (and hierarchical) division between Woman/women and Man/men which is in turn the very thing much feminism wishes to overcome'. On the other hand, Alcoff points to the danger of 'nominalism: the idea that the category "women" is a fiction and that feminist efforts must be directed towards dismantling this fiction ... an effective feminism could only be a wholly negative feminism, deconstructing everything and refusing to construct anything.'[12]

CONCLUSION

If equality is seen as being more than adapting women, it requires measures which have a focus which extends beyond women. There is a need to remember that men are part of gender equality. Hence, it is not necessarily a simple matter to identify particular measures unequivocally as promoting 'equality'. The critique of equality which has just been presented demonstrates that different assessments may be reached depending in part on the analysis of the problem/causes of women's current inequality in employment, and in part on needing to place measures in their context, including their operation in practice. Some measures, which are often taken at face value to be equal opportunity provisions, in fact may be double-edged for women's equality, with negative potential in terms of promoting equality, as well as positive.

An example of this is provided by measures which (in form or practice) reinforce the premise that women have, and should continue to have, primary responsibility for childcare (and other dependent care) with a consequent intermittent (and less 'committed') attachment to the workforce than men, who are not seen as carers. On this analysis, enhanced maternity or childcare leave for women, although facilitating women's continued participation in wage work, may be problematic for equality. Provisions targeted at men, such as paternity leave, which could help foster a greater sharing of social and occupational responsibilities as between men and women, and help challenge the 'male norm' in the organisation of paid work, might be considered (potentially) to offer more in terms of gender equality.

A second example is provided by flexibility arrangements including part-time schedules. Although flexible work arrangements may be valued as an aid to combining domestic responsibilities and paid work, the existence of part-time or

---

11   C Smart 'Law's Power, the Sexed Body and Feminist Discourse' (1990) 17 *Journal of Law and Society* 194, at 200.

12   Alcoff, op cit, (1988) 13 *Signs*, No 3, p 405 at pp 417–18.

other 'non-standard' working may be a problematic indicator of equal opportunities. Gender equality is unlikely to be served where part-time work is
ghettoised into low graded 'women's jobs' or detached from an organisation's
internal labour market and remuneration system. One would need to know, not
simply that there was provision for part-time work, but at what levels, available
to whom, on what conditions etc to form an assessment.

Always an issue in considering gender quality is that 'women' and 'men' are
not homogeneous categories; differences exist in terms of ethnicity, class, age,
etc. Equal opportunity provisions may be concerned with a particular group of
women rather than women in general. This is a general principle which increasingly characterises EU labour law's regulation of different categories of worker.[13]

---

13   As demonstrated in Part VIII, Chapters 28–32 of this book.

Chapter 14

EC Equality Law in Context: Collective Bargaining

INTRODUCTION

The inspiration of EU equality law was Article 119 of the Treaty of Rome requiring equal pay for equal work:[1]

'Each Member State shall during the first stage ensure and subsequently maintain the application of the principle that men and women should receive equal pay for equal work.

For the purpose of this Article, "pay" means the ordinary basic or minimum wage or salary and any other consideration, whether in cash or in kind, which the worker receives, directly or indirectly, in respect of his employment from his employer.

Equal pay without discrimination based on sex means:
  (a) that pay for the same work at piece rates shall be calculated on the basis of the same unit of measurement;
  (b) that pay for work at time rates shall be the same for the same job.'

Thus formulated, the Article was held to have direct effect by the decision of the European Court in *Defrenne*:[2]

'The principle that men and women should receive equal pay, which is laid down by Article 119, may be relied on before the national courts. These courts have a duty to ensure the protection of the rights which that provision vests in individuals, in particular in the case of those forms of discrimination which have their origin in legislative provisions or collective labour agreements, as well as where men and women receive unequal pay for equal work which is carried out in the same establishment or service, whether private or public.'

---

1   A slightly different formulation was substituted by the Maastricht Treaty:
  '1.   Each Member State shall ensure that the principle of equal pay for male and female workers for equal work is applied.
   2.   For the purpose of this Article, "pay" means the ordinary basic or minimum wage or salary and any other consideration, whether in cash or in kind, which the worker receives directly or indirectly, in respect of his employment, from his employer.
        Equal pay without discrimination based on sex means:
        (a)   that pay for the same work at piece rates shall be calculated on the basis of the same unit of measurement;
        (b)   that pay for work at time rates shall be the same for the same job.
   3.   This Article shall not prevent any Member State from maintaining or adopting measures providing for specific advantages in order to make it easier for women to pursue a vocational activity or to prevent or compensate for disadvantages in their professional careers.'
2   Case 43/75: *Defrenne v SABENA* [1976] ECR 455, as stated in paragraph 40.

As such it became the basis for numerous claims before national courts and references to the European Court. The development and analysis of the law on equal pay and equal treatment in employment, not surprisingly, has been focused on legislation and case law.

Yet it is acknowledged that, in most Member States of the EU, pay and conditions of employment of men and women workers are largely determined by collective agreements. It is through collective bargaining, conducted by trade unions and employers and their associations, that the payment systems and structures, and other terms and conditions of employment, are fixed. Litigation through national courts, basing claims on EU legislation and decisions of the Court of Justice, directly affects only a tiny number of litigants. Any legal rules so established have to be mediated through the collective bargaining system.

It is that system which interprets and applies, for better or worse, the legal rules in the actual determination of pay and conditions of employment of men and women workers. If most workers in the EU experience the EU law on sex equality only through the collective bargaining activity of employers and trade unions, it is that context which really determines the application of EU law. An understanding of that context becomes essential to an understanding of the legal rules on equality.

This chapter focuses on the relatively under-developed area of EU equality law as it interacts with collective bargaining. It is arguably as, if not more, important to analyse the legal rules as they relate to the reality of collective determination of pay and employment conditions, as to apply them to the circumstances of an individual case of sex discrimination. To that end, it is an essential skill for the EU labour lawyer to comprehend the collective dimension of the law on equality.

National systems of collective bargaining are embedded in industrial relations systems of great variety. The *actors* involved, trade unions and employers' organisations, the *processes* of collective bargaining and social dialogue at different levels (national, sectoral, enterprise, workplace), and the *outcomes* in the form of collective agreements differ widely from country to country. The EU law on equal pay and equal treatment in employment interacts with these national industrial relations contexts to produce an outcome which belies any pretence to a uniform EU law. To understand the significance of the EU labour law on equality, it has to be considered in the industrial relations and collective bargaining context in which it operates.

This chapter begins with a general account of the interaction of collective bargaining and equal opportunities. There follow outlines of five different national contexts (France, Italy, Germany, Denmark and the UK) which illustrate the variety of this interaction in the EU.

COLLECTIVE BARGAINING AND EQUALITY

The legal implementation of equal opportunities policy has frequently encountered collective bargaining.[3] But collective bargaining as a concept is not

---

3   Case 143/83: *EC Commission v Denmark* [1985] ECR 427; Case 165/82: *EC Commission v UK* [1983] ECR 3431; Case 235/84: *EC Commission v Italy* [1986] ECR 2291; Case 237/85: *Rummler* [1986] ECR 2101; Case 109/88: *Danfoss* [1989] ECR 3199; Case C-33/89: *Kowalska* [1990] ECR I-2591; Case C-127/92: *Enderby v Frenchay Health Authority* [1993] ECR I-5535.

particularly focused on equal opportunities.[4] Hence, mutual understanding has not been easy to achieve. There is a well developed literature on equal opportunities and on collective bargaining in Europe, but relatively little which aims to link the two.

It has already been pointed out that there are many differences between countries as regards the composition and structure of the social partners, the nature of the negotiation processes between them, and the character of the various outcomes which emerge in the form of collective agreements. Collective agreements, including those on equal opportunities, possess very different characteristics because of different national contexts: legal, industrial relations, economic and social. For example, different formats, different legal effects, different nature of the entitlements (specific and general) described in agreements and whether agreements are 'representative' or constitute 'good practice'. Agreements may articulate among themselves at different levels: national, sectoral, regional, enterprise, workplace, and also with laws and management practices. Collective agreements on equal opportunities have to be analysed in their national context in order to make sense of collective bargaining on equal opportunities in each country.

The two concepts of collective bargaining and equality combine at the national level due to the growth in women's labour force participation and their presence within the trade unions. The sophisticated concepts of equal opportunities policy contrast with the relatively restricted agendas of trade unions' bargaining platforms and employers' personnel practices. This has already led to legal clashes before the European Court of Justice.

The two concepts combine at EC level due to the development of social policy regulation towards European social dialogue. Equal opportunities policy at EC level has to adjust to the new form of regulation. But also, the new form of social regulation at EC level – the European social dialogue articulated with different national industrial relations systems – has to accommodate the sophistication of EC equal opportunities policy as it has developed.

Dimensions of equal opportunities and collective bargaining

The *combination* of equal opportunities and collective bargaining has several dimensions: scope/content, regulatory form, coverage/diffusion, actors/motives, and process/result.[5]

Scope/content

The wide range of *potential* topics for collective bargaining on equal opportunities policy highlights the relatively impoverished content of most collective

---

4   There is a parallel with law: law too is not particularly focused on equal opportunities, and it too is the subject of analysis as to its utility in achieving equal opportunities objectives. A major focus of research has been on the issue of the limitations of legal processes. See the Report on the 1992 Louvain-la-Neuve Conference on procedures and remedies: access to equality between women and men in the EC, C McCrudden (1993) 22 *Industrial Law Journal* 77 (March).

5   These dimensions were sketched in a memorandum by Dr Hubert Krieger of the European Foundation for the Improvement of Living and Working Conditions, Dublin, and were developed in a Background Report by B Bercusson for the International Research Group on Equal Opportunities and Collective Bargaining in Europe, 1994.

agreements, when compared to the scope and content of equal opportunities policy as it has been developed at EC and national levels. If the regulation of equal opportunities in the EC is to depend more on social dialogue and collective bargaining at EC and national levels, this gap assumes great importance. For the purpose of achieving a uniform implementation of equal opportunities, it becomes all the more important to spread knowledge of collective agreements which have sought to encompass less common areas of equal opportunities policy.

Regulatory form

EC equal opportunities law and policy has repeatedly clashed with the regulatory form of *collective bargaining*. The contradiction has affected the actors, processes and outcomes of collective bargaining.

Actors	The separation of bargaining units into categories producing agreements more favourable to men has been declared discriminatory (*Enderby*[6]).
Processes	Pay bargaining processes which lack transparency as regards lower paid women (*Danfoss*[7]) or include criteria which discriminate against women (*Rummler*[8]) are declared unlawful.
Outcomes	Collective agreements which contain clauses which directly or indirectly discriminate against women are unlawful (*Kowalska*[9]) or must be capable of being so declared (*EC Commission v UK*[10]).

On the other hand, the regulatory *legal* strategies of implementation of equal opportunities policy have been criticised, and collective bargaining has been proposed as a possibly more effective strategy.[11] The emergence of the European social dialogue as a primary form of EC regulation highlights the potential of collective bargaining as a regulatory strategy for equal opportunities policy.

Coverage/diffusion

At the level of legislation, the coverage of equal opportunities policy is EC-wide and national. At the level of collective bargaining, the coverage is patchy. It varies among countries and sectors and by topic. Coverage and diffusion of equal opportunities in collective agreements is not necessarily the same as that of collective bargaining in general.

For example, collective bargaining might be expected to be more developed as regards equal opportunities policy in those sectors where there is high female employment. However, an ILO study demonstrates that in countries where a sector is highly feminised, union density for women may be low or high.[12] It is argued that there is no correlation between female predominance

---

6 Case 127/92: *Enderby v Frenchay Health Authority* [1993] ECR I-5535.
7 Case 109/88: *Handels-og Kontorfunktionaerernes Forbund i Danmark v Dansk Arbejdsgiverforening* [1989] ECR 3199.
8 Case 235/84: *Rummler v Dato-Druck GmbH* [1986] ECR 2101.
9 Case C-33/89: *Kowalska v Hamburg* [1990] ECR I-2591.
10 Case 165/82: [1983] ECR 3431.
11 McCrudden, op cit.
12 S Hastings and M Coleman *Women Workers and Unions in Europe: An Analysis by Industrial Sector*, ILO, Geneva, IDP Women/WP-4, p 22.

and union density. Equal opportunities collective bargaining may be focused not only on sectors which are highly feminised, but on those which have high union density.[13]

Actors/motives

The focus on collective bargaining means special regard must be had to trade unions. However, employers may be involved in equal opportunities policy where there are women workers even in the absence of collective bargaining. Equal opportunities policy cannot ignore employers' unilateral policies, and how this affects equal opportunities and collective bargaining. But the emphasis on collective bargaining means looking closely at unions. It is their role in pushing on women's issues that is crucial. Employers may take initiatives – but they are unlikely to push for them against union opposition.

That the social partners through collective bargaining may play a positive role in the pursuit of equality is clear, but it should be noted also that collective bargaining may pose problems for achieving that objective. Collective bargaining is itself a gendered process and collective agreements may reflect, embody or perpetuate discriminatory practices:[14]

> 'Most unions, whatever their egalitarian pretensions, have typically been biased in the composition of their officials and activists towards relatively high status, male, native born, full-time employees. Intentionally or otherwise, the programmes developed in collective bargaining, and even more crucially, those issues assigned real priority, reflect the dominant concerns of these hegemonic groups.'

That collective agreements may be discriminatory was acknowledged in, for example, the Equal Treatment Directive. Measures which the Member States are required to take under that Directive include those necessary to ensure that:[15]

> 'any provisions contrary to the principle of equal treatment which are included in collective agreements, individual contracts of employment, internal rules of undertakings . . . shall be, or may be declared, null and void or may be amended.'

The precise ways in which discrimination may be embodied in collective bargaining and collective agreements have been revealed by research in different Member States,[16] while in a number of legal cases the development of the European concept of discrimination and equal opportunities has contrasted with the relatively restricted agendas of trade unions' bargaining platforms and employers' personnel practices.

The ILO study noted that growth of employment in a sector, combined with a rising proportion of women workers in the sector and a low and falling general

---

13 However, where a sector is highly feminised in two countries but with different union density in each, it may be that the country with low density still has relatively high density in that sector compared to other sectors in that country. So the criterion is not absolute density, but relative union density of a sector in the country. Ibid, Tables 17–20, pp 22–5 show this for different sectors.

14 R Hyman 'Changing Trade Union Identities and Strategies', in R Hyman and A Ferner (eds) *New Frontiers in European Industrial Relations*, Blackwell 1994.

15 Council Directive 76/207/EEC of 9 February 1976, OJ L39/40, Article 4(b).

16 In the UK, L Dickens et al *Tackling Sex Discrimination Through Collective Bargaining*, London 1988.

level of union density created the conditions for a potentially important area of union membership recruitment. This factor is indicative of potential union interest in equal opportunities policy in order to attract new members. This is so especially because the ILO study argues that union density is not lower for women because of feminised sectors, but because these sectors have general low union density and many women work in them.[17]

Process/result

Collective bargaining on equal opportunities in Member States – the collective agreements – provides a starting point for developing the process of the European social dialogue. This does not mean that national processes of negotiating equal opportunities agreements will be replicated at European level. The question is what lessons may be learned from national experience. The European social dialogue may produce agreements which have to be articulated with national systems of collective bargaining.[18] The importance of collective bargaining on equal opportunities lies in its significance at:

–   the pre-EC social dialogue phase; by drawing on experience of collective bargaining over equal opportunities policy within the Member States, ideas and inspiration may be obtained, and valuable lessons about what not to do may be learned;
–   the post-EC social dialogue phase: as national collective bargaining systems may likely become the means of implementing EC-level agreements on equal opportunities, it is essential to understand the present practice of collective bargaining on equal opportunities.

Feminisation of the labour force and scope of collective bargaining

The interaction of collective bargaining and equal opportunities has additional importance given the increased feminisation of the European labour market and the need for employment policies and trade union strategies to respond to such change. This is not surprising given the increase in women's share of the labour market and the rise in women's participation rates in the labour force during the 1980s,[19] though unemployment among women was rising faster.[20] Women's activity rates have consistently increased over the last 20–30 years. Between 1960 and 1990 the recorded labour force in the EC increased by just under 29 million, of which over 20 million were women.[1]

The increasing number of economically active women is reflected in female trade union membership. Surveys show that women's share of union membership is steady or rising, though there is great variation among countries in

17   Hastings and Coleman, op cit, pp 25–6.
18   See generally C Cockburn *Women and the European Social Dialogue: Strategies for Gender Democracy*, Doc V/5465/95-EN, European Commission, 1995; C Cockburn, M C Alemany Gomez, M Bergamaschi, H M Nickel and C Rogerat *Women in the Europeanizing of Industrial Relations: A Study in Five Member States*, Doc V/664/94-EN, European Commission, December 1993.
19   S Hastings and M Coleman *Women Workers and Unions in Europe: An Analysis by Industrial Sector*, ILO, Geneva, IDP Women/WP-4, Table 1, p 5, Table 2, p 6.
20   *Women in the European Community*, Eurostat, Luxembourg 1992, Chapter VII, p 72.
1   Commission of the EC *Employment in Europe* (1992) COM (91) 354.

Western Europe with respect to overall union density, female union density, and ratio of female to male union density.[2] Issues of internal equity (the position of women within trade unions) are connected to issues of external equity (including collective bargaining for equality). This has been recognised in initiatives taken by a number of organisations to facilitate the articulation and representation of women's particular interests and to increase the number of women in leadership positions in the trade unions.[3] It is, however, still the case that women are under-represented on decision-making structures and in leadership positions.[4]

The focus on collective bargaining recognises the importance of joint regulation in the determination of terms and conditions of work for large numbers of citizens in Europe, and its potential as a mechanism for progress towards the achievement of gender equality. The extent of this potential, however, is linked to various features, including those concerned with the scope, content, coverage and diffusion of joint regulation and its outcomes.

The degree of union density (proportion of eligible workforce in membership of unions) and coverage of collective bargaining (the number of workers covered by collective agreements as a percentage of those wage and salary earners) varies as between Member States. So, too, does the scope, content, and form of collective bargaining and collective agreements. There is variation too, although to differing degrees, in these factors within any country by such variables as sector, industry, occupational group, firm size, etc. There are also differences in patterns of unionisation and collective bargaining coverage as between women and men.

Great Britain has a collective bargaining coverage of 39% of the workforce; figures for other countries in Europe are in excess of 60%; in many the proportion of workers covered is over 80% (eg Austria, Belgium, France, Finland, Germany, Sweden).[5] It should be noted that the coverage of collective bargaining may be considerably greater than union density in countries (for example, France and Spain) where there is provision for the extension of collectively agreed terms to those who are not members of the contracting organisations.

Any consideration of the potential role for collective bargaining in promoting women's equality inevitably raises questions about the health and future of collective bargaining in general. In some countries (perhaps notably in the UK) there has been a shift away from joint regulation towards a more individualised approach to the employment relationship. The 1980s were marked by union decline in Europe, particularly in the private sector, often reversing membership gains made in the 1970s. In some countries (Britain, France, Ireland, Netherlands, Spain, Portugal) there was severe decline. Although such developments clearly have negative potential for the role of collective bargaining as a

2   Hastings and Coleman, op cit, pp 10–12 and Table 16 on p 21. For recent data on UK unions, see 'Women in the unions', *Equal Opportunities Review* No 59, January/February 1995, p 38.
3   A Trebilcock 'Strategies for strengthening women's participation in trade union leadership' (1991) 130 *International Labour Review*. No 4, 407.
4   See eg M Braithwaite and C Byrne *Women in decision-making in trade unions*, ETUC and European Commission, 1994.
5   Figures from OECD, Employment Outlook, July 1994, and R Hyman and A Ferner (eds), op cit. The collective bargaining coverage figures are adjusted to take account only of those employees who are not excluded from bargaining rights.

mechanism for promoting equality, they also contain within them some positive aspects in that, faced with a range of internal and external challenges, unions in many countries in Europe have been forced to reconsider their role and strategies.

One among many facets of this concerns their actual and potential female membership and the extent to which union interest representation 'can genuinely include constituencies formerly marginalised as a result of such factors as gender, ethnicity and employment status'.[6] This raises questions to do not only with women's representation among the membership of trade unions, and mechanisms of interest representation and how they connect with collective bargaining mechanisms, but also questions concerning women's representation in leadership and decision-making positions, including among negotiators. Research within some national contexts indicates a positive link between women's presence in leadership positions and in collective bargaining arenas and the development and prioritising of equality agendas.[7]

In discussing the potential for collective bargaining as a mechanism for promoting gender equality it is necessary to observe that, even where collective bargaining is securely established and extensive, there will be areas outside the scope of joint regulation and within employer prerogative which are crucial for equal opportunities. Employers' opportunities to tackle discrimination and promote gender equality in the workplace are, therefore, potentially greater than those open to trade unions, since employers can act not only through collective bargaining but also by unilateral action in their employment strategies and human resource policies.[8]

In practice, the line between unilateral employer action on the one hand and collective bargaining and agreement on the other may not be easy to draw. The nature or form of some unilateral action taken by an employer may be affected by previous bargaining with the union, or be influenced by consultation short of negotiation with worker representatives, or by anticipation of union reaction, etc. Further, collective bargaining may seek to develop upon unilateral employer policies, or employer action may seek to implement something upon which it has proved difficult to secure agreement. The concept 'collective bargaining' is located on a continuum ranging from unilateral employer action, through informal arrangements, information, consultation, negotiation and collective agreement to unilateral union action.

Collective agreements on equality

How does the EU law on sex equality manifest itself in collective agreements? These may take a variety of forms. One type of equal opportunities agreement seems easy to identify. Its contents declare it to be a good practice

6   R Hyman, op cit.

7   E Heery and J Kelly 'Do female representatives make a difference?' (1988) *Work, Employment and Society* (December) 487; T Colling and L Dickens *Equality bargaining: why not?* (1989); P Kumar 'Collective bargaining and workplace concerns', in L Briskin and P McDermott *Women – Challenging Unions* (1993).

8   Scope for *unilateral* union action to determine terms and conditions within the workplace may exist but to a lesser extent. An example might be where the union controls entry to a particular trade or job. Unions have greater scope for unilateral action in respect of their own internal structures.

agreement, or an innovative agreement. It is the result of a successful process of collective bargaining on equal opportunities. Illustrations include self-declared 'equal opportunities agreements', which may be procedural (for example setting up structures; monitoring arrangements) and/or substantive;[9] positive action for women agreements (eg as in Germany in respect of access to particular forms of vocational training; or specific jobs); single issue agreements on areas with a stated or assumed relevance to gender equality (eg sexual harassment procedures); or provisions within more general collective agreements which are intended to contribute to equal opportunities. These cover a range of topics, eg sexual harassment, family leave, equal pay, atypical working, access to training, etc.

Collective bargaining is often active in the equal opportunities area by way of specific reference to legal rules on equal opportunities. Examples include agreements picking up on legal requirements, such as the case law on the need for transparency in pay systems (*Danfoss*[10]) particular approaches to pay determination/job evaluation (*Nimz*,[11] *Rummler*[12]); treatment of part-time workers (*Nimz, Rinner-Kühn*,[13] *Kowalska*,[14] etc; filling gaps where there is no legal regulation (eg as in the case of paternity leave in the UK); or going beyond legal provision (ie using legal provision as a floor on which to build through collective bargaining).

There is a more complex category of collective agreements which *appear* to be equal opportunities agreements, in that they ostensibly favour women workers, but, in light of the critique of the equality concept presented earlier, are arguably negative in their consequences for women. The case law of the European Court has encountered and challenged such agreements.[15] Illustrations include collective agreements and provisions within agreements which appear not to be of any direct relevance to equal opportunities. These provisions (for example on pay and pay opportunities, working time, access to benefits, job security) appear neutral, but may in effect (intentionally or not) serve to underpin or perpetuate gender inequalities in the workplace. Here the discriminatory dimension is *invisible* in the agreement and only made visible when the agreement or provision is seen in the context of sex segregation in the workplace where it has effect.[16] It is also necessary to consider the relationship between separate collective agreements, especially where bargaining units are sex segregated (as in *Enderby*[17]). Of course, there are agreements which even on their face are discriminatory; again, national case law provides examples.

Perhaps the most interesting category of collective bargaining bearing on

9 For examples, see Appendices to L Dickens *Collective Bargaining and the Promotion of Equality: The Case of the United Kingdom*, ILO, Geneva 1993.
10 Case 109/88: *Handels-og Kontorfunktionaerernes Forbund i Danmark v Dansk Arbejdsgiverforening* [1989] ECR 3199.
11 Case C-184/89: *Nimz v Hamburg* [1991] ECR I-297.
12 Case 237/85: *Rummler v Dato-Druck GmbH* [1986] ECR 2101.
13 Case 171/88: *Rinner-Kühn v FWW GmbH* [1989] ECR 2743.
14 Case C-33/89: *Kowalska v Hamburg* [1990] ECR I-2591.
15 For example, Case 312/86: *EC Commission v French Republic* [1988] ECR 6315, which concerned collective agreements providing leave for mothers in connection with childcare. Or agreements prohibiting women from working certain hours.
16 A range of examples of this can be found in L Dickens et al *Tackling Sex Discrimination Through Collective Bargaining* (1988).
17 Case C-127/92: *Enderby v Frenchay Health Authority* [1993] ECR I-5535.

equal opportunities comprises those agreements which do not appear to be equal opportunities agreements at all. There is nothing about them which appears to be specifically relevant to women. Yet their effects, or the way they are applied, are discriminatory.

It is the 'equality dimension' of collective agreements in general – for example, indirect discrimination in payment systems, seniority systems, dismissals procedures – which is the real problem. The most difficult issue is to discern the discriminatory effect of apparently neutral agreements, such as wage scales and pay structures. Such agreements are *not* obviously equal opportunities agreements. Yet they present the law on equality with perhaps its greatest challenge. The problem for the law is to identify those agreements and expose their discriminatory effects. In a sense, the task of the law is to make the invisible visible. The invisible is not easy to locate. The problem lies in the process of application of the agreement, which renders the agreement discriminatory. The objective is to make the application process visible.

Some agreements themselves seek to avoid discrimination in the application of their apparently neutral provisions. Innovative agreements attempt to explicitly address the invisibility of the process which leads to discrimination. Illustrations of 'invisible' agreements, those making visible hidden discrimination, include:

(a) agreements which explicitly attempt to address discrimination identified in previous processes, which attempt to inject an equality dimension into general provisions on pay, terms and conditions etc;
(b) agreements seeking to remove present discrimination by eg identifying and eliminating provisions which resulted in inequitable terms as between men and women;
(c) agreements redressing past discrimination (eg providing for positive action);
(d) agreements which have been 'equality-proofed', guarding against discriminatory outcomes by assessing outcomes from a gender perspective; injecting an 'equality dimension';
(e) agreements providing for implementation (monitoring/enforcement provisions).

Such agreements address *formerly* hidden discrimination, and attempt to bring the issue into the open. This is done by making it the subject of explicit provision in the agreement – explaining how earlier processes discriminated, and hence how the agreement (often in the form of a procedure) aims to remedy this. They have the advantage of having a strong and sophisticated reinforcement in the EU law on sex discrimination, manifested in various ways:

(i) the requirement of *transparency* articulated in the *Danfoss* case is precisely aimed at making the invisible visible.[18] Employers using apparently neutral criteria for pay systems are required to explicitly articulate the process of application of these criteria;
(ii) the concept of equal pay for work of equal value creates a pressure in favour of *job evaluation* procedures, which can reveal the discrimination inherent in traditional payment systems. Job evaluation systems themselves can be scrutinised;[19]

---

18   Case 109/88: [1989] ECR 3199.

19   As in the *Rummler* case, which held that if ostensibly neutral factors in job evaluation discriminate against women, they must be compensated for by other factors which favour women. Case 237/85: [1986] ECR 2101.

(iii)   the concept of *indirect discrimination* is based precisely on the discriminatory application or effects of ostensibly neutral criteria. It incorporates the requirement that employers articulate *justifications* for such discriminatory effects and prescribes strict conditions over what justifications are acceptable in EC law.

In conclusion, collective agreements best reflecting the EU law on equality are those which are most explicit, elaborate, detailed and persuasive about how to overcome the invisible discrimination which occurs in the application of the agreement.[20]

NATIONAL CONTEXTS OF COLLECTIVE BARGAINING ON EQUALITY

It must always be borne in mind, however, that collective agreements within each Member State have to be considered in their particular national context, without prejudging the nature of any provisions. The ways in which pay discrimination is tackled and pay equity is sought can be expected to differ and, similarly, the nature of provisions dealing with employment conditions other than pay. In this section, a number of different national contexts are briefly explored to demonstrate the complexities confronting equality law in the EU in the national context of collective bargaining.

France

In France, collective bargaining takes place at both industry-wide and enterprise levels. There is a legal duty to bargain, though there is no obligation to reach an agreement. Bargaining at industry level is obligatory and must cover minimum wages (annual negotiations) and job classifications (every 5 years). Bargaining at enterprise level is obligatory on, among other subjects, wage bargaining by categories of employees and working time. It is possible to extend the legal effect of a collective agreement by an administrative procedure to all employers and employees in a sector ('erga omnes').

A law of 13 July 1983 made it obligatory for those collective agreements capable of extension to include new provisions concerning equal treatment in employment and for pregnant and nursing mothers. These were to be added to those clauses already required regarding the application of the principle of equal pay for equal work.

The *Commission Nationale de la Négociation Collective* has the duty to secure the elimination of all elements in collective agreements that are discriminatory and to check that all new national agreements take into account, and include provisions on the issues of promotion, hiring and compensatory measures for

---

20   Illustrations can be found in specific areas; for example, pay. Pay agreements may incorporate mechanisms to achieve equal opportunities. Examples would be agreements reviewing pay structures, remarking on discriminatory effects, and proposing measures to combat them: eg abolishing the bottom grades of a structure, comprising mainly women; reducing percentage wage increases in favour of flat rate increases favouring low-paid women; higher increases for the lowest paid categories (often women).

indirect discrimination. Beginning in 1984 there has been published an annual report.[1]

Soon after the law of 1983, the report published in 1985 described the state of collective agreements on the principles of equal pay and equal treatment between women and men, as well as women and work generally. The conclusion was that the texts of agreements in force at the end of 1983 were virtually silent as regards equal pay and, above all, as regards equal treatment. There were relatively frequently clauses concerned with consequences of pregnancy and maternity on the working lives of women, but even these clauses needed to be updated and generalised. A review of developments over the four years following the law demonstrates the contextual impact of the law.

During 1984, compared to the previous year, the situation had developed very little. Of 927 agreements in force in 1984, less than 4% (32) involved one or more of the three topics (equal pay, equal treatment, maternity); 16 agreements included a clause concerning equal treatment between men and women; the principle of 'equal pay for equal work', even though enacted by the legislature in 1973, appeared in only 12 agreements.

The content of these clauses on equal treatment or equal pay was always very brief: a simple statement of the principle prohibiting all discrimination on grounds of sex and specifying some areas of application of the principle: hiring, promotion, dismissal, training, etc. There was also a tendency to abolish discriminatory clauses which reserved certain more favourable rights to women: leave to care for a sick child, leave to raise children after maternity or adoption.

The report made two general observations. First, the law of 13 July 1983 on equality in employment had not given rise to a significant development of collective bargaining at industry level on this issue. Secondly, the contents of the negotiations that did take place were modest. On the other hand, two positive points can be highlighted. Clauses on equal treatment were introduced in most of the new or replaced agreements, and discriminatory provisions were being eliminated.

The *bilan* published in June 1986, covering developments the following year, 1985, was similarly not very optimistic. Of 33 agreements analysed, 11 agreements included a clause concerned with equal treatment; equal pay appeared in 19 agreements, and the tendency continued to eliminate discriminatory clauses which reserve certain rights to women only. The percentage of texts providing for working conditions related to pregnancy and for maternity leave was almost identical to 1984: 14 provided for reductions of hours for pregnant women; 9 provided for ante-natal visits; 11 provided for a temporary change of job; 20 provided additional remuneration during maternity leave.

The *bilan* published in June 1987, covering developments in 1986 reviewed 16 agreements: 7 of the 16 contained a clause concerned with equal treatment in employment; the equal pay principle was introduced in only one agreement; 8 agreements dealt with facilities to care for a sick child, of which 2 agreements reserved it to mothers and 3 agreements extended it to fathers. As regards leave to raise children, of the 16 agreements, 3 eliminated the exclusive rights of the mother as beneficiary, one newly provided for such exclusivity; 3 maintained this exclusivity. Three agreements contained clauses favouring women: one barred women from working on Sundays; one provided for rest periods for

---

1   *Bilan Annuelle sur l'Egalité Professionnelle entre les Femmes et les Hommes.*

femmes mécanographes; and one provided different holiday entitlements for men and women.

In the *bilan* published in June 1988 and covering 1987, of the 18 agreements analysed, 8 contained a clause concerned with equal treatment in employment; the equal pay principle figured in 11; and, as regards pregnancy and maternity, the position is described in relation to 1986 in the following chart:

CLAUSES	NUMBER OF AGREEMENTS		%	
	1986	*1987*	*1986*	*1987*
Reduction of working hours	5	12	32	66
Ante-natal visits	2	10	12	55
Temporary change of job	3	8	19	44
Pay during pregnancy	11	8	68	44

This review of sectoral level agreements does not touch upon enterprise agreements. But it is the sectoral level which has tended to be more important in collective bargaining in France. Albeit their coverage of a sector is extensive, the issue of equality does not appear to have made great inroads immediately following the enactment of legislation intended to achieve that effect.

Italy

Collective bargaining in Italy also takes place at different levels. Collective bargaining at plant level is informal, often limited to specific issues, and there is relatively little organised documentation. However, national or regional sectoral bargaining and agreements appear to be particularly rich in provisions on equality, and are relatively well documented.

One publication prepared by the trade unions was dedicated to provisions in collective agreements on equal opportunity.[2] It included provisions of agreements renegotiated in 1986–87 in ten industries: food, agriculture, chemicals, commerce, media, metalworking, civil service, research, textiles and road transport; also agreements still in the stage of renegotiation in the air and rail transport and construction industries, as well as contracts renegotiated in 1984–86: banking and telecommunications. Significantly, the volume concludes with the text of the Council Recommendation on positive action.[3]

Another volume presented the negotiating demands adopted by the three trade union confederations (CGIL, CISL and UIL) and the national collective agreements concluded in six industries (metalworking, chemicals, textiles, food, printing and agriculture).[4] The contents of these demands and agreements were classified under various headings, and included headings which had significant impact on women.

For example, a section on occupational training included an extract from the national collective agreement in agriculture which explicitly covered training

2   G Gilardi *Le pari opportunità nei contratti*, Ediesse, Roma 1987.
3   Ibid, pp 143–5. Recommendation no 84/635 of 12 December 1984, OJ 331/84.
4   F Sabbatucci (ed) *Contratti a confronto*, Ediesse, Roma 1988.

for women.[5] Another section contained extracts from collective agreements under the heading 'positive action for equal opportunity', which contained extracts from the national agreements in private and public sector metalworking, public sector chemicals, textiles and agriculture. Each of these agreements included, inter alia, an explicit reference to the Council's 1984 Recommendation on Positive Action.[6]

The complexity of collective bargaining on issues of equality in Italy can be illustrated by the case of equal pay. In the perspective of Italian trade unions, the labour law on equal pay is influenced by the changing pattern of collective bargaining. The inter-confederal (all sector) agreement of 1960 reduced the existing wage differential between men and women workers for the same jobs, but maintained an explicit wage gap of about 10%. This was subsequently annulled by the courts on the basis of the principle of equal pay for equal work in Article 37 of the Constitution. The result was a progressive upward adjustment of women's pay in industry-wide agreements.

Direct discrimination does not appear in agreements, but indirect discrimination persists: women remain concentrated at the lowest wage levels; classification systems operate so that female-dominated jobs are undervalued. The egalitarian wage policies of Italian unions have aimed less at realising equal pay, than at eliminating low pay, and thus aim to reduce the impact of this indirect discrimination.

On the other hand, although the concept of 'pay' has been generally construed to include all types of benefits, some agreements have excluded certain items (eg special bonuses linked to individuals' or groups' seniority or responsibility or qualifications). The indirectly discriminatory effects of this are still not widely appreciated. The growth of productivity linked bargaining in certain sectors threatens a policy of equal pay for work of equal value. As it allows for variations in pay among individuals according to productivity, it becomes more difficult to compare men and women when the productivity bonus is linked to groups or individuals. As with other premium payments, the application of the bonus system can become discriminatory, as in the food processing industry productivity agreement of 1987.

Following judicial interpretations, different sectoral agreements, negotiated by different unions and resulting in different wage structures, cannot be compared. This allows for a classification of jobs having similar characteristics, even within a sector (let alone in different sectors) even when signed by the same unions and employers' associations, which allocates lower grades to jobs in women dominated subsectors. An example is in textiles: male dyeing v female hosiery.

Job evaluation is largely unknown. Attempts during the 1960s failed because the mobility entailed in their application (reclassification of jobs as re-evaluated, including downwards where male jobs are re-evaluated) encountered legally guaranteed protections against such downward mobility. There have been calls for rethinking of job evaluation factors, but implementation is not considered likely through judicial processes. Rather, progress will be likely to come through collective bargaining, stimulated by legal pressures. Though not systematically

---

5   Ibid, pp 228–9.
6   Ibid, pp 231–6.

addressed by Italian unions, some developments may be found.[7]

For example, the passage of groups of women from one wage level to another in the textile industry, recognising the irrelevance of presumed heavier work and maintenance duties, done through a combination of rotation of tasks, short training courses, promotions and reorganising job descriptions. The case of Perfetti in the food sector confirmed the inadequacy of general clauses affirming the value of women's work without specific implementing mechanisms, and the positive results of union activity analysing and condemning discriminatory situations. Some 244 of the 249 women were employed at level 5, with only 12 men at that level despite the 1981 declaration of willingness to value women's work. There continued the assignment of all higher jobs to men and continued use of male-oriented classification factors (physical effort, ignoring the responsibility attached to women's work). The preparation by workplace union organisations, in conjunction with those based on the region, analysing and condemning this discrimination, together with the declared intention to take legal action, led the company to withdraw its previous refusal to negotiate and to indicate willingness to undertake training to improve the position of women. Finally, in December 1985, there was a plant agreement providing for the passage from level 5 to level 4 of 75 women.

There were some significant changes after Law No 903 of 1977, which gave collective bargaining specific competence in 'flexibilising' the rules governing female labour as regards prohibitions on heavy work, the possibility of night working, and the relationship between maternity absence and career progression. Use of these provisions was, however, relatively rare, for reasons of the limitations imposed and the delicacy involved in removing restrictions which, in the absence of controls on positive action, might have negative results. In the metal-working sector, retraining courses aimed at enabling women to move to higher classifications (Italtel, 1978); initiatives, supervised jointly by the management and plant union representatives, to retrain female employees (E Marelli, 1980); feasibility studies to examine the possibility of reorganising production lines to enhance the qualifications of female workers (Ellettrocondutture, 1980); enriching the tasks fulfilled by women to improve their qualifications (Ellettrocondutture, GTE Phillips, Face Standard, 1977; IBM, 1978). The Borletti agreement of 6 December 1977, which anticipated the 1977 law, proposed to guarantee equal pay, both by eliminating the different piece-rates of men and women, and by recognising the qualifications of female employees. It not only sought to do this by abolishing the barriers which blocked women's access to higher levels or certain jobs, but also aimed at changing the labour process to assist the gaining of qualifications and through specific training courses.

The implications of introducing new technology for women's work and remuneration have led to negotiated agreements on positive action for women, mainly in large enterprises – La Rinascente, ENI, Italtel – to ensure maintenance

---

7   F Borgogelli and T Treu 'Parità e pari opportunità nella contrattazione collettiva', in *Donne e Lavoro: Analisi e Proposte* Ministero del Lavoro e della Previdenza Sociale, Comitato Nazionale per la Parità, 2nd ed, Roma 1986, pp 159–74. F Borgogelli *Il Lavoro Femminile tra Legge e Contrattazione: Una Ricerca sulla Contrattazione Collettiva in Tema di Lavoro Femminile,* Franco Angeli, Milano 1987. For a recent review, M Bergamaschi 'Valutazione del lavoro femminile e contrattazione', in *Pari e dispari,* Annuario 5, Franco Angeli, Milano 1995, pp 105–19.

of career training for women, which has led slowly to the presence of women in the middle levels of management. These efforts may be limited to declarations of principle (eg Basile, 1985 in the textile sector), but may also be effectively implemented, eg the agreement in Tubettificio Ligure, 1980. This agreement on the reorganisation of work and technological change included provisions for plant level meetings and efforts to identify the measures needed, inter alia, to train groups of female employees to ensure they are compatible with the new production process, and to introduce initiatives aimed at a flexible use of female workers in the new processes.

There are not many such agreements, but they show what was possible to achieve through collective bargaining building on an otherwise less than effective legal basis.

Germany

There are two different kinds of agreements between collectives of workers and employers. The first are collective agreements between unions and employers or an organisation of employers; the second are agreements between works councils and an employer: works council agreements, which are not regarded as 'collective agreements' in German law. Collective agreements proper are usually based on regional bargaining: an organisation of employers on one side and a union, normally affiliated to the central union confederation (DGB), on the other. Sometimes the collective agreement, regional or national, is only a framework agreement, filled in by enterprise level bargaining.

Many important cases decided by courts in the area of equal pay have involved collective agreements.[8] In the 1950s, most cases resulted from collective agreements on pay, according to which women doing the same work as men received only 70–80% of the male wage. The Federal Labour Court declared such provisions void. In spite of the number of judgments against these *Frauenabschlagsklauseln*, they continued to exist until 1972, when they were replaced by the so-called *leichtlohngruppen* (light wage group) – a group of usually female workers paid less than male workers in comparable jobs because their work was physically lighter. One of the last cases dealing with a directly discriminatory provision in a collective agreement was decided by the Federal Labour Court as recently as 1985.[9] The Berlin Metalworkers' wage agreement provided that only married men could receive a monthly married person's wage supplement (10DM). The Federal Labour Court declared this provision void.

A number of agreements can illustrate the advantages and disadvantages of collective agreements for women. An agreement in the paper producing industry includes wage groups I and II, which cover 'easy or light work'; only from group III on does the agreement speak of 'employees of full worth'. In practice, male jobs start with group III. In chemicals, the agreement unified conditions for blue and white collar workers and formed 13 new wage groups. But the

---

8   Discriminatory provisions in the normative part of a collective agreement can be attacked relying on Article 3 II of the Basic Law. Norms of the agreement have the same legal effect as other legal norms. When an employer applies a discriminatory provision contained in a collective agreement, the worker can bring a claim based on section 611a ff BGB against the employer.

9   13 November 1985. DB 86,542.

division between technical and commercial white collar workers continued to favour technical workers despite unified wording. In practice, the male–female gap increases because of higher evaluation of 'typically male jobs'. Six years seniority is necessary to reach the top wage. Additional pay is only for 'nasty' work – typically male work.

In the agreement in MTV clothing there is to be found discriminatory treatment of part-time workers, seniority rules, exemption of mothers from excess hours, leave for the care of sick children, but also counting of former periods of employment for mothers interrupting work to care for children. In metal-working, the agreement does not discriminate on its face: it applies to part-time workers, and there are no light-wage groups. Section 5 requires gender-neutral job evaluation and uses analytical job evaluation with the following criteria (in diminishing importance): knowledge, dexterity, additional thought process, responsibility for work, strain on senses and nerves, strain on muscles, and environmental influences.

Denmark

There are special features of the Danish welfare state and industrial relations system which characterise the relationship between collective bargaining and sex equality.

Within the largest umbrella organisation, the Confederation of Danish Trade Unions (LO), there are some 31 unions, of which some 3–5 unions cover the majority of the female work force. Whereas in Germany, organisation is by industry, in Denmark it is by qualification, in principle, and, to some degree, by sex. Unskilled workers organise by sex: men are members of one union, women of another. On the employers' side, more than half of working women are employed in the public sector.

The social security system includes legislation protecting women during pregnancy and after childbirth, including provisions for parental leave. Collective agreements provide additional benefits. These benefits are not necessarily better in the agreements negotiated by the unskilled women's union. The best maternity provisions are found in the male-dominated sectors. These have very progressive provisions on parental leave and childcare. Childcare provisions are usually sex-neutral in their formulation, and are available to men also. Otherwise they would be unlawful as discriminatory. Collective agreements may also provide benefits not allowed under legislation: there were no statutory provisions for leave to care for sick children, but clauses providing for this were found in collective agreements.

On equal pay, prior to 1973 there were different rates for men and women in collective agreements. Since 1973, specific provisions have abolished the differences. Agreements do not explicitly provide for equal pay – it is implicit. Hence, there are no equal pay clauses. Unions are opposed to job evaluation and it is practically never used. Instead, unions in Denmark favour low wage policy – to raise the level of the low paid. Flat rate increases or the abolition of the lowest rates in an agreement or wage structure would usually be called a low pay policy, even though it benefited women disproportionately.

This does not mean that unequal pay does not exist in collective agreements in Denmark. The issue manifests itself in two forms. First, different collective agreements; differentials in an enterprise's wage structure are not determined by job evaluation between grades in one collective agreement. Different jobs come under different agreements. Unions negotiate wage rates for their members based on their qualifications. Each union has its own collective agreement. The differentials arise from different collective agreements.

Secondly, it is possible to have differentiation among workers covered by one collective agreement, though the differential is not fixed in the agreement. This results from what is called the 'minimum wage system'. The agreement only lays down a minimum – usually exceeded in practice. Every employee has an individual wage, which in principle is negotiated on an individual basis. Collective agreements are not usually negotiated at workplace level in Denmark, but by the national or regional union. On the basis of these agreements, the individual employee negotiates individual supplements.

The unions and employers saw it as important to deal with equal pay without State intervention. They opposed the Equal Pay Directive's provisions on enforcement. The unions retain control by taking what they see as breaches of the Directive to arbitration. The machinery to ensure compliance with the EU Directive is that if a women or a union feels there has been discrimination, they can take the case, not to the civil courts, but to arbitration, claiming that it is a violation of the Danish implementing legislation. Only very few individuals outside the collective industrial relations system go to the civil courts.

The proliferation of collective agreements within one establishment, each negotiated by a different union representing an occupational grouping, means that it can happen that exactly the same job is done by women paid under one agreement and men paid under another agreement. An unskilled woman member of the women's union may be under one collective agreement: an unskilled male worker doing the same or approximately the same work under another. Since equal value is accepted as binding in Denmark, if the same job or jobs of equal value are covered by two separate agreements, and the male workers' union has been able to negotiate better rates than the women workers' union, the women workers' union has, on occasion, gone to arbitration claiming that their own agreement is not valid because it violates the Equal Pay Act and the employer must now give what it could not achieve at the negotiating table.

The first such case was won in 1977[10] and another succeeded in 1987.[11] After these cases, the existing practice was changed and there were many voluntary settlements out of court by individual companies. After the 1987 case the biggest employers' organisation circulated its members with a letter telling them to correct such arrangements. If not, the letter informed the members that they would receive no support in the event of a court case.

The employers had to raise the wage level for women workers. The difference usually consisted of some kind of basic rate, typically the same for men and women, but with some increments in the male collective agreement. These now had to be added to the female collective agreement. There was some activity regarding merit increments, described in the male agreement, but not found in the female agreement (eg lifting). After the case, if there were provisions in the male agreement which were not in the female agreement, employers had to include the same kind of provision (the 'lifting' clause, for example).

10   Arbitral award of 8 December 1977, the *FDB* case.
11   Arbitral award of 19 April 1987, the *Premier-IS* case.

United Kingdom

Collective agreements in the UK are negotiated at national, enterprise and workplace levels, by full-time national and regional officials of trade unions with senior management, and by local shop stewards representing the employees in a workplace with local management. Although the decline of multi-employer, industry-wide agreements had already begun in the 1950s, a survey by the Confederation of British Industry found that during the period 1979–86 there was a 'marked diminution' in the influence of such agreements, matched by a pronounced growth in single-employer bargaining at company or establishment level. By 1986, 87% of employees in plants with collective bargaining had their basic rates of pay negotiated at establishment or company level.

This had implications for collective bargaining and equal pay. A decision of the European Court had condemned the UK for:[12]

> 'failing to introduce into its national legal system in implementation of the provisions of Council Directive 75/117/EEC of 10 February 1975 such measures as are necessary to enable all employees who consider themselves wronged by failure to apply the principle of equal pay for men and women for work to which equal value is attributed and for which no system of job classification exists to obtain recognition of such equivalence . . .'

British law was changed so as to allow for claims that women's work was of equal value to that of men only with effect from 1 January 1984, when the Equal Pay (Amendment) Regulations 1983 came into force. The law became a potential basis for negotiations between unions and management with the objective of equal pay agreements.

In the first three years, there were over 2,000 formal claims made to industrial tribunals. Over the first 10 years, almost 8,000 equal value applications were made to industrial tribunals. This impressive quantitative impact is belied by putting it in context. Only just over 560 employers are or have been involved in equal value proceedings over this 10-year period, with just over a quarter in the health sector alone. The large total of claims included large numbers of multiple claims from women working for the same employer. In 1986, of 1,481 applications, 1,115 were against British Coal; in 1987, of 1,738 applications, 1,395 were from speech therapists.[13] This large number of multiple claims against single employers demonstrates the vital role of trade unions and collective bargaining as a factor in equal value claims, whether as a support or a target for litigation.

In a context of extreme decentralisation of pay bargaining, coordination among unions in pursuing equal pay strategies was both important and extremely difficult. A review of the equal pay strategies pursued by 16 unions revealed a wide variation.[14] A few unions provided for centralised direction of equal pay claims; others preferred to allow local officials to take the initiative, with varying attempts at coordinating these local efforts. Some unions did not attempt any centralised coordination, or have any specific strategy on equal pay.

12 Case 61/81: *EC Commission v United Kingdom of Great Britain and Northern Ireland* [1982] ECR 2601, paragraph 14.
13 'Equal value update', *Equal Opportunities Review*, No 58, November/December 1994, p 11.
14 *Equal Opportunities Review*, No 11, January/February 1987, pp 10–18.

Negotiations on equal pay were related to the law on equal value in different ways. The legal claim might be launched as a prelude to negotiations; or negotiations and litigation might be linked in a deliberate strategy; or might be perceived as separate but parallel strategies, as when test case litigation strategies were used. In some cases litigation was discouraged by unions, with the emphasis placed solely on negotiating equal pay agreements. However, as one observer commented: [15]

> 'Reliable and detailed information concerning out-of-court equal value settlements is difficult to obtain. Having elected to resolve a particular claim internally, both management and trade union are likely to adopt and maintain a low profile approach, at the very minimum, until an agreement is reached. Thereafter, information might be more forthcoming, but this will often be superficial and might be misinterpreted by those unfamiliar with the structure, practices and procedures of the specific organisation.'

One major undertaking, however, received a great deal of deserved attention: a job evaluation exercise for local authority manual workers agreed in 1986.[16] The agreement affected about one million workers, three-quarters of whom were women. Basic wage rates were negotiated nationally in the National Joint Council comprising the organisation of local authority employers and the three major trade unions.

The previous grading structure was the result of a job evaluation exercise carried out at the end of the 1960s. The result was that the majority of the women, working part-time, were in the lower grade jobs with lower basic rates, whereas workers in the higher grades with higher basic rates were mainly men, who also had greater opportunities to increase their basic rate through overtime payments and various bonuses.

By 1985 the scheme was criticised as discriminatory and the new Equal Value Regulations allowed for individual complaints, the results of which were unpredictable, and could undermine the collective bargaining machinery. Rather than support individual claims by dissatisfied members, therefore, the unions undertook to achieve equal pay for work of equal value through the negotiating machinery. The job evaluation scheme was agreed at the beginning of 1986.

A team was engaged and drew up 540 job descriptions based on a breakdown into six factors: skill, responsibility, initiative, mental and physical effort, and working conditions. Care was taken to ensure that these factors were not skewed so as to reflect considerations which favoured one sex. For example, the factor of skill took account not only of traditional formal training and qualifications but also informal training, acquired experience, caring as well as communicative skills and literacy and numeracy. The factor of responsibility took account of women's jobs having more responsibility for people and men's having more responsibility for resources. So this factor was divided into three sub-factors: responsibility for people, for resources and for supervision. Physical

15   D Collinson, describing an equal value agreement in the UK financial sector (Eagle Star Insurance Group and the Banking, Insurance and Finance Union); *Equal Opportunities Review*, No 11, January/February 1987, p 18.
16   A detailed account, from which the following is derived, is in *Equal Opportunities Review* No 13, May/June 1987, pp 21–4.

effort was not limited to heavy lifting, which unduly favours men's jobs, but also included bending and kneeling and continuity of effort, which ensured that jobs frequently undertaken by women were not undervalued. Similarly, working conditions were defined so that they included not only traditionally considered unfavourable working conditions, such as noise and dirt, but also noise and people, and that working conditions inside could be as unpleasant as working outside.

The analytical breakdown of different jobs having been completed, the task of evaluating the jobs involved allocating values to them. This was undertaken by panels representing equally employers and unions, and with equal numbers of men and women. The panels evaluated 40 major occupations, covering approximately 90% of the labour force. Each was analysed in terms of the factor headings, with each factor having 4 or 5 possible levels. For example, a job might be allocated to level 3 for skill and level 2 for responsibility and level 4 for working conditions, and so on.

A coordinating panel, comprising seven employer and six union representatives, and including five women, then applied weights to the different factor levels, so as to reach a potential overall total of 1000 points. Not all factors were deemed to be worth an equal number of points, nor, within each factor, an equal number of points at different levels. Each manual worker's job had to be allocated factor weights and points with a view to satisfying the requirements of equal value considerations. This meant that traditional emphasis on physical effort and formal training had to be balanced out.

The coordinating panel decided that the major factors in local government manual jobs were skill and responsibility, and awarded each a factor weighting of 36%. Responsibility was subdivided into responsibility for people, resources and supervision, with 12% each. Initiative, considered to overlap with responsibility, was allocated 6%, as was working conditions. To balance out, mental and physical effort were each allocated 8%. The outcome of the exercise could be represented in the following table: [17]

WEIGHTING BY LEVEL AND FACTOR						
Factor	*Evaluation level*					*Factor weighting*
	1	2	3	4	5	
Skill	26	72	108	306	360	36%
Responsibility:						
for people	12	30	90	120		
for resources	12	30	90	120		36%
for supervision	6	12	54	108		
Initiative	6	18	36	60		6%
Mental effort	8	24	48	80		8%
Physical effort	8	24	48	80		8%
Working conditions	6	18	36	60		6%

17   Ibid, Table 2 on p 23.

Each job was allocated its quota of points according to the factors it was deemed to comprise and their weighting. This produced a rank order of jobs for local authority manual workers as in the following table:[18]

THE JOB EVALUATION RESULTS	
Rank/occupation	*Score*
1. School caretaker 2	690
2. Home help	630
3. School caretaker 1	612
4. Cook 4	606
5. Social services driver/attendant	600
6. Refuse driver	588
7. Roadworker 3	582
8. Gardener 4	570
9. Care assistant	558
10. Waste disposal operative	546
11. Driver 2	540
12. Roadworker 2	486
13. Gardener 3	468
14. Cook 3	462
15. Sewer operative	438
16. Housing caretaker	432
17. School cleaner in charge	426
18. Leisure attendant 2	414
19. Assistant school caretaker	396
20. Driver 1	384
21. Security attendant/porter	378
22. Roadworker 1	374
23. Grave digger	374
24. Gardener 2	336
25. Leisure attendant 1	330
26. Cook 2	330
27. Domestic assistant 2	294
28. School crossing patrol	284
29. Refuse collector	272
30. Supervisory assistant	272
31. Cook 1	210
32. Dining room assistant	210
33. General cleaner	200
34. Road sweeper	198
35. Gardener 1	176
36. School cleaner	176
37. Domestic assistant 1	158

18   Ibid, Table 1 on p 22.

Of the outcome it was stated that some 'caring' jobs, such as home helps, predominantly female, had been evaluated more highly than was the case in the previous job evaluation, whereas other jobs, such as refuse collectors, predominantly male, had moved down. But there remained difficult negotiating tasks involving the drawing up of pay grade boundaries and consequent allocation of jobs to different grades, and, not least, the negotiating of pay rates for each new grade. A major problem regarded the bonus earning schemes so important to the predominantly male jobs.

Apart from such major coordinated collective endeavours, individual unions undertook initiatives. The then second largest trade union in Britain, the General, Municipal and Boilermakers' Union, as of 1987 developed a new head of claim: 'eliminating sex bias'. This was presented to all employers on the occasion of the review of a collective agreement. The new head of claim encompassed 13 items and stated that its aim was to achieve, among other things: overtime payments for part-time workers, unsocial hours payments for twilight shift workers, equal access to bonus schemes, an end to job segregation which places women in low paid, low status jobs, and paid leave for family circumstances. Progress on the elimination of sex bias was monitored by the union's National Industry Conferences and its National Equal Rights Advisory Committee. Agreements were to be collected and made accessible through a computerised database.

On the negative side, the UK had been condemned again by the European Court for:[19]

'failing to adopt in accordance with Directive 76/207 of 9 February 1976 (Article 4(b)) the measures needed to ensure that any provisions contrary to the principle of equality of treatment contained in collective agreements ... are to be, or may be declared void or be amended ...'

The Sex Discrimination Act 1986, section 6, rendered void discriminatory provisions in collective agreements. Under section 3 of the Equal Pay Act 1970, a collective agreement containing a term which applied specifically to men only or to women only could be referred to the Central Arbitration Committee for amendment or to remove the discrimination. This provision appeared to hold great potential following the award of the Committee in *ASTMS and the Norwich Union Insurance Group.*[20] In this decision, the Committee relied on Article 119 to extend its jurisdiction under section 3 to amending indirectly discriminatory (as well as directly discriminatory) provisions in collective agreements.

Unfortunately, this was the Committee's last award before repeal of this jurisdiction by the 1986 Act. In the event, the decision was later overruled by the High Court in *R v Central Arbitration Committee, ex p Norwich Union.*[1] There remains no specific mechanism whereby allegedly discriminatory collective agreements can be challenged.

CONCLUSION

The significance of this exercise in sketching national contexts is to demonstrate how much the European law on equal pay for work of equal value was integrated

19 Case 165/82: *EC Commission v United Kingdom of Great Britain and Northern Ireland* [1983] ECR 3431, paragraph 21.
20 Award 87/2, 30 January 1987.
 1 (8 June 1988, unreported).

into the national context of collective bargaining, and its associated qualities of multiple actors on both employer and trade union sides, complex negotiating procedures and outcomes. The collective bargaining context could not afford to ignore the EU law on equality, but that law had to accommodate the national context, which allowed for a distinctive shaping of the law in its application.

Chapter 15

Equality and (Re)conciliation of Work and Family Life

INTRODUCTION

The *theoretical* critique of equality demonstrates the deficiencies of the EC legislation and case law. The *operational* context of the law – collective bargaining – demonstrates the wider network of regulation to which it must accommodate. The tension between the traditional orientation of equality law in the EC and the future evolution of social policy in the EU has emerged with startling clarity in the aftermath of the negotiation of the Maastricht Treaty. The problem with equality law has been its boundaries. In its *substance* it is cut off from the context of women's and men's lives – a broader concern with the promotion of gender equality in general. In its *operation* it has been cut off from the industrial relations context in which it applies.

Thus, for example, given the economic orientation of the EC, it is the world of paid work, and access to it, and not the domestic sphere which has been central to the EC law on equality. The domestic sphere as such, and large areas of debate concerning women and the family, did not fall centrally within its concern. The two-way link between women's (and men's) domestic and wage labour roles was often discounted, as was the extent to which particular strategies, policies or provisions took for granted women's unpaid work in the home and their domestic and caring roles, and failed to consider those issues which are at the work/family interface.

It is impossible to completely ignore the domestic context of women workers, as is evident in the case law on indirect discrimination. But this context was not directly confronted by EC policy. Rather, it was uneasily accommodated by attempts to balance a policy against sex discrimination with justifications for employer and State policies having discriminatory consequences. This context can no longer be ignored. The work/family interface is central to the Commission's plans for the future social policy of the EU.

The Commission's Green Paper of 17 November 1993 began by raising fundamental questions about the concept and definition of work, including paid and voluntary work:[1]

'. . . work has other functions in addition to providing income: purposeful activity and personal fulfilment, dignity, social contacts, recognition and a basis for organising

---

1 Green Paper, *European Social Policy: Options for the Union* (1993) Section II.C.3, 'The role of work in society', p 19.

daily or weekly time. The massive entry of women into the labour market is partly a reflection of this reality. Their role in the economy and in society will have a decisive influence in the future.'[2]

Attention was focused on the work/leisure dichotomy in light of more complex patterns of use of time over the life cycle. The Green Paper poses the question not solely in terms of paid work:[3]

'. . . modern production systems permit more flexible work/family/leisure/education patterns. On the other hand, the greater flexibility required by enterprises is leading to more insecurity for those who, rather than being in the "core" workforce, are in the "contingent" labour force which is needed to adjust output when demand falls. Thus, both sides of the equation have to be looked at if we are to answer the question whether these varied and more flexible forms of working time and participation in work represent an opportunity to reconcile efficiency with both a higher quality of life and more widely spread working opportunities.'

The background of the fragmentation of the workforce into categories characterised by different working time regimes has been a focus of labour law regulation in Europe during the past decade. Close attention to the patterns and distribution of working time among industries and occupations and between men and women reveals the prevalence of relatively high levels of working hours among male workers, and the predominance of women in the part-time workforce. Women workers were seen as a, if not the critical factor:[4]

'Social and labour market structures continue to operate on the assumption that women are primarily responsible for home and child care while men are responsible for the family's economic and financial well-being . . .

The gender-based division of family and employment responsibilities not only constrains women's lives but also deprives men of the emotional rewards resulting from the care and development of children.

There needs to be a combined labour market and social policy to develop the rights and opportunities of women, one which reflects their role in society and their needs throughout their lives. The strategic objective should be to go from equal rights to equal treatment in the labour market through equality of opportunities in society, thereby making better use of women's experience and skills for the benefit of society as a whole, including increased participation in the decision-making process.'

2   Publication of the Green Paper was accompanied by a 'Reference Document' showing its key ideas, published in *Europe Documents* No 1861, 20 November 1993. A similar quotation is on p 3. The Green Paper put it elsewhere as follows (p 15):

'. . . citizens of advanced, industrialised democracies such as those in the European Community have difficulty in forging a personal and social identity when they are part of the "non-active" population. As new jobs are created in Europe, new groups enter the labour market because there is a latent "social" demand for work, as well as the economic demand arising from the wish to maintain or expand family income. Many women, for example, seek work for reasons of emancipation, dignity, social identity and the ordering of their lives, as well as income. Beyond paid work there is a demand for voluntary activity, as witnessed by the rapid and healthy growth of community organisations and associations, and by the active involvement of older people in them. People want to participate and need to have that activity recognised, whatever it is and whether it is carried out inside or outside the home.'

This section in the Green Paper, entitled 'What sort of a society do Europeans want?' concludes with the question (p 16): 'What is the next stage in equality of opportunity, without which European democracy will falter?'

3   Ibid, Section II.H.8, 'Quality of output, quality of work and quality of life', p 31.
4   Ibid, Section II.F, 'Women's rights and opportunities', p 25. See also Section III.C.2, 'Promoting equal opportunities for women and men in a changing European society', pp 55–8.

The Green Paper also raised the question:[5]

'Should the social partners strengthen their involvement in the following issues:
. . . equal opportunities, reconciliation between work and family . . .'

The subsequent 1994 White Paper, *European Social Policy – A Way Forward for the Union*, was, in some respects, more succinct and reticent in its follow-up.[6] In a section entitled 'Investing in a World Class Labour Force', the Commission merely agreed:[7]

'There are some signs too of a new approach to the organisation of working life, with a higher degree of alternation between work, training and leave.'

However, in the Section entitled 'Equality of Opportunity between Women and Men', it was more expansive. An entire section was dedicated to 'Reconciling Employment and Household/Family Life':[8]

'10. The growing participation of women in the economy has been one of the most striking features of recent decades, suggesting that there is now an urgent need, in the interests of society as a whole, for working life and family life to be more mutually reinforcing. Technological production and societal trends are leading enterprises to be at the forefront of such social changes, in some respects ahead of legislation and public policy. The latter is now confronted with major issues such as the relationship between working time and care time. Changing demographic trends mean that the responsibility for elderly dependants is moving up the social agenda, although childcare is still the major problem for working parents in many Member States. New social infrastructures are needed to support the household and the family, and the question of how families can be helped to carry the costs remains to be addressed.

11. Progress towards new ways of perceiving family responsibilities may slowly relieve the burden on women and allow men to play a more fulfilling role in society. However, greater solidarity between men and women is needed if men are to take on greater responsibility for the caring role in our societies and if flexibility in employment is not to lead to new pressures on women to return to the ranks of the non-salaried population or be obliged to accept paid work at home in isolation from the community. This solidarity will be assisted by the implementation of the 1992 Council Recommendation on Childcare,[9] which calls for the provision of leave arrangements for fathers as well as mothers throughout the Union. Positive policy action is also needed to help the process of change and to promote a more nearly equal sharing of parental responsibilities, another element in the Childcare Recommendation.'

A more concrete commitment was made in Section III, when referring to completing the existing Social Action Programme:[10]

'. . . the Commission will also examine the possibility of a framework directive covering the issues of reconciling professional and family life, including career breaks such as parental leave. Such a proposal would seek gradually to encourage the development of new models better suited to the changing needs of European

5   Ibid, Section III.C.5.c, 'Reinforcing the social dialogue: The changing industrial relations agenda', p 64. See the more categoric Green Paper Reference Document, p 8: 'There could be a number of issues where social partners may if they wish usefully strengthen their involvement . . . equal opportunities, reconciliation between work and family . . .'
6   COM (94) 333.
7   Ibid, Section II.8.
8   Section V.B, paragraphs 10–12.
9   92/241/EEC, OJ L123 of 8.5.92.
10 Op cit, White Paper, paragraph 8.

society, and be specifically designed to facilitate the full integration of women into the labour market. It would set minimum standards within a framework designed to encourage competitive solutions in a changing world. In this event the existing proposal on Parental Leave will be withdrawn.'

In Section VIII.A on 'Promoting and Strengthening the Social Dialogue', the Commission also reiterated its intention to make proposals to:[11]

'stimulate the involvement of the social partners at European level in actions to . . . address major new issues such as reconciling family and work . . .'

The Commission's Medium Term Social Action Programme 1995–1997 duly confirmed this in Section V on 'Equality of Opportunity for Women and Men':[12]

'In February 1995, the Commission launched consultations with the social partners under the Agreement on Social Policy to consider the possibility of negotiating an agreement on the reconciliation of professional and family life. The aim of such a proposal will be to promote equal opportunities and encourage the introduction of new, flexible models better suited to the changing needs of European society. Future action will depend on the outcome of the current consultations. Now that this consultation process is under way, the Commission's existing proposal on parental leave has been overtaken, and will therefore be withdrawn at the appropriate stage.'

This consultation proposal, produced by the Commission on 22 February 1995, is worthy of close attention, both because it attempts to use the Maastricht machinery, implying the potential use of the social dialogue process, and for the light it throws on the evolution of the EU policy on equality.

EQUAL OPPORTUNITIES IN CONTEXT

In its Introduction, the Consultative Document begins with an acknowledgement that its inspiration was equal opportunities, but immediately shifts attention to the context of reconciliation:[13]

'The Commission's interest in this area derives from its policy of equal opportunities for women and men. Since the early 1980s, reconciliation has been a Commission priority in this area. On 24 November 1983, the Commission submitted a proposal for a Council Directive on parental leave and leave for family reasons. The aim of the proposal was to provide workers with a minimum leave entitlement following the birth or adoption of a child. It also foresaw the granting of leave to workers for other family reasons.'

After reviewing the failure of the parental leave proposal to achieve the requisite approval of the Council of Ministers, there is a Section II entitled: 'The General Socio-Economic Context'. There are, in fact, multiple contexts.

The first is that equal opportunities means reconciliation for all workers, though the emphasis is on relieving women from the demands of their working and family lives:[14]

'Reconciliation is a concept which is still developing within the EU. In recent years, experience in different Member States has highlighted the importance of this idea in

11 Ibid, paragraph 11.
12 COM (95) 134 final, Brussels, 12 April 1995, paragraph 5.1.2.
13 Consultative Document, *Reconciliation of Professional and Family Life*, February 1995, paragraph 2.
14 Ibid, paragraph 6.

several contexts. The first of these contexts is equal opportunities. There will be no substantial progress towards greater equality between men and women until a comprehensive reconciliation policy is put in place for all workers. It will be instrumental in relieving women in particular from unreasonable and conflicting demands in their working and family lives.'

A second context emphasised is that of new employment opportunities. The paragraph concludes with the sentence: 'It may also open up new employment opportunities for men and women'. No further detail is given in this paragraph and, in particular, it is not specific about whether this is to be achieved through changing employers' and/or men's patterns.

The third context is that reconciliation can improve the functioning of European labour markets. Here the emphasis is on flexibility, encouraging women's labour market participation, with specific reference to working time arrangements:[15]

> 'In a similar vein, reconciliation should be seen as an integral part of the attempt to improve the functioning of European labour markets. There is broad agreement on the need to provide for greater flexibility in work. Enabling workers to reconcile their family lives with their work obligations will allow more women to become economically active. Reconciliation can help to bring this about through periods of leave and varied or reduced working hours.'

The connection is then made with the earlier context of employment policy:[16]

> 'National experience has shown the employment potential of such measures. However, the issue of costs arising out of such a policy needs to be considered. The situation needs to be avoided where individual employers have to bear all direct and indirect costs as this could be an incentive against employing particular workers.'

A fourth context is that of family policy. Heretofore, equal opportunities policy was considered not to have any implications for family responsibilities and relationships.[17] This is not the case with a social policy based on reconciliation. There is less reticence regarding the potential of policy intervention; possibilities canvassed include public recognition and encouragement:[18]

> 'Another social context where reconciliation is important is the family. The policy of reconciliation aims to uphold family relationships and responsibilities. The benefits for workers who can achieve greater harmony between their professional and family lives will be felt by their families too. In particular, men will be able to take a greater role in the raising of children and the care of other family members where the need arises. As a family support measure, reconciliation offers much to society generally and denotes public recognition of the value of personal relationships.'

The fifth and final context is that of training and education: improving the quality of human capital:[19]

> 'Finally, the context of training and education deserves mention. The future of the European economy rests upon the quality of its human capital. In face of ever-increasing levels of skill and expertise across the world, European workers need all possible support in upgrading their own skills. Reconciliation, which could take the form of training leave or sabbaticals, should be an important component of any

15 Ibid, paragraph 7.
16 Ibid.
17 Case 184/83: *Hofmann v Barmer Ersatzkasse* [1984] ECR 3047.
18 Consultative Document, paragraph 8.
19 Ibid, paragraph 9.

scheme designed to raise the level of professional ability within the EU. Every effort should be made to ensure that education and training provision takes into account the varying needs and convenience of all sectors of the population by ensuring maximum possible access in terms of timing and location. Certain sectors have already made progress in this area, notably the public sector, but there is a need to involve the whole spectrum of employment.'

It is not spelled out how training and education is specifically linked to reconciliation of work and *family* life (as contrasted with the more familiar exigency of reconciling work and occupational training in general). Is it that training and education, linked to work, are somehow easier to accommodate with family responsibilities? Or are education and training to be used as an incentive to people to undertake family responsibilities, and at the same time such education and training would be particularly easy to achieve in that context? The decisive break with traditional equality policy is that it seems to imply more than ensuring that women with family responsibilities are not denied (equal) access to training. Rather, training may be an incentive to undertake such responsibilities (for men).

The multiple contexts of reconciliation include, therefore, equal opportunities, employment policy, improving labour markets, family relationships and training and education. But the pathbreaking evolution is really that of contextualising equal opportunities policy in the EU so that it goes beyond the confines of equality law. It is neatly summarised as follows:[20]

'It is submitted therefore that a policy rooted in equal opportunities has developed into one focussed on quality. Quality of family life, quality of working life and quality of human resources.'

The inspiration may have been equality law. But other contexts have usurped its place as the main concern, such as policies on employment and flexibility. Attention has switched to the relationship of families and work.

This is a different and wider issue than equal opportunities for women. It potentially implies, on the one hand, concern for the family: children and older people. On the other hand, it has significance in diversifying priorities. The substantive content of the proposal affects not only women but the organisation of work and family structures. The form and wording will place less emphasis on equal opportunities and concepts of direct and indirect discrimination. It will probably relate more to substantive issues and concepts which arise in the implementation of the Working Time Directive. It may come to be affected by EU policy concerned with different forms of employment, such as part-timers. In sum: it presages a fundamental shift in EU law away from equality as the central issue and towards other concerns. These were reflected in subsequent sections of the Consultative Document.

IMPLICATIONS FOR EU LABOUR LAW

The implications for labour law of a policy centred on reconciliation of work and family life were spelled out in Section III: The changing employment roles of men and women. It began by emphasising inequality:[1]

---

20 Ibid, paragraph 10.
1 Ibid, paragraph 11.

'11. ... unemployment among women is higher, on average, than among men. And relatively few women, outside those with high levels of education and skill, enter, or progress in, the labour market on equal terms with men.'

Moreover, new working arrangements are said in practice to reinforce existing gender divisions, especially with regard to part-time work, where there is no equality in protection, terms and conditions or training and career development.[2]

The question, however, is whether equality is at issue. Or whether it is using new working arrangements, including part-time, to counter gender divisions. The objective is *not* to make part-timers equal to full-timers (adopting the male standard), but to recast working arrangements – the standard employment relationship and traditional family structures – to achieve specific policy objectives. This is the import of the following paragraphs:[3]

'The significant and rapid changes in the labour market which have taken place in recent years, in terms of women's participation and its implications for working and family structures and patterns, have developed in the context of labour market policies and frameworks still based to a great extent on old assumptions of mass manual and semi-skilled production processes; cyclical, mainly male, unemployment; and traditional household structures.'

There is a subtle recasting of equal opportunities policy in terms not simply of equality in the labour market, but to accommodate other contexts. The objective is not equality, but reconciliation – for both men and women:[4]

'Therefore, the totality and direction of labour market changes tend not to have the effect required, of meeting the more general objective of ensuring a more equal sharing of work and family and household roles and responsibilities. All too often, the increase in participation by women in the labour market results in additions to their existing family or caring responsibilities, rather than enabling a more effective reconciliation of these various demands between men and women.'

The implications are that policy seeks not simply to ease the burden on women, but rather to increase the burden on others: of sharing on men; and, on employers, to accommodate this by recasting the standard employment relationship:[5]

'The wide-ranging reform of Member States' employment systems – as foreseen in the White Paper on Growth, Competitiveness and Employment – needs to take on board these basic policy challenges in a way which places reconciliation as an integrated part of the overall strategy of increased access to employment and incomes for all.'

The White Paper on 'European Social Policy: A Way Forward for the Union' referred to the Delors 'White Paper on Growth, Competitiveness and Employment':[6]

'The (Delors) White Paper stresses the need to widen considerably access to work, to widen the concept of work, and to build a new solidarity ... particularly in view of

2   Ibid, paragraph 12.
3   Ibid, paragraph 13.
4   Ibid, paragraph 14.
5   Ibid, paragraph 15.
6   Section I, paragraph 9.

the increasing participation rates of women, changing family structures and roles, and the need to maximise the potential of all the Union's human resources . . .'

In general the White Paper emphasised that:[7]

'6.   . . . It will be necessary to reassess the value given to jobs traditionally performed by women, jobs like childcare, care of elderly people, work in family enterprises and care in the home local services. In addition, new forms of work organisation will tend to create more flexible jobs not only for women but also for men. Policies are necessary which will lead to both sexes taking advantage of the potential benefits of flexibility . . .'

The White Paper concluded:[8]

'1.   . . . the traditional social protection systems of Europe – based on the concept of the welfare state – are an important achievement that needs to be maintained. But . . . (t)his means giving a top priority to employment, securing new links between employment and social policies by developing a "trampoline" safety net, and recognising that those who are not in the labour market also have a useful role to play in society. While the European social model provides a good foundation, it needs to be developed to provide a new synergy between the welfare and wealth-creating functions of society.
2.   This is all the more important because the EU will experience significant changes in its demographic structure within the next 20 years . . .'

The future of European social policy requires a vision of social roles involving not only paid work, but also other activities constituting the social identity of citizens. This was the inspiration of the Commission's initial Green Paper:[9]

'The industrial revolution and the technology of the production line not only separated the work and welfare functions but also rigidified the separation of work from other activities. Yet work has other functions in addition to providing income: purposeful activity and personal fulfilment, dignity, social contacts, recognition and a basis for organising daily or weekly time . . . changes could mean that the division between "working time" and "other time" will again fade, so that work is reintegrated into a wider pattern of activities. They present the challenge of realigning work and welfare in ways that help as many as possible to participate actively in their societies, while taking advantage of the greater flexibility that new modes of production allow.'

This approach raises fundamental questions for EU labour law. Is it only the employment patterns of women which require adjustment; or those of both men and women? If employment patterns are to be adjusted to accommodate women's patterns, this could imply no change in women's work, but only a change in employers' patterns to allow them to be reconciled with women's patterns. Or should men's employment patterns also be adjusted, as a matter of obligation, to allow for the requisite policy of reconciliation?

But reconciliation of what? Employers' patterns do not need to be adjusted to men's patterns – they *are* men's patterns. What does reconciliation mean here – unless it means requiring changes in employers' patterns to accommodate men and women. If employers' patterns have to reflect a plurality of options to

---

7   Section 5, paragraph 6.
8   Section VI, paragraphs 1–2.
9   Section II.C.3.

accommodate *both* types of working patterns, however, the lessons of the past are that this means men will not change; rather, women will accommodate, and employers' adjustment will be forced, minimal and difficult to monitor. Effectively, discrimination in career development and opportunities will continue.[10]

THE POTENTIAL OF LEGISLATION AND SOCIAL DIALOGUE

The Consultative Document then drops back to consider the situation in Member States.[11] There are outlined the legal measures at Member State level. These take the form of parental leave schemes of varying duration, part-time or full time, taken consecutively or in blocks, and may be available to both parents. But above all, they are still linked to birth, maternity and young children, though it is noted that family leave may in some cases be extended beyond childbirth, though in practice only regarding a child's illness, except by special agreement in other circumstances.

The emphasis so far is on *legal* measures. But there are two questions. First, what other means of policy expression are available; secondly, are *parental leave* schemes the only or best expression or means of achieving the objective of reconciliation?

The answers are sought first by looking 'at the social partner level'.[12] The point is made that the social partners have progressed beyond the legislative provisions, especially in the public sector. The Commission sees in this 'a positive indication of the possibility of an agreement on reconciliation at European level between the social partners'. There follows an explicit attempt to link all the contexts explored in the Document through the EU social dialogue:[13]

> '*In summary*, the Commission believes that the social partners should explore the widest possible range of issues relating to reconciliation ... Successful discussion could have major implications for equal opportunities, employment opportunities, the quality of individual working life and increased efficiency of a world class labour force.'

Legislation does not seem to be promoted as an avenue for expanding beyond equal opportunities, but social dialogue is.[14] Here it should be recalled that the Document began with the invocation of the social dialogue procedure laid down in Article 3 of the Agreement on Social Policy annexed to the Treaty on European Union.[15] This is reiterated in a section entitled 'Issues of Subsidiarity'.[16]

---

10 A similar dilemma is anticipated with the Working Time Directive's prohibition on working more than 48 hours a week on average. In the face of demands by the workers for highly remunerated overtime, and employers' willingness to continue to accommodate this, how is the EU law's prohibition to be enforced?

11 Section IV, paragraphs 16–17.

12 Section V, paragraphs 18–19.

13 Ibid, paragraph 19.

14 Is this because social dialogue is considered to have more potential, or because the social partners are not trusted to accommodate equal opportunities policy alone?

15 Paragraph 1.

16 Section VI, paragraphs 20–21.

The Commission cites *both* the 1989 Community Charter concerning reconciliation, but with an equal opportunities emphasis, *and* the Maastricht Agreement
on Social Policy, Article 1 of which concerns working conditions *as well as*
equality – thus expanding the agenda by bring in other contexts. The implication
is that EU competence extends not only to equality, but to wider contexts also. It
then incants the subsidiarity definition in Article 3B of the Treaty on European
Union and states: [17]

> 'The Commission believes that action in the field of reconciliation between pro-
> fessional and family life is directly linked to the achievement of the abovementioned
> objectives. It also considers that the specific objectives of promoting reconciliation
> between family and professional life, laying down minimum standards of protection
> and establishing common rules ensuring fair competition within the Community
> cannot be sufficiently achieved by the Member States acting alone and can therefore
> by reason of the scale and effects of the proposed action, be better achieved by gen-
> eral framework arrangements operating at Community level.'

The culmination of this careful expansion of the policy agenda beyond equality
is the next section, headed: 'What is being asked of the social partners in this
consultation?' The answer is blunt: [18]

> 'The terms of discussion are wider than the issue of time off work for workers with
> children. The Commission wishes to draw attention to the Council Recommen-
> dation on Childcare,[19] adopted in 1992. This instrument indicates the other issues
> which might be included in discussions on reconciliation. Apart from leave, the
> Recommendation favours action at enterprise level, especially within the framework
> of collective agreements, which create an environment, structure and organisation of
> work which take into account the needs of parents with children. It underlines the
> necessity of childcare services being widely available and accessible. It also favours
> the greater involvement of men in the upbringing of children. In general, the
> Recommendation emphasises the need for flexibility and partnerships at all levels.'[20]

As if this was not comprehensive enough, the Commission adds: [1]

> '... there are several contexts which need to be taken into account. During the
> course of these discussions the social partners are invited to explore, in addition to
> the issues described above, what other elements should be on the agenda.'

17   Ibid, paragraph 21.
18   Ibid, paragraph 22.
19   Council Recommendation 92/241/EEC on child care of 31 March 1992, OJ L123/16 of
      8.5.1992.
20   The 1992 Recommendation on Childcare does indeed refer to other issues. It emphasises
      initiatives in the following four areas (Article 2(3)):
>   '1.   The provision of children-care services while parents:
>   –   are working,
>   –   are following a course of education or training in order to obtain employment, or
>   –   are seeking a job or a course of education or training in order to obtain employment.
>   For the purposes of this Recommendation, "child-care services" means any type of
>   child care, whether public or private, individual or collective.
>   2.   Special leave for employed parents with responsibility for the care and upbringing of
>   children.
>   3.   The environment, structure and organisation of work, to make them responsive to the
>   needs of workers with children.
>   4.   The sharing of occupational, family and upbringing responsibilities arising from the
>   care of children between women and men.'
1   Op cit, paragraph 24.

In the replies from the social partners responding to the Commission's Consultative Document, many of these issues were taken up. It was disappointing therefore, that the Commission itself, in its follow-up document, produced a much less ambitious and more ambiguous proposal. Having undertaken the first round of consultations of the social partners mandated by the Protocol and Agreement on Social Policy, the Commission produced a second paper:[2]

> 'to consult management and labour on the content of a Community measure on reconciliation of professional and family life, pursuant to Article 3(3) of the Agreement on Social Policy annexed to the Treaty on European Union.'

On the one hand, the Commission's Paper reiterated that:[3]

> 'On many occasions, the Commission has argued that formal equality in the workplace needs to be supplemented by measures supporting real equality of opportunity embracing both the professional and family lives of workers. This requires consideration of the employment patterns of men and women and the choices which they may be encouraged to make about working time and the organisation of work. This issue is at the heart of current debates about employment and unemployment in Europe.'

On the other hand, the proposal put forward was 'for a binding framework measure (directive) which could develop a number of principles'.[4]

These principles, however, focused mainly on individual employment rights to leave for both mothers and fathers, with some genuflections to the myriad other issues. The only prospect for a return to the wider horizons of the original Consultative Document is the Commission's insistence that 'the exact modalities for taking the leave ... should be determined by employers and employee representatives'.[5] The onus of exerting the effort to secure accommodation of employment structures to achieve 'real equality of opportunity' is left to the social partners.

CONCLUSION

The EU policy on equal opportunities began ostensibly with modest proposals concerned with parental leave. But the Consultative Document makes it clear that the context is much wider and the policy objectives more ambitious. It signals a breakthrough from narrow equality issues to wider labour market, labour relations and gender roles issues.

The starting point is the standard employment relationship – the prototype of labour market regulation. In labour law, workers' rights are the rights of workers who are permanent, full-time and (disproportionately) male. This prototype is breaking down due to management's flexibilisation strategies applied to labour and increasing female labour market participation, particularly in the area of part-time work.

Their interaction produces a combustion point where flexibilisation in the form of different treatment of part-timers confronts the EC law on indirect sex

---

2 Commission Paper on 'Reconciliation of Professional and Family Life', May 1995.
3 Ibid, paragraph 6.
4 Ibid, paragraph 7.
5 Ibid, paragraph 7.1.

discrimination. The problem with this interaction is that the only norms applicable are those of EC equality law. The consequences are negative: it only addresses inequality; it does not require positive measures; it allows for (objective) justifications; it affects only part-timers, and only so long as (and because) these are disproportionately women.

The proposals on reconciliation of work and family life aim to meet all these weaknesses, expanding the norms applicable to include positive measures aimed at men and women. That is not to say there is a concept of an ideal working time regime which allows for reconciliation. There is no single model in a Europe with different cultural contexts; and not even in one Member State where life styles and child-rearing patterns can vary. What is called for is a choice of models: the availability of different working time schedules.

These alternative schedules could be developed in various ways. They could be devised unilaterally by employers, with the risk of private interest predominating. Legislative fiat might be too rigid. Individual bargaining yields results reflecting unequal bargaining power. Collective bargaining depends on the strength of and the risk of sexism in unions. It may be that what is required is some combination of these: collective bargaining backed by legislation; or a hierarchy of norms: individual agreement, based on a collective agreement, supported by Member State legislation, backed by an EU level guarantee in the form of the Charter of Fundamental Social Rights.

So far, the emphasis has been on reconciliation of professional and *family* life. This inspiration is owed to the longstanding preoccupation in EU labour law with women through equality policy, in particular, the EU law on indirect discrimination. But the question may be asked: why should the *family* be the determining factor? One cannot assume a typical family, just as one cannot assume typical work. It should be open to 'non-family' workers to apportion their 'family equivalent' time to other ends.

There are other social concerns demanding to be reconciled with working life: care for the aged, community care, social and other interests. Further, there are wider issues of unemployment and work-sharing, requiring the reconciliation of the interests of employed workers and the unemployed. All have claims to justify new EU policies, many involving changes, in the words of the Recommendation on Child-care, in the 'environment, structure and organisation of work'.

This is not to say that family concerns are irrelevant, or secondary. Merely that the inspiration for the EU policy on reconciliation may be purely the chance of previous EC law on sex discrimination. This incorporates all the limitations of that EC law. But the concept of reconciliation offers the prospect of integrating wider contexts and perspectives into the EU regulation of working life.

Part V

European Labour Law and the Enterprise

Chapter 16

Labour and the Enterprise

ORIGINS

Labour in the enterprise began in EU law as a factor of production. The four freedoms classed labour along with goods, services and capital as one of the factors guaranteed free circulation in the common market. For the rest, there was the undertaking regarding equal pay in Article 119 of the Treaty of Rome, and a gesture in the direction of labour market intervention in the form of vocational training. Beyond this, the commitment to labour took the form of a principle of improvement of living and working conditions, to be achieved through the benefits of the common market, but without any concrete mechanisms engaging the workers in the enterprise themselves.

The provisions on free movement of labour did not address issues of collective concern to workers in the enterprise. Indirectly, however, the common market logic, though confined to harmonisation of working conditions, could be extended to embrace these matters. Given this oblique perspective, it was perhaps not surprising that the first major initiative proposed by the Commission only emerged in 1972, and took the form of the draft Fifth Directive on harmonisation of company structure and administration. This proposal sought to require companies with over 500 employees to include employee representatives on an obligatory supervisory board. It was unsuccessful in obtaining the approval of the Council of Ministers.

Shortly afterwards, the position was transformed under the impetus of the Social Action Programme following the Paris Summit of 1972, finally adopted in 1974. It came to be applied in the context of the economic dislocation in Western Europe consequent on the rise in oil prices following the 1973 Middle East war. Within the constraints of the logic of harmonisation in a common market, this led to two Directives: on collective dismissals and protection of employees in transfers of undertakings. Both these Directives included provisions requiring the information and consultation of workers' representatives. In Council Directive 75/129/EEC of 17 February 1975 on the approximation of the laws of the Member States relating to collective redundancies:[1]

'Article 2:
1. Where an employer is contemplating collective redundancies, he shall begin consultations with the workers' representatives *in good time* with a view to reaching an agreement.

---

1 Directive 75/129, OJ L48/29 of 22.2.1975, as amended by Directive 92/56/EEC of 24 June 1992, OJ L245/3 of 26.8.92, Article 1(2). The amendments inserted to the original directive are italicised.

2. These consultations shall, at least, cover ways and means of avoiding collective redundancies or reducing the number of workers affected, and *of* mitigating the consequences *by recourse to accompanying social measures aimed, inter alia, at aid for redeploying or retraining workers made redundant.*

   Member States may provide that the workers' representatives may call upon the services of experts in accordance with national legislation and/or practice.

3. To enable workers' representatives to make constructive proposals, the employers shall *in good time during the course of the consultations*:

   (a) supply them with all relevant information and

   (b) shall in any event *notify them* in writing *of*:

   (i) the reasons for the *projected* redundancies;

   (ii) the number of *categories of* workers to be made redundant;

   (iii) the number *and categories* of workers normally employed;

   (iv) the period over which the *projected* redundancies are to be effected;

   (v) the criteria proposed for the selection of the workers to be made redundant in so far as national legislation and/or practice confers the power therefor upon the employer;

   (vi) the method for calculating any redundancy payments other than those arising out of national legislation and/or practice.

   The employer shall forward to the competent public authority a copy of, *at least, the elements of* the written communication *which are provided for in the first subparagraph, point (b), subpoints (i) to (v).'*

In Council Directive 77/187/EEC of 14 February 1977 on the approximation of the laws of the Member States relating to the safeguarding of employees' rights in the event of transfers of undertakings, businesses or parts of businesses:[2]

'Article 6:

1. The transferor and the transferee shall be required to inform the representatives of their respective employees affected by a transfer within the meaning of Article 1(1) of the following:
   – the reasons for the transfer,
   – the legal, economic and social implications of the transfer for the employees,
   – measures envisaged in relation to the employees.

   The transferor must give such information to the representatives of his employees in good time before the transfer is carried out.

   The transferee must give such information to representatives of his employees in good time, and in any event before his employees are directly affected by the transfer as regards their conditions of work and employment.

2. If the transferor or the transferee envisages measures in relation to his employees, he shall consult the representatives of the employees in good time on such measures with a view to seeking agreement.'

These Directives might have been the beginning of a sustained development towards a role for labour in the enterprise. The following years saw a number of initiatives by the Commission which attempted to expand their scope: two drafts of a Directive on procedures for informing and consulting employees in large national and multinational firms in 1980 and 1983 (the so-called 'Vredeling' Directive, named after the then Commissioner for Social Affairs); a revised draft Fifth Directive on company structure and administration in 1983; and a revised draft Regulation and Directive on the Statute for a European Company, in 1979 (amending earlier drafts of 1970 and 1975).

2   Directive 77/187, OJ L61/26 of 5.4.77.

However, all these initiatives came to naught. The requirement of unanimity in the Council of Ministers congealed any movement they might have represented. Progress was only made in the sphere of health and safety at work, where a number of Directives were adopted regarding information and consultation over hazards at work (lead and ionic compounds in 1982,[3] asbestos in 1983,[4] noise in 1986[5]), culminating in the Framework Directive in 1989.[6]

SPILL-OVER EFFECT

The inability of the EU to expand the scope of the issues to be regulated by labour in the enterprise led to a familiar development of 'spill-over' from those Directives which had been adopted, so as to require information and consultation in an increasingly wide range of circumstances. A number of issues illustrating this 'spill-over' effect will be explored briefly (privatisation, transnational issues).

The legislative log-jam was finally broken under the impact of the Member States' desire for a social dimension to accompany the 1992 Single Market Programme, which led to the adoption of the Protocol and Agreement on Social Policy of the TEU. The result was the Directive on European Works Councils. The Directive will require detailed analysis, as it manifests a general strategy towards labour in the enterprise which has long-term consequences.

These Directives, then, should be seen not as individual and isolated cases of special situations or circumstances where EU policy was exceptionally supportive of labour in the enterprise. Rather, they are part of a general evolution of policy in the EU towards labour in the enterprise. The specific individual measures embodying this policy have been shaped by the contingent difficulties of social policy formation at particular conjunctures in the development of the EU. But they should be seen in this general context. The Maastricht Protocol and Agreement on Social Policy are particularly significant, as is evident in the approval of the European Works Council Directive.

It is this context which produces the spill-over effect whereby Directives apparently covering only narrowly defined situations involving labour in the enterprise (collective dismissals, transfers of undertakings, transnational enterprises) raise general and momentous issues of workers' representation, the role of collective agreements, adequacy of sanctions, dismissal of strikers, privatisation policies and, ultimately, managerial prerogative.

---

3   Council Directive 82/605/EEC of 28 July 1982, Article 11(2)(b); OJ L247/82.
4   The Asbestos Directive 83/477/EEC, OJ L263/83, Articles 11(2), 14(2)(b) as amended by Council Directive 91/382/EEC of 25 June 1991.
5   Council Directive 86/188/EEC of 12 May 1986, Article 3(4), OJ L137/86.
6   Council Directive 89/391/EEC of 12 June 1989, OJ L183/1.

Chapter 17

The Collective Dismissals Directive 1975

INTRODUCTION

The requirements of the 1975 Directive were implemented in Member States in a variety of formulations, not all of which were deemed acceptable. Infringement proceedings launched by the Commission under Article 169 led to the European Court upholding complaints against Italy,[1] Belgium[2] and the UK.[3]

The detailed findings in these cases regarding whether certain provisions of domestic law complied with the Directive are less important than the light they throw on general issues in EU labour law. Some of these are explored elsewhere in this book: for example, that implementation of Directives could be achieved through collective agreements (Italy); that a system for securing the presence of worker representatives to be informed and consulted was mandatory, and that sanctions prescribed must be effective (UK). Three further issues specific to this Directive are worthy of note: the European Court's view of the role of labour in the enterprise, the scope of dismissals covered ('personal to the worker'), and the transnational dimension added to the Directive by amendments in 1992.

THE EUROPEAN COURT OF JUSTICE AND LABOUR'S ROLE IN THE ENTERPRISE

Legislative policy in the EU is subject to its being interpreted by the European Court. Much, therefore, depends on the perception by the Court of the policy being pursued. The results of applying teleological techniques of interpretation depend on which teleology is being applied. Pro-EC-integration bias does incorporate a tendency to uphold Commission complaints against Member States for failure to comply with EU legislative policy by limiting the scope of Directives. In furtherance of its mission to secure EU legislative objectives, the European Court has upheld complaints by the Commission against non-complying Member States in six decisions on the 1975 Directive.[4]

However, pro-integration bias will not always provide an obvious solution to questions raised for preliminary rulings on the interpretation of EU labour law.

---

1   Cases 91/81: [1982] ECR 2133, and 131/84: [1985] ECR 3531.
2   Case 215/83: [1985] ECR 1039.
3   Case C-382/92: [1994] ECR I-2435.
4   Italy three times, Belgium twice, UK once.

Indeed, in the one case of a preliminary ruling under Article 177 on the 1975 Directive, the European Court acted all too like a national court giving a judgment in a labour law case.

Case 284/83 (*Nielsen*) was a reference to the Court under Article 177 by the Specialarbejderforbundet i Danmark (Supreme Court of Denmark) for a preliminary ruling.[5] The case concerned a company in financial difficulties which informed the bankruptcy court that it was suspending payments of its debts. The employer was thereupon asked by the trade unions to provide a guarantee for future payment of wages. When this was not forthcoming, on the advice of their unions, the workers stopped work. Two questions were referred to the Court:

'(1) May a termination of employment which is effected by the employees because the employer has notified the bankruptcy court that he is suspending payment of his debts be treated as dismissal by the employer with the consequences that the employment falls within the scope of Council Directive No 75/129/EEC of 17 February 1975 . . . ? The reply should be based on the assumption that the employees' termination of their employment was justified under Danish law.
(2) Does Council Directive No 75/129/EEC apply not only where the employer in fact contemplated large-scale redundancies, but also where he ought to have contemplated large-scale redundancies and to have given advance notice thereof but failed to do so?'

As regards the first question, the Supreme Court of Denmark took the view that:[6]

'the objective of the directive, which is to strengthen the protection of workers in the event of collective dismissal, implies that the termination by the workers of their employment on the ground that payment of their wages is no longer guaranteed should be treated as dismissal effected by the employer.'

The European Court objected:[7]

'That argument cannot be accepted. The directive does not affect the employer's freedom to effect or refrain from effecting collective dismissals. Its sole object is to provide for consultation with the trade unions and for notification of the competent public authority prior to such dismissals. Article 2(2) provides that consultation with the trade unions must, at least, cover "ways and means of avoiding collective redundancies or reducing the number of workers affected, and mitigating the consequences". Article 4 provides that projected collective redundancies notified to the competent authority are to take effect only after a particular period has elapsed. The competent public authority is to use that period to seek solutions to the problems raised by the projected collective redundancies. As the Guarantee Fund and the Commission rightly observe, to treat termination of their employment by the workers in the manner advocated by Specialarbejderforbundet i Danmark (Supreme Court of Denmark) would give the workers the possibility of bringing about dismissals against the will of the employer and without his being in a position to discharge his obligations under Articles 2 and 3 of the directive. It would lead to a result precisely contrary to that sought by the directive, namely to avoid or reduce collective redundancies.'

5　Case 284/83: *Dansk Metalarbejderforbund and Specialarbejderforbundet i Danmark v H Nielsen & Son, Maskinfabrik A/S* [1985] ECR 553.
6　Ibid, paragraph 9.
7　Ibid, paragraph 10.

On the second question the Supreme Court of Denmark contended:[8]

> 'that the effectiveness of the directive would be impaired if the employer were not obliged, by implication, to foresee collective redundancies as soon as he encounters serious financial difficulties.'

Again the European Court objected:[9]

> 'As the Guarantee Fund and the Commission rightly state, there is no implied obligation under the directive to foresee collective redundancies. It does not stipulate the circumstances in which the employer must contemplate collective redundancies and in no way affects his freedom to decide whether and when he must formulate plans for collective dismissals.'

The Court is concerned to establish what it regards as the object of, or result sought by, the Directive, and to exclude implied obligations. Looking to the wider issue of labour in the enterprise, it asserts that '(i)ts sole object is to provide for consultation with the trade unions'. The striking feature of this judgment is the emphasis by the Court on 'the employer's freedom to effect or refrain from effecting collective dismissals', and 'his freedom to decide whether and when he must formulate plans for collective dismissals'. This is not seen as inconsistent with the obligation to consult with trade unions.

The Court's vision of labour in the enterprise is one which views the EU obligation of 'consultation' as not affecting the employer's freedom of decision-making. Protection of the employee by this mechanism is seen as subordinate to the employer's freedom of action. This is a fundamental issue in labour law. What place does it have in the future construction of EU labour law?

One way of approaching this question is to consider how labour in the enterprise could interact with the pro-integrationist bias of the Court manifest in other cases. The answer may be to take the long view of the development of EU labour law. In so far as labour plays an ever more important role in the process of European integration, it will increase its potential attraction to the Court. The European social dialogue, institutionalised through the Maastricht Protocol and Agreement on Social Policy, will be a powerful instrument, in so far as labour in the enterprise is articulated with social dialogue as a means of formulating and implementing EU labour law. Additionally, the role of labour in the enterprise will be powerfully assisted by the transnational dimension explicitly inserted into the 1975 Directive by the amendments introduced in 1992.

The fragility of the European Court's commitment to managerial prerogative may be illustrated by the Court's additional justification of its answer to the second question as to whether the employer ought to have contemplated collective redundancies because of the financial state of the undertaking:[10]

> 'Moreover, as the Commission rightly observes, the effect of the interpretation proposed by the Specialarbejderforbundet i Danmark would be that any employer who ceased to trade as a result of insolvency and who failed to notify the public authority of any projected collective redundancy would incur the penalties laid down by national law, since he would not have foreseen collective redundancies in sufficient time. Such an interpretation would run counter to the wording of Article 1(2), which excludes from the scope of the directive collective redundancies caused "by the termination of an establishment's activities where that is the result of a judicial decision".'

---

8   Ibid, paragraph 14.
9   Ibid, paragraph 15.
10   Ibid, paragraph 16.

It was precisely this paragraph that was deleted by the amending Directive of 1992.[11] The Explanatory Memorandum accompanying the Commission's proposal stated that:[12]

'The general exclusion of the current directive in cases where an establishment's activities are terminated as a result of a judicial decision no longer appears to be appropriate. There seems no reason why employees' information and consultation rights . . . should not apply in such cases.'

If anything, impending insolvency increases the urgency and should accelerate the process of information and consultation of those directly affected – employees and their representatives.

This isolated decision is significant, not in what it actually decides, but as an indication of how the judges in the European Court may decide issues of EU labour law which are, or appear to be, relatively abstracted from general issues of European integration. The insistence upon managerial freedom is not supported by any reference to either EU or national law or policy. It is pure managerial ideology.

It may be contrasted with the judgment of 8 June 1994 in *EC Commission v UK*, in which the European Court cited *Nielsen* for the proposition that:[13]

'Admittedly, the directive carries out only a partial harmonisation of the rules for the protection of workers in the event of collective redundancies . . . (citing *Nielsen*) . . . and is for that reason not designed to bring about full harmonisation of national systems of worker representation in undertakings. However, the limited character of such harmonisation cannot deprive the provisions of the directive, and especially Articles 2 and 3, of their effectiveness. In particular, it cannot prevent Member States from being required to take all appropriate measures to ensure that worker representatives are designated with a view to complying with the obligations laid down in Articles 2 and 3.'

The point at issue in the case touched precisely on the question of managerial discretion with regard to recognition of workers' representatives:[14]

'The United Kingdom itself recognises that, as United Kingdom law now stands, workers affected by collective redundancies do not enjoy protection under Articles 2 and 3 of the directive in cases where an employer objects to worker representation in his undertaking.

In those circumstances, United Kingdom law, which allows an employer to frustrate the protection provided for workers by Articles 2 and 3 of the directive, must be regarded as contrary to those articles.'

Unlike *Nielsen*, managerial freedom is here explicitly subordinated to the requirement on Member States 'to take all appropriate measures to ensure that worker representatives are designated with a view to complying with the obligations laid down . . .' The role of labour in the enterprise takes priority.[15]

The judgment in *Nielsen* is a vision of the 1975 Directive as an exceptional interruption of normal discretionary managerial decision-making by requiring

11 Council Directive 92/56/EEC of 24 June 1992 amending Directive 75/129/EEC, OJ L245/3 of 26.8.92, Article 1(1)(b) deleting Article 1(2)(d).
12 Document of 16.9.91, paragraph 18.
13 Case 382/92: [1994] ECR I-2435, paragraph 25.
14 Ibid, paragraphs 26–7.
15 This reinforces the point that a Commission complaint seems to be regarded as more persuasive on issues of Community policy than references under Article 177.

consultation of workers' representatives. This vision of exceptionality is questionable as the scope of consultation required by other Directives becomes increasingly wider, and as obligatory consultation and social dialogue become a permanent element at the highest levels of formulation and implementation of EU labour law.

SCOPE OF THE DIRECTIVE

The Collective Dismissals Directive, despite its rubric, has come to be perceived as providing *individual* protection against a certain type of dismissal. The 1975 Directive has tended to be seen through the lens of protection of individual rights,[16] even though, unlike the Acquired Rights Directive, it provides only for information and consultation of worker representatives and includes no provisions guaranteeing individual rights. The individualistic characterisation of the 1975 Directive has contributed to a perception of its scope as limited to dismissals of a particular kind, economic, redundancy, technical, reflected in various national implementing provisions.[17]

These alleged attributes limiting its scope need to be reassessed. The emphasis on dismissals of this particular kind is understandable in the context in which the Directive came to be *applied*: the economic difficulties following the first oil crisis led to many closures and restructuring involving collective dismissals for just such economic reasons. But the *proposals* for the Directive were produced in the wake of a report by the Commission of July 1972.[18] Moreover, the English language version of the Directive refers not to collective dismissals, but to collective 'redundancies'. The term 'redundancy' in UK domestic law has attributed to it a very specific meaning by virtue of earlier legislation, the Redundancy Payments Act 1965, which defined redundancy as:[19]

'(a) the fact that the employer has ceased, or intends to cease, to carry on the business for the purposes of which the employee is or was employed by him, or has ceased, or intends to cease, to carry on that business in the place where the employee is or was so employed, or
(b) the fact that the requirements of that business for employees to carry out work of a particular kind, or for employees to carry out work of a particular kind in the place where he is or was employed, have ceased or diminished or are expected to cease or diminish.'

However, the definition of collective redundancies in the Directive was quite different from that in the UK legislation:[20]

'"collective redundancies" means dismissals effected by an employer for one or more reasons not related to the individual workers concerned . . .'

---

16   For example, in R Blanpain and J-C Javillier *Droit du Travail Communautaire*, Litec, Paris 1991, Part II, entitled 'Individual Labour Law' includes the Directive on collective dismissals; similarly, Part III, 'Individual Relations' in M Rocella and T Treu *Diritto del Lavoro della Comunità Europea*, Cedam, Padova 1992; and Chapter 4, 'The Protection of Employment Rights', in R Nielsen and E Szyszczak *The Social Dimension of the European Community*, 2nd ed, Handelshojskolens Forlag, Copenhagen 1993.
17   See the account in Chapter 4.
18   (1972) Bulletin of the EC (No 9), paragraph 42.
19   Re-enacted in the Employment Protection (Consolidation) Act 1978, s 81(2).
20   Article 1(1)(a).

Nonetheless, the UK legislation implementing the Directive, the Employment Protection Act 1975, incorporated the 1965 Act's definition of 'redundancy'.[1] It has taken almost twenty years for the UK to amend its legislation bringing it into line with the Directive,[2] and even this did not preclude the European Court formally condemning this distortion.[3]

The general issue raised by the Directive is whether dismissals are to be dealt with on an individual or a collective basis. The argument has been made that dismissal of employees is an issue which requires distinctions to be made between different *types* of dismissal, in particular, with regard to procedures to be followed.[4] The distinctions followed the reasons for the dismissal. Dismissals by reason of misconduct, incompetence, ill-health and so on require procedures tailored to the specific circumstances of each type of dismissal.

A fundamental distinction is apparent in the Collective Dismissals Directive: *certain* dismissals are a *collective* issue, to be dealt with through a procedure of information and consultation of worker representatives. The context in which the Directive emerged, the reluctance of Member States to take on board its implications for their domestic labour law, and perhaps the very bluntness of its message has tended to obscure its policy significance.

The Directive poses a direct challenge to the concept of dismissals being an issue of concern only as regards *individual* employment protection. Certain dismissals are excluded from its scope: '. . . dismissals effected by an employer for one or more reasons . . . related to the individual workers concerned . . .'[5] Impliedly, such dismissals are to be dealt with by other procedures. As yet, EU law has not prescribed rules, though the Maastricht Protocol explicitly now gives the EU competence to approve Directives concerning dismissals.

The *collective* dimension of dismissals is highlighted. It is acknowledged as a matter of EU law concern that 'dismissals effected by an employer for one or more reasons not related to the individual workers concerned' are *deemed* to have a collective dimension. EU law requires that certain procedures involving collective representatives of the workers be engaged.

This goes *beyond* mere *representation* of the individual worker. The collective interests of *other* workers are affected. Information and consultation is a process in which these collective interests can be articulated and taken into account. That the potential scope of this has been underestimated is evident in the European Court's decision making the presence of workers' representatives mandatory. Collective issues do not only arise where there are previously collective representatives present and able to identify them and take them up.

Inevitably, this will require a process of elaboration of the meaning of 'dismissals effected by an employer for one or more reasons not related to the individual workers concerned', which are *deemed* to have a collective dimension. How criteria will be devised and applied as between the European Court and national courts is territory as yet unexplored. It will not be easy. Dismissals

---

1   Employment Protection Act 1975, s 125(6), now TULR(C)A, s 195.
2   The Trade Union and Labour Relations (Consolidation) Act 1992, s 195, as amended by the Trade Union Reform and Employment Relations Act 1993.
3   Case C-382/92: *EC Commission v UK* [1994] ECR I-2435.
4   R Benedictus and B Bercusson *Labour Law: Cases and Materials*, Sweet & Maxwell, London 1987, Chapter 10, Section 1, 'Rules on Termination: Sources and Structure', pp 296–300 and pp 316 ff.
5   Article 1(1)(a).

are not always self-evidently individual or collective.

An example drawn from UK experience is particularly illuminating. The UK courts drew a distinction between dismissals by reason of redundancy, and dismissals by reason of changes in the work resulting from a reorganisation.[6] The latter were deemed to fall *outside* the scope of redundancy and hence did not engage the provisions of the UK law introduced to implement the 1975 Directive. Yet few will dispute that a reorganisation of the enterprise involves collective issues, and that dismissals which result from such a reorganisation are 'dismissals effected by an employer for one or more reasons not related to the individual workers concerned'.

Other cases will be less easy to resolve. For example, dismissals by reason of ill-health or incompetence are often linked with collective issues involving other employees. Before workers are dismissed for ill-health, there may be questions raised as to the possibility of temporary cover or replacement by other employees. Alleged incompetence of a worker threatened by dismissal may raise issues of the adequacy of training and supervision provided, probation periods, or alternative posts available as an alternative to dismissal. Even dismissals by reason of employee misconduct raise issues of collective concern: the consistency of management practice and procedures, or general issues of discipline, as when an employee is dismissed by way of setting an example to the workforce as a whole.

The extension of the scope of the Directive to bring more dismissals under the umbrella of collective protection was evident in the amendments to the 1975 Directive in 1992.[7] To be covered by the Directive, the number of redundancies ('dismissals effected by an employer for one or more reasons not related to the individual workers concerned') taking place had to reach thresholds stipulated in Article 1(1)(a) of the 1975 Directive. These were altered by the 1992 amending Directive adding:[8]

> 'For the purpose of calculating the number of redundancies provided for in the first subparagraph of point (a), terminations of an employment contract which occur to the individual workers concerned shall be assimilated to redundancies, provided that there are at least five redundancies.'

In this way, terminations of individual contracts per se are perceived potentially to raise issues of collective concern when they take place contemporaneously with dismissals which are 'for one or more reasons not related to the individual workers concerned'.

The specifically *collective* dimensions of individual dismissals were further emphasised in other amendments introduced in 1992. These built on the requirements of consultation aimed at 'ways and means of avoiding collective redundancies or reducing the number of workers affected, and mitigating the consequences' by adding a reference to:[9]

> 'recourse to accompanying social measures aimed, inter alia, at aid for redeploying or retraining workers made redundant.'

---

6   See the cases and discussion in Benedictus and Bercusson, op cit, pp 67–88.
7   Council Directive 92/56/EEC of 24 June 1992 amending Directive 75/129/EEC on the approximation of the laws of the Member States relating to collective redundancies, OJ L245/3 of 16.8.92.
8   Ibid, Article 1(1).
9   Ibid, Article 1(2) substituting new Article 2(2).

The dismissal of workers deemed incompetent or suffering from disabling ill-health may thus fall within the scope of consultations aimed at redeployment or retraining. Arrangements for redeployment and retraining are often the subject of collective negotiation; dismissal of workers involving such considerations inevitably raise issues not related to the individual workers alone.

The same can be said of the new requirement inserted by the 1992 amendments that employers notify workers' representatives of:[10]

'(v) the criteria proposed for the selection of the workers to be made redundant in so far as national legislation and/or practice confers the power therefor upon the employer;

(vi) the method for calculating any redundancy payments other than those arising out of national legislation and/or practice.'

Again, selection of workers implies the consideration of other workers and possible reasons for dismissing them instead of the worker concerned. Hence, the reasons for eventual dismissal are 'for one or more reasons not (wholly) related to the individual workers concerned'. Similarly, redundancy payments are often a matter of collective practice, and the application of this practice raises collective issues.

In sum, the scope of the Collective Dismissals Directive has general implications going far beyond the narrow vision of it as confined to specific economic circumstances. It imports a policy of collectivisation of decision-making on dismissals in general, requiring involvement of workers' representatives on this key issue in industrial relations.[11]

The 1975 Directive was an early harbinger of a general policy in EU labour law which differentiates it from national labour law policies in this field. EU law did not attempt to lay down substantive rules for which reasons and circumstances justify dismissal. Rather it proceduralised decision-making over dismissal, in a highly specific way, not by individualised procedures requiring a quasi-judicial proceeding internal to the workplace, with the employer often prosecutor and judge.[12] Rather, as the title of the Directive indicates, through recognition of the collective dimension of dismissals, reinforced most recently by the European Court's decision interpreting the Directive as requiring mandatory worker representation.

This EU labour law policy is not unique to dismissals, though the Collective Dismissals Directive was one of the earliest manifestations of it. The requirement of involvement of workers' representatives is apparent in numerous proposals and increasingly in Directives. For example, the Framework Directive on Health and Safety and the 'daughter' Directives include detailed provisions requiring consultation on health and safety matters. The Working Time Directive is striking in its incorporation of collectively agreed standards, but also in numerous provisions including requirements of involvement of workers' representatives.

The corollary to dismissals is hiring practices. Interestingly, the Health and Safety Framework Directive requires consultation when temporary workers are imported into the enterprise, as does the Directive on health and safety of

---

10 Ibid, Article 1(2) inserting a new Article 2(3)(v) and (vi).
11 For a highly dramatic illustration of the potential scope of the Directive, see its application to strike dismissals in Chapter 33.
12 See the critique of the UK law in Benedictus and Bercusson, op cit, pp 351 ff.

temporary workers.[13] Proposed Directives on part-time workers included provisions requiring consultation of workers' representatives when part-timers were to be hired.[14]

The European Works Councils Directive has as its raison d'être the policy of consultation over a wide range of issues deemed to be of collective concern to employees. The policy has extrapolated from the point where decision-making regarding an individual worker affects other workers, to where decision-making affecting employees in an establishment in one Member State affects employees in establishments of the same enterprise in another Member State. This last example of the way in which transnational decision-making brings in its train the EU policy of involvement of the collective representatives of workers was particularly evident in the 1992 amendments to the 1975 Directive.

TRANSNATIONAL DIMENSION

The transnational dimension of decision-making on collective dismissals was not addressed in the original Directive in 1975. However, the profile of the issue had been raised sufficiently high to register on the eleven Member States who approved the Charter of Fundamental Social Rights of December 1989. Points 17 and 18 of the Charter state:[15]

'Information, consultation and participation for workers must be developed along appropriate lines, taking account of the practices in force in the various Member States.

This shall apply particularly in companies or groups of companies having establishments in two or more Member States of the European Community.

Such information, consultation and participation must be implemented in due time, particularly ... in cases of collective redundancy procedures ...'

The Commission's Action Programme, which aimed to implement the 1989 Charter, followed this recognition of the transnational dimension of dismissal decisions by proposing revision of the 1975 Directive with specific emphasis given to this dimension:[16]

'The directive on collective redundancies should be completed so as to cover cases where the redundancy decision is taken by a decision-making centre or an undertaking located in another Member State.

... There will most certainly be cases of transfrontier restructuring which, justified though they may be, will have to be accompanied by appropriate information and consultation. A response at Community level appears the most appropriate approach especially since the directive should apply in cases where the decision concerning collective redundancies is taken by a decision-making centre or an undertaking located in another Member State.

This legal loophole should be eliminated.'

---

13   Directive 91/383 of 25 June 1991 supplementing the measures to encourage improvements in the safety and health at work of workers with a fixed-duration employment relationship or a temporary employment relationship. See Chapter 31.
14   See Chapter 30.
15   The significance of this, and developments described hereafter, is apparent in their explication in the Explanatory Memorandum of 16 September 1991, which accompanied the proposed amendment to the 1975 Directive.
16   Action Programme, quoted ibid, paragraph 4.

The Explanatory Memorandum of the proposed Amending Directive gave details on the impact of the internal market on corporate reorganisations within the Community and the resulting significant increase in mergers, takeovers, transfers and joint ventures, leading to the growing concentration of company ownership. A report on the acquisitions (majority holdings or mergers) effected by the top 1,000 European industrial enterprises showed that, over the 1980s, the number of such operations had doubled every three years, rising from 108 in 1984–85 to 492 in 1988–89. These operations were not only national, but increasingly transnational:[17]

> 'National-type operations (between two enterprises belonging to the same Member State) largely dominated between 1983 and 1987. Almost two-thirds of the number of acquisitions recorded involved this type of operation. Since 1987, more rapid growth has been noted in the number of acquisitions involving Community enterprises belonging to two different Member States. In 1988–89, such operations represented 40% of the total number of acquisitions effected. International-level operations involving two enterprises – the one Community, the other non-Community – accounted for approximately 15% of the total number of operations recorded.'

The implications of these developments for the EU policy on collective dismissals were spelled out in the Explanatory Memorandum:[18]

> 'In the context of this accelerating corporate restructuring, an increasing number of employees will be affected by key corporate decisions taken at a level higher than their immediate employer, or at group level by controlling undertakings situated either within or, increasingly, outside the country where their own establishment or undertaking is located. Despite the growing complexity in company organisation, ownership and control, the existing procedures for informing and consulting employees and employee representatives are still confined to enterprise level (though there is legislation concerning national group-level works councils or equivalent bodies in a few Member States). This means that, although employees may be part of an undertaking whose headquarters are located in a different country or which belongs to a group of undertakings whose controlling undertaking is located abroad, the scope and effectiveness of their information and consultation rights could be endangered if the decision-making centre chooses not to provide the employer with the required information.
> The 1975 Directive ... does not make specific provision for situations in which redundancies among an employing undertaking's employees are proposed by its controlling undertaking whether the controlling undertaking is situated in the same Member State as the controlled undertaking (the employer) or in a different State. However, it cannot be assumed that "all relevant information" (Article 2(3)) held by a controlling undertaking concerning the proposed redundancies will always be provided to the employing undertaking for the purposes of consulting worker representatives.
> Similarly, where the central administration of a multi-establishment undertaking proposes to make workers redundant in one of its establishments, the existing directive does not make specific provision for the disclosure to local management of all relevant information held by the central administration where it is situated outside the Member State in which the establishment concerned is situated.'

Corporate decision-making processes which are outside the establishment or undertaking in which the employees are being dismissed will usually involve

---

17 Ibid, paragraph 6. Detailed figures for the years from 1983–84 to 1988–89 were given in paragraph 7.
18 Ibid, paragraphs 8–10.

consideration of factors extraneous to that establishment or undertaking. Information regarding other establishments and undertakings, including their workforces, will be relevant to the dismissal decision. The dismissal decision is a matter of collective concern to employees outside the undertaking, and possibly also outside the Member State.

The amendment proposed and eventually approved was modest: [19]

'The obligations laid down ... shall apply irrespective of whether the decision regarding collective redundancies is being taken by the employer or by an undertaking controlling the employer.

In considering alleged breaches of the information, consultation and notification requirements laid down by this Directive, account shall not be taken of any defence on the part of the employer on the ground that the necessary information has not been provided to the employer by the undertaking which took the decision leading to collective redundancies.'

The Explanatory Memorandum observed that: [20]

'The main changes proposed are to fulfil the aim of ensuring the enforcement of the existing directive in cases of transnational undertakings and associated undertakings, Thus, it is provided that the information and consultation requirements laid down by the directive apply irrespective of whether the decisions entailing collective redundancies are taken by the employer himself, by a controlling undertaking or by the central administration of a multi-establishment undertaking. In order to reinforce this central obligation it is also established that an employer's failure to comply with the directive's requirements can not be condoned on the ground that the undertaking taking the decision leading to collective redundancies failed to inform the employer in due time.'

The Memorandum was careful to point out, however, that: [1]

'... the revised text does not directly impose any obligation on controlling undertakings as such. Problems of extraterritoriality are therefore avoided. It should also be noted that the Commission is not proposing a mechanism (as envisaged under the original draft of the "Vredeling" directive) whereby employees would have the right to seek consultation with the undertaking's central administration or with the management of a controlling undertaking (the so-called "by-pass" system).'

The amendment builds on the foundation of the employer's obligation. The employer remains the subject of the obligation. But it is recognised that the legal structure of the employer may be articulated with other undertakings nationally and transnationally, so that dismissals in the employer's undertaking may be decided by, or be the consequence of decisions by, other undertakings.

The obligations of the employer dismissing the workers are likely to be affected in significant ways as a consequence. Breach of the obligation to provide information is not to be excused by reason of lack of information due to failure of the other undertaking to provide it. But the requirement of consultation is also not to be excused by reason of lack of information. One possible consequence is the undermining of the *Nielsen* decision, which rejected the argument that the employer was liable for failure to consult where he ought

19   New Article 2(4) substituted by the 1992 Amending Directive, Article 1(2).
20   Op cit, paragraph 14.
 1   Ibid, paragraph 16.

reasonably to have contemplated dismissals.[2] After the 1992 amendment, no account is to be taken of any defence to liability where the employer pleads he has not been provided with the necessary information. If, thereafter, the reason the employer produces for not having consulted is failure to contemplate dismissals due to lack of information, this defence will not be taken into account. He will be deemed to have known, even where he might not reasonably have been expected to know.

This is reinforced by the reference to the role of 'the undertaking which took the decision leading to collective redundancies'. This decision is not necessarily the decision to dismiss, but is a 'decision leading to collective redundancies', a decision which has that consequence. Many decisions of other undertakings, controlling undertakings and others, may affect the employment decisions of an employer.[3] It is the employer's task to keep abreast of developments by awareness of decisions affecting him. If he fails to do so, he cannot plead ignorance.

Once again, the feature which stands out is the Directive's emphasis on dismissal not being the problem of an isolated individual, but an event linked with other decisions, even those taken in other undertakings and other countries. This is consistent with the general move towards treating dismissals as a collective issue.

The Directive is still contingent on the employer 'contemplating collective redundancies', even if he may not be able to defend himself where it is lack of information which led to breach of his obligations. There are many other individual employment issues which are as potentially collective in their causes and interrelated to other decision-makers as dismissals. This is recognised in the Council Directive on European Works Councils, which expands the obligations of the 1975 Directive to a wide range of such issues. The lineaments of Community policy on labour and the enterprise are emerging with some degree of clarity.

---

2 Case 284/83: *Dansk Metalarbejderforbund and Specialarbejderforbundet i Danmark v H Nielsen & Son, Maskinfabrik A/S* [1985] ECR 553.
3 Subparagraph 2 of the amended Article 2(4), unlike subparagraph 1, does not refer to controlling undertakings.

Chapter 18

The Acquired Rights Directive 1977

INTRODUCTION

The 1977 Directive has generated a much greater volume of case law by the European Court than the 1975 Directive. This included infringement proceedings under Article 169 where Commission complaints were upheld against Belgium, Italy and the UK, but also a number of references by national courts to the European Court for preliminary rulings under Article 177 to interpret provisions of the Directive.

The 1977 Directive sits uneasily on the cusp between the EU's policy on labour in the enterprise and the free labour market policy of the common market origins of the EU. It is not concerned with labour *in* the enterprise; its subject matter is rather labour mobility *between* enterprises. The free movement of labour is constrained by the Directive's prescribing collective labour rights going beyond the information and consultation obligations in the 1975 Directive, and adding to these individual employment protection rights for workers concerned. Common market inspiration is compromised by the inherent conflict between a policy of free labour markets and harmonisation policy aimed at a level playing field for competing employers. By going beyond labour *in* the enterprise, the Directive has confronted a number of issues which cast a new light on the mobility of labour in the common market. Mobility of labour between enterprises is to be regulated in a way unthinkable in relation to labour on the open market.

The Directive also addressed fundamental issues in the law of competition. Competition spawns the phenomenon of takeover or merger of enterprises. In competition between enterprises, the role played by labour costs is often central. The Directive imposed a limit on the use of labour costs as a factor in competition law. Three issues illustrate these themes:

1. The policy of reducing the role of labour costs in competition between enterprises was given a high profile in a context of fashionable privatisation.
2. The shifting focus of the Directive between regulation of transfers of undertakings and protection of employees created tensions when definitions of the 'enterprise' were found by the European Court to be too rigid, a cause of such unease on the part of some Member States as to provoke attempts at amendment of the Directive.
3. The blurring of boundaries between protection of labour *in* the enterprise and outside it raises the question of the relevance of the Directive's policy to transformations *within* the enterprise.

LABOUR STANDARDS AND COMPETITION

The Acquired Rights Directive, as its title indicates, aims at 'the approximation of the laws of the Member States relating to the safeguarding of employees' rights in the event of transfers of undertakings, businesses or parts of businesses'. Competition between enterprises can be based on many factors: technology, product quality, and so on. Labour costs are another factor which will affect an employer's competitive performance. Where labour costs are not a relevant factor in a transfer, the Directive may be less critical in ensuring that labour standards are maintained for the employees affected.

It is where labour costs *are* a factor in transfers that the Directive's impact may be significant. It aims to regulate transfers of undertakings in which labour costs play a role. The transfer of an undertaking from one employer to another, when an object of the exercise is to cut labour costs, encounters the safeguards of the Directive. In the words of Article 3(1):

'The transferor's rights and obligations arising from a contract of employment or from an employment relationship existing on the date of a transfer ... shall, by reason of such transfer, be transferred to the transferee.'

Further, Article 3(2) provides:

'Following the transfer ... the transferee shall continue to observe the terms and conditions agreed in any collective agreement on the same terms applicable to the transferor under that agreement, until the date of termination or expiry of the collective agreement or the entry into force or application of another collective agreement.

Member States may limit the period for observing such terms and conditions, with the proviso that it shall not be less than one year.'

Terms and conditions of employment in contracts and collective agreements are to be safeguarded; but employment itself is not always guaranteed where the transfer brings with it changes in the numbers employed:[1]

'The transfer of an undertaking, business or part of a business shall not in itself constitute grounds for dismissal by the transferor or the transferee. This provision shall not stand in the way of dismissals that may take place for economic, technical or organisational reasons entailing changes in the workforce.'

The safeguarding of terms and conditions of employment by the Directive is not permanent. The Directive does not preclude changes being introduced subsequently to the transfer, subject to the one-year guarantee of collectively agreed terms and conditions. But the uncertainty of when, how and whether reductions in labour costs could be achieved following a transfer may deter those transfers undertaken with the aim of profiting from lower labour standards.

The scope of the Directive is confined to situations where employees are involved in the transfer of an undertaking. However, the principle it expresses is of fundamental importance to labour in the enterprise: competition, at least in this specific situation, is not to include labour costs. Labour standards are to be protected by ensuring that where competition leads to transfers of undertakings, labour standards are maintained.

---

1   Article 4(1).

The significance of the EU policy on labour standards and competition embodied in the Acquired Rights Directive has been most marked in the case of enterprises 'contracting out' parts of their business to other employers. This was possible where it was considered that certain parts of the business could be separated off to be performed by other employers at lower cost. Bidders competing for such contracts were subject to the Directive. Bids based on lower labour costs were unable, due to the Directive's requirements, to guarantee that the labour costs of employees transferred to them would be lower. So where labour costs related to labour standards *were* a significant factor in a contract, the Directive operated to obstruct the contracting-out process by guaranteeing the maintenance of labour standards after the transfer.

The most vivid application of the principle excluding labour costs from competition between enterprises was the case of privatisation policy in the UK. 'Contracting-out' policies were aggressively pursued by the Conservative government elected in the UK in 1979, both at central and local government level. The contracting-out to private enterprises of services previously undertaken by public authorities was undertaken voluntarily by Conservative local administrations and then made a matter of legal obligation by legislation ('compulsory competitive tendering' – CCT).[2]

As the name indicates, the essence of the policy was competition among enterprises for contracts. This competition among bidders potentially included competition over labour costs. In many cases, the existing workforce would be taken over by the successful bidder. The transfer of a part of the business with its workforce would normally have meant that the employees transferred benefited from the protection of the Directive. Bids would have to specify that employees transferred to the successfully bidding contractor would continue to benefit from their existing terms and conditions of employment. Bids based on the calculation of lower labour costs through a reduction in labour standards and a lowering of terms and conditions of employment would be violating the Directive.

However, the Transfer of Undertakings (Protection of Employment) Regulations 1981 (TUPE), which transposed the 1977 Directive into UK law, defined an 'undertaking' covered by the Regulations as follows:[3]

'"undertaking" includes any trade or business but does not include any undertaking or part of an undertaking which is not in the nature of a commercial venture.'

This exclusion of non-commercial ventures was taken to mean that the contracting-out by central and local governments of services they provided was not the transfer of an 'undertaking' and not covered by the Regulations or the Directive. Hence, bids providing for a reduction in labour standards to the detriment of terms and conditions of employees transferred were accepted and often successful. Thousands of employees transferred suffered from worse conditions of employment.

That this exclusion of transfers of undertakings 'not in the nature of a commercial venture' was not warranted by the Directive gradually became clear, in

---

2   B Napier *CCT, Market Testing and Employment Rights; The Effects of TUPE and the Acquired Rights Directive*, Institute of Employment Rights, London 1993.
3   SI 1981 No 1794, reg 2(1).

particular, in the decision of the European Court in *Dr Sophie Redmond Stichting* which concerned the transfer of activities of a foundation financed wholly out of public funds.[4] These were held to be of an economic nature in the sense that the same type of activity could equally have been carried on by a profit-making body:[5]

'. . . the fact that in this case the origin of the operation lies in the grant of subsidies to foundations or associations whose services are allegedly provided without remuneration does not exclude that operation from the scope of the directive. The directive . . . is designed to ensure that employees' rights are safeguarded, and covers all employees who enjoy some, albeit limited, protection against dismissal under national law . . .'

The exclusion in the UK Regulations was subsequently removed by the Trade Union Reform and Employment Rights Act 1993.[6] However, the Commission of the EC had meanwhile complained to the European Court that the UK Regulations violated the Directive as not applying to transfers of non-profit-making undertakings.

The UK government maintained that the Directive did not apply to transfers of non-profit-making undertakings on the ground that such undertakings 'which are not engaged in "economic activities" within the meaning of the Treaty, do not come within its scope'. This argument was rejected by the Court:[7]

'. . . the fact that an undertaking is engaged in non-profit-making activities is not in itself sufficient to deprive such activities of their economic character or to remove the undertaking from the scope of the directive.'

One consequence of this judgment is that where employees transferred with worse conditions have suffered loss, they may be able to claim compensation from the UK government for its failure to properly implement the Directive under the ruling in *Francovich*. Even before the European Court's judgment, the TUC had written to the government in July 1993 pointing out the failure of the Regulations adequately to transpose the Directive and seeking compensation for those who had suffered. It was reported in January 1994 that five public sector trade unions had issued 128 writs against the government in connection with employees affected by CCT exercises by local authorities and contracting-out exercises in the civil service and health service. The claim was that these employees either lost their jobs or were re-employed by contractors at lower rates of pay or on less favourable terms and conditions by the exclusion in the Regulations.[8]

The 1977 Directive was conceived in a context far removed from privatisation policies. Nonetheless, the principle it embodied – no competition over labour standards in the enterprise – was of profound significance.[9] The extent to which, albeit belatedly, EU law in the form of this Directive may circumscribe UK government policy on privatisation is an eloquent reminder of the supranational regulatory potential of EU labour law.

4 Case C-29/91: *Dr Sophie Redmond Stichting v Bartol* [1992] ECR I-3189.
5 Ibid, paragraph 18.
6 Section 26.
7 Case C-382/92: *EC Commission v UK* [1994] ECR I-2435, paragraph 45.
8 IRS, *Industrial Relations Law Bulletin*, No 488, January 1994, p 16.
9 Another manifestation of this policy is in the EU regulations governing public procurement policy, which also constrains bidders to adhere to specified labour standards. See Chapter 27.

LABOUR AND THE DEFINITION OF THE ENTERPRISE

The Directive refers to the 'transfer of an undertaking, business or part of a business'. The definition of these terms became crucial when what was being *transferred* comprised *wholly or mainly employees*, whose rights were to be safeguarded by the Directive. The question became whether labour activities could be a, or, indeed, *the* criterion of what constitutes an undertaking or enterprise within the meaning of the Directive. The resultant definitions of the undertaking by the European Court were a cause of such unease on the part of some Member States as to provoke attempts at amendment of the Directive.

The European Court's perception of labour in the enterprise surfaced in a number of cases on the 1977 Directive. *Botzen* concerned whether the Directive applied to employees who:[10]

'although not belonging to the part of the undertaking which was transferred, carry on certain activities using the assets assigned to the transferred part, or who, being assigned to the administrative department of the undertaking which was not itself transferred, carried out certain duties for the benefit of the transferred part of the undertaking.'

The Court answered in the negative. It held:[11]

'An employment relationship is essentially characterised by the link existing between the employee and the part of the undertaking or business to which he is assigned to carry out his duties. In order to decide whether the rights and obligations under an employment relationship are transferred under Directive No 77/187 . . . it is therefore sufficient to establish to which part of the undertaking or business the employee was assigned.'

In the European Court's view, therefore, Article 3(1) of the Directive did not cover employees who performed duties involving use of assets transferred, but who were not themselves employed in the part of the undertaking transferred. To be part of a transferred undertaking, activities by employees need to be connected by an employment relationship with the transferred undertaking.

An employment relationship with the transferred undertaking may be *necessary* for the employees to be protected by the Directive. But are such employment relationships and activities *sufficient* to constitute an undertaking? Can labour in the enterprise qualify as a, or, indeed, *the* constituting element in an enterprise, so that transfer of employees is equivalent to transfer of an undertaking?

In *Spijkers*, this possibility was acknowledged as the European Court chose to qualify the criterion for an undertaking covered by the Directive in the following terms:[12]

'. . . the decisive criterion for establishing whether there is a transfer for the purposes of the directive is whether the business in question retains its identity.

Consequently, a transfer of an undertaking, business or part of a business does not occur merely because its assets are disposed of. Instead it is necessary to consider, in a case such as the present, whether the business was disposed of as a going concern,

---

10 Case 186/83: *Botzen v Rotterdamsche Droogdok Maatschappij BV* [1985] ECR 519, paragraph 11.
11 Ibid, paragraph 15.
12 Case 24/85: *Spijkers v Gebroeders Benedik Abbatoir CV and Alfred Benedik en Zonen BV* [1986] ECR 1119, paragraphs 11–14.

as would be indicated, inter alia, by the fact that its operation was actually continued or resumed by the new employer, with the same or similar activities.

In order to determine whether those conditions are met, it is necessary to consider all the facts characterising the transaction in question, including the type of under-taking or business, whether or not the business's tangible assets, such as buildings and movable property, are transferred, the value of its intangible assets at the time of the transfer, whether or not the majority of its employees are taken over by the new employer, whether or not its customers are transferred and the degree of similarity between the activities carried on before and after the transfer and the period, if any, for which those activities were suspended. It should be noted, however, that all those circumstances are merely single factors in the overall assessment which must be made and cannot therefore be considered in isolation.

It is for the national court to make the necessary factual appraisal, in the light of the criteria for interpretation set out above, in order to establish whether or not there is a transfer in the sense indicated above.'

On this ruling, it seemed that the labour activities of employees transferred could in themselves constitute an undertaking, if they constituted a 'business (which) retains its identity', and this 'would be indicated, inter alia, by the fact that its operation was actually continued or resumed by the new employer, with the same or similar activities'.

The possibility of labour activities being sufficient to qualify as an undertaking falling under the Directive seemed to be reinforced by the European Court in *Rask*.[13] The case concerned the contracting out of the operation of four canteens owned by Phillips. Under the contract, ISS undertook all the planning, purchasing, preparation and other tasks involved in the running of the canteen, and also agreed to take over the staff previously employed by Phillips on the same conditions. Phillips paid a monthly sum related to the running of the canteen – pay, work clothes, management, products such as place settings and linen and so on, and placed at the disposal of ISS all premises, equipment and facilities needed for running the canteen.

On these facts, the European Court held that, although the only items transferred to ISS were the contracts of employment of employees previously employed by Phillips, there had been a transfer of a business retaining its identity – the business in question being the provision of canteen services.

Nonetheless, the decision as to whether a transfer has taken place remains one for the national court. The difficulty of the British courts confronted with this possible identification of the enterprise with the labour of its employees was evident in the *Dines* case.[14]

The Local Government Act 1988 required local authorities to put certain of their services out to competitive tendering. The health authorities for some years had been obliged to invite private contractors to tender to undertake certain ancillary work, including general cleaning of hospitals. These contracts were awarded on a periodical basis. In *Dines*, Initial Services had a 3-year contract for cleaning a hospital which expired on 30 April 1991. In January 1991 the authority invited tenders for cleaning the hospital from 1 May. Pall Mall Services was awarded a 3-year contract from 1 May.

All the applicant employees were declared redundant and their employment

---

13   Case C-209/91: *Rask v ISS Kantineservice A/S* [1993] IRLR 133.
14   *Dines v Initial Health Care Services Ltd and Pall Mall Services Group Ltd* [1993] IRLR 521, EAT; on appeal [1994] IRLR 336, CA.

terminated on 30 April. Under the new contract, Pall Mall Services introduced its own management, equipment, stock and supplies, but offered the applicants new employment starting 1 May. The question was whether they were covered by the Transfer Regulations. The Industrial Tribunal concluded:[15]

'. . . looking at all the circumstances in this case we are satisfied there was no transfer of equipment, materials or goodwill from (Initial) to (Pall Mall) and that there was not a transfer of an undertaking or . . . an "economic unit" to which the Regulations apply. (Initial), when they had the cleaning contract, carried on their business at the hospital premises. That business ceased when their contract expired and the Authority permitted a new business to provide the services when they contracted with Pall Mall. We appreciate that it is immaterial having regard to the provisions of 3(2) of the Regulations, whether a business is sold. The fact that a business is not sold does not mean there cannot be a transfer within the meaning of the Regulations.[16]

However, when one company enters into competition with a number of other companies to obtain a contract as happened in this case and a different company wins the contract from the contractor that was previously providing the services then this is a cessation of the business of the first contractors on the hospital premises, and the commencement of a new business by (Pall Mall) when they are awarded the contract. The fact that (Pall Mall) employed the same workforce at the same workplace is not in this case a factor giving rise to a transfer under the Regulations for the reasons given in this Decision.'

The EAT upheld the Tribunal's decision; but, despite argument that the cleaning services did not constitute an undertaking, declined to make a ruling on this point.

The EAT delivered its decision on 31 August 1993. On 14 April 1994, the European Court delivered its judgment in *Schmidt.*[17] Christel Schmidt was employed as the only cleaner in a branch of a German bank. The bank decided to contract out the cleaning and the contractor offered to employ Mrs. Schmidt on an hourly rate of pay which she claimed was inferior to her previous wage. The Labour Court referred the following preliminary questions to the European Court:

'1. May an undertaking's cleaning operations, if they are transferred by contract to a different firm, be treated as part of a business within the meaning of Directive 77/187/EEC?

2. If the answer to question 1 is in principle in the affirmative, does that also apply if prior to the transfer the cleaning operations were undertaken by a single employee?'

The European Court answered both questions in the affirmative. As to the first:[18]

'The protection provided by the Directive applies in particular, by virtue of Article 1(1), where the transfer relates only to a business or part of a business; that is to say,

---

15 Paragraph 10 of the judgment of the Tribunal, quoted in the decision of the EAT, ibid.
16 Reg 3(2) provides: 'Subject as aforesaid, these Regulations so apply whether the transfer is effected by sale or by some other disposition or by operation of law'. It is the transfer of the undertaking which is important, not the legal mechanism through which this transfer is accomplished. Case 287/86: *Landsorganisationen i Danmark for Tjenerforbundet i Danmark v Ny Molle Kro* [1987] ECR 5465; Case 324/86: *Foreningen af Arbejdsledere i Danmark v Daddy's Dance Hall A/S* [1988] ECR 739.
17 Case C-392/92: *Schmidt v Spar- und Leihkasse der Fruheren amter Bordesholm, Kiel und Cronshagen* [1994] IRLR 302.
18 Ibid, paragraphs 13–14.

a part of an undertaking. In those circumstances the transfer relates to employees assigned to that part of the undertaking since, as the Court held in its judgment in *Botzen v Rotterdamsche Droogdok Maatschappij BV*: 186/83 [1985] ECR 519 at paragraph 15, an employment relationship is essentially characterised by the link between the employee and the part of the undertaking or business to which he is assigned to carry out his duties.

Thus, when an undertaking entrusts by contract the responsibility for operating one of its services, such as cleaning, to another undertaking which thereby assumes the obligations of an employer towards employees assigned to those duties, that operation may come within the scope of the Directive. As the Court held at paragraph 17 of its judgment in *Rask* ... the fact that in such a case the activity transferred is for the transferor merely an ancillary activity not necessarily connected with its objects cannot have the effect of excluding that operation from the scope of the Directive.'

On the second question the Court emphasised: [19]

'It should be noted that one of the objectives of the Directive, as clearly stated in the second recital in the preamble thereto, is to protect employees in the event of a change of employer, in particular to ensure that their rights are safeguarded. That protection extends to all staff and must therefore be guaranteed even where only one employee is affected by the transfer.'

Both the German and the UK Governments, intervening in the case, had argued that the absence of any transfer of tangible assets excluded the possibility of the transfer of a business. Their arguments followed the logic of defining the enterprise in terms other than the activities of the employees. The Court rejected their arguments: [20]

'The fact that in its case law the Court includes the transfer of such assets among the various factors to be taken into account by a national court to enable it, when assessing a complex transaction as a whole, to decide whether an undertaking has in fact been transferred does not support the conclusion that the absence of these factors precludes the existence of a transfer. The safeguarding of employees' rights, which constitutes the subject-matter of the Directive, as is clear from its actual title, cannot depend exclusively on consideration of a factor which the Court has in any event already held not to be decisive on its own (judgment in *Spijkers v Benedik*: 24/85 [1986] ECR 1119 at paragraph 12).

According to the case law of the Court (see the judgment in *Spijkers*, cited above, at paragraph 11, and the judgment in *Dr Sophie Redmond Stichting v Bartol*: C-29/91 [1992] IRLR 366 at paragraph 23), the decisive criterion for establishing whether there is a transfer for the purposes of the Directive is whether the business in question retains its identity. According to the case law, the retention of that identity is indicated inter alia by the actual continuation or resumption by the new employer of the same or similar activities. Thus, in this case ... the similarity in the cleaning work performed before and after the transfers – which is reflected, moreover, in the offer to re-engage the employee in question – is typical of an operation which comes within the scope of the Directive and which gives the employee whose activity has been transferred the protection afforded to him by that Directive.'

One month after the judgment in *Schmidt*, on 19 May 1994, the Court of Appeal allowed the appeal against the decision of the EAT and the Industrial

19 Ibid, paragraph 15.
20 Ibid, paras 16–17.

Tribunal in *Dines*. Reviewing the decisions of the European Court, Neill LJ, delivering the judgment of the Court of Appeal, stated that:[1]

> 'It will be seen that a possible transfer of an undertaking can take place in a number of different circumstances, including the following . . .
> (a) The undertaking may be sold direct by A to B,
> (b) A may carry on certain activities as part of its business and then decide to contract these activities out to B,
> (c) A may be carrying on an undertaking on B's premises and then, at the expiration of a lease or for some other reason, a similar undertaking may be carried on thereafter either by B or by a new lessee, C. Effectively, the reason for the cessation of A's activities on B's premises may be as a result of a system of competitive tendering whereby after the cessation of A's contract the activities are carried on by C.'

He then referred to the European Court's judgment in *Schmidt* and quoted from paragraph 12 of that judgment:[2]

> 'According to the case law of the Court (*Rask* at paragraph 15) the Directive is applicable where, following a legal transfer or merger, there is a change in the legal or natural person who is responsible for carrying on the business and who by virtue of that fact incurs the obligations of an employer vis-à-vis the employees of the undertaking, *regardless of whether or not ownership of the undertaking is transferred*' (italics added).

He then went on to declare the Industrial Tribunal's view as to competitive tendering bringing the losing contractor's business to an end so as to preclude a transfer, quoted above in paragraph 10 their judgment, to be a misdirection:[3]

> 'The European cases demonstrate that the fact that another company takes over the provision of certain services as a result of competitive tendering does not mean that the first business or undertaking necessarily comes to an end . . . a transfer may take place in two phases.'

The *Schmidt* case, confirmed in the British context by the Court of Appeal in *Dines*, was a severe blow to the privatisation process in so far as it was founded on competitive undercutting of labour costs by contractors. It was not the death knell, however, as the European Court made clear the limits of the protection extended to employees by the Directive:[4]

> 'It may, however, be noted that while Article 4(1) of the Directive provides that the transfer of an undertaking or part of an undertaking cannot in itself constitute grounds for dismissal by the transferor or the transferee, that provision does not stand in the way of dismissals for economic, technical or organisational reasons entailing changes in the workforce.
> Finally, it should also be borne in mind that the Directive does not preclude an amendment to the employment relationship with the new employer, in so far as national law allows such an amendment otherwise than through a transfer of the undertaking . . .'

Despite these inherent limitations on the Directive's potential impact on employers' labour cost-cutting, the response of some Member States was fast

---

1 *Dines v Initial Health Care Services Ltd and Pall Mall Services Group Ltd* [1994] IRLR 336, at paragraph 42.
2 Ibid, paragraph 44.
3 Ibid, paragraphs 47–48.
4 *Schmidt*, paragraphs 18–19.

and furious. It surfaced in documents of the Commission which emerged proposing amendments to the Directive. In a Background Report, the Commission explained its intention to 'update' the Directive with a replacement for the original Directive in its entirety. Among other proposals, the updated Directive was to 'clarify' the term 'undertaking':[5]

'The Directive does not apply where only an activity of an undertaking is transferred and there is no transfer of an economic entity in its own right. On this point the directive follows case law. For the avoidance of doubt an economic entity means a self contained set of elements pursuing a specified economic objective. The Court considers each case should be taken on its merits looking at the characteristics of the transaction, tangible and intangible assets transferred, the number of employees transferred, the transfer of customers and principally whether the entity transferred was self contained and different from the other activities of the undertaking.'

The proposed revision lays down that the Directive:[6]

'shall not apply in the event of the transfer of only an activity of an undertaking, unless an economic entity which retains its identity is also transferred at the same time'.[7]

The Commission's proposed revision of the Transfer of Undertakings Directive narrowed its scope by subtly distinguishing three situations:

(a) an activity *only* is transferred: the Directive does not apply;
(b) an activity is transferred, which *also* constitutes an entity: the Directive applies;
(c) an activity is transferred *together* with an economic entity: the Directive applies.

The danger lies in the first of these situations. It misleadingly implies that an activity alone *cannot* fall under the Directive. This is wrong. The Commission tries to cover itself by allowing that an activity which is *also* an entity is covered. But the damage is done by the implication that an 'activity' may not be covered. The proposed revision can be attacked on three grounds.

First, it ignores the wording of the Directive: 'part of a business'. The Directive covers the transfer of any 'undertaking, business or *part* of a business'. The gloss of 'economic entity' put on the Directive by Court decisions does not diminish the Directive's coverage of transfers of *parts* of a business. As the Commission says:

'the business consists of several parts operating autonomously and pursuing a specific economic objective, even if a partial one.'

---

5 Background Report, *The Acquired Rights Directive*, ISEC/B2/95, p 5.
6 File Note of the Commission.
7 The focus on *activities*, in contrast to *economic entities* has potential discriminatory consequences due to *occupational* sex segregation in the workforce. Sex segregation means that certain activities are carried out predominantly by men or women. Designating activities as excluded from the scope of the Directive will disproportionately affect women engaging in those activities characterised by occupational sex segregation. This has to be justified in accordance with objective criteria which satisfy the requirements, inter alia, of proportionality. The indirect sex discrimination resulting from contracting-out was highlighted by a report published by the UK Equal Opportunities Commission in 1995: K Escott and D Whitfield 'The gender impact of CCT in local government'; see the summary in *IRS Employment Trends*, No 585, June 1995, p 14.

The 'economic entity' transferred is characterised by the Commission as 'the continuation or restarting by the new management of the same or similar economic *activities*'. The Commission concedes:

> 'From an intellectual point of view it is difficult to imagine the transfer of an activity involving workers without the simultaneous transfer of an "economic entity".'

Is it possible to imagine the transfer of an *activity* without the 'continuation or restarting by the new management of the same or similar economic *activities*'?

Secondly, it contradicts the decisions of the European Court. The Commission presents a distinction of:

> 'two completely different situations:
> (a) transfer of an *activity only* and
> (b) transfer of an activity *and* of an economic entity,
> without, however, diminishing the level of protection which workers currently enjoy'.

The Court had confined the scope of the Directive to the transfer of an 'economic entity'. It had *not* explicitly recognised any distinction with 'activities', so as to exclude 'an activity only'. The Commission's case is that an activity *on its own* is not enough; there must *additionally* also be an entity – either because the activity itself consists of one, or is accompanied by one.

But the Commission gives three examples (catering, document reproduction, cleaning) which betray its case by contradicting the Court's definition of an entity. In each example, the sole factor distinguishing an entity from an activity is the presence of machinery or equipment:

- serving meals with 'all elements necessary for the preparation of such meals';
- document reproduction 'with photocopiers and all necessary equipment';
- cleaning 'with trolleys, auxiliary equipment, etc.'

Yet the Commission cites the Court as defining an entity by taking into account 'all the facts characterising the transaction in question': property, employees, intangible assets, activities, customers, etc. The Court does *not* single out *any* of these as *not* being capable of constituting, or being *essential* to constitute an economic entity. The Commission does.

By singling out an 'activity' as *not* sufficient for a transfer to be covered, it contradicts the Court. The Court has not excluded the possibility that activities alone may constitute an entity. Similarly, by singling out machinery and equipment as a *necessary* element, it contradicts the Court. The Court has clearly ruled out the need for machinery and equipment to accompany an activity in order to constitute an entity.

Thirdly, it is contrary to the objective of the Directive, which is the protection of employees' rights, not the protection of employers who transfer activities. In asserting that the Directive applies to both public and private entities, the Commission states: 'It is the legal status of the workers which counts'.

It is the transfer of the activities of employees which above all engages the Directive. Only then does the provision in Article 3: maintenance of the continuity of contractual rights and obligations, apply.[8] In so far as activity means labour, to exclude 'only activities' from the scope of the Directive runs the risk of contradicting its objective. This is the logic of the *Schmidt* case. Transfer of

---

8 Transfer of machinery, assets, buildings, customers, etc does not affect such rights, though it may engage other obligations upon the transferor employer vis-à-vis the employees.

the labour of even a single employee is to be protected.

It may be true on a set of facts that 'The mere fact that employees are transferred is not sufficient'. But it is equally true that it *may* be sufficient. The Commission's proposal that the Directive not apply in the event of transfer of only an activity misleadingly implies that an activity alone *cannot* be sufficient to fall under the Directive. This is wrong. An activity alone can be an economic entity. The Commission admits as much when it allows that an activity which is also an entity is covered. Any amendment which undermines the potential of an activity alone constituting an economic entity contradicts the present objective, structure and wording of the Directive.

In conclusion, the key issue is whether the proposed revision of Article 1(1) does overturn *Schmidt*. The effort to narrow the scope of the Directive can be portrayed as dividing a spectrum composed as follows:

COVERED   NOT COVERED

undertaking . . . entity . . . parts of undertaking . . . activity/entity . . . . activity only

The proposed separation of 'activity/entity' from 'activity only' is a subtle distortion of the Court's decisions. These *do* require the transfer of an entity. The nature of such an entity depends on the facts. It is clear, however, that an activity does *not* require machinery or equipment to constitute an economic entity. Also, it *may* be composed of an activity only.

It is incorrect to state that the Directive:

'shall not apply in the event of the transfer of only an activity of an undertaking, unless an economic entity which retains its identity is transferred at the same time.'

It is incorrect in implying a distinction between activity and entity, and requiring *both* to be transferred at the same time. This is misleading since activity and entity can be one and the same. The correct formulation would be that the Directive:

'shall apply in the event of the transfer of only an activity of an undertaking, when it constitutes an economic entity which retains its identity.'

Amendments to or replacements of the Directive require unanimity among the Member States voting in Council. It is by no means clear that such unanimity will be forthcoming on the Commission's proposal.

The wider significance of this debate over the Court's interpretation of the Directive is that it highlights the EU policy towards labour in the enterprise. The Court expresses this policy by its insistence that the activity of employees can be a central and defining element of the undertaking, and that the objective of the 1977 Directive is to protect employees.[9] The protection extended by the

---

9   After this passage was written, the Court appears to have raised doubts over its position by the decision in *Rygaard* (Case C-48/94: *Ledernes Hovedorganisation (acting for Rygaard) v Dansk Arbejdsgiverforening (acting for Stro Molle Akustik A/S)* [1996] IRLR 51, decided 19 September 1995. The Court cited *Spijkers* and *Schmidt*, but stated (paragraphs 20–2):

'The authorities cited above presuppose that the transfer relates to a stable economic entity whose activity is not limited to performing one specific works contract.

That is not the case of an undertaking which transfers to another undertaking one of its building works with a view to the completion of that work. Such a transfer could come within the terms of the directive only if it included the transfer of a body of assets enabling the activities or certain activities of the transferor undertaking to be carried on in a stable way.

That is not so where, as in the case now referred, the transferor undertaking merely makes available to the new contractor certain workers and material for carrying out the works in question.'

1977 Directive applies only to transfers, and even then is not comprehensive: dismissals and changes in terms of employment may eventually follow. But it is a significant starting point. How far this policy could reach if taken to its logical conclusion is the subject of the next section.

THE OBJECTIVE OF THE DIRECTIVE: EXTENDING ITS SCOPE

The scope of the Directive is defined by the requirement that there has been a transfer within the meaning of Article 1(1), which reads:

> 'This Directive shall apply to the transfer of an undertaking, business or part of a business to another employer as a result of a legal transfer or merger.'

It is also necessary that the business preserves its autonomy.[10]

The essence of the transfer is less the legal *quality* of the transaction than the fact that a change has occurred regarding the employer, and 'the business preserves its autonomy'[11] or 'maintains an identity distinct'.[12] Both UK law and the EC Directive refer to 'another employer'. Formally, this seems to mean another legal person in the relationship of employment.

For example, it is generally accepted that the Directive, which applies only where there is a transfer to another employer, fails to achieve its objective when the undertaking is transferred through a share purchase. The employees are under contract with the company. The transfer of shares in the company does not legally alter their employment status with that company. So although there is *effectively* a change of ownership – in that the company is now owned by another person – the transaction falls outside the scope of the Directive.

The scope of the Directive, as interpreted by the European Court in *Schmidt* and accepted by the Court of Appeal in *Dines*, is much wider than a narrow interpretation might indicate. A transfer may be deemed to have occurred where more than one transaction may be involved; or where there is no direct link between transferor and transferee.

As appears through the case law of the European Court, an undertaking, business or part of a business may be a bundle of premises, equipment, services and employees without a separate legal identity. The object of the transfer is an autonomous function with a distinct identity. The logical thrust of the European Court judgments on the Directive is towards holding that the Directive applies when an autonomous *function* is transferred. This logic can be applied to the Directive's requirement that there be a transfer to another employer.[13]

The logic would dictate that an employer is defined not only in terms of separate legal existence, but rather in terms of a distinct legal relationship to the employee. A change of employer occurs, arguably, when the quality of this relationship with the employee changes. This is a *functional* transfer in the position of the employer, even though, formally, the employer's relationship with the employee has not terminated and been transferred to another employer.

---

10   Article 5(1).
11   Article 5(1).
12   TUPE, Reg 9(1).
13   This argument was applied to the case of 'derecognition', discussed in Chapter 11.

The *policy* of the Directive is that a major *change* in the employer's relationship with employees should *not* change arrangements regarding, for example, information and consultation of workers' representatives. 'If the business preserves its autonomy', so should collective recognition arrangements.

Empirical research has shown that, in Britain today, derecognition attempts frequently accompany employer moves to performance related pay, major changes in working conditions and job cuts which do not involve changes in the legal identity of the employer.[14] However, major changes in the functional relationship between employer and employees are equivalent to the effects of a 'transfer'. The Directive's policy would require that the EU objective of legal protection by way of information and consultation of workers' representatives be extended to employees in these circumstances.

14 See G Gall and S McKay, op cit, in Chapter 11.

Chapter 19

The European Works Councils Directive 1994

INTRODUCTION

The Council of Ministers of the European Union (EU) approved Directive 94/45/EC (hereafter the EWCs Directive) on 22 September 1994.[1] This requires the establishment of a European Works Council (EWC) or a procedure in Community-scale undertakings and Community-scale groups of undertakings for the purposes of informing and consulting employees. The Directive is a significant step in the development of EU labour law. It is particularly so for the domestic labour law of the UK.

The Directive is the first measure to be approved under the Protocol and Agreement on Social Policy of the Treaty on European Union. The significance of the UK opt-out from this 'social chapter' of the Union Treaty will be tested first through the implementation of this Directive. It is already seen to have had an impact as UK multinational enterprises voluntarily accept its provisions.

The Directive raises crucial questions in the context of worker representation. The EU is prescribing specific transnational representation structures. These are bound to interact with national systems of worker representation. They are likely to lead the European Court of Justice into pronouncements on this issue at a time when questions of representativeness, for example, in the social dialogue at European level, are being addressed. In the UK, as a result of the European Court's decision on 8 June 1994, representation issues are a critical point with the government having produced proposals in order to comply with European law.

A transposition committee of Member States' representatives has been set up to discuss and, if possible, agree on the substance, form and timing of Member State implementation of the Directive into national law. This has important implications for future coordination and the effective implementation and enforcement of EU law. Significantly, despite its opt-out, the UK is participating on this committee.

With a calculated 1,200 multinational enterprises covered, each with a European Works Council comprising 30 members,[2] aided by an expert, the Directive

---

1 Council Directive 94/45/EC of 22 September 1994 on the establishment of a European Works Council or a procedure in Community-scale undertakings and Community-scale groups of undertakings for the purposes of informing and consulting employees, OJ L254/64 of 30.9.94.
2 A single enterprise may have more than one EWC, if different divisions of the company have separate councils, as well as an overall EWC. This has been the proposed structure for Coats Viyella, the second UK-based multinational enterprise (MNE) to establish a voluntary EWC. See the text in 'European-wide information and consultation initiatives on the increase', *IRS Employment Trends*, No 587, July 1995, p 10 at p 12.

has the potential to make a decisive step towards a transnational industrial relations system. The activities of some 36,000 representatives and 1,200 experts in developing transnational information and consultation procedures are not likely to be overlooked. At a conference organised by the TUC on 27–28 March 1995, the representative from the European Trades Union Confederation, Willi Buschak, pointed out:

> 'European works councils will bring together the workers' representatives from the company, mostly people who normally do not frequent international meetings or congresses or at least not so often. They will have a chance to learn in direct meetings what their colleagues in other countries think, why they think so, why they behaved in one way and not in another. Workers' representatives will no longer read or hear about each other, they will talk to each other and get to know each other.'

The Directive is characterised by a stratagem which is assuming ever greater prominence in European labour law: the delegation to the social partners, management and labour, of the competence to negotiate the relevant European labour law standards. The delegation, however, is not complete. It is subjected to a subtle structuring process which shapes the strategies pursued by the social partners. The outcome of such negotiations depends, as always, first on the balance of forces between the social partners. However, there is much scope for tactical manoeuvring within the often ambiguous framework laid down by the Directive. Strategies of litigation and negotiation may be exploited by the parties, aided and abetted by labour lawyers. The Directive is a worthy exemplar of an underlying deep structure of European labour law, and of its potential for analysis by labour lawyers.

Finally, and not least, the importance of the Directive lies simply in the fact that, by applying to large multinational undertakings and groups of undertakings, it is of immense economic significance, and not least to the trade union and labour movement.

GROUPS OF COMPANIES AND UK INDUSTRIAL RELATIONS

The influence of groups of companies as a category of business enterprise on industrial relations in the UK is likely to increase, not least as a result of developments on the European level: specifically, the European Works Council Directive of 1994.[3] The importance of industrial relations policies in the *large* company sector is evident in the *contrast* it presents with industrial relations in the rest of the economy.

The most recent national Workplace Industrial Relations Survey (WIRS), carried out in 1990,[4] looked at 2,061 workplaces employing over 1,450,000 people. It was a nationally representative sample with over half the establishments surveyed employing between 25 and 49 people and another 25%

---

3   Council Directive 94/45/EC of 22 September 1994 on the establishment of a European Works Council or a procedure in Community-scale undertakings and Community-scale groups of undertakings for the purposes of informing and consulting employees, OJ L254/64 of 30.9.94. It is asserted that the prominence of large companies has increased as the influence of multi-employer bargaining has declined in recent years. 'The impact of financial controls and other changes in company-level industrial relations', *IRS Employment Trends*, No 557, April 1994, p 7.

4   N Millward, M Stevens, D Smart, W R Hawes *Workplace Industrial Relations in Transition*, Dartmouth Publishing, 1992. Earlier surveys were carried out in 1980 and 1984.

employing between 50 and 99 people. Less than 10% of the establishments surveyed employed more than 200 people and less than 1% had more than 1,000
people. The WIRS found that over all the establishments surveyed, the proportion of workplaces recognising one or more trade unions fell from 52% in 1984
to 40% in 1990.

This contrasts with the results of a survey carried out in mid-1992 among a
representative sample of 176 large companies, defined as multi-site companies
with 1,000 or more UK employees.[5] This found that 69% of companies recognised trade unions for the largest employee group within the workforce, and in
25% of the companies, trade union recognition covered all UK establishments.[6]
This contrast is confirmed by the 1990 WIRS, which found that the decline in
union recognition was largely confined to establishments with fewer than 200
employees.

Union recognition was most common in the manufacturing sector (84% of
enterprises) followed by other production sectors (60%) and services (54%). It is
significant that companies which recognised unions employed considerably
more employees that those which did not. Meetings were reported to take place
between lay union representatives from different sites in 46% of companies, and
47% of companies which recognised unions reported that single-table bargaining arrangements (involving co-operation between different trade unions) were
in place on at least one site within the enterprise.

The higher prevalence of union recognition in large firms is particularly significant for the European dimension because of the notable extent to which
large firms operating in Britain are multinationals: a total of 60% of large firms
in the UK are multinationals, both overseas-owned (one-fifth of large firms)
and UK-owned companies with operations overseas (half the British owned
large firms).[7]

This trend can be illustrated by industrial relations in the food industry,
which represents one of the UK's largest sectors of manufacturing industry.[8]
This industry has been characterised by a trend towards concentration, through
mergers and acquisitions, and is now dominated by a few large companies, frequently multinationals.

In March 1994 it was estimated that a total of 396,500 people were employed
in the food industry. The leading unions representing manual workers in the
industry are general workers' unions: the Transport and General Workers'
Union (TGWU) representing an estimated 100,000 workers and the General,

5   P Marginson, P Armstrong, P Edwards, J Purcell, N Hubbard 'The control of industrial
    relations in large companies: an initial analysis of the second company-level industrial
    relations survey', *Warwick Papers in Industrial Relations*, No 45, December 1993. The total of
    176 represents about one-fifth of such companies in the UK, the total of 975 companies char-
    acterised as employing 1,000 or more people and having two or more operating sites within
    the UK.
6   In 17% unions were recognised in most establishments, and in 27% unions were recognised in
    some establishments only.
7   The survey found that multinational companies were less likely to recognise unions at all UK
    sites than UK domestic companies, and, related to this, were more likely to bargain on a
    decentralised, site-by-site basis and to have decentralised pay bargaining. See main findings
    from the 1992 survey summarised in *IRS Employment Trends*, No 557, April 1994, p 8.
8   'Industrial Relations in the Food Industry', *IRS Employment Trends*, No 567, September 1994,
    p 12. The following paragraphs are based on this survey.

Municipal and Boilermakers' Trade Union (GMBTU) with approximately 60,000 members. Other unions are the Bakers', Food and Allied Workers' Union (BFAWU), with 32,000 members in the food and baking sector, and the Union of Shop, Distributive and Allied Workers (USDAW), with some 30,000 members in the food industry.

The European dimension of the food industry in Britain is evidenced through the increased presence of European multinationals. Where these are based in the other Member States of the European Union, the significance of the movement towards information and consultation structures has also affected their UK subsidiaries. Three examples may be used to illustrate this.

BSN/Danone, a French-based food multinational has British subsidiaries among its operations in Europe. Since 1987, on the basis of an exchange of letters between BSN management and IUF, the international union organisation for foodworkers (with British members including the GMBTU, TGWU, MSF (the Manufacturing, Science and Finance Trade Union) and USDAW) an annual information meeting has been held, which includes both lay and full-time union officials and IUF officials. In the meeting of May 1994, three British shop stewards and three full-time union officials attended. This meeting led to a joint declaration on trade union rights between BSN and IUF which recognises the right of employees to belong to a trade union, affirms the value of trade union organisation in the company, and encourages local management and unions to negotiate and publicise collective agreements.

The Swiss Nestlé corporation owns British subsidiaries and has been attending international meetings with union representatives organised by the IUF since the 1970s. Annual joint information meetings have been held since an exchange of letters between IUF and management in 1990. The meetings involve both lay representatives and union officials and five shop stewards and one official from the UK attended the April 1994 meeting.

A US-based multinational, CPC, has operations in 21 European countries and numerous subsidiaries in the UK. In early 1994, on its own initiative and without any prior arrangement with trade unions, the company established a 'European Employees Council' made up on the employee side by representatives from each Western European country in which the company had at least 100 employees, including the UK. The IUF claimed the management attempted to by-pass trade unions, especially in the UK. Its first meeting was held on 1 July 1994, and represented the first US-based multinational in any sector to have launched a formal European-level employee information structure.

The initiatives by overseas multinationals in the food industry may be contrasted with UK-owned food multinationals. By late 1994, no such UK-based company had established a European Works Council, despite pressure on the largest of them, Unilever (a UK/Dutch owned multinational with the largest food group with British involvement). The IUF had organised European-level meetings of union and employee representatives in a number of British food and drink multinationals (United Biscuits, Guinness and Cadbury Schweppes). It was not surprising, therefore, that the first 'agreement on Europe-wide information and consultation' was signed by United Biscuits on 9 November 1994.

These considerations make it necessary to undertake a detailed and exhaustive analysis of the Directive's provisions and its implications. In what follows these, and other themes, will be developed more fully.

WHO IS COVERED?

As the first Directive to be approved under the Protocol and Agreement on Social Policy of the Maastricht Treaty on European Union, it followed the procedure laid down in the Agreement annexed to the Protocol – consultation of management (UNICE and CEEP) and labour (ETUC) at EU level. The negotiations between these 'social partners' came close to producing the first EU collective agreement, but were fatally undermined by the British CBI's last-minute rejection of the compromise agreed by UNICE. Following the breakdown of negotiations, the issue reverted to the Agreement's legislative procedure, which culminated in the Directive.

Under the Agreement, the Directive applies to fourteen Member States, not including the UK.[9] However, despite the UK's 'opt-out', multinational enterprises (MNEs) with establishments located in the UK will not escape its effects.

Moreover, although it is clear that the Directive does not apply in the UK, it is not clear whether employees in the UK are to be counted in deciding which MNEs are covered. The UK is a Member State of the EU. The question is whether it can be considered a non-Member State for the purposes of Article 2(1), so that employees in the UK do not count.

The language throughout the Articles of the Directive refers simply to Member States. Only the Preamble, referring to the Protocol, lists the 11 Member States and concludes: '(hereinafter referred to as "the Member States")'.[10] This means the Directive does not apply to the UK as provided in the Protocol.

But it is open to question, and may be arguable in the European Court, that the 11 Member States can provide in their national law that the threshold criteria defining the MNEs covered are to include in the count employees in the UK, even if the Directive's provisions do not apply in the UK.

UK workers' representation in European multinationals

The enterprises affected are 'Community-scale undertakings' and a 'Community-scale group of undertakings' with at least 1000 employees in the Member States and at least 150 employees in each of at least two Member States (Art 2(1)(a) and (c)).

An early estimate was that, even if employees in the UK are not included in the calculations, the Directive will apply to 102 UK-based MNEs with 1000+ employees in other Member States and 150 employees in each of at least two Member States.[11] It will also apply to continental-based MNEs and non-EU based MNEs with establishments in the UK – some of whom will have the requisite numbers of employees in the Member States.

Up to now, the UK and Ireland were the only countries in the EU without legislation providing a generally applicable system of workplace employee representation with information and consultation rights. Although the European

---

9   The eleven Member States at the time it was approved, plus the three new Member States (Austria, Finland, Sweden) as of 1 January 1995. It also applies in the three EEA countries, Iceland, Liechtenstein and Norway.

10   Recital 5.

11   See TUC, Multinationals Information Project, *European Works Councils*, Information Pack, pp 11–13 for a list of the names of the MNEs and sectors concerned.

Works Councils Directive will not apply directly to UK employers, it will have consequences for UK workers' representation on such Councils established by multinationals, whether UK or other, which have UK subsidiaries. The European Works Councils Directive is bound to have repercussions on UK employers generally, especially when taken together with the effects of the European Court's judgment of 8 June 1994 and the government's proposed legislation to bring UK law into compliance with EC law.

The requirement on UK-based multinationals to establish EWCs where they fall under the provisions of the Directive as having two or more subsidiaries in EU Member States employing at least 150 employees and an overall number of employees exceeding 1,000 means it is unlikely they will seek to exclude their UK employees (often a majority) from participation in such EWCs. Similarly, those multinationals based outside the UK with UK establishments are unlikely to exclude the employees of their UK subsidiaries.

Even if not legally required, this inclusion of UK employees in representative bodies of multinationals is dictated by political and practical reasons. It may be that national legislation implementing the Directive in other Member States may require such representation; industrial relations with workers' representatives from establishments outside the UK will be made more difficult if UK establishments are not represented and their interests are engaged. It will be in management's interest to have the interlocutors of these interests represented in consultations with representatives of the rest of the workforce.

Representation of UK workers in existing structures is already well-established. Examples include those at BSN, Bull, Continental Can/Schmalbach-Lubeca, Elf-Aquitaine, Générale des Eaux, Kone, Nestlé, Pechiney, Renault, Thomson CE and Thomson CSF.[12]

For example, in 1992 the Compagnie Saint Gobain signed an agreement with the recognised unions in its subsidiary companies throughout the EU establishing a 'Conference for the European Social Dialogue', which formalised the annual meetings held since 1988 with employee representatives. The main Saint Gobain subsidiaries in the UK are the steel company Stanton plc and the industrial ceramics manufacturer TSL Group, which have 1,200 and 400 employees respectively. The agreement was translated into English by TSL's personnel manager, approved by the group company, and the text signed by senior lay representatives of the GMBTU, MSF and AEEU (Amalgamated Engineering and Electrical Union) at TSL, and the AEEU, GMBTU, MSF and the Steel Industrial Management Association (SIMA) at Stanton.

Saint Gobain's UK operations are too small for a group delegate, so the selection of the four UK representatives was shared proportionately: three from Stanton and one from TSL. At TSL, the GMBTU negotiates for a majority of the employees, so that union nominated the company's representative. As the GMBTU thus has a representative, the representatives from Stanton are usually chosen by the other unions: AEEU, MSF and SIMA. In practice the representatives have been senior lay officials of the unions. The GMBTU representative

---

12 This and the following information is derived from 'Cross-border talks: European Consultation and Information Arrangements', *IRS Employment Trends*, No 561, June 1994, p 6; 'The UK and "European Works Councils"', *European Industrial Relations Review*, No 246, July 1994, p 14.

who attended two meetings was quoted as saying that, although the rank and file membership does not display great interest in European matters: [13]

'. . . the information provided by the Conference on changes in strategy and plans for research and development and safety are of interest to shop stewards and union activists.'

Another example is Allianz, one of the largest insurance multinationals in Europe, with around 73,000 employees worldwide. The Allianz Company Council was formed more than 10 years ago on the initiative of the International Federation of Commercial, Clerical, Professional and Technical Employees (EURO-FIET). In the UK, the main Allianz company is Cornhill Insurance, which has approximately 3,000 employees. The recognised union is MSF which sends one of its regional officers and a lay representative to the annual two-day meeting. The MSF officer writes to the management and informs them of the draft agenda of the meeting and requests paid time off for the union's workplace representative to attend the Council, which has always been granted. The MSF official normally makes a report on the Council to the union's national executive council and circulates a newsletter summarising events to MSF members in Cornhill.

A third example is Rhône-Poulenc, a French based multinational with approximately 86,000 employees, whose main UK subsidiaries employ 4,400 at 11 main sites. An informal annual meeting, the 'President's European Dialogue' between senior executives of the group and employee representatives from six European States was established in 1990. The UK sends four representatives consisting of one from each of Rhône-Poulenc's main UK businesses, chosen using varying consultative structures in the subsidiaries, but also the four main unions recognised by Rhône-Poulenc: AEEU, GMBTU, MSF and TGWU.

Research undertaken by the Trades Union Congress [14] demonstrates that such involvements are not exceptional. Results produced in March 1994 found that transnational steering committees of union/employee representatives had been established in 12 UK-based multinationals, including Coats Viyella, Reed International, Cadbury Schweppes, Watmoughs Holdings, Redland, BPB, Lucas Industries, GKN, United Biscuits Holdings and Guinness. There had been initial seminars/meetings of representatives (though no steering committees) established in nine UK-based multinationals, including BET, Rolls-Royce, Pilkington, BAT Industries, Securicor Group, Hillsdown Holdings and ICI. UK unions were involved on steering committees of representatives in 37 multinationals based elsewhere in Europe, including Digital Equipment Corporation, Philips, Rothmans, Heinz, Coca-Cola, Jefferson/Smurfit, Tupil International, Pirelli, Pepsico, Levi Strauss, Springer, Crédit Lyonnais, Rank Xerox and Otis. UK unions were involved in initial meetings of representatives in 14 multinationals based elsewhere in Europe, including Philip Morris, Triumph, Svenska Cellulosa, L'Oréal, Siemens and Colgate Palmolive.

---

13   Ibid, *IRS Employment Trends*, at p 7. He said 'we are still trying to convince the membership that the company is French-owned'.

14   In 1993, the TUC's application for 260,000 ECU funding to the European Commission under budget line B3 4004 for a project on 'information and consultation in multinational companies' was granted. This included establishing a database to identify multinationals and representatives involved in EWCs or transnational meetings and of relevant trade union personnel.

In addition to these European multinationals, there are UK unions involved in multinationals based outside Europe. Japanese multinationals come second only to the USA of those which will have to establish a EWC under the Directive. Of 27 Japanese-owned companies which will be covered,[15] 25 have operations in the UK and in nine of these, the UK is the home of the largest single EU workforce.[16] In December 1994, Honda became the first to establish an information and consultation structure at European level for its European operations employing some 5,000 workers, including a car and engine plant in the UK, motorcycle plants in Belgium, Italy and Spain, a power equipment company in Italy, and numerous sales operations. The employee side has one representative for each location in Europe with over 50 permanent full-time employees.[17] However, the identity of the representatives in the UK is being contested; while the representatives from Belgium are elected trade union representatives, and the Chair from the German works council, Honda's largest European operation, the plant at Swindon in England, is not unionised.

The first UK-based European Works Councils

Although not covered by the EWCs Directive, it was unlikely that UK based multinationals could avoid its impact on their operations. Despite this, there were few who actively sought to take the lead. The first to do so was United Biscuits (UB), which, on 9 November 1994, signed an agreement with the GMBTU on 'Europe-wide information and consultation'. UB employs some 40,000 workers worldwide, including 17–18,000 in the UK and around 5,000 in operations throughout Europe.[18]

The agreement established a UB European Consultative Council as a forum for the 'exchange of information and views between management and employees with the aim of establishing a transnational dialogue'. The agreement states that the Council:[19]

'2.2 ... will focus principally on the performance of the United Biscuits Group (and in particular its European operations), the direction of the overall strategy of the group, on jobs and employment policy, and broad commercial factors affecting its operations ...

2.3 The (Council) will not involve itself in matters that are the prerogative of national or local negotiating or consultative processes.'

On the employee side there are 20 representatives, 13 from the UK and 7 from non-UK operations, all nominated by national trade unions or works council

15 A report identified from among the Fortune 500 list of the world's largest companies by turnover, 17 Japanese-owned companies covered: Asahi Glass, Canon, Fuji, Fujitsu, Honda, Kao, Komatsu, Konica, Matsushita, Minolta, Nissan, Pioneer, Ricoh, Sharo, Sony, Toshiba and Yamaha. M Hall, M Carley, M Gold, P Marginson, K Sisson *European Works Councils: Planning for the Directive* (1995). The TUC research project adds a further 10 companies: Bridgestone, Dainippon, Hitachi, Mitsubishi, NEC, Olympus, Sumitomo, TDK, Yakazi and Yoshida Kogyo. 'European Works Councils update – trends and issues', *European Industrial Relations Review*, No 256, May 1995, p 14 at p 16.
16 Including Canon, Fujitsu, Hitachi, Matsushita and NEC.
17 For details, see *European Industrial Relations Review*, op cit, at p 17.
18 'The first UK European Works Councils', *European Industrial Relations Review*, No 251, December 1994, p 20.
19 Articles 2.2 and 2.3.

type bodies. The UK representatives are allocated by group company. The employee representatives are 'accompanied by four full-time officials from unions with a formal relationship with the company': two represent UK unions (USDAW and TGWU), one represents non-UK unions and one represents both GMBTU and ECF-IUF, the European food industry committee affiliated to the ETUC.

The second EWC established by a UK-based multinational was particularly significant as it was the first such agreement in the European Textile and Clothing Industry. It was signed by Coats Viyella at the end of February 1995, and covers 34,000 employees in the EU, of which approximately 27,000 are employed in the UK. The UK trade unions were authorised to initiate negotiations by the European Industry Secretariat for the textile and clothing industry, ETUC:TCL. However, the negotiations leading to the agreement were founded upon long-standing agreements and procedures between the company and the three main UK unions (KFAT, GMBTU and TGWU). As explained by the official from the TGWU, existing agreements already provided for a national level annual meeting between senior directors of the company and union representatives, which covered issues including information on the company's development and general business performance.[20]

The Works Councils Agreement provides for a two-tier structure of European Committees. The first of these are Divisional Committees covering each of the six Divisions of the Company. The second tier is the group European Forum with membership from each Division. One agreement covers the whole of the Company's operations, but there will be six further agreements for each Division.

During 1994 negotiations were taking place, with a first draft of the agreement being discussed at a meeting in November 1994, and final agreement being reached in February 1995. Throughout this period, coordination was necessary both within the UK between the UK unions and across Europe with all the main unions involved. This co-operation was carried out by the ETUC: TCL. Within the UK, with the largest body of employees, it was necessary to establish contact with textile and non-textile unions, which became increasingly important as the number of seats on the Divisional Councils and Group Council was discussed. While the vast majority of union members were in the three main unions, where appropriate, seats were allocated to other unions on a pro rata basis.

The problems to be resolved in constructing European Works Councils comprising workers' representatives in a relatively fragmented trade union movement as in Britain are compounded by the difficulties encountered when non-union multinationals seek to establish EWCs.

The most contentious case so far as been that of Marks & Spencer, the UK retailer, which announced on 9 March 1995 in a letter to all European employees the establishment of a 'European Council' explicitly as a response to the EWCs Directive, and calling on employees to nominate themselves as representatives.[1]

20   Paper by P Booth, National Secretary, Textiles, TGWU, at the TUC Conference, 'European Works Councils: What will they mean in Britain?', 27–28 March 1995, Stoke Rochford.
1   'European Works Councils update – trends and issues', *European Industrial Relations Review*, No 256, May 1995, p 14 at p 19. 'European Works Councils and the UK', *IRS Employment Trends*, No 581, April 1995, p 13 at p 15.

Marks & Spencer is a UK-owned retail group employing over 50,000 workers in Europe, the vast majority in the UK (around 46,300) with the remainder in France (1,570), Ireland (540), Spain (500), Belgium (200) and the Netherlands (120). The company does not recognise a trade union for collective bargaining purposes in the UK, with over 90% of its employees. In the other European countries, according to EURO-FIET, the Geneva-based trade union organisation which represents commercial workers' unions in Europe, the company has collective agreements with trade unions. This is the case in France and Ireland, and the company is covered by sectoral agreements in Belgium and the Netherlands. In Ireland, the MANDATE union claims 100% membership, while there is reported to be substantial union membership in Belgium and France. EURO-FIET has denounced the company's unilateral initiative, which it claims pre-empted a meeting with union affiliates from four countries who were due to meet to establish a EWC in line with the Directive.

The company called upon employees to approach their personnel department by 1 April 1995 to nominate themselves. Where more than one did so for a constituency, the company proposed that selection would be by 'focus teams', 'house committees' and management. Allocation of places on the 'European Council' will vary with the number of employees per country: one place for up to 1,499 staff, two for 1,500–2,999 staff, and one additional place for each additional 3,000 staff, up to a maximum of 13 places.

EURO-FIET has asked the company to refrain from appointing the council pending consultations. The Irish union MANDATE has instructed its members not to make nominations to the Council until the issues have been resolved, and EURO-FIET has asked its other affiliates not to participate in the initiative.

Another such initiative was the proposal in April 1995 by the management of Unilever, the UK/Dutch-owned personal products multinational, for the establishment of a 'European employee forum' covering the whole group, a European workforce of some 100,000, including 23,000 in the UK. This was countered by a joint resolution of a steering committee organised by the European organisation of food workers (ECF–IUF) and chemical workers (EFCGU) which met on 24 April comprising representatives from Austria, Belgium, Germany, Ireland, Italy, the Netherlands, Norway, Spain, Sweden and the UK. The resolution set up a bargaining committee to reach an agreement based on much more rigorous requirements than those set out in the company's proposal. UK unions were particularly dissatisfied with the company's proposal as regards the management's selection of the UK's three representatives. One was to be nominated by the consultative forum for management staff, while the other two would be selected through an 'electoral college' made up of representatives elected or appointed by consultative councils.[2]

A report published in 1995 distinguished three groups among those multinationals covered by the Directive. Those with their headquarters in the 16 States in the European Economic Area (EEA), having 1000+ employees within the 16 and a subsidiary in at least one other of the 16 countries affected, numbered 458. Those of which it could be confirmed that the subsidiary employed

2 'European-wide information and consultation initiatives on the increase', *IRS Employment Trends*, No 587, July 1995, p 10 at p 16.

at least 150+ people numbered 216. Of 326 companies with headquarters in the UK with the requisite 1000+ employees and one subsidiary in another State, 83 were confirmed as meeting the 150+ threshold for the subsidiary.[3] Of the remainder, unavailability of data made it difficult to confirm that they met the threshold. But it was calculated that, if as few as one quarter of those companies which are unconfirmed turn out to meet the criteria of the Directive, the resulting total would be some 140 UK companies.[4]

Workers' representation in these enterprises is currently undergoing considerable upheaval. The reasons for this include the impact of the Directive on the readiness of corporate groups to accept representative structures, and the potential effects of the decision of the European Court of Justice in *EC Commission v UK* on 8 June 1994 and the consequent legislative plans of the UK government. There are also the proposals on trade union recognition put forward by the Trades Union Congress and pressed upon the opposition Labour Party as a priority for legislation if the Labour Party wins the next election (due before spring 1997).[5]

British delegates participating in representative structures established in corporate groups have reported the advantages to be gained from contacts established between workers' representatives from different entities within the group: the sharing of information, the exchange of experience and ideas, countering perceived management attempts to 'play off' national workforces against one another, and the possibility of a more coordinated approach to collective bargaining among national unions.[6] The pressures for improving workers' representation across groups of companies in the UK are likely to increase.

CONTEXT: REPRESENTATION ISSUES

The specific issue of who is to represent workers on EWCs is of critical importance because the general issue of worker representation has reached a turning point in EU labour law. The law on worker representation which emerges from the EWCs Directive will have effects going beyond the specific case of multinational enterprises. This is because it will be taking shape in advance of, or contemporaneously with, the EU law on workers' representation which is currently attracting attention in the following three other contexts.

First, on 8 June 1994 the European Court of Justice condemned the UK for:[7]

'failing to provide for the designation of workers' representatives where an employer does not agree to it.'

---

3   Overall, taking into account companies headquartered both inside and outside the 16 EEA States covered by the Directive, the report estimates that some 860 corporate groups qualify as having 1000+ employees and subsidiaries in at least two of the 16 EEA States, many of which each probably employ at least 150+ employees. M Hall, M Carley, M Gold, P Marginson, K Sisson *European Works Councils: Planning for the Directive* (1995).
4   'European works councils and the UK', *IRS Employment Trends*, No 581, April 1995, p 13 at p 16.
5   'Your voice at work: TUC proposals for rights to representation at work', Trades Union Congress, July 1995. See the summary in *IRS Employment Trends*, No 590, August 1995, p 3.
6   'Cross border talks: European consultation and information arrangements', *IRS Employment Trends*, No 561, June 1994, p 6 at p 10.
7   Cases C-382/92 and C-383/92: *EC Commission v UK* [1994] ECR I-2435 and [1994] ECR I-2479.

The restriction of the right to consultation to where the employer recognised trade unions was held to contravene the EC Directives on consultation of workers' representatives in situations of collective dismissals or transfers of undertakings. In the words of the Advocate-General:[8]

'It is, however, for the Member States to adopt the laws, regulations and administrative provisions necessary, if no consensus can be reached, to ensure the designation of workers' representatives for the application of the directives.'

As a result of this decision, the UK government is required to introduce a law on worker representation. This domestic law will be scrutinised to ensure it complies with EC law.

Secondly, the EC Framework Directive 89/391/EEC of 12 June 1989[9] on safety representatives, which are defined in Article 3(c), is probably inadequately transposed in the Health and Safety at Work etc Act 1974, s 2(4), and the Safety Representatives and Safety Committees Regulations 1977, Reg 3(1), which again limit the appointment of safety representatives to where there are recognised unions.[10]

Thirdly, at the same time, the European social dialogue at EU level, given a major role in the Protocol and annexed Agreement on Social Policy of the Maastricht Treaty on European Union, raises questions of who represents labour at EU level. The Commission's Communication of 14 December 1993[11] began to develop criteria for identifying representatives of labour for the purposes of the procedure of consultation and dialogue at European level. Decisions over criteria of representativeness at EU level are likely to be contentious and may end up in the European Court of Justice.[12]

All these developments converge on the general issue of workers' representation in European labour law. If they do reach the European Court, the decisions of that body are likely to influence not only the EU law, but also the general debate over worker representation in Member States, including the UK.

The EWCs Directive is just one of several attempts at EU legislation on worker representation. Others have failed to achieve the approval of the Council of Ministers and have remained draft proposals. Examples include the draft Fifth Directive on Company Law, which proposed worker representation on company boards; the so-called 'Vredeling' draft Directive, which proposed obligatory information and consultation of workers' representatives in enterprises with complex structures; and the proposals for an EC Company Statute, which included provisions for worker representation.[13]

---

8   Opinion of Advocate-General Van Gerven on Cases C-382/92 and C-383/92, delivered on 2 March 1994, paragraph 14.
9   OJ L183/1.
10 This is dealt with in Chapter 24.
11 COM (93) 600 final.
12 See the Opinion of the Economic and Social Committee, adopted on 24 November 1994 on the Commission's Communication regarding implementation of the Protocol on Social Policy, ECOSOC 1310/94, doc COM (93) 600 final, Brussels 23–24 November 1994. See also J J Van Dijk (Rapporteur for the Committee) and B Bercusson (Expert to the Rapporteur) in (1995) *International Journal of Comparative Labour Law and Industrial Relations.*
13 See 'The EWCs Directive and previous participation initiatives', *European Industrial Relations Review* No 207, April 1991, p 23.

THE IMPLICATIONS OF THE DIRECTIVE FOR UK DOMESTIC LAW

The EWCs Directive is thus a breakthrough in the stalemate. The way it is implemented in practice will be of crucial importance in debates seeking to make progress on these other proposals at EU level, as well as on UK domestic law on worker representation.

Its impact on UK domestic law may emerge as a result of litigation. At first sight, this seems problematic because of the UK opt-out; the EWCs Directive need not be implemented in UK law. However, as indicated above, many UK multinational enterprises, and others, will be affected by legislation on EWCs in other Member States. This may allow for claims against UK multinational enterprises for failure to set up EWCs. The relevant law may impose obligations on the UK multinational enterprises, for example, to provide information to their continental subsidiaries required to set up EWCs. UK employees may acquire rights to be represented on the EWCs, to have time off and facilities to carry out trade union duties in connection with the EWCs. The possibilities will doubtless be explored.

A second indirect impact of the EWCs Directive on domestic law is through the UK government's legislative proposals on worker representation following the European Court's judgment of 8 June 1994.[14] There are substantive criteria inherent in the Court's judgment. Arguments as to what is implicit in EC law on worker representation (eg that representatives must be effective and independent) will be the basis for potential challenges to the government's legislative proposals implementing the Directive so as to comply with the Court's judgment.

The EWCs Directive prescribes how worker representation on EWCs is to be constituted. The rules laid down may affect the UK government's proposals, since these proposals are likely to include criteria which could be used also in defining the composition of EWCs. As such, presuming some future legislation on EWCs in the UK, they will have to be consistent with the requirements of the Directive. Otherwise, separate legislation on worker representation in EWCs will be necessary. The Directive is thus likely to be influential in the fate of the government's legislative proposals.

Finally, trade unions are very soon going to become engaged in the first steps towards the establishment of EWCs. As will be seen below, the first stage involves the establishment of a Special Negotiating Body, which is to negotiate the creation of the EWC with the multinational enterprise's central management. The negotiation of a successful EWC will greatly depend on who seizes the initiative and the tactics adopted by management and by the workers' representatives.

In particular, the obligations arising from the Directive do not apply to multinational enterprises where, in the immediate future, before the coming into effect of the Directive on 22 September 1996:[15]

> 'there is already an agreement, covering the entire workforce, providing for transnational information and consultation of employees.'

---

14   'Consultation about collective redundancies and business transfers: a legislative proposal', Department of Employment, March 1995. For a summary, see *Industrial Relations Law Bulletin*, No 520, May 1995, p 15.
15   Article 13.

Multinational enterprises, including UK multinationals, may seek to negotiate voluntary arrangements to avoid the EWCs Directive in the future. Trade union negotiators will be taking legal advice to ensure their rights under the Directive are safeguarded.

The Commission of the EC has allocated large sums of money towards meetings of workers' representatives in transnational enterprises: UK£22m in the two-year period 1991–93. The TUC has been allocated substantial funding for this purpose. Within this programme, there has been careful consideration of the legal implications of the EWCs Directive.

THE DIRECTIVE'S IMPACT: THREE PHASES

The Directive is to be implemented by the Member States no later than 22 September 1996.[16] Its impact will be felt in three phases.

1. Immediate: the initial phase will involve the *establishment* of the Special Negotiating Bodies (SNBs) which negotiate the creation of the EWCs. This is the most immediate and practical issue.
2. Medium-term: once the SNB is established, the next phase is the *negotiation* of an agreement creating a EWC and defining its composition, functions, and so on.
3. Long-term: once the EWC is established, its functioning needs careful attention.

The first two phases are most crucial at present:

Phase 1:   The functioning of EWCs is contingent on their successful negotiation by the SNB. The initiative to create the SNB, its composition and procedure of negotiation will be critical to the future structure of the EWCs. It is possible that litigation will erupt to forestall moves by management deemed to violate requirements of the Directive.

Phase 2:   Once established, the SNB negotiates the EWC. Member States are required to introduce national legislation implementing the fall-back subsidiary requirements in the Annex to the Directive. These requirements will become the basis of negotiations by the SNB in creating the EWC. The requirements of the Annex therefore play a crucial role. They will be exploited at this stage both in government strategy in formulating any legislation, and also for negotiating purposes with management. Again, there may be litigation to forestall certain moves by government and management.

Phase 3:   Once agreement is reached on the EWC, attention will be paid to ensuring that maximum advantage is obtained from the agreement and any relevant provisions of the Directive.

16   Article 14(1).

Chapter 20

Negotiating with European Labour Law: Creating a European Works Council

INTRODUCTION

The UK is not a Member State covered by the Directive. Nonetheless, the Directive may be used to induce UK multinational enterprises to establish Special Negotiating Bodies (SNBs), Member State multinational enterprises to involve UK unions and workers in their EWCs, and non-Member State multinational enterprises to involve UK unions and workers in their EWCs in proportion to their relative importance in the EC. There may already be a voluntarily established agreement in force providing for transnational information and consultation.[1] The Directive may raise the issue whether this should be built on and improved, or challenged and replaced with a EWC. If there is no agreement in force, following the Directive, a EWC needs to be created.

The law will affect the strategies of the various actors involved, the processes they engage in and their outcomes. In each case, the law will be an instrument in determining who seizes the initiative, and how this initiative is controlled to achieve desired objectives. For example, central management has initiating powers to set up the SNB and negotiate the EWC, Member States have the power to determine means of election or appointment of the SNB, employees have power to trigger the process, unions, or other workers' representatives may be engaged. Processes engaged include triggering the SNB, the creation of the SNB, initiation of negotiations to create the EWC, determination/negotiation of the EWC and initiation of the EWC functions of information and consultation. The outcomes for workers and their organisations should be representation rights and rights of information and consultation. The opportunities for different legal strategies arising from the Directive are explored in this chapter.

THE IMMEDIATE PRIORITY: SPECIAL NEGOTIATING BODIES

Section II (Articles 4–7) of the Directive is entitled 'Establishment of a EWC or Employee Information and Consultation Procedure' (ICP). Article 4 is entitled: 'Responsibility for the establishment of a EWC or an employee ICP'. The Directive appears to envisage an alternative to a collective representative body, the EWC, in the form of an individual employee ICP.

---

1 Article 13.

The choice as to which of these alternatives is selected as the form of workers' information and consultation in multinational enterprises will be the first objective of the strategies of the different actors involved. In these strategies, the establishment and functioning of the Special Negotiating Body (SNB) is of critical importance. Article 5 on the SNB is not very clear. A number of issues need to be analysed separately.

Preconditions for the process as a whole: central management's responsibility

The first step engages 'the central management'. It is responsible:[2]

'for creating the conditions and means necessary for the setting up of a EWC or an ICP.'

Who is 'central management'?

'The central management' is defined in Article 2(1)(e). The usual case is of a Member State multinational enterprise. The problem in the UK (not a Member State for the purposes of the Directive) arises from Article 4(2):

'Where the central management is not situated in a Member State, the central management's representative agent in a Member State, to be designated if necessary, shall take on the responsibility . . .

In the absence of such a representative, the management of the establishment or group undertaking employing the greatest number of employees in any one Member State shall take on the responsibility . . .'

As regards *UK multinational enterprises covered by the Directive*, the question is whether the central management by definition is *not* situated in a Member State. As with the question of counting UK employees in calculating thresholds, it is open to question, and may be challenged in the European Court, whether the other 14 Member States can provide in their national laws that the central management responsible is that of the UK multinational enterprise, even if the Directive's provisions do not apply in the UK.

If they do not, *responsibility for the EWC does not lie with UK central management.* Either:

– the UK central management must designate a representative agent in a Member State (eg where it has a subsidiary); or
– in the absence of a designated representative agent, the responsibility lies with the management of the establishment or undertaking in the Member State employing the most employees.

The central management of UK multinational enterprises may want to retain effective control, but the *formal* responsibility 'for creating the conditions and means necessary for the setting up of a EWC or an ICP' (Article 4(1)) is elsewhere.

As regards *non-EC MNEs covered by the Directive*, they must designate a representative agent in a Member State, or in its absence, the management of whichever *Member State* subsidiary has most employees is responsible. Unless

2   Article 4(1).

the UK is deemed a Member State for these purposes by the law of the Member States, even if the UK subsidiary has most employees, the management responsible:

'for creating the conditions and means necessary for the setting up of a EWC or an ICP'

will be in another Member State – either designated, or that with the greatest number of employees after the UK. Both these risk taking management responsibility outside the UK even where it is a UK multinational enterprise or the UK has the largest subsidiary of a non-EC multinational enterprise. This makes for potential problems of enforcing the Directive's obligations if there is a breach of the multinational enterprise's responsibilities towards UK employees or their representatives.

One way of avoiding this may be through Article 13: where there are agreements in force, the obligations arising from the Directive shall not apply. One strategy would aim to achieve, with UK multinational enterprises or non-EC multinational enterprises with large establishments in the UK, a voluntary 'agreement, covering the entire workforce, providing for the transnational information and consultation of employees'. The arguments in favour of such an agreement are that:

– otherwise the *UK multinational enterprise* management must delegate responsibility to the management of one of its foreign subsidiaries. Looking to the future, when the Directive applies to the UK, the central management of UK multinational enterprises will have to assume responsibility in any event.

– otherwise the *non-EC multinational enterprise* will have to delegate responsibility under the Directive to the management of a smaller subsidiary when its major operation is in the UK.

Most of Article 4 is concerned with identifying the central management responsible under the Directive for the obligations of a non-EC multinational enterprise. It does not address possible problems in identifying 'the central management'. This is not a formal organ in corporate law. It assumes that industrial relations is a centralised management function, which is not the clear finding of much of the literature on multinational enterprise labour relations.[3] This potentially creates legal problems of attributing responsibility or liability for failures of central management to respect the obligations of the Directive.

What are central management's responsibilities?

The responsibility of central management is:[4]

'for creating the conditions and means necessary for the setting up of a EWC or an ICP.'

---

3 Generalisations about the exercise of centralised power in multinational groups of companies must be refined in order to precisely reflect the concerns of labour. One study of manpower policy decisions within multinational corporations in the UK demonstrated that different types of decisions tended to be taken at different levels. For example, decisions on numbers employed were made primarily by the parent company/registered headquarters in 22 out of 30 cases, whereas recruitment of management staff was decided mainly by the UK subsidiary in 24 out of 30 cases. J Hamill 'Labour relations decision making within multinational corporations', (1984) 15 *Industrial Relations Journal*, No 2, at p 30.

4 Article 4(1).

This is in addition to the procedural obligations set out in Article 5: to initiate negotiations with the SNB,[5] to convene a meeting with the SNB[6] and to bear the expenses of negotiations with the SNB.[7]

'CREATING'

The EWC is something new. 'Creating' implies that *new* circumstances have to be created, and, perhaps, that pre-existing conditions may have to change. Central management have to remove any obstacles and provide facilities. Over time, a list of requirements will emerge from practice.

'CONDITIONS AND MEANS'

The conditions and means required to be created depend on the functions and objectives of the EWC. The Directive speaks of the conditions and means necessary for the *setting up*, not the actual functioning, of the EWC. But setting one up *implies* that conditions and means must include those necessary to achieve the performance of these functions. Again, a list of resources will emerge from practical experience in the setting up of EWCs.

One basic condition is the freedom of workers and their representatives to associate for the purpose of negotiating the EWC or ICP. This may include a right to trade union facilities. Arguably, failure of central management to allow this violates its obligations under Article 4(1).

'NECESSARY'

Conditions and means must be those needed to set up a EWC or ICP. Experience in different national circumstances of setting up representative bodies, and the hazards of employer intervention, as well as existing multinational enterprise practice, should indicate whether the *transnational* dimension adds anything else to the list of conditions and means necessary to the setting up a EWC or an ICP.

Enforcement

How is Article 4's responsibility/obligation to be enforced? If a EWC or ICP is *not* created, is it arguably a violation of Article 4? Or does central management merely need to follow the steps laid out in Article 5? National legislation implementing the Directive will further define these obligations.

If there is arguably a failure of central management in 'creating the conditions and means necessary for the setting up of a EWC or an ICP', there is the question of who is the potential plaintiff, and what remedies are available. Effective remedies are one of the standards required of national legislation by EC law. National legislation implementing the Directive may further define management obligations and remedies for their non-fulfilment.

Establishing the SNB (Article 5): the role of employees' representatives

The central management is responsible for creating the conditions and means for setting up a EWC (Article 4(1)), initiating negotiations with the SNB (Article

5 Article 5(1).
6 Article 5(4).
7 Article 5(6).

5(1)), convening a meeting with the SNB (Article 5(4)) and bearing the expenses of negotiations with the SNB (Article 5(6)). However, the actual *establishment* of the SNB is *not* necessarily controlled by the central management.

The *composition* of the SNB is determined by Member State rules (Article 5(2)(a)). The *timing* of the establishment of the SNB may influence the application of these rules. It is not entirely clear how the establishment of the SNB is triggered.

How is the establishment of the SNB triggered?

Article 5(1) begins by stating that:

> '... the central management shall initiate negotiations for the establishment of a EWC or an ICP
> – on its own initiative or
> – at the written request of at least 100 employees or
> – their representatives
> in at least two undertakings or establishments in at least two different Member States.'

Central management, either on its own initiative or at the request of others, *always* initiates negotiations with the SNB. This raises potential problems when more than one actor wishes to act. The request of others is for no more than initiation of *negotiations* with the SNB.

However, the *initiation* of negotiations is *not* to be confused with the *establishment* of the SNB. Article 5(2) (establishment) is arguably independent of Article 5(1) (initiation of negotiations). It may be that the establishment of the SNB precedes the initiation of negotiations. The order of the first two paragraphs of Article 5 should be reversed. There seem to be two possible procedures:

PROCEDURE 1:

1. Article 4(1): the central management 'shall be responsible for *creating* the conditions and means necessary for the *setting up* of a EWC or an ICP'.
2. Article 5(1): the central management 'shall *initiate* negotiations for the establishment of a EWC or an ICP' at the request of one of those entitled to initiate.
3. Article 5(2): 'For this purpose, a SNB shall be *established* in accordance with the following guidelines...'
4. Article 5(4): 'With a view to the conclusion of an agreement in accordance with Article 6, the central management *shall convene* a meeting with the SNB.'

PROCEDURE 2:

1. Article 4(1): the central management 'shall be responsible for *creating* the conditions and means necessary for the *setting up* of a EWC or an ICP'.
2. Article 5(2): 'For this purpose, a SNB shall be *established* in accordance with the following guidelines...'
3. Article 5(4): 'With a view to the conclusion of an agreement in accordance with Article 6, the central management *shall convene* a meeting with the SNB'.
4. Article 5(1): the central management 'shall *initiate* negotiations for the establishment of a EWC or an ICP' at the request of one of those entitled to initiate.

The initiation of negotiations thus either:

Procedure 1: *triggers* the establishment of the SNB; or
Procedure 2: *engages* an already established SNB.

The *composition* of the SNB is predetermined by Member State rules (Article 5(2)). The *timing* of establishment of the SNB depends on the decision to initiate of central management, *or* employees, *or* their representatives.

In *practice*, the composition of the SNB may be influenced by the *timing* of the initiative. The timing may give *tactical advantages* in determining the election or appointment of representatives to the SNB, reflecting shifts in trade union or management strength. Either side, management or workers' representatives who can initiate negotiations, will be ready to trigger the establishment of the SNB at a favourable moment.

What rules determine the composition of the SNB?

Article 5(2) provides:

> '. . . a SNB shall be established in accordance with the following guidelines:
> (a) The Member States shall determine the method to be used for the election or appointment of the members of the SNB who are to be elected or appointed in their territories . . .'

This appears to mean that there may be no common criteria agreed among the Member States for their members of the SNB. Article 5(2)(c) (first paragraph) requires at least one representative from each Member State with an establishment or undertaking. The SNB members-representatives from each Member State will reflect national criteria of election or appointment of employees' representatives.

Nonetheless, it is arguable that one common criterion is that the members of the SNB should be employees' representatives. In the UK context, this means trade union representatives.

It is not clear that employees' representatives-members of the SNB must be employees of the multinational enterprise. Employees' representatives may themselves be employees, but need not be. This is reinforced by Article 10, paragraph 2 concerning protection of employees' representatives:

> 'This shall apply *in particular* to attendance at meetings of SNBs . . . and the payment of wages for members *who are on the staff* of the Community-scale undertaking or the Community-scale group of undertakings for the period of absence necessary for the performance of their duties.'

By implication, some of the employees' representatives on the SNB may not be on the staff of the undertaking, and hence not entitled to payment of wages. It seems that when Member States determine the method to be used for the election or appointment of the members of the SNB, they may not exclude employees' representatives who are not themselves employees of the undertaking.

The process is further complicated by Article 5(2)(c) (second paragraph) which provides for:

> 'supplementary members in proportion to the number of employees working . . . as laid down by the legislation of the Member State within the territory of which the central management is situated.'

A contradiction arises because the *method* of election or appointment of SNB members is determined by the rules of the Member State where the establishment is located; but the *number* of SNB members is determined by the rules of the Member State where the central management is situated. There is a possibility that the designation of the central management by UK multinational enterprises or non-EC multinational enterprises could be influenced by the different rules on proportional representation of different Member States.

SNB members: employees' representatives

The method of election or appointment of SNB members appears to be by *unconditional* delegation to Member State rules. If so, it is possible that a Member State, such as the UK, could try to legislate rules for the election or appointment of members of the SNB which ignore or exclude trade union representatives.

Whether Member State discretion in enacting rules for election or appointment of SNB members is unconditional is a fundamental issue in EU labour law. For example, could the UK enact rules challenging trade union representation on SNBs? Legislation along these lines in the UK could be questioned by way of litigation based on four grounds.

A PRESUMPTION IN SUBPARAGRAPH (2) OF ARTICLE 5(2)(A) THAT SNB MEMBERS ARE TO BE, OR TO BE ELECTED OR APPOINTED BY, EMPLOYEES' REPRESENTATIVES

One challenge would be based on subparagraph (2) of Article 5(2)(a), which provides:

> 'Member States shall provide that employees in undertakings and/or establishments in which there are no employees' representatives *through no fault of their own,* have the right to elect or appoint members of the SNB'.[8]

It is arguable that this creates a presumption either:

(i)   that the members of the SNB *are to be* the employees' representatives under Member State rules; or

(ii)   that employees' representatives are to *elect* or *appoint* the members of the SNB.

Employees *only* elect or appoint where 'there are no employees' representatives *through no fault of their own . . .*' Otherwise, it is employees' representatives who are, or elect or appoint, the SNB.

The composition of the SNB, according to Article 5(2)(a), should be determined as follows:

(i)   the Member States are to determine the method of election or appointment, which is to produce the employees' representatives on the SNB (subparagraph 1);

(ii)   if the method does not produce employees' representatives through no

---

8   This provision appears to envisage the alternative, that employees do *not* elect or appoint SNB members, where:

1. there are employee representatives;

2. there are no employee representatives through the employees' fault.

The argument is that in alternative 1 employee representatives elect or appoint SNB members. What happens in alternative 2 (indeed, what constitutes 'employees' fault') is not immediately clear.

fault of the employees, then the employees have the right to elect or appoint the SNB (subparagraph 2).

The meaning of 'through no fault of their own' becomes clear in light of the following subparagraph 3 of Article 5(2)(a):

'This second subparagraph shall be without prejudice to national legislation and/or practice laying down thresholds for the establishment of employee representation bodies.'

There may be no representatives as national rules may lay down thresholds for the establishment of employee representation bodies. This is *not* the fault of employees. Hence, employees have the right to elect or appoint the SNB. But apart from that case, employees' representatives must be designated under national rules. It is they who are to be, or to elect or appoint, the members of the SNB.[9]

The objective, structure and wording of the Article which produces this result is consistent with the logic of Cases C-382/92 and C-383/92: *EC Commission v UK*, decided by the Court on 8 June 1994.[10] The Commission complained that the UK had not provided rules for the designation of workers' representatives where this did not take place on a voluntary basis, as was required by Article 1(1)(b) of the 1975 Directive on Collective Dismissals and Article 2(c) of the 1977 Transfers of Undertakings (Acquired Rights) Directive:

'"workers' representatives" means the workers' representatives provided for by the laws or practices of the Member States.'

The Court held that this language:[11]

'leaves to Member States only the task of determining the arrangements for designating the workers' representatives . . .'

Member States are:[12]

'required to take all appropriate measures to ensure that workers' representatives are designated with a view to complying with the obligations laid down . . .'

In the words of the Court's judgment:[13]

'United Kingdom law, which allows an employer to frustrate the protection provided for workers/ employees by . . . the directive, must be regarded as contrary to (EC law).'

The argument that the EWCs Directive does not explicitly designate employee representatives as the members of the SNB, or provide for such representatives to elect the members parallels an argument rejected by the Court in Case C-382/92. The UK invoked Article 6(5) of the Transfers of Undertakings Directive:

'Member States may provide that where there are no representatives of the employees

---

9   Recognition of this is provided by Article 10, paragraph 1, which provides that members of SNBs 'shall, in the exercise of their functions, enjoy the same protection and guarantees provided for employees' representatives by the national legislation and/or practice in force in their country of employment.'
10 [1994] ECR I-2435.
11 Case C-383/92, paragraph 19; Case C-382/92, paragraph 18.
12 Case C-383/92, paragraph 25; Case C-382/92, paragraph 28.
13 Case C-383/92, paragraph 27; Case C-382/92, paragraph 30.

in an undertaking or business, the employees concerned must be informed in advance when a transfer within the meaning of Article 1(1) is about to take place.'

The UK argued:[14]

'that it follows from the very wording of Article 6(5) of the directive that the Community legislature envisaged the possibility that national legislation or practice might not provide for employee representation in circumstances other than the very limited cases contemplated by the Commission since it authorised Member States, without any restriction, to provide that the employees concerned may be directly informed in advance when a transfer is about to take place where there are no employee representatives in an undertaking or business.'

The Court rejected this argument:[15]

'22. Article 6(5) of the directive does, admittedly, envisage the possibility of there not being any employee representatives in an undertaking or business. However, that provision cannot be read in isolation and independently of the other provisions of Article 6.

23. As mentioned above, paragraphs 1 and 2 of Article 6 of the directive lay down the obligation to inform and consult employee representatives in the event of the transfer of an undertaking. Paragraphs 3 and 4 of Article 6 specify the cases in which Member States may, under certain conditions, limit that obligation. Paragraph 4, in particular, allows Member States to exempt from that obligation undertakings or businesses which, in respect of the number of their employees, do not fulfil the conditions for the election or designation of a collegiate body representing employees. In order to prevent employees being thereby deprived of all protection, paragraph 5 of Article 6 allows Member States to provide that employees must none the less be informed in advance when a transfer is about to take place.

24. The intention of the Community legislature was not therefore to allow the different national legal systems to accept a situation in which no employee representatives are designated since such designation is necessary to ensure compliance with the obligations laid down in Article 6 of the directive.'

Similarly, the intention of the Community legislature in the EWCs Directive is arguably that employee representatives are to be designated as the members of the SNB, or for such representatives to elect the members of the SNB.

The provision in Article 5(2)(a), subparagraph 2, which appears to allow for employees directly to elect the members of the SNB where 'there are no employees' representatives through no fault of their own' is not to be read 'in isolation and independently of the other provisions of Article (5)'. It is explicable through the provisions of subparagraph 3 of Article 5(2)(a) which, as in Article 6(4) of the Transfers of Undertakings Directive 'allows Member States to exempt from that obligation undertakings or businesses which, in respect of the number of their employees, do not fulfil the conditions for the election or designation of a collegiate body representing employees'. As stated above, apart from that case,[16] employees' representatives must be designated under national rules. It is they who are to be, or to elect or appoint, the members of the SNB.

---

14   Paragraph 21.
15   Paragraphs 22–24.
16   The nature of the thresholds for the establishment of employee representation bodies will also require scrutiny.

THE CRITERIA FOR WORKERS' REPRESENTATIVES-MEMBERS OF THE SNB IMPLICIT IN THE COURT'S JUDGMENT IN CASES C-382/92 AND C-383/92: *EC COMMISSION V UK*

In *EC Commission v UK*, the UK government argued that: [17]

> 'the directive does not require Member States to provide a specific mechanism for worker representation merely in order to comply with the requirements of the directive where an undertaking has no workers' representatives by virtue of national law.'

The Court nonetheless imposed the requirement on the UK to designate worker representatives because of the consequences this would have for the rights of workers under the provisions of the Directive: [18]

> 'which require Member States to take all measures necessary to ensure that workers are informed, consulted and in a position to intervene through their representatives in the event of collective redundancies (or the transfer of an undertaking).'

The argument is that to undertake the tasks of information and consultation specified in the Directives, worker representatives must possess certain qualities. These would arguably include the experience, independence and resources required to protect the interests of the workers they represent. National laws or practices providing for their designation must secure these qualities, otherwise they do not attain the objective of the EC Directive.

Similarly, in the case of the EWCs Directive, to secure that workers are properly represented on the SNB, the workers' representatives concerned will have to possess the experience, independence and resources to fulfil the task of the SNB. Member State legislation implementing the Directive will be scrutinised, and, if necessary, challenged by way of litigation, including, if necessary, a reference to the European Court if it proposes workers' representatives as SNB members who cannot fulfil their designated function by virtue of lacking the necessary qualities.

The quality of workers' representatives is especially sensitive and significant because of the earlier mentioned alternatives envisaged by the Directive. Both the headings to Section II and Article 4 refer to the 'establishment of a EWC *or* an employee ICP'. Similarly, Article 5(3) specifies that the task of the SNB is to determine the EWC or the ICP. The choice of a collective representative body, the EWC, rather than the individualised ICP, is more likely to follow from an SNB composed of workers' representatives than from SNB members elected or appointed in some other way.

As argued above, in parallel to the decision of the European Court in Cases C-383/92 and C-382/92, the EWCs Directive requires that *employees' representatives* be designated under national rules. It is *they* who are to be, or to elect or appoint, the members of the SNB. The only exception is the case provided in subparagraph 2 of Article 5(2)(a) – where thresholds preclude the establishment of employee representation bodies. Member States, including the UK government, which make legislative proposals for designating members of the SNB which do not satisfy the standards implicit in the Court's judgment, necessary to attain the EC objective, may be challenged.

---

17 Case C-383/92, paragraph 22; Case C-382/92, paragraph 25.
18 Case C-383/92, paragraph 23; Case C-382/92, paragraph 26.

In theory, the method for election or appointment of employees' representatives-members of the SNB could differ from those required for designation of workers' representatives by the 1975 and 1977 Directives. For example, the Advocate-General took the view that these latter Directives did not create:[19]

> 'an obligation to introduce a general system of worker representation going beyond the scope of the directives ... the Member States would even in my opinion be doing enough if they were to provide for an ad hoc system, by which I mean an arrangement enabling the affected workers, or a majority of them, to designate ad hoc representatives in a particular case in which the provision of information and/or consultation are required under the directives (even if the application of such a system might give rise to numerous difficulties). The essential point ... is that the designation of workers' representatives must not depend exclusively on the free choice or recognition of the employer.'

Legislation determining the method for the election or appointment of the members of the SNB could in theory designate employees' representatives who are different from those elected or appointed for other purposes.[20] They would still have to possess the qualities necessary to achieve the objectives of the Directive.

It is questionable whether legislation providing for different representatives would be legally compatible with the Directive's requirements, and hence acceptable to the European Court. Realistically, would a government find it practicable to enact, or employers welcome, a variety of laws on workers' representatives for different purposes?[1] In the UK context, the prime candidates to be employees' representatives on the SNB are the trade union representatives.

COMPETITION WITH OTHER REPRESENTATIVES WITHIN THE
MULTINATIONAL ENTERPRISE

Member State rules might seek to provide that the (employees' representatives-) members of the SNB are selected on the basis of criteria which diverge from established employee representation structures within the multinational enterprise – at workplace, company, divisional or group levels. These established representatives often have consultation or negotiation rights under national (and EU) rules. The result of a separate channel of representation for the SNB negotiations could be potential competition and conflict between different representatives with bargaining competences.

---

19   Opinion of Advocate-General Van Gerven on Cases C-382/92 and C-383/92, delivered on 2 March 1994, paragraph 14.
20   Criteria specific to a particular function of workers' representatives were also evident in the Commission's Communication on Implementation of the Protocol and Agreement on Social Policy of the Maastricht Treaty. According to the Commission, the social partners engaged in the social dialogue process who are to be consulted should have the following qualities (paragraph 24):
    a. be cross industry or sectoral at EC level;
    b. consist of Member State social partners and with capacity to negotiate agreements and representative of all Member States, as far as possible;
    c. be adequate to ensure effective consultation.
For comment, see the Opinion of the Economic and Social Committee on the Commission's Communication, discussed in Chapter 36.
1   Such as different representatives for the purposes of collective dismissals (the 1975 Directive), for transfers of undertakings (the 1977 Directive), for safety purposes (the 1989 'Framework' Directive) and for the EWCs Directive – as well as for future prospective Directives.

It is unlikely that the EU legislator intended that SNB members who are to negotiate the EWC were to be different from established employee representation channels. Again, the provision in subparagraph 2 of Article 5(1)(a) appears to link the rules on election or appointment of SNB members with the:

'national legislation and/or practice laying down thresholds for the establishment of employee representation bodies',

as does the definition of 'employees' representatives' in Article 2(1)(d):

'means the employees' representatives provided for by national law and/or practice.'

In the UK, where employee representation structures are established in workplaces, the representatives are trade union representatives. This may be argued to be the 'practice' which is to shape the Member State rules on the election or appointment of members of the SNB.

Some support for this argument may be found in the judgment of the High Court in *Griffin v South West Water Services Ltd.*[2] This case considered the meaning of Article 1(1)(b) of the 1975 Directive on collective redundancies in the context of whether the Directive was 'unconditional and sufficiently precise' to be capable of direct effect under EU law. The Article provides:

'"Workers' representatives" means the workers' representatives provided for by the laws or practices of the Member State.'

It was submitted that this provision:[3]

'allows existing practice or existing law to be substituted for implementing legislation in a State that does not enact such legislation or enacts defective legislation. If such a practice exists . . . (it) merely involves identifying who, in accordance with that practice, the representative is.'

The judge stated:[4]

'I do not agree. I confess I have great difficulty in understanding exactly what is meant by "practices" in Article 1.1(b) if it means something other than a procedure agreed between the particular employer and his employees for discussing matters of redundancy and the like. Since it is contrasted with the word "laws", it would appear to refer to a means of designating who an employee's representative is other than by reference to the laws of the Member State. In my view, where there is no agreement between employer and employee as to who the employee's representative is for the purpose of consulting over collective redundancies, the Directive requires that the Member State should bring into force laws, regulations or administrative provisions, in compliance with Article 6 of the Directive, to enable the workers' representatives to be identified. Since the Directive gives to the member state such a wide discretion in designating who the "workers' representatives" are to be, it cannot in my view be said that Article 2 is "unconditional and sufficiently precise".

If that conclusion is correct it follows that the Directive cannot be enforced directly . . .'

However, in the event that he was wrong on this point, the judge went on to state his conclusions on the issue of who were the 'workers' representatives' provided for by the laws or practices of the UK within the meaning of Article

---

2   [1995] IRLR 15.
3   Ibid, submission of John Hendy QC, paragraph 139.
4   Ibid, paragraphs 140–1.

1(1)(b) in a case where there were rival claimants: a staff council established by the employer (South West Water) for the purpose, and trade union representatives (UNISON in the case in the question). After hearing evidence from industrial relations experts (who disagreed) the judge concluded:[5]

'... that the consultative machinery established by South West Water in the shape of the staff council and area consultative committees was very much the exception in the field of modern-day industrial relations and that, despite an increasing trend towards de-recognition of trade unions for collective bargaining purposes, many employers still continue to recognise trade unions for other purposes including dealing with collective redundancies ...

If, therefore, the expression "practices", as used in Article 1.1(b), refers to the practices followed in industry generally in the United Kingdom (if not at South West Water) with regard to consultation between management and workforce over matters such as collective redundancies, and I am concerned to identify who, on the basis of such practices, are to be regarded as the representatives of those members of staff employed by South West Water whom South West Water is contemplating making redundant and who are members of Unison, my answer is Unison and not the staff side representatives on the staff council.'

The case is being appealed, and, in all probability, will be referred to the European Court. It provides some support, however, for the argument that, where there is an established practice of trade union representation, it is trade union representatives who are to be, or to elect or appoint, the members of the SNB.

THE SUBSIDIARY REQUIREMENTS IN THE ANNEX TO THE DIRECTIVE

The function of the SNB is to establish the EWC by agreement with the central management. The composition of the EWC is likely, therefore, to reflect the composition of the SNB. An SNB elected or appointed in accordance with methods determined by the Member State, which does not include employees' representatives, such as trade unions, could agree to a EWC unacceptable to trade unions. Could a EWC negotiated by such an SNB be challenged?

The Directive provides that:[6]

'1. In order to achieve the objective in Article 1(1), the subsidiary requirements laid down by the legislation of the Member State in which the central management is situated shall apply ...
2. The subsidiary requirements referred to in paragraph 1 as adopted in the legislation of the Member States must satisfy the provisions set out in the Annex.'

The Annex to the Directive prescribes:[7]

'The EWC shall be composed of employees ... elected or appointed from their number by the employees' representatives, or, in absence thereof, by the entire body of employees.

The election or appointment of the EWC shall be carried out in accordance with national legislation and/or practice.'

The Annex thus envisages a EWC composed of, or elected or appointed by, the employees' representatives. An SNB which agrees to a EWC *not* so elected

---

5   Ibid, paragraphs 150–1.
6   Article 7.
7   Paragraph 1(b).

or appointed is arguably not achieving the objective of the Directive.

The Annex's subsidiary requirements apply where:[8]

- the SNB and the central management so decide;
- central management refuses to commence negotiations within six months of a request;
- three years elapse after a request without an agreement.

The latter two situations automatically require that the EWC comprise, or be elected or appointed by, the employees' representatives. Does the first situation allow an agreement by the SNB which ignores the choices of the employees' representatives?

Normally the SNB 'shall act by a majority of its members' (Article 6(5)). It might seem, therefore, that an SNB elected or appointed by a method determined by the Member State, which does *not* include employees' representatives, could agree on a EWC *against* the wishes of the employees' representatives. However, the Directive provides that a decision by the SNB to exclude the subsidiary requirements in the Annex requires a two-thirds majority (Article 5(5)). It could be argued that the majority vote allowed by Article 6(5) does not allow for the exclusion of the subsidiary requirements. Arguably, an SNB which agrees to a EWC not composed of, or elected or appointed by, employees' representatives is acting inconsistently with the objective of the Directive.

The structure and objective of the Directive, and, in particular, the subsidiary requirements of the Annex support the view that the SNB should reflect the eventual composition of the EWC: it 'shall be composed of employees ... elected or appointed from their number by the employees' representatives, or, in absence thereof, by the entire body of employees.'

Conclusion

The structure and wording of the three subparagraphs of Article 5(2)(a) should be read as giving, in the first place, to employees' representatives the right to elect or appoint the members of the SNB. Employees' representatives, as defined in Article 2(1)(d):

'means the employees' representatives provided for by national law and/or practice.'

As interpreted by the European Court in *EC Commission v UK*, Member States must provide for such representation.[9]

This interpretation of the Court is reflected in the provision in Article 5(2)(a), first subparagraph, that:

'The Member States shall determine the method to be used for the election or appointment of the members of the special negotiating bodies who are to be elected or appointed in their territories.'

The Member States have the choice of method with regard to providing for employees' representatives, but shall secure that employees' representatives are themselves, or elect or appoint, the members of the SNB.

8 Article 7(1).
9 Cases C-382/92 and C-383/92: [1994] ECR I-2435 and [1994] ECR I-2479.

In sum: the composition of the SNB to be established under Article 5(2) is as follows:

(i)   the method of election or appointment of members of the SNB is determined by the Member States;[10]

(ii) this method shall ensure that the members of the SNB are, or are elected or appointed by, employees' representatives (as provided for by national law and/or practice;[11] if there are no employees' representatives through no fault of the employees, the employees have the right to elect or appoint members of the SNB;[12]

(iii) thresholds on provision for employees' representatives are acceptable;[13]

(iv) representativity across Member States where employees are employed is guaranteed;[14]

(v) there are supplementary members in proportion to the number of employees working in establishments, as laid down by the Member State where central management is located;[15]

(vi) there is a minimum of three and a maximum of 17 members of the SNB.[16]

Convening the SNB and initiating negotiations with the SNB to establish a EWC or ICP

Whichever procedure involves the *establishment* of the SNB (independent of or contemporaneous with the initiation of negotiations over the EWC), *negotiations* appear to *follow*:

1.   an initiative by one of the three eligibles (central management, 100 employees or their representatives) (Article 5(1));

2.   establishment of the SNB as provided for by Member State rules (Article 5(2)).

The next step appears to be the convening of the SNB:[17]

> 'With a view to the conclusion of an agreement in accordance with Article 6, the central management shall convene a meeting with the SNB . . .'

Central management controls *only* the convening of a meeting with the SNB. *Convening* is *not* the same as *initiating* negotiations[18] or *establishing* the SNB.[19] *Others* may dictate the timing of the initiation of negotiations or establishment of the SNB. This timing may be of critical importance.

Timing the initiation of negotiations

It appears that the SNB, as well as the three named eligibles in Article 5(1) (central management, 100 employees or their representatives), can initiate

---

10   Article 5(2)(a), subparagraph 1.
11   Article 2(1)(d).
12   Article 5(2)(a), subparagraph 2.
13   Article 5(2)(a), subparagraph 3.
14   Article 5(2)(c), subparagraph 1.
15   Article 5(2)(c), subparagraph 2.
16   Article 5(2)(b).
17   Article 5(4).
18   Article 5(1).
19   Article 5(2).

negotiations. Awkwardly, Article 5(5) allows that:

'The SNB may decide, by at least *two-thirds* of the votes, *not* to open negotiations in accordance with paragraph 4, *or* to terminate the negotiations already opened.'

The implication is that the SNB too may decide to open negotiations – in accordance with paragraph 4 'with a view to the conclusion of an agreement'. If so, there appear to be *four* eligible parties who may seize the initiative and open negotiations.

Another view is that the power of initiation of negotiations towards the EWC granted in Article 5(1) serves *only* to stimulate the establishment of the SNB. After this, only either central management or the SNB may initiate the actual negotiations. The SNB takes the place of the employees or their representatives, as these representatives are, or elect or appoint, the members of the SNB (unless there are no employees' representatives, in which case the members of the SNB are elected or appointed by employees directly).[20]

Either the SNB or the central management may seize the initiative to begin negotiations. As with the establishment of the SNB, negotiations in practice may be influenced by the *timing* of their initiation The timing may give *tactical advantages* reflecting shifts in trade union or management strength. Both sides will seek to initiate negotiations at a favourable moment.

Strategic and tactical voting

The potential danger to the trade union side is illustrated by Article 5(5), which provides that:

'The SNB may decide, by at least *two-thirds* of the votes, not to open negotiations in accordance with paragraph 4, or to terminate the negotiations already opened.

Such a decision shall stop the procedure to conclude the agreement referred to in Article 6. Where such a decision has been taken, the provisions in the *Annex shall not apply.*

A new request to convene the SNB may be made at the earliest two years after the abovementioned decision unless the parties concerned lay down a shorter period.'

The dangerous situation might arise since, first, the timing of the establishment of the SNB may be dictated by central management initiative. Secondly, Member State rules determine the method of election or appointment of the SNB (though, as argued above, the SNB is to be composed of employees' representatives 'provided for by national law and/or practice'). And, thirdly, a two-thirds majority of the SNB so elected or appointed could terminate negotiations.

Theoretically, it might be possible to delay any agreement on a EWC for up to eight years. The subsidiarity requirements of the Annex do not automatically apply until three years have elapsed following a request to initiate negotiations (Article 7(1), 3rd indent). A last minute decision to stop the procedure means a new request to (re-)convene the (existing) SNB must wait at least two years (Article 5(5), subparagraph 3). A further three years might elapse without agreement. At that point (but perhaps earlier) an initiative to establish a new SNB may be taken.

Hence, the importance of seizing the initiative. If central management dictates the timing, it might be able to influence the composition of the SNB and hence

20   Article 5(2)(a), subparagraph 2.

the conduct of negotiations so as to kill off a EWC by a two-thirds majority,[1] or agree to a weak EWC agreement or even an ICP by a simple majority.[2] To the contrary, the objective of the employees' representatives would be to secure a majority to avoid any agreement for a weak EWC or an ICP; or at least a one-third minority to block a decision terminating negotiations.

In reality, the SNB is unlikely to divide easily into a majority and minority group. A multi-national SNB composed of employees' representatives from different Member States will likely be much more fragmented. To avoid the negative consequences of excessive fragmentation, much preparatory work will be required at European level to secure the necessary coordination and co-operation between employees' representatives in the same multinational enterprise in different countries. This would aim to seize the initiative at the most favourable moment to establish the SNB, initiate negotiations and conclude a EWC agreement.

The objective could be to secure a trade union majority. But, failing this, the aim could be to secure strategic coalitions blocking any anti-trade union majority emerging, and, if necessary, to hold out for three years until the subsidiary requirements of the Annex automatically apply.

Resources

A final consideration of practical importance concerns the resources of the SNB. The Directive lays down an EU standard in Article 5(6), subparagraph 1:

> 'Any expenses relating to the negotiations (conducted by the SNB) shall be borne by the central management so as to enable the SNB to carry out its task in an appropriate manner.'

The EU standard requires resources adequate 'to enable the SNB to carry out its task in an appropriate manner'. Member State rules providing resources to employees' representatives differ. They must *at least* satisfy the EU standard.

In contrast, the role of Member State standards is indicated by Article 10, paragraph 1:

> 'Members of SNBs ... shall, in the exercise of their functions, enjoy the same protection and guarantees provided for employees' representatives by the national legislation and/or practice in force in their country of employment.'

This implies *different* levels of protection and guarantees between Member States. But these are *minimum* standards. The EU standard is the entitlement of SNBs in all Member States.

Member State provisions vary. For example, in the UK, there are provisions now in the Trade Union and Labour Relations (Consolidation) Act 1992 on time off for trade union duties and activities. Adjusted to the SNB operations of negotiating a EWC agreement, these should include time off (paid and unpaid) for members of the SNB, pre-meeting expenses, training, liaising with other EWCs already established in the sector, facilities and expert advice.

The 'operation of the SNB' (Article 5(6), subparagraph 2) in carrying out its task 'in an appropriate manner' implies relevant protection and guarantees. There are some more specific provisions.

---

1   Article 5(5).
2   Article 6(5).

Experts

Article 5(4), subparagraph 2, provides:

'For the purpose of the negotiations, the SNB may be assisted by experts of its choice.'

Experts 'to enable the SNB to carry out its task in an appropriate manner' could include lawyers to provide advice on the legal entitlements and obligations of the SNB and its members, as well as a range of others helpful in negotiating a EWC adapted to the specific nature of the industry, structure of the multinational enterprise, and so on. The SNB can draw up its proposed list of experts for submission to central management for funding.

However, the Member State may limit funding to cover one expert only (Article 5(6), paragraph 2). Apparently, one paid expert is appropriate. What is not specified is how much of the expert's time will be needed if only one can be hired. It might make more sense for the central management to agree to short-term funding of a number of specialists for specific purposes, rather than long-term funding of one expert who will have to cover a number of areas.

Budgetary rules

Following the stipulation of the EU standard requiring the funding of expenses 'so as to enable the SNB to carry out its task in an appropriate manner', Article 5(6), subparagraph 2, provides:

'In compliance with this principle, Member States may lay down budgetary rules regarding the operation of the SNB.'

The meaning of *budgetary* rules is not clear. They must comply with the principle of enabling the SNB to carry out its task in an appropriate manner. However, the following sentence, that Member States 'may in particular limit the funding to cover one expert only', implies that some substantive limits are possible. Member State budgetary rules appear to be limited to the quantifying of paid time. They do not cover the amount of unpaid time, or its purposes or any conditions to be attached.

Time off: paid and unpaid

Article 10, paragraph 1, provides members of SNBs with:

'the same protection and guarantees provided for employees' representatives by the national legislation and/or practice in force in their country of employment.'

Article 10, paragraph 2 continues:

'This shall apply *in particular* to attendance at meetings of SNBs . . . and the payment of wages for members who are on the staff of the Community-scale undertaking or the Community-scale group of undertakings for the period of absence necessary for the performance of their duties.'

'In particular' attendance at meetings of SNBs implies that SNB members may be absent, justifiably, for *other* reasons, such as education and training, meetings with other SNBs or EWCs in the sector, meetings with experts, and so on. It may be that the time off for these absences is necessary 'so as to enable the SNB to carry out its task in an appropriate manner', and hence is eligible for funding by central management.

THE MEDIUM TERM: NEGOTIATING A EWC

Introduction

Once established, the Special Negotiating Body:[3]

> 'shall have the task of determining, with the central management, by written agreement, the scope, composition, functions, and term of office of the European Works Councils (EWCs) or the arrangements for implementing a procedure for the information and consultation of employees (ICP).'

Article 6 of the Directive is concerned with the content of the agreement. Article 7 prescribes subsidiary requirements contained in the Annex, to apply in certain situations. A number of issues raised by these Articles, and the Annex, require analysis.

The priority as between a EWC and an ICP

An innocuous, but fundamental, ambiguity emerges from Article 6(1):

> 'The central management and the SNB must negotiate in a spirit of cooperation with a view to reaching an agreement on the detailed arrangements for implementing the information and consultation of employees provided for in Article 1(1).'

The emphasis is on the information and consultation of *employees*. Albeit *one* of the alternative ways of achieving this is through a EWC, this appears not to be the necessary result. The strategic objective of some employers, and some Member State governments, including the UK, and especially after the European Court's decision in *EC Commission v UK*,[4] may be to use the Directive as a launchpad for direct consultation of and information to *individual* employees – minimising *collective* representation.

The determining factor in the success of such a strategy will be *not* the EWC, which may never emerge, but the SNB. This is the one collective representative body which the Directive *requires* to be created and negotiated with. Countervailing trade union strategies of negotiation and litigation will aim to control the SNB and ensure that the outcome of its negotiations with the central management is a EWC, not an ICP. For an ICP could, potentially, minimise collective representation and become a procedure for consultation of and information to individual employees with few, if any, representation rights for trade unions. An ICP has this threatening potential for two reasons.

Discussion v consultation

There is a long list of issues to be determined by agreement between the SNB and central management regarding information and consultation of the EWC (Article 6(2)). In contrast, those to be determined regarding the ICP are relatively meagre:[5]

> 'The agreement must stipulate by what method the employees' representatives shall have the right to meet to discuss the information conveyed to them.

---

3   Article 5(3).
4   Cases C-382/92 and C-383/92: [1994] ECR I-2435 and [1994] ECR I-2479.
5   Article 6(3), subparagraphs 2–3.

This information shall relate in particular to transnational questions which significantly affect workers' interests.'

The objective of the Directive is 'consultation', as defined in Article 2(1)(f), which

'means the exchange of views and establishment of dialogue between employees' representatives and central management or any more appropriate level of management.'

In the ICP, this becomes a right of the representatives 'to discuss the information conveyed to them'. Information may be conveyed to individual employees for their representatives to then discuss it.

This is a potential threat to the collective representation of employees which is the function of trade unions. An agreement which provided only for such discussion would be vulnerable to challenge as so far from the concept of consultation, as defined in the Directive, that it does not satisfy the requirement that there be established an ICP capable of fulfilling the objective of the Directive.

Subsidiary requirements

Article 7 prescribes the subsidiary requirements set out in the Annex, which must be adopted in the Member State legislation implementing the Directive. Significantly, *all* of the paragraphs of the Annex refer to EWCs and do not refer to an ICP. The relatively meagre requirements of Article 6(3), subparagraphs 2–3 on the ICP may be contrasted with the detailed provisions on consultation and information of the EWC in paragraphs 2 and 3 of the Annex.

As a result of this omission to specify the ICP in the Annex, Member State implementing legislation may fail to even stipulate subsidiary requirements regarding an ICP. Negotiating an ICP thus offers advantages to employers in that there are no legislative requirements against which to measure the agreement on an ICP.

Does a EWC have priority over an ICP?

The relative disadvantages of an ICP, as compared with a EWC, are such that it is likely that litigation will erupt should the former be adopted. A legal challenge to an ICP would be based on the argument that Article 6, and in particular Article 6(2), prescribes a *priority* in favour of a EWC over an ICP.

Article 6(1), which does not refer to a EWC but rather to 'the detailed arrangements for implementing the information and consultation of employees provided for in Article 1(1)', seems to be neutral as between a EWC or an ICP. This apparent neutrality, however, is controverted by the following paragraphs.

Article 6(2) begins by providing that 'the agreement *referred to* in paragraph 1 ... shall determine' – and there follow details *only* of a EWC, *not* an ICP. This seems to imply that the *first* point of reference is a EWC. This is reinforced by Article 6(3) which begins by providing that:

'The central management and the SNB may decide, in writing, to establish one or more ICPs *instead* of a EWC.'

The word 'instead' implies that a EWC must at least have been already considered, and may be deemed to have priority over an ICP. Article 6(3) stipulates requirements for an ICP which are meagre relative to those imposed on a EWC. An ICP agreement confined to these requirements might be open to challenge as not satisfying the objective of the Directive.

In sum, the argument is that the wording, structure and objective of Article 6 of the Directive gives priority to a EWC over an ICP: first, the structure, in that the order of the paragraphs prioritises the EWC; secondly, the wording, in that the ICP is to be established only 'instead' of a EWC; and, finally, the objective, given the relatively meagre content of agreements for an ICP compared to a EWC. All these point in the direction of recognition that the first priority of an agreement negotiated by the SNB and the central management is to be a EWC. An ICP requires justification. If accepted, such an argument has implications for the procedure of negotiation between the SNB and central management.

The Directive's stratagem: bargaining in the shadow of the Annex

Article 6(1) provides:

> 'The central management and the SNB must negotiate in a spirit of co-operation with a view to reaching an agreement . . .'

The obligations of central management

It has been argued that the Directive grants priority to an agreement on a EWC over an ICP. The behaviour of central management may be assessed in light of this priority. The obligation to negotiate in a spirit of co-operation entails concrete actions which central management must undertake with a view to reaching an agreement on a EWC. This may involve meetings, providing information, putting forward reasoned positions, giving reasoned replies to arguments, with supporting evidence, and so on. A spirit of co-operation may be contrasted to one of conflict. Central management's behaviour will be scrutinised in light of this.

Management conduct must be consistent with a desire to reach an agreement, perhaps with priority to a EWC. If no agreement is reached, it may be necessary to justify the behaviour which failed to achieve the agreement. For example, a continual refusal by central management to entertain a proposal by the SNB to create a EWC would seem to require explanation. A failure to make any concessions in response to concessions by the other side arguably would not be consistent with a spirit of co-operation.

Alleged violations by central management of the obligation to negotiate in a spirit of co-operation on a EWC – for example, its refusal to consider other than an ICP – could be subject to challenge by way of litigation. Such litigation will inevitably raise the question of appropriate remedies. These might include the imposition of a EWC on central management. For a EWC is the outcome envisaged where the subsidiary requirements of the Annex apply. The application of the subsidiary requirements in the Annex, creating a EWC, operates in two situations:[6]

> '–   where the central management refused to commence negotiations within six months of the request referred to in Article 5(1) (to initiate negotiations), or
> –   where, after three years from the date of this request, they are unable to conclude an agreement . . .'

---

6   Article 7(1), 2nd and 3rd indents.

The failure of central management to negotiate in a spirit of co-operation can lead to the first scenario where, after only six months, this *failure* is characterised as a *refusal* to commence negotiations.

The role of the subsidiary requirements in the Annex

The subtlety of the Directive's stratagem lies in *apparently* leaving all to the unfettered negotiations of the SNB and central management. The Directive even goes so far as to explicitly allow for the exclusion of the Annex requirements in any agreements reached:[7]

> 'The agreements referred to in paragraphs 2 and 3 shall not, unless provision is made otherwise therein, be subject to the subsidiary requirements of the Annex'.[8]

Formally, the content of the agreement is not confined by the Annex. But the Annex's subsidiary requirements apply where[9] the SNB and the central management so decide;[10] central management refuses to commence negotiations within 6 months of a request; or 3 years elapse after a request without an agreement.[11] *In practice*, central management will have to offer incentives to persuade the SNB to make an agreement offering less than the subsidiary requirements in the Annex.

On the other side, the employees' representatives on the SNB also are not bound by the Annex. Negotiations can flexibilise Annex requirements. Both sides have an incentive to treat it as the basis for negotiations. The Annex should be examined closely – not as a minimum entitlement, but as a package which could be negotiated and varied, if enough incentives are offered.

In practice, therefore, the structure of negotiations between the SNB and central management is such that the subsidiary requirements in the Annex become the effective threshold for agreements. This is done by determining the composition of the SNB to comprise employees' representatives; and bringing the Annex to bear where the SNB is not willing to settle for less than the subsidiary requirements. The argument is that the Directive does not lay down explicit formal minimum requirements for a EWC. Rather it provides the framework for a negotiating strategy of the SNB.

The Directive does not make this a simple task. The SNB can act by a majority of its members.[12] A simple majority on the SNB could, by agreement with central management, determine the composition, functions, procedures,

---

7 Article 6(4).
8 There is a transitional provision in Article 13 whereby the obligations arising from the Directive do not apply to certain agreements which are in existence on 22 September 1996 or the date of transposition of the Directive in the Member State in question, where this is earlier. Such agreements must satisfy various criteria, analysed below. Arguably, an agreement which does *not* meet these qualifications cannot claim exemption from the subsidiary requirements under Article 6(4).
9 Article 7(1).
10 It may be that the central management and SNB are agreed that only some parts of the subsidiary requirements apply, but conclude an agreement on other issues listed in Article 6.
11 It is not clear whether the subsidiary requirements apply when the central management and SNB are unable to conclude an agreement on *all* the issues listed in Article 6. It may be that where agreement is not reached on some issues, the relevant parts of the subsidiary requirements apply.
12 Article 6(5).

resources and so on of the EWC apparently in any way the parties wished. It will be up to trade unions from the different countries represented on the SNB to develop co-operative strategies to secure an effective EWC.

The scope of the EWC: excluding establishments or undertakings

The apparent autonomy granted to the central management and the SNB is illustrated by Article 6(2)(a), which provides that they shall determine:

'the undertakings of the Community-scale group of undertakings or the establishments of the Community-scale undertaking which are covered by the agreement.'

This appears to imply that the EWC or ICP may *not* cover all undertakings or establishments.

The SNB, however, necessarily includes at least one member representing each Member State with an establishment or undertaking, and supplementary members proportionate to the numbers of employees working in those establishments or undertakings.[13] To exclude from the EWC representatives from establishments or undertakings in a Member State, or failure to reflect proportionately the numbers of employees working in certain establishments or undertakings contradicts the principles of the SNB's own composition.

A majority of the SNB could apparently decide to do so, as Article 6(5) provides that:

'For the purposes of concluding the agreements referred to in paragraphs 2 and 3, the SNB shall act by a majority of its members.'

However, an agreement with central management excluding establishments or undertakings from representation on the EWC could be challenged on at least two grounds. First, a decision by a majority of the SNB to contradict its own mandatory composition by excluding some of its representatives from the EWC requires justification in light of the duty to 'negotiate in a spirit of co-operation' which applies also to the SNB. Secondly, the *threshold* requirements for the application of the Directive are:[14]

'– at least 1,000 employees within the Member States,
– at least two group undertakings in different Member States, and
– at least one group undertaking with at least 150 employees in one Member State and at least one other group undertaking with at least 150 employees in another Member State.'

An agreement for a EWC covering less than this threshold would seem to require justification.

Structuring negotiations on the composition of the EWC

The composition of the EWC, as in the case of the SNB, is a crucial issue. Article 6(2)(b) leaves it to be determined by the central management and the SNB. The apparently total freedom to determine the composition of the EWC is reinforced by the opening phrase of Article 6(2): 'Without prejudice to the

---

13   Article 5(2)(c).
14   Article 2(1)(c).

autonomy of the parties . . .' This provision seems to leave the composition of the EWC surprisingly unregulated, and hence open to manipulation by the SNB and central management. There is here a potential risk of conflict not only between trade unions and central management, but among trade unions and employees' representatives from different countries on the SNB.

Article 6(2)(b) provides that:

'the agreement . . . between the central management and the SNB shall determine . . .

. . .

(b) the composition of the EWC, the number of members, the allocation of seats and the term of office.'

The absence of explicit rules is in striking contrast with the Directive's specific provisions on the composition and method of election and appointment of the SNB.[15] The composition of the EWC is to be negotiated and is not subject to any express criteria. The implication is that the SNB, itself constrained as to its membership, is unlikely in practice to agree to a EWC out of line with its own composition.

In contrast with the Directive's rules on the composition of the SNB, there are no express formal limitations on the composition of the EWC in terms of election or appointment (eg by employees or their representatives) or representation of establishments or undertakings along geographical or numerically proportionate lines. The absence of explicit formal criteria for membership of the EWC implies that it is not limited in its composition to employees. This appears to allow for co-opting of outsiders from, eg the European Trade Union Confederation (ETUC), EU-wide sectoral organisations, or other experts. There is not even an express requirement that the EWC include 'employees' representatives', as defined in Article 2(1)(d) by national law and/or practice.

Arguably, however, as with the apparent freedom to determine the establishments or undertakings covered by the agreement, the SNB and central management's agreement on the composition of the EWC is subject to certain implicit limitations. These limitations may be deduced from, first, the provisions[16] determining the composition of the SNB, which, in a spirit of co-operation, is to negotiate the composition of the EWC; and, secondly, the subsidiary requirements for the EWC set out in the Annex, which are to apply in certain circumstances '(i)n order to achieve the objective in Article 1(1)' of the Directive ('to improve the right to information and to consultation of employees'). These subsidiary requirements for the EWC resemble those applicable to the SNB: employees elected or appointed from their number by the employees' representatives or, in the absence thereof, by the entire body of employees.[17]

These two sets of provisions, Article 5(2)(a–c) and paragraph 1(b) of the Annex, provide a framework for the composition of the EWC to be negotiated between the SNB and central management. In practice, the negotiations are structured so that the subsidiary requirements in the Annex become the effective threshold for agreements. The Annex is brought to bear where the SNB is not willing to settle for less than the subsidiary requirements.

Both parties are bargaining in the shadow of the Annex. Specifically, the

15   Article 5(2)(a–c).
16   Article 5(2)(a–c).
17   Paragraph 1(b) of the Annex.

Directive structures the negotiations between the SNB and central management so that the agreement which results is effectively subject to the Annex requirement that the EWC be composed of employees' representatives. This is due to the composition of the SNB, which the Directive mandates to comprise employees' representatives. A second requirement, less clear, is that these representatives also be employees.

EWC to be composed of employees' representatives

It was argued above that the method of election or appointment of members of the SNB is determined by the Member States;[18] and this method shall ensure that the members of the SNB are, or are elected or appointed by, employees' representatives.[19] If there are no employees' representatives through no fault of the employees, the employees have the right to elect or appoint members of the SNB.[20]

Similarly, paragraph 1(b) of the Annex provides:

'The EWC shall be composed of employees of the Community-scale undertaking or Community-scale group of undertakings elected or appointed from *their number* by the employees' representatives or, in the absence thereof, by the entire body of employees.

The election or appointment of members of the EWC shall be carried out in accordance with national legislation and/or practice.'

There is some ambiguity as to whether the phrase 'their number' refers (back) to employees, or (forward) to employees' representatives. In either case, it is clearly the employees' representatives who elect or appoint the members of the EWC. It is most likely they will elect or appoint employees from among themselves.

The absence of employees' representatives allows for election or appointment of members of the EWC by 'the entire body of employees'.[1] Employees have the right to elect or appoint the members of the SNB where 'there are no employees' representatives through no fault of their own'.[2] In the normal case, the SNB will comprise employees' representatives. So will a EWC created under the subsidiary requirements in the Annex.

The subsidiary requirements of the Annex apply where the SNB and the central management so decide; central management refuses to commence negotiations within six months of a request; or three years elapse after a request without an agreement.[3] The negotiating strategy inherent in the structure of the Directive is based on an SNB composed of employees' representatives. The SNB is in a strong negotiating position. If central management does not agree with the SNB, effectively, the employees' representatives on the SNB alone will determine the composition of the EWC. If central management refuses to negotiate, or refuses to agree to employees' representatives nominated by the SNB, after three years the EWC will be set up comprising those elected or appointed by the employees' representatives alone.

---

18   Article 5(2)(a), subparagraph 1.
19   As provided for by national law and/or practice (Article 2(1)(d)).
20   Article 5(2)(a), subparagraph 2.
1   Paragraph 1(b), subparagraph 1.
2   Article 5(2)(a), subparagraph 2.
3   Article 7(1).

Some hypothetical examples

The negotiating positions of the employees' representatives can be illustrated by some hypothetical cases.

1. A UK MNE with subsidiaries in France and Germany. The UK MNE's central management designates either a subsidiary in France or Germany as its representative agent to take on the responsibility of negotiating the EWC.[4] French and German employees' representatives are elected or appointed to the SNB in accordance with the methods determined by the Member States.[5]

   (a) The French and German employees' representatives insist on the inclusion of UK employees' representatives on the SNB, if allowed by national rules implementing the Directive.[6]

   (b) An SNB composed only of French and German employees' representatives negotiates a EWC agreement with central management which includes on the EWC UK employees' representatives.[7]

   (c) Central management rejects the demand of the SNB for UK employees' representatives on the EWC. After three years,[8] the employees' representatives elect or appoint the EWC including UK employees' representatives.[9]

   Unresolved questions include whether UK employees' representatives on an SNB or EWC can enforce legal rights under a EWC agreement, or, in the absence of an agreement, any legal rights – in UK courts or elsewhere.

2. An MNE (UK or other) with most of its employees in one or two Member States. The SNB, acting by a majority of its members from the one or two Member States, could agree on a EWC packed with employees' representatives contrary to the wishes of employees' representatives from other Member States.

   Normally the SNB 'shall act by a majority of its members'.[10] However, the Directive provides in the Annex that the EWC necessarily include at least one member representing each Member State with an establishment or undertaking, and supplementary members proportionate to the numbers of employees working in those establishments or that undertaking.[11]

   The importance of representation from different establishments and enterprises is also evident in paragraph 3 of the subsidiary requirements in the Annex. This concerns the rights of the EWC in 'exceptional circumstances' involving 'measures significantly affecting employees' interests'. It makes special provision for 'those members of the EWC who have been elected or appointed by the establishments and/or undertakings which are directly concerned by the measures.'

   In certain circumstances, a decision by the SNB to exclude the subsidiary requirements in the Annex requires a two-thirds majority.[12] It could

---

4 Article 4(2).
5 Article 5.
6 Article 5(2)(a).
7 Article 6(2)(c).
8 Article 7(1).
9 Annex, paragraph 1(b).
10 Article 6(5).
11 Annex, paragraph 1(d).
12 Article 5(5).

be argued that an agreement (not normally subject to the Annex by Article 6(4)) excluding the subsidiary requirements in the particular circumstances of national and proportionate representation, requires more than the normal majority vote allowed by Article 6(5).

3.   An MNE with employees distributed over a number of Member States. The SNB, acting by a majority of its members, could agree on a EWC *against* the wishes of some of the other employees' representatives.

A multi-national SNB composed of employees' representatives from different Member States will likely be fragmented. The trade unions' objective would be to secure a majority. But, failing this, the aim would be to secure strategic coalitions blocking any anti-trade union majority emerging, and, if necessary, to hold out for three years until the subsidiary requirements of the Annex automatically apply.

4.   An MNE central management persuades a majority of the SNB to establish a EWC manifestly lacking effective employees' representation.

Normally the SNB 'shall act by a majority of its members'.[13] Arguably, an SNB which agrees to a EWC without effective employees' representation is acting inconsistently with the objective of the Directive. The subsidiary requirements arguably may be read as the minimum threshold requirements for an effective EWC. It could be argued that the majority vote allowed by Article 6(5) does not allow for the exclusion of the subsidiary requirements.

Much will depend on the provisions in the laws of the other Member States and the strategies of their trade union movements. Transposition in all countries is still in the preparatory stage and no draft legislative texts have been drawn up. But in two countries, Denmark and Norway (which has accepted the Directive under the EEA Treaty) the transposition will be through an agreement between the social partners. In Sweden the trend is towards legislation and in Finland the Directive will be transposed via a law drawn up in the course of tripartite talks. In Germany, talks are going on between social partners in the metalworking industry regarding a joint recommendation, but an initial draft bill will be prepared by the Ministry of Labour in September 1995. In France and Italy the governments have started consulting the social partners. The strategies of the social partners, and that legislation, may affect the rights of UK employees of UK MNEs, and their trade union representatives on EWCs.

EWC to be composed of employees?

The subsidiary requirements for the EWC prescribe: 'The EWC shall be composed of employees ... elected or appointed from their number by the employees' representatives...'[14] There is no such explicit provision regarding membership of the SNB. There thus appears to be a difference between the two sets of provisions as to whether the members must also be employees.

In accordance with the subsidiary requirements, membership of the EWC, as with the SNB, appears to be restricted to employees' representatives. The argument was made above that members of the SNB are employees' representatives,

13   Article 6(5).
14   Paragraph 1(b) of the Annex.

who may themselves be employees, but need not be. This may be the case also for the EWC negotiated by the SNB with central management.

The ambiguity is reflected in Article 10, paragraph 2 concerning protection of employees' representatives:

'This shall apply *in particular* to attendance at meetings of SNBs or EWCs ... and the payment of wages for members *who are on the staff* of the Community-scale undertaking or the Community-scale group of undertakings for the period of absence necessary for the performance of their duties.'

By implication, some of the employees' representatives on the EWC (as with the SNB) may not be on the staff of the undertaking, and hence not entitled to payment of wages. There is an argument, therefore, that when central management and the SNB negotiate the composition of the EWC, they may include employees' representatives who are not themselves employees of the undertaking.

The functions and procedure of the EWC

The SNB and central management are to negotiate an agreement determining:[15]

'(c) the functions and the procedure for information and consultation of the EWC;
(d) the venue, frequency and duration of meetings of the EWC;
(e) the financial and material resources to be allocated to the EWC.'

Two preliminary points should precede analysis of the Directive's provisions. First, according to Article 1(1):

'The purpose of this Directive is to improve the right to information and to consultation of employees in Community-scale undertakings and Community-scale groups of undertakings.'

The implication is that the Directive aims to improve, to go beyond the status quo. Secondly, according to the 'Definitions':[16]

'"consultation" means the exchange of views and establishment of dialogue between employees' representatives and central management or any more appropriate level of management.'

The meaning of 'consultation' goes beyond the conventionally understood limitations of the term and extends into the 'establishment of dialogue.'

As with the other issues to be agreed between the SNB and central management, the Directive's stratagem structures the negotiations so that the subsidiary requirements in the Annex become the effective threshold for agreements. The provisions of the Annex on the functions and procedures of the EWC therefore require close analysis. They cover the scope of the topics to be covered by the information and consultation procedure, and the nature of the information and consultation process. The provisions of the Annex may be regarded as the minimal basis for negotiations; they can be varied, if enough incentives are offered.

---

15   Article 6(2).
16   Article 2(1)(f).

The scope of the topics to be covered by the information and consultation procedure

Formally, there is no limitation on the topics to be subject to the procedure of information and consultation of the EWC. The subsidiary requirements of the Annex provide a comprehensive indication. The EWC is:[17]

> 'to be informed and consulted ... on the progress of the business ... and its prospects.
> ... *in particular* ... the structure, economic and financial situation, the probable development of the business and of production and sales, the situation and probable trend of employment, investments, and substantial changes concerning organisation, introduction of new working methods or production processes, transfers of production, mergers, cut-backs or closures of undertakings, establishments or important parts thereof, and collective redundancies.'

A general characterisation of the scope of topics to be covered is added by paragraph 3 of the subsidiary requirements of the Annex:

> 'Where there are exceptional circumstances affecting the employees' interests to a considerable extent, particularly in the event of relocations, the closure of establishments or undertakings or collective redundancies ... the EWC shall have the right to be informed. It shall have the right to meet ... so as to be informed and consulted on measures significantly affecting employees' interests.'

The *general* scope of topics requiring information and consultation include the progress of the business and its *prospects*, where there are exceptional *circumstances* affecting the employees' *interests* to a considerable extent, and *measures* significantly affecting employees' *interests*. All the rest are *particular* illustrations, *not exclusive* of other topics related to the progress and prospects of the business or affecting employees' interests.

Certain qualities should be noted. As regards the progress of the business and its prospects, *prospects*, as evident in the illustrations, means the information and consultation process is to be concerned not only with past events but also with *future* developments. As to exceptional *circumstances*, these include conditions *external* to the undertaking; it is management's duty to inform the EWC when such exceptional circumstances exist which affect employees' interests. As regards measures significantly affecting employees' interests, *measures* requiring information and consultation imply that the measures concerned are not yet implemented, but only *contemplated*. *Interests* of employees are not defined; the illustrations of relocations, closures and collective redundancies reflect the employment concerns of the 1975 and 1977 Directives. The EWC Directive's purpose is to improve on this to require information and consultation when *other* interests of employees (eg changes in working methods or production processes, working time organisation, pay systems and structures) are considerably or significantly affected.

The question is whether, in order for the EWC to be involved, the topic has to affect the interests of all employees, or most, or a relatively large number; employees in two or more Member States, or in two or more establishments in one Member State, or only a relatively small number of employees. The implication of the following subparagraph 2 of paragraph 3:

> 'Those members of the EWC who have been elected or appointed by the establishments and/or undertakings which are directly concerned by the measures in question shall also have the right to participate ...'

---

17 Annex, paragraph 2.

is that *not all* employees need be concerned for the process of information and consultation to be engaged.

Employees' representatives on the SNB can draw on these guidelines as the starting point for their demands in a negotiating strategy with central management. Apart from the general headings, a shopping list of specific information desired might be considered under each heading. This might be preferable to leaving the initiative to management to decide what to include.

The nature of the information and consultation process

Again, there are no *formal* limitations on the procedure of information and consultation of the EWC which may be agreed between the SNB and central management. One constraint, however, is that an agreement may not provide for less than the 'consultation' defined in Article 2(1)(f): an 'exchange of views and establishment of dialogue.'

In the Directive's definition, the process of consultation goes beyond a mere 'exchange of views'. A static, formal, ad hoc, one-way process is incompatible with the purpose of the Directive. The nature of the process mandated by the Directive is encapsulated in the concept of 'dialogue'. The qualities indicated by this concept are those of an active and continuous process of communication and interaction between the EWC and management. The agreement between the SNB and central management must allow for the *establishment of dialogue* required by the Directive. The subsidiary requirements of the Annex provide an indicative framework of the minimum procedures required.

FREQUENCY OF MEETINGS

The SNB and the central management are to determine the 'frequency . . . of meetings of the EWC'.[18] A consultation process of exchanges of views and dialogue cannot, save in the most unusual case, be limited to a rare and predetermined meeting. The dynamic nature of Community-scale undertakings demands regular and frequent meetings, as well as those ad hoc meetings responding to unexpected developments.

This is reflected in the list of *illustrations* in the subsidiary requirements in the Annex of the scope of the topics to be covered by the information and consultation procedure: the structure, economic and financial situation, the probable development of the business and of production and sales, the situation and probable trend of employment, investments, and substantial changes concerning organisation, introduction of new working methods or production processes, transfers of production, mergers, cut-backs or closures of undertakings, establishments or important parts thereof, and collective redundancies.

The subsidiary requirements of the Annex reflect this. First:[19]

'The EWC shall have the right to meet with the central management once a year, to be informed and consulted, on the basis of a report drawn up by the central management on the progress of the business of the Community-scale undertaking or Community-scale group of undertakings and its prospects.'

---

18   Article 6(2)(d).
19   Paragraph 2, subparagraph 1.

But also:[20]

> 'Where there are exceptional circumstances affecting the employees' interests to a considerable extent ... the EWC shall have the right to be informed. It shall have the right to meet, at its request, the central management, or any other more appropriate level of management within the Community-scale undertaking or group of undertakings having its own powers of decision, so as to be informed and consulted on measures significantly affecting employees' interests.'

Minimum frequency is an annual meeting plus ad hoc meetings. It would seem more sensible to have a regular schedule of meetings throughout the year, which might avoid some of the potential disruption of unscheduled ad hoc meetings.

TIMING OF MEETINGS

The timing of the annual meeting is linked with the 'report drawn up by the central management on the progress of the business ... and its prospects', which is the basis of the annual meeting. As regards ad hoc meetings, the subsidiary requirements of the Annex specify:[1]

> 'This information and consultation meeting shall take place as soon as possible on the basis of a report drawn up by the central management or any other appropriate level of management of the Community-scale undertaking or group of undertakings ...'·

In exceptional circumstances, to await the preparation of a special report would often nullify the effectiveness of any consultation process. The requirement that the meeting 'take place as soon as possible' requires that the information process be engineered so that it meets at least the subsidiary requirements of the Annex.

Undertakings of the size covered by the Directive maintain systems which generate a constant flow of information on the progress and prospects of the business. The systems are aimed at continuously informing management at different levels. What is now required is to *integrate* the Directive's requirement, the 'establishment of dialogue' with the EWC, into the normal corporate information flow. Ad hoc meetings will follow whenever this information flow generates the need for the consultation required by the Directive.

PARTICIPANTS

The EWC and central management are the main protagonists. But the nature of a Community-scale undertaking or groups of undertakings engages many others among employees' representatives and management at lower levels who should be integrated into the information and consultation process to achieve an effective exchange of views and establish a dialogue. This is recognised in the subsidiary requirements. As regards the annual meeting, it is provided that: 'The local managements shall be informed accordingly'.[2] The number of employees' representatives on the EWC may make it unwieldy as an instrument for effective information and consultation in all circumstances. Hence, the subsidiary requirements provide:[3]

> 'The EWC shall have a minimum of three members and a maximum of 30.
> Where its size so warrants, it shall elect a *select committee* from among its members,

---

20   Paragraph 3, subparagraph 1.
1   Paragraph 3, subparagraph 3.
2   Paragraph 2, subparagraph 1.
3   Paragraph 1(c).

comprising at most three members.
It shall adopt its own rules of procedure'.[4]

The need to involve others than the central management and full EWC is particularly likely in the case of ad hoc meetings. Hence, the subsidiary requirements provide that in such exceptional circumstances:[5]

'. . . the *select committee* or, where no such committee exists, the EWC shall have the right to be informed, It shall have the right to meet, at its request, the central management, or *any other more appropriate level of management* within the Community-scale undertaking or group of undertakings *having its own powers of decision*, so as to be informed and consulted . . .

Those members of the EWC who have been elected or appointed by the *establishments or undertakings which are directly concerned* by the measures in question shall also have the right to participate in the meeting organised with the select committee.

This information and consultation meeting shall take place as soon as possible on the basis of a report drawn up by the central management or *any other appropriate level of management* . . .'

The agreement on the procedure for information and consultation of the EWC between the SNB and central management should recognise the necessary involvement of different participants, reflecting the structure of the undertaking and of employees' representation.

CONDUCT OF MEETINGS

The primary consideration is to remember the purpose of the Directive: '. . . to improve the right to information and to consultation . . .'[6] The purpose is *not* a meeting. It is, as defined in Article 2(1)(f): '. . . the exchange of views and establishment of dialogue . . .' The objective of meetings is to establish this dialogue. This involves exchanges of opinions, arguments and counter-arguments, proposals and counter-proposals, and so on. A meeting may involve a number of sittings over a period of days.

The SNB and central management are to determine 'the venue . . . and duration of meetings of the EWC'.[7] It is not easy to see how this can be done in advance. The duration of meetings will depend on the agenda, and given the indications in the Annex's subsidiary requirements of the topics to be covered in the annual meeting,[8] or in ad hoc meetings,[9] this is potentially lengthy. The basis of meetings is a report by management. It takes time to prepare, for an exchange of views and for a dialogue to develop. It must also take account of translation into different languages, and so on.

This indeterminacy implies a very rough determination of duration, perhaps days rather than hours, minimum and maximum duration, rather than precise calculation. Ultimately, the test of whether the conduct and duration of a meeting

---

4   It has been already noted that the subsidiary requirements guarantee representation of all
    Member States in which there is an establishment or undertaking, with provision for supplementary members in proportion to the number of employees working in the establishments or
    undertakings (paragraph 1(d)).
5   Paragraph 3, subparagraph 1.
6   Article 1(1).
7   Article 6(2)(d).
8   Paragraph 2, subparagraph 2.
9   Paragraph 3, subparagraph 1.

is adequate to meet the requirements of the Directive is if it succeeds in '... the exchange of views and establishment of dialogue ...'[10]

The subsidiary requirements in the Annex provide that: 'The Member States may lay down rules on the chairing of information and consultation meetings'.[11] Where the subsidiary requirements do not apply, the SNB and central management are to negotiate and agree on the conduct of the meeting. This includes important issues such as drawing up the agenda, drafting and circulating minutes, and providing documentation. The subsidiary requirements in the Annex further provide:[12]

'Before any meeting with the central management, the EWC or the select committee, where necessary enlarged ... shall be entitled to meet without the management concerned being present.'

Again, issues of venue and duration must be agreed.

FINANCIAL AND MATERIAL RESOURCES

The SNB and central management are to negotiate and agree: 'the financial and material resources to be allocated to the EWC'.[13] Further:[14]

'... members of EWCs ... shall, in the exercise of their functions, enjoy the same protection and guarantees provided for employees' representatives by the national legislation and/or practice in force in their country of employment.'

Unlike the SNB, where the Directive lays down an EU standard for resources,[15] it is the Member State standards which provide the *minimum* standard of guaranteed resources which cannot be derogated from by the agreement negotiated by the central management and SNB under Article 6. This implies different levels of protection and guarantees, as Member State provisions vary.[16] Adjusted to the EWC's functions, these should include time off (paid and unpaid) for members of the EWC, pre-meeting expenses, training, liaising with other EWCs already established in the sector, facilities and expert advice.

In the absence of agreement between the SNB and the central management, the subsidiary requirements do provide an EU standard. The subsidiary requirements in the Annex provide:[17]

'6. The EWC or the select committee may be assisted by experts of its choice, in so far as this is necessary for it to carry out its tasks.
7. The operating expenses of the EWC shall be borne by the central management.
   The central management concerned shall provide the members of the EWC with such financial and material resources as enable them to perform their duties in an appropriate manner.
   In particular, the cost of organising meetings and arranging for interpretation facilities and the accommodation and travelling expenses of members of the

---

10   Article 1(f).
11   Paragraph 4, subparagraph 1.
12   Paragraph 4, subparagraph 2.
13   Article 6(2)(e).
14   Article 10, paragraph 1.
15   Article 5(6), subparagraph 1.
16   In the UK, the relevant provisions on time off for trade union duties and activities are in the Trade Union and Labour Relations (Consolidation) Act 1992.
17   Paragraphs 6 and 7.

EWC and its select committee shall be met by the central management unless otherwise agreed.

In compliance with these principles, the Member States may lay down budgetary rules regarding the operation of the EWC. They may in particular limit funding to cover one expert only.'

These requirements reflect what the negotiations between the SNB and central management must accommodate: the financial and material resources necessary for the EWC.

Unlike the SNB, which only negotiates the one agreement on the EWC, the EWC is not dedicated to a one-off task. It is an enduring and ambitious enterprise. To sustain its activities there is likely to be required a permanent secretariat providing the continuity necessary to maintain an effective instrument of information and consultation. Careful and detailed consideration is required of the resources and personnel required.

The 'operating expenses of the EWC'[18] are a separate item from the resources.[19] They include:[20] 'In particular, the cost of organising meetings and arranging for interpretation facilities and the accommodation and travelling expenses of members of the EWC and its select committee'. To appropriately fulfil its tasks of information and consultation, the EWC will need operating expenses to provide it with the continuity guaranteed to the central management of the undertaking with its permanent staff. Resources will be needed to cover the maintenance of a permanent secretariat providing the services required by a fluctuating membership of the EWC.

In language similar to the Directive's provisions on resources to be supplied to the SNB,[1] the subsidiary requirements stipulate resources adequate 'to enable (the members of the EWC) to perform their duties in an appropriate manner'.[2] Member State rules providing resources to employees' representatives differ. Financial and material resources beyond operating expenses include the provision of relevant training and facilities. In the absence of agreement between the SNB and central management, Member State provisions must *at least* satisfy this EU standard. There are further more specific provisions.

The subsidiary requirements in the Annex provide:[3]

'The EWC or the select committee may be assisted by experts of its choice, in so far as this is necessary for it to carry out its tasks.'

As with the similar provision for the SNB,[4] experts 'necessary for it to carry out its tasks' could include lawyers to provide advice on the legal entitlements and obligations of the EWC and its members, as well as a range of others helpful in enabling the EWC to develop its role in the information and consultation process adapted to the specific nature of the industry and undertaking. It is important for the EWC to prepare a list of experts for submission to central management for funding.

---

18 Paragraph 7, subparagraph 1.
19 Stipulated in the following subparagraph.
20 As indicated in subparagraph 3.
1   Article 5(6), subparagraph 1.
2   Paragraph 7, subparagraph 2.
3   Paragraph 6.
4   Article 5(4), subparagraph 2.

However, as with the SNB[5] the Member State may limit funding to cover one expert only.[6] Apparently, one paid expert is appropriate. Again, what is not specified is how much expert's time will be needed if only one can be hired. It might make more sense for the central management to agree to short-term funding of a number of specialists for specific purposes, rather than long-term funding of one expert who will have to cover a number of areas.

In the absence of an agreement between the central management and the SNB, the subsidiary requirements stipulate as the EU standard that 'central management . . . provide the members of the EWC with such financial and material resources as enable them to perform their duties in an appropriate manner'.[7] Similarly to the provision for the SNB's funding of expenses,[8] however, the subsidiary requirements continue: 'In compliance with these principles, the Member States may lay down budgetary rules regarding the operation of the EWC'. Again, the meaning of *budgetary* rules is not clear. They must comply with the principle of enabling the EWC to carry out its task in an appropriate manner. However, the following sentence, that Member States 'may in particular limit funding to cover one expert only', implies that some substantive limits are possible.

At worst, Member State budgetary rules are limited to the quantifying of *paid* time. They should not cover the amount of *unpaid* time, or its purposes or any conditions to be attached. Article 10, paragraph 1, provides members of EWCs with 'the same protection and guarantees provided for employees' representatives by the national legislation and/or practice in force in their country of employment', and continues:[9]

> 'This shall apply *in particular* to attendance at meetings of . . . EWCs . . . and the payment of wages for members who are on the staff of the Community-scale undertaking or the Community-scale group of undertakings for the period of absence necessary for the performance of their duties.'

'In particular' attendance at meetings of EWCs implies that EWC members may be absent, justifiably, for other reasons, such as education and training, meetings with other EWCs in the sector, meetings with experts, and so on. It may be that the time off for these absences is necessary[10] 'to enable (the members of the EWC) to perform their duties in an appropriate manner', and hence is eligible for funding by central management.

REPORT BACK

The communication of the *results* of the process established by the Directive to participants *other* than central management and the EWC is not the subject of any provision in the Directive. In the absence of agreement, however, the subsidiary requirements in the Annex provide some obligations. On the management side, as regards the SNB's negotiation of the EWC: 'The central management and any other more appropriate level of management shall be informed of the

5 Article 5(6), paragraph 2.
6 Paragraph 7, subparagraph 4.
7 Paragraph 7, subparagraph 2.
8 Article 5(6), subparagraph 2.
9 Article 10, paragraph 2.
10 Paragraph 7, subparagraph 2.

composition of the EWC'.[11] As already mentioned, as regards the annual meeting, it is provided that: 'The *local managements* shall be informed accordingly'.[12] Report back is not relevant where the process of information and consultation involves an 'appropriate level of management'.[13]

On the employees' side there is explicit provision in the subsidiary requirements:[14]

'... the members of the EWC shall inform the representatives of the employees of the establishments or of the undertakings of a Community-scale group of undertakings or, in the absence of representatives, the workforce as a whole, of the content and outcome of the information and consultation procedure carried out in accordance with this Annex.'

Exemption: voluntary agreements in force

The Directive contains a provision which can potentially pre-empt the creation of a EWC:[15]

'... the obligations arising from this Directive shall not apply to Community-scale undertakings or Community-scale groups of undertakings in which, on the date laid down in Article 14(1) for the implementation of the Directive (22 September 1996) or the date of its transposition in the Member State in question, where this is earlier than the abovementioned date, there is already an *agreement*, covering the *entire workforce*, providing for the *transnational* information and consultation of employees.'

Agreements qualifying under this provision are exempt from the obligations of the Directive. It is important, therefore, to scrutinise any agreements to see if they qualify under the provision.

The reference to 'agreement', in the singular, appears to exclude the possibility that agreements with individual employees qualify under this provision. Rather, it appears to parallel provisions in other Directives allowing for derogation through collective agreements negotiated by organisations of workers and employers. Since the UK will not be transposing the Directive, the earlier of the two dates, 22 September 1996, would seem to be conclusive as regards agreements with UK MNEs. Any agreements after that date do not qualify. It is arguable that an agreement which does not include the workforce employed in the UK by MNEs, UK-based or other, is not an 'agreement, covering the entire workforce' and so does not qualify as exempt from the obligations of the Directive.

Any agreements claiming exemption would have to demonstrate that they provided for 'the transnational information and consultation of employees' consistently with the purpose of the Directive 'to improve the right to information and to consultation of employees in Community-scale undertakings and Community-scale groups of undertakings'.[16] This might be tantamount to respect for many of the obligations prescribed by the Directive. Article 13(2) provides that

11   Annex, paragraph 1(e).
12   Annex, paragraph 2, subparagraph 1.
13   Annex, paragraph 3, subparagraphs 1 and 3.
14   Annex, paragraph 5.
15   Article 13(1).
16   Article 1(1).

the Directive applies where an exempt agreement expires and is not renewed by joint decision of the parties. It is implicit that to qualify, the agreement must allow for expiry.

There are already agreements on information and consultation in force in some MNEs. Following the approval of the Directive, other MNEs will seek to negotiate agreements for a EWC before the Directive comes into effect on 22 September 1996.[17] There is a risk that such agreements might find that the obligations arising from the Directive do not apply to them due to Article 13. Existing agreements should be scrutinised as to whether they qualify for exemption under Article 13. If they do not, then the obligations of the Directive apply. If they do, when they expire, they should not be renewed. Trade unions may wish to renew such agreements, to avoid disrupting existing arrangements. Trade unions may also wish to negotiate agreements prior to 22 September 1996. To ensure that such agreements are not exempt from the Directive under Article 13, it would suffice to ensure that they do not qualify. Perhaps the easiest method is to insert a clause formally excluding from coverage a small group of workers.

The European Commission Working Party comprising representatives of the Member States has been meeting to discuss the legal status of the voluntary agreements on information and consultation concluded under Article 13. These agreements are exempt from the obligations of the Directive. However, they are subject to the criteria in Article 13(1). They must cover the entire workforce and provide for transnational information and consultation of employees.

These are minimum requirements. National laws transposing the Directive must include at least these criteria, in order to enable national courts to assess whether pre-existing agreements are exempt. The Working Party discussed whether further minimum requirements for exempt agreements could be added by national laws. It seems there is no need for total harmonisation. But there was a consensus that any agreement valid under Article 6 would be protected under Article 13.

If accepted by the Member State laws transposing the Directive, this is potentially an important point. It is said to embody a 'principle of equivalence' between the agreements concluded under Article 6 and those concluded under Article 13. Although there is no reference in Article 13 to the provisions of Article 6, the latter is considered a reference model to certify the acceptability of agreements concluded under Article 13.

Agreements under Article 6 cover the composition, functions, procedure, venue, frequency and duration of meetings of and the financial and material resources to be allocated to the EWC. If agreement is not reached under Article 6, the requirements in the Annex apply.[18] Member State laws to this effect should apply equivalent criteria to Article 13 agreements. So, for example, the Commission Working Party agreed that Article 13 agreements should at least stipulate by what methods the employees' representatives shall have the right to meet to discuss the information conveyed to them. It is clear that it must be the outcome of a negotiation process; if dictated by management or not reached by

---

17   In December 1994, the European Foundation for the Improvement of Living and Working Conditions produced a collection of the texts of 35 agreements in European multinationals on information and consultation structures.

18   Article 7.

a representative body defending the interests of the entire workforce, it would not qualify.

The validity of a voluntary agreement will be questioned when the negotiation procedure is triggered at the written request of 100 employees or their representatives[19] calling for the establishment of an SNB. This is likely to raise the question of whether a voluntary agreement is valid to exclude the requirement of the Directive to establish an SNB and for central management to negotiate a EWC.

For example, what of an existing agreement which does not cover the whole group of undertakings but only a part of it? Does a request to establish an SNB entail the invalidation of that agreement, or do the procedures concern only the part of the group excluded from the agreement? The practical solution would be for the parties to the agreement to allow a period of 2–3 months to clear up such problems.

Another issue being discussed by the Working Party is the question of the representativeness of those negotiating and signing a voluntary agreement. One possibility discussed by the Working Party was the establishment of legal presumptions of representativeness.

Finally, there is the question of which national courts are competent to deal with legal disputes connected with the Directive. The trend is to see disputes concerning issues of individual worker protection as being a matter for the courts of the country of origin of the relevant worker representative, whereas litigation concerning the collective rights of information and consultation would be dealt with in the jurisdiction where the multinational undertaking had its registered office. These proposed solutions raise many questions regarding UK multinationals and representatives of UK employees on EWCs.

CONCLUSION: NEGOTIATING THE END OF MANAGEMENT PREROGATIVES

The Directive begins: 'The purpose of this Directive is to improve the right to information and to consultation of employees . . .'[20] By consultation is meant: '. . . the exchange of views and establishment of dialogue between employees' representatives and central management or any more appropriate level of management'.[1] The outcome of the process prescribed by the Directive is the exchange of views and establishment of dialogue.

On more concrete outcomes there are scanty provisions in the subsidiary requirements in the Annex. In relation to ad hoc meetings with the EWC 'where there are exceptional circumstances affecting the employees' interests to a considerable extent':[2]

> 'This information and consultation meeting shall take place as soon as possible on the basis of a report drawn up by the central management or any other appropriate level of management of the Community-scale undertaking or group of undertakings, on which an *opinion* may be delivered at the end of the meeting or within a reasonable time.
>
> This meeting shall not affect the prerogatives of the central management.'

---

19 Article 5(1).
20 Article 1(1).
1   Article 2(1)(f).
2   Annex, paragraph 3, subparagraphs 3 and 4.

It would be contrary to the purpose of the Directive to regard this opinion as the conclusive outcome of the process. The Directive has more fundamental and long-term objectives.

The argument is that the Directive's stratagem is to provide the framework for a negotiating strategy of the SNB, based on the minimum procedures prescribed in the subsidiary requirements of the Annex. The outcome of this stratagem is the creation of a EWC for the purposes of information and consultation.

The levers of corporate power depend on access to information and swiftness of decision making.[3] The Directive's strategy for the EWC is to provide it with these levers of corporate power. Information is to be provided; consultation takes time. The EWC, equipped with information, may influence the decision-making of central management. But influence requires power. Power means the ability to impose costs. Delay is costly. Delay is the currency with which the EWC can buy influence. The EWC's influence is to be exercised not simply for cash payments to the employees it represents, pay-offs by management to avoid delay. The EWC is to use the threat of delay to influence management decisions.

The process of influencing management decision-making is complex. Comparative analysis has provided some guidance. A study carried out by Ruskin College stipulated certain conditions to successful influence: early access to the decision-making process, a predetermined decision-making procedure, and coordination of employees' representative structures.[4] The Directive provides one legal instrument for developing these conditions of influence over management decision-making.

This is evident in the apparently paradoxical provision in the subsidiary requirements regarding the ad hoc meeting with the EWC required in exceptional circumstances: 'This meeting shall not affect the prerogatives of the central management'.[5] What *are* these prerogatives? This provision of the Directive may provide at last an opportunity to clarify the meaning of this phrase.

The apparent paradox lies in that, whatever these prerogatives are, this provision cannot stop the process of information and consultation prescribed by the Directive. Management decisions on the topics specified by the Directive are now irrevocably subject to the process of exchange of views and establishment of dialogue. This has implications for management prerogatives. If it means anything, management prerogatives mean the right to act without restraints. The whole purpose of the Directive is to *subject* management decision-making to a procedure of information and consultation. This must *preclude* unilateral action.

The *procedure* involving information and consultation of the EWC cannot stop unilateral management action: 'This meeting shall not affect the prerogatives of

---

3   These are argued to be the essence of corporate power by E H Herman *Corporate Control, Corporate Power*, Cambridge 1982.

4   Final Report presented to the Directorate General for Internal Market and Industrial Affairs and the Directorate General for Employment, Social Affairs and Education of the European Commission, *The Control of Frontiers: Workers and New Technology: Disclosure and Use of Company Information*, Ruskin College, Oxford, October 1984. See also Appendix to Final Report: Summaries of Case Studies. The conclusions of the Final Report are reproduced in (1984) *European Industrial Relations Review* No 134, p 22. On the policy implications of this Report, see paper by H Levie to Directorate General V/A/2 of the Commission (1985).

5   Annex, paragraph 3, subparagraph 4.

the central management'. But the *Directive* can: *breach* of the procedure leads to a *remedy* capable of restraining unilateral management action. The Directive contains a special Article on 'Compliance with this Directive' which goes further than usual:[6]

'1. Each Member State shall ensure that the management of establishments of a Community-scale undertaking and the management of undertakings which form part of a Community-scale undertaking which are situated within its territory and their employees' representatives or, as the case may be, employees abide by the obligations laid down by this Directive, regardless of whether or not the central management is situated within its territory . . .

. . .

3. Member States shall provide for appropriate measures in the event of failure to comply with this Directive; in particular, they shall ensure that adequate administrative or judicial procedures are available to enable the obligations deriving from this Directive to be enforced.'

The Directive's obligations imply that management action be subject to the prescribed process of information and consultation. To secure this, it is not enough to rely on sanctions on central management. Internal corporate controls are insufficient to ensure that lower management's action is subject to the process. Member States are obliged to intervene in the internal management structures of MNEs to secure compliance.

Management prerogatives to take action cannot be stopped. But, following the Directive, they are to be subject to procedures of information and consultation of the EWC, procedures which are to be enforced by effective remedies.

The future of the European Works Council Directive will be dominated by three developments. First, scrutiny of Member State legislation to ensure that it satisfies the requirements of the Directive. Secondly, litigation to test the obligations on management to inform and consult, to restrain unilateral management action, and, in case of violation, to claim the necessary remedies to ensure that management abides by them. Finally, negotiation of agreements developing the Directive's stratagem of building on the subsidiary requirements prescribed in the Annex.

6   Article 11(1) and (3).

Part VI

European Labour Law and Health and Safety in the Working Environment

Chapter 21

The European Concept of Health and Safety: the Case of the Working Time Directive

INTRODUCTION

The law on health and safety and the working environment in Europe has a long and fascinating history and a mountain of technical literature analysing the wealth of legislative and judicial material. The EU since its beginnings has contributed to this law. On 20 July 1962 there were adopted two Commission Recommendations, one on company medical services and another aimed at harmonising the conditions for the recognition and notification of occupational diseases.[1]

The decades that followed betrayed uncertainty as to the future of the EU law on health and safety. During the few years after 1962, two further Recommendations were adopted, but for ten years after 1967 there was no further action, and, it has been said of the subsequent period from 1974 to 1985:[2]

'The impression of a determined drive for all-out regulation and control conveyed by the documents of the period from 1974 to 1985 (ie from the first Social Action Programme and the setting up of the Advisory Committee on Safety, Hygiene and Health Protection at Work – ACSH – to the adoption of the "new approach" and the Single Act) sits ill with the extremely mediocre level of actual achievements.'

The insertion of a new Article 118A into the Treaty of Rome by the Single European Act of 1986 gave the opportunity for new legally binding measures to be adopted. Prior to this provision coming into effect in 1987, only six Directives on health and safety at work had been adopted. The complex development of Community policy on health and safety during the 1980s culminated with the adoption of the Framework Directive 89/391/EEC of 12 June 1989,[3] followed by a further six 'daughter' directives, to come into effect by 1 January 1993, with still further Directives to come.

The implications for UK labour law on health and safety cannot be overstated. As stated in the editors' preface to the latest edition of a leading practitioners' text on health and safety law:[4]

'The current edition marks a revolution as great if not greater than the Health and Safety at Work etc Act 1974. The European Directives have landed. They have

---

1 OJ EC of 31 August 1962. See generally, L Vogel *Prevention at the Workplace*, European Trade Union Technical Bureau for Health and Safety, Brussels 1994, pp 63 ff. Also *Social Europe* (1990) No 2.
2 L Vogel, ibid, p 67.
3 Council Directive 89/391/EEC of 12 June 1989 on the introduction of measures to encourage improvements in the safety and health of workers at work. OJ L183/1.
4 J Hendy and M Ford, Redgrave Fife & Machin's *Health and Safety*, 2nd ed, London 1993, p v.

changed the face of British health and safety law. The principal Regulations to implement the Directives become law on 1 January 1993 and much of our old legislation has gone in consequence.'

They quote the Health and Safety Commission's Annual Report for 1991–92 to the effect that European and international developments 'continue to set the agenda for developments in health and safety law and standards'.[5]

The four chapters of Part VI will focus on four central features of the European labour law on health and safety which reflect the 'European revolution' in British health and safety law. Each of these involves an aspect of this European labour law which has impinged upon a fundamental feature of UK health and safety law and, arguably, could transform domestic law. They concern the *scope*, the *standards*, the *strategy* and the *implementation* of the European labour law on health and safety at work.

The first feature is the *scope* of the European labour law on health and safety. The scope is not constrained by the traditional vision of accidents and disease at work. Rather, it is characterised by an overall view of the working environment. The Framework Directive expressly refers to 'the safety and health of workers in every aspect related to the work'.[6] The view is taken that '(i)t therefore covers both risks arising out of the use of physical, chemical and biological agents, and aspects related to work organisation and job content. Mental stress and well-being at work fall within the scope of the directive'.[7] The clearest manifestation of this is the Working Time Directive, which will be analysed in detail.

The Working Time Directive is an exemplar of a second feature of the emerging European labour law on health and safety: the role of collective bargaining and collective agreements in the formulation of health and safety *standards*. Rather than imposing general and/or more or less specific and detailed standards regarding the organisation of working time compatible with health and safety, the Working Time Directive systematically delegates to the social partners, the workers and managements concerned, the task of elaborating the relevant standards. This concept of setting European labour standards through social dialogue is a characteristic of European labour law which has appeared in other contexts, but is particularly vivid here.

The third feature is the *strategy* of the Directive. The approach of European labour law to health and safety at work may be characterised as preventative through the specific mechanism of risk assessment. This has been said to be the point at which 'the framework Directive is most innovative and the employers most critical of it'.[8]

The fourth feature addresses *implementation and enforcement*. This is an element which has been noted in other contexts of this book but which is particularly significant in the European labour law on health and safety. It involves the Directive's view of workers' participation through safety representatives. The particular interest of this feature lies in its interaction with the existing UK law on safety representatives, dating back to the Robens reforms of the Health and Safety at Work etc Act 1974. It highlights the Europeanisation of UK labour law and hence will be the subject of a detailed analysis.

---

5   Ibid, p lxi.
6   Article 5(1).
7   European Trade Union Technical Bureau for Health and Safety, *A User's Guide to European Community Directives on Health and Safety at Work*, Brussels 1993, p 12.
8   L Vogel, op cit, p 79.

THE WORKING ENVIRONMENT AND THE WORKING TIME DIRECTIVE

On 25 July 1990, the Commission of the European Communities adopted a proposal for a Council Directive concerning certain aspects of the organisation of working time.[9] Following consultation of the European Parliament,[10] an amended proposal was submitted to the Council on 23 April 1991.[11] A common position was reached by the Ministers of Social and Labour Affairs at a meeting on 1 June 1993, with all Member States voting in favour, bar the UK, which abstained and announced its intention to challenge the legal basis of the proposed Directive in the European Court.[12] Nonetheless, the Directive was adopted by the Council at a meeting on 23 November 1993 and has become the law of the EU.[13]

The legal basis of the Directive is Article 118A of the EC Treaty which stipulates that:

'the Member States shall pay particular attention to encouraging improvements, especially of the working environment, as regards the safety and health of workers, and shall set as their objective the harmonisation of conditions in this area.'

The Commission's Explanatory Memorandum quoted the Council Framework Directive on health and safety of 12 June 1989, which stresses that 'the incidence of accidents at work and occupational diseases is still too high' and 'preventative measures must be introduced or improved without delay to safeguard the safety and health of workers and ensure a higher degree of protection'.[14] The Commission also emphasised the World Health Organisation's definition that:[15]

'health is a state of complete psychic, mental and social wellbeing and does not merely consist of an absence of disease or infirmity.'

In this, the Commission appears to have taken a liberal approach to the interpretation of the scope of Article 118A. It is not necessary for working time to create *serious* health hazards to fall within Article 118A. There is rather movement towards the Nordic countries' concept of physical, psychological and social aspects such as monotony, lack of social contacts at work or a rapid work pace.[16]

The UK government takes the view that there is no reliable evidence linking working time with health and safety, and that the working time proposal relates rather to working conditions and should be adopted on a legal basis which requires unanimous voting. Hence the working time proposal was an 'inappropriate precedent' and the UK government will lodge an appeal with the European Court of Justice to challenge the legal basis selected. The UK government has

9   COM (90) 317 final – SYN 295, Brussels, 20 September 1990; OJ C254 of 9 October 1990, p 4. The text may be found in *European Industrial Relations Reports* No 202, November 1990, p 27.
10   OJ C72 of 18 March 1991, p 95.
11   *European Industrial Relations Reports* No 210, July 1991, p 27.
12   *European Industrial Relations Reports* No 233, June 1993, p 2; *Industrial Relations Law Bulletin*, No 475, June 1993, p 12.
13   Council Directive 93/104/EC of 23 November 1993 concerning certain aspects of the organisation of working time. OJ L307/18 of 13.12.1993. *Europe* No 6113, 24 November 1993, p 10.
14   Council Directive 89/391/EEC, quoted in the Explanatory Memorandum, p 17, paragraph 33.
15   Ibid.
16   For an acute and detailed analysis by a Danish labour lawyer of the scope of Article 118A in light of various Community labour law initiatives, see the LLM dissertation by Jacob Sand 'The Social Dimension of the Internal Market: Health and Safety at Work' (1993) on file at the European University Institute, Florence.

asserted that it will not introduce implementing legislation until the Court has reached its decision.[17] After the Council of Ministers adopted the Directive on 23 November 1993, the British delegation again announced that the UK would bring the Directive before the Court of Justice, considering the legal basis to be erroneous. The Social Affairs Commissioner, Padraig Flynn, commented that:[18]

> 'This does not mean that it does not have to respect the implementation of the directive while waiting for a Court of Justice's decision. The UK has no chance of winning the case for reasons of worker health and safety, according to our legal services.'

The final text of the Directive includes provisions on daily and weekly rest periods, maximum weekly working hours, minimum annual holidays and night work, shiftworking and patterns of work. The provisions of the Directive, particularly those of the earlier two drafts, may give the initial impression of setting standards too innocuous to merit attention, let alone praise. But the final text may prove that this is an under-estimation of their potential impact. This will be demonstrated by a detailed analysis of the standards specified in these provisions, and consideration of their application in the context of working time in Europe, and, in particular, in the UK.

'WORKING TIME'

'Working time' is defined in Article 2(1):

> 'any period during which the worker is working, at the employer's disposal *and* carrying out his activity or duties, in accordance with national laws and/or practice' (my italics).

'Rest period' is defined as 'any period which is not working time'.[19] It is not always clear when a worker is considered to be 'working'. In the past, this issue has been the subject of controversy with regard to the law on vicarious liability – whether the worker was 'working' when injuring another so as to engage the employer in liability – and the law on health and safety – whether the worker was 'working' when he sustained an injury.

Also problematic is the fact that many workers are entitled to time off work for various reasons: to carry out trade union activities, health and safety responsibilities and public duties.[20] It is not clear whether periods spent on these count as 'working time', or a 'rest period', or neither for the purpose of calculating entitlements to rest periods and limitations on working time.

DAILY AND WEEKLY REST PERIODS

One of the most important developments in working time has been the dissociation between working time and plant operating hours. The Commission noted the increase in operating hours of plants, and the more varied opening hours in

---

17   See the accounts in *Industrial Relations Law Bulletin*, No 475, June 1993, p 12; Agence *Europe* No 5991 of 2 June 1993, p 7.
18   *Europe* No 6114, 25 November 1993, p 10.
19   Article 2(2).
20   Employment Protection (Consolidation) Act 1978, s 29; Safety Representatives and Safety Committee Regulations 1977, reg 4(2); TULR(C)A, ss 168, 170.

the retail trade sector. It argued that, on the one hand, these increase capacity utilisation and productivity, enhance flexibility, are conducive to investment in modernisation and create savings in relation to fixed productive capital for a given output. On the other hand, it argued, the resulting flexibility of working time arrangements tends to reflect the aspirations of employees to reconcile work and family responsibilities, helps integrate more people into the labour market and enhances employment opportunities.[1] The following two Tables reproduce data on the dissociation of operating hours and individual working time in general and in the retail trade in particular in the Member States:[2]

WORKING HOURS AND OPERATING HOURS PER WEEK IN INDUSTRY[3]		
Member State	*average operating hours*	*working hours (full time)*
Belgium	77	37
Federal Republic of Germany	53	38
Greece	64	40
Spain	69	40
France	69	40
Ireland	61	41
Italy	73	39
Netherlands	74	39
Portugal	54	44
United Kingdom	76	37
EUR 10	66	39

OPENING HOURS AND CONTRACTED WORKING HOURS PER WEEK IN RETAIL TRADE[4]		
Member State	*opening hours*	*working hours (full time)*
Belgium	51	38
Federal Republic of Germany	48	39
Spain	45	43
France	56	38
Italy	49	38
Netherlands	52	40
Portugal	51	44
United Kingdom	58	39
EUR 8	53	39

1 Commission's Explanatory Memorandum, op cit, p 4, paragraph 4.
2 Ibid, Tables 1 and 2, p 5.
3 Source: Special EC labour market survey, results published in European Economic Supplement B, 11, 1989.
4 Ibid, European Economic Supplement B, 2, 1990.

The risks to health and safety which result from the very long individual working hours now possible with increased operating or opening times induced the Commission to consider imposing rules concerning minimum rest periods to protect workers against excessively long working hours detrimental to health and safety. This was done against the background of existing Member State provisions for rest periods. The Commission produced a Table illustrating these provisions:[5]

DAILY AND WEEKLY REST PERIODS (HOURS) AND DAILY MAXIMUM WORKING TIME				
	STATUTORY PROVISIONS			
Member State	*daily rest period*	*maximum daily working time*	*weekly rest period*	
			statutory	CA[6]
Belgium		12 with CA	24	48
Denmark	11		24	48
Federal Republic of Germany		10	24	48
Greece		12	24	36–48
Spain	12	9	36	48
France		12 with CA	24	48
Ireland		12	24	48
Italy		10	24	48
Luxembourg		10	44	48
Netherlands	9–11	10	24	48
Portugal		10	24	36–48
United Kingdom	no general statutory provisions			48

Minimum daily rest period

The Commission's first draft of 20 September 1990 proposed a minimum daily rest period of eleven consecutive hours per period of 24 hours.[7] The European Parliament on 20 February 1991 voted to strengthen the Directive to increase this to 12 consecutive hours in a period of 24 hours, and this was reflected in the second draft submitted by the Commission to the Council on 23 April 1991. However, the common position agreed by the Council on 1 June 1993 reinstated the previous standard of 11 consecutive hours of rest in a 24 hour period, which is now in the Directive:[8]

Daily rest

'Member States shall take the measures necessary to ensure that every worker is entitled to a minimum daily rest period of eleven consecutive hours per 24-hour period.'

5   Commission's Explanatory Memorandum, Table 3, p 9.
6   CA = collective agreements, which cover most workers. The weekly rest period may not fall at the weekend. In that case, equivalent rest periods are normally granted. In addition, many collective agreements provide for more rest periods in the form of roster-free days, additional days where the working week is concentrated into less than five days per week etc.
7   Article 3.
8   Article 3.

The stipulation of a minimum 11 hours of rest in a 24 hour period implies potentially a lawful 13 hour working day. However, this is unlikely to be allowed by reason of other provisions of the Directive.

The principle of the humanisation of work

The imposition of a minimum 11 hours of rest (implying a maximum working day of 13 hours) was supplemented, in the first two drafts proposed by the Commission, by a general provision (albeit not in Section II on 'Daily, weekly and yearly rest', but rather in Section III on 'Night work, shift work and patterns of work') that:[9]

'Member States shall ensure that employers take the necessary measures to ensure that changes made to patterns of work take account, according to the type of activity, of health and safety requirements, especially as regards breaks during working hours.'

This text was changed in the common position adopted by the Council on 1 June 1993, so the Directive now reads:[10]

Pattern of work

'Member States shall take the measures necessary to ensure that an employer who intends to organise work according to a certain pattern takes account of the general principle of adapting work to the worker,[11] with a view, in particular, to alleviating monotonous work and work at a predetermined work-rate, depending on the type of activity, and of safety and health requirements, especially as regards breaks during working time.'

This new provision contains new requirements. First, the obligation arises not only when the employer *changes* patterns of work. It applies to the *initial* organisation of working time. Secondly, the obligation refers back in time to when the employer *intends* to organise work according to a certain pattern. Thirdly, the exclusive reference to health and safety is replaced by *two* factors which must be taken into account: the general principle of adaptation of work to the worker, to a human being; *and* health and safety requirements, a second and separate factor.[12] Finally, the principle of humanisation of work is to have particular regard to alleviating monotonous work and work at a predetermined work-rate – factors which are not related to health and safety requirements narrowly considered.

Both drafts emphasise breaks during working hours. However, the first draft's required provision of such breaks aimed at avoiding health and safety risks is transformed by the final text's inclusion of the principle of the humanisation of work. The above-quoted WHO definition and the Nordic countries' emphasis on psychological and social aspects of working time such as monotony, lack of

---

9   Article 11.
10 Article 13.
11 The French version speaks rather of the 'principe général de l'adaption du travail a l'homme'. Hence my preference for the general principle of humanisation of work.
12 Contrast Article 6, which imposes requirements regarding maximum weekly working time, and mentions only that these are necessary 'in keeping with the need to protect the health and safety of workers.'

social contacts at work or a rapid work pace here receive explicit recognition. Breaks at work are not aimed solely at avoiding dangers to health and safety: they are to be integrated as a means of humanising work patterns.

Rest breaks during working hours

In addition, the common position adopted by the Council on 1 June 1993 and approved on 23 November imposed two further constraints: maximum weekly working time;[13] and rest breaks during daily working hours.[14]

The duration of the rest break during working hours is not specified:[15]

Breaks

'Member States shall take the measures necessary to ensure that, where the working day is longer than six hours, every worker is entitled to a rest break, the details of which, including duration and the terms on which it is granted, shall be laid down in collective agreements or agreements between the two sides of industry or, failing that, by national legislation.'

This is slightly ambiguous. It could be read as requiring a rest period, but leaving it wholly unspecified when this is to be taken (not necessarily, for example, *during* the first six hours of work). This seems inconsistent with the requirement of Article 13 to have regard to breaks in working time as an element in the humanisation of work. At the least, this would support a reading of the provision as requiring at least one rest period during the first six hours of work, and a further rest period during any subsequent six-hour work period. For example, in the event of a 13-hour working day, there could be at least a one-hour break between two six-hour working periods, or, if the single break was shorter than one hour, at least one further rest period after a second six-hour period had elapsed.

The requirement of rest periods during working hours effectively reduces the maximum 13-hour working day by the amount of the rest periods. It is unclear whether daily breaks for rest count towards daily working hours within the meaning of 'working time' as defined in Article 2(1) of the Directive. But whether the duration of the working day includes rest periods or not, it cannot be prolonged beyond 13 hours, as this would violate the requirement of 11 *consecutive* hours of rest.[16]

The minimum EU standard for the duration of the working day is, therefore, 11 consecutive hours of rest, and a maximum 13 hours of work punctuated by at least one long break or two or more shorter breaks, the intervals being not more than six hours apart. However, a working time regime which opted for such long working days would be constrained by the provisions on maximum hours in a working week.[17]

---

13 Article 6, see below.
14 Article 4.
15 Article 4.
16 Technically, a working day of six hours' work, followed by one minute's rest, followed by a further six hours' work and another one minute break, and then another 58 minutes' work, could comply with the requirement of a break for 11 consecutive hours. But it is questionable whether two one-minute breaks in a 12-hour 58-minute working day is healthy and safe, let alone human. The required break during working hours is likely to be much more substantial.
17 Article 6, see below.

Negotiated rest breaks during working hours

The EU standard is to be determined by *collective bargaining*, though without specifying the appropriate level, and in its absence, by legislation. The duration of rest breaks is not indicated, but certain criteria may be expected to emerge following precedents involving the balancing of employer and worker interests in the EU law on indirect sex discrimination.[18] These criteria might require that the *duration* of the rest period responds to the human needs of the worker, be appropriate, having regard to the length of the preceding and subsequent work periods, and takes into account all the different possibilities of organising the working time of the workforce as a whole so as to provide adequate rest periods for all workers.

These will be supplemented by the Directive's requirement in Article 13 that the employer:

'who intends to organise work according to a certain pattern takes account of the general principle of adapting work to the worker ... especially as regards breaks during working time.'

Member States must require employers to organise working time taking into account this principle of humanisation of work. Working time regimes which aim to avoid risks only to health and safety, understood as limited to the physical well-being of workers, but do not 'alleviate monotonous work and work at a predetermined work-rate' are not adequate. If it can be shown that an organisation of working time including work breaks would ameliorate these problems, it is arguable the employer has at least to justify not introducing them.

To determine the extent of the employer's obligation to organise working time so as to include work breaks, again the law on justification of indirect sex discrimination may be invoked as a precedent. A working time regime which fails to include work breaks reflecting the worker's human needs would have to be justified by the employer demonstrating that it responds to a real need of the enterprise, it is appropriate in that the benefit to the employer is proportionate to the unpleasantness, stress or damage to the workers affected by it, and it is necessary in order to achieve this objective, ie no alternative working time regime could achieve it. Daily rest breaks which do not respond to the worker's human needs, and which cannot be justified by the employer, violate the EC standard. Member State legislation which does not secure that such rest breaks are provided would arguably be in violation of the duty to implement the Directive's requirements, and State liability might be imposed to compensate the workers affected.[19]

---

18 Compare the criteria laid down by the European Court of Justice in Case 170/84: *Bilka-Kaufhaus GmbH v Weber von Hartz* [1986] ECR 1607, 13 May 1986, at 1628, paragraph 36: 'It is for the national court, which has sole jurisdiction to make findings of fact, to determine whether and to what extent the grounds put forward by an employer to explain the adoption of a pay practice which applies independently of a worker's sex but in fact affects more women than men may be regarded as objectively justified (on) economic grounds. If the national court finds that the measures chosen by Bilka correspond to a real *need* on the part of the undertaking, are *appropriate* with a view to achieving the objectives pursued and are *necessary* to that end, the fact that the measures affect a far greater number of women than men is not sufficient to show that they constitute an infringement of Article 119' (my italics).
19 Cases C-6/90 and C-9/90: *Francovich and Bonifaci v Italian Republic* [1992] ECR I-5357, 19 November 1991.

Weekly rest periods

In addition to daily rest periods, the first two drafts of the Directive provided:[20]

> 'Member States shall adopt the necessary measures to ensure compliance, in every seven-day period, with the minimum period of one rest day on average following without interruption the daily rest period as defined in Article 3 over a reference period of not more than 14 days.'

The final Directive, as in the common position adopted on 1 June 1993, changed the wording:[1]

Weekly rest period

> 'Member States shall take the measures necessary to ensure that, per each seven-day period, every worker is entitled to a minimum uninterrupted rest period of 24 hours plus the eleven hours' daily rest referred to in Article 3.'

The weekly rest period must follow on from one of the 11 hour daily rest periods, so as to constitute a continuous break of 35 hours at least once a week, averaged over 14 days.[2]

The language is changed from Member States ensuring compliance to a worker being entitled. The emphasis is on rights to be provided, rather than enforcement to be guaranteed. This may allow for the possibility of 'direct effect', so that the Directive could be invoked before national courts to override contrary provisions in laws, collective agreements or individual contracts.[3]

Sunday working

A further qualification is added by the final text of Article 5 to the requirement of a weekly rest period:

> 'The minimum rest period referred to in the first paragraph shall in principle include Sunday.'

The legal implications of the reference to Sunday as a day of rest, as expressed in this Article, are unclear in the event that Sunday is *not* adopted as a day of rest. Technically, the possibilities range from placing Sunday first in the order of priority, requiring justification if Sunday is not chosen, to merely requiring consideration of Sunday rest. The Preamble is helpful here in stating explicitly in the ninth Recital that:

> 'Whereas, with respect to the weekly rest period, due account should be taken of the diversity of cultural, ethnic, religious and other factors existing in the Member

---

20 Article 4.

1   Article 5.

2   Article 16(1): 'Member States may lay down: (1) for the application of Article 5 (weekly rest period), a reference period not exceeding 14 days.'

3   See, with regard to 'direct effect', Chapter 10. The question arises whether direct effect could also be claimed in the case of Article 4 (rest breaks) where: (a) the duration is not so precisely specified; and (b) implementation is left first to collective agreements. It could be argued as regards (a) that once the duration was specified in collective agreements, the Directive itself becomes a source of enforceable rights. Failure on the part of the parties to the agreement to lay down rest periods would not expose them to liability, as the Member State is then under an obligation to act. Direct effect is less clear in that case.

States; whereas, in particular, it is ultimately for each Member State to decide whether Sunday should be included in the weekly rest period, and if so to what extent.'

Whatever else it may mean, this provision on Sunday as, in principle, a day of rest is interesting because it demonstrates the acceptance by the Council of Ministers of a scope for proposals based on Article 118A which go beyond purely health and safety requirements.[4]

24 or 35 consecutive hours?

There is an ambiguous provision tacked on to the end of Article 5:

'If objective, technical or work organisation conditions so justify, a minimum rest period of 24 hours may be applied.'

The meaning of this exception is not clear. There are two possibilities. Each eliminates one of the qualifications attached to the provision in the first paragraph: either, that 24 hours is to be added to the 11 hours of daily rest; or that the 24 hours be without interruption. Most likely, it refers to the requirement that the 24 hour weekly rest period be connected to a previous 11 hour rest period, so as to constitute a solid block of 35 hours rest per week. Apparently, a minimal 24 hour period may be justified in some circumstances. The only other possibility would seem to be that the provision for a 24 hour rest period is not to be a consecutive period, but is to be added to the 11 hours minimum daily rest and distributed throughout the week so that there is no consecutive 24 hour period.

The justifications possible are not specified. They apparently are not among the explicit derogations to Article 5 allowed by Article 17(1)–(3) regarding certain types of work, occupations, risks or collective bargaining arrangements. Nor is there provision for compensatory measures, as in Article 17(2). However, the exceptional regimes allowed for by this last paragraph of Article 5 require *regular* justification as new techniques or work organisation may invalidate or attenuate the original justification. Moreover, they have to accommodate the Directive's specification of a maximum working week of 48 hours.[5]

Derogations

Member States may derogate from the requirements as to daily and weekly rest periods[6] in the case of *certain activities*.[7] In the case of *some* of these, 'Member States may derogate' – *with* 'due regard for the general principles of

---

4 This is consistent with an argument as to the scope of measures eligible for qualified majority voting under Article 100A(2). That article requires unanimity in the Council of Ministers for measures relating to the rights and interests of employed persons. Nonetheless, it has been argued that measures which relate *both* to such rights *and* also to other issues might nonetheless be approved by qualified majority vote. B Bercusson 'The European Community's Charter of Fundamental Social Rights of Workers' (1990) 53 *Modern Law Review* 624, at pp 633–4.

5 Article 6.

6 Articles 3, 4 and 5.

7 Article 17(1) and (2).

the protection of the safety and health of workers' – but *without* the specific requirement for provision of equivalent compensating periods:[8]

Derogations

'1. With due regard for the general principles of the protection of the safety and health of workers, Member States may derogate from Articles 3, 4, 5, 6, 8 or 16 when, on account of the specific characteristics of the activity concerned, the duration of the working time is not measured and/or predetermined or can be determined by the workers themselves, and particularly in the case of:
(a) managing executives or other persons with autonomous decision-making powers;
(b) family workers; or
(c) workers officiating at religious ceremonies in churches and religious communities.'

In the case of *other* activities, Member States may derogate 'by means of laws, regulations or administrative provisions', but, equally, derogation may occur, *without* the need for Member State authorisation, 'by means of collective agreements'. However, these cases *are* subject to provision of 'equivalent periods of compensatory rest or . . . appropriate protection':[9]

'2. Derogations may be adopted by means of laws, regulations or administrative provisions or by means of collective agreements or agreements between the two sides of industry provided that the workers concerned are afforded equivalent periods of compensatory rest or that, in exceptional cases in which it is not possible, for objective reasons, to grant such equivalent periods of compensatory rest, the workers concerned are afforded appropriate protection;
2.1 from Articles 3, 4, 5, 8 and 16:
(a) in the case of activities where there is a considerable distance between the worker's usual place of work and the place where he is required to work or, where there is no usual place of work, between different workplaces;
(b) in the case of security and surveillance activities requiring a permanent presence in order to protect property and persons, particularly security guards and caretakers or security firms;
(c) in the case of activities involving the need for continuity of service or production, particularly:
(i) services relating to the reception, treatment and/or care provided by hospitals or similar establishments, residential institutions and prisons;
(ii) dock or airport workers;
(iii) press, radio, television, film production, postal and telecommunications services, ambulance, fire and civil protection services;
(iv) gas, water and electricity production and distribution, household refuse collection and incineration plants;
(v) industries in which work cannot be interrupted on technical grounds;
(vi) research and development activities;
(vii) agriculture;
(d) where there is a foreseeable surge of activity, particularly in:
(i) agriculture;
(ii) tourism;
(iii) postal services;
2.2 from Articles 3, 4, 5, 8 and 16:
(a) in the circumstances described in Article 5(4) of Directive 89/391/EEC, ie where occurrences are due to unusual and unforeseeable circumstances,

8   Article 17(1).
9   Article 17(2).

beyond the employers' control, or to exceptional events, the consequences of which could not have been avoided despite the exercise of all due care;
(b) in cases of accident or imminent risk of accident;
2.3 from Articles 3 and 5:
(a) in the case of shift work activities, each time the employee changes shift and cannot take daily and/or weekly rest periods between the end of one shift and the start of the next one;
(b) in the case of activities involving periods of work split up over the day, particularly those of cleaning staff.'

General derogations covering *all activities,* in the case of daily and weekly rest periods, are also possible through collective agreements between the social partners, *subject* to provision of 'equivalent compensating rest periods . . . or . . . appropriate protection'.[10]

Finally, in the case of the requirement as to 11 hours minimum daily rest[11] and 24 hours minimum weekly rest[12] – but *not* in the case of the requirement of daily rest breaks[13] – certain derogations are possible:[14]

'from Articles 3 and 5:
(a) in the case of shift work activities, each time the employee changes shift and cannot take daily and/or weekly rest periods between the end of one shift and the start of the next one;
(b) in the case of activities involving periods of work split up over the day, particularly those of cleaning staff.'

MAXIMUM WEEKLY HOURS

The first two drafts of the Directive did not mention a maximum limit to weekly working hours.[15] However, the European Parliament proposed such an amendment, and this provision is now to be found in the final text:[16]

Maximum weekly working time

'Member States shall take the measures necessary to ensure that, in keeping with the need to protect the health and safety of workers:
(1) the period of weekly working time is limited by means of laws, regulations or administrative provisions or by collective agreements or agreements between the two sides of industry;
(2) the average working time for each seven-day period, including overtime, does not exceed 48 hours.'

The reference period over which the average 48 hour weekly working time is to be calculated is not to exceed four months, periods of paid annual leave and sick leave not being included in the calculation of the average.[17]

---

10 Article 17(3).
11 Article 3.
12 Article 5.
13 Article 4.
14 Article 17(2.3).
15 Article 6 of the first two drafts of the Directive did so obliquely by requiring that: 'The performance of overtime must not interfere with the minimum rest periods laid down in Articles 3 and 4' (daily and weekly rest periods).
16 Article 6.
17 Article 16(2).

Health and safety and humanisation of work

The point of reference specified in this Article is health and safety. However, with respect to breaks during working time, the general principle of humanisation of work is required to be taken into account.[18] It is not easy to see how such a principle can fail to affect maximum weekly working hours. Rest breaks mandated by such a principle, and not only by health and safety, imply limits on weekly working hours.

Derogations

The EU standard stipulates that weekly working time must be limited by national law, or by collective agreements reached by the social partners.[19] However, the weekly working time specified in these instruments is subject to a maximum of 48 hours working, including overtime, per week on average, calculated over a maximum four-month period.[20] Member States *are* permitted to derogate from this standard 'with due regard for the general principles of the protection of the safety and health of workers' in some specified activities.[1] However, derogations are *not* permitted as regards *maximum weekly working time* (though it *is* allowed as regards daily and weekly breaks) in the longer list of specified activities in Article 17(2); nor through the general power to derogate through collective agreements in Article 17(3).

With regard to these specified activities, or the general power to derogate through collective agreements, the sole derogation possible is *not* to the 48 hour maximum, but only to the *reference period* over which it may be calculated. Article 17(2) and (3) allows for derogations from Article 16(2)'s fixing of a maximum four-month reference period. But even then, Article 17(4) limits the possible extension of this reference period to a maximum of six or 12 months:

> 'The right to derogate from Article 16(2), provided for in (Article 17(2) and (3)) may not result in the establishment of a reference period exceeding six months.
>
> However, Member States shall have the option, subject to compliance with the general principles relating to the protection of the safety and health of workers, of allowing, for objective or technical reasons or reasons concerning the organisation of work, collective agreements or agreements concluded between the two sides of industry to set reference periods in no event exceeding twelve months.'

Also, the qualification of 'compliance with the general principles relating to the protection of health and safety of workers' requires that Member States justify any derogations.

Derogation, or delay?

Article 18 of the Directive contains 'Final provisions' and prescribes the standard obligation of Member States to comply (as envisaged in Article 189 of the EC Treaty). The period specified for compliance is three years after adoption of the

---

18   Article 13.
19   Article 6(1).
20   Article 16(2).
 1   Article 17(1).

Directive.[2] Exceptionally, Article 18(1)(b)(i) begins: 'However, a Member State shall have the option not to apply Article 6 . . .', and ends:

> 'Before the expiry of a period of seven years counted from the expiry of the period of three years referred to in (a), the Council shall, on the basis of a Commission proposal accompanied by an appraisal report, re-examine the provisions of this point (i) and decide on what action to take.'

This might seem to read as a *permanent* power of Member States to derogate from Article 6, subject to conditions specified. If so, it is not clear why it falls under the heading 'Final provisions',[3] rather than the heading 'Derogations'.[4] On this reading it is simply another form of derogation, though one subject exceptionally to review after seven years.

Alternatively, however, it could be read as granting *only* a further seven year period before compliance is required. The seven years may be renewed on the basis of a Commission proposal. On this reading it could be read as a *temporary* derogation facility, lasting seven years and subject to review (and possible renewal on the basis of a Commission proposal). This reading is reinforced by the provision which follows in Article 18, and which regards Article 7:[5]

> '*Similarly*, Member States shall have the option, as regards the application of Article 7, of making use of a transitional period of not more than three years starting from the end of the three-year period referred to in (a) . . .' (my italics).

This appears to regard the option of Member States with regard to Article 6 as *similarly* subject to a transitional period, though of seven years, not three, and subject to review.

Individual agreement and collectively agreed derogation

Article 17 ('Derogations') allows for *general* derogation from the Directive's labour standards on daily and weekly rest breaks and periods[6] 'by means of *collective* agreements'.[7] Article 18 ('Final provisions') allows for *general* derogation from maximum weekly working hours if the employer 'has first obtained the worker's agreement'.[8] Both kinds of derogation are subject to equivalent compensating rest periods or appropriate protection. Individual agreement to work more than 48 hours (including overtime) per week is additionally subject to respect for 'the general principles of the protection of the safety and health of workers' and a host of other conditions:

> 'However, a Member State shall have the option not to apply Article 6, while respecting the general principles of the protection of the safety and health of workers, and provided it takes the necessary measures to ensure that:
> – no employer requires a worker to work more than 48 hours over a seven-day

---

2   Article 18(1)(a).
3   Article 18.
4   Article 17.
5   Article 18(1)(b)(ii).
6   Articles 3, 4 and 5.
7   Article 17(3).
8   Article 18(1)(b)(i).

period, calculated as an average for the reference period referred to in Article 16(2), unless he has first obtained the worker's agreement to perform such work;
- no worker is subjected to any detriment by his employer because he is not willing to give his agreement to perform such work;
- the employer keeps up-to-date records of all workers who carry out such work;
- the records are placed at the disposal of the competent authorities, which may, for reasons connected with the safety and/or health of workers, prohibit or restrict the possibility of exceeding the maximum weekly working hours;
- the employer provides the competent authorities at their request with information on cases in which agreement has been given by workers to perform work exceeding forty-eight hours over a period of seven days, calculated as an average for the reference period referred to in Article 16(2).'

These provisions are only relevant if the Member State opts *not* to apply the requirement as to maximum working hours. This is no easy option. The measures necessary raise many potential difficulties:

- Under what conditions is the consent of the worker to be obtained and expressed? Given the need to ensure respect for 'the general principles of the protection of the health and safety of workers', what steps are required to ensure that the consent given is a fully informed one, free of pressures adverse to health and safety?
- Is the consent to be expressed orally or in writing?
- Is the consent irrevocable, and, if not, how may the worker withdraw consent once given?
- What constitutes 'detriment' suffered by a worker who is not willing to give his agreement: loss of a job or of promotion, transfer, denial of access to training?
- What information needs be maintained in the records required to be kept by the employer of the workers exceeding the 48-hour weekly limit: names, occupations, number of hours worked, health and accident records?
- Who are the 'competent authorities' to review the records required to be kept of workers exceeding the 48-hour limit; how are they to exercise their powers other than by regular inspection; what are the procedures whereby they exercise their powers effectively?
- What is the information about workers' individual agreements to work more than 48 hours which is to be provided by employers at the request of the competent authorities, and on which occasions may it be requested?

The list of bureaucratic requirements on the State, and compensatory obligations for the employer, necessitated by a Member State's opting out of the Directive's 48-hour maximum weekly working hours is formidable. It constitutes a powerful incentive both for Member States to apply the EU standard, and for employers to make the attempt to organise working time so as to enable workers not to exceed 48 hours work per week.

The legal position is made ambiguous since there is no clear provision for *collective* agreements on overtime working which exceed the 48 hours limit. Two sets of problems are likely to emerge as a result of frequently complicated collective agreements regulating overtime working.

Can individual agreement be deduced from a collective agreement between the employer and the union representing the workers? This is questionable since it would have been simple to include Article 6 in the list of standards allowing for derogation by collective agreement in Article 17(2). This was not done, and the implication is that individual agreement is necessary.

Even if collective agreements can stand in for individual agreement, can an individual worker still opt out of a collective agreement? Individual workers might opt out by refusing to work the overtime agreed to by their union. They might also agree individually to work hours in contradiction to the agreement. Different national labour laws contain varying rules regarding the inderogability of collective agreements.[9]

A hypothetical illustration raising legal questions about the effects of the Directive is the following:

1. The UK opts out of Article 6 prescribing the 48-hour limit.
2. A collective agreement is made imposing overtime exceeding the 48-hour weekly limit.
3. An individual worker refuses to work the overtime prescribed by the agreement:
   - ever;
   - on one occasion;
   - because he feels tired and fears for his health and safety.

If the employer subjects the worker to any detriment, can the worker:

- claim compensation against the employer on the grounds that individual agreement to perform such work was not obtained;
- claim compensation against the State for not taking the necessary measures of protection?[10]

These questions are likely to become of great practical importance. Overtime working for long hours is one of the distinguishing features of working time in the UK.

SHIFT WORK

The Commission's Explanatory Memorandum to the proposed Directive calculated that the percentage of employees doing shiftwork, both regular and occasional, was as shown in the table on page 322 overleaf.[11]

---

9 Prohibiting it, permitting it when in melius or subjecting it to conditions. See generally, Lord Wedderburn 'Inderogability, Collective Agreements and Community Law' (1992) 21 *Industrial Law Journal* 245.

10 Cases C-6/90 and C-9/90: *Francovich and Bonifaci v Italian Republic* [1992] ECR I-5357. Rejecting one of the Parliament's amendments to the Council's common position, the Commission wished 'to make clear to the Council that it considers that, where a Member State uses the option set out in Article 18.1(b)(i), workers' representatives should be consulted, where they exist, before agreement is reached for a worker to work more than 48 hours a week on average; it also considers that such a Member State will have to ensure that any individual who believes he has been subjected to any detriment, because he was not willing to give his agreement to perform such work, will be able to seek redress through the judicial procedure in place in that Member State with regard to individual employment rights.'

11 Explanatory Memorandum, p 10, paragraphs 17–18.

PERCENTAGE OF EMPLOYEES DOING REGULAR AND OCCASIONAL[12] SHIFTWORK	
UK	29%
Spain	29%
Belgium	24%
Greece	23%
Ireland	17%
Italy	17%
Netherlands	17%
Germany	15%
Portugal	12%
Denmark	11%

The same source shows that the percentage of employees in manufacturing doing shift work varies considerably among Member States:

PERCENTAGE OF EMPLOYEES IN MANUFACTURING DOING REGULAR AND OCCASIONAL[13] SHIFTWORK	
UK	64%
Italy	46%
Spain	45%
Belgium	39%
Ireland	36%
Greece	32%
Netherlands	29%
France	25%
Germany	22%
Portugal	10%

Shift work is defined in the Directive:[14]

'"Shift work" means any method of organising work in shifts whereby workers succeed each other at the same work stations according to a certain pattern, including a rotating pattern, and which may be continuous or discontinuous, entailing the need for workers to work at different times over a given period of days or weeks.'

Shift work is subject to the Directive's general requirements as to: minimum daily rest periods, maximum daily working hours, minimum rest periods during working hours, weekly rest periods, and maximum weekly hours.

Occasionally, these are *less* favourable to shift workers. *Derogation*, by laws, regulations or administrative provisions, or by means of collective agreements

---

12   Occasional shift work given 50% weighting.
13   Ditto.
14   Article 2(5).

(though with equivalent compensatory periods) *is possible* with respect to otherwise mandatory minimum 11-hour daily rest periods[15] and minimum 24 + 11 = 35-hour weekly rest periods:[16]

> '(a) in the case of shift work activities, each time the employee changes shift and cannot take daily and/or weekly rest periods between the end of one shift and the start of the next one;
> (b) in the case of activities involving periods of work split up over the day, particularly those of cleaning staff.'[17]

Where shift work also entails night work, the relevant provisions will apply, sometimes with special force. The first two drafts explicitly provided:[18]

> 'In the event of shift work involving night work the working of two consecutive fulltime shifts shall be prohibited.'

This was dropped from the final draft. The Directive now contains a more general provision requiring that:[19]

> 'night workers whose work involves special hazards or heavy physical and mental strain do not work more than eight hours in any period of 24 hours during which they perform night work.'

Shift work is also linked together with night work in the general provisions of Article 12:

Safety and health protection

> 'Member States shall take the measures necessary to ensure that:
> (1) night workers and shift workers have safety and health protection appropriate to the nature of their work;
> (2) appropriate protection and prevention services or facilities with regard to the safety and health of night workers and shift workers are equivalent to those applicable to other workers and are available at all times.'

'Equivalent' does not mean equal services and facilities. They must be appropriate to the nature of the shift work.

The extent to which new rhythms of shift work have proliferated was indicated in the Table produced by the Commission introducing its original proposed Directive:[20] its figures are shown overleaf (page 324).

The Commission also gave details of research presenting the consequences for health and safety of shift work. In light of this, it was not surprising that the first two drafts included a general provision specific to shift work:[1]

> 'The scheduling and total length of breaks for rotating shift workers ... shall take account of the more demanding nature of those forms of working time.'

But this provision did not survive to the final text. Although Section III of the Directive is headed 'Night work, shift work and patterns of work', the final text

15 Article 3.
16 Article 5.
17 Article 17(2.3).
18 Article 7(2).
19 Article 8(2).
20 Explanatory Memorandum, Table 4 on p 11.
 1 Article 7(4).

SHIFTWORK IN INDUSTRY (AS % OF ENTERPRISES)[2]										
	B	*D*	*GR*	*E*	*F*	*IRL*	*I*	*NL*	*P*	*UK*	*EUR*
yes	80	65	52	68	74	53	83	63	19	73	70
– continuous	22	6	14	17	10	16	9	11	4	14	10
– interrupted each day	37	42	14	27	40	15	35	19	6	22	33
– interrupted each week	21	16	24	24	24	14	38	33	9	17	22
with – 2 shifts	19	46	21	1	25		37	27	10	34	32
with – 3 shifts	22	19	24	25	19		31	21	7	29	23
with – 4 shifts	7	0	4	33	8		12	2	2	6	7
with – 5 shifts	6	0	2	6	4		1	5	0	4	2
with – 6+ shifts	5	0	0	3	1		2	5	0	0	1
– other patterns	4	0	0	1	2		0	2	0	0	1
average number of shifts	3.3	2.3	2.8	3.8	2.9		2.8	3	2.6	2.7	3
number	20	35	47	31	26	45	17	37	81	27	30

retains little specific regulation of shift work. Instead, there is in this Section only the general provision already heavily emphasised:[3]

Pattern of work

'Member States shall take the measures necessary to ensure that an employer who intends to organise work according to a certain pattern takes account of the general principle of adapting work to the worker, with a view, in particular, to alleviating monotonous work and work at a predetermined work-rate depending on the type of activity, and of safety and health requirements, especially as regards breaks during working time.'

This is clearly applicable to shift work. But it is short on prescribing specific obligations. It is important to reiterate the earlier conclusions. It applies to the *initial* organisation of shift working, when the employer *intends* to organise work according to a certain pattern. *Two* factors must be taken into account when organising shift work: the general principle of adaptation of work to the worker, to a human being; and health and safety requirements, a second and separate factor. The principle of humanisation of work is to have particular (but not exclusive) regard to alleviating monotonous work and work at a predetermined work-rate – factors which are not related to health and safety requirements narrowly considered. Shift work entails many other disruptions.

The mere avoidance of health and safety risks is transformed by the principle of the humanisation of work. The translation of this new EC law principle into measures which must be adopted by Member States poses a challenge. For example, the obligation focuses on the employer who envisages organising work according to a certain rhythm. He is to be required to take account of the general principle of adaptation of work to human beings. This could be read as implying a requirement of consultation and participation of workers and their representatives. The Directive in many places emphasises the role of the social

2   Source: Special EC labour market survey, results to be published in *European Economy*.
3   Article 13.

dialogue in setting standards. This is in line with the Commission's general duty to promote social dialogue.[4] The second draft of the proposed Directive required that:[5]

'Consultation and participation of workers and/or their representatives shall take place in accordance with Article 11 of Directive 89/391/EEC on the matters covered by this Directive.'

This disappeared, though the Preamble to the final text contains in the third recital:

'Whereas the provisions of Council Directive 89/391/EEC of 12 June 1989 on the introduction of measures to encourage improvements in the safety and health of workers at work are fully applicable to the areas covered by this Directive without prejudice to more stringent and/or specific provisions contained there.'[6]

Moreover, Article 1(4) provides:

'The provisions of Directive 89/391/EEC are fully applicable to the matters referred to in paragraph 2,
(which reads: "This Directive applies to: (a) minimum periods of daily rest, weekly rest and annual leave, to breaks and maximum weekly working time, and (b) certain aspects of night work, shift work and patterns of work.")
without prejudice to more stringent and/or specific provisions contained in this Directive.'

The substance of the requirement in the second draft may therefore survive in the measures to be adopted by Member States, in accordance with their obligation under the Directive, to secure that employers do take into account the general principle of adaptation of work to human beings. The obvious way to achieve this is to consult those human beings and engage them in the process of organising working time.

ANNUAL HOLIDAYS

The first draft of the Directive required provision for annual paid holidays, but did not attempt to specify any common duration:[7]

'Member States shall adopt the necessary measures to ensure that all workers are afforded an annual paid holiday for a minimum period; the procedures relating to duration and any splitting shall be determined in accordance with national practices.'

The statutory regulation of annual paid holidays in the Member States at this time was as shown in the table overleaf (page 326).

The European Parliament's proposed amendments specified that there must be at least four weeks' annual paid holidays, and five for workers who work

---

4   Article 118B of the Treaty of Rome.
5   Article 9.
6   The first of the Statements for entry in the Council Minutes attached to the final text reads that the Council and the Commission stated: 'Although this Directive is not an individual Directive within the meaning of Article 16(1) of Directive 89/391/EEC, the provisions of that Directive are applicable in this field insofar as they affect aspects regulated in this Directive and, in addition, when they are applicable by their nature.'
7   Article 5.

STATUTORY REGULATION OF ANNUAL PAID HOLIDAYS[8]	
Country	*Statutory Provision*
Belgium	4 weeks
Denmark	5 weeks
France	5 weeks
Germany	3 weeks
Greece	4 weeks/4 weeks 2 days
Ireland	3 weeks
Italy	–
Luxembourg	5 weeks
Netherlands	4 weeks
Portugal	3–4 weeks
Spain	5 weeks
UK	–

nights for at least the 12-month reference period. The second draft proposed by the Commission adopted the provision of a minimum four weeks' paid holiday, but not the extra week for night workers:[9]

'Member States shall adopt the necessary measures to ensure that all workers are afforded an annual paid holiday for a minimum period of four weeks in respect of every period of 12 months for which they work for their employer. It shall not be possible to replace the minimum period of annual paid holiday with financial compensation.'

The text of the Directive as finally adopted reflects these preceding provisions:[10]

'1. Member States shall take the measures necessary to ensure that every worker is entitled to paid annual leave of at least four weeks in accordance with the conditions for entitlement to and granting of such leave laid down by national legislation and/or practice.
2. The minimum period of paid annual leave may not be replaced by an allowance in lieu, except where the employment relationship is terminated.'

Unlike other requirements of daily and weekly rest periods,[11] the Directive does not allow for any derogation from the requirement for an annual rest period. It is an absolute entitlement that cannot be reduced. Conditions for entitlement and granting are subject to national regulation. But this cannot replace the minimum period of paid annual leave by an allowance in lieu.

The final text does provide for a transitional period:[12]

'Similarly, Member States shall have the option, as regards the application of Article 7, of making use of a transitional period of not more than three years starting from the end of the three-year period referred to in (a), provided that during that transitional period:
– every worker receives three weeks' paid annual leave in accordance with the

8 Source: *European Industrial Relations Reports* No 210, July 1991, p 26.
9 Article 5.
10 Article 7.
11 Articles 3 and 5.
12 Article 18(1)(b)(ii).

conditions for entitlement to and granting of such leave laid down by national legislation and/or practice, and
- the three-week period of paid annual leave may not be replaced by an allowance in lieu, except where the employment relationship is terminated.'

The three week annual paid leave entitlement will come into effect at once; before it becomes four weeks, a Member State may insist on a six-year transitional period (three years after the initial three-year period for compliance).

NIGHT WORK

The Commission's Explanatory Memorandum to the first draft of the proposed Directive calculated that the percentage of employees engaged in regular and occasional night work (50% weighting being applied to the latter to make the two percentages compatible) was as follows: [13]

PERCENTAGE OF EMPLOYEES IN REGULAR AND OCCASIONAL[14] NIGHT WORK	
UK	25%
Greece	17%
France	15%
Ireland	15%
Spain	14%
Belgium	13%
Denmark	13%
Netherlands	12%
Portugal	12%
Germany	9%
Italy	9%

Nightwork in industry is less widespread than in the economy as a whole, and its distribution among Member States is different: 23% in Spain, 17% in the Netherlands, 16% in the UK, 13% in Italy, 10% in Belgium and less than 10% in the other five Member States, dropping to 4% in Portugal.

Four articles in the final Directive impose restrictions on night working and provide safeguards for night workers. But the definition of 'night workers' itself was revised by consecutive drafts.

Who are 'night workers'?

In the first draft: [15]

'3. "night work" means all work performed during a period of not less than 7 consecutive hours comprised between 8.00pm and 9.00am . . .
. . .

---

13 Explanatory Memorandum, p 11, paragraph 19.
14 Occasional night work given 50% weighting.
15 Article 2(3) and (5).

5. 'night worker' means an employee who performs night work, whether through shift work or otherwise on a regular basis.'

In the second draft, the definition of 'night worker' was enlarged to include employees who perform night work:[16]

'regularly or in excess of a certain number of hours a year, the number to be defined by each Member State after consultation with representative employers' and workers' organisations.'

To qualify as a night worker it was necessary to spend most working hours at night (8pm – 9am). Those who worked fewer than seven consecutive hours during this period did not qualify. Also, night workers were those who did so regularly. Occasional night work did not qualify.

The requirement of regular night working was retained in the final draft. But, as regards the duration of night work, the requirement of seven consecutive hours during a 13-hour period was altered by limiting it to three hours in the five-hour period between midnight and 5am,[17] and the final draft allowed even these parameters to be altered:[18]

'(3) "night time" means any period of not less than seven hours, as defined by national law, and which must include in any case the period between midnight and 5am;
(4) "night worker" means:
  (a) on the one hand, any worker who during night time works at least three hours of his daily working time as a normal course, and
  (b) on the other hand, any worker who is likely during night time to work a certain proportion of his annual working time, as defined at the choice of the Member State concerned:
    (i) by national legislation, following consultation with the two sides of industry, or
    (ii) by collective agreements or agreements concluded between the two sides of industry at national or regional level.'

This would allow for expansion of the category 'night worker' to include also *occasional* night workers. It also gives freedom to reduce the duration and temporal incidence of night working. Both may be done by legislation (after consultation) or by collective agreement. Where employers demand night work, they can only circumvent the Community standards by reaching agreement.

Maximum night work over a reference period

The first two drafts limited night working by reference to the average night work performed over a reference period:[19]

'Normal hours of work for night workers shall not exceed an average of eight hours in any 24-hour period calculated over a reference period not longer than fourteen days in which they perform night work.'

16   Article 2(5).
17   Article 2(3) and (4)(a).
18   Article 2(4)(b)(i) and (ii).
19   Article 7(1).

These proposals were altered in the final draft. The new EU standard still prohibits more than eight hours night working in a 24-hour period *on average*.[20]

> 'Member States shall take the measures necessary to ensure that:
> (1) normal hours of work for night workers do not exceed an average of eight hours in any 24-hour period.'

However, the reference period over which the average is calculated is to be specified as follows:[1]

> 'Member States may lay down:
> (3) for the application of Article 8 (length of night work), a reference period defined after consultation of the two sides of industry or by collective agreements or agreements concluded between the two sides of industry at national or regional level.
>   If the minimum weekly rest period of 24 hours required by Article 5 falls within that reference period, it shall not be included in the calculation of the average.'

The position is unclear if a reference period is *not* defined by the Member State, and/or if the social partners have *not* reached agreement on one. It could be argued then that the limit becomes eight hours in a reference period of 24 hours. Member States can extend this reference period, or can authorise derogations by collective agreement on a longer period. On the other hand, the reference to eight hours *on average* could imply that there is no reference period unless one is so defined.

Night work and overtime, hazardous and onerous work

Further protection from night working of a particularly onerous kind (overtime, shifts, hazardous, physically or mentally onerous occupations) appeared to be envisaged in the remainder of the provisions in Article 7 of the first two drafts:[2]

> '2. In the event of shift work involving night work the working of two consecutive full-time shifts shall be prohibited.
> 3. Subject to the provisions contained in paragraph 1, no overtime shall be performed by night workers before or after a daily period of work which includes night work in occupations involving special hazards or heavy physical or mental strain.
> 4. The scheduling and total length of breaks for rotating shift workers and for night workers shall take account of the more demanding nature of those forms of working time.'

The final draft does not contain the prohibition on consecutive full-time shifts involving night work. Instead, there is a general provision banning more than eight hours' work including night work in any 24-hour period, allowing again a role for collective bargaining in defining the circumstances when this restriction applies:[3]

> 'Member States shall take the measures necessary to ensure that . . .
> (2) night workers whose work involves special hazards or heavy physical or mental

---

20 Article 8(1).
1 Article 16(3).
2 Article 7(2), (3), (4).
3 Article 8(2).

strain do not work more than eight hours in any period of 24 hours during which they perform night work.

For the purpose of this point, work involving special hazards or heavy physical or mental strain shall be defined by national legislation and/or practice or by collective agreements or agreements concluded between the two sides of industry, taking account of the specific effects and hazards of night work.'

A further provision in the second draft, and retained in the final text, does not regulate the timing of work. Rather it simply prescribes an obligation on employers to secure the health and safety of night workers and to ensure a certain level of protection and prevention facilities:[4]

Safety and health protection

'Member States shall take the measures necessary to ensure that:
(1) night workers and shift workers have safety and health protection appropriate to the nature of their work:
(2) appropriate protection and prevention services or facilities with regard to the safety and health of night workers and shift workers are equivalent to those applicable to other workers and are available at all times.'

Again, 'equivalent' does not mean equal services and facilities. They must be appropriate to the nature of the night work.

Health assessments

In the first draft, an entitlement by night workers to a free health assessment was envisaged. In the final draft it was formulated as follows:[5]

'1. Member States shall take the measures necessary to ensure that:
(a) night workers are entitled to a free health assessment prior to their assignment and thereafter at regular intervals.'

However, the final draft inserted a new provision that:[6]

'3. The free health assessment referred to in paragraph 1(a) may be conducted within the national health system.'

This formulation, while not affecting the entitlement to a free health assessment, renders the nature of the employer's obligation ambiguous. Would an employer satisfy the requirement if he obliged the worker to undertake such an health assessment using public health facilities? What is the position if using public facilities entails expense (travel, time off work) or they are not immediately or promptly available?

Job security

Provision is made for night workers 'suffering from health problems recognised to be connected with the fact that they perform night work' to be transferred to day work. However, the formulation of this provision appears to have changed.

---

4   Article 12.
5   Article 9(1)(a).
6   Article 9(3).

In the first and second drafts, it was for transfer '*as soon as possible* to day work for which he is fit'.[7] In the final draft, it is transfer: '*whenever possible* to day work to which they are suited'.[8]

General guarantees

The final draft allows Member States to provide general guarantees for certain workers:[9]

Guarantees for night-time working

'Member States may make the work of certain categories of night workers subject to certain guarantees, under conditions laid down by national legislation and/or practice, in the case of workers who incur risks to their safety or health linked to night-time working.'

This general power has to be exercised with care in light of the past history of using general restrictions to either single out women or have greater impact on women, thus violating the fundamental principle of equal treatment in EC law.

Informing competent authorities

This provision started off in the first draft as a vague requirement:[10]

'The employer who regularly uses night workers shall duly inform the authorities competent in matters of health and safety.'

The nature, frequency and form of information required was not defined, nor were the authorities to be informed identified. The second draft merely added:[11]

'He shall also inform them when night workers work overtime.'

The final draft deleted this later addition and reverts to the original formula, with two changes. First, there is the crucial qualification that the information is to be provided to the authorities 'at their request'.[12] Secondly, the relevant authorities are merely indicated as those 'competent', not necessarily those 'competent in matters of health and safety'. It is not clear whom these competent authorities are to be: for example, whether they need be public authorities, or could be designated as the trade unions.

Consultation and participation of workers

There was provision in the second draft to require 'consultation and participation of workers and/or their representatives . . . in accordance with Article 11 of the (Framework) Directive 89/391/EEC on the matters covered by this Directive'.[13] Although this disappeared in the final draft, it may still apply by virtue of Article 1(4).

7   Article 8(2).
8   Article 9(1)(b).
9   Article 10.
10   Article 9.
11   Article 9.
12   Article 11.
13   Article 9.

Derogations

A variety of derogations are permitted from the restrictions on night working. In general, for certain occupations;[14] by collective agreements,[15] subject to compensatory periods; for certain activities, subject to equivalent compensatory periods.[16]

CONCLUSION

The seismic shift in the UK law on health and safety at work entailed by EC law is illustrated by the Working Time Directive. From a situation where working time is virtually unregulated in domestic law, the UK will now have to incorporate into its labour law detailed regulations governing daily and weekly rest periods, maximum weekly hours, shift work, annual holidays and night work.

Nor is this simply an exercise in (re-)regulation. The nature of the European law being imported is qualitatively different from domestic law on health and safety. It addresses not merely the concerns of accident and disease prevention and avoidance, but also the welfare and well-being of the worker. This is illustrated in particular in the provisions of Article 13 of the Directive regarding the principle of 'humanisation of work'. The requirement that the employer 'takes account of the general principle of adapting the work to the worker' is potentially revolutionary in its implications for the health and well-being of workers, so much determined by the organisation of working time patterns.

An employer intending to organise work according to a certain pattern may now be confronted by a worker or group of workers who claim that the proposed pattern does not suit their needs. The employer who rejects their claim may face a complaint based on the Directive that s/he has not taken account of the need to adapt work to the workers concerned.

A court faced by such a legal claim might respond by enquiring of the employer what evidence there was that such account had been taken: specifically, whether the refusal to adapt the proposed working time pattern was substantiated – that the employer had considered adapting the work to the workers, but had rejected their complaint for justifiable reasons. The employer may then be called upon to produce justifications (perhaps following those already recognised in EU law for indirect sex discrimination); for example, that the proposed working time pattern was adapted to the needs of the enterprise. However, the complainant workers may be able to demonstrate that their alternative proposed working time pattern is *both* better adapted to them, *and* satisfies the exigencies of the employer. Principles of proportionality and necessity may be invoked. The upshot is that the organisation of working time is no longer the exclusive managerial prerogative of the employer, but is a process of mutual accommodation, subject ultimately to adjudication.

The implications of this process for the UK are particularly salutary in light of the relatively high levels of night work and shift work in the UK. They are likely to be extraordinarily significant taken together with the Directive's prescription of a maximum working week averaging 48 hours. British workers

14   Article 17(1)(a)–(c).
15   Article 17(3).
16   Article 17(2.1) and (2.2).

have the highest number of weekly working hours in Europe; the UK has by far the highest proportion of workers normally working more than 48 hours per week. The adjustments necessary to accommodate the European standard prescribed in the Directive are likely to be dramatic.

The European concept of health and safety, extended to the well-being of the worker, is manifest in the regulation of working time. The adaptation of working time patterns, towards mutual accommodation, away from shift-working, night work and towards reduced working hours demonstrates European labour law's commitment to a different concept of workers' welfare.

Chapter 22

Collective Bargaining and Health and Safety Standards

INTRODUCTION

The EU labour law on health and safety reflects the evolution of a European labour law which draws upon the national traditions of Member States and proposes a model both recognisable by its inspiration in national experience and yet different in its synthesis of the elements of different traditions. It reflects the traditional model of stipulating labour standards through precise legislative formulations. It also recognises the trend, more marked in some countries than others, towards attributing to the social partners an active role in the formulation of labour standards.

In the result, the EU labour standards prescribed are relatively general; the necessary precision is obtained through the activities of those most closely involved in the field: labour and management. The role of collective bargaining in determining the EU standards of health and safety is particularly striking in the Working Time Directive.

The significance of this Directive in the evolution of European law on health and safety cannot be over-estimated. Its origins are disputed as being not in health and safety, but rather the regulation of working conditions. As such, the character of its regulation sharply divided the UK, with its tradition of collective bargaining, from continental systems of legislative regulation of working time, though neither system was undiluted.

The political constraints of qualified majority voting contributed to its, perhaps opportunistic, characterisation as a health and safety measure, but this was also consistent with a wider concept of health, safety and welfare being promoted by the Commission. The outcome was a health and safety measure inspired by the differing traditions of regulation of working conditions, which also challenged the traditional dividing line between health and safety and working conditions. The potential consequences for the future development of health and safety law in Europe are profound.

THE ORIGINS OF THE WORKING TIME DIRECTIVE

The origins of the Working Time Directive are particularly illuminating in revealing the development of the specific European labour law approach to health and safety. Its origins were decidedly mixed. The impetus to health and safety initiatives provided by the enactment of a new Article 118A by the Single

European Act 1986 has already been noted. But the issue of working time had been the subject of attention by the Commission in the form of a draft Recommendation on the reduction and reorganisation of working time in 1983. This was followed by specific provision in the Community Charter of Fundamental Social Rights of Workers of December 1989.[1] When the Commission put forward its Action Programme to implement the Charter, the ambiguous quality of its motivation for legislation, and its choice of the instrument for standard setting on working time was evident.

The Community Charter and Action Programme

The Community Charter of Fundamental Social Rights had two separate drafts before the final text was approved in Strasbourg in December 1989. All three drafts provided for rights to 'a weekly rest period' and to 'annual paid leave'. The second draft (Article 12), however, added a specific reference, as regards the right to a 'weekly rest period', to standards '*to be agreed jointly by the two sides of industry*'. The final draft's Article 8 extended this reference to a specific standard to *both* the weekly rest period and annual paid leave. However, it replaced the earlier reference to a standard 'agreed jointly' with a standard which 'must be harmonised in accordance with *national practices* while the improvement is being maintained'.

In the Preamble to the Charter, the reference to 'practices' specifies that 'implementation (of social rights) may take the form of laws, collective agreements or existing practices', appearing to distinguish among these. However, other Articles of the final draft seem to counter the implication that Article 8 *substitutes* practices for jointly agreed standards.[3] If 'national practices' include

---

1 Article 8: 'Every worker of the European Community shall have a right to a weekly rest period and to annual paid leave, the duration of which must be progressively harmonised in accordance with national practices'.

2 See B Bercusson 'The European Community's Charter of Fundamental Social Rights of Workers' (1990) 53 *Modern Law Review* 624, at pp 632–8.

3 Comparison may be made with the second draft's provisions on remuneration (Article 8). This Article also made a distinction between standards to be set 'by law or by collective agreements at national, regional, interoccupational, sectoral or company level or in accordance with national practices'. This was changed in the final draft (Article 5) to read standards fixed 'in accordance with *arrangements* (cf "national practices") applying in each country' – so as to include all methods of standard setting.

  Despite the Preamble, the context of the final draft's reference in Article 8 to 'practices' seems to include laws *and* collective agreements. On the one hand, unlike 'arrangements', it seems to have a bias towards informality: less law than industrial relations. Perhaps, given the change from the second draft's 'two sides of industry', 'practices' are not limited to *industry* level agreements, but include practices at all levels. As in the second draft's Article 8 on remuneration, '*national* practices' presumably refers to their quality as pertaining to one of the Member States, not their scope. The final draft's provision in Article 21 for 'equitable remuneration' for young people also specifies the standard as that 'in accordance with national practice'.

  Other Articles in the final draft also refer to 'practice' in the sense of standards set through informal collective autonomous action. The section of the Charter on 'Freedom of Association' (Articles 11–14) emphasises this. Article 12 refers to rights to negotiate and conclude agreements under conditions laid down by 'national legislation and practices'. Article 13 encourages dispute settlement 'in accordance with national practice'. The section on 'Information, Consultation and Participation' (Articles 17–18) advocates such developments 'taking account of the practices in force in the various Member States' (Article 17).

standards set by collective agreements, the Article's requirement that harmonis-ation take place while maintaining the improvement implies Community-wide coordination of collectively bargained standards.

The Commission's proposals in the Action Programme to implement the Charter were in line with this interpretation. The Action Programme refers to the Council's failure to adopt the Commission's 1983 draft recommendation on the reduction and reorganisation of working time. It reiterates that 'the adap-tation, flexibility and organisation of working time . . . play a not inconsiderable role in determining the situation of the labour market', and emphasises its important role in competitiveness. The proposal, therefore, was for a Directive on the adaptation of working time. Significantly, the Commission noted:[4]

> 'Moreover, collective agreements on this matter are increasing in number in many industrial sectors throughout the Community.
>
> In order to avoid excessive differences in approach from one sector or country to another, the basic conditions which these agreements should comply with ought therefore to be clearly defined.
>
> The Commission considers moreover that as regards this diversity care should be taken to ensure that these practices do not have an adverse effect on the wellbeing and health of workers.
>
> For this reason, as regards the maximum duration of work, rest periods, holidays, night work, week-end work, systematic overtime, it is important that certain mini-mum requirements be laid down at Community level.
>
> For the Commission it would be a matter of proposing minimum reference rules without entering into details as regards their implementation.'

Collective agreements as a source of Community regulation of working time

The most daring aspect of the Commission's proposal was the focus on collec-tive agreements as the source setting the standards to be harmonised. The Commission acknowledges the role of collective agreements in regulating flexi-bility of working time. It does not explicitly refer to the hotly contested issue in many Member States as to whether flexibility of working time *ought to be* sub-ject to collectively agreed regulation. Nor is any comment made on the extent to which flexibility is *in practice* subjected to collectively agreed regulation. The existence of some collective agreements and the inevitable diversity in their approaches is sufficient to introduce the considerations of harmonisation and health and safety which justify the Commission defining 'the basic conditions which these agreements should comply with'. This approach was bound to come into conflict with governments opposed to collectively agreed regulation of working time flexibility, and would have a substantial impact in Member States and on industrial sectors where such regulation is relatively uncommon. The Commission further proposes 'minimum reference rules without entering into details as regards their implementation'. This implies that the proposed Directive would stipulate standards, but not implementation mechanisms.

Article 8 of the Charter led to an Action Programme proposal on working

---

4 Communication concerning the Commission's Action Programme relating to the implemen-tation of the Community Charter, COM (89) 568 final, Brussels, 29 November 1989, pp 18–19. The Explanatory Memorandum to the first draft of the Working Time Directive included quo-tations from the Charter and Action Programme; p 2, paragraph 1.

time with potentially far-reaching implications for the relation of collective bargaining agreements to Community standards. These can be summarised under two headings following the Action Programme's own words:

- What are 'the basic conditions which these agreements should comply with'?
- How are the 'minimum reference rules' to be formulated?[5]

Basic conditions with which collective agreements should comply

The aim of defining the basic conditions with which collective agreements should comply is 'to avoid excessive differences in approach from one sector or country to another'. The equal weight attached to *sectoral* differences contrasts with the frequent focus in the comparative literature on *national* differences in approach. 'Basic conditions' could refer to a number of different features which characterise national practice of collective agreements on working time. Two features of industrial relations are said to be of primary importance: the *relationship* between statutory law (or action by the State) and collective bargaining (action by the social partners); and the degree and type of *centralisation* of industrial relations institutions, particularly collective bargaining and trade unions.[6]

The Commission *Comparative Study on Rules Governing Working Conditions in the Member States* reported that in most countries legislation had set a general standard of normal weekly working time.[7] Recently, however, measures had been introduced to allow for the possibility of regulating working hours other than on a weekly basis. The main instrument for this 'flexibilisation' was collective bargaining. The formulas included daily and weekly ceilings, normal average working hours over a specified period and reductions in working time in return for flexibility. Following this flexibility model, nightwork was in some countries generally forbidden, but derogation was allowed, whereas in other countries it was generally allowed, unless explicitly forbidden. While there are problems in defining 'overtime working' nine Member States (apart from Denmark, Italy and the UK) had laid down ceilings per day, week or year. The ceilings are often replaced through collective bargaining.

Flexibilisation through collective bargaining takes a variety of forms, some of which are described in the following extract:[8]

'. . . a minimum core of protection, of substantive regulation . . . may become smaller but it may also be different . . . most legislations are not moving towards a short simple list of basic protective provisions, but may move to greater complexity in the

---

5   The discussion of these issues is here confined to the topic of working time. But Article 7 of the Charter postulates a right to improvement, through approximation, of living and working conditions in general, 'in particular the duration and organisation of working time and forms of employment other than open-ended contracts'. The issues addressed here, therefore, may become relevant when Commission proposals on topics other than working time are forthcoming.

6   T Treu 'Introduction' to Chapter II, 'New Trends in Working Time Arrangements', in A Gladstone (ed) *Current Issues in Labour Relations: An International Perspective*, Walter de Gruyter, Berlin and New York 1989, pp 149–60, at pp 155–6.

7   Synopsis, Commission Staff Working Paper, SEC(89) 1137, Brussels, 30 June 1989.

8   R Blanpain 'General Report', in R Blanpain and E Kohler (eds) *Legal and Contractual Limitations on Working-Time in the European Community Member States*, European Foundation for the Improvement of Living and Working Conditions, Office for Official Publications of the EC: Kluwer (1988) at pp 83–4.

regulation. For instance, flexibility has been realised by adding exceptions to the existing legislation, by establishing new complicated rules for calculating "averages" etc. The core is not one in the classic sense, but one of great diffusion and this may even be the case with collective bargaining.

In discussing the core, different methodological possibilities come to mind. The first is the more classical one, a statutory legal core, reduced but more complex, with many exceptions; another is a derogatory possibility given either to the collective or to the individual parties. A further possibility might be that the law or (national) bargaining sets only a border limit (40-hour-week) over a certain period of time and leaves parties free to do what they like inside the boundaries ...

The role, however, of public powers (as legislators and employer) remains important ... on the one hand "controlled" deregulation; on the other, and more important, financial support of the most significant forms of work reorganisation.'

A Directive on working time flexibility aimed to outline basic procedural conditions for the regulation of working time by collective agreements.

From the Explanatory Memorandum to the final Directive

Introducing its first proposal for a Directive on Working Time, the Commission explained that:[9]

'Accordingly, pursuant to the Charter and as announced in its action programme, the Commission intends to propose a groundwork of basic provisions on certain aspects of the organisation of working time connected with workers' health and safety at work which relate to:
- minimum daily and weekly rest periods,
- minimum annual paid holidays;
- minimum conditions determining the recourse to shift and especially night work;
- protection of workers' health and safety in the event of changes in working patterns resulting from adjustments in working time.'

However:[10]

'other issues mentioned in the action programme in the field of the adaptation of working time should be left to both sides of industry and/or national legislation. In addition these matters should be dealt with in depth within the framework of the dialogue between both sides of industry at Community level without prejudice to the Commission's prerogative to submit proposals should it see fit to do so.'

In particular, the Commission emphasised that 'the question of *systematic overtime* is a subject best dealt with by the two sides of industry and by national provisions'. The role of working time in achieving flexibility of capacity utilisation was seen to be due to the social partners:[11]

'In many cases legislation, but above all the conclusion of a large number of collective agreements have supported the trend towards more flexible use of productive equipment ...'

Explicit reference was made to recent draft laws on the regulation of working time in Germany, to collective agreements (or even enterprise agreements) in

9   Explanatory Memorandum, p 2, paragraph 2.
10   Ibid, p 3.
11   Ibid, p 4, paragraph 4.

the Netherlands which made it possible to amend or adjust statutory maxima, and to experience in Belgium where very high numbers of hours can be worked in a week provided the average weekly working time over a 13-week period does not exceed 38 hours.[12] Even with night work, collective agreements may derogate from a general ban, as is often the case in Germany, Greece, France, Italy and Portugal.[13]

The delicate balance between legislation and collective bargaining was spelled out twice in the Explanatory Memorandum in almost identical terms; once at the beginning and again in its final provisions:[14]

'. . . given the differences arising from national practices, the subject of working conditions in general falls to varying degrees under the autonomy of both sides of industry who often act in the public authorities' stead and/or complement their action. To take account of these differences and in accordance with the principle of subsidiarity the Commission takes the view that negotiation between the two sides of industry should play its full part within the framework of the proposed measures, provided that it is able to guarantee adherence to the principles set out in the Commission's proposals . . . In other words, it is important in this field to take into consideration the fact that such agreements concluded by management and labour can in principle make a contribution to the application of Community directives, without, however, releasing the Member States concerned from the responsibility for attaining the objectives sought via these instruments.'

In light of this explicit, even enthusiastic, recognition of the role of collective bargaining in the Community Charter's Action Programme and Explanatory Memorandum, the first two drafts of the Working Time Directive took an important, if cautious, initiative. There was no mention of collective bargaining in the Preambles, but both drafts provided for the possibility of general derogation in Article 12(3):

'In case of collective agreements made between employers and representatives of the workers at the appropriate levels, aiming at setting up a comprehensive set of provisions regarding the adjustment of working time corresponding to the specific conditions of the enterprise, including daily and weekly rest periods as well as night- and shift-work, subject to the condition that on these specific points equivalent periods of compensatory rest are granted to the workers within a reference period that must not exceed six months.'

Both drafts also allowed for the possibility of implementation of the Directive through collective agreements:[15]

'Member States shall comply with this Directive . . . by bringing into force the laws, regulations or administrative provisions necessary or by ensuring that the two sides of industry establish the necessary provisions through agreement, without prejudice to the obligation on the Member States to achieve the results to be obtained by this Directive.'

12 Ibid, p 8, paragraphs 12, 14.
13 Ibid, p 13, paragraph 25.
14 Ibid, p 4, paragraph 3 and again in paragraph 32 on pp 16–17. The former added at the beginning of the extract quoted: 'While acknowledging the need for certain basic rules with regard to working time at Community level it should be emphasised that . . .' The latter began: 'Finally, it should be emphasised that . . .'
15 Article 14.

In addition, the second draft added an Article 9:

> 'Consultation and participation of workers and/or their representatives shall take place in accordance with Article 11 of Directive 89/391/EEC on the matters covered by this Directive.'

This initial caution was overcome in the final draft. The Preamble of the Directive incorporates a new penultimate paragraph:

> 'Whereas it is necessary to provide that certain provisions may be subject to derogations implemented, according to the case, by Member States or the two sides of industry . . .'

The final text of the Directive also included a large number of new provisions which made collective bargaining an element in the setting of EC standards on working time. In the final text, the role of collective bargaining in determining *some* of the EU standards on working time has undergone a significant *qualitative* change. In the past, it was largely confined to allowing for derogations to prescribed standards. The present Directive also allows for collective agreements themselves to fix or define relevant standards, usually only with the consent of the Member State concerned, but in one exceptional case, with *priority* over Member State legislation.[16]

NIGHT WORK: NIGHT WORKERS, REFERENCE PERIODS, KINDS OF WORK

Collective bargaining plays a role in *defining* who are night workers; 'night worker' means:[17]

> 'any worker who is likely during night time to work a certain proportion of his annual working time, as defined at the choice of the Member State concerned:
> (i) by national legislation, following *consultation with the two sides of industry, or*
> (ii) *by collective agreements* or agreements concluded between the two sides of industry at national or regional levels.'

Article 8 prescribes for night workers normal hours not exceeding an average of eight hours in any 24-hour period. However, the reference period over which the average is calculated is not specified and Member States may provide for the *reference period* to be *defined* by collective bargaining:[18]

> 'for the application of Article 8 (length of night work), a reference period defined after *consultation of the two sides of industry or by collective agreements* or agreements concluded between the two sides of industry at national or regional level.'

Collective bargaining may also *define* the *kind of work* which prohibits averaging out the maximum eight hours' work in any 24-hour period:[19]

> 'Member States shall take the measures necessary to ensure that:
> . . .
> (2) night workers whose work involves special hazards or heavy physical or mental

16   Daily rest periods, Article 4.
17   Article 2(4)(b).
18   Article 16(3).
19   Article 8(2).

strain do not work more than eight hours in any period of 24 hours during which they perform night work.

For the purpose of this point, work involving special hazards or heavy physical or mental strain shall be defined by national legislation and/or practice *or by collective agreements* or agreements concluded between the two sides of industry, taking account of the specific effects and hazards of night work.'

The provisions of Article 8 may be derogated from by collective agreements under the general derogation provisions already prefigured in the first two drafts,[20] but now assuming a larger scope.[1] There is also a general provision allowing Member States to provide guarantees for night workers by law or '*practice*':[2]

Guarantees for night-time working

'Member States may make the work of certain categories of night workers subject to certain guarantees, under conditions laid down by national legislation and/or *practice*, in the case of workers who incur risks to their safety or health linked to night-time working.'

Finally, Article 11 contains the terse statement:

'Member States shall take the measures necessary to ensure that an employer who regularly uses night workers brings this information to the attention of the competent authorities if they so request.'

No indication is given of who these authorities are. The role of trade unions in many Member States could easily qualify them as a competent authority.

REST BREAKS: PRIORITY TO COLLECTIVE AGREEMENTS

As regards *rest breaks* during working hours, the Directive gives *priority* to collective agreements over legislation in *determining* the EC standard:[3]

Breaks

'Member States shall take the measures necessary to ensure that, where the working day is longer than six hours, every worker is entitled to a rest break, the details of which, including duration and the terms on which it is granted, shall be laid down in *collective agreements* or agreements between the two sides of industry or, failing that, by national legislation.'

The EU standard is to be determined by collective bargaining, (though without specifying the appropriate level) and, only in its absence, by legislation.

Again, the provisions of Article 4 may be derogated from by collective agreements under the general derogation provisions of Article 17((2) and (3)). The effect of such derogation is rendered more problematic by the fact that the standard being derogated from by collective agreements may also have been established by collective agreements. This raises complex questions of the relations between different levels of collective agreements. The law governing

---

20 Article 14.
1 Article 17(2) and (3).
2 Article 10.
3 Article 4.

these questions is not homogeneous across the Community. National labour laws which purport to structure collective agreements in an articulated hierarchy may come into conflict with the EC provisions authorising derogation.

MAXIMUM WEEKLY HOURS: LIMITS, REFERENCE PERIODS

Article 6 provides:

Maximum weekly working time

'Member States shall take the measures necessary to ensure that, in keeping with the need to protect the health and safety of workers:
(1) the period of weekly working time is limited by means of laws, regulations or administrative provisions *or by collective agreements* or agreements between the two sides of industry;
(2) the average working time for each seven-day period, including overtime, does not exceed 48 hours.'

The reference period over which the average 48-hour weekly working time is to be calculated is not to exceed four months.[4] Unusually, derogations are *not* permitted by collective agreement as regards maximum weekly working time. The sole derogation possible is *not* from the 48-hour maximum, but only from the *reference period* over which it may be calculated. Article 17(2) and (3) allows for derogations from Article 16(2)'s fixing of a maximum four-month reference period. But, even then, Article 17(4) limits the possible extension of this reference period to a maximum of six or 12 months:

'The right to derogate from Article 16(2), provided for in (Art 17(2) and (3)) may not result in the establishment of a reference period exceeding six months.

However, Member States shall have the option, subject to compliance with the general principles relating to the protection of the safety and health of workers, of allowing, for objective or technical reasons or reasons concerning the organisation of work, *collective agreements* or agreements concluded between the two sides of industry to set reference periods in no event exceeding twelve months.'

ANNUAL HOLIDAYS: PRACTICE

Article 7(1) provides:

'Member States shall take the measures necessary to ensure that every worker is entitled to paid annual leave of at least four weeks in accordance with the conditions for entitlement to and granting of such leave laid down by national legislation and/or *practice.*'

The reference to 'practice' (as in Article 10 with respect to night work) arguably includes collective bargaining agreements, despite Article 8's apparent distinction between 'national legislation and/or practice or by collective agreements'. The same language is used in the option to postpone introduction of the EC standard in Article 18(1)(b)(ii).

---

4   Article 16(2).

PATTERN OF WORK: CONSULTATION

Article 13 provides:

Pattern of work

'Member States shall take the measures necessary to ensure than an employer who intends to organise work according to a certain pattern takes account of the general principle of adapting work to the worker . . .'

As already demonstrated, the Directive emphasises the role of collective bargaining in setting many *specific* standards. This Article could be read as implying a *general* requirement of consultation and participation of workers and their representatives. Article 1(4) provides:

'The provisions of Directive 89/391/EEC are fully applicable to the matters referred to in paragraph 2,[5] without prejudice to more stringent and/or specific provisions contained in this Directive.'

Member States are obliged to secure that employers take into account the general principle of adaptation of work to human beings. The obvious way to achieve this is through consultation of workers and their representatives.

OTHER COMMUNITY INSTRUMENTS

Article 14 provides:

More specific Community provisions

'The provisions of this Directive shall not apply where other Community instruments contain more specific requirements concerning certain occupations or occupational activities.'

The reference here is to instruments such as Regulations. But, following the Maastricht Protocol and Agreement on Social Policy, there is the possibility of collective agreements at Community level.[6] EU level agreements may also constitute 'other Community instruments'.

MORE FAVOURABLE COLLECTIVE AGREEMENTS

Article 15 provides:

More favourable provisions

'This Directive shall not affect Member States' right to apply or introduce laws, regulations or administrative provisions more favourable to the protection of the safety and health of workers or to facilitate or permit the application of *collective agreements* or agreements concluded between the two sides of industry which are more favourable to the protection of the safety and health of workers.'

---

5   Paragraph 2 reads: 'This Directive applies to: (a) minimum periods of daily rest, weekly rest and annual leave, to breaks and maximum weekly working time, and (b) certain aspects of night work, shift work and patterns of work.'
6   Article 4 of the Agreement.

'COLLECTIVE AGREEMENTS OR AGREEMENTS BETWEEN THE TWO SIDES OF INDUSTRY'

This formula, with minor variations, appears in all the Directive's provisions incorporating collective bargaining as an instrument in the formulation of EC standards on working time.[7] The question is: is there a difference between 'collective agreements' and 'agreements (concluded) between the two sides of industry (at national or regional, at lower, or at the appropriate collective levels)'? And if so, what is the difference? Possibilities include that the latter term 'agreements' may include tripartite agreements, or agreements between the social partners which do not fall within the term of art 'collective agreements' as defined in national law. Examples might be works council agreements in Germany; or neo-corporatist agreements at the highest levels. But the Directive gives no hint as to what the difference is.

DEROGATIONS: FRAMEWORK AGREEMENTS AND STATE REGULATION

The first two drafts provided for derogation through collective agreement. This was already a breakthrough in that it authorised EU standards to be formulated, albeit only by way of derogation:[8]

> 'In case of collective agreements made between employers and representatives of the workers at the appropriate levels, aiming at setting up a comprehensive set of provisions regarding the adjustment of working time corresponding to the specific conditions of the enterprise, including daily and weekly rest periods as well as night- and shift-work, subject to the condition that on these specific points equivalent periods of compensatory rest are granted to the workers within a reference period that must not exceed six months.'

But the derogation clause, and the role of collective agreements in derogations, became much more complicated in the final text.

Member State derogation from Articles 3, 4, 5, 6, 8 or 16 is permitted in general, for certain activities and occupations (Article 17(1)). Derogation by collective agreements or agreements between the two sides of industry is permitted: from Articles 3, 4, 5, 8 and 16 for certain other activities, subject to equivalent compensatory periods;[9] and from Articles 3 and 5 in the case of shift work activities or others involving split periods of work. The most complex provision allowing for derogation is Article 17(3):

> 'Derogations may be made from Articles 3, 4, 5, 8 and 16 by means of collective agreements or agreements concluded between the two sides of industry at national or regional level or, in conformity with the rules laid down by them, by means of

---

7   Articles 4, 6(1), 17(2): 'collective agreements or agreements between the two sides of industry'; Articles 8(2), 15, 17(4): 'collective agreements or agreements concluded between the two sides of industry'; Articles 2(4)(b)(ii), 16(3), 17(3): 'collective agreements or agreements concluded between the two sides of industry at national or regional level'; Article 17(3): 'collective agreements or agreements concluded between the two sides of industry at a lower level'; Article 17(3): 'collective agreements or agreements concluded between the two sides of industry at the appropriate collective level'.

8   Article 12(3).

9   Article 17(2.1 and 2.2).

collective agreements or agreements concluded between the two sides of industry at a lower level.

In Member States where there is no statutory system assuring the conclusion of collective agreements or agreements concluded between both sides of industry at national or regional level, on the matters covered by this Directive, or in Member States in which a specific legal framework exists for this purpose and within the limits thereof, the Member State concerned may, in accordance with national legislation and/or practice, allow derogations from Articles 3, 4, 5, 8 and 16 by way of collective agreements or agreements concluded between both sides of industry at the appropriate collective level.

The derogations provided for in the first and second subparagraphs shall be allowed only on condition that equivalent compensating rest periods are granted to the workers concerned or, in exceptional cases where it is not possible for objective reasons to grant such periods, the workers concerned are afforded appropriate protection.

Member States may lay down rules:
– for the application of this paragraph by the two sides of industry, and
– for the extension of the provisions of collective agreements or agreements concluded in conformity with this paragraph to other workers in accordance with national legislation and/or practice.'

Rendered down, what Article 17(3) permits is derogation by:

1. national or regional agreements;[10] or
2. lower level agreements in conformity with rules laid down by national or regional agreements.

This gives primacy to national or regional levels of collective agreements. Other levels may only derogate in conformity with these.

The autonomy of this bargaining is limited by the provision that Member States 'may lay down rules for the application of this paragraph by the two sides of industry'. It is not clear how interventionist such rules may be. Rules simply prohibiting derogations by the two sides of industry are unlikely to be permitted. The question is how far rules regulating the actors entitled to bargain (representativeness), the process of bargaining (rules on strikes), or the outcomes (the legal effect of agreements) can impinge on the autonomy of the two sides of industry without violating the Directive's clear intention that the two sides of industry be able to agree on derogations by means of collective agreements.

Member States are not obliged to lay down such rules. And where a statutory system does *not* assure national or regional agreements on working time, or there is another legal framework specifically for working time, Member States may allow derogations by agreements 'at the appropriate collective level'. In any event, all derogations must allow for equivalent compensating rest periods.

The meaning of this complex provision can be better understood by seeing how it differs from its predecessor. In the former provision, priority was not given to any particular level: it referred to agreements 'at the appropriate levels'. The aim of agreements was 'the setting up of a comprehensive set of provisions' – consistent with a framework agreement, but not exclusively so – 'regarding the adjustment of working time corresponding to the specific conditions of the *enterprise*'. The later provision more strictly *confines* enterprise

10 Unless 'collective agreements' are something apart from 'agreements concluded between the two sides of industry at national or regional level'.

level agreements to the *framework* established by national or regional agreements. It also allows for regulation – to an unspecified extent – of the two sides of industry in creating this framework.

A concrete illustration of what this provision means may emerge as the result of the Statement for Entry in the Council Minutes re Article 17 by the Council and the Commission:

> 'On transposition of this Directive into their national legislation, Member States may regard collective agreements or agreements between the two sides of industry in force prior to the date of adoption of this Directive, until they expire, as meeting the minimum requirements of this Directive, if they guarantee at least an equivalent level of protection.
>
> Member States wishing to avail themselves of this option will forward to the Commission no later than six months prior to the scheduled date of implementation of this Directive a description of the collective or other agreements in question.'

The agreements provided should indicate the level and scope of agreements considered by the Member States, and then the Commission, as falling within the parameters of derogations permitted by Article 17(3).

IMPLEMENTATION OF THE DIRECTIVE THROUGH COLLECTIVE AGREEMENTS

Article 18(1)(a) of the final draft reiterates the previous draft's provision[11] allowing for Member States to comply by ensuring 'that the two sides of industry establish the necessary measures by agreement'. Article 18(4) provides:

> 'Member States shall report to the Commission every five years on the practical implementation of the provisions of this Directive, indicating the viewpoints of *both sides of industry.*'

CONCLUSION

Most of the working time standards specified in the first two drafts of the Directive ignored the role of collective agreements, except by way of potential *derogations* from EU standards, and as a means of implementing the Directive. In contrast, the final draft *additionally* incorporates collective bargaining in *setting* substantive EU standards in relation to night work, daily rest breaks, maximum weekly working hours, including overtime and annual holidays.

The most likely immediate effects of the Directive in the UK are the following. First, the employer is under a legal obligation to organise *work patterns* so as to take account of 'the general principle of adapting work to the worker, with a view, in particular, to alleviating monotonous work and work at a predetermined work-rate depending on the type of activity, and of safety and health requirements, especially as regards breaks during working time'.[12] This will have important consequences for shift-workers, as well as for daily and weekly rest periods.

11　Article 14.
12　Article 13.

Second, *overtime working* above the 48-hour weekly limit (normally averaged over a four-month reference period) will be unlawful.[13] A high proportion of workers in the UK normally work a week which *exceeds* the 48-hour limit. A Member State may allow a worker to give individual agreement to work more hours, if this respects general principles of protection of safety and health; but the worker is to be subject to no detriment for refusal to work more than 48 hours. Careful records must be kept by the employer of such working, to be monitored by competent authorities.

Third, *shift work* will be subject to the Directive's general requirements as to maximum daily working hours, mandatory breaks, and minimum weekly rest periods. It is also subject to the general requirement of humanisation of work in Article 13. Fourth, *night workers* are defined broadly to include also those who do only brief spells of night work. The Directive fixes maximum night work over a reference period, provides special protection for night working of a particularly onerous kind, and includes special health and safety provisions, including health assessments, job security and other guarantees. Fifth, the provision in Article 5 that 'The minimum (weekly) rest period . . . shall in principle include *Sunday*' is unclear in its mandatory effects, but indicative of a need for justification. Sixth, *annual paid leave* may be set at a minimum of three weeks for a six-year transition period, after which the minimum will be four weeks.

Finally, there is an important role for *collective bargaining* in *setting* substantive EC standards in relation to night work, daily rest breaks, maximum weekly working hours, including overtime and annual holidays. There is explicit provision requiring Member States to consult the social partners before legislating standards on night work. There is an argument that the principle of humanisation of working time contained in Article 13 requires consultation of workers and their representatives when the employer 'intends to organise work according to a certain pattern'.

Collective bargaining has received a major stimulus in the Working Time Directive. This reflects a general trend in European labour law, to which the UK tradition has made a fundamental contribution. The emergence of a European model of working time regulation exemplifies the dynamic process of evolution of a European labour law.

13   Article 6.

Chapter 23

The Preventative Strategy: Risk Assessment

INTRODUCTION

The new European law on health and safety is characterised by a specific strategy:[1]

'(it) is based on concepts relatively novel in our law, in particular "risk assessment". The emphasis is very heavily on suppression of dangers before they arise wherever that can be achieved rather than guarding against risks which have been allowed to occur.'

A crucial factor is the identification and assessment of hazards, with responsibility for the control of these hazards.[2]

THE EU AND UK LAW

The 1989 Framework Directive, in Article 6, prescribes:

'1. Within the context of his responsibilities, the employer shall take the measures necessary for the safety and health protection of workers, including prevention of occupational risks and provision of information and training, as well as provision of the necessary organisation and means . . .

2. The employer shall implement the measures referred to in the first sub-paragraph of paragraph 1 on the basis of the following general principles of prevention:
   (a) avoiding risks;
   (b) evaluating the risks which cannot be avoided;
   (c) combating the risks at source;
   (d) adapting the work to the individual, especially as regards the design of workplaces, the choice of work equipment and the choice of working and production methods, with a view, in particular, to alleviating monotonous work and work at a predetermined work-rate and to reducing their effect on health;
   (e) adapting to technical progress;
   (f) replacing the dangerous by the non-dangerous or the less dangerous;
   (g) developing a coherent overall prevention policy which covers technology,

---

1   J Hendy and M Ford, Redgrave Fife & Machin's *Health and Safety*, 2nd ed, London, 1993, Preface, p v.
2   S Dawson, P Willman, A Clinton and M Bamford *Safety at Work: the limits of self-regulation*, CUP, Cambridge 1988.

348

organisation of work, working conditions, social relationships and the influence of factors related to the working environment;
(h) giving collective protective measures priority over individual protective
measures;
(i) giving appropriate instructions to the workers.
3. Without prejudice to the other provisions of this Directive, the employer shall,
taking into account the nature of the activities of the enterprise and/or establishment:
(a) evaluate the risks to the safety and health of workers, inter alia in the choice
of work equipment, the chemical substances or preparations used, and the
fitting-out of workplaces.
Subsequent to this evaluation and as necessary, the preventative measures
and the working and production methods implemented by the employer
must:
– assure an improvement in the level of protection afforded to workers
with regard to safety and health,
– be integrated into all the activities of the undertaking and/or establishment and at all hierarchical levels;
(b) where he entrusts tasks to a worker, take into consideration the worker's
capabilities as regards health and safety;
(c) ensure that the planning and introduction of new technologies are the subject of consultation with the workers and/or their representatives, as regards
the consequences of the choice of equipment, the working conditions and
the working environment for the safety and health of workers;
(d) take appropriate steps to ensure that only workers who have received
adequate instructions may have access to areas where there is serious and
specific danger.'

As implemented in Regulation 3(1) of the Management of Health and Safety at
Work Regulations 1992:[3]

'Every employer shall make a suitable and sufficient assessment of –
(a) the risks to the health and safety of his employees to which they are exposed
whilst they are at work; and
(b) the risks to the health and safety of persons not in his employment arising out of
or in connection with the conduct by him or his undertaking,
for the purpose of identifying the measures he needs to take to comply with the
requirements and prohibitions imposed upon him by or under the relevant statutory
provisions.'

Risk assessments are required also under other sets of Regulations, such as the
Control of Substances Hazardous to Health (COSHH) Regulations 1988, as
amended in 1992, the Manual Handling Operations Regulations 1992 and the
Health and Safety (Display Screen Equipment) Regulations 1992.[4]

WHAT IS A RISK ASSESSMENT?

The Approved Code of Practice to the Management of Health and Safety at
Work Regulations provides that a suitable and sufficient risk assessment should:

– identify the significant risks arising out of work;

3 SI 1992 No 2051.
4 For details, see *Occupational Health Review*, January/February 1993, pp 6–14.

–   enable the employer to identify and prioritise the measures that need to be taken to comply with the relevant statutory provision;

–   be appropriate to the nature of the work and such that it remains valid for a reasonable period of time.

However, the overlapping sets of requirements covering risk assessments have been criticised as a source of confusion:[5]

'present risk assessment requirements exhibit marked differences with regard to such matters as when assessments are required, the legal standards with which assessments must comply, the extent to which they must be recorded in writing, the circumstances in which they must be reviewed, and whether assessments are explicitly required to be carried out by competent persons.'

The European labour law injected into the UK system of health and safety is, therefore, characterised by its emphasis on the anticipation of risk, rather than on protection against danger. The advantages of this approach were spelled out by one commentator as follows:[6]

'The main reason for inclusion of assessments in recent legislation is, along with the introduction of self-regulation, the need to draft requirements which are applicable to a vast number of diverse work locations. For example, manual handling requirements existed in workplace-specific legislation such as the Factories Act and Agricultural Acts. The Manual Handling Operations Regulations 1992 however are made under the Health and Safety at Work Act and apply to all workplaces to which the main Act applies.

It is difficult to draw up specific requirements that apply to such a wide variety of manual handling tasks: community nurses lifting patients in to and out of baths; check-out operators in a supermarket; assembly line workers loading goods on to conveyor belts and construction workers unloading cement bags from a lorry on a building site. So the approach has been to provide guidance material and to require each employer to assess the risks caused by manual handling operations within his or her organisation.'

The approach can be illustrated through two sets of Regulations.

Display screen equipment

Under the Management of Health and Safety at Work Regulations 1992 an employer has a duty to make a 'suitable and sufficient' assessment of the risks to the employees while at work. This assessment should attempt to identify potential risks to the user's workstation with a view to providing suitable remedies. These are further specified in the Health and Safety (Display Screen Equipment) Regulations 1992, which require a workstation analysis for all computer installations which have been installed or refurbished since 1 January 1993. A workstation analysis requires that the impact of the computing equipment on its environment be assessed, and that a satisfactory working environment be provided, addressing heat, noise, light, reflections and space, as well as the ergonomic design of the workstation, the equipment and the software.

Evidence indicates that using a computer keyboard and screen for long periods can result in a number of symptoms, including musculoskeletal symptoms, headaches and eye problems. Bad positioning of screen, keyboard, desk

5   *Health and Safety Information Bulletin*, No 224, August 1994, pp 7–8.
6   M Everley 'Why risk it?' *Health and Safety at Work*, October 1994, p 14 at p 15.

and chair can lead to upper limb disorders. The Health and Safety Executive reports that over a million working days a year are lost due to work-related upper limb disorders. These had led to litigation claiming damages for repetitive strain injury (RSI), and it has been argued that RSI is related to the working environment.[7]

Pregnancy

Regulations to implement the 'daughter' Directive on pregnant workers came into effect on 1 December 1994[8] and apply to workers who are pregnant, have recently given birth or are breastfeeding. Under the regulations employers must assess risks to the health and safety of these workers and ensure that they are not exposed to the risks identified by the risk assessment which would present a danger to their health and safety. If a risk remains after taking whatever preventative action is reasonable, the employer should change the worker's hours or conditions to avoid the risk; or offer alternative work; or if neither is possible, give her paid leave from work for as long as is necessary to protect her health and safety. The Health and Safety Executive has estimated that the additional costs of implementing the new measures will be between £46m and £74m.[9]

LIABILITY FOR RISKS

The concept of risk as a central element in European health and safety law has a number of implications. It is the fact that the risk was avoidable, but was not avoided by various measures, which becomes the source of the liability when injury occurs. It is not the defective workplace or work process, but the failure to assess and avoid the risk. This in turn has implications in terms of the spread of responsibility. If prevention is the essence of the EU law, then who else, besides the employer, is potentially responsible for avoiding the risk? In particular, what is the responsibility of the State and those agencies charged with enforcing the law?

Remedies against the State for violations of EU law are currently looming large on the agenda of European law. Questions are raised as to the liability of the State and the agencies responsible for enforcing EU law on health and safety. There could be separate heads of liability for failures to avoid risk, and failure to adopt the adequate and effective measures necessary to secure that employers are avoiding risks. Procedurally, they could be linked through legal actions against the employer and the State or its agencies as joint tortfeasors. It might be sufficient for the injured plaintiff to establish liability against one of them, and leave it to that defendant to share out the allocation of damages among the others.

This raises the question of the potential of 'risk assessments' as a basis of civil liability. In UK domestic law, there are a number of possibilities. The substantive elements of the claim would be those necessary to establish independently a cause of action for breach of statutory duty. Has the failure resulted in injury to a person of a class which the legislation was designed to protect, of whom

---

7   See *Health and Safety at Work*, April 1994, pp 12–13; and July 1993, p 14.
8   Council Directive 92/85, OJ L348/1.
9   *Health and Safety at Work*, June 1994, p 10.

the plaintiff was one? If the law was violated and the plaintiff suffered damage of a kind against which the provision was designed to give protection, caused by the breach, then liability is made out.

Alternatively, the failure to carry out a risk assessment could become an element in negligence actions. As it was put in one management briefing:[10]

> 'Under common law, the employer has a duty to take reasonable steps to prevent injury to employees or others who, with reasonable foresight, are likely to be injured by the employer's activities. The employer's duty, with regard to employees, extended to both avoiding injury through positive acts of negligence and through failure to act. It is obvious that risk assessments fit into this framework. They deal with both the issue of "reasonable foresight" and that of "acts and omissions".'

Again, failure to carry out the risk assessment required could constitute in itself a failure to provide a safe system of work in violation of the UK domestic legislation on health and safety. The Association of Personal Injury Lawyers has indicated the importance of linking risk assessments and the duty of care: employers are to be asked to produce records of risk assessments in both criminal and civil litigation.

IS UK IMPLEMENTATION ADEQUATE?

It is in this light that the UK's implementation of the Directive's requirements on risk assessments must be scrutinised. The Management of Health and Safety at Work Regulations 1992, which implement the Directive's requirements on risk assessments, form part of the criminal law. Failure to undertake the appropriate risk assessments is a criminal offence for which employers can be prosecuted.

It has been argued that the requirement of risk assessments will undermine employer's defences to prosecution, which have often been based on the fact that most duties placed upon them are qualified by the phrase 'so far as reasonably practicable'. When an employer claims that an action is not reasonably practicable, it will be necessary to demonstrate at least that there was carried out a proper risk assessment:[11]

> 'An employer claiming that an action was not reasonably practicable, therefore, needs to take an assessment of the risk along to the courtroom together with an accountant's figures relating to the cost of the control measures.'

The key to the effectiveness of this central element of EU law, therefore, is enforcement. There is no doubt as to the costs of non-enforcement. A Health and Safety Executive document, said to provide the most comprehensive estimate of the costs of accidents at work in the UK, calculates the cost to employers as between £4 billion and £9 billion annually, equating to between five and ten per cent of all UK industrial companies' gross trading profits in 1990. The cost to individual workers and their families is estimated to be almost £5 billion per annum, after making allowances for social security payments and civil compensation.[12]

The cost of accidents has not been matched by anything like the resources

---

10   *Health and Safety at Work,* October 1994, p 16.
11   Ibid.
12   Health and Safety Executive, 'The costs to the British economy of work accidents and work-related ill health' (1994) *Occupational Safety and Health,* April 1994, p 2. See also 'What do accidents cost?', *Health and Safety at Work,* January 1995, pp 12–14.

dedicated to ensuring compliance with the law, as the following summary shows:[13]

'After the few years in the late eighties during which the HSE's (Health and Safety Executive) budget had been temporarily stabilised, a 2.6 per cent cut was imposed in 1994–95 to be followed by a 5 per cent cut in 1995–96, along with the freezing of the grant thereafter. Over the two years 1994–96 this would amount to a £15 million reduction in HSE's budget and the loss of up to 230 out of about 4,800 staff.'

The cuts led the HSE Director General to state that, 'In 1993, against a background of an increasingly tight public expenditure situation, the Executive was required for the first time for some years to plan reductions in provision, both against previous plans and in real terms, over the next three years'. It was reported that funding cuts were forcing the HSE to lose a further 100 specialist posts, including scientists, doctors and certain inspectors by April 1995.[14] The effects are qualitative as well as quantitative:[15]

'Not only is there likely to be growing early retirement among experienced inspectors, but as a result of previous restrictions on recruitment during the 1980s, the overall organisational profile of the inspectorate is becoming a less experienced one with over one third of its staff having less than five years' experience. Its ability to meet its responsibilities has therefore increasingly been undermined ... By the mid-80s Dawson was already noting that overall the number of visits by HSE inspectors had "declined markedly" over the previous decade. The fall in the number of visits has been linked to increasing reliance on a priority system whereby the "more responsible" establishments are visited less than before and a more "targeted" inspection approach is adopted. As Dawson points out, however, the reduction in the number of visits and inspections tends to lead to a "reactive" rather than "proactive" strategy and thus directly detracts from the HSE's "educative function".'

A review of Health and Safety Regulation by the UK Health and Safety Commission concluded that enforcement was not excessive: 'Firms are far more likely to suffer the costs and other losses of an accident (1 in 4.5 chance of reportable injury, 1 in 27 chance of major injury, and 1 in 7,300 chance of fatality) than to be subject to legal sanctions (1 in 80 chance of administrative sanction, and 1 in 800 chance of prosecution)'.[16]

If the enforcement machinery through administrative or criminal sanctions is relatively weak, it makes the possibility of civil claims all the more important. The argument has been made that the new regulations provide 'a genuine opportunity for the civil law to act as a complementary force to criminal sanction'.[17] It is argued that:[18]

'In the past, ignorance about occupational disease, a reluctance to litigate, difficulties in accessing civil justice and the absence of a reliable legal framework on which to

13   C Woolfson *Deregulation: The Politics of Health and Safety*, Glasgow 1994, p 14.
14   Quoted in *Health and Safety Bulletin*, No 229, January 1995, p 4.
15   Woolfson, op cit, pp 14–15.
16   *Occupational Safety and Health*, October 1994, p 39.
17   With reference to the Control of Substances Hazardous to Health (COSHH) Regulations 1988; W Davies 'COSHH and Employers' Civil Liability – I: a potent force for change', *Occupational Health Review*, October/November 1991, p 20 at p 23.
18   Ibid, pp 22–3. In part two of his analysis the author compares civil liability at common law, under the Factories Act 1961 and under the COSHH Regulations, and concludes 'that COSHH emerges as the superior instrument from the viewpoint of the employee seeking compensation through the civil courts for occupational disease or injury caused by hazardous substances'. W Davies 'COSHH and Employers' Civil Liability – II: actions more likely to succeed', *Occupational Health Review*, December 1991/January 1992, p 10 at p 15.

pursue a claim generally kept the overall cost of compensation to levels that were tolerable for employers and manageable for insurers. In future, employers' conduct will come under greater scrutiny, particularly in the wake of occupational illness. A more enlightened and litigious labour force, encouraged by knowing that employers cannot escape a clear duty to have up-to-date knowledge of hazards and backed up by an effective legal framework with improved legal services, is likely to pursue compensation more vigorously – the price that will be paid by insurers, and ultimately employers, for the consequences of non-compliance could be much greater...

...If only an additional 0.5% of UK annual cancers were identified as occupationally related to hazardous substance exposure, and assuming the victims were successful in obtaining compensation through the civil courts, then the ten-year period between 2000 and 2010 would involve 7,500 settlements.

...Such developments would introduce new considerations within the civil liability deterrent equation.'

This makes it all the more surprising that the Management of Health and Safety at Work Regulations 1992, intended to implement the Framework Directive, provide in Regulation 15:

'Exclusion of civil liability. Breach of a duty imposed by these Regulations shall not confer a right of action in any civil proceedings.'

It has been stated that 'this limitation may be argued to amount to a deficient implementation of the Directive'.[19]

There does not appear to be consistency in the UK government's approach. The Management of Health and Safety at Work (Amendment) Regulations 1994,[20] which came into force on 1 December 1994, implement the health and safety aspects of the 1992 Pregnant Workers Directive. The Regulations add a new Regulation 13A to the 1992 Regulations. This requires that the general risk assessment under Regulation 3(1) includes an assessment of risk where the persons working in an undertaking include women of childbearing age; and the work could involve risk, by reason of her condition, to the health and safety of a new or expectant mother, or to that of her baby, from any processes or working conditions or physical, biological or chemical agents.

However, amendments introduced to the final version of the Regulations provided that the new risk assessment provisions *can* confer a right of action in civil proceedings, a right absent from the remainder of the Regulations. The Health and Safety Commission had raised this issue as one which might be necessary for full compliance.[1] The question remains open regarding the exclusion of civil liability in Regulation 15 of the 1992 MHSW Regulations.

In EU law, the question arises whether any requirements of the Framework Directive could be regarded as having direct effect (at least as regards emanations of the State). Specifically, the requirement to undertake risk assessments, as a central element in EU health and safety law, would be a prime candidate for consideration as having direct effect. In accordance with now established principle, the Directive should shape the interpretation of any UK regulations. In domestic law, it could be argued to constitute a new tort of breach of EU law duty. Whether it is an independent head of liability or a contributory element to other heads of liability, EU law requires that all available domestic actions

19   Hendy and Ford, op cit, p 433.
20   SI 1994 No 2865.
1   *Health and Safety Information Bulletin*, No 228, December 1994, p 2.

should be used to secure the effective enforcement of EU law.

The issue of whether the UK law on health and safety adequately implements the requirements of the new EU Directives is of critical importance. Apart from the possibility of a complaint by the Commission under Article 169 of the Treaty, there is now the prospect of claims against the government from individuals who have suffered damage consequent on the failure to adequately implement EU law.

Chapter 24

Implementation and Enforcement: Safety Representatives

INTRODUCTION

Comparison of national and EU legal provisions often produces a culture shock. EU law emerges from a process of negotiation involving fifteen Member States, the EU institutions (Parliament, Commission, and so on) and many special interest groups. Directives which result reflect a much wider range of pressures than laws operating in one country.

This is evident also in a comparison of the UK legislation on safety representatives with the provisions of the Framework Directive 89/391/EEC on health and safety of 12 June 1989.[1] The requirements of the Directive may seem extremely, even excessively complex and detailed. This has to be tolerated as the price to be paid for accommodating all the parties, States and institutions involved.

But comparison also offers the opportunity for scrutiny of national law to ensure it complies with the requirements of the Directive – another chance for interest groups to secure their objectives. The purpose of this section is to indicate what the Directive requires of a UK law on safety representatives, and to raise issues relating to bringing the UK into compliance with EU law. This involves an extended analysis of whether, and, if so, how the UK law falls short of the requirements of EU law.

The UK law is mainly in the Health and Safety at Work etc Act 1974 (hereafter HSWA)[2] and the Safety Representatives and Safety Committees Regulations 1977 (hereafter SRSCR),[3] as amended by the Management of Health and Safety at Work Regulations 1992 (hereafter MHSW),[4] which inserted a new Regulation 4A. Relevant provisions are also in the Employment Protection (Consolidation) Act 1978 (hereafter EPCA),[5] as amended by the Trade Union Reform and Employment Rights Act 1993 (hereafter TURER), s 28, Schedule 5, paragraphs 1 and 3.[6] The UK provisions have received further elaboration in the Code of Practice approved by the Health and Safety Commission under Section 16 of the HSWA 1974, and the Guidance Notes supplementing the statutory framework,

---

1   OJ L183/1.
2   1974, c 37.
3   SI 1977 No 500.
4   SI 1992 No 2051.
5   1978, c 44.
6   Quotations are from the relevant provisions: section (s), Regulation (Reg), Article (Art).

also issued by the Health and Safety Commission.[7]

This chapter aims to set out the differences between the UK and EU law on safety representatives under the following headings: appointment, functions, facilities and assistance, protection and enforcement. The objective is to demonstrate how the enforcement of health and safety law has been 'Europeanised' by EU law, and the extent to which the UK has adapted to this process. .

APPOINTMENT

Single v multiple safety representatives

The UK law *restricts* legal provision to safety representatives and safety committees.[8] The functions of safety committees are specified only in the most general terms in the HSWA, s 2(7). There is also provision for appointment by the employer of 'competent persons' under MHSW 1992.[9] Those appointed under Reg 6 are only to assist the employer, and those nominated under Reg 7 are only concerned with evacuation from premises.[10]

The EU law provides for a *variety* of persons, with different, sometimes overlapping, functions, entitlement to facilities and assistance, protection against employer sanctions and methods of enforcement. The limited provision in UK law can only stand if safety representatives incorporate *all* the functions, entitlements to facilities and assistance, protection against employer sanctions and methods of enforcement prescribed for workers and workers' representatives with safety responsibilities in EU law.

Even if UK safety representatives were so comprehensively endowed, it is questionable whether the objective of the Directive can be achieved in a system which concentrates in one set of representatives all the separate categories which can be identified in the Directive. The logic of the EU law appears to be that functional differentiation and specialisation requires appointment of, at least, workers with specific responsibilities for safety and health, designated workers, general workers' representatives, and workers' representatives with specific responsibility for the safety and health of workers. The objective, structure and

---

7 These, together with the SRSCR 1977 are contained in the so-called 'Brown Book' published by HMSO. Citations will refer to pages in the 'Brown Book', 1988 edition.

8 The Management of Health and Safety at Work Regulations 1992 provide in Reg 12(2):

'Every employee shall inform his employer or any other employee of that employer with specific responsibility for the health and safety of his fellow employees . . .'

It is not clear whether under UK law these 'other *employees*' are confined to the appointed safety *representatives.*

9 Regs 6(1) and 7(1)(b).

10 In the case of the 'competent persons' appointed under Reg 6, it is expressly anticipated that the person concerned might not be an employee of the employer (Reg 6(4)(a)). This is also possible, but less likely in practice, in the case of the 'competent persons' nominated under Reg 7. The appointment of non-employees is questionable in light of the equivalent in EU law: 'designated workers'. The only appearance of 'designated workers' in UK law is in EPCA, s 22A(1)(a) (as amended by TURER 1993, s 28, Sch 5, para 1), which protects an employee from any detriment on the ground that 'having been *designated* by the employer to carry out activities in connection with preventing or reducing risks to health and safety at work, he carried out, or proposed to carry out, any such activities . . .'

wording of the Framework Directive imply a variety of representatives. The Directive appears to support a distinction between:

1. *representatives*:
    – general representatives, who fulfil certain functions in health and safety, and
    – specialist representatives in health and safety.
2. *workers*:
    – with specific responsibilities, and
    – designated workers.

The implication is that appointment of the different workers and workers' representatives is *not* identical. A survey of national practice indicates that this is commonly to be found.[11]

For example, general representatives have other representative functions which *complement* their health and safety functions. Hence:[12]

'... the employer shall ... ensure that the planning and introduction of new technologies are the subject of consultation with the workers and/or their representatives, as regards the consequences of the choice of equipment, the working conditions and the working environment for the safety and health of workers.'

The issue of new technology has too many general implications to be left to specialist safety representatives. Again:[13]

'Employers shall consult workers and/or their representatives and allow them to take part in discussions on all questions relating to safety and health at work.
   This presupposes ...
– the right of workers and/or their representatives to make proposals,
– balanced participation in accordance with national laws and/or practices.'

There must be a remit to general negotiating machinery of safety and health questions, as, again, specialists may not have a broad enough overview. Also:[14]

'Workers' representatives must be given the opportunity to submit their observations during inspection visits by the competent authority.'

Again, the overall perspective of general representatives must be recognised.[15]

Who is empowered by the Directive?

EU law prescribes different methods of *appointment* for each category of worker and workers' representative:

– designated *workers* – by the employer;
– general workers' *representatives* – in accordance with the laws or practices

11 See European Trade Union Technical Bureau for Health and Safety (TUTB), *A User's Guide to European Community Directives on Health and Safety at Work*, Brussels 1993, Annex on Workers' Representation in Western Europe with particular emphasis on workplace health and safety, pp 29–36.
12 Framework Directive, Article 6(3)(c).
13 Article 11(1).
14 Article 11(6).
15 A reflection of the Directive's distinction between general workers' representatives and workers' representatives with specific responsibility for the safety and health of workers is evident in the Directive's explicit protection of the activities of the latter (Article 11(4)), but not those of the former.

of the Member States;
- workers' *representatives* with specific responsibility for the safety and health of workers – in accordance with national laws and/or practices;
- *workers* with specific responsibilities for safety and health – no method of appointment indicated.

UK law restricts safety representatives to cases where there is a trade union *recognised* by the employer.[16] There is no such limitation in EU law. Following the decision of the European Court of Justice in *EC Commission v UK*,[17] this limitation is probably unsustainable. What does EU law require in its place?

There are two separate issues. First, do the repeated references to 'workers *and/or* their representatives' in the Framework Directive[18] imply an *option* for employers to inform or consult *either* workers *or* their representatives? Is an individual consultation system consistent with EU law? Secondly, *if* workers' representatives are mandatory, *how* must they be appointed? What is the meaning of 'national laws and/or practices'?

Is an individual information and consultation system consistent with EU law?

The argument that a system of information and consultation of individual employees satisfies the requirements of the Directive is based on the interpretation of the repeated references to 'workers and/or their representatives' (or variations thereon) in the Directive[19] as implying *choice. Either* workers *or* their representatives are entitled to the rights conferred of information, consultation and participation. But there are at least two arguments that an individual consultation system is inconsistent with EU law.

First, the objective, structure and wording of the Directive imply a logic of involvement of *both* employees *and* their representatives. Hence, the multiple categories of persons engaged in health and safety activities envisaged by the Directive. The language is not otherwise explicable in those provisions where one[20] or the other,[1] or *both*,[2] have rights. This language is only explicable in terms

---

16 HSWA, s 2(4); SRSCR, Reg 3(1).
17 Cases C-382/92 and C-383/92: [1994] ECR I-2435 and [1994] ECR I-2479.
18 Or variations thereon in Articles 6(3)(c), 6(4), 10(1), 10(3), 11(1), 11(2) and 11(6).
- Article 6(3)(c): 'planning and introduction of new technologies are the subject of consultation with the workers and/or their representatives . . .'
- Article 6(4): '. . . inform . . . workers and/or workers' representatives.'
- Article 10(1): information for 'workers and/or their representatives . . .'
- Article 10(3): '. . . workers with specific functions in protecting the safety and health of workers or workers' representatives with specific responsibility . . .'
- Article 11(1): 'Employers shall consult workers and/or their representatives . . .'
- Article 11(2): 'Workers or workers' representatives with specific responsibility . . . shall take part in a balanced way, in accordance with national laws and/or practices, or shall be consulted . . .'
- Article 11(6): 'Workers and/or their representatives are entitled to appeal . . .'
19 The relevant provisions are Articles 6(3)(c), 6(4), 10(1), 10(3), 11(1), 11(2) and 11(6).
20 Article 11(5): 'Employers must allow workers' representatives . . .'
    Article 11(6): 'Workers' representatives must be given the opportunity to submit their observations during inspection visits . . .'
    Article 12(3): 'Workers' representatives with a specific role . . . shall be entitled to appropriate training.'
1 Article 13(2)(d), (e), (f): workers (in general) are to inform/co-operate with the employer and/or the workers with specific responsibility in certain situations.
2 Article 11(4): 'workers referred to in paragraph 2 and the workers' representatives referred to . . .'

of these multiple categories. Sometimes one, sometimes others must be informed and consulted. They are not alternatives. Which is engaged depends on which has the functions envisaged and the rights conferred by a particular provision.

Secondly, the choice offered by the word *or* is applicable only where there are *no* workers' representatives. There may be no representatives as national rules may lay down thresholds for the establishment of employee representation bodies.[3]

The Directive envisages 3 situations:

(i)   there are *no* representatives (due to thresholds); only *workers* are engaged;
(ii)   there *are* representatives: the employer may engage representatives only;
(iii) there *are* representatives: the employer may engage representatives *and* workers.

The definition of representatives is persons:[4]

'elected, chosen or designated in accordance with national laws and/or practices to represent workers.'

There is now authority from the European Court's decision in *EC Commission v UK*[5] that this *obliges* Member States to provide for a system of worker representation. In the words of the Court's judgment:[6]

'26.   . . . as United Kingdom law now stands, workers affected by (collective redundancies/the transfer of an undertaking) do not enjoy protection under . . . the directive(s) in cases where an employer objects to worker representation in his undertaking.

27. In those circumstances, United Kingdom law, which allows an employer to frustrate the protection provided for workers by . . . the directive(s), must be regarded as contrary to those (directives) . . .'

In this, the Court subscribed to the views of Advocate-General Van Gerven, in an Opinion delivered on 2 March 1994:[7]

'. . . to make the activity of workers' representatives totally dependent on voluntary recognition by employers is incompatible with the protection of workers as apparent from the directives in the light of their objective, structure and wording.'

The Court imposed the requirement on the UK to designate worker representatives because of the consequences this would have for the rights of workers under the provisions of the Directive:[8]

'which require Member States to take all measures necessary to ensure that workers are informed, consulted and in a position to intervene through their representatives in the event of collective redundancies (or the transfer of an undertaking).'

Similarly, such a mandatory system of representatives would be negated if employers, by confining the Framework Directive's rights to individual employees, were free to ignore workers' representatives upon whom the Directive had conferred rights to be informed and consulted.

---

3   This is foreseen under the Acquired Rights Directive of 1977, Article 6(5), and under the European Works Councils Directive of 1994, Article 5(2)(a). See Cases C-382/92 and C-383/92: *EC Commission v UK* [1994] ECR I-2435, at paragraphs 22–4.
4   Article 3(c).
5   Cases C-382/92 and C-383/92: [1994] ECR I-2435 and [1994] ECR I-2479.
6   Case C-383/92, paragraphs 26–27, in terms identical to those of Case C-382/92, paragraphs 29–30.
7   Paragraph 9.
8   Case C-383/92, paragraph 23; Case C-382/92, paragraph 26.

If workers' representatives are mandatory, how must they be appointed? What is the meaning of 'national laws and/or practices'?

Implicit in the Court's judgment is the argument that, to undertake the tasks of information and consultation specified in the Directives under examination, workers' representatives must possess certain qualities. These would arguably include the experience, independence and resources required to protect the interests of the workers they represent. National laws or practices providing for their designation must secure these qualities, otherwise they do not attain the objective of the Directive.

Similarly, in the case of the Framework Directive, to secure that workers are properly informed and consulted on health and safety, the workers' representatives concerned will have to possess the experience, independence and resources to fulfil this task. UK government legislative proposals for designating health and safety representatives which do not satisfy the standards implicit in the Court's judgment, necessary to attain the EU objective, could be challenged.

Legislation determining the method for the election or appointment of health and safety representatives could, in theory, designate workers' representatives who are different from those elected or appointed for other purposes. Realistically, would a government find it practicable to enact, or employers welcome, a variety of laws on workers' representatives for different purposes? A separate channel of representation for health and safety purposes could lead to potential conflict between different representatives, such as different representatives for the purposes of collective redundancies (the 1975 Directive), for transfers of undertakings (the 1977 Directive), for the purposes of the European Works Councils Directive, and for safety purposes (the 1989 Framework Directive) – as well as for future prospective Directives. It is unlikely that the EU legislator intended that safety representatives were to be different from established employee representation practice. Here too, the provisions link the rules with 'national laws and/or practices'.

In the UK, where employee representation is established in workplaces, the representatives are from trade unions. This is arguably the 'practice' which is to shape the UK rules on the election or appointment of safety representatives.[9]

Must safety representatives be employees?

The SRSCR, Reg 3(1) provides that:

'a recognised trade union may appoint safety representatives from amongst the employees . . .'[10]

---

9 Some support for this argument may be found in the judgment of the High Court in *Griffin v South West Water Services Ltd* [1995] IRLR 15; Mr Justice Blackburne. See the discussion in Chapter 19.

10 Reg 3(3)(b) provides that 'a person shall cease to be a safety representative for the purposes of these Regulations when – (b) he ceases to be employed at the workplace . . .' Reg 3(4) provides that the representative 'shall so far as is reasonably practicable either have been employed by his employer throughout the preceding two years or have had at least two years' experience in similar employment'. The exceptions, where safety representatives 'need not be employees of the employer concerned' are cases in which 'the employees in the group or groups the safety representatives are appointed to represent are members of the British Actors' Equity Association or of the Musicians' Union' (Reg 8(2)).

The Directive, however, does not specify that safety representatives be employees:[11]

> 'Workers' representative with specific responsibility for the safety and health of workers: any person elected, chosen or designated in accordance with national laws and/or practices to represent workers where problems arise relating to the safety and health protection of workers at work.'

Whether safety representatives are employees depends on which of the four categories of persons indicated by the Directive as involved in health and safety matters is concerned. Two categories: *workers* with specific responsibility and designated *workers*, appear from the structure of the Directive's provisions to be employees. However, as regards two others: (general) workers' *representatives*, and workers' *representatives* with specific responsibility for safety and health, neither appears to need be employees.

It is arguable that the UK law's restriction of safety representatives to employees is not permissible. The delegation to national laws and/or practices does not confer total discretion. Presumably, Member States could not provide for the employer to be the workers' representative. It is interesting that the Guidance Notes on Safety Committees in the Brown Book[12] provide that its composition includes management.[13] Paragraph 10(b) implies that management aims to ensure the necessary knowledge and expertise on technical matters.

There are circumstances where non-employee safety representatives – full-time union officials or other experts – could be desirable: workplaces where unions are recognised but poorly organised, with union members but no recognition, or with neither recognition nor members, small establishments, dispersed workforces, requiring special expertise, and so on.

The TUC has proposed to remove the requirement in Reg 3(1) that safety representatives be appointed from 'amongst the employees' of the employer concerned to allow unions to appoint non-employees, possibly through a system of regional safety representatives. It has been said that such a reform would require a change in the Regulations.[14] But this may not be necessary if Reg 3(1) is inconsistent with the Directive.

Summary – appointment

UK law allows for safety representatives to be appointed by recognised trade unions and safety committees to be established at their request. EU law requires appointment of different categories of workers and workers' representatives involved in health and safety issues and specifies different methods of appointment for each category.

The UK law limiting safety representatives to where trade unions are recognised is inconsistent with EU law. But the requirement that safety representatives be appointed by trade unions – as is the practice in the UK – is consistent with

---

11   Article 3(c).
12   Pages 47 ff.
13   Paragraph 9.
14   P James *The European Community: A Positive Force for UK Health and Safety Law?*, The Institute of Employment Rights, London 1993, p 17.

EU law, even where unions are not recognised. UK law does not provide for appointment of the different categories specified by the Directive.

FUNCTIONS

Under UK law, the functions of safety representatives are spelled out in detail. Nonetheless, does UK law cover *all* the functions specified for the multiple persons prescribed by EU law? Health and safety functions prescribed under UK and EU law will be systematically compared.

'Workers ... with specific responsibility for the safety and health of workers'

For *'workers* ... with specific responsibility for the safety and health of workers', the functions prescribed in the Directive often *overlap* with those of safety *representatives* under UK law. Article 11(2) provides that:

> 'Workers or workers' representatives with specific responsibility for the safety and health of workers *shall take part in a balanced way*, in accordance with national laws and/or practices, or shall be consulted *in advance* and in good time by the employer with regard to ...'

The list which follows is reflected in new Reg 4A of SRSCR:

> '(1) ... every employer shall consult safety representatives in good time with regard to – ...'

However, the UK law's formulation is different, and arguably deficient, in that:

- it does not prescribe an alternative to consultation 'shall take part in a balanced way, in accordance with national laws and/or practices';
- the words 'in advance' are absent;
- it is not clear that, under Reg 4A(1)(b) ('arrangements for appointing or ... nominating'), UK safety representatives must be consulted with regard to 'the enlistment, where appropriate, of the competent services or persons outside the undertaking and/or establishment, as referred to in Article 7(3) (to organise protective and preventive measures where these cannot be organised for lack of competent personnel in the undertaking and/or establishment)'.[15]

Again, the Directive in Article 13(2)(d),(e),(f) states that 'workers must in particular, in accordance with their training and the instructions given by their employer' inform and co-operate with the employer or 'workers with specific responsibility for the safety and health of workers' at certain times and in certain tasks. The MHSW partially reflect this by providing in Reg 12(2):

> 'Every employee shall inform his employer or any other employee of that employer with specific responsibility for the health and safety of his fellow employees ...'

It is not clear whether under UK law these *'other employees'* are the appointed safety *representatives.* Further, there is no mention of their prescribed function of

15   Article 11(2)(d).

co-operating with workers who have been trained to inform and co-operate on safety and health. Is it feasible for the safety representatives to undertake this when the Directive appears to envisage a separate person for this task?

Designated workers

These workers have two functions under the Directive:

'. . . the employer shall designate one or more *workers* to *carry out* activities related to the protection and prevention of occupational risks for the undertaking and/or establishment'.[16]

'. . . the employer shall, inter alia, for first aid, fire-fighting *and* the evacuation of workers, designate the *workers* required to *implement* such measures'.[17]

The MHSW partially reflect this by providing in Reg 6(1):

'Every employer shall . . . appoint one or more competent *persons* to *assist* him in undertaking the measures he needs to take to comply with the requirements and prohibitions imposed upon him by or under the relevant statutory provisions.'

The relevant statutory provisions would include Reg 4(1) which provides:

'Every employer shall make and give effect to such arrangements as are appropriate . . . for the effective planning, organisation, control, monitoring and review of the preventive and protective measures.'

Also Reg 7(1)(a) and (b):

'Every employer shall –
(a) establish and where necessary give effect to appropriate procedures to be followed in the event of serious and imminent danger to persons at work in his undertaking;
(b) nominate a sufficient number of competent *persons* to *implement* those procedures insofar as they relate to the evacuation from premises of persons at work in his undertaking . . .'

There are at least three discrepancies between the Directive and the Regulations as regards the functions of 'designated workers'. First, the UK provisions raise the question whether the employer may appoint '*persons*' other than '*workers*'. The following paragraphs of Article 7 make it clear that the workers concerned are employees of the employer and only:[18]

'If such protective and preventive measures cannot be organised for lack of competent personnel in the undertaking and/or establishment, the employer shall enlist competent external services or persons.'

To the contrary, Reg 6(4)(a) envisages appointment under Reg 6(1) of a person 'who is not in his employment' and gives no priority to employees.

Secondly, according to the Directive, the function of these designated workers is 'to *carry out* activities related to the protection and prevention of occupational risks'. It is arguable that this is not the same as what Reg 6(1) prescribes: 'to *assist* (the employer) in undertaking the measures he needs to take to comply with the

16   Article 7(1).
17   Article 8(2).
18   Article 7(3).

requirements and prohibitions imposed upon him'.

Finally, the Directive states that these workers are required to implement measures 'inter alia, for first aid, fire-fighting *and* the evacuation of workers'. Reg 7(1)(b) only requires nomination of persons to implement procedures for 'evacuation from premises of persons'.

Workers' representatives (general) and safety representatives

The UK Regulations make no provision for a role for workers' representatives in general on safety matters, as contrasted with specifically appointed safety representatives. This is arguably a major failing of the UK law. The argument is that the Directive distinguishes the *two types of representatives* according to their different functions. *General workers' representatives* are the subject of the following provisions:

'... the employer shall ... ensure that the planning and introduction of *new technologies* are the subject of consultation with the workers and/or their representatives, as regards the consequences of the choice of equipment, the working conditions and the working environment for the safety and health of workers'.[19]

'Employers shall consult workers and/or their representatives and allow them to take part in discussions on *all questions relating to safety and health at work.*
This presupposes ...
- the right of workers and/or their representatives to make proposals,
- balanced participation in accordance with national laws and/or practices.'[20]

'Workers' representatives must be given the opportunity to submit their observations during *inspection visits* by the competent authority.'[1]

Workers' representatives with specific responsibility for the safety and health of workers are given more specific functions by the following provisions:

'Workers or workers' representatives with specific responsibility for the safety and health of workers shall take part in a balanced way, in accordance with national laws and/or practices, or shall be consulted in advance and in good time by the employer with regard to:
(a) any measure which may substantially affect safety and health;
(b) the designation of workers referred to in Articles 7(1) and 8(2) and the activities referred to in Article 7(1);
(c) the information referred to in Articles 9(1) and 10;
(d) the enlistment, where appropriate, of the competent services or persons outside the undertaking and/or establishment, as referred to in Article 7(3);
(e) the planning and organisation of the training referred to in Article 12.'[2]

'Workers' representatives with specific responsibility for the safety and health of workers shall have the right to ask the employer to take appropriate measures and to submit proposals to him to that end to mitigate hazards for workers and/or to remove sources of danger.'[3]

19 Article 6(3)(c).
20 Article 11(1).
1 Article 11(6).
2 Article 11(2).
3 Article 11(3).

Do the UK Regulations prescribe for safety representatives *all* the functions laid down in the Directive – for workers' representatives (general) as well as those with specific responsibility for safety and health?[4] The UK Regulations are questionable in four respects.

Is the 'consultation' provided for in UK law adequate?

UK Law prescribes 'consultation',[5] 'make representations',[6] 'represent',[7] 'attend meetings',[8] and 'consult . . . in good time'.[9] The Directive provides for informing, consultation, balanced participation,[10] consultation *and* taking part in discussions of workers' general representatives,[11] consultation *or* taking part in a balanced way of representatives with specific responsibility for safety and health,[12] asking for measures and submitting proposals by representatives with specific responsibility for safety and health,[13] and submitting observations by workers' general representatives.[14] There is no precise definition of these terms in the Directive. A distinction appears to be made between consultation of workers' *general* representatives and consultation of workers' representatives *with specific responsibility for safety and health.*

With respect to workers' *general* representatives, it is stated that employers:[15]

'shall consult workers and/or their representatives *and* allow them to take part in discussions on all questions relating to safety and health at work.
This *presupposes*:
– the consultation of workers,
– the right of workers and/or their representatives to make proposals,
– balanced participation in accordance with national laws and/or practices.'

On 'balanced participation', there is the statement entered in the record by the Council and Commission at the conclusion of the Council discussions on the common position on the Directive:[16]

'The notion of balanced participation embraces a range of multiple forms of worker participation which vary considerably between Member States. The present directive places no obligation on the Member States to provide a specific form of balanced participation.'

---

4 Even if they do, is it consistent with the Directive to exclude general representatives from any role in health and safety and load all the responsibility on to safety representatives alone? This will be addressed later when the question is asked whether EU law requires more than one set of representatives to perform the functions specified.
5 HSWA, s 2(6).
6 SRSCR, Reg 4(1)(c),(d).
7 SRSCR, Reg 4(1)(f).
8 SRSCR, Reg 4(1)(h).
9 SRSCR, Reg 4A(1).
10 Article 1(2).
11 Article 11(1).
12 Article 11(2).
13 Article 11(3).
14 Article 11(6).
15 Article 11(1).
16 Council Document 9869/88 RESTRICTED SOC 82 of 12 December 1988, p 22, quoted in Laurent Vogel *Prevention at the Workplace*: an initial review of how the 1989 Community Framework Directive is being implemented. European Trade Union Technical Bureau for Health and Safety (TUTB), Brussels 1994, p 83.

It seems clear, however, that balanced participation is *not* the same as consultation and must include some new element of involvement of workers' representatives. It is arguable that the omission of any reference to balanced participation, in addition to consultation, in the UK law is not acceptable. Article 11(1) presupposes *both* 'on all questions relating to safety and health at work'. Further, the right to consultation 'on all questions relating to safety and health at work' should not be confined to safety representatives.

In relation to workers' representatives *with specific responsibility for safety and health*, the Directive appears to provide for alternatives: [17]

'... workers' representatives with specific responsibility for the safety and health of workers shall take part in a balanced way, *or* shall be consulted in advance and in good time by the employer, with regard to (the items listed).'

As to 'consultation', there is now a definition in the European Works Councils Directive 94/45/EC of 22 September 1994. The Directive begins: [18]

'The purpose of this Directive is to improve the right to information and to consultation of employees ...'

By consultation is meant: [19]

'... the exchange of views and establishment of dialogue between employees' representatives and central management or any more appropriate level of management.'

The process is the exchange of views and establishment of dialogue, not a static, formal, ad hoc, one-way process. The *establishment of dialogue* implies an active and continuous process of communication and interaction between labour and management. On issues as vital as safety and health this should be the minimum expected of the consultation required under the Framework Directive.

Do the Regulations cover all the matters specified for consultation in the Directive?

UK law provides: [20]

'It shall be the duty of every employer to *consult* any such representatives with a view to the making and maintenance of *arrangements* which will enable him and his employees to *co-operate* effectively in promoting and developing *measures* to ensure the health and safety at work of the employees, and in checking the effectiveness of such measures.'

The Directive provides: [1]

'Employers shall consult workers and/or their representatives and allow them to take part in discussions on *all questions* relating to safety and health at work.'

Arguably, the UK law is much narrower in its scope of mandatory consultation. The closest UK law gets to satisfying this requirement of the Directive is the provision which allows for safety representatives to make representations on general matters affecting health, safety or welfare. [2]

---

17 Article 11(2).
18 Article 1(1).
19 Article 2(1)(f).
20 HSWA, s 2(6).
1 Article 11(1).
2 SRSCR, Reg 4(1)(d).

New Reg 4A added a requirement of consultation on a wide range of specific matters, but falls short of the requirement to consult on *all questions* relating to safety and health at work. Some of the specific provisions in the new Reg 4A on the *matters to be consulted upon* are different from, and in some cases arguably also narrower than, those requiring consultation and participation under the Directive. This will be demonstrated by contrasting the provisions of the Directive with those in the Regulations under the following headings.

MEASURES WHICH MAY SUBSTANTIALLY AFFECT SAFETY AND HEALTH

Compare Reg 4A(1)(a): '... *introduction* of any measure...' with Article 11(2)(a): '... any measure...' Consultation should cover issues going beyond the introduction of the measures, and include also their maintenance, effectiveness and so on.

DESIGNATED WORKERS

Compare Reg 4A(1)(b):

'... *arrangements* for appointing or ... nominating
– competent persons to assist him in undertaking *measures* ... to comply with the requirements and prohibitions imposed on him;'[3]

and

'– competent persons to implement ... *procedures* insofar as they relate to the *evacuation* from premises ...'[4]

and Article 11(2)(b):

'... the *designation* of
– workers to carry out *activities* related to the protection and prevention of occupational risks;'[5]

and

'– workers required to implement ... *measures* (for *first-aid, fire-fighting* and the *evacuation* of workers).'[6]

The priority of *workers* to be designated is not made clear. Nor is the scope of their activities precisely congruent with those requiring consultation by the Directive.

ENLISTMENT OF OUTSIDE COMPETENT SERVICES OR PERSONS

Compare Reg 4A(1)(b): '... *arrangements* for appointing or ... nominating ("competent persons")' and Article 11(2)(d): 'the enlistment ... of the competent services or persons outside the undertaking and/or establishment...' These external persons are to be enlisted where workers 'to carry out activities related to the protection and prevention of occupational risks'[7] cannot be designated 'for lack of competent personnel'.[8] The UK law does not specify this. It is

3 Reg 6(1) of MHSW.
4 Reg 7(1)(b) of MHSW.
5 Article 7(1).
6 Article 8(2).
7 Article 7(1).
8 Article 7(3).

inconsistent with the Directive, except in so far as 'persons' could include workers, and workers are given priority over external persons or services.

INFORMATION

Compare Reg 4A(1)(c):

> 'any health and safety information he is required to provide to the *employees* ... by or under the relevant statutory provisions;'

(for example, hazards,[9] identified risks, preventative and protective measures, procedures, persons nominated to implement evacuation procedures, risks notified,[10] and fixed term employment),[11] with Article 11(2)(c):

> 'the information referred to in:
> - Article 9(1):
>   (- risks;
>   - protective measures and equipment;
>   - list of accidents, accident reports); and
> - Article 10:
>   (- risks and protective and preventative measures and activities in respect of the undertaking, establishment and each type of workstation and/or job;
>   - workers designated to implement measures on first aid, fire-fighting and evacuation;
>   - information provided to employers of outside undertakings engaged in work in the undertaking;
>   - information *available to* workers with specific health and safety functions and workers' safety *representatives*, including information yielded by protective and preventive measures, inspection agencies and bodies).'

For example, SRSCR Reg 7 entitles safety *representatives* to inspect and take copies of documents, and Reg 8 is a general requirement on the employer to make available to *representatives* 'the information, within the employer's knowledge, necessary to enable them to fulfil their functions'.

Neither of these comes within the scope of the mandatory consultation requirements of Reg 4A(1)(c). But the Directive would require consultation over what information is required to be provided to representatives.[12]

TRAINING

Compare Reg 4A(1)(d):

> 'the planning and organisation of any health and safety training he is required to provide to the *employees* ... by or under the relevant statutory provisions';

and Article 11(2)(e):

> 'the planning and organisation of the training referred to in Article 12.'

The UK law prescribes training for employees roughly equivalent to that prescribed by the Directive in Article 12.[13] Article 12 prescribes training for

---

9   MHSW, Reg 7(2)(a).
10 MHSW, Reg 8.
11 MHSW, Reg 13(1).
12 Article 11(2)(c).
13 MHSW, Reg 11.

employees, but *also* for:

'workers from outside undertakings ... engaged in work in (the employer's) undertaking';[14]

and

'workers' representatives with a specific role in protecting the safety and health of workers'.[15]

The UK law provides that the employer's duty to ensure the health, safety and welfare of his employees includes:[16]

'the provision of such ... training as is necessary to ensure, so far as is reasonably practicable, the health and safety at work of his employees.'

The SRSCR, Reg 4(2) requires the employer to:

'permit a safety representative to take such time off with pay during the employee's working hours as shall be necessary for the purposes of – ... (b) undergoing such training in aspects of those functions as may be reasonable in all the circumstances ...'

Reg 4A(2) requires the employer to 'provide such facilities and assistance as safety representatives may reasonably require for the purpose of carrying out their functions'.

It is not clear whether these provisions together are equivalent to the entitlement to training (and not only time off) of workers' representatives guaranteed by the Directive.[17] If not, there is both a violation of Article 12 and, also, UK law fails to oblige the employer to consult on the planning and organisation of this training, as required by Article 11(2)(e) of the Directive.

NEW TECHNOLOGY

Compare Reg 4A(1)(e):

'the health and safety consequences for the employees ... of the introduction (including the planning thereof) of new technologies into the workplace';

and Article 6(3)(c)):

'... the employer shall ... ensure that the planning and introduction of new technologies are the subject of consultation with the workers and/or their representatives, as regards the consequences of the choice of equipment, the working conditions and the working environment for the safety and health of workers.'

The failure of the UK law to explicitly indicate 'choice of equipment, the working conditions and the working environment' as specific issues requiring consultation for their safety and health consequences may not satisfy EU law requirements.

---

14 Article 12(3).
15 Article 12(4).
16 HSWA, s 2(2)(c).
17 The Directive, Article 12(3), specifies an entitlement to 'appropriate training' for workers' representatives, and Article 12(4) provides that it 'may not be at the ... expense ... of the workers' representatives'. Article 11(5) prescribes 'adequate time off work, without loss of pay and ... the necessary means to enable such representatives to exercise their rights and functions deriving from this Directive'.

Are there other functions under the Directive for representatives, and, if so, which representatives?

The UK law specifies further functions for safety representatives in SRSCR Reg 4(1):

'(a) to investigate potential hazards and dangerous occurrences ... and to examine the causes of accidents ...
(b) to investigate complaints ...
(c) to make representations to the employer on matters arising out of ... (a) and (b) ...
(d) to make representations to the employer on general matters ...
(e) to carry out inspections ...'

The Directive simply provides in Article 11(3):

'Workers' representatives with *specific responsibility for the safety and health of workers* shall have the right to ask the employer to take appropriate measures and to submit proposals to him to that end to mitigate hazards for workers and/or to remove sources of danger.'

The provisions in the SRSCR are more specific. But the Directive allows for initiatives covering a potentially wider range of measures and action proposals.

For example, Regs 5, 6 and 7 prescribe a number of conditions which must be fulfilled if there is to be entitlement to inspect the workplace (notice, frequency, consultation, employer's agreement, specified circumstances, employer's presence) or documents (notice, exceptions). This cannot restrict the safety representatives' right under Article 11(3) to 'ask the employer to take appropriate measures and to submit proposals to him to that end to mitigate hazards for workers and/or to remove sources of danger'.[18]

What are the consequences of the employer refusing to take the measures or the action specified in the proposals of the representatives with specific responsibility for safety and health? The Directive seems to allocate to *general* workers' representatives the responsibility for enforcement of the employer's obligations. Thus, in Article 13(6):

'Workers and/or their representatives are entitled to appeal ... to the authority responsible for safety and health protection at work if they consider that the measures

---

18   That the Regulation is arguably restrictive is apparent in the Guidance Notes (Brown Book) (p 29, paragraph 16):

'In some circumstances where a high risk activity or rapidly changing circumstances are confined to a particular area of a workplace or sector of an employee's activities it may be appropriate for more frequent inspection of that area or sector to be agreed.'

The Guidance Note remains within the confines of the Regulation as it still requires the agreement of the employer. Similarly, paragraph 17 attempts to mitigate the need for formal notice to the employer: '... it is desirable that the employer and the safety representatives should plan a programme of formal inspections in advance, which will itself fulfil the conditions as to notice'. Again, Reg 6(1) provides:

'Where there has been a notifiable accident or dangerous occurrence in a workplace or a notifiable disease has been contracted ... those safety representatives *may* carry out an inspection of the part of the workplace concerned and so far as is necessary for the purpose of determining the cause they *may* inspect any other part of the workplace ...'

However, the Guidance Note in the Brown Book says (p 35, paragraph 23):

'For the purpose of ascertaining the circumstances of a notifiable accident, dangerous occurrence, or notifiable disease, it *will* be necessary for the representatives to examine ...'

taken and the means employed by the employer are inadequate for the purposes of ensuring safety and health at work.'

UK law which restricts the entitlements of safety representatives, and the corresponding obligations of employers, and reserves enforcement of these rights and obligations to safety representatives, is out of line with the Directive's vision. It may be more appropriate for certain safety functions to be allocated to general workers' representatives.

Thus, SRSCR, Regs 5, 6 and 7, regarding inspections of the workplace, and, in particular, following notifiable accidents, occurrences and diseases, provide that the entitlement to carry out these inspections is reserved to *safety* representatives. This may not be acceptable where it is more appropriate for *general* workers' representatives to have the function in question. For example, the SRSCR specifies that *safety* representatives shall: [19]

'... represent the employees ... in consultations ... with inspectors of the Health and Safety Executive or of any other enforcing authority.'

In contrast, the Directive appears to see this as a function of the *general* representatives: [20]

'Workers' representatives must be given the opportunity to submit their observations during inspection visits by the competent authority.'

Do the Regulations cover all employees?

The UK law limits the scope of the functions of safety representatives to matters which affect the health and safety *only* of the employees 'the safety representatives concerned represent'; in Reg 4(1):

'(b) to investigate complaints by any employee he represents relating to that employee's health, safety or welfare at work;
(c) to make representations to the employer on matters arising out of (b);
...
(f) to represent the employees he was appointed to represent in consultations at the workplace with inspectors...'

and in Reg 4A(1):

'... every employer shall consult safety representatives in good time with regard to –
(a) the introduction of any measure at the workplace which may substantially affect the health and safety of the employees the safety representatives concerned represent;
...
(c) any health and safety information he is required to provide to the employees the safety representatives concerned represent; ...
(d) the planning and organisation of any health and safety training he is required to provide to the employees the safety representatives concerned represent; ...
(e) the health and safety consequences for the employees the safety representatives concerned represent of the introduction (including the planning thereof) of new technologies into the workplace.'

This is the logical counterpart to the restriction on appointment of safety representatives to where trade unions are recognised. Safety representatives only

---

19   Reg 4(1)(f).
20   Article 11(6).

operate where, and in so far as, employers recognise trade unions. This restriction has been condemned by the European Court in *EC Commission v UK* (8 June 1994). The Framework Directive contains no such limitation. The functions of representatives, both general and safety representatives, are carried out with respect to all workers, not just those whom the employer recognises they represent.

SOME CONCLUSIONS

Can one set of representatives perform all health and safety functions adequately, or does EU law require certain functions to be performed by others? It has been argued that safety representatives appointed under UK law are not granted *all* the requisite functions stipulated under EU law for a multiplicity of persons. These include a variety of functions for general workers' representatives, designated workers and workers with specific responsibilities for safety and health – as well as for safety representatives.

The UK law does prescribe the duty of the employer to establish a safety committee:[1]

'... it shall be the duty of every employer, if requested to do so by the safety representatives ... to establish ... a safety committee having the function of keeping under review the measures taken to ensure the health and safety at work of his employees and such other functions as may be prescribed.'

But there is nothing in the Regulations[2] as to its functions, powers or rights. Nor is there anything in the Approved Code of Practice. Only the Guidance Notes provide some indications. Indeed, at six pages, this is the longest section by far in the Brown Book.[3] Paragraph 7 outlines its 'specific functions'. These could be said to cover much of what is expected of various categories stipulated by the Directive (though, of course, the Brown Book predates the Directive).

But they are only Guidance Notes. They have no legal force in UK law and provide no legal basis for entitlements. It is not clear how a safety committee, a collective body, could fulfil the responsibilities of designated workers and workers with specific responsibilities, or even general representatives – all empowered individually by the Directive. The Directive does not empower committees.

Even if the UK provisions designating safety representatives *were* to grant them the *full* range of functions provided under the Directives, it is arguable that this would still not satisfy the requirements of EU law. The Directive expressly adopts the approach of proposing a variety of persons to deal with the complex nature of the prevention and protection measures needed for workers' safety and health. A single category, safety representatives, as defined under UK law, is unlikely to be deemed adequate compliance – unless their nature is radically changed to encompass the multiple roles and functions envisaged by the Directive.

This is evident in management structures responsible for health and safety. The Guidance Notes (Brown Book) reflect this when they speak of the need for

---

1 HSWA, s 2(7).
2 Reg 9.
3 The Brown Book, pp 47–52.

ready access by safety representatives to management – the employer and his representatives:[4]

> 'who those should be, will be determined in the light of local circumstances. It may not be desirable to specify one individual for all contacts, bearing in mind that hazards could involve differing degrees of urgency and importance.'

If multiple management representatives are envisaged as desirable given the variety of circumstances, it is equally evident that multiple persons on the workers' side are necessary – as recognised in the Framework Directive. This is simply the reflection at EU level of the national experience of the Member States.[5] The UK law needs to be reformed to reflect this 'European' model of safety representatives.

FACILITIES AND ASSISTANCE

In UK law, safety representatives are entitled to:[6]

> 'such time off with pay during the employee's working hours as shall be necessary for the purposes of –
> (a) performing his functions under section 2(4) of the 1974 Act and (those listed in paragraph 1 of this Regulation);
> (b) undergoing such training in aspects of those functions as may be reasonable in all the circumstances . . .'

With the additional function of being consulted under the new Reg 4A came further provision:[7]

> 'every employer shall provide such facilities and assistance as safety representatives may reasonably require for the purpose of carrying out their functions . . .'

The provisions entitling safety representatives to carry out inspections also included an entitlement to:[8]

> 'such facilities and assistance as the safety representative may reasonably require (including facilities for independent investigation by them and private discussion with the employees) . . .'

In so far as the functions specified for safety representatives under UK law do *not* include *all* the health and safety functions of the various categories of persons specified under EU law (as described above), the UK provision is inadequate.

The Framework Directive imposes 'General obligations on employers' which include in Article 6(1):

> '. . . the employer shall take the measures necessary for the safety and health protection of workers, including . . . provision of information and *training*, as well as provision of the necessary organisation and *means*',

---

4   Page 23, paragraph 13.
5   See the TUTB User's Guide, op cit, which reports on the division of general and safety representatives, and the multiplicity of forms of safety representatives and committees.
6   SRSCR, Reg 4(2).
7   Reg 4A(2).
8   Regs 5(3) and 6(2).

and Article 6(5):

> 'Measures related to safety, hygiene and health at work may in no circumstances involve the workers in financial cost.'

The Directive's health and safety functions *not* currently allowed for by UK law must be incorporated into UK law, along with employer provision of necessary means, and at no cost to the workers. In such cases, and even when the UK law does allow for functions mandated by EU law, the UK law provision for paid time off, training, facilities and assistance may still fall below that provided by EU law.

Cost of information

The Directive provides for various information to be received by workers and/or their representatives,[9] and for workers with specific functions in protecting the safety and health of workers or workers' representatives with specific responsibility for the safety and health of workers to 'have access, to carry out their functions and in accordance with national laws and/or practices' to specified information.[10] SRSCR, Reg 7 provides:

> '(1) Safety representatives shall ... be entitled to inspect and take copies of any document relevant to the workplace ... which the employer is required to keep by virtue of any relevant statutory provisions ...
> (2) An employer shall make available to safety representatives the information ...'

Information which the Directive requires to be received by workers is to be provided at the expense of the employer. The SRSCR, Reg 7 recognises that information to which safety representatives have access, to be useful, may have to be copied. Under UK law, it is not clear who pays the cost. It is arguable that the Directive's Article 6(5) applies: it should 'in no circumstances involve the workers in financial cost'.

Paid time off, facilities and assistance, and 'the necessary means' and 'expense'

UK law prescribes for safety representatives time off with pay during working hours to perform certain functions and, undergo training,[11] or 'facilities and assistance'.[12] For the 'competent persons' appointed under MHSW, there is provision that 'the time available for them to fulfil their functions and the means at their disposal are adequate'.[13]

EU law prescribes a variety of provisions for different categories of persons with health and safety functions. For '*designated workers*' given functions with respect to protective and preventive services (inter alia, first aid, fire-fighting, evacuation of workers), the Directive specifies in Article 7(2):

> 'Designated workers shall be allowed adequate *time* to enable them to fulfil their obligations arising from this Directive',

---

9 Article 10(1).
10 Article 10(3).
11 SRSCR, Reg 4(2).
12 SRSCR, Reg 4A(2).
13 MHSW, Reg 6(3).

and in Article 7(5):

> 'the workers designated must have the necessary *capabilities* and the *necessary means* . . .'

'*General*' workers' representatives, consulted on planning and introduction of new technologies,[14] or 'all questions relating to safety and health at work',[15] are to receive information,[16] which should 'in no circumstances involve the workers in financial cost'.[17] Workers' representatives with *specific responsibility* for the safety and health of workers are provided for by the Directive as follows:[18]

> 'Employers must allow workers' representatives with specific responsibility for the safety and health of workers adequate *time off work, without loss of pay*, and provide them with the *necessary means* to enable such representatives to exercise their rights and functions deriving from this Directive.'

Means necessary to safety functions

In the case of the *functions* of workers' representatives with specific responsibility for the safety and health of workers, the entitlement is to *more* than time off work without loss of pay. They must be provided with 'the necessary means'. Similarly, 'designated' workers. If the UK law's provision of 'facilities and assistance as safety representatives may reasonably require'[19] does not provide for these additional necessary means, it is deficient. In so far as 'competent persons' appointed under MHSW Reg 6(1) are equivalent to the Directive's 'designated workers', their entitlement to adequate means may be sufficient.

Experts

One *means* necessary to safety representatives is the assistance of experts. The Guidance Note in the Brown Book provides:[20]

> '(if) expertise is not available within the undertaking. The employer and the safety representatives may wish to seek advice from outside the undertaking, for example from appropriate universities or polytechnics . . . arrangements should be *agreed*. If the representatives wish to have advice from their own technical advisers, such advisers may be called in where this has been *agreed* in advance with the employer. A copy of any report . . . made to the safety representatives should also be available to the employer.'

The Directive does not make the entitlement to means necessary 'to enable such representatives to exercise their rights and functions deriving from this Directive' conditional on employer agreement, even though they are at the expense of the employer.

Training

Given their 'specific role in protecting the safety and health of workers', *both* '*general*' workers' representatives *and* workers' representatives with *specific responsibility*

---

14   Article 6(3)(c).
15   Article 11(1).
16   Article 10(1).
17   Article 6(5).
18   Article 11(5).
19   Reg 4A(2).
20   Page 36, paragraph 26.

for the safety and health of workers[1] are entitled to 'appropriate *training*', which 'may not be at (their) *expense*'.[2] Further, '[T]he training . . . must take place *during working hours* or in accordance with national practice either within or outside the undertaking and/or the establishment'.[3]

Expenses of training

As regards *training*, as it must take place during working hours and is not to be at the workers' expense, it is *at least* paid time off. But there may be additional expenses associated with training, for example, if it takes place away from the establishment or undertaking. The implication of the Directive is that these are to be paid by the employer.

Content of training

The Code of Practice approved by the UK Health and Safety Commission provides:[4]

'Trade unions are responsible for appointing safety representatives and . . . should inform management of the course it has approved and supply a copy of the syllabus, indicating its contents, if the employer asks for it . . . The number of safety representatives attending training courses at any one time should be that which is reasonable in the circumstances, bearing in mind such factors as the availability of relevant courses and the operational requirements of the employer . . .'

None of these conditions are to be found in the Directive. They may not detract in any way from the right to training guaranteed by the Directive.

PROTECTION

In UK law, safety representatives, members of safety committees, 'designated' employees and employees acting in a situation of serious and imminent danger are protected from being 'subjected to any detriment'[5] or dismissed.[6]

Similarly, in EU law, 'designated workers may not be placed at any disadvantage',[7] nor may 'workers or workers' representatives with specific responsibility for the safety and health of workers',[8] or workers acting in a situation of serious and imminent danger.[9] There is no specific mention of protection from dismissal – presumably included in the concept of disadvantage.

Whether not being 'subjected to any detriment' is equivalent protection to not being 'placed at any disadvantage' is questionable. It goes to the issue of remedies. Detriment may imply a limitation to compensatory claims. Disadvantage may allow for more open-ended remedies.

---

1 Query: also 'designated' workers and workers with specific responsibilities?
2 Article 12(3) and (4).
3 Article 12(4).
4 The Brown Book, page 21, paragraph 5.
5 EPCA, s 22A.
6 EPCA, s 57A.
7 Article 7(2).
8 Article 11(4).
9 Article 8(4) and 8(5).

A surprising omission is the protection of general workers' representatives. The protection of *general* workers' representatives undertaking the functions indicated for them in the Directive does not seem to be explicitly addressed by the Directive. The protection provided in Article 11(4) is expressly limited to 'the activities referred to in (Article 11(2) and (3))', which excludes other health and safety functions prescribed for workers' representatives.[10]

This is a serious defect in EU law. UK law, insofar as it protects trade union activities which could include the health and safety functions prescribed in Article 6(3)(c), Article 11(1) and Article 11(6), is still in advance of the law of the EU.

ENFORCEMENT

The enforcement of the UK law on workers' health and safety representatives is through criminal and civil processes. The criminal process is in the hands of the Health and Safety Executive.[11]

The civil process is limited in three respects. First, enforcement is by complaint to an industrial tribunal.[12] Secondly, the grounds of complaint are confined to protection of certain persons and activities; for example, the employer's failure to permit paid time off for certain activities;[13] the employer subjecting persons to a detriment;[14] the employer dismissing certain persons.[15] Thirdly, the remedies available are a declaration and compensation,[16] with the additional possibility of interim relief in dismissal cases.[17]

The Directive's provisions are rather more general:[18]

'1. Member States shall take the necessary steps to ensure that employers, workers and workers' representatives are subject to the legal provisions necessary for the implementation of this Directive.

2. In particular, Member States shall ensure adequate controls and supervision.'

There is no explicit provision for the different categories of workers and workers' representatives with health and safety functions. But presumably they could all invoke Article 11(6):

'Workers and/or their representatives are entitled to appeal, in accordance with national law and/or practice, to the authority responsible for safety and health protection at work if they consider that the measures taken and the means employed by the employer are inadequate for the purposes of ensuring safety and health at work.'

There is no explicit reference to remedies, but it is implicit that the appeal has some potential remedial result.

It is arguable that UK law is deficient in the following respects. First, the Health and Safety Commission and Executive are unable to 'ensure adequate

---

10 Article 6(3)(c), Article 11(1) and Article 11(6).
11 See the critique in Chapter 23.
12 SRSCR, Reg 11; EPCA, ss 22B, 71.
13 SRSCR, Reg 11.
14 EPCA, s 22B.
15 EPCA, s 57A.
16 SRSCR, Reg 11(3); EPCA, s 22C.
17 EPCA, ss 71–78.
18 Article 4.

controls and supervision' of the rights conferred by the Directive. Specifically, the criminal law process is not able to secure the health and safety functions of workers and workers' representatives prescribed by the Directive. The gaps in the Regulations cannot be compensated for by Codes of Practice and Guidance Notes. Their legal status is such [19] that only the provisions of the Regulations can be regarded as adequate implementation.

Secondly, the civil law process through the industrial tribunals is not adequate to 'ensure adequate controls and supervision' of the rights conferred by the Directive. Specifically, no provision is made for complaints on grounds of failure to provide the various entitlements to facilities and assistance, apart from paid time off, guaranteed by the Directive. Civil liability for breach of MSHW Regulations is excluded.[20] In so far as the Directive's provisions are implemented through the MSHW,[1] no remedy is available for breach. Finally, the remedies of a declaration and compensation are not effective to secure the rights guaranteed by the Directive.

Developments in EU law may be available to remedy some of these deficiencies. These include enforcement of provisions of the Directive having 'direct effect' against an employer who is an emanation of the State, 'purposive' interpretation of UK law to give effect to the result envisaged by the Directive, and, last but not least, liability of a Member State for damages caused by failure to implement the Directive and provide effective means of enforcement.[2]

CONCLUSION

The UK law on safety representatives is in many cases clearly, and in some arguably, not in compliance with the EU Framework Directive. UK legislation on worker representation is to follow the European Court's judgment in *EC Commission v UK* of 8 June 1994. This will be the occasion for renewed controversy regarding the substantive requirements of EC law on worker representation. The defects in the UK's compliance with the EU law on workers' representation in matters of health and safety will be relevant to this debate. The defects highlighted demonstrate that any general legislative proposals on worker representation need to be scrutinised carefully in light of EU requirements. Moreover, EU law offers potential means of redress – through domestic and European litigation.

The Framework Directive is thus likely to become involved in any legal strategy aimed at influencing the government's legislative proposals on general worker representation. Any such proposals may well affect the UK law on safety representatives. Specific defects in UK law allow for potential litigation using recent developments in EU law. Litigation attacking these defects could avail itself of:[3]

– direct enforcement of provisions of the Directive having 'direct effect' against an employer who is an emanation of the State;

19 HSWA, s 17.
20 MSHW, Reg 15.
1 As regards 'designated workers' under Regs 6 and 7.
2 Joined Cases C-6/90 and C-9/90: *Francovich and Bonifaci v Italy* [1991] ECR I-5357.
3 For details, see J Hendy and M Ford, Redgrave, Fife & Machin's *Health and Safety*, 2nd ed, Butterworths, London 1993, pp lxv–lxxiv.

- 'purposive' interpretation of UK law to give effect to the result envisaged by the Directive;
- liability of a Member State for damages caused by failure to properly implement the Directive.[4]
- the availability of remedies, including injunctive relief, for the enforcement of rights in EU law.

The explosion of claims from part-time women workers denied access to occupational pensions, contrary to EU law, has demonstrated the potential of Euro-litigation. The defects in the implementation of the Framework Directive may offer similar opportunities.

For example, one major defect highlighted is that UK law only allows for appointment of safety representatives where trade unions are recognised. Even when appointed, they are empowered to act only for the employees they represent. This is arguably non-implementation of the clear requirements of the Framework Directive, and as such a violation of EU law. A worker injured at a workplace without the benefit of safety representatives (eg union members where the union was not recognised, or a non-union member not represented) may argue that the injury was caused or contributed to by the failure to take measures which might have been taken had there been a safety representative, which could have prevented the accident or injury.

Actions against emanations of the State, or against the State on the *Francovich* principle, could produce salutary effects on government action to properly implement the Framework Directive. Other litigation seeking to exploit EU law could include:

- injunctive relief preventing employers obstructing the appointment by trade unions of (regional) safety representatives (non-employees), and the exercise of their rights and functions for union members;
- injunctive relief where there has been a failure to consult workers' representatives over 'the planning and introduction of new technologies ... as regards the consequences of the choice of equipment, the working conditions, and the working environment for the safety and health of workers';[5]
- compensation where expense has been incurred by safety representatives undertaking training which has not been reimbursed by employers;[6]
- compensation where 'the necessary means' have not been provided to workers' representatives to enable them to exercise their rights and functions.[7]

Legal strategies can do no more than contribute to an overall political strategy aimed, at least, at bringing the UK law into line with EU law. But their potential should not be overlooked or underestimated.

---

4 Joined Cases C-6/90 and C-9/90: *Francovich and Bonifaci v Italy* [1991] ECR I-5357.
5 Article 6(3)(c).
6 Article 12(4).
7 Article 11(5).

Part VII

Free Movement of Workers and European Labour Law

Chapter 25

The Changing Context of Free Movement in the European Union

INTRODUCTION

The free movement of workers usually takes pride of place in general treatments of the labour law and social policy of the European Community.[1] Implicit in neo-liberal conceptions of a European Common Market, free movement of labour takes its place alongside the other fundamental freedoms established in the Treaty of Rome: freedom of movement of capital, goods and services. Free movement of workers is perceived as a keystone of the social dimension of the Rome Treaty.

As applied in the context of the European labour market, free movement of workers led to many problems which could be characterised as being of a social nature. The movement of workers from one Member State to another led to questions of entitlement to social security benefits of various kinds, the transfer of acquired entitlements to such benefits, including pensions, issues concerning the families of such workers and their entitlements to education, housing and so on. As it developed, the labour market issue of free movement acquired a social baggage in the form of EC law on these myriad social issues.

However, the perception of free movement of workers as a social issue is questionable. Embedded in its labour market context, it is an economic, not a social concept. Social policy issues arose in the context of whether Member States' restrictions on entitlement to various social provisions infringed the EC law guarantee of free movement of workers. The ambivalence resulting from this was evident in a number of contexts.

A social measure might be adopted by a Member State which denied access to a benefit to non-nationals, and thus arguably had the effect of inhibiting free movement of foreign workers. But could an EC social policy be invoked to contest such a discriminatory measure even when no effect could be demonstrated as regards the free movement of workers? When the Commission proposed social policy measures, did it have to demonstrate their relevance to free movement of workers in order to be anchored on the Treaty provisions regarding free movement? The Treaty provisions on free movement were subject to limitations justified on grounds of public policy, public security or public

---

1 See the lengthy chapters devoted to it in textbooks on the subject, reviewed in Chapter 1. Outside the labour law context, though still considered to be within the social policy dimension, the issue of free movement of persons has been the subject of extensive commentary; see D O'Keeffe 'The Free Movement of Persons and the Single Market' (1992) *European Law Review* 3.

health – social policy grounds excluded from EC competence and reserved to national authorities.[2] Should provisions on free movement be dealt with as part of Community labour law even when they had no social policy but only purely labour market implications?

The EC law on free movement of workers which dominated the field for potential development of EC social policy during its first decade and a half, had the potential to make major contributions to the development of European labour law. For example, the law on free movement of workers proceeded from the principle of non-discrimination on the basis of nationality. The principle of non-discrimination fed into the later development by the European Court of EC law on sex equality. The legal definition of 'worker' for the purposes of free movement was developed independently of national law definitions, and expanded beyond the limitations imposed by those national labour laws, in the interests of eliminating constraints on free movement of all workers within the European labour market.

But the main focus of attention in the labour law on free movement remained the social protection of migrant workers. Social policy is again driven by the free movement imperative. The social security policies of the Member States are to be subjected to Community law intervention with this objective in mind. EC law dictates the principle of equal treatment of all nationals of the Member States, and their families, in relation to the social security law of the Member States. Further, the free movement of workers is to be facilitated by principles allowing for the aggregation of periods of insurance and employment within the whole of the Community regarding entitlement to social security rights, and the export of benefits to workers who take up residence in another Member State.

The body of law which emerged implementing these principles is technically formidable and the policy issues seemingly intractable. The Community social security rules have been:[3]

'criticised as being complicated to a point where their basic function, namely to guarantee the fundamental Community right of free movement of persons, has been obliterated.'

The Member States have refused to endorse a policy of harmonisation of domestic social security systems rooted in national traditions and the Commission has sought at most to move to a policy of convergence of basic social security objectives and policies.[4]

THE CHANGING CONTEXT

The underlying problem of the EC law on free movement of workers is that the context in which it was formulated has changed:[5]

'. . . it was conceived at a time of full employment, when most of the social protection was assumed by state schemes and when the typical migrant was a male blue-collar

2   Article 48(3).
3   C Laske 'The impact of the single European market on social protection for migrant workers' (1993) 30 *Common Market Law Review* 515, at 517.
4   Council Recommendation on the convergence of objectives and policies on social protection, OJ 1991 C194.
5   Laske, op cit, p 521.

worker, employed full-time and usually moving from south to north. Today's situation (and that of post-1992 Europe) is very different: the whole of the Community is struggling with high unemployment, Member States increasingly opt out of social security responsibilities by shifting the burden of insuring against certain risks onto the individual, and an increasingly genuine Internal Market has seen a steep migration of white-collar workers in particular from the middle management.'

Though this still focuses on social security issues, high unemployment threatens as much, if not more, the labour standards of workers. Migration of workers from areas of the Community with lower labour standards can undermine higher labour standards established elsewhere with 'social dumping'. The migration of highly qualified workers depends on whether their qualifications will be recognised outside the Member State where they were acquired.

For European labour law, two critical issues have become whether the policy of free movement can threaten workers' conditions of employment; and whether free movement of professional workers is inhibited by lack of recognition of professional qualifications. Each will be treated in its context. The former involves not only isolated individuals, but also the movement of workers from areas with low labour standards to those with higher labour standards. The latter raises questions of professional control of qualifications and its challenge by supranational regulation.

Chapter 26

Free Movement of Professional Workers

LEGAL PROVISIONS ON FREE MOVEMENT OF WORKERS

The Treaty of Rome seeks to guarantee the free movement of workers:[1]

'1. Freedom of movement for workers shall be secured within the Community by the end of the transitional period at the latest.

2. Such freedom of movement shall entail the abolition of any discrimination based on nationality between workers of the Member States as regards employment, remuneration and other conditions of work and employment.

3. It shall entail the right, subject to limitations justified on grounds of public policy, public security or public health:
   (a) to accept offers of employment actually made;
   (b) to move freely within the territory of the Member States for this purpose;
   (c) to stay in a Member State for the purpose of employment in accordance with the provisions governing the employment of nationals of that State laid down by law, regulation or administrative action;
   (d) to remain in the territory of a Member State after having been employed in that State, subject to conditions which shall be embodied in implementing regulations to be drawn up by the Commission.

4. The provisions of this Article shall not apply to employment in the public service.'

Council Regulation 1612/68 of 15 October 1968 on freedom of movement for workers within the Community provided:[2]

'1. Any national of a Member State shall, irrespective of his place of residence, have the right to take up an activity as an employed person, and to pursue such activity within the territory of another Member State in accordance with the provisions laid down by law, regulation or administrative action governing the employment of nationals of that State.

2. He shall, in particular, have the right to take up available employment in the territory of another Member State with the same priority as nationals of that State.'

The free movement of workers is confined to the scope of the definition of 'workers'. The European Court has defined 'worker' in EC law independently of

---

1   Article 48.
2   Article 1 of Regulation 1612/68/EEC, OJ 1968 L257/2; OJ Special Edition 1968–69 475; as amended by Council Regulation 2434/92, OJ 1992 L245/1.

the national laws of the Member States, though with elements clearly derived from national experience:[3]

> 'That concept must be defined in accordance with objective criteria which distinguish the employment relationship by reference to the rights and duties of the person concerned. The essential feature of an employment relationship, however, is that for a certain period of time a person performs services for and under the direction of another person in return for which he receives remuneration.'

The Court made clear that 'the nature of the legal relationship between employee and employer, whether involving public law status or a private law contract, is immaterial as regards the application of Article 48'. Hence, in the case of *Lawrie-Blum*:[4]

> '... a trainee teacher, who, under the direction and supervision of the school authorities, is undergoing a period of service in preparation for the teaching profession during which he provides services by giving lessons and receives remuneration must be regarded as a worker within the meaning of Article 48(1) of the EEC Treaty, irrespective of the legal nature of the employment relationship.'

LEGAL PROVISIONS ON FREE MOVEMENT OF PROFESSIONALS

Notwithstanding the already generous scope of the EC law definition of 'worker', the Treaty went on to guarantee the right to free movement also of those who supply services as self-employed persons or seek the right of establishment in other Member States.[5] The activity in question may not be clearly that of a worker or a person supplying services or seeking the right of establishment, but the Treaty and the Court have sought to extend the same freedoms equally to all three categories of economic activity. With specific regard to the latter categories, it was provided in Article 57 of the Treaty:

> '1. In order to make it easier for persons to take up and pursue activities as self-employed persons, the Council shall, acting in accordance with the procedure referred to in Article 189b, issue directives for the mutual recognition of diplomas, certificates and other evidence of formal qualifications.
>
> 2. For the same purpose, the Council shall, before the end of the transitional period, issue directives for the coordination of the provisions laid down by law, regulation or administrative action in Member States concerning the taking up and pursuit of activities as self-employed persons. The Council, acting unanimously on a proposal from the Commission and after consulting the European Parliament, shall decide on directives the implementation of which involves in at least one Member State amendment of the existing principles laid down by law governing the professions with respect to training and conditions of access for natural persons. In other cases the Council shall act in accordance with the procedure referred to in Article 189b.

---

3 Case 66/85: *Lawrie-Blum v Land Baden-Württemberg* [1986] ECR 2121. This EC law definition of worker, however, was applicable only to the area of policy of free movement; for the purposes of other areas of policy, notably in labour law, the Court deferred to national law definitions: Case 105/84: *Mikkelsen v Danmols Inventar A/S* [1986] 1CMLR 316.
4 Ibid.
5 Articles 52–57.

3. In the case of the medical and allied and pharmaceutical professions, the progressive abolition of restrictions shall be dependent upon coordination of the conditions for their exercise in the various Member States.'

However, as one review commented:[6]

'whereas the free movement of workers was implemented ahead of schedule ... little headway has been made so far on the right of establishment and the freedom to provide services. In an economic unit such as the Community ... it is essential to maximise not only the use of labour but also the expertise and services of professionals who should be able to move wherever they wish or where they are most needed.'

With specific reference to the coordination prescribed in Article 57(2), the author of this review observed:[7]

'In the early years, there was great disagreement as to how much coordination was to be effected ... Since the professions are usually highly-regulated the problem of coordination is a very complex one.'

Laslett cites by way of example a Commission proposal for the medical profession drawn up in 1969, which declared that existing codes of professional conduct would need to be supplemented by 'rules relating to the socio-economic and community facets of health policy and aiming at safeguarding the interests of the State, the profession, and, above all, the population at large'. Although it was supported by the Standing Committee of Doctors in the EEC, it did not gain Council support.

The progression towards a general system allowing for the free movement of professionals was slow and painful, encountering the obstacles posed by national systems of qualification and regulation of professional activity. First, there was a Council Resolution of 6 June 1974 on the mutual recognition of diplomas, certificates and other evidence of formal qualifications.[8] This set the tone for, secondly, the drafting of sectoral Directives in various professions. These covered doctors,[9] other major health care professions (nurses, dentists, veterinary surgeons, midwives, pharmacists), which followed the broad lines of the provisions on doctors,[10] architects,[11] and lawyers.[12]

Hence, Council Directive 77/249/EEC to facilitate the effective exercise by lawyers of freedom to provide services, adopted on 22 March 1977, did not provide for any coordination whatsoever of training requirements. Nor did it provide for 'recognition' as such of national diplomas. Recognition is based on the fact that a person is legally entitled to practice in another Member State. As to the conditions of legal practice:[13]

'1. Activities relating to the representation of a client in legal proceedings or before public authorities shall be pursued in each host Member State under the conditions

---

6　Julia M Laslett 'The mutual recognition of diplomas, certificates and other evidence of formal qualifications in the European Community' (1990/91) *Legal Issues of European Integration* 1.
7　Ibid, p 9.
8　OJ 1974 C98/1.
9　Council Directive 75/362/EEC of 16 June 1975 on the mutual recognition of diplomas in medicine, OJ 1975 L167/19.
10　Council Directives 77/452/EEC and 77/453/EEC, OJ 1977 L176; 78/686/EEC and 78/687/EEC, OJ 1978 L233; 78/1026/EEC and 78/1027/EEC, OJ 1978 L362; 80/154/EEC and 80/155/EEC, OJ 1980 L33; and 85/432/EEC and 85/433/EEC, OJ 1985 L235.
11　Council Directive 85/384/EEC, OJ 1985 L223, not adopted until 1985.
12　Council Directive 77/249/EEC, OJ 1977 L78/17.
13　Article 4.

laid down for lawyers established in that State, with the exception of any conditions requiring residence, or registration with a professional organisation, in that State.

2. A lawyer pursuing these activities shall observe the rules of professional conduct of the host Member State, without prejudice to his obligations in the Member State from which he comes.

3. When these activities are pursued in the United Kingdom, "rules of professional conduct of the host Member State" means the rules of professional conduct applicable to solicitors, where such activities are not reserved for barristers and advocates. Otherwise the rules of professional conduct applicable to the latter shall apply . . .'

Finally, in the period during which these Directives were being considered and adopted, the Court of Justice established further important principles regarding recognition of diplomas and the interpretation of the Directives.

This piecemeal, sectoral and casuistic approach was overtaken by the momentum generated by the Single European Market programme in the mid-1980s. A proposal for a Council Directive was formulated on 9 July 1985 and a Directive was finally adopted on 21 December 1988 on a general system for the recognition of higher education diplomas awarded on completion of professional education and training of at least three years' duration.[14]

The Directive follows the principle of 'mutual recognition' applicable to the free movement of other factors of production,[15] which underlay the Commission's White Paper setting out the Single European Market programme. The principles underlying the approach of the Directive, as outlined by Laslett, include the principle of mutual trust:[16]

'The new system has no mandatory coordination of training requirements for the various professions in question, but relies wholly on the comparability of certificates and on mutual trust between Member States.'

This is expressed in Article 3 of the Directive:

'Where, in a host Member State, the taking up or pursuit of a regulated profession is subject to possession of a diploma, the competent authority may not, on the grounds of inadequate qualifications, refuse to authorise a national of a Member State to take up or pursue that profession on the same conditions as apply to its own nationals:
(a) if the applicant holds the diploma required in another Member State for the taking up or pursuit of the profession in question in its territory, such diploma having been awarded in a Member State . . .'

Similarly, with regard to proof of good character or repute:[17]

'the host State shall accept as sufficient evidence, in respect of nationals of Member States wishing to pursue that profession in its territory, the production of documents issued by competent authorities in the Member State of origin or the Member State from which the foreign national comes showing that those requirements are met.'

One critical question, however, concerned the position where the professional activity in question was regulated not by State authorities but by professional associations or organisations of an ostensibly private character, the rules of

---

14 Council Directive 89/48/EEC of 21 December 1988, OJ 1989 L19/16.
15 Case 120/78: *REWE-Zentral AG v Bundesmonopol-verwaltung für Branntwein* [1979] ECR 649 ('Cassis de Dijon').
16 Op cit, p 31.
17 Article 6(1).

which did not fit the model of laws, regulations or administrative provisions laid down by State authorities. Accordingly, the Directive defined 'regulated professional activity' as one governed by laws, regulations or administrative provisions, but, where this was not the case:[18]

'... a professional activity shall be deemed to be a regulated professional activity if it is pursued by the members of an association or organisation the purpose of which is, in particular, to promote and maintain a high standard in the professional field concerned and which, to achieve that purpose, is recognised in a special form by a Member State and:
- awards a diploma to its members,
- ensures that its members respect the rules of professional conduct which it prescribes, and
- confers on them the right to use a title or designatory letters, or to benefit from a status corresponding to that diploma.

A non-exhaustive list of associations or organisations which, when this Directive is adopted, satisfy the conditions ... is contained in the Annex ...'

The legal definition of professional activity is thus recognised to be a highly *contextual* one, contingent on national circumstances. Laslett noted that the Rome Treaty refers sometimes to 'activities', sometimes to 'professions', and that in the chapter on establishment the term 'self-employed activities' was more frequent. In the provisions on freedom to supply services, Article 60 defined services to include, in particular, '(d) activities of the professions'. She comments:[19]

'a "profession" may be an idea which does not necessarily cover the same activities in every Member State since it is a more subjective concept, calling into play national characteristics and a certain professional climate.'

The national context of professions and their governance, clearly appreciated in Article 57(2), is here hinted at. The Treaty does not define 'profession', and Laslett goes on to outline 'some general characteristics of the professions, which should be true for all the Member States'.[20] These are said to include:

1. regulated training to a high standard, linked to some form of higher education;
2. subjection to a code of practice demanding high ethical standards and discipline; closely allied to this is the independence of members of the professions, free from third party influence prejudicial to the client;
3. personal contact between practitioner and client, based on mutual trust and responsibility to act in the client's best interests.

The concept of 'professional activity' which emerges from these elements seems also to permeate the Community instruments seeking to regulate free movement of professional workers. Its adequacy, however, is questionable, as its contingency, the dependence on national context, undermines the effort to apply principles of mutual recognition. Even more important, the logic of free movement in a Single European Market may be antithetical to the raison d'être of the professions.

---

18 Article 1(d).
19 Laslett, op cit, p 3, referring to de Crayencour *The Professions in the European Community*, Commission of the EC: European Perspectives, Brussels, Luxembourg 1981, p 37.
20 Ibid, p 5.

A CONTRADICTION: THE CONCEPT OF PROFESSIONAL ACTIVITY AND FREE MOVEMENT

It has been argued that the 'professions' as a social formation were far from universal, and, indeed, were peculiar to the English-speaking world, mainly the Anglo-American world:[1]

'It was enough that both their countries clearly had professions while it was not at all certain that there were any professions in continental Europe or anywhere else. They knew for certain that continental societies had intellectuals, indeed a superfluity of them, since many landed on their shores. They could reasonably presume that these societies had abundant legal, medical and engineering expertise, but professions were a different matter. In part this was another example of "Fog in channel: Continent isolated", and the fog obscured from British view all the associations and collective action of the lawyers, doctors and engineers of continental Europe. French and German scholars did not help the situation since few of them thought the professions worthy subjects to investigate. Indeed, they could hardly understand or translate the concept . . .

In the 1970s, the fog finally began to clear, as more and more evidence was collected about continental professions. The British themselves had little part in this. The OECD and EEC played a minor role, by discussing the practical issues of the free movement of professionals . . .'

In his analysis of the defining qualities of professional activity, Torstendahl also claims that 'Professionalism and professionalisation are . . . bound to the English language . . . There is no immediate counterpart to these concepts in other countries'.[2] However, to theorise about professions requires a break with this:[3]

'The "essential properties" of professionals must not be decided by how the concept is used in English. It is argued that essential properties must, instead, be connected with knowledge (abstract knowledge), and both education and certificates have been discarded as the basis for the groups that ought to be considered. These groups may be called "knowledge-based" groups.

If knowledge-based groups are recognised as the basis around which a theory of professionalism has to be formed . . . the next problem is what it means to act professionally. Here it has been argued that professional activity has to be connected with exclusionary closure as a strategy for collective action'.[4]

The elements of collective action and exclusionary closure are more familiar in studies of workers' organisations and trade unions. As Collins put it:[5]

'Instead of seeing occupations as having fixed positions on a market, we see that occupations themselves can become status groups in the realm of work. Instead of merely responding to market dynamics, as in the model of class conflict stemming

---

1 M Burrage 'The professions in sociology and history', in R Torstendahl (ed) *Professions in Theory and History*, 1990, at p 4.
2 Torstendahl 'Three approaches to theories of professionalism', ibid, at p 59.
3 Ibid, pp 59–60.
4 Torstendahl goes on to say: 'It is further argued that there is no logical link between the knowledge-based group as such and the exclusionary closure strategy . . . Knowledge-based groups have not acted and will not act only from the exclusionary closure strategy. To what extent do they rely on this strategy, and which other groups use this strategy? These are important questions'.
5 R Collins 'Market closure and the conflict theory of the professions', in Torstendahl (ed), op cit, p 24 at p 25.

from Marx, occupations attempt to control market conditions. Some occupations are relatively successful at this, others less so. Those which are especially successful are the ones which we have come to call "the professions".'

If a defining quality of the professions is the exclusionary closure of an occupation in the market, there is evident a potential conflict with the liberal economic theory behind free movement of workers in the European Community. The prospects of a clash, however, depend on the extent to which the occupational market closure achieved by professions is threatened by the free movement of professional workers in the EU.

The facts on the ground may be the saving grace. For reports of the death of nationally based professional activity are highly exaggerated. Laslett points out in her conclusions that a considerable break-through in the work on mutual recognition of diplomas in the framework of realising freedom of movement in the Community was made in the mid-to-late seventies in the health sector. Yet, despite this, the number of doctors who actually choose to live and work in another Member State remains low. She cites a 1988 study which showed that only 4,500 doctors had availed themselves of the advantages of the Directives in the space of ten years, of a total of nearly 600,000 doctors practising in the Community.[6]

An illustration: the legal profession

Among the groups mentioned above as benefiting from Directives promoting the mutual recognition of qualifications were, apart from doctors and other health care professionals and architects, also lawyers. Free movement of lawyers among the Member States might be considered optimistic, as law is thought to be archetypically nationally bound.

In the case of some legal professions, indeed, even movement *within* national boundaries is constrained. For example, the regulations governing the legal profession in Germany have been characterised as being of a 'quasi-medieval conservatism'.[7] The German legal profession is organised into regions, a form of mandatory decentralisation, as every German lawyer is admitted to only one civil court in Germany and may not reside or establish his business outside the district in which that court is situated. It was claimed that the small firms and sole practitioners who make up the bulk of the privately practising profession welcome the protection from competition afforded by this restrictive practice. The irony was pointed up that whilst 53,000 German lawyers are restricted to practising in one locality, EC rules of freedom of establishment would allow any French or UK firm to choose its locality and to have offices in more than one city.

In the legal professions of other countries, it might seem easier to achieve freedom of movement *among* the Member States than movement *between* the branches of the legal profession in one country. The traumas of the divided profession in the UK are well known.

An example is the position of solicitor-advocates in Scotland. Provision for

---

6   Laslett, op cit, p 50, citing a study reported in *Europe*, 7 April 1988, p 10. She concludes: 'Such figures seem to show that other barriers, perhaps linguistic, psychological or social, also play an important role'.

7   C Morton 'Can German lawyers break the chains', *International Financial Law Review*, March 1989.

extended rights of audience for solicitors was made in 1990.[8] At the end of June, the Dean of the Faculty of Advocates issued a ruling binding on all his members banning working solicitor-advocates and advocates working together.[9]

Council Directive 77/249/EEC of 22 March 1977[10] was intended 'to facilitate the effective exercise by lawyers of freedom to provide services'. Lawyer is defined, in the UK, as Advocate, Barrister and Solicitor,[11] and Article 2 provides that:

'Each Member State shall recognise as a lawyer for the purposes of pursuing the activities (by way of provision of services) any person listed (within the definition of "lawyer") ...'

So a 'lawyer' covered by the Directive can, on a temporary basis, perform the work of a 'lawyer' in any other Member State.

Moreover, Article 5, as an exception, allows Member States to require foreign lawyers 'to work *in conjunction* with a lawyer who practises before the judicial authority in question'. The UK law states that an EC lawyer who is not a barrister or solicitor (or in Scotland, an advocate) must be instructed by, and act in conjunction with, an advocate, barrister or solicitor entitled to practise before the court in question.[12]

Presumably the Dean of the Faculty of Advocates would not, or could not, prohibit an advocate appearing with a 'lawyer' from another Member State equivalent to a solicitor, let alone equivalent to a solicitor-advocate. Restrictive practices such as those reflected in the Dean's ruling on solicitor-advocates contradict the spirit of these provisions.

Restrictive practices limiting foreign lawyers have been struck down.[13] For example, in *Gullung*,[14] a local Bar in France prohibited any lawyer from assisting Mr Gullung in representing clients on grounds that he did not have the integrity, good repute and dignity to become an *avocat*. The Court held that Gullung could not rely on the Directive as he had violated professional rules of conduct set down by the host State. Gullung had a chequered history and the Court said of the local Bar's ban:[15]

'The requirement seeks to ensure the observance of moral and ethical principles and the disciplinary control of the activity of lawyers and pursues an objective worthy of protection.'

8   Law Reform (Miscellaneous Provisions) (Scotland) Act 1990, s 24, inserting a new section 25A into the Solicitors (Scotland) Act 1980.
9   'No advocate shall appear in any court with a solicitor-advocate instructed for the same client'. The Dean subsequently said he would consider applications to allow this, but without any indication of the reasons or parameters which would govern the exercise of his discretion. A report on Scotland's law firms in 1993 stated that there were 32 such solicitor-advocates thus prohibited from 'mixed doubles'. *International Financial Law Review*, October 1993, p 19.
10 OJ 1977 L78/17.
11 Article 1(2).
12 European Communities (Services of Lawyers) Order 1978, SI 1978 No 1910, Article 9. There is some doubt whether this could apply to a case where the law of the Member State does not require representation by a lawyer, as where the client could conduct his own case. Case 427/85: *EC Commission v Germany* [1988] ECR 1123.
13 For example, Case 107/83: *Ordre des Avocats au Barreau de Paris v Klopp* [1984] ECR 2971: the Paris Bar's refusal to admit lawyers because they have practices in other Member States was struck down.
14 Case 292/86: *Gullung v Conseil de l'Ordre des Avocats du Barreau de Colmar et de Saverne* [1988] ECR 111.
15 Ibid, at 139, paragraphs 28, 29.

One would not expect the Court to be so sympathetic to the Dean's ban.

The right of establishment in EC law is also concerned with free movement of professionals and services. It might be relevant if the Dean's ruling were adversely to affect other Member State nationals, thus hindering free movement. Thus Council Directive 89/48/EEC[16] on a general system for the recognition of higher-education diplomas awarded on completion of professional education and training of at least three years' duration stipulates that possession of such a diploma entitles a Member State national to take up professional activity in another Member State on the same conditions as apply to its own nationals. A migrant lawyer is entitled to use the professional designation 'solicitor' or 'advocate' – and cannot be refused membership on the ground that he is not qualified. Though they can be required to undergo special training or an adaptation period where this can be justified.[17]

Suppose a French or German lawyer was seeking to practice in Scotland, and they possessed the qualifications to be both solicitor and advocate, or 'solicitor-advocate'. It is arguable that the Dean's ruling is contrary to EC law if the foreign 'solicitor-advocate' was hindered in his practice by the Dean's ruling.

The Dean's argument is said to be based on the advocate's non-contractual relationship to the client.[18] The advocate holds an office engaging him in a duty to the court, his profession and the public, independent of the client, in contrast to the solicitor's contract of employment with the client.

This position may be criticised in light of the view taken by the European Court of Justice in interpreting the scope of the right of establishment of professionals in the EC Treaty. Article 55 provides that the right does not apply:

'so far as any given Member State is concerned, to activities which in that State are connected, even occasionally, with the exercise of official authority.'

Reyners v Belgian State[19] was a challenge to Belgian legislation admitting only Belgians as legal practitioners. The Court rejected the Belgian government's argument that Article 55 applied to exclude lawyers from the right of establishment:[20]

'Professional activities involving contacts, even regular and organic, with the courts, including even compulsory co-operation in their functioning, do not constitute, as such, connexion with the exercise of official authority.

The most typical activities of the profession of avocat, in particular, such as consultation and legal assistance and also representation and the defence of parties in court, even when the intervention or assistance of the avocat is compulsory or is a legal monopoly, cannot be considered as connected with the exercise of official authority.'

The justification put forward by the Dean is at odds with EC law, which rejects the special position of advocates in relation to the courts as justifying exclusion

---

16   OJ 1989 L19/16.
17   Article 4(1)(b).
18   As explained by Ian Willock in *SCOLAG Journal,* July 1993, p 104, relying on *Batchelor v Pattison and Mackersy* (1876) 3 R 914, cited in *Brodt v King* [1991] SLT 272. Willock is critical of these authorities.
19   Case 2/74: [1974] ECR 631.
20   Ibid, at 655.

from practice before them.[1]

The problem remains of finding a Member State national qualified in their own country practising as a solicitor in Scotland who might challenge the Dean's ruling. The principle of 'reverse discrimination' might be an obstacle to a native solicitor-advocate making a complaint. When a Member State treats its own citizens less favourably than those of other Member States, this is not necessarily a violation of EC law![2]

The travails of the legal profession in the UK are not unique in the Community. In Paris, in 1971, in an attempt to regulate legal advice given by persons who were not qualified as *notaires* or *avocats*, the profession of *conseil juridique* was created by statute. *Conseils juridiques* were required to be qualified by having studied French law. All lawyers practising international law in Paris are either *avocats* or *conseils*. Traditionally, the status of *avocat* has been higher, having rights of audience in the French courts which the *conseil* does not, although *conseils* can appear before tribunals and in arbitrations.

The Paris Bar, on 23 April 1988, adopted a resolution to fuse the two branches, *avocats* and *conseils juridiques*, into the single profession of *avocats conseils*. The requisite legislation to implement such a fusion caused a storm. In June 1990, the French Communist Party sided with conservative forces to reject the draft legislation. The fusion was finally passed and came into effect on 1 January 1992. The new law was restrictive regarding establishment, favouring only those foreign firms set up prior to 31 December 1990. This led the UK Lord Chancellor, Lord Mackay, to denounce the French legislation as contrary to the spirit of 1992.[3]

In so far as EU law has contributed to free movement in the legal profession in Europe, the movement has been almost all in one direction – to Brussels. At the start of 1988 there were just five UK law firms with offices in Brussels. By October 1990, it was reported that there were at least 30 UK law firms, and some 18 US law firms, with increasing numbers of Germans, Dutch, French, and Scandinavians.[4] This did not mean establishment was easy: an example concerned the Belgian bar's restrictions on advertising in 1989–90. Belgium has dozens of local bars, including a double bar in Brussels, one for French and one for Flemish speakers. Only in November 1989 did the Flemish Bar decide to permit publicity; the French Bar followed suit shortly after. But it was reported that many lawyers were still frustrated.[5]

1   The Chairman of the General Council of the English Bar, Robert Seabrook QC has been quoted as follows: 'The director of DG IV (EC Competition Directorate) is on record as having said that if any one Member State has a liberal rule of practice without any obvious adverse effects the same should prevail in the other Member States. If competition policies were to be framed with that approach there could be quite far-reaching consequences'. *International Financial Law Review*, February 1994, p 48.
2   Case 175/78: *R v Saunders* [1979] ECR 1129. In the general context of life in the Scottish legal profession, this limitation was considered to be a relatively minor adversity, R Shiels 'The inevitable decline of the Solicitor Advocate', *SCOLAG Journal*, March 1995, p 37.
3   This account is drawn from C Morton 'Paris lawyers – preparing to take on the world?', *International Financial Law Review*, November 1988, Law Firm Supplement; P Stewart 'Of sheep and lawyers', *International Financial Law Review*, November 1990; 'French lawyers law denounced', *International Financial Law Review*, February 1991. See generally, V R Brotski 'European Community Law and the EC Lawyer's Right to Practice in France after the Enactment of Loi No 90–1259', (1993) 25 *Case Western Reserve Journal of International Law* 333.
4   *Financial Times*, 19 October 1990, p 24.
5   C Griffiths 'Battling with the Belgian Bar', *Legal Business*, July/August 1990, pp 24–6.

CONCLUSION

It is instructive to compare the debate over free movement of professionals with that over regulation of working conditions for workers moving to another country. The free movement of workers is said to be undermined by regulations which restrict the conditions upon which those workers can be employed. Against this, it is argued that free movement without some regulatory protection could lead to social dumping, as workers from countries with low wages and social protection standards are dumped into those with higher wages and standards. The argument is that national labour standards, such as those set by organisations of workers through collective agreements, should be mandatory for all workers working in the national territory, including those moving from elsewhere in the Community.

The threat of social dumping is less likely to affect professional workers. Occupational market closure is still the reality for many professions in Europe. National law often grants professions the capacity to maintain their grip through self-regulation. Liberalisation of the labour market through supranational regulation encounters the double resistance of national tradition and organised professional clout. Successful implementation of the free movement principle would threaten the defining feature of professional organisations. Professional dumping is much easier to stop than social dumping. The professionals see to that. Maybe that is why they are called professionals.

Chapter 27

Free Movement and Social Dumping

INTRODUCTION

The decline in the traditional sources of labour mobility in the EU from areas of high unemployment, mainly in the south, has been accompanied by a rise in labour mobility in a different form. The Commission pointed out that the completion of the Single European Market will bring about a considerable number of employment relationships which will be temporarily performed in a Member State other than the State in the territory of which they are habitually performed. The Commission anticipates that:[1]

'Thus, a new intra-Community mobility of workers within their jobs, different from the traditional mobility in search for new employment, is increasingly growing within the European Community in the framework of the economic freedoms, in particular, of the freedom to provide services.'

The Commission highlighted the potential of the services industry, which accounts for half the Community's production and 40% of jobs, in a wide range of activities. In particular, transnational subcontracting is developing in the construction sector and public works:[2]

'There are more and more instances of firms based in one Member State and moving with their staff to another State to provide a service, or of firms sending their workers from their country of origin to another Member State to work for a legally distinct undertaking.'

The increase in the number of transnational acquisitions by top European industrial enterprises was noted as liable to stimulate the temporary expatriation of workers within groups of companies or within companies with multiple operations throughout Europe.[3]

Free movement of workers in the Community has focused on the right to seek and take up employment. *Conditions* of employment for migrant workers have not heretofore been regulated – subject to the overriding requirement of

---

1 Explanatory Memorandum to the Proposal for a Council Directive concerning the posting of workers in the framework of the provision of services, COM (91) 230 final – SYN 346, Brussels, 1 August 1991, paragraph 1. The Memorandum cites the article by A Lyon-Caen 'Le droit, la mobilité et les relations du travail: quelques perspectives' (1991) *Revue du Marché Commun*, No 334, pp 108–113.
2 Ibid, paragraph 5.
3 Ibid, paragraph 8.

non-discrimination on grounds of nationality. The principle of equal treatment of migrant workers has now received a further impulse, however, as a result of a further initiative of the Commission which has been identified as part of its plan of 'encouraging high labour standards as part of a competitive Europe': the proposal concerning the posting of workers in the framework of the provision of services.[4]

This proposal repays close analysis for two reasons. First, it demonstrates how interrelated labour law issues at EU level have become; a proposed Directive on working conditions of migrant workers has raised fundamental issues to do with collective labour standards in the EU. Secondly, it demonstrates the complexity of European labour law's attempts to accommodate very different systems of collective bargaining and collective agreements. To posit as EU labour standards those of collective agreements, a formulation has to be found for the EU instrument which will encompass this range of different systems and their outcomes.

THE ORIGINS OF THE PROPOSED DIRECTIVE

On 1 August 1991, the Commission published a Proposal for a Council Directive concerning the posting of workers in the framework of the provision of services.[5] This was concerned to implement the commitment in the Commission's Action Programme relating to the Community Charter of Fundamental Social Rights of Workers, as regards the 'working conditions applicable to workers from another State performing work in the host country in the framework of the freedom to provide services, especially on behalf of a subcontracting undertaking'.[6] This protects local working conditions where workers are imported by foreign subcontractors.

The Commission posed the question 'as to which national labour legislation should be applied to undertakings which post a worker to carry out temporary work in a Member State'.[7] Formally, the solution depends on conflict of law rules, but given that these vary among Member States, the outcome may give rise to distortions of competition between national and foreign undertakings. The Commission therefore proposed to coordinate the laws of the Member States 'to eradicate practices which may be both detrimental to fair competition between undertakings and prejudicial to the interests of the workers concerned'.[8] The element of competition between firms as regards labour conditions was described as follows:[9]

'A particular problem arises, however, where a Member State places obligations, notably with regard to pay, on firms based in and working on its territory, and these

---

4   Medium Term Social Action Programme 1995–97, COM (95) 134 final, Brussels, 12 April 1995, p 16, paragraph 4.2.2. The Commission states that 'in view of the progress made in Council discussions on this proposal, the Commission will continue to press for its adoption in 1995. If this does not happen, the Commission will initiate consultations with the social partners to identify how best to resolve the problems in this field'.

5   COM (91) 230 final, SYN 346, Brussels, 1 August 1991.

6   Action Programme, Part II, Section 4B.

7   Explanatory Memorandum, paragraph 2.

8   Ibid, paragraph 3.

9   Ibid, paragraph 9 bis.

firms are faced with competition – for a specific task carried out within that same Member State – from a firm based elsewhere and not subject to the same obligations. Legitimate competition between firms is then overlaid by potentially distortive effects between national requirements.

The question is therefore one of finding a balance between two principles which find themselves in contradiction. On the one hand, free competition between firms, including at the level of subcontracting across borders, so that the full benefits of the single market can be realised, including by firms based in Member States whose main comparative advantage is a lower wage cost. On the other, Member States may decide to set and apply minimum pay levels applicable on their territory in order to ensure a minimum standard of living appropriate to the country concerned.'

This competition between firms would not occur, of course, if national labour laws were harmonised. The fact is, however, that the disparities among Member States regarding labour standards are such as to produce what has been termed 'social regime competition' – competition among Member States as to the costs imposed on employers by national regimes of social and labour regulation.[10] The Commission's Explanatory Memorandum elaborates this difference as regards pay levels and working time standards. The conclusion was:[11]

'National differences as to the material content of working conditions and the criteria inspiring the conflict of law rules may lead to situations where posted workers are applied lower wages and other working conditions than those in force in the place where the work is temporarily carried out. This situation would certainly affect fair competition between undertakings and equality of treatment between foreign and national undertakings; it would from the social point of view be completely unacceptable.'

The legal framework proposed by the Commission to combat this problem drew upon a number of sources of inspiration. One in particular is of interest, the decision in *Rush Portuguesa Lda v Office National d'Immigration*,[12] not least because it derives from the European Court, which may eventually be faced with interpretation of the Community instrument regulating this issue.

Rush Portuguesa Lda, a building and public works undertaking, was a company governed by Portuguese law, whose registered office was in Portugal. It entered into a subcontract with a French company for works in France and, to carry out these works, brought its Portuguese workforce from Portugal. However, it failed to obtain work permits for these workers, as prescribed by the French Labour Code, and was therefore informed by the Director of the *Office National d'Immigration* that it was required to make certain payments. The company challenged this before the French Administrative Tribunal, arguing that the effect of applicable provisions of the EEC Treaty[13] was that a provider of services may move freely from one Member State to another with his employees. The Tribunal considered that their decision depended on the interpretation of the applicable Community law and referred the issue to the European Court. One of the questions put to the Court was the following: 'May the right of a Portuguese company to provide services throughout the Community be made subject . . . to

---

10   W Streeck 'La dimensione sociale del mercato unico europeo: verso un'economia non regolata?' (1990) *Stato e Mercato*, No 28, pp 31–68.
11   Op cit, paragraph 12.
12   Case C-113/89: [1990] ECR I-1417.
13   Articles 59–66.

conditions, in particular relating to the engagement of labour in situ, the obtaining of work permits for its own Portuguese staff or the payment of fees to an official immigration body?'[14]

The issue was complicated by the fact that the transitional provisions regarding Portuguese accession were still in force, so that free movement of workers was not available, whereas the freedom to provide services was available. The Portuguese company argued that 'a person providing services may go from one Member State to another with his workforce. The application to that workforce of the restrictive provisions of the code du travail is therefore contrary to Community law'.[15] The French Government argued:[16]

> 'that right does not impede the application of all national rules concerning the economic activity in question ... an undertaking cannot be allowed, under the cloak of subcontract work, to evade national provisions concerning the supply of labour, in particular those relating to temporary work ... a distinction must be drawn between the activity of the undertaking, which is entitled to freedom to provide services, and the status of the undertaking's employees.'

The Portuguese Government argued against the French Government's position:[17]

> 'The availability of such an undertaking's workforce as a whole determines its production capacity and therefore its capacity to provide the service in question. Any condition restricting the use of a company's workers consequently limits its freedom to provide services ... The terms of their employment are, moreover, governed entirely by Portuguese law.'

The Commission sought an intermediate position by seeking to distinguish among the workforce those workers who, by virtue of their special position can be associated with the employer's freedom to provide services, and other workers who cannot.[18]

Advocate-General Van Gerven in his Opinion emphasised that the French national legislative provisions, which effectively restricted the freedom to provide services, could be justified in terms of the general good: 'the restriction introduced by the national provision must be objectively necessary in order to protect an interest which is acceptable from a Community point of view'.[19] The Advocate-General then proposed to differentiate among the workforce, albeit using criteria differing from those suggested by the Commission.

The Court of Justice, on the one hand, accepted that the Portuguese company could not be precluded from bringing its workers into France by:[20]

> 'making the staff subject to restrictions such as conditions as to engagement in situ or an obligation to obtain a work permit. To impose such conditions on the person providing services established in another Member State discriminates against that person in relation to his competitors established in the host country who are able to use their own staff without restrictions, and moreover affects his ability to provide the service.'

14   Op cit, at 1420.
15   Ibid, at 1421.
16   Ibid.
17   Ibid, at 1422.
18   Ibid, at 1422–4.
19   Ibid, at 1429.
20   Ibid, at 1443, paragraph 12.

On the other hand, the Court made the following profoundly important state-ment:[1]

> 'Finally, it should be stated, in response to the concern expressed in this connection by the French Government, that Community law does not preclude Member States from extending their legislation, or collective agreements entered into by both sides of industry, to any person who is employed, even temporarily, within their territory, no matter in which country the employer is established; nor does Community law prohibit Member States from enforcing those rules by appropriate means.'

The substantive outcome of the judgment is that restrictions on entry would not be permitted, but regulation of terms and conditions of employment, by law or collective agreement, was permissible.

Unlike the Commission in its later proposal, the Court did not address the implications of this judgment, and particularly the statement as to the possibility of regulating employment conditions of foreign contractors, for freedom to pro-vide services. Effectively, such regulation would undermine foreign contractors, since it eliminated their main competitive advantage, derived from less costly labour and social regulation of working conditions. The Commission obviously appreciated this. But it clearly opted to subordinate the competition imperative to a social policy – a profoundly important policy choice:[2]

> 'the need to eradicate discrimination between national and non-national undertak-ings and workers with respect to the application of certain working conditions, justify a Community proposal which ... intends to create a hard core of mandatory rules laid down by statutes or by erga omnes collective agreements, without disrupting the labour law systems of the Member States and particularly their legislative or volun-taristic approach and their collective bargaining systems.'

Hence, Article 3(1) of the proposed Directive provided:

> 'Member States shall see to it that, whatever the law applicable to the employment relationship, the undertaking does not deprive the worker of the terms and conditions of employment which apply for work of the same character at the place where the work is temporarily carried out, provided that:
> (a) they are laid down by laws, regulations and administrative provisions, collective agreements or arbitration awards, covering the whole of the occupation and industry concerned having an "erga omnes" effect and/or being made legally binding in the occupation and industry concerned, and
> (b) they concern the following matters:
>   (i) maximum daily and weekly hours of work, rest periods, work on Sun-days and night work;
>   (ii) minimum paid holidays;
>   (iii) the minimum rates of pay, including overtime rates and allowances, but excluding benefits provided for by private occupational schemes;
>   (iv) the conditions of hiring out of workers, in particular the supply of work-ers by temporary employment businesses;
>   (v) health, safety and hygiene at work;
>   (vi) protective measures with regard to the working conditions of pregnant women or women who have recently given birth, children, young people and other groups enjoying special protection;

---

1   Ibid, p 1445, paragraph 18.
2   Explanatory Memorandum, op cit, paragraph 18.

(vii) equality of treatment between men and women and prohibition of discrimination on the grounds of colour, race, religion, opinions, national origin or social background.'

There remain many issues of interpretation and application of the requirement that certain collective agreements be observed – not least arising from the differences in the nature and legal effects of collective agreements in different Member States. But the proposal by the Commission requiring employers to adhere to collectively agreed standards as those which Community law demands is of fundamental significance.

The origins of the Commission's proposed Directive lie, therefore, in the European Court's decision in *Rush Portuguesa.* The Court had declared:[3]

'. . . in response to the concern expressed in this connection by the French Government, that Community law does not preclude Member States from extending their legislation, or collective labour agreements entered into by both sides of industry, to any person who is employed, even temporarily, within their territory, no matter in which country the employer is established; nor does Community law prohibit Member States from enforcing those rules by appropriate means.'

This language is repeated almost verbatim in recital 8 of the Preamble of the proposed Directive.[4] The judgment of the Court reflects the French labour law experience of reliance on compulsory adherence to collective agreements by all employers. This is accomplished through formal procedures such as administrative extension of their legal effect beyond the parties to them, or by doctrines precluding individual contracts derogating from collectively agreed standards. This reliance on compulsory effects is a reflection of the low level of unionisation and employer resistance to union recognition. Hence, the proposed Directive had provided:[5]

'Member States *shall see to it* that, whatever the law applicable to the employment relationship, the undertaking does not deprive the worker of the terms and conditions of employment which apply for work of the same character at the place where the work is temporarily carried out, provided that (a) they are laid down by laws, regulations and administrative provisions or collective agreements or arbitration awards, covering the whole of the occupation and industry concerned having an "erga omnes" effect and/or being made legally binding in the occupation or industry concerned . . .'

What is significant is that the proposed Directive seeks to go *beyond* the principle enunciated in *Rush Portuguesa.* It is not surprising that Member States could require persons employed on their territory to be subject to their *legislation.* It is not so common, however, for States to insist on the extension of *collective agreements* to all workers on their territory. There was nothing in the Court's decision which made it *mandatory* for Member States to extend collective agreements; the Court merely declared that nothing in EC law precluded them from doing so or from enforcing the rules in those agreements.

---

3   Case C-113/89: *Rush Portuguesa Lda v Office National d'Immigration* [1990] ECR I-1417, at 1445, paragraph 18.
4   COM (91) 230 final, SYN 346, Brussels, 1 August 1991.
5   Article 3(1).

BEYOND *RUSH PORTUGUESA*: MANDATORY WORKING CONDITIONS FOR MIGRANT WORKERS

The potential of this proposed Directive, therefore, is that it goes beyond the principle in *Rush*. The first draft of the proposed Directive prescribed in Article 3(1) that:[6]

> 'Member States *shall see to it* that, *whatever the law applicable* to the employment relationship, the undertaking does not deprive the worker of the terms and conditions of employment which apply for work of the same character at the place where the work is temporarily carried out . . .'

National law is irrelevant, except where more favourable.[7] This is an *EC* guarantee of labour standards: it does not depend on *national* law. This Article does *not* determine the *national law* applicable to the contract, which will regulate the migrant worker's terms of employment. It may be the foreign law or the domestic law. It does not matter. What the proposed Directive *does* is to impose on the undertaking, '*whatever the law applicable to the employment relationship*' the obligation not to deprive the migrant worker of the terms laid down by law or collective agreements.

It is important to appreciate that this EC rule does not depend on either the law of the home or the host country. If the migrant worker is governed by the law of his *home* country, not that where he is working, s/he is *still* entitled to a guarantee of terms not less favourable than those of laws and collective agreements applicable in the host country. But even if the law applicable to the worker *is* that of the *host* country, *that law may not guarantee him the conditions laid down in collective agreements*. It is *EC law* which now provides that guarantee.

In this sense, the proposed Directive is revolutionary. It *prescribes* collectively agreed standards, apparently even in circumstances where the worker might not normally be covered by collectively agreed standards.

THE REVISED DRAFT DIRECTIVE

The problem with the first draft of the proposed Directive was that it too consciously reflected the French labour law tradition of extension of legally binding agreements. European labour law, however, must accommodate the labour law traditions of other Member States. The Explanatory Memorandum to the amended proposal explains the need 'to clarify the original text by deleting the term "erga omnes" which is unknown in some Member States'.[8] Such agreements are not to be found in Germany where regional bargaining predominates, and are thought to be contrary to the Italian constitution. Hence the proposed Directive, as amended, stipulates as mandatory labour standards applicable to

---

6   COM (91) 230 final, SYN 346, Brussels, 1 August 1991.
7   The law applicable, whether of the home or host country, remains in effect. Article 3(3) 'does not prevent application of terms and conditions of employment provided for by the law applicable which are more favourable to workers'.
8   Amended proposal for a Council Directive concerning the posting of workers in the framework of the provision of services (presented by the Commission pursuant to Article 149(3) of the EEC Treaty), dated 10 May 1993. OJ C187 of 9 July 1993.

migrant workers coming from another country, collective agreements:[9]

> 'which must be observed by all undertakings in the geographical area and in the profession or industry concerned. In the absence thereof, Member States may include those collective agreements or awards which are generally applicable in the area or in the profession or industry in question . . .'

The devil is in the small print. The proposed amended Directive contains a contradiction. It first provides that the relevant collective agreements are those:[10]

> 'observed by *all* undertakings in the geographical area and in the profession or industry concerned'.[11]

It goes on to provide that, in the *absence* of agreements observed by *all* undertakings:

> 'Member States *may* include those collective agreements or awards which are generally applicable in the area or in the profession or industry in question . . .'

Mandatory collective agreements?

The question is whether Member States are *obliged* to include the latter agreements among the standards imposed on undertakings employing posted workers. Or merely, as put by Explanatory Memorandum:

> 'to *allow* Member States, in the absence of the abovementioned collective agreements (or awards), to include those which are complied with . . .'

Although the word '*may*' would seem to preclude an obligation to observe generally applicable collective agreements, there are arguments that the Member States are so obliged.

First, the result of leaving such inclusion to the discretion of Member States could be that *no* collectively agreed standards are applied to such undertakings (though laws, regulations and administrative provisions would be); no agreements are observed by *all* undertakings, and generally applicable agreements (eg those observed by the vast majority) are not included.

If so, Article 3(4) would have no effect. The collectively agreed standards specified there would not benefit posted workers. Article 3(1) would be negated:

> 'Member States *shall see to it* that . . . the undertaking does not deprive the worker of the terms and conditions of employment which apply for work of the same character at the place where the work is temporarily carried out . . .'

If Member States were permitted to choose *not* to include otherwise generally applicable agreements, the proviso that follows could exclude any collectively agreed standards, in the absence of agreements applicable to *all* undertakings.

Secondly, the origins of this provision lie in an Amendment (No 33) proposed by the European Parliament. This did *not* make it optional for Member States to include collective agreements among the relevant standards required to be observed. It simply *added* to the *mandatory* list of collective agreements covering (as then drafted) 'the whole of the occupation and industry concerned having an

9   Ibid, Article 3(1)(a) and (4).
10   Article 3(4).
11   In which case *all* workers presumably benefit. The proposed Directive does not really add anything by imposing mandatory standards which, to apply, must *already* be observed by all undertakings.

erga omnes effect and/or being made legally binding in the occupation or industry concerned' those:

'being customary locally and not representing discrimination against undertakings established in other countries.'

The draft of the proposed Directive does *not* make it so clearly *mandatory* for Member States to extend the effect of 'generally applicable' agreements to the undertakings.

Thirdly, the apparent possibility not to make agreements mandatory for posted workers could be read as covering the situation where there are no generally applicable agreements. Then Member States may not include such agreements. But where there *are*, Member States may not refuse to make such provision. Otherwise posted workers would be left with no protection even where relevant standards have been designated by the Directive. This may not be the most elegant way of expressing this, but elegant drafting is not the Commission's strong point.[12]

Finally, Article 4(3) provides:

'Member States shall ensure that official information on the collective agreements which are generally applicable within the meaning of Article 3(4) is published by a competent authority and readily available to the undertakings referred to in Article 2. Failing such information, the undertaking in question shall not be bound by the abovementioned collective agreements.'

This refers only to 'generally applicable agreements', not those observed by all undertakings. This requirement seems to be mandatory. There is no indication that it depends on whether the Member State *chooses* to include these agreements among the standards imposed on undertakings employing posted workers.[13] Once the competent authority has collected and published the information, the Member State is obliged to include these agreements among the standards mandatory for posted workers.

What are the consequences of the ambiguous status of 'generally applicable' agreements? If the Directive stops short of the mandatory extension of generally applicable agreements, it allows *some* Member States to insist on adherence to generally applicable agreements, but also allows *others* to undermine those standards by allowing foreign enterprises not to adhere to them and compete with home enterprises. There are powerful incentives on home employers to prevent unfair competition.

However, it is important to remember that the proposed Directive is not exclusively about freedom of *services*; it is about the posting of *workers* in that framework. Article 1 changed the scope of the Directive. In the first draft it applied to:

'. . . undertakings . . . which exercise their activities in the framework of the provision of services . . .'

---

12   This follows the example of Council Directive 91/533/EEC of 14 October 1991 on an employer's obligation to inform employees of the conditions applicable to the contract or employment relationship, OJ L288/32 of 18.10.1991. As there, the provision that written information is to be given to employees on collective agreements 'where appropriate' (Article 2(2)(j)) is not to be read as optional, but mandatory *where such agreements exist*.

13   Otherwise, it would have been easy to begin: 'Where the Member State includes collective agreements which are generally applicable within the meaning of Article 3(4), it shall ensure that official information on these agreements is published . . .'

In the second draft, it applied to:

> '. . . employment relationships carried out in the framework of the provision of services . . .'

This change of emphasis implies that the scope of the Directive is aimed at employment relationships, not freedom of enterprises to provide services.

Some substance is required for the injunction of Article 3(1), that 'Member States *shall see to it* that . . . the undertaking does not deprive the worker of the (relevant) terms and conditions of employment'. Member States cannot have been intended to be allowed to eviscerate the Directive by, in the absence of collective agreements applicable to all undertakings, declining to extend the scope of generally applicable agreements to posted workers. The lack of clarity in this provision could be fatal to the impact of the Directive.

Of course it does raise delicate problems. Formally, a *requirement* that generally applicable agreements be made erga omnes would encounter difficulty – even if they were limited to geographical areas. As yet, the requirement is *only* that such agreements be made mandatory for *posted* workers. Once this is done, the further issue may be addressed of whether other, non-posted workers, not covered by generally applicable agreements, should also be covered. This requires a closer look at what is meant by '*generally applicable agreements*'.

Generally applicable agreements

The word used is 'applicable', not 'complied with'. Does 'applicable' require actual compliance? This could be construed as *either* applicable in *practice,* ie complied with/observed; *or* applicable *formally,* ie covers the undertakings in general. The question is whether the intention was to reduce the strictness of the requirement that *all* enterprises observe, by allowing (a) for when only a few did not 'observe'; or (b) for when the agreements purport to cover the relevant undertakings generally, regardless of compliance.

The Explanatory Memorandum stated:

> '. . . by the great majority of national-level undertakings in the occupation or industry in question. The fact that an economically insignificant number of national-based undertakings do not observe the collective agreements (or awards) in question, would not necessarily impede their application to the undertaking referred to in Article 2 . . .'

The quantitative element implied by 'generally' is here interpreted in a double and potentially contradictory sense: the great majority of enterprises, *or* an economically significant number. The latter might not be the great majority, or even the majority at all, depending on the structure of the industry. What percentage constitutes great majority? What constitutes economic significance? Is it related to the factor mentioned in the following sentence of the new Article 3(4)?

> '. . . provided that their application to the undertaking referred to in Article 2 ensures equality of treatment on matters itemised under paragraph 1 point (b) between that undertaking and national-based undertakings being in a similar position.'

The Explanatory Memorandum elaborates:

> '. . . A key factor will be the extent to which those undertakings are real potential competitors relative to undertakings referred to in Article 2. The term "national-based undertakings being in a similar position" should be construed as enterprises

established in the Member State concerned, which undertake similar activities or operations and are equivalent in volume or size.'

On this reading, the collective agreements to be relevant need only be generally applicable to undertakings in a similar position, regardless of numbers or economic significance, so as to preclude discrimination.

To summarise: the objective is to eliminate competition on labour conditions. The instrument is to establish relevant standards applicable to all those competing for a contract. The relevant measure establishing the standard is a collective agreement observed by all undertakings in the area in the profession or industry concerned. In the absence of such agreements, Member States *may* provide for undertakings to comply with agreements generally applicable in the area or profession or industry, so as to ensure equality of treatment (equal competition) between foreign and national-based undertakings in a similar position.

It is unclear whether Member States may refuse to make such provision. Such a reading would leave posted workers with no protection even where relevant standards have been designated by the Directive. The apparent facility not to make provision may be read as covering the situation where there are no generally applicable agreements. Where Member States do designate agreements applicable to contractors generally, they will be relevant agreements to be enforced through the Directive. This is the case whatever the law applicable to the worker's employment.

One-month qualification period: uncertainty

The importance of invoking collective agreements as the EU labour standard for posted workers is highlighted by the original draft's one-month qualification period for entitlement to pay and holidays under local conditions. This has given rise to some of the toughest negotiating over the proposed Directive. The Explanatory Memorandum to the second draft conceded a reduction from three months to one month at the request of Parliament. But it justified one month on grounds of flexibility, and as being in line with Article 4(3) of Council Directive 91/533/EEC of 14 October 1991 on the employer's obligation to inform workers.[14]

That provision refers to posted workers and their right to information in writing about certain working conditions related to that posting, such as its duration and any special conditions. However, it does not deny any *entitlements* under working conditions prevailing in the country to which they are posted. It only excludes them from the right to be *informed* in writing of certain conditions related to their posting: its duration, special payments, which currency, repatriation. It does not seem to follow from the exclusion of the right to be *informed* that they should be excluded from *substantive* rights as well.

What is the consequence of this exclusion? The proposed Directive does *not* apply to these workers as regards holidays and pay, though it *does* as regards other terms specified (hours, conditions of hiring out by temporary employment businesses, health and safety, pregnancy protection, equality). The result is that these workers are thrown back on conflict of laws rules.

Which law applies to their contract? The position is one of great uncertainty.

---

14 Council Directive 91/533/EEC of 14 October 1991 on an employer's obligation to inform employees of the conditions applicable to the contract or employment relationship, OJ L288/32 of 18.10.1991.

It was described in the Explanatory Memorandum to the first draft of the proposed Directive. It depends on Articles 6 and 7 of the Brussels Convention of 1980.[15] One of the justifications for the Directive was the need for legal *certainty*. The *non*-applicability of the proposed Directive does not produce certainty. It does *not* mean that the standards specified do *not* apply to those workers. Their position is simply uncertain.

Indeed, the exclusion of workers of less than one month could be said to have made the situation even more uncertain. Article 7 of the Brussels Convention provides for the application of *mandatory* rules of the law of the forum State and of other countries with which the situation has a close connection. While it is unclear what are mandatory rules, they might include rules providing guarantees also to workers employed for less than one month.

In sum: the exclusion of workers posted for less than one month means their position depends on the Brussels Convention rules. It does not mean they do not benefit from the standards stipulated by the proposed Directive, through the Brussels Convention rules, not the proposed Directive. These may entitle them to the Directive's proposed standards. The position is unclear. Indeed, under the Brussels rules, the proposed Directive makes their position much more uncertain than it was before.

CURRENT DEBATES AND FURTHER DRAFTS

The potential revealed by earlier drafts has been rendered even more complex and problematic by later drafts informally discussed in the Council of Ministers under successive Presidencies. The principal change appears to allow more flexibility in what the Directive covers in a number of respects. First and foremost, regarding the labour standards applicable, current drafts provide different labour standards for different *activities/sectors* in which posted workers may be engaged. It makes much more difficult and complex the application of collective agreements to posted workers.[16] The most important issue, again, is that of which labour standards are applicable and, in particular, what is the role of collective agreements.

The labour standards for posted workers were specified by the second draft, of 10 May 1993, as collective agreements, as well as laws, regulations and administrative provisions. In subsequent drafts, this second draft has suffered two major changes. First, relevant collective agreements as prescribed EU labour standards are restricted to the activities listed in an Annex (mainly the construction industry); secondly, the relevant collective agreements are defined in a very complex fashion. As a result, it is not clear which collective agreements are relevant, or whether they are always obligatory standards for posted workers in the Member States.

In the subsequent draft, the relevant standards are those:[17]

'laid down:
– by laws, regulations and administrative provisions, and/or

---

15 Explanatory Memorandum, pp 11–12.
16 Specifically, the current drafts try to limit the role of collective agreements to activities/sectors specified in an Annex; there is an attempt to limit the application of labour standards to workers who have worked beyond a specified time threshold; and to apply different standards to different working conditions.
17 Article 3(1)) (my translation from the French text).

– by collective agreements or arbitration awards declared to be of general application within the meaning of paragraph 4 to the extent that they concern the
activities listed in the Annex . . .'

It appears that for activities *not* listed in the Annex, the labour standards specified
are *only* those specified in the first indent: 'laws, regulations and administrative
provisions'. The principle of *Rush Portuguesa* appears to be safeguarded by an
Article 3(6) *allowing* Member States to apply collective agreements to other
activities. But the proposed Directive's revolutionary extension of the principle by
mandating collective agreements is confined to the activities listed in the Annex.[18]

Which collective agreements are specified as labour standards for the activities
listed in the Annex? Article 3(1) specifies 'collective agreements or arbitration
awards declared to be of general application within the meaning of paragraph
4'. Article 3(4) specifies, in order of priority:[19]

(i) 'collective agreements or arbitral awards declared to be of general application';
(ii) in the absence of a system of declaration of general application, Member
States '*may take as a threshold*'
  – agreements having a general effect, and/or
  – agreements agreed by most representative social partners and widely
applied throughout the national territory.

Beginning with the standard having first priority, 'collective agreements or arbitral awards declared to be of general application', there are two approaches which
can make sense of this provision. The first approach is that it does *not* imply a *formal* system of declaration of general application of collective agreements. The
standards required are agreements. Article 3(4) defines these agreements as:[20]

'must be *observed* by all the enterprises belonging to the sector or to the occupation
concerned and falling within the field of territorial application of these (agreements).'

This may be contrasted with an amendment which sought to define them as those
'which are legally enforceable and binding'. This latter amendment regards collective agreements as civil law contracts, a relatively narrow interpretation.

The argument is that the term '*observed*' means the agreement is an instrument with *varying legal* effects in different national legal contexts, in both their
public and labour law dimensions. For example, that it may be incorporated
into individual contracts of employment in practice, extended by administrative order, inderogable, and so on. The conditions of detached workers must be
those in agreements so observed.

The second approach *assumes* a *formal* system of declaration of general application of collective agreements. The problem is that if an agreement is already
formally declared of general application and respected by all enterprises, the
proposed Directive is irrelevant; it does not add anything by making it a
mandatory standard for posted workers. Following the logic of *this* argument,
the only way the proposed draft of the Directive can make sense is if it *requires*
the system of formal declaration of general application to be used. Agreements,
where they exist, must be declared of general application as regards (at least)

---

18 Unless collective agreements can be fitted under 'laws, regulations and administrative provisions' – a point to be discussed later.
19 My translation from the French text.
20 Ditto.

posted workers. That this interpretation is at least arguable or foreseeable is evidenced by the proposed Declaration 5.2 of the Council and Commission on Article 3 of this particular draft:[1]

'Article 3 does not imply any obligation on Member States to extend declarations of general applicability, as regards their content and the field of application.'

Turning to the standard having second priority,[2] where a system of declaration of general application of collective agreements does not exist, the two possibilities above are not available: there are no generally applicable agreements. There are two issues which must then be addressed. First, are the Member States free to ignore collective agreements 'in the absence of a system of declaration of general application'? Secondly, if they must, or choose to, adopt collective agreements as the standard, which collective agreements are the relevant labour standards for detached workers?

The word '*may*' might seem to allow Member States to ignore collective agreements. There are various arguments that they cannot: that where there are agreements, Member States are *obliged* to regard them as labour standards for detached workers.

First, if they could ignore them, the result could be that *no* collectively agreed standards are applied (though laws, regulations and administrative provisions would be) 'in the absence of a system of declaration of general application'. Article 3(4) would have no effect. Also, Article 3(1) would be negated:

'Member States *shall see to it* that, whatever the law applicable to the employment relationship, the undertaking ... does not deprive the worker of the terms and conditions of employment which apply for work of the same character at the place where the work is carried out ...'

If Member States could choose *not* to include any collectively agreed standards, there would be no need for a second priority.

Secondly, where there are *no* relevant collective agreements, the Member States may not use such agreements as standards. But, as argued earlier, where there *are*, Member States may not refuse to use them. Otherwise posted workers would be left with no protection even where relevant standards have been designated by the Directive. As noted above, Directive 91/533 similarly provides that information is to be given on collective agreements 'where appropriate'. This is not to be read as optional, but mandatory *where such agreements exist.*

Thirdly, the last paragraphs of Article 3(4) stipulate equal treatment between enterprises covered by the relevant collective agreements and the enterprises employing the posted workers. This insistence on equality would be absurd if Member States could refuse to apply the agreements only to the enterprises employing the posted workers.

Finally, again as argued earlier, Article 4(3) provides:

'Member States shall take the necessary measures to ensure that information regarding the terms of employment and working conditions provided in Article 3 are readily accessible.'

---

1   My translation from the French text.
2   'ii. in the absence of a system of declaration of general application, Member States "*may* take as a threshold"
   – agreements having a general effect, and/or
   – agreements agreed by most representative social partners and widely applied throughout the national territory.'

This includes information on the collective agreements which are referred to in Article 3. There is no indication that the obligation depends on whether the Member State *chooses* to include these agreements among the standards imposed on undertakings employing posted workers. Otherwise, it would have been easy to provide:

> 'Where there are agreements declared to be generally applicable or, in the absence of a system of declaration of generally applicable agreements, where the Member State adopts collective agreements within the meaning of Article 3(4), it shall ensure that information on these agreements is generally accessible . . .'

It is arguable that this information should be published by a competent authority and be accessible to those concerned: workers, unions and undertakings. Failing such information, the Member State may be liable to compensate for damage caused by its failure.

To summarise the position on labour standards applicable to posted workers under this draft. Collective agreements are relevant only to the Annex activities.[3] Priority is given to agreements having some legal consequences, or a formal system of declaring agreements to be of general application.[4] If no such system exists,[5] it is arguable that Member States are obliged to apply agreements having a general effect on all similar enterprises (indent 1), or agreements negotiated by the most representative social partners and widely applied (indent 2), being agreements which are equally applicable to similar enterprises.[6]

CONCLUSION: EUROPEAN LABOUR LAW AS APPLIED COMPARATIVE LABOUR LAW

The current proposed draft Directive presents singular features. First, laws and collective agreements may be deemed to be alternative standards, not cumulative. Secondly, collective agreements are specified as relevant to activities/sectors (mainly construction) listed in the Annex. There may be required a formal system of declaration of the general application of agreements with legal effects. In the absence thereof, it may be only optional for Member States to apply collective agreements having general effects or application.

A major question of comparative labour law arises out of this proposal.[7] Can some collective agreements fall within the enumerated categories of 'laws, regulations and administrative provisions' applicable to all other activities? And, if so, do such collective agreements apply generally (ie also to non-Annex activities/sectors)?

The answer to this question may be illuminated by a closer look at what the proposed Directive prescribes as the labour standards for activities/sectors listed in the Annex. These standards were, first, *collective agreements* 'declared of general application'.[8] This means either the *presence* of a *formal* system of declaration of

---

3   Article 3(1), indent 2.
4   Article 3(4), paragraph 1.
5   Article 3(4), paragraph 2.
6   Article 3(4), paragraph 3.
7   This issue was first elaborated at a meeting of trade union officials from Member State federations of building workers, held by the European Federation of Building and Wood Workers, in Brussels, on 11 January 1995.
8   Article 3(4).

general application of collective agreements; or the *absence* of a *formal* system of declaration of general application of collective agreements, *but* agreements are '*observed* by all the enterprises belonging to the sector or to the occupation concerned and falling within the field of territorial application of these (agreements)'. Secondly, *collective agreements* having a general effect or concluded by most representative social partners and widely applied; and arguably to be made mandatory. Are *these types* of collective agreements distinguishable from 'laws, regulations and administrative provisions'?

Collective agreements relevant to the Annex activities/sectors turn out to be, first, those declared to be of general application. This may be either formally, by some legislative procedure – hence indistinguishable from 'laws, regulations and administrative provisions'; or as de facto respected generally – ie having the same *effects* as 'laws, regulations and administrative provisions'. Secondly, the agreements are of general effect or most representative and widely applied – ie again having the same *effects* as 'laws, regulations and administrative provisions'.

The distinction becomes very difficult to make in practice between, on the one hand, those collective agreements designated for Annex activities, given the qualities attributed to them by the draft Directive, and, on the other, 'laws, regulations and administrative provisions' applicable to all other activities/sectors. '(L)aws, regulations and administrative provisions' applicable to all activities will often *include* the types of *collective agreements* applied by the proposed draft Directive to Annex activities.

The proposed draft Directive is caught in a circular argument. First, it proposes an apparent fragmentation of standards as between Annex and non-Annex activities. But then the standards applicable to non-Annex activities ('laws, regulations and administrative provisions') turn out to be remarkably similar in their effects, and perhaps even formally, to those applicable to Annex activities ('collective agreements') because of the specific characteristics of these agreements. The proposed draft Directive is thus a reminder of the conceptual ambiguities of collective agreements as regulations: are they laws or agreements? Where they are equivalent to regulations, they should be applied under the proposed draft Directive *both* to Annex activities, and to all others.

The proposed draft Directive's collective agreements are those most like laws, and are often formally declared to have the status of laws. The Commission tries to operationally distinguish them from laws. It may be a mistake to try to apply different standards ('collective agreements' and 'laws, regulations and administrative provisions') to different activities. The European Court in *Rush Portuguesa* was wiser: it declared *both* agreements and laws to apply, and avoided any operational need to distinguish between them.[9]

9　The draft should support labour standards which apply to all activities, not just those in the Annex, and include collective agreements more clearly and widely defined. An example of such a proposal was one amendment proposed to Article 3(4). Relevant agreements are confined to the Annex activities(Article 3(1), indent 2). But relevant agreements are defined more simply as those agreements which cover the territory where the services are being performed (by the detached workers); and which must be applied by all enterprises, national and foreign, which can provide the same service. There is no need for a formal system of declaration of general application or legal effects of agreements. And agreements are not an optional standard for Member States. Another example is inspired by Article 3(5) of the proposed draft. This makes it optional for the host Member State to require that temporary workers from enterprises in other Member States benefit from conditions which are applicable to *temporary* workers in the host Member State. The labour standard specified is very simple. The same conditions apply regardless of legal source: law, agreement, or whatever.

Title III

Twin Pillars of European Labour Law

Part VIII

Individual Employment in European Labour Law

Chapter 28

Legal Concepts and New Forms of Work

INTRODUCTION

A specific quality of European labour law derives from the emergence of two pillars.[1] These are, first, a typology of individual employment relationships regulated by EC law; and, secondly, the social dialogue and collective agreements as definitive features in the EC regulation of labour.

These are called pillars because they constitute the poles of attraction around which the future European labour law will crystallise. Formulation of this law will involve techniques increasingly linked to collective bargaining and social dialogue. Substantive content will reflect the exigencies of protection of a fragmented workforce requiring a regulatory framework appropriate to its particular circumstances. The challenge for European labour law will be to find a structure which reconciles general collective regulation with diversified categories of individual employment.

This chapter begins with an account of how fragmentation of the workforce has become a central concern of European labour law in the past two decades. There follows an elaboration of the emerging typology of workers. This is explored through the substantive law of the EC on different categories of workers, especially part-time workers, where a European strategy through regulation and collective bargaining at national and EU level is most developed, but also temporary workers, workers without a contract but with an 'employment relationship', workers with long hours and so on. Finally, I speculate on how and why this feature is emerging as a pillar of EU labour law. Recently, there may be discerned a new, and more radical, approach to the issue, which has much more profound implications, including, at one level, citizenship, and, at another, reconciliation of work and family life.[2]

THE LEGAL CONCEPT OF WORKERS AND EMPLOYEES[3]

The modern legal concept of work and workers is shaped by the ideology of classical liberalism. As put by Alan Fox:[4]

'To insist that a man's labour is his own is not only to say that it is his to alienate in a wage contract; it is also to say that his labour and its productivity is something for

---

1 Proposed in B Bercusson 'Maastricht: A fundamental change in European labour law' (1992) 23 *Industrial Relations Journal* 177.
2 This latter aspect is dealt with in more detail in Chapter 15.
3 The following section is derived from R Benedictus and B Bercusson *Labour Law: Cases and Materials*, Sweet & Maxwell, London 1987, pp 6–9.
4 A Fox *Beyond Contract: Work, Power and Trust Relations* (1974), pp 164–7.

which he owes no debt to civil society – a further perspective on the separation of economics and ethics. The traditional view that property and labour were *social* functions with *social* obligations was thereby undermined' (my italics).

The failure to appreciate the social function of labour, for example housewives' domestic labour,[5] and the focus solely on its quality as a market commodity have implications for relations at work:[6]

> 'as with all market relationships, the interests of buyers and sellers are antagonistic ... Issues of control inevitably pervade this relationship.'

While, therefore, different *legal* formulations of the concept of the worker are possible, the labour law of the States of Western Europe starts with the relationship of employment being characterised as a contract of service, with a clear ideological foundation.[7]

> '(As regards the definition of the "employee" and the "contract of employment") There is ... a convergence in modern legal doctrine towards the recognition of *submission* of the employee to the employer's command or control as to the time, place and manner in which the work is to be done as a necessary criterion' (my italics).

The emphasis on subordination in *labour* law may be contrasted with different approaches in other legal contexts. The worker as such may be an object of taxation, a subject of social security, protected by legislation on health and safety, a member of a trade union – as well as being related to the employer through a contract of service. The legal concept of the worker may vary according to the policy pursued by the legal rules affecting the workers.[8] For example, in the British law on unemployment benefit, *income* is a more important criterion than subordination.[9]

Laws affecting workers, despite the very different contexts in which they function, and the diverse policies pursued, frequently adopt the contract of employment and subordination as the criteria defining the objects of their attention. Increasingly, however, the incongruence of the contract of employment with the objectives of the law in question requires reconsideration of the ideological element of subordination.[10]

---

5   O Clarke and A I Ogus 'What is a wife worth?' (1978) 5 *British Journal of Law and Society* 1.
6   R Hyman 'Trade unions, control and resistance', in G Esland and G Salaman (eds) *The Politics of Work and Occupations* (1980), pp 303–7.
7   H Barbagelata 'Categories of workers and labour contracts', in R Blanpain (ed) *Comparative Labour Law and Industrial Relations in Industrialised Market Economies*, 4th edition (1990), p 37.
8   For example, the concept of the worker in the law of vicarious responsibility (liability for the acts of third parties) has been characterised as follows: '... the classification of a particular factual situation must always be considered in the light of the purpose for which the classification is being made. Thus in a case of vicarious liability the enquiry is always whether one person is legally responsible for the acts of another. The relationship between the parties may therefore be classified as a master–servant relationship *for this purpose* even though the relationship might not be so classified for other purposes ... [This] approach has the merit of emphasising that legal concepts are tools to be used intelligently for the purpose in hand and not to be applied blindly to a variety of uses': P S Atiyah *Vicarious Liability in the Law of Torts* (1967), pp 31–3.
9   A I Ogus and E Barendt *The Law of Social Security* (1978), pp 82–3.
10   R W Rideout *Principles of Labour Law*, 3rd edition (1979), p 11: 'It may be that the next stage should be to say that certain elements pointing to or from service should be weighted according to the purpose for which the distinction is required. So, if vicarious liability is the issue, control should be of primary importance, whilst if qualification to receive industrial injury benefits is to be decided the main consideration should be the worker's lack of capital and his economic dependence on the payment he receives from a regular employer for his work'.

NEW FORMS OF WORK

The use of labour law tools to analyse the concept of the 'worker' has been challenged as never before by the disintegration of the standard employment relationship and the emergence of new forms of work.[11] It is necessary to determine which elements of the contract of employment should be emphasised for different social purposes.

The debate has been influenced less by labour lawyers than by economists and industrial relations experts. In the labour law literature, the issue of 'new forms of employment' is situated in the context of a debate in which the focus of attention tends to be on the distinction between *typical* and *atypical* employment. The distinction is between a model of a standard employment contract, and new forms involving part-time, casual, fixed-term, self-employed, independent or home workers, to name but a few. The literature focuses on the implications for labour and social security law of legal relations which deviate from the standard model.

The industrial relations literature places the issue of new forms of employment in the context of the debate over *labour market flexibility*. Specifically, 'new forms of employment' is included in that part of employers' strategies on flexibility concerned with external or numerical flexibility. The employer changes the numbers and types of employees' relationships to the enterprise in order to achieve the desired flexibility of response to changing market conditions. Another part of the same strategy is internal or functional or task flexibility, where existing employees are required to change their jobs at the workplace where necessary to meet market demands. Strategies on new forms of employment cannot be considered without also considering strategies on task flexibility.

In the economic literature, 'new forms of employment' is part of the more general debate on *segmentation of the labour market*. This examines broad cleavages in the workforce: between large employers and small employers, unionised and non-unionised workers, firms using advanced technology and firms using low technology, low-paying and high-paying sectors, and so on. These cleavages do not correspond to the 'typical/atypical' employment distinction, nor to the contours of the flexibility debate. As with the other disciplines, economists see new forms of employment as only one component of the changing labour force.

---

11   U Mückenberger and S Deakin 'From deregulation to a European floor of rights: Labour law, flexibilisation and the European single market' (1989) 3 *Zeitschrift für ausländisches und internationales Arbeits- und Sozialrecht* 153. See also U Mückenberger 'Non standard forms of work and the role of changes in labour and social security regulation' (1989) *International Journal of the Sociology of Law* 381. Yota Kravaritou elaborates two basic legal models of employment: (1) the classic job with its traditional employment contract, and (2) work under new forms of great variety, among which she distinguishes (a) those jobs which may be termed employment without an employer – the status of fake self-employed, subcontracting, possibly homeworking and teleworking, clandestine work in the grey or black economy – and (b) new forms under a non-permanent employment contract, notably the fixed-term contract, the temporary employment contract, the employment-training contract: 'it is in this type of contract that one finds the greatest lack of traditional guarantees, and this is the place where "new" rights and minimum standards are beginning to be defined – although this has not yet happened in all countries'. Y Kravaritou *New Forms of Work: labour law and social security aspects in the European Community*, European Foundation for the Improvement of Living and Working Conditions: Office for Official Publications of the EC, Luxembourg 1988.

Each of these formulations by different disciplines includes the issue of 'new forms of employment' as a component of a broader problematic. The question as to strategies of the actors on new forms of employment will be answered differently depending on whether the legislator addresses the problem as one of typical/atypical employment, labour market flexibility, or labour market segmentation.[12]

Legal mechanisms

Law offers a number of specific mechanisms and strategies on new forms of employment. For example, legislation providing protection based on continuity or duration of employment, or the number of employees in the establishment, operates to exclude from legal protection (or rather, did so until recently in the UK) part-timers or temporary workers, or those in small establishments. Other workers are excluded through legal doctrine distinguishing employees from the self-employed.

Other legal mechanisms are more *general*. For example, France and Italy share the legacy of a *system* of law, in the form of legal codes, which provide a legal context into which labour law protection of new forms of employment has to be inserted. This creates problems for systems which require the logic and symmetry of *principles*, unlike other systems which are less comprehensive and systematic (the British common law). Certain types of new forms of employment in France and Italy – for example, solidarity contracts and training contracts – are easier to protect, through application of established principles of the labour law framework. In contrast, the British Youth Training Scheme was brought into existence without considering its relation to the wider labour law system. This led to great difficulties in defining the rights of young workers under these training schemes as compared with similar workers outside the schemes.

In German labour law too there are legal principles of equality and generality to which certain actors' strategies for dealing with new forms of employment will be attracted. There has developed an important role for statutory law which cannot be derogated from by the contracting parties. On the other hand, the contract of employment as the starting point of much labour law in a market economy provides a pole of attraction for other actors' strategies. These opposing poles of attraction can be seen in different strategies adopted by the same actor: judges, for instance. Broadly speaking, the strategy of a minority is to favour statutory rights, to 'normalise' the status of employment in the sense of integrating all workers into the standards of the labour law system. This has clear implications for new forms of employment. On the contrary, the majority of judges are keenly aware of the tension between contract and statute. It resolves this tension by distinguishing issues concerned with hiring and dismissal – where freedom of contract is more important than equal treatment – from issues arising within an existing employment relationship – where equality

---

12   For further argumentation on this point, see B Bercusson 'Legal, Political and Industrial Relations Strategies Regarding New Forms of Employment', in *L'Evolution des Formes d'Emploi*, Actes du colloque de la revue 'Travail et Emploi', 3–4 Novembre 1988. See also C Hakim 'Core and periphery in employers' workforce strategies: evidence from the 1987 ELUS Survey', in (1990) 4 *Work, Employment and Society*, No 2, p 157.

is more important. This strategy sometimes comes into conflict with government strategies of deregulation.

The significance of this can be seen by comparing the British case, where there is no such general principle of equality. In Germany, unequal treatment of even two male workers in terms of wages, fringe benefits, promotion, etc is prohibited as discrimination. This affects the issue of fragmentation, or new forms of employment, because in almost every form of atypical work one finds less favourable treatment of this kind. The principle of equality becomes an element in a strategy for dealing with new forms of employment. However, in Britain there is no such principle. Employers are free to treat workers differently (save on grounds of sex, race, etc). The strategy for dealing with new forms of employment cannot avail itself of a general equality principle.

Another legal strategy is evident in the debate in Italy, and to a lesser extent in France, over flexibility of sources of labour law. At first sight, the debate is concerned with the articulation between different levels of collective agreements, and between such agreements and legislation. To this extent, individual freedom of contract is less evident than is the case in Germany. However, the element of normalisation, standardisation, equality is still the essence of the debate. The more devolution of terms and conditions of employment is permitted, from legislation down through levels of collective bargaining, the less standardisation results, down to the point where new forms of employment may (or may not) be permitted under workplace agreements.

Quite a different legal strategy looks to the relationship between the social security system and these new forms of employment. In Britain, one of the reasons for employers using new forms of employment is to avoid the burden of social security contributions payable for typical employees. In Scandinavia, however, the social security system is not generally based on the labour market, but is financed out of general taxation. Everybody is covered whether or not they are in the labour market. Similarly, most employment protection covers virtually everybody, through collective agreements covering the vast majority of the workforce which is unionised. In this way new forms of employment are in less danger of exploitation – and actors' strategies consequently change.

Industrial relations mechanisms

Collective agreements may protect only union members. Trade union movements organised on industrial, occupational, geographical or political lines may lead to different levels of protection for different groups depending on the strength and policy of the union organisations to which they are affiliated. The Scandinavian experience demonstrates the use of industrial relations strategies towards new forms of employment to avoid fragmentation. Nearly half the total workforce is employed on a typical contract, if by typical is meant full-time, indeterminate contracts. More than half the female workforce is on part-time and about 10% of the male workforce is on part-time; so about 25–30% of the total are on part-time contracts and another 10% is on fixed-term contracts.

However, the rate of unionisation is very high both for typical and so-called atypical workers. Traditionally, nearly everybody – almost 90% of workers – is in a union. This means that almost all workers are covered by collective agreements: the traditional source of labour law. Indeed, some studies indicate that generally it is well-qualified women, not the low-paid unskilled workers, who are part-time. Unskilled low-paid workers are in typical work – full time – because they need to be in order to earn enough money. The 'atypical' forms of employment are not a pathological condition of the labour market. Paradoxically, one finds rather a correlation between low pay and 'typical' employment. And not only from the point of view of low pay: the increase in employment opportunities also comes in the 'atypical' labour market, whereas the 'typical' labour market is shrinking.

Scandinavia presents us with a situation where one can easily identify the 'new forms of employment', because there are so many of them. But from the point of view of labour law they are not the subjects of a special strategy. They are covered by collective agreements as part of the unionised workforce. They are just workers who have particular hours or certain kinds of contracts. But the whole rest of the framework of labour law does not distinguish them in any way.

It is interesting that, for example, in Denmark during the 1950s there was a debate in the unions whether or not to open up to these new forms of employment, particularly part-time work. The initial attitude, particularly from the male-dominated unions, was that they would not accept it. This is still the attitude of some unions. But during the 1960s and 1970s the women-dominated unions started allowing it in their collective agreements. The trade union confederation stopped opposing it. The reason was that the unions had to choose between getting the part-time women as members, or watching an entire labour market develop outside the unions' control. If unions and collective agreements excluded part-time workers, and by law employers are bound by collective agreements, employers would be tempted to try to operate through a non-unionised part-time labour market. The unions would not take the risk of thus losing control.

Political mechanisms

In France, State/political regulation of the forms of employment is very strong. Each time in France there appears in large numbers a new form of employment, historically legislation appears to regulate it. In the 20th century, this was the case with domestic labour, then fixed term contracts, part-time work and casual labour. There is a strong tradition of State intervention in the labour market, a stronger role than is found in other areas of labour regulation, for example, wages, where collective agreements are primary. This regulatory intervention of the State has the function of rendering these new forms of employment socially acceptable. The intervention makes possible and legitimate the use of this form by employers, while affording at the same time a minimum protection. There is a search for an equilibrium.

In Britain, the current State/political strategy towards new forms of employment may be said to have gone even further: toward the provision of incentives towards fragmentation of the workforce, making it disadvantageous for the employer to employ workers in typical rather than atypical forms. A significant aspect of the British State/political strategy is that, on the face of it, the amount of formal legal intervention is very small. It is at the opposite end of the spectrum from France. The strategy towards new forms of employment is not through traditional labour law, but through political intervention in the labour market, using measures which do not necessarily assume the form of traditional labour legislation. This occurs in a variety of ways. For example, when the government decides to use public resources to fund the training of workers, or to help young people come into the labour market. Another example is when public sector work is compulsorily required to be put out to private tender, in the knowledge that certain forms of sub-contracted labour will be used (with pay and conditions below public sector standards). Similarly, when government contracts are made without the safeguards as to pay and conditions and union membership protection which had originated in the Fair Wages policy dating back to 1891.

At some point the question becomes: is the focus of State policy 'new forms of employment'? Or is it rather a policy concerned with employment promotion, labour market flexibility, or enterprise assistance? In each of these, 'new forms of employment' is but one element of a grander strategy. Employers and unions are likely to be aware, and often are involved in the development of these macro-economic strategies. The problem for labour lawyers is that their perspectives may not encompass these wider political visions. Constrained by their limited views of 'forms of employment', they adopt strategies which focus on the narrower issues of 'new forms of employment', using only the instruments of labour law and labour legislation. The result is contradictory when applied in the context of the wider State/political strategy.

NEW FORMS OF EMPLOYMENT IN THEIR CONJUNCTURAL CONTEXT

These different perspectives all relate the issue of atypical work to the enactment of legislation concerned with *termination* of employment.[13] The origins of this linkage lie in the economic crisis of the 1970s and 1980s, mass redundancies and restructuring leading to unemployment reaching new heights in Western Europe.[14] Earlier responses of the 1970s and 1980s aimed mainly at trying to force new forms of employment into old models, and tried to slow down, regulate or prevent *terminations*.[15] Analysis of the new forms of work aimed to

13 This is not a new phenomenon: the enactment of legislation concerned with termination of employment was designated some time ago by Kahn-Freund as the most noteworthy and important extension of regulatory legislation in the field of labour law: *Labour and the Law*, 3rd ed (1983), p 38.

14 As in the case of new forms of employment, there is an interesting point to be made about the concentration of labour law on the termination of employment as *the* issue, a focus which demonstrates something of the ideological constraints imposed by the concept of the contract of employment in the classical sense outlined above. The enactment of statutory provisions on unfair dismissal has resulted in an inordinate amount of attention being paid to and emphasis placed upon termination of work. Instead of being perceived as only one of a variety of solutions, and by far the least desirable in many ways, to problems of workers who are ill, incompetent, unco-operative, insubordinate, inefficient, etc, termination has become accepted as such a solution, subject only to occasional challenge. A different approach would question whether termination is the best solution to these problems. The industrial practice of the social partners provides examples of many other measures which can deal with sickness or injury, incompetence and misconduct much more efficiently than termination: B Bercusson 'Labour Law and the Public Interest: A Policy Approach', in Lord Wedderburn and W T Murphy (eds) *Labour Law and the Community: Perspectives for the 1980s*, Institute of Advanced Legal Studies, London 1982, p 179 at p 180. Also, B Bercusson 'Labour Law', in A Martin and P Archer (eds) *More Law Reform Now* (1983).

15 See 'Restructuring Labour in the Enterprise', (1986) 15 *Bulletin of Comparative Labour Relations* for a comparative survey.

develop some alternative model or classification of the individual employment relationship to replace the threatened standard contract of employment model – so far without much success.[16]

National labour laws later came to demonstrate quite different approaches to these same issues. First, there was a fundamental attack on the standard employment relationship through the regulation of working-time, mainly part-timers, temporary work, and various forms of 'atypical' work. Secondly, the response to recession and economic slowdown was less termination of employment than flexibility, mobility and retraining.

One of the key strategies for the avoidance of termination as a solution to the specific problems of economic recession has been reduction of working hours. This strategy was taken up by many national trade union movements, often with considerable success. It has been noted that 'the reduction of working time becomes the means of exchange for the flexibility demanded by employers'.[17] The outcome is the much remarked upon separation of working time from the operating time of workplaces.[18]

The strategy of reduction of hours and reorganisation of working time produces severe distortions in the standard employment relationship, which nonetheless remains in the legal form of the contract of employment. This can take two forms. First, the reduction of working time down to 35 hours a week or less renders any difference in employment protection with part-time workers working between 25–30 hours a week less defensible. Secondly, the variety of working time regimes resulting from attempts to increase operating time is remarkable. Complicated shift systems whereby employees work different numbers of days and hours in different weeks produced work patterns not so very different from the casual or temporary workers ostensibly 'atypical'.[19]

The focus on the concept of work takes two directions in European labour law. One is an attempt to formulate a new legal concept of worker/employee. A second is to focus attention on the issue of *working time*. The starting point is that workers with different work time schedules should not be a priori excluded from consideration when labour standards are in question. But that is not to say that all should a priori benefit from the *same* labour standards. It is probable that different working time schedules imply different needs and hence different standards may be applicable. What is important is that the legal category of 'employment' and the criterion of subordination should not be used as the

16 See the papers presented in the volume of the Actes du colloque de la revue 'Travail et Emploi', 3–4 Novembre 1988: *L'Evolution des Formes d'Emploi*, op cit. Also M Pedrazzoli (ed) *Lavoro subordinato e dintorni: comparazioni e prospettive*, Il Mulino, Bologna 1989. Compare G and J Rodgers (eds) *Precarious jobs in labour market regulation: The growth of atypical employment in Western Europe*, International Institute for Labour Studies/Free University of Brussels, Geneva 1989.

17 J Bastien 'Les syndicats européens face au temps de travail: le marché unique comme défi pour le reformulation de revendications syndicales' (1989) *Sociologie du Travail*, No 3, p 283 at p 295.

18 T Treu 'Introduction' to Chapter II, 'New Trends in Working Time Arrangements', in A Gladstone (ed) *Current Issues in Labour Relations: An International Perspective*, Walter de Gruyter, Berlin 1989, p 149 at pp 155–6.

19 See arrangements in the auto industry described in 'Seven-day 24-hour working at Rover' (UK), *European Industrial Relations Review*, No 201 (October 1990), p 11; 'Working time arrangements at BMW Regensburg' (Germany), *European Industrial Relations Review*, No 197 (June 1990), p 11; 'Creation of a third shift at Renault-Flins' (France), *European Industrial Relations Review*, No 196 (May 1990), p 5; 'Flexible working time referendum at General Motors' (Belgium), *European Industrial Relations Review*, No 188 (September 1989), p 4.

crude instrument for distinguishing among workers. The search for a solution by way of adoption of different criteria to define 'work' overlaps with the focus on working time. It would attend closely to differences in the *working time* schedules of all workers – employees or whatever – and formulate labour standards appropriate for different working time schedules.

These two directions are evident in a number of EU labour law instruments. The Council Directive on an employer's obligation to inform employees of the conditions applicable to the contract or employment relationship[20] is an attempt to extend the boundaries of labour law beyond the conventional contract of employment. The emerging EU labour law on part-time workers is an attempt to tackle the problem from the perspective of regulation of working time. The driving logic is one of employment policy and redistribution of working time. Finally, the Directive on health and safety of temporary workers is an illustration of an attempt to craft rules specifically for a particular category of workers. In examining these, an attempt is made to demonstrate how European labour law has addressed the fundamental issue of new forms of work and employment.

---

20   Council Directive 91/533/EEC of 14 October 1991, OJ L288/32 of 18.10.91.

Chapter 29

Contracts and Employment Relationships

INTRODUCTION

The concept of an 'employment relationship' distinct from a relationship founded on a contract of employment was already to be found in various pieces of EC legislation: the Acquired Rights Directive of 1977, the Directive on protection of employees in the event of insolvency of 1980, the 1989 Framework Directive on health and safety.[1] However, it was not until after the Community Charter of Fundamental Social Rights of 1989 that there was an initiative directed explicitly to this aspect of the problem of new forms of work.

On 8 January 1991, the Commission presented a proposal for a Council Directive 'on a form of proof of an employment relationship'.[2] In the accompanying Explanatory Memorandum, the Commission referred to the current situation which had 'encouraged the introduction and development of various forms of work, some of which are designed to meet the personal and family requirements of employees'.[3] However:[4]

'Certain long-standing forms of work, such as part-time or home working, have now been supplemented by such new forms as "part-time vertical work", ie work organised on a daily, weekly, monthly or annual basis, job-sharing, job-splitting, on-call work, work-training contracts and training schemes. The traditional growth in different forms of contract is also tending to be submerged by the growth in different forms of contract causing enterprises to change their employees' status to make them

---

1   The Acquired Rights Directive of 1977 referred to rights and obligations 'arising from a contract of employment or from an employment relationship': Article 3(1); also Article 4(2) which refers to where the 'contract of employment or the employment relationship is terminated'. The Directive on protection of employees in the event of insolvency of 1980 referred to 'employees' claims arising from contracts of employment or employment relationships' (Article 1(1)) (repeated in Articles 3(1), 3(2), and 4(2)). However, it goes on to say that the Directive 'is without prejudice to national law as regards the definition of the terms "employee" . . .' (Article 2(2)). Moreover, Article 1(2) allows Member States to 'exclude claims by certain categories of employee from the scope of this Directive, by virtue of the special nature of the employee's contract of employment or employment relationship . . .' An Annex to the Directive specifies who in various Member States is deemed to fall into a category of employees having a contract of employment or an employment relationship of a special nature. The 1989 Framework Directive on health and safety refers instead to 'workers', defined as 'any person employed by an employer, including trainees and apprentices but excluding domestic servants' (Article 3(a)).
2   COM (90) 563 final, Brussels, 8 January 1991.
3   Ibid, paragraph 3.
4   Ibid, paragraph 4.

426

self-employed or small-scale sub-contractors, and leading also to an erosion of the criteria defining the traditional status of an employee. In the same perspective, the introduction of new forms of distance work, such as telework, can equally contribute to the shift away from the conventional master–servant relationship.'

This proliferation of new forms of employment and its implications for traditional legal criteria of employment status were exacerbated by other developments noted by the Commission:[5]

'New production methods and the explosive development of the service industry have both played a part in making the labour market considerably more flexible, thus generating new possibilities for "black work" and other illicit practices the development of which, in the medium term, is likely to penalise workers as much as employees by distorting the rules of the game.

These developments, to which must be added the greater flexibility in the time reference frame (adaptation of working time or development of intermittent and maintenance work), have also tended to cloud the position of many workers, leading to confusion, uncertainty and instability. They tend, a fortiori for those workers without written proof of their working relationship, to make workers unaware of certain social and professional rights linked to this relationship.'

For guidance in seeking to combat the negative consequences of these developments in the labour market, the Commission looked to the experience in the Member States. It found that there were to be found formal requirements which made it easier for employment contracts and relationships to be identified. In continental legal systems, there was required a compulsory written employment contract establishing primarily *particular forms* of employment. On the other hand, in the United Kingdom and Ireland, employers were required to inform employees in general in writing of the main conditions of their employment contract.[6]

The Commission's objective was stated as follows:[7]

'The provision of a written declaration relating to a form of proof of an employment relationship is designed ... to clarify the legal position of employees who are not covered by a written employment contract or letter of appointment, and, in particular, to give them a better idea of when, where and for whom they are supposed to be working, and, more generally, to give them written proof of the essential elements of this relationship. This will do a lot towards improving the transparency of the Community labour market, while at the same time giving workers more security, a better idea of their rights and more mobility within the Community. Moreover, the more general provision of a written proof of the working relationship may constitute an element in the fight against "black work".'

The disparities in Member State regulation of the problem were said to 'constitute an obstacle to the effective functioning of the Common Market. It would appear essential ... to bring provisions into line to enable workers to obtain proof of their employment relationship'.[8] The appropriate legal basis for Community action was, therefore, Article 100 of the EEC Treaty, allowing for proposals for approximation of provisions having a direct effect on the functioning of the Common Market.

5   Ibid, paragraphs 5–6.
6   Ibid, Tables on pages 6–7 of the Explanatory Memorandum.
7   Ibid, paragraph 7.
8   Ibid, paragraph 9.

The EU intervention was therefore aimed at accomplishing a number of overlapping objectives. First, to combat the uncertainty as to the legal status of new forms of work, it was necessary to find some means of proving the existence of an employment relationship. Secondly, the uncertainty extended beyond the existence of the relationship itself into what the terms and conditions of the relationship were. Hence, there was a need for information about the terms of employment. Thirdly, it was necessary to ascertain which were the legal entitlements of the parties to the employment relationship. The Commission expressed the view that the proposal would contribute to ensuring the greater transparency of the labour market, and emphasised that it 'specifically concerns those workers who have neither a written contract of employment nor a letter of appointment explaining the elements of the employment relationship or referring to a collective agreement or any other easily accessible written document'.[9]

Of particular interest was the Explanatory Memorandum's declaration on the scope of the proposed Directive:[10]

'This Directive concerns any working relationship emanating from a contract of employment or any other legal form of recruitment (eg teleworking, training, employment-training, etc) which links a worker to an employer and which is subject to the legislation in force in a Member State. The concepts of employee and employer are based on Member States' national law.'

The breadth of coverage was diminished, however, by the exclusion of employment relationships where fewer than eight hours per week were worked on average. As regards those workers within its scope, however, the Explanatory Memorandum declared:[11]

'The proposal for a Directive has as its objective the creation of an instrument to make employers responsible for providing precise information on the nature and content of working relationships in the company.

To this end, it makes provision for an obligation to provide all workers covered by this Directive with a document setting out the details of the conditions and elements of their employment relationships with their employer. As such it does not relate to the rules of national law concerning the conclusion of employment contracts. The document in question is designed to be a declaratory element and written proof of the employment contract or relationship established in accordance with the national law of a Member State. The employer must sign the declaration and keep a copy.

The proposal also sets out the points for inclusion in the written declaration: standardisation of the main elements of the document should prevent any differences between national legislation in this field. Finally, the proposal provides for employees to be informed by their employers of any substantial changes affecting their working conditions as described in the written declaration . . .'

The initial proposal advanced by the Commission was the subject of amendment. The initial proposal defined its scope as applying 'to any employment relationship which is subject to the legislation in force in a Member State'. This might have been interpreted as applying only to those employment relationships recognised by national laws as contracts of employment. This possibility

9   Ibid, paragraph 2.
10 Ibid, paragraph 11.
11 Ibid, paragraphs 12–13.

was eliminated by the introduction in the final draft of the Directive of the crucial distinction between employees 'having a contract *or* employment relationship defined by the law in force in a Member State and/or governed by the law in force in a Member State'.[12]

The significance of the Directive for UK law is potentially great. Here, the focus is on those aspects of the Directive demonstrating the twin pillars of European labour law: individual employment, and the collective dimension.

SCOPE: WHO ARE 'WORKERS/EMPLOYEES'?

The first draft of the Directive defined its scope by stating that it applied to 'any employment relationship'. The final draft refined this, so that Article 1 of the Directive defines its scope as follows:

'1. This Directive shall apply to every paid employee having a contract or employment relationship defined by the law in force in a Member State and/or governed by the law in force in a Member State.'

So whereas the first draft's provision regarding 'any employment relationship' could have been interpreted as including, but limited to, employment contracts, the final Directive makes a clear distinction between contractual and other employment relationships – and includes *both* within the scope of the Directive.

The significance of this can be illustrated by comparing the equivalent provision in the UK legislation. The EPCA 1978 provided for written particulars of terms of employment to be given to the 'employee', defined as:[13]

'an individual who has entered into or works under (or, where the employment has ceased, worked under) a contract of employment.'

Instead of 'employee', defined in UK domestic law as a person having a contract of employment, the scope of the Directive includes also paid employees having an employment relationship. Emphasising the point, Article 1(2) of the Directive provides that Member States may exclude from the scope of the Directive employees with a contract or employment relationship:[14]

'(a) – with a total duration not exceeding one month, and/or
  – with a working week not exceeding eight hours;[15] or
 (b) of a casual and/or specific nature provided, in these cases, that its non-application is justified by objective considerations.'

The significance of the Directive is that it impliedly includes within its scope workers who do *not* have a *contract* of employment, and thus do not fall within the definition of 'employee' in UK domestic law. Rather, it also includes those with a *relationship* of employment.

---

12 Council Directive 91/533/EEC of 14 October 1991 on an employer's obligation to inform employees of the conditions applicable to the contract or employment relationship, OJ L288/32 of 18.10.91; Article 1(1).
13 EPCA, s 153(1).
14 This was watered down from the first draft's clear prohibition that: 'The provisions of this Directive shall not apply . . .'
15 The first draft of the Directive stipulated 'eight hours' work on average a week'.

The potential of this was not lost on the Member States, though different reactions followed. For example, the Italians took exception to the possibility of non-application of the Directive to certain categories of workers by virtue of Article 1(2). When the Directive was approved, the Italian delegation insisted that there be inserted the following statement in the Declarations to be inserted into the Minutes of the Council of Ministers with respect to Article 1:

'Italy has serious reservations about both paragraphs 1 and 2 because the exceptions neutralise the effect of the directive. This is not the best way of Community harmonisation, especially as it regards an elementary right (a letter of appointment).'

To the contrary, the British delegation required to be inserted into the Minutes of the Council the following:

'The definition in UK legislation of the expression "employment relationship" imports the exclusion of civil servants and independent workers from the field of application of the present directive.'

Neither of these Declarations has any legal consequences.

What constitutes a 'relationship of employment'?

The question is: what elements constitute a 'relationship of employment', which is not also a contract of employment. One obvious category is that of independent contractors/self-employed workers – in domestic law considered as having not a contract of employment or of service, but a contract for services. These are paid workers; they have a relationship of employment. This relationship, contrary to the title of self-employment, is with the paying client or customer.

But there are obviously others. This emerges with clarity from Article 1(2)(b) – which states that the Directive applies to casual and/or specific workers, unless its non-application is justified. The problem of classifying such workers as employees has been encountered in domestic UK law.[16] But that case law is irrelevant for the purposes of the Directive. The coverage of the Directive is dependent not on classification, but on justification.

By definition, therefore, the scope of the Directive includes a variety of workers whose legal classification falls outside the familiar category of employees with a contract of employment. The question then becomes: who are the others covered? What are the criteria of 'employees having an employment relationship'?

First, they must be 'paid'. That is not the same as saying there is a contract,[17] although being paid makes it likely. The Directive clearly envisages paid employment relationships which are not contractual. Moreover, the Directive does not specify from whom the payment comes. Contrast may be made with the definition of 'pay' in Article 119 of the Treaty (equal pay), 'which the worker receives ... from his employer'. In contracts of employment, payment will normally be received from the employer. But in employment relationships,

---

16 See R Benedictus and B Bercusson *Labour Law: Cases and Materials*, Sweet & Maxwell, London 1987, Chapter 1, pp 13–24.

17 It might be argued that being 'paid' implies consideration, hence a contract. As seen, this does not necessarily mean a contract of service, as it would cover a contract for services. Moreover, consideration is not an element in continental civil law contract doctrine.

the nexus is not as direct as in contract. The worker will receive pay, but who from? Here one may recall the extremely wide definition given to this term by Article 119:

> '... "pay" means the ordinary basic or minimum wage or salary and any other consideration, whether in cash or in kind, which the worker receives, directly or indirectly, in respect of his employment ...'

The rewards for employment 'relationships' may be quite differently constructed from those for contracts of employment. The use of the term 'relationship' requires EU law to take cognisance of a multitude of forms of work which never acquire contractual status, but are nonetheless carried out in the expectation of some form of reciprocal benefit, which may fall short of the common law concept of contractual 'consideration'.

The first element of an employment relationship is, therefore, some expectation of reciprocal benefit, with the broadest possible construction of the form which reward may take for work performed.

Secondly, the information required by the Directive to be provided must be that of the 'essential aspects of the contract or employment relationship'.[18] There is no formal checklist. What is an essential aspect of the employment relationship is, presumably, not necessarily identical to what would be assumed to be essential to an employment contract. It will rather vary with the nature of the relationship.

However, the information provided 'shall cover at least' certain items listed in Article 2(2). These prescribe some degree of specification, in that the employment must be capable of a degree of definition in terms laid down by the Directive's obligation to provide information. Scrutinised closely, the requirements are not excessively exigent. The place of work need not be fixed;[19] there need be no work title – a brief description of the work will suffice;[20] leave and notice entitlements may be indicated through a procedure or method of determining them;[1] and relevant collective agreements only where appropriate.[2] However, there is required information on the date of commencement of the relationship;[3] if a temporary relationship, the expected duration;[4] remuneration entitlement,[5] within the broad sense of rewards described above, and normal working time.[6]

The second element of an employment relationship concerns the definable quality of an employment relationship. The Directive prescribes that only some aspects of the relationship require a degree of definition. On the other hand, all 'essential aspects' must be notified. These less familiar aspects may be specific to the qualitatively different nature of certain employment relationships compared with contracts of employment.

Thirdly, employment relationships 'of a casual and/or specific nature' may be excluded, but only if this is 'justified by objective considerations'.[7] In a preemptive

---

18   Article 2(1).
19   Article 2(2)(b).
20   Article 2(2)(c).
 1   Article 2(2)(f),(g).
 2   Article 2(2)(j).
 3   Article 2(2)(d).
 4   Article 2(2)(e).
 5   Article 2(2)(h).
 6   Article 2(2)(i).
 7   Article 1(2)(b).

move, without formal legal significance, the Council and Commission inserted the following Declaration into the Minutes of the Council:

> 'The Council and Commission agree that the option opened by point b) applies to specified and limited situations resulting from the particular and casual nature of the employment relationship, such as those of domestic service, students and pupils.'

To the contrary, the wording of the paragraph creates a *presumption* that casual and specific employment relationships *are* within the scope of the Directive. The casual and/or specific nature of work does not preclude it being an employment relationship (or even a contract). The Directive clearly excludes the possibility that the parties themselves could subjectively decide to exclude the relationship from the scope of the Directive. Its non-application must be justified by 'objective considerations'. Objective reasons must be stipulated and excessively wide definitions could be challenged.

It is not easy to formulate purely objective considerations. Exclusion may be in the interests of employers, but not those of workers, as even casual and/or specific workers could benefit from the Directive's provisions. To assist it in deciding a challenge, the European Court might draw on the definition of 'objective justification' it has developed in the law on 'indirect' sex discrimination:[8]

> 'the means chosen for achieving that objective correspond to a real need on the part of the undertaking, are appropriate with a view to achieving the objective in question and are necessary to that end.'

So if other measures are available to compensate for depriving workers of the information required by the Directive, this might justify non-application. Otherwise, not.

The third element of an employment relationship is, therefore, that it may be casual and/or specific and still fall within the scope of the Directive.

What these elements of an employment relationship comprise is the recognition by EU labour law that work has taken new forms which may not fall within the classical common law definition of contracts of employment. These employment relationships include some expectation of reciprocal benefit, with the broadest possible construction of the form which reward may take for work performed; they require only some aspects of the relationship to be defined, but require all 'essential aspects' to be explicitly notified; and may be casual and/or specific. Such employment relationships will fall within the scope of the EU labour law laid down in this Directive. That EU labour law is prepared to extend employment protection outside the scope of contracts of employment, to cover workers outside the normal confines of UK labour law is significant. Its significance is apparent from the protection extended to these employment relationships outside the UK legislation's scope.

PROTECTION AVAILABLE TO *ALL* EMPLOYMENT CONTRACTS/RELATIONSHIPS

The objectives of the Commission were set out in the Explanatory Memorandum. The growth of new forms of employment produces a situation where workers often lack information about their terms and conditions of employment

---

8   Case 170/84: *Bilka-Kaufhaus GmbH v Weber von Hartz* [1984] ECR 1607, paragraph 37.

and their employment rights. This situation is aggravated when doubt exists about whether certain work is covered by labour law at all, or whether it is so-called 'black work'. By extending the scope of the workers covered to include employment relationships outside the normal contract of employment, even casual work, the Directive imposes EU labour law obligations which domestic law must now incorporate. The additional protections now available to all employment relationships should be noted.

Information to be provided in writing

While only some items are prescribed to be notified by the Directive, the information provided must cover all 'essential aspects' of the employment relationship.[9] One problem of workers engaged in the new forms of employment relationship is precisely, as the Explanatory Memorandum put it, that they:[10]

'have neither a written contract of employment nor a letter of appointment explaining the elements of the employment relationship or referring to a collective agreement or any other easily accessible written document.'

The Directive requires that:[11]

'1. The information referred to in Article 2(2) may be given to the employee, not later than two months after the commencement of employment, in the form of:
   (a) a written contract of employment; and/or
   (b) a letter of engagement; and/or
   (c) one or more other written documents, where one of these documents contains at least all the information referred to in Article 2(2)(a), (b), (c), (h) and (i).
2. Where none of the documents referred to in paragraph 1 is handed over to the employee within the prescribed period, the employer shall be obliged to give the employee, nor later than two months after the commencement of employment, a written declaration signed by the employer and containing at least the information referred to in Article 2(2).
   Where the document(s) referred to in paragraph 1 contain only part of the information required, the written declaration provided for in the first subparagraph of this paragraph shall cover the remaining information.
3. Where the contract or employment relationship comes to an end before expiry of a period of two months as from the date of the start of work, the information provided for in Article 2 and in this Article must be made available to the employee by the end of this period at the latest.'

Information of itself is a valuable resource. Lack of it, in the case of new forms of employment, was one inspiration for the Commission's initiative. However, the impact of the provision of written information upon the employment relationship remains to be considered. Here something can be learned from the UK experience, which, as the Commission noted, with Ireland, was the primary source inspiring this EC legislation.[12]

---

9 Article 2.
10 Op cit, paragraph 2.
11 Article 3.
12 Op cit, paragraph 8. The following paragraphs are derived from Annotations by B Bercusson to the relevant legislation in C D Drake and B Bercusson *The Employment Acts 1974–1980 with Commentary*, Sweet & Maxwell, London 1981.

The UK legislation of 1963, the Contracts of Employment Act, was not intended to secure written contracts for workers. Rather, as in the case of the Directive, its concern was for the provision of written information. Despite this, there has been a tendency by lawyers and judges, tempted as a result of the uncertainties of unwritten contracts, to seize upon the written statement of particulars required by the UK legislation as the *written contract*. Signature of the statement by one or both of the parties has only added to the irresistibility of the temptation.[13] The requirement in the Directive that the employer sign the written declaration[14] is likely to increase this tendency.

However, there was some judicial resistance to the direct assimilation of written statements into written contracts of employment.[15] Where a direct transformation of written statement into contract has seemed too robust, the objective of resolving judicial uncertainty as to contractual terms of employment has been achieved by attaching to the written statement the status of *almost incontrovertible proof* of the terms of the (unwritten) contract – virtually estopping a denial of its terms.[16]

The Department of Employment Guide to the legislation advised the employee not to 'put his signature to any form of words which might imply agreement with the terms and conditions stated', since the signature might bind him regardless of other terms agreed orally. Employees were advised, if asked to sign, to 'confirm that they are only being asked to sign for *receipt* of the written statement'.

Early research on the impact of the legislation[17] indicated that, of the employers surveyed, many did comply with the requirement to provide written particulars of terms of employment, at least to some extent. A British Institute of Management survey of 1980 on company practice relating to the written employment contracts of managers and specialist staff found that 96% of the companies surveyed provided written contracts for some or all of those staff.

Of those employers who did comply, the forms of compliance were many: there was a myriad of documents purporting to comply, ranging from letters of appointment, offers of employment on specified terms, documents intended to be written statements of particulars, and others intended to be written contracts – both of which might be headed with the title of the legislation, and follow the pattern of terms required to be laid out by the legislation; and numerous other documents, complete and incomplete as to the requisite employment terms, and headed by various titles: Contract, Statement of Particulars, Terms of Employment, Conditions of Work etc, sometimes requiring signature of either or both parties and sometimes not.

---

13   In *Gascol Conversions Ltd v Mercer* [1974] ICR 420, the employee's signature was the decisive factor to Orr and Lawton LJJ in transforming the document in question into a contract.
14   Article 3(2).
15   eg Lord Parker in *Turiff Construction Ltd v Bryant* (1967) 2 KIR 659; and as to the effect of signature, Lord Denning in *Secretary of State for Employment v ASLEF (No 2)* [1972] 2 QB 455, CA.
16   eg *Smith v Blandford Gee Cementation Co Ltd* [1970] 3 All ER 154, where the employer was estopped from denying what was said in the written statement; *W P M Retail Ltd v Lang* [1978] IRLR 243, EAT, where the employer's failure to pay an agreed bonus was not treated as a variation of the contract; rather the employer was still bound, and the employee's continuing to work over two years was not a waiver of his contractual rights – he was entitled to his accumulated unpaid bonus payments.
17   P Leighton and M Dumville 'From Statement to Contract' (1977) 6 *Industrial Law Journal* 133.

Given the extremely varied forms of response by employers to the legislation, the English lawyer's approach was as follows: classify the various documents into one of the categories: contract/statement of particulars. Then, as a matter of discretion – if contract, parol evidence may be allowed to amplify (though not contradict) it, and doctrines of mistake, misrepresentation, intention to create legal relations etc, may be relevant. If a statement of particulars, evidence is allowed to amplify or contradict it, and doctrines of, eg, estoppel may apply.

Either way, written documents are in this way given some primary role, and employees are usually at a disadvantage in this respect. The documents are invariably drawn up by the employer – the employee only 'consents'. As Sir Otto Kahn-Freund said: [18]

> 'This is the reality of things, in the language of the law that reality is concealed. There the unilateral rule- and decision-making power of management is presented as based on a "contract", on the free will of the employer and the employee.'

Employers with superior bargaining power and access to professional expertise on personnel management and legal advice naturally exploit these resources in drafting statements – geographical mobility or job flexibility clauses in employment documents are usually a good illustration of this.

An alternative approach would seek to redress this imbalance: any evidence as to terms of employment would be allowed, including, without any special significance, any written documents, whatever their nature. The key-stone of this approach would be collective custom and practice. It partially avoids the practical problems for workers of acceptance or signature of documents being held against them, and of maintaining adequate records over long periods – such written records being deemed conclusive. The requirement of the written statement of particulars would be retained to fulfil its original purpose – written information for employees – but no more. [19]

This UK national experience is reflected in the otherwise mysterious provisions of Article 6 of the Directive:

> 'This Directive shall be without prejudice to national law and practice concerning:
> – the form of the contract or employment relationship,
> – proof as regards the existence and content of a contract or employment relationship,
> – the relevant procedural rules.'

Formally, this provision appears to maintain any national law regarding the existence, form and content of any contract or employment relationship unaffected by the Directive. What the UK experience with the parallel written statement of particulars demonstrates is how this formal abstinence is belied by its practical impact.

The situation was complex enough when the written statement interacted with an acknowledged existing contract of employment, whatever its form and content. The position becomes even more interesting when the existence itself of a contract is in doubt. The Directive applies also to employment relationships which may not be contracts of employment. In practice, it is often the vagueness and uncertainty of any obligations engaged in such relationships

---

18 *Labour and the Law* (1977) p 12.
19 Judicial support for this approach emerged in *System Floors (UK) Ltd v Daniel* [1982] ICR 54, EAT, and *Mears v Safecar Security Ltd* [1982] ICR 626, CA.

which preclude them from reaching the quality of a contract of employment. In such a case, the provision of detailed information about essential aspects of the employment relationship may be, in practice, sufficient to cause the employment relationship to cross the threshold and become a contract of employment.

Formally, the written information is neutral in its impact: in practice this neutrality may be difficult to sustain. As the UK practice shows, a judge may find it more difficult to maintain that an employment relationship was so informal and casual as not to constitute an employment contract if there is available written information about essential aspects of the relationship, including pay, working time, job description, place of work, and so on.[20]

The Directive's goal is thus achieved in an indirect and subtle way. The objective is to attack the problems associated with new forms of work which lack the clarity and certainty associated with formal contracts of employment. The Directive explicitly abstains from interfering with national labour laws regarding the form, proof of existence and content or even procedural rules relevant to the contract of employment. However, by imposing the *same* requirements regarding provision of written information on *both* contracts *and* relationships of employment, the latter is potentially raised to the status of the former.

The UK experience suggests that in these circumstances it becomes difficult to argue that a form of employment with written prescribed terms and conditions falls outside the protection traditionally ascribed to employees with contracts of employment. If this is replicated as a result of the EU Directive's implementation in other Member States, progress will have been made in assimilating to all employment relationships the protection formerly accorded only to workers with contracts of employment.

Similarly, in the case of informal employment relationships of the type which concerned the Commission and led to the Directive, the terms of the employment relationship may be located in a variety of sources, written and oral, or in the form of custom and practice. Article 6 affirms that national law shall continue to prevail in determining terms and conditions of employment, including the hierarchy of sources of such terms. However, here also the Directive's requirement of a written document specifying terms and conditions will be difficult to ignore. Formally outside the hierarchy of sources, as UK experience shows, it will be almost irresistible as a source of information when there is any dispute about the terms and conditions of employment.

A final point: given the obligation imposed by the Directive on the employer, the written information will be prepared by the employer. This does give the employer an advantage in that the document purporting to set out the required information about terms and conditions of employment is unilaterally drafted by the employer. Its accuracy may be questioned when, in the context of a dispute, the employer produces the written document as evidence of the terms and conditions of employment. Challenges to the accuracy, and hence validity of the document purporting to comply with the Directive's requirements are likely in the absence of any worker input to the document. This might be obviated if the document itself cites a collective agreement as the source for terms and conditions. The potential link of individual employment relationships and collective agreements is relevant here.[1]

---

20   As stated above, in the UK the employer's signing the written declaration containing the information (Article 3(2)) might well be decisive.
1   See Chapter 33.

Modification of the relationship

The document with the requisite information will be prepared by the employer and must be given to the employee not later than two months after the commencement of employment.[2] It is highly probable that changes will occur in aspects of the employment at various times in the course of its duration. To maintain the Directive's objective of keeping the employee informed, the original document will have to reflect these changes. This is provided for in Article 5(1):

> 'Any change in the details referred to in Articles 2(2) and 4(1) must be the subject of a written document to be given by the employer to the employee at the earliest opportunity and not later than one month after the date of entry into effect of the change in question.'

Again, the experience of the parallel legislation in the UK demonstrates the potential difficulties.

The notification required here is of an *agreed* change. The common law rule is that an employer cannot change terms of employment without the consent of the employee. So merely informing the employee by a written statement is not conclusive of the existence of an *agreed* change in the terms. Unfortunately, it was all too easy to transform the *knowledge* of a powerless worker that a change was being proposed into binding consent. Nonetheless, where the employer has not the right in the contract, if he tries to alter rates of pay, hours of work, or the status or grade of the employee – he must obtain the employee's consent before the change can have any legal effect. The *existence* of a written statement does not mean that it has been agreed and is thus binding.[3]

Remedies

Breach by an employer of obligations under the Directive may take many forms: failure to provide some or all of the information, in good time, in the proper

---

2 Article 3(1).
3 *Jones v Associated Tunnelling Co Ltd* [1981] IRLR 477, per Browne-Wilkinson J:

> 'If, as in the present case, there is no evidence of any oral discussion varying the original terms, the fact that a statement of terms and conditions containing different terms has been issued cannot be compelling evidence of an express oral variation. The most that can be said is that by continuing to work without objection after receiving such further statement, the employee may have impliedly agreed to the variation recorded in the second statement or is estopped from denying it.
>
> In our view, to imply an agreement to vary or to raise an estoppel against the employee on the grounds that he has not objected to a false record by the employers of the terms actually agreed is a course which should be adopted with great caution . . . it is asking too much of the ordinary employee to require him either to object to an erroneous statement of his terms of employment having no immediate practical impact on him or be taken to have assented to the variation'.

There is a further query raised by the provision in Article 5(1) of the Directive regarding the words 'date of entry into effect'. Does this mean legal effect or practical effect? If the latter, it may not be necessary to provide information until it actually is implemented. A recent UK case on mobility clauses allowed for a declaration of illegality of a mobility clause, on the grounds that it indirectly discriminated against women, as it had legal effect even though not implemented in practice: *Meade-Hill v British Council* [1995] IRLR 478, CA.

form, or providing inaccurate information. For the defence of the rights of the employee, the Directive provides:[4]

> 'Member States shall introduce into their national legal systems such measures as are necessary to enable all employees who consider themselves wronged by failure to comply with the obligations from this Directive to pursue their claims by judicial process after possible recourse to other competent authorities.'

The appropriate remedies are not easily conceived. The UK parallel legislation provides for recourse to an industrial tribunal which may itself provide the information. This falls short of the requisite efficacy demanded for the enforcement of EC law. The employer loses nothing by failing to comply. The employee has the burden of bringing a claim against an employer with whom he is in a continuing relationship. This is likely to suffice to deter any contentious proceedings, which can only prejudice any future employment relationship. The authors of some early research on the workings of the UK legislation concluded:[5]

> '... if an employer of, say, 5,000 employees fails to provide written statements, the only recourse the work-force has is by way of individual complaint to a tribunal. It is not open to a trade union or a group of employees to bring a group action, and although there is, of course, the possibility of a "test case", contacts with local trade union officials suggest that a successfully brought "test case" does not always produce a response on the part of the employer towards the rest of the work-force.'

The Directive envisages recourse to other competent authorities. Comparative experience may reveal better alternatives. The Commission may well consider whether inadequate and ineffective sanctions constitute failure properly to implement the Directive.

The 1991 Directive is only a beginning. But it is a significant milestone on the path to consolidating within European labour law the expanding sphere of employment relationships falling outside the traditional confines of national labour laws.

---

4   Article 8(1).
5   P Leighton and M Dumville 'From Statement to Contract' (1977) 6 *Industrial Law Journal* 133, at pp 138–9.

Chapter 30

Part-time Workers

INTRODUCTION

In every Member State of the European Community, the majority of part-time workers is female. As a consequence, any treatment of part-time workers which is less favourable than that accorded to full-time workers constitutes indirect discrimination and is unlawful under EC law unless it can be justified. This has already had major consequences for part-time women workers. The European Court has upheld claims to equal treatment with respect to occupational pensions, sick benefits, wage adjustments and severance pay.

While the gender dimension is significant and, indeed, crucial, it has had the major drawback of importing the principle of equality into EU labour law's treatment of part-timers, without reflection on whether it is appropriate. Constructing the foundation for a labour law governing part-time workers on a criterion drawn from EU law on sex discrimination has a major disadvantage. Indirect discrimination can be justified.

This means that less favourable treatment of part-time workers is justifiable in an EU labour law premised on the equality principle, provided the treatment is on grounds unrelated to sex discrimination. Once sex discrimination is eliminated, there is no further guiding principle on how part-time workers should be treated under EU labour law. On this principle, any EU labour law on part-time workers would disappear if men and women were equally distributed among part-time workers – regardless of how part-timers were treated.

Yet part-time employment is impossible to ignore as a specific category of employment relationship, for reasons related to its gender composition, but also for wider reasons. These have become increasingly evident in EU labour law proposals related to working time. Part-time work has to be examined in the context of working time in Britain in general.

WORKING TIME IN THE UK: EXCEPTIONAL FEATURES

Analysis of working time in the UK, using evidence from the 1991 Labour Force Survey, throws up a number of features which distinguish Britain from other EU Member States.[1]

1 The analysis which follows draws on G Watson 'Hours of work in Great Britain and Europe: Evidence from the UK and European Labour Force Surveys', (1992) *Employment Gazette* (November), pp 539–57, who states: '. . . probably the greatest advantage of the LFS over all other sources of hours data is that a comparable survey is conducted in all other EC member states' (p 540).

Atypical hours for full-timers and part-timers

The account in the 1992 *Employment Gazette* included a Table which showed the *average* hours worked by employees in each Member State in 1990 (the most recent year's data available):[2]

EMPLOYEES AVERAGE TOTAL USUAL WEEKLY HOURS 1990[3]			
	Part-time	*Full time*	*All*
Belgium	20.7	38.0	35.8
Denmark	19.0	39.0	34.2
France	21.8	39.6	37.5
Germany	19.5	39.9	36.8
Greece	20.8	40.1	39.5
Holland	16.3	39.0	31.9
Ireland	18.1	40.4	38.6
Italy	25.2	38.6	38.0
Luxembourg	23.0	39.9	38.7
Portugal	20.0	41.9	41.2
Spain	18.1	40.7	39.7
UK	17.6	43.7	37.8
Europe 12	19.0	40.4	37.4

It was observed that 'there are not great differences between many countries'; considering the largest economies, the UK average hours of 37.8 per week was not out of line with average hours of 37.5 in France, 36.8 in Germany and 38.0 in Italy. The UK average is only achieved, however, by conflating the average hours of part-time and full-time workers. When these are taken separately, the UK emerges as distinctively different from the 11 other EU Member States.

The *average* hours worked by *full-time* employees in the UK is the *highest* in the EC at 43.7 hours. Only Portugal comes close with an average 41.9 hours. Comparing the other big economies, full-time workers in the UK work on average 5.1 hours more per week than Italian full-timers, 4.1 hours more than the French, and 3.8 hours more than German full-time workers.

At the same time, the *average* hours worked by *part-time* employees in the UK is, next to the Netherlands, the *lowest* in the EU at 17.6 hours. Comparing the other big economies, part-time workers in the UK work on average 7.4 hours less per week than Italian part-timers, 4.2 hours less than the French, and 1.9 hours less than German part-time workers.

This is further illustrated by contrasting the differences between Member States in the proportions of employees usually working long hours (defined as over 48 hours per week) and the proportions working in jobs involving only a

2 Ibid, Table 15 on p 553. Based on the 12 Member States at that time.
3 Source: EUROSTAT 1990. Full and part-time status is generally determined by respondents own assessment, not by hours worked. In Greece, Italy and Holland slightly different definitions are used (see EUROSTAT 1988).

small number of hours (defined as less than 16 hours per week).[4] At the lower end of weekly hours worked, the UK is not alone: the Netherlands (15.1%), the UK (9.7%) and Denmark (9.5%) have the highest proportions of employees working in small hours jobs (reflecting the higher overall proportion of women in employment in these countries). Each of these countries, however, is far above the proportion working in such small hours jobs in the other nine Member States, ranging from 0.8% in Greece to 4.2% in Germany. And the UK's 9.7% is far above the other three largest economies (Germany: 4.2%, France, 2.6%, Italy: 1.7%).

At the upper end of weekly hours worked, however, the UK stands alone with 16% of employees usually working more than 48 hours weekly. This is far above the proportion working such long hours in the other Member States, ranging from 1.7% in the Netherlands to 8.3% in Ireland. The UK proportion is more than three times the proportion working such long hours in each of the other three largest economies: France: 5.3%, Germany: 4.8%, Italy: 3.5% The number working such long hours in the UK is probably more than all those working similar long hours in the other three countries combined![5] The *Employment Gazette* survey observes:[6]

'In Britain overtime has historically been an important element of employees' working time in manufacturing industry and in particular for manual workers ... overtime hours whether paid or unpaid are, for many people, an integral part of their working week.'

Some 9.5 million employees (43.8%) usually work some form of overtime each week. Some 23.4% (over 5 million) work basic hours and *paid* overtime averaging 7.1 hours per week, and 17% (about 3.7 million) work basic hours plus *unpaid* overtime averaging 7.3 hours per week.[7] 'Working long hours in a paid job ... is very much a male phenomenon'.[8] Some 2.9 million male employees (24.8%) usually work more than 48 hours per week compared with only 0.5 million women (4.8%). Full-time men work the highest levels of overtime: on average 5 hours overtime per week (3 hours paid and 2 hours unpaid).

Unpaid overtime working is very common amongst managerial and professional workers: some 25–40%, with the highest incidence among teaching professionals (63.7%). These occupations, with a higher proportion of women workers, illustrate the fact that the proportion of *unpaid* overtime worked by women is considerably higher (58%), compared to men (40%).

The long hours and overtime working by full-time men in the UK can be characterised in the EU context as *atypical* work. In this light, the Directive on

4   Op cit, Figure 4 on p 554.
5   The exceptional length of the working week in the UK coincides with other features already noted: the UK shares with Spain the highest overall proportion of employees doing regular and occasional shiftwork (29%); it has by far the highest proportion of employees in manufacturing doing regular and occasional shiftwork (64%). The second highest proportion of employees in manufacturing doing regular and occasional shiftwork is Italy, with 46%. In France it is 25% and in Germany, 22%. The UK also has the highest proportion of employees in regular and occasional night work: 25%. The next highest is Greece with 17%; in France it is 15% and in Germany, 9%.
6   *Employment Gazette*, p 544.
7   3.4%, 0.75 million work both; ibid, pp 550–1.
8   Ibid, p 549.

Working Time, which prohibits normal working exceeding 48 hours weekly,[9] can be seen as the functional corollary of other EU initiatives aimed at regulating atypical work.[10]

Working time: the gender dimension

Not only do part-time workers work shorter hours in the UK, there are also many more of them than in any of the other three larger economies. The 1990 Labour Force Survey shows that the proportion of workers in the UK usually working up to 30 hours a week is 22.5%, as compared with 14.8% in Germany, 14.4% in France and 11.5% in Italy. In the EU, part-timers comprise a larger proportion of workers only in the Netherlands (28.6%) and Denmark (22.8%).[11]

The striking feature of part-time work throughout the EU is the predominance of *women part-time workers*: over 80% of persons employed part-time in 1988 were women; the figure for men was only 18.2%. The UK was above the average: 85.7% of part-time workers were women. The chart below provides a break-down by country:[12]

MEN/WOMEN BREAKDOWN OF PART-TIME WORK BY COUNTRY – 1988 (%)			
	Total	*Men*	*Women*
Europe 12	100.00	18.2	81.8
Belgium	100.00	12.9	87.1
Denmark	100.00	20.5	79.5
Germany	100.00	9.5	90.5
Greece	100.00	34.2	65.8
Spain	100.00	26.3	73.7
France	100.00	16.3	83.7
Ireland	100.00	31.5	68.4
Italy	100.00	37.8	62.2
Luxembourg	100.00	19.4	80.6
Netherlands	100.00	30.2	69.8
Portugal	100.00	32.9	67.1
UK	100.00	14.3	85.7

9   Council Directive 93/104/EC of 23 November 1993 concerning certain aspects of the organisation of working time, OJ L307/18 of 13.12.1993, Article 6.
10   Council Directive 91/383 of 25 June 1991 supplementing the measures to encourage improvements in the safety and health at work of workers with a fixed-duration employment relationship or a temporary employment relationship, OJ 1991 L206/19; Council Directive 91/533 of 14 October 1991 on an employer's obligation to inform employees of the conditions applicable to the contract or employment relationship, OJ 1991 L288/32.
11   For a chart illustrating the growth of part-time employment between 1983 and 1988, see *A Social Portrait of Europe*, Statistical Office of the European Communities (Eurostat), Luxembourg 1991, Table 5.6 on p 62.
12   Ibid, Table 5.11 on p 63.

Again, the UK, Denmark and the Netherlands, with the highest proportion of part-time workers also have the highest proportions of women workers in the part-time workforce:[13]

PROPORTIONS OF MEN/WOMEN WORKERS IN THE PART-TIME WORKFORCE			
	Total	*Women*	*Men*
Europe 12	13.2	28.1	3.9
Belgium	9.8	23.4	2.0
Denmark	23.7	41.5	8.9
Germany	13.2	30.6	2.1
Greece	5.5	10.3	2.9
Spain	5.4	13.0	2.1
France	12.0	23.8	3.4
Ireland	8.0	17.0	3.7
Italy	5.6	10.4	3.2
Luxembourg	6.4	15.0	1.9
Netherlands	30.4	57.7	14.5
Portugal	6.5	10.5	3.6
UK	21.9	44.2	5.5

In March 1989, almost one in four of all employees in the UK worked less than full-time:[14]

	All employees	*Of which part-time employees*
Total:	22,235,000	5,295,000 (23.8%)
Women:	10,255,000	4,394,000 (43%)
Men:	11,980,000	901,000 (8%)

In spring 1992, 45% of all women in work in the UK, but only 6% of men, worked part-time in their main job.[15] Two salient facts characterise women's part-time employment. First, women employees with dependent children aged 1–15 work an average of 25.1 hours, compared to 32.7 for those with no dependent children.[16] Secondly, only 40% of part-time workers are women with one or more dependent children under 16.[17]

The first fact indicates that children dictate the hours of work of working women. Although overall only 19.4% of women work less than 16 hours a

---

13 Ibid, Table 5.7 on p 62.
14 Industrial Relations Services *Employment Trends* No 449, 10 October 1989, p 6. See also (1990) *Employment Gazette* (December), p 619.
15 G Watson and B Fothergill 'Part-time employment and attitudes to part-time work', (1993) *Employment Gazette* (May), pp 213–20. Over 80% of the men were over 50 or under 25, compared to less than 40% of the women whose age distribution is more even.
16 (1992) *Employment Gazette* (November), at p 549 and Table 9 on p 550.
17 (1993) *Employment Gazette* (May), p 214, Table 1.

week, the figure for women with children aged under five is nearly twice as high at 34.3%. For women without dependent children only 11.7% work fewer than 16 hours, that is less than a third the rate for women with children.

The second fact indicates that the *absence* of children does *not* preclude women choosing to work part-time. This is significant because more than one in three (35.2%) of women *without* dependent children work the standard 35–39 hour week. The working pattern of this group of women only differs from that of male workers when it comes to those working beyond 45 hours: 52.6% of women without dependent children have working hours of between 35–44 hours a week. The corresponding figure for men is almost exactly the same at 52.9%.

The conclusion to be drawn is that working women's hours of work are, like men's, spread over a large spectrum. There is a substantial overlap in the range of working hours of the two groups, but the range of women's hours begins much lower down and that of men extends much higher up:[18]

EMPLOYEES' TOTAL USUAL WEEKLY HOURS BY SEX AND FOR WOMEN BY FAMILY STATUS						
	0–15	*16–24*	*25–34*	*35–44*	*45–48*	*49+*
All men	3.0	1.6	2.1	**52.9**	15.5	24.9
All women	18.4	16.7	11.7	44.0	4.4	4.8
Women with dependent children aged 0–15	28.0	25.8	14.5	26.2	2.5	3.3
Women with no dependent children	13.7	12.2	10.5	**52.6**	5.3	5.5

Comparing both ends of the range we see huge concentrations of either sex at the ends of the range of working hours: women at the lower end and men at the higher end:

EMPLOYEES' TOTAL USUAL WEEKLY HOURS BY SEX AND FOR WOMEN BY FAMILY STATUS			
	0–34	*35–44*	*45+*
All men	6.7	52.9	40.4
All women	46.8	44.0	9.2
Women with dependent children aged 0–15	68.2	26.2	5.8
Women with no dependent children	36.4	52.6	10.8

Certain conclusions may be drawn from the predominance of women in part-time employment and the concentration of men with longer working hours. Before expounding these, a third feature which distinguishes working time in the UK from working time in other Member States should be noted.

18   Data derived from (1992) *Employment Gazette* (May), Table 9, pp 548–9.

The distribution/dispersion of working hours

The UK has a very different distribution of working hours to other Member States of the EU. Employees in every other country are heavily concentrated within a narrow range of hours. In most other Member States, a narrow hours band accounts for a significant segment of employees. The Table presents the single hour band with the densest concentration in each country:[19]

PROPORTION OF EMPLOYEES IN A SINGLE HOUR BAND				
Luxembourg	83 %	work	40	hours
Spain	71		40	
France	50		39	
Denmark	49		38	
Ireland	49		40	
Belgium	49		38	
Greece	49		40	
Italy	48		40	
Portugal	38		45	
Germany (W)	30		38	
Netherlands	30		38	
UK	10		40	

In eight of the 12 Member States, very close to half or more of all employees work within a single hour band. When the hours band is widened to include the most common range between 38–40 hours, the result is as follows:[20]

PROPORTION OF EMPLOYEES WORKING 38–40 HOURS WEEKLY	
Luxembourg	83.4 %
Spain	75.0
Belgium	68.6
France	64.4
Greece	64.4
Germany (W)	63.4
Netherlands	57.2
Ireland	54.8
Denmark	53.2
Italy	52.8
UK	45.9
Portugal	24.7[1]

19 Table derived from ibid, Figure 5, p 556.
20 Ibid, derived from Table 16, pp 554–5.
 1 In Portugal, a further 41.7% work 45–48 hours.

In all Member States except the UK and Portugal more than half of all employees work within the 38–40 hours band. The *Employment Gazette* explains:[2]

> 'What the data clearly show is the extent and influence of labour market regulation on the hours worked by employees. With the exception of the UK, and, to some extent, Ireland and Denmark, all other EC states have wide-ranging regulation of their labour markets, either through direct legislation or through legally binding collective agreements. It is this which, no doubt, explains in part the concentration of working time within these countries. If we consider France, for example, where the statutory working time for many employees is set at 39 hours, we see that there is indeed a heavy concentration of employees working at exactly this number of hours.
>
> Consequently, it is possible to see that the UK with its highly de-regulated labour market has a greater diversity of working time than elsewhere in the EC. In other countries where the majority of employees work within a small range of hours it is quite feasible to talk of a 'standard' employee. However in the UK the idea of standard amount of working time is less appropriate and even potentially misleading.'

Yet even in Ireland and Denmark almost half of employees work within a single hour band. In Italy, the country closest to the UK in terms of the proportion of employees working 38–40 hours weekly, 48% of employees work a 40-hour week. The dispersion of hours around the average worked by employees is wider in the UK than any other Member State.[3] The dispersion of hours in the UK may be due in part to the absence of national regulation and legally binding collective agreements, but it may also owe something to the decentralisation of the processes of regulation of working time in the UK, including collective bargaining.

If the factor of national regulation by legislation or collective agreement is critical, it highlights the potential role of EU legislation in the form of the Working Time Directive and EU level collective agreements in developing a European model.

Conclusion

Working time in the UK is characterised by three features. First, nearly half of all employees, whether male or female, work a 'typical working week' in a relatively narrow band of hours: 52.9% of men and 44.0% of women usually work between 35–44 per week. Secondly, a large group of full-timers usually works much longer hours: 16% of employees, mainly men,[4] usually work more than 48 hours per week. Thirdly, a large group of part-timers: 22.5% of employees, 85.7% of whom were women[5] usually work below 30 hours per week; 9.7% of employees usually work less than 16 hours per week.

THE NATURE OF PART-TIME WORK

The UK has an unusually large number of part-time workers. Most of these are women.[6] The common stereotype of these women is that they have dependent

2 (1992) *Employment Gazette* (May), p 555.
3 Ibid, Table 16, p 555.
4 2.9 million, 24.8% of male employees.
5 43% of female employees were part-timers.
6 85.7%; 45% of women but only 6% of men work part-time in their main job.

children. However, the data show that *slightly more* (ie *most*) women part-timers do *not* have dependent children:

WOMEN EMPLOYEES' TOTAL USUAL WEEKLY HOURS BY FAMILY STATUS						
	1000s	*0–15*	*16–24*	*25–30*	*Total*	*1000s*
All women	10,224	18.4	16.7	8.2	43.3	4,427
Women with dependent children aged 0–15	3,318	28.0	25.8	11.1	64.9	**2,153**
Women with no dependent children	6,906	13.7	12.2	6.9	32.8	**2,265**

A majority of women who do *not* have the constraints of child-care responsibilities *nonetheless* work part-time. Most men also do not have the constraints of child-care responsibilities, but very few work part-time. An examination of the attitudes of part-time employees to their work may illuminate why many *women without* child-care responsibilities *do*, and most *men without* child-care responsibilities *do not*, work part-time.[7]

Recent research found that 'the main factors motivating respondents to work part-time, and the things they looked for in a job were: money, social contact and self esteem'.[8] A key finding of the research was 'that most people have a variety of reasons for working part-time and for women in particular motivations may have changed over time'.[9] For many, 'the main reason they worked part-time was to balance work with other (usually domestic) responsibilities'. However, the research also found that 'many respondents said their initial reasons for working part-time (for example looking after child(ren) were no longer valid or as relevant. Now they were used to working part-time, the benefits outweighed the disadvantages. What had started as a transition had become a satisfactory end in itself'.[10]

The research referred to a number of respondents, who tended to be older and/or those financially better off, who described part-time working as 'the best of both worlds'. The satisfaction was derived 'not so much from the qualities of the job itself but rather from the overall benefits part-time work had on an individual's life-style'. This was said also possibly to help explain the 'generally higher levels of job satisfaction found amongst part-timers in surveys such as the BSA (British Social Attitudes) ... the 1989 survey found that 91% of part-time employees compared to 81% of full-timers were satisfied with their jobs'.[11]

Finally, the research commented on factors which hindered workers taking up part-time work and specified two in particular. First: 'it was usually lower

---

7 G Watson and B Fothergill 'Part-time employment and attitudes to part-time work', (1993) *Employment Gazette* (May), pp 213–20.

8 Ibid, p 216. This is echoed in the statements in the Commission's Green and White Papers regarding the importance of work to the social identity of men and women.

9 Ibid, p 215.

10 Ibid, p 215: 'Also the nature of domestic responsibilities can change over time and may not only involve looking after young children. Older children (now adults themselves) or ill/disabled partners could also involve a great deal of work ...'

11 Ibid, p 220.

skilled jobs which were offered on a part-time basis ... the recession had adversely affected many of the innovations designed to "tempt" people back into work – eg flexitime, workplace nurseries, jobshares etc'. But probably the key issues for part-timers 'were the number of hours involved in a job and the times of day they could work'. The 1989 British Social Attitudes Survey found the largest difference between full- and part-timers as regards important aspects of a job was in relation to 'flexible hours': there was a 20% difference (62% to 42%) in the proportion of full and part-time employees saying these were important. The research in question 'adds to the BSA findings ... that convenient or flexible hours were the sine qua non for some part-timers'.[12]

Three conclusions may be drawn from these findings. First, the initial experience of part-time working, early exposure/socialisation to this form of work, is important. Most men, and many women, never work part-time and are never in a position to assess whether the benefits outweigh the disadvantages. If a person easily obtains part-time employment and becomes used to working part-time, it may become a satisfactory end in itself. Not necessarily for everybody, but for a great many more men and women than is now the case.

Secondly, part-time work is not an end in itself. In many cases, it is undertaken to balance work with other (usually domestic) responsibilities. Socialisation to part-time work must ensure that other responsibilities are not ignored. There are many forms of community service, vocational training and creative and leisure forms of activity, as well as domestic responsibilities: housework, childcare, caring for the disabled or elderly, which could and should accompany working part-time. Such activities beneficially complement the formation of a social identity beyond work and increase the general welfare of society.

Thirdly, a worker willing to undertake part-time work as well as other social responsibilities confronts the barriers to part-time working in the labour market. There is a lack of skilled and satisfying part-time jobs, or such jobs providing for flexitime, workplace nurseries and job shares, without demands for extra hours at short notice, travel and transport difficulties, and so on.[13]

EU POLICY TO DATE: EQUAL RIGHTS FOR WOMEN PART-TIMERS

EU law has made considerable progress in the prohibition of discrimination against part-time workers. This is due to the fact that in *every* Member State of the EU a *majority* of part-time employees is *female*.[14] The consequence is that if an employer treats part-time workers less favourably than full-timers, such treatment is more likely to have a negative impact on women than on men – as most part-timers are women. Such treatment therefore constitutes 'indirect discrimination' and is unlawful under Community law.[15] The inestimable contribution of EU law is that it has drawn attention to, and, in part, remedied the grosser forms of discrimination against women part-time workers.

---

12 Ibid, p 217.
13 Other barriers mentioned include the attitudes of others to part-time workers, particularly prevalent amongst husbands of inactive women. Ibid, p 217.
14 *A Social Portrait of Europe*, Statistical Office of the EC (Eurostat), Luxembourg, 1991, see Table above, p 442.
15 Case 170/84: *Bilka-Kaufhaus v Weber von Hartz* [1986] ECR 1607.

But EU law has two critical limitations. First, part-time workers are only the incidental beneficiaries of a policy and principle aimed at equal opportunity for women part-timers. If male workers join the ranks of part-timers, EU law will become inapplicable. Less favourable treatment of part-timers will not be discriminatory, since male and female part-timers are treated equally badly. Secondly, given discriminatory effects against female part-timers, their maximum entitlement under EU law is to equal treatment with male full-timers, on a pro rata basis.

THE NEW EUROPEAN MODEL: REDISTRIBUTION, RIGHTS AND INCENTIVES

EU law and policy are taking two important and linked steps towards a European model of working time. They have in common an attempt to deal with two 'atypical' forms of work. First, employment for 'atypically' very long hours is to be prohibited. Secondly, part-time employment is to be protected.

Redistribution of working time

The first step, of banning 'atypically' long working hours, is to cut off the longer end of the range of working hours. The Working Time Directive imposes a 48-hour limit on the average working week.[16] The provisions of the Directive will preclude employers offering work exceeding the 48 hours average weekly maximum. Even in the case of countries opting to delay introduction of this provision for seven years, employees will be entitled to refuse to work more than 48 hours.[17]

Not least because of high levels of unemployment, there is an argument for the redistribution of hours, at least from those working very long hours, into shorter-time employment; in particular, more part-time jobs could be created.

Rights for part-timers: beyond equality

The law on indirect discrimination precludes less favourable treatment for women part-time workers. The Commission has long proposed Directives to extend this entitlement to equal treatment to all part-time workers. The earliest proposals contained this entitlement by way of a prohibition on discrimination in labour and social security entitlements.[18] But they went beyond the formal equality principle by providing also the right of full-time workers to change to

---

16 Article 6.
17 This will affect case law in the UK; for example, where an employee obliged under the terms of his employment to work overtime 'as required' was held fairly dismissed for persistently refusing to do weekend standby duty. *Kirkpatrick v Lister-Petter Ltd, Industrial Relations Legal Information Bulletin* No 415, 21 December 1990, p 12. This is one illustration of how EC labour law spills over into labour law in general, here on unfair dismissal, despite absence of specific EC competence.
18 Draft Directives on voluntary part-time work were presented by the Commission as long ago as 4 January 1982, OJ C/62, p 7, and 5 January 1983, OJ C/18, p 5, Articles 2 and 3.

part-time work, and vice-versa.[19] Two later proposals added entitlement of part-timers to equal treatment with full-timers specifically with regard to access to vocational training, benefits in cash and in kind granted under social assistance and social security schemes (statutory and occupational), annual holidays, dismissal and seniority allowances and social services within the undertaking.[20]

These entitlements to equal treatment are important. But measures are required which encourage or require employers to go beyond equal treatment: to offer jobs with flexible hours and provide for the special needs of workers with other responsibilities.

Such provision has already been adopted by some employers in the UK seeking to attract women workers. A survey of 96 organisations employing 800,000 people found that of possible measures to improve the recruitment and retention of women, flexible working provisions were used by the largest number of organisations. This was followed in descending order by recruitment and selection measures, consultation with and research into women employees' needs, job-sharing, maternity leave provisions, career breaks and family leave. Childcare provision was the least popular measure, although many organisations said they were considering the introduction of childcare measures.[1]

A survey of 120 employers employing over one million workers found that one in five employers had agreements which provided more than the minimum statutory maternity provision, and that the average return to work rate of women covered by these agreements was almost twice that of women who did not benefit from additional maternity pay or leave. Paternity pay was available to male employees in one third of the surveyed organisations. Only four (3%) organisations provided childcare facilities for their employees, although such provision was under consideration or planned by six others. Thirty per cent of employers gave women the opportunity to work part-time when they returned to work after maternity leave; in most cases this could be a permanent arrangement if the woman wished.[2]

In a survey of 2,000 employees, 53.5% said they combined work with caring responsibilities for children, elderly, ill or disabled relatives or friends who need support or attention on a regular basis. The percentage of women in employment who were also carers, 54%, was the same as the percentage of male carers, 54%. Caring responsibilities caused difficulties for employees. Some 42% of men and women had had to take time off work during the previous year because of childcare responsibilities, with 36% having to leave work early and 31% having to arrive late. The percentage of men who said they had to take time off because of childcare responsibilities was very similar to that for women. Caring for an adult had adversely affected the working lives of 47% of female and 35% of male employees surveyed.[3]

---

19   Article 6.
20   Proposal for a Council Directive on certain employment relationships with regard to working conditions; Proposal for a Council Directive on certain employment relationships with regard to distortions of competition, COM (90) 228 final – SYN 280, Brussels, 13 August 1990, OJ C/224, p 6, as amended by COM (90) 533 final – SYN 280, Brussels, 31 October 1990. The proposal contained also a measure with ambiguous consequences for part-timers: requiring employers intending to have recourse to part-time work to inform workers' representative bodies within the undertaking (Article 2(3)).
1   Industrial Relations Services (IRS) *Recruitment and Development Report* No 6, 19 June 1990, p 2.
2   IRS *Employment Trends* No 439, 10 May 1989, p 6; No 442, 27 June 1989, p 12.
3   IRS *Employment Trends* No 468, 17 July 1990, p 4.

A survey found that, despite the projected fall in the number of young people coming into the labour market, few employers had adopted 'family friendly' policies aimed at attracting and keeping people with caring responsibilities in their workforce. In particular, none of the private sector employers offered their employees any specific help with caring for elderly dependents. Yet, as the age profile of the labour force changes, with an increasingly large proportion likely to be concentrated in the 45–55 age bracket, the factor determining the ability of many workers to take on paid employment may well be the availability of 'eldercare'.[4]

The EU law on sex discrimination does not provide adequate protection for part-time workers. For example, an employer's insistence that an employee should work at certain times of the day can, in some circumstances, amount to indirect sex discrimination. But the court has to strike a balance 'between the discriminatory effect of the condition and the reasonable needs of the party who applied the condition'. In a case where the employee refused to work certain hours required to teach sport to school children because of her childcare responsibilities, the court held the school children's needs outweighed the discriminatory effect on the woman employee.[5]

There is, therefore, a need for measures to encourage the provision of part-time work and to recognise the family and other responsibilities of workers. This will include rights in labour law to require employers to make special provisions. It will also impose obligations on Member State social welfare systems to assist part-timers and workers with special caring responsibilities.

The solution is not only the redistribution of working time by constricting the upper range of working hours. It requires incentives to adopt a lower range of working hours by providing benefits to part-timers who do socially useful work like childcare or caring for the aged and disabled, or who undergo education and training, undertake community service, perform public functions, and so on.

This is a theme consistent with the thrust of the Commission's Green and White Papers on the future of European social policy. The stark work/leisure dichotomy should give way to more complex patterns of the use of time incorporating the elements of social responsibility, education and training. New patterns of working time offer the possibility of new combinations of work, education, social responsibility and leisure in a more integrated life cycle.

The measures required will therefore go beyond the traditional labour law rights and social security law entitlements. They will include rights and entitlements to training, caring responsibilities, community service, and provide incentives to workers to undertake these activities. The objective is to make paid work not the sole, nor always the central activity of human life.

Work is traditionally separated from the rest of life by time. Labour law does not formally and directly regulate non-working time. But the availability of non-working time, and the uses to which it can be put, depend on the regulation of working time. The development of a European model of working time is central to the lives of all those who live in Europe.

---

4   IRS *Employment Trends* No 457, 6 February 1990, p 4.
5   *Briggs v North Eastern Education and Library Board* [1990] IRLR 181.

IMPLEMENTING THE EUROPEAN MODEL: THE ROLES OF LEGISLATION AND SOCIAL DIALOGUE

EU *legislation* in the form of the Directive on Working Time is potentially a major step forward in the evolution of a European model of working time. However, working time is an area in which both the European Union and the Member States have competences. Following the Maastricht Treaty on European Union, this competence may be exercised also by the social partners in the form of social dialogue at EU level or by the social partners within Member States through collective bargaining. Within this general framework, much of any progress towards the new European model of working time will be made within Member States. It falls to national legislatures, trade unions and employers and their organisations within Member States to undertake this task.

Implementing the European model within the UK

Within the UK, the *sectoral* level of regulation, whether by law or collective bargaining, may be critical. The extremes of the range of working hours are highly concentrated in certain industries. Among those working long hours, 'Other Transport', with only 3.8% of all employees, includes the single largest number of employees usually working 60 or more hours per week – 10.3% of the total number in the UK. Other sectors with common long hours jobs include agriculture, forestry and fishing with 15.2% of employees usually working 60 or more hours per week. The coke, oil, gas extraction and nuclear industries, with 17.4% of employees usually working 60 or more hours per week, also have the highest average employee hours at 48.6 per week.[6] These sectors are clearly candidates for careful attention when the Working Time Directive comes into effect.

Among those working very short hours, less than 16 per week, some 60% work in just four industrial sectors, employing only 26% of all employees: retail distribution (25.4%), hotels and catering (14.3%), schools (10.3%) and other services (10.4%).[7] The *Employment Gazette* points out that in such industries – hotels and catering, retail distribution, cleaning and other services industries – there are definite times of greater demand which account for large numbers of short hours jobs. However:[8]

'it is clear that in other industries where there are peaks in demand there are few part-time jobs. For example both train and bus services have peaks and troughs in demand during each day and also across the week. However very few employees in the transport sector work part-time, and although peaks and troughs may be covered by shift working including split shifts, it is possible that regular variations in demand could also be covered by part-time workers as in many other service industries.

What is also interesting is the fact that in recent years many companies in both the service sector and in manufacturing have extended their opening/operating hours. This means that it is often not possible to work "full-time" ie work all the hours a company is operating. The need for cover or shifts to be organised across longer time periods should increase the opportunities for employees to be able to work a

6   (1992) *Employment Gazette* (November), p 547.
7   Ibid.
8   Ibid, pp 547–8.

wider variety of hours. However in many areas there still appears to be a continuing tradition of employing mainly full-time workers, ie over 30 hours per week, and of employing few people to work part-time.'

Industries at both extremes of the range of working hours are likely to be affected by the introduction of the new European model of working time. Industries with many part-timers will be the target of measures providing these workers with protection – at least rights equal to those of full-time workers. But also, if the Green and White Papers' logic is pursued, measures recognising the family and other responsibilities of workers, providing training opportunities and ensuring the requisite social welfare.[9]

Those industries with a concentration of long hours workers will be faced with the need for compliance with Article 6 of the Directive: the maximum weekly working time of 48 hours on average, including overtime. These industries are candidates for the application of the obligation foreseen in Article 13:

> 'an employer who intends to organise work according to a certain pattern takes account of the general principle of adapting work to the worker, with a view, in particular, to alleviating monotonous work and work at a predetermined work-rate depending on the type of activity, and of safety and health requirements, especially as regards breaks during working time.'

It was argued above that this provision implied an obligation to take into account the views of workers and their representatives. It provides an opportunity for trade unions to negotiate over the restructuring of working time in line with the new EU standard of humanisation of work. At the same time it provides them with the opportunity to rethink traditional bargaining packages and promote the new European model including rights and entitlements to training, caring responsibilities, community service, and providing incentives to workers to undertake these activities.

Occupations in which there are concentrations of long hours workers will offer trade unions opportunities for recruitment and mobilisation as they face the problems of renegotiating traditional working time patterns: health service professionals (with the longest hours) average 51 hours per week, managers in agriculture and services (46.8), drivers and mobile machine operators (46.4) and those working in other occupations in agriculture, forestry and fishing.[10] In so doing, trade unions have an opportunity to resolve the dilemma which has been confronting them for many years: declining membership in traditional sectors and inability to recruit among the categories of new forms of employment. This has raised problems of representativeness which owe much of their urgency to the fact that standard employment relationships are decomposing; as a result, the internal constitutional structures of unions are under challenge.

Resolving these problems will test the capacity of unions in many ways: to

---

9 One measure is indicated by the fact that of the 14.6% of male part-timers, 52.7% are over 50, and 30.5% are between ages 16–19 ((1993) *Employment Gazette* (May), Table 2 on p 214). One policy proposal would be for a combination of partial retirement with youth training: a legal requirement (in the form of a law or collective agreement) on employers of maximum part-time weekly working hours for workers over 50, with a guarantee of previous earnings, coupled with a requirement to engage a part-timer aged 16–19, with a guarantee of training. Not only does it ease the burden on older people: more important, it may socialise younger people into part-time work.

10 Op cit, p 548.

carry their traditional members to support the new trade-offs resulting from changes in working hours; to integrate the new categories of workers; to accommodate the involvement of women in unions; to organise 'atypical' workers and successfully engage in collective bargaining on issues relevant to them. The next section explores how the sectoral social dialogue in the EU has the potential to make a particular contribution on the issue of working time.

Sectoral level bargaining and the Working Time Directive

Sectoral level bargaining in the Member States

It was highlighted earlier that the sectoral level of bargaining is becoming more important in Europe, with the exception of the UK. A study carried out for the Commission by Vaughan-Whitehead[11] suggested that within the majority of Member States sectoral bargaining has moved into the position once occupied by multi-sector national level bargaining. This is particularly important for an EU-wide framework for bargaining, as areas within the competence of sectoral bargaining could be translated into European agreements.

Vaughan-Whitehead emphasised in particular that reduction and adjustment of working hours and various flexibility issues had begun to be discussed at sectoral level.[12] He gives numerous indicative examples:[13]

Netherlands: Sectoral bargaining was extended in 1987 to cover working hours (in the banking and engineering sectors).

Italy: In 1987 shorter working hours was one of the main topics of sectoral bargaining.

Denmark: There has been a marked increase in the number of sectoral agreements covering a shorter working week (fixed at 37 hours until 1990) in the public and engineering sectors.

France: An agreement on shorter working hours was signed for the first time in the French hotel industry, and other agreements covered such matters as part-time working and the employment of seasonal workers in the foodstuffs industry.

Belgium: The return to free collective bargaining in 1986 led to the identification of new needs with regard to working hours in the glassmaking and building industries.

Spain: The General Workers' Union (CGT) and the employers' confederation (CEOE) agreed in March 1988 to extend sectoral negotiations to new topics, and subsequent sectoral agreements have resulted in the adjustment of working hours for bank staff and shorter working hours in the hotel industry.

Vaughan-Whitehead concluded that 'It is only in the UK, where collective bargaining has declined both with regard to wages and other topics, that this trend has not been noted'.[14]

---

11   D Vaughan-Whitehead 'Wage Bargaining in Europe: continuity and change', *Social Europe*, Supplement 2/90.
12   Ibid, at p 13, and see the examples quoted in Table 3, pp 26–32.
13   Ibid, pp 13–14.
14   Ibid.

Sectoral agreements in the Working Time Directive

The Working Time Directive appears to make room for sectoral agreements through its many references to 'collective agreements or agreements between the two sides of industry' – a formula which, with minor variations, appears in all the provisions incorporating collective bargaining as an instrument in the formulation of EU standards.[15]

It was argued that a preference for the sectoral level could be perceived in the most complex provision allowing for derogations:[16]

'Derogations may be made from Articles 3, 4, 5, 8 and 16 by means of collective agreements or agreements concluded between the two sides of industry at national or regional level or, in conformity with the rules laid down by them, by means of collective agreements or agreements concluded between the two sides of industry at a lower level.'

Article 17(3) permits derogation by national or regional agreements or lower level agreements in conformity with rules laid down by national or regional agreements. This gives primacy to national or regional levels of collective agreements, where sectoral agreements are most common. Other levels may only derogate in conformity with these. Moreover, Article 17(3) continues:

'Member States may lay down rules . . .
– for the extension of the provisions of collective agreements or agreements concluded in conformity with this paragraph to other workers in accordance with national legislation and/or practice.'

These procedures of extension already exist, but apply almost everywhere to sector level agreements only.

The growth of sector level bargaining on working time within Member States fits into the space opened up by the Working Time Directive's espousal of collective agreements as EU labour standard setting instruments. The question is whether a further link can be established between sectoral agreements at Member State level and agreements at EU-level in the same sectors. An illustration of the possibilities comes from the metalworking sector.

Sectoral agreements on working time in the metalworking industry[17]

There are 26 trade unions in the EU Member States affiliated to the European Metalworkers' Federation (EMF) representing about half of the EC Member State workforce in engineering. Affiliates to the EMF retain their autonomy 'as far as their own trade union activities are concerned', while the EMF endeavours 'to achieve common action by all metalworkers' unions in the Community'. Members 'pledge themselves to respect and support, as far as possible, the decisions and principles of the competent EMF organs'.[18]

EMF strategy emphasises *coordination* of national collective bargaining efforts. Sectoral bargaining at Member State level retains primacy: EU-level sectoral activity focuses on coordinating Member State sectoral bargaining objectives and action.

---

15 Articles 2(4)(b)(ii), 4, 6(1), 8(2), 15, 16(3), 17(2),(3) and (4).
16 Article 17(3).
17 Some of the material from this section appears in B Bercusson 'European Labour Law and Sectoral Bargaining', (1993) 24 *Industrial Relations Journal* (December) 257.
18 Statutes of the European Metalworkers' Federation (EMF) in the Community, Chapter I.

The period of the formation of the EMF as a separate organisation for metal-workers in Europe was also a time of struggle for the shorter working week. In a 1969 paper the EMF identified the reduction of working time as having the potential to 'serve as starting points or basis for the coordination of the collective bargaining policy in the metal trade unions in the EEC'.[19] Between 1967 and 1972 hours' reductions were won in all the then Member States.

WORKING HOURS' CAMPAIGN 1967–1972		
Country	*New maximum ·hours*	*Date of agreement*
Belgium	42.0	1.7.70
France	44.0	1.9.69
Germany	40.0	1.1.67
Italy	44.5	Unions raising demands for 40-hour week in 1969 negotiations
Luxembourg	40.0	1.1.72
Netherlands	42.5	1972

Negotiations began in Germany with the first concession in 1967, spread through France, Italy and Belgium and were then followed by agreements in Luxembourg and the Netherlands.

The recent round of reductions in the working week appears to have had a similar history. Within the engineering sector collective agreements in general fix the working week at below 48 hours, with most agreements around 36–40 hours.

WEEKLY HOURS IN ENGINEERING AS FIXED BY LAW AND COLLECTIVE AGREEMENT (C/A)[20]					
Country			*weekly working time*		
	by law	doa	by C/A		actual hours worked
Belgium	40	1975	36–38	(by region)	38.4
Denmark	–	–	37	(1.9.90); 39 ('87)	37.4
France	39	1982	38.5		39.5
Germany	48	1938	36	(1993); 35 (10.95)	38.0
Greece	40	1984	37–40		40.3
Ireland	48	1938	39	(by end 1990)	40.6
Italy	48	1923	40	(1985/1989)	40.1
Luxembourg	40	1975	40		40.2
Netherlands	48	1919	38	(1982)	36.8
Portugal	44	1991	44	(manual); 40 (non-man)	43.3
Spain	40	1983	38–40		40.2
UK	–	–	37	(by end 1991)	43.1

19 'Structure and Development of Collective Bargaining. Negotiations in the Metal Industries of the EEC', *Information Bulletin* of the European Committee for the Metalworkers' Unions, No 4/69 (September–December), at p 12.

20 Source: EMF Comparative Tables on Working Time in the Metalworking Industry, (June 1990) and Eurostat Labour Force Survey, 1989.

THE CAMPAIGN IN GERMANY

The campaign for reduction in working hours in Germany began in the late 1980s. In 1990 the deal in engineering was struck by a two stage process, from 37 to 36 hours as of 1 April 1993 and to 35 hours as from 1 October 1995. One notable feature of the German agreement, which also formed part of the UK experience, was that the hours' reductions were traded against new flexibility proposals, introduced as 'taking into account the economic situation'.[1] One way this was achieved was by extending the working week (to up to 40 hours) for a proportion of employees at any given time. This gave employers greater freedom to allocate employees according to the demands of production. Thus concession of the demand for the shorter working week gave employers the opportunity to extend productive working.

One German study, by the independent research institute DIW, found that reductions in the working week had a positive effect on the German economy. Moderate/long term pay agreements had been concluded in return for the hours' reductions and these had reduced German labour costs. There had been an extension in the use of equipment and an increased use of shift work/flexible day/weekend work. Sunday and holiday working had increased from 10% (1965) to 18% (1991); nightwork from 11% to 14%.

The most famous example of this was the Volkswagen agreement of November 1993 which reduced working time for production staff to an average of 28.8 hours per week without any compensatory increase in pay rates. This was credited with the avoidance of some 30,000 redundancies, which meant that VW did not have to make massive redundancy payments. This model gained wide notoriety in Germany and in Europe in general. In the following months, Gesamtmetall, the German metal industry employers' association, conducted a survey of 1,259 firms in the metal and electronics industries in Germany of which 110 had reduced working time temporarily to a minimum of 30 hours. The unused volume of work was said to be enough to avoid 50,000 redundancies.[2]

THE CAMPAIGN IN THE UK

In the UK the claim for a 35 hour week had been submitted even earlier, in 1983, although it was not finally settled until after the German claims. The UK submission came five years after a previous hours' reduction had cut the working week in engineering from 40 to 39 hours. That one-hour cut had been accompanied by productivity deals aimed at reducing its cost. When the new claim was submitted in 1983 unions accepted that changes to working practices might form part of the deal. But talks dragged on over several years without any real progress and eventually collapsed when the employers, demanding that no company should be obliged to reduce hours unless there was a trade-off of greater flexibility, pulled out of national negotiations.[3]

With the collapse of the national agreement the CSEU (Confederation of Shipbuilding and Engineering Unions) had no alternative but to pursue the

1 'Collective Bargaining in the West in 1990'. *European Industrial Relations Review* No 210, July 1991.
2 Handelsblatt, 25 August 1994, cited in 'Flexibility and work organisation', *Social Europe* Supplement 1/95, at p 18.
3 R Richardson and M Rubin *The Shorter Working Week in Engineering: surrender without sacrifice*, CEP Discussion Paper, January 1993, at page 3. This paper provides a fairly detailed account of the working time negotiations in the UK.

claim on a firm by firm basis. The strategy which it chose was to target a limited number of companies, call the members in those firms out on strike and pay a high level of strike pay financed by a general levy of the whole membership.

By April 1991 the CSEU claimed that it had successfully concluded the first stage of its programme with agreements in 1,666 companies covering 600,000 workers,[4] and that, as with the German experience, these reductions were at least partly financed by changes to working practices, cuts in breaks, bell to bell working, increased flexibility and a tightening up of procedures on sickness and lateness. According to Richardson and Rubin the apparent success of the campaign was not as great, when the extent of the concessions is taken into account.[5]

Moreover, *actual* hours now worked by employees in engineering, compared to those worked prior to the new agreements, may not differ greatly; indeed, there is evidence that in some cases they have actually increased. There has been a *decline* in the proportion of employees whose basic *contractual* weekly hours were 40, from 22% in 1984 to 14.8% in 1991. As would be expected, at the same time the proportion of workers whose basic *contractual* hours were 37 *increased* from 6.5% to 11.3%.

But these *contractual* reductions have not necessarily led to employees *actually* working fewer hours. Although the proportion of those *working* 40 hours did decline, from 13.9% in 1984 to 9.7% in 1991, that fall is *less* than the fall in contractual hours. The rise in the proportion of those *actually* working 37 hours, from 4.8% to 6.5%, does not reflect fully the changes in *contractual* hours. The proportion of workers who work 37 hours (6.5%) is the same as the proportion whose contractual hours were 37 before the start of the latest round of negotiations. The reduction in the contractual working week comes hand in hand with an increase in the proportion of workers actually working more than 48 hours, from 12.2% in 1984 to 15.5% in 1991.

The prospects for future sectoral bargaining on working time

It has been demonstrated that it is possible for unions with differing histories and traditions to focus on the same issue and bargain on it. There has not so far been coordinated bargaining; however, there are in place procedures and practices which could allow it to develop. The Western European Metal Trades Employers' Organisation (WEM) believes that what has taken place has not been the result of a strategic campaign, internationally coordinated; rather, there

4   There is some argument as to the actual numbers covered. The EEF (Engineering Employers Federation) disputes the CSEU figures and states that just 595 out of its 5,000 member companies, employing 135,000 workers (about a third of the manual workforce) did settle.

5   Op cit, at page 33. In every Member State where deals have been concluded there have been trade-offs between hours and flexibility, either through shift working or round the clock working and these have occurred both within and outside the engineering sector. With the exception of Luxembourg, in every Member State there have been hours reductions negotiated in the last decade. Usually these were achieved through cuts in weekly hours, but annual hours agreements have also been concluded. *Working Time in Europe, European Industrial Relations Review* Report No 5, 1991.

6   The Western European Metal Trades Employers' Organisation (WEM) was founded on an ad hoc basis in 1962 and formalised in 1970. It represents engineering employers' organisations in nine of the Member States (there is no representation from Greece, Ireland and Portugal), and others outside the EU. Its federated members are recognised as 'being responsible for the conclusion of the collective agreements in the metal industry of the countries concerned'.

were claims oriented to national priorities.[6] The present lack of coordination should not obscure the fact that the emergence of a Single European Market may lead to a convergence of national priorities on working time, if factors which favour such bargaining are more powerful than those which impede it.

The Council Directive on Working Time could be a catalyst in this direction. The text allows for sectoral level collective agreements to derogate from the standards prescribed there. In this way it opens the way to a campaign by the EMF to coordinate such demands. An EU-sectoral level agreement on working time could provide a number of advantages. Sectoral agreements at Member State level could adapt the procedures agreed at *EU-level* in line with national requirements. This flexibility would not affect the fundamental guarantees provided in the Directive on Working Time. Sectoral agreements at Member State level would adapt to local conditions the rules agreed at EU-sectoral level. EU-sectoral agreements would guarantee Member State sectoral compliance with the EC standards. It would ensure that Member State sectoral bargaining excludes competition through the undermining of basic working conditions.

CONCLUSION

The emergence of a European model of working time exemplifies the dynamic process of evolution of a European labour law. The emergent European model of working time is not that of one or other Member State. It draws on the experience of *various* Member States so that to each it is both familiar in some of its elements and yet different in its entirety. This can be exemplified through the the the impending encounter of the European model of working time with UK experience.

As regards the UK, the Directive and resulting European model curtail the tradition of very long working hours in certain industries and occupations. The impulse is towards a redistribution of working hours from longer to shorter hours. This reflects the narrower range of working hours, with high concentrations in specific hours bands, to be found in many other Member States, quite different from the exceptionally wide distribution currently to be found in the UK.

On the other hand, the Directive and European model introduce a potentially dynamic role for collective bargaining both for derogation and for standard setting which is familiar to the UK, but less so to many other Member States, where legislation plays the key role in regulating working hours. This is an important opportunity for trade unions to rethink traditional bargaining packages and promote the new European model, including rights and entitlements to training, caring responsibilities, community service, and providing incentives to workers to undertake these activities.

The distinctive EU contribution may be perceived, first, in the law on indirect sex discrimination. Through the statistical fact of female predominance in part-time working, this has led to extensive legal interventions to ensure equal treatment for part-timers. Going further, the Green and White Papers promise a more dynamic approach: providing incentives for part-time employment, guaranteeing part-timers equal protection and recognising family and other social responsibilities of workers. The centrality of part-time work to a European model of working time is a manifestation of the new European labour law.

Chapter 31

Specific Categories of Employment

INTRODUCTION

EU labour law's attempts to come to terms with the fragmentation of the work-force and the development of new forms of work took different directions. Those already dealt with include extending the boundaries of labour law beyond the contract of employment to include a wider range of employment relationships, and developing a policy on the distribution of working time, with particular emphasis on part-time workers.

A third alternative strategy is to directly acknowledge and regulate specific new forms of work. The initiatives in this direction took the form of proposals for Council Directives on certain employment relationships in the aftermath of the approval of the Charter of Fundamental Social Rights in December 1989.[1] One proposal introduced at the same time[2] was eventually approved and became Council Directive 91/533 of 25 June 1991 supplementing the measures to encourage improvement in the safety and health at work of workers with a fixed-duration employment relationship or a temporary employment relationship.[3]

The three proposals were accompanied by a lengthy Explanatory Memorandum which pointed out differences between Member States in the numbers and proportion of the workforce employed in such relationships. It was estimated that the workers concerned by the Directives accounted for some 20% of total employment.[4] As regards *part-timers*, in 1988 these were over 30% of the working population in the Netherlands, and more than 20% in Denmark (23.7%) and the UK (21.9%), some 13.2% in the Germany, but around 5% in Spain (5.4%), Italy (5.6%), Greece (5.5%) and Portugal (6.5%) (8% in Ireland).[5] The Community average was 13.6%, more than 14 million part-time employees.

As regards *temporary employment*, in 1988, employees with a temporary contract were 22.4% in Spain, 18.5% in Portugal and 17.6% in Greece, but fell from just over 11% in Germany and Denmark, to 8.7% in the Netherlands,

1 Proposal for a Council Directive on certain employment relationships with regard to working conditions; Proposal for a Council Directive on certain employment relationships with regard to distortions of competition, COM (90) 228 final – SYN 280, Brussels, 13 August 1990.
2 Proposal for a Council Directive supplementing the measures to encourage improvements in the safety and health at work of temporary workers, COM (90) 228 final – SYN 281, Brussels, 13 August 1990.
3 OJ 1991 L206/19.
4 Explanatory Memorandum, paragraph 20.
5 *A Social Portrait of Europe*, Luxembourg 1991, p 62, Table 5.6; also ibid, paragraph 15.

7.8% in France and 5.9% in the UK.[6] A 1989 survey showed that 30% of employment relationships in Spain were limited in time, but the figure was around 10% in Italy, Greece, Ireland and Portugal and below 10% in all other Member States.[7]

Eight main issues were considered to call for particular attention:[8]

- access to training;
- taking into account such employees in calculating numbers of persons in employment with a view to the setting up of representative bodies for workers;
- information for workers' representative bodies in the event of recourse to the workers concerned;
- grounds for recourse to temporary employment;
- information for the temporary workers employed where the employer intended to recruit full-time employees for an indefinite period;
- rules concerning access to social assistance;
- access to the social services of undertakings;
- the specific situations of workers employed through temporary employment businesses.

Instead of being incorporated into one Directive, however, these issues were divided among three different draft Directives, each ostensibly concerned with a different theme: (1) working conditions, (2) distortions of competition, and (3) health and safety, and each with a different legal basis. The significance of the legal basis lies in the capacity of the Council of Ministers to approve proposed Directives either by qualified majority voting or by unanimity. The working conditions draft Directive was based on Article 100 of the Treaty of Rome, requiring unanimity. The draft Directive on distortions of competition was based on Article 100A, and that on health and safety on Article 118A – both of which require only qualified majority voting.

The working conditions draft Directive (Article 100) applies to temporary and part-time workers and covers:

- access to training, services and social assistance/social security schemes;[9]
- calculation of employee numbers relating to employee representative bodies;[10]
- information and consultation of employee representatives;[11]
- informing about full-time open-ended vacancies;[12]
- contents of temporary employment contracts;[13]
- temporary work agencies and user companies;[14] and
- obligations of temporary employment agencies.[15]

6   Ibid, p 64, Table 5.13.
7   Explanatory Memorandum, paragraph 16.
8   Ibid, paragraph 48.
9   Articles 2.1, 3 and 4.
10 Article 2.2.
11 Article 2.3.
12 Article 5.
13 Article 2.4.
14 Article 6.
15 Article 7.

The distortions of competition draft Directive (Article 100A) also applies to temporary and part-time workers and deals with:

- entitlement to social protection under statutory and occupational social security schemes;[16]
- holidays, dismissal payments and seniority allowances;[17] and
- termination of a temporary contract before term.[18]

The health and safety draft Directive (Article 118A) applied only to temporary workers and concerns:

- contents of the contract between the user company and the temporary work agency;[19]
- user companies' responsibilities;[20]
- information and training of temporary workers;[1] and
- work requiring special medical supervision.[2]

The proposals regarding these specific categories of employment can be better understood less through detailed analysis of their substantive provisions than through the context in which they emerged and in which they were considered in the early 1990s.

SPECIFIC CATEGORIES OF WORKERS, LABOUR COSTS AND SOCIAL DUMPING

The approval of only one of the three proposed Directives specifically addressing particular forms of work was significant for a variety of reasons. Two of the three proposals, the two that were not approved, related to *both* part-timers *and* non-permanent workers. The third applied *only* to non-permanent workers, and it was this proposal only which was approved.

Prior to their presentation, there was an intense debate on which Articles of the Treaty of Rome should constitute their legal basis. The two proposed Directives on certain employment relationships were based respectively on Article 100 and Article 100A of the Treaty. Article 100 required unanimous approval in the Council of Ministers. This was not forthcoming. Article 100A allowed for qualified majority voting, but not, according to Article 100A(2), if it related to 'the rights and interests of employed persons'. The interpretation of this phrase would have been stringently tested by an attempt to extend qualified majority voting to the second proposal. The third proposal, however, was based on Article 118A of the Treaty, inserted by the Single European Act 1986, which allowed for qualified majority voting on proposals concerning 'the working environment, as regards the health and safety of workers.'

The draft Directives were accompanied by considerable dispute as they progressed through the legislative procedure. Within the Commission, the Legal

---

16   Article 2.
17   Article 3.
18   Article 4(b).
19   Article 3.
20   Article 4.
 1   Article 5.
 2   Article 6.

Service and Directorate-General V (Social Affairs) had differences over the appropriate legal bases for the draft Directives. Parliament and the Economic and Social Committee objected to the division of issues among different drafts with different legal bases. In the case of ECOSOC, a tripartite body, the employer members approved the substantive content of the draft Directives on atypical work, but objected to the legal basis allowing for qualified majority voting. On the contrary, Parliament objected to the draft Directives where approval required unanimity in the Council of Ministers. Parliament put forward amendments inserting the content of the working conditions draft directive (based on Article 100) into the other two.

Only the third proposal, relating to the health and safety of temporary workers, was approved by the Council of Ministers. The implications of the approval of a Directive affecting only temporary workers by qualified majority voting in the Council are particularly interesting, given the composition and distribution of the labour force within the EC. Unlike part-timers, there is no general preponderance of women workers in the non-permanent workforce.[3] However, with respect to both part-timers and non-permanent workers, there is a clear North–South cleavage within the Community.

The northern European Member States have a disproportionately high number of part-timers compared to the southern European Member States. In 1988, part-timers were over 30% of of the working population in the Netherlands, and more than 20% in Denmark (23.7%) and the UK (21.9%), some 13.2% in Germany, but around 5% in Spain (5.4%), Italy (5.6%), Greece (5.5%) and Portugal (6.5%) (8% in Ireland).[4] The opposite is true for non-permanent workers, who are concentrated more densely in the south. In 1988, employees with a temporary contract were 22.4% in Spain, 18.5% in Portugal and 17.6% in Greece, but fell from just over 11% in Germany and Denmark, to 8.7% in the Netherlands, 7.8% in France and 5.9% in the UK.[5]

The implications of a specific category of employment regulated by EC labour law are that the *costs* of such regulation are borne by the employers of that category of employees, and appear as a form of competitive disadvantage vis-à-vis employers not subject to such regulation. In so far as part-time employment is predominantly concentrated in northern Europe, employers in those countries have to bear a disproportionate cost of the equality law of the EC. Conversely, the enactment of EC regulations specifically aimed at non-permanent employment imposes costs disproportionately on southern European employers, where such employment is concentrated. The early adoption by the Council of such regulation has significance for the general debate over 'social dumping', given the generally lower labour costs of southern European employers.

SPECIFIC CATEGORIES OF WORKERS IN THE CONTEXT OF AN EVOLVING EC LABOUR LAW

The 1990 draft Directives had been preceded by earlier Commission proposals. A draft Directive on 'temporary employment businesses' and 'fixed duration

---

3 See *A Social Portrait of Europe*, Statistical Office of the European Communities (Eurostat), Luxembourg 1991, p 64, Table 5.13.
4 Ibid, p 62, Table 5.6.
5 Ibid, p 63, Table 5.13.

contracts' was presented in 1982 and revised in 1984;[6] another on 'voluntary part-time work' was also presented in 1982 and revised in 1983.[7] Neither was ever adopted by the Council. However, their formulation at a time when the debate on 'atypical' work was still in its infancy was significant.

The implications of dramatic growth in new forms of employment, the consequent fragmentation of the labour market and the relative, and potential longer-term, decline in the 'typical' employment model had not yet sunk in. The constraints on social legislation in the Rome Treaty meant that proposals had to find a legal basis supported by the common market ethos of Article 100; in particular, on the basis of distorting competition through uneven labour standards. This combined with the then dominant theme in EU labour law: anti-discrimination, derived from the provisions in the Treaty and the then recent plethora of Directives on sex equality. This ethic affected other social policy initiatives. Not surprisingly, therefore, the initiatives of the early 1980s focused on prohibiting discrimination, eliminating different standards which distorted competition, and regulating the transition from 'atypical' to 'typical' work. Despite the passage of several years before the new proposals of 13 August 1990 emerged, perhaps due to the inactivity on social policy due to the UK veto on initiatives, the same thinking continued to dominate.

The proposed Council Directive on certain employment relationships with regard to working conditions (the Article 100 Directive) in its Preamble emphasised that certain workers 'do not always enjoy within the undertaking treatment equal to that of other employees in respect of employment and working conditions'.[8] It proposed to ameliorate this situation by provisions in a number of Articles:

> '2.1 Employees covered by an employment relationship for part-time work and/or a fixed duration shall enjoy access to vocational training initiated by the undertaking under conditions comparable to those enjoyed by workers employed in full-time employment of an indefinite duration, account being taken of the duration of work and the nature of the tasks to be carried out . . .
>   3. Employees covered by this Directive shall be entitled to enjoy the same treatment as workers employed in full-time employment of an indefinite duration as regards benefits in cash and in kind granted under social assistance schemes or under non-contributory social security schemes.
>   4. Employees covered by this Directive shall have access within the undertaking to the social services normally made available to the other employees.'

Equal treatment emerged also in the proposal for a Council Directive on certain employment relationships with regard to distortions of competition (the Article 100A Directive). In this case, however, as its title indicates, the rationale for equal treatment was two-fold: 'the elimination of distortions of competition and at the same time promotion of economic and social cohesion in the Community'.[9] Equal treatment was the subject of the following Articles:

> '2. Member States shall take the necessary measures to ensure that employees covered by this Directive (Article 1: part-time and temporary employment relationships) are afforded, vis-à-vis employees employed full-time for an indefinite duration, social

---

6   OJ C128/2, 7 May 1982 and OJ C133/1, 6 April 1984.
7   OJ C62/7, 4 January 1982; OJ C18/5, 5 January 1983.
8   Recital 3.
9   Recital 1.

protection under statutory and occupational social security schemes rooted in the same foundations and the same criteria, account being taken of the duration of work and/or pay.

3. Member States shall take the necessary measures to ensure that part-time workers are accorded the same entitlements to annual holidays, dismissal allowances and seniority allowances as full-time employees, in proportion to the total hours worked.'

In an important extension of scope, both Directives provided: 'This Directive shall apply to seasonal workers in so far as the special features of this form of work allow'.[10]

The *qualified* application of the equality principle to these categories of employment, particularly with respect to part-time workers, sits uneasily with the highly developed case-law of the European Court on indirect discrimination with respect to part-time workers, a majority of whom are women.

Further variations on the theme of equality were evident in numerous drafts subsequently proposed by Member States to revise the proposed Directive in an attempt to secure its passage through the Council of Ministers. A draft in 1993 proposed a minimum level of remuneration for such workers, related proportionately to the basic pay of full-time and/or indefinite duration workers.[11] Another draft of early 1994 proposed a general principle of equal treatment, with explicit justifications for deviating from the principle:[12]

'(1) The labour law provisions of the member states shall not contain less favourable regulations for part-time employees than for full-time employees in a comparable situation on account of the part-time nature of the employment. Furthermore, the member states shall take the measures required to ensure that employers do not treat part-time employees less favourably than full-time employees in a comparable situation in the same undertaking on account of the part-time nature of the employment.

(2) The labour law provisions of the member states shall not contain less favourable regulations for employees with fixed-duration contracts than for employees with open-ended contracts in a comparable situation on account of the fixed-duration nature of the employment. Furthermore, the member states shall take the measures required to ensure that employers do not treat employees with fixed-duration contracts less favourably than employees with open-ended contracts in a comparable situation in the same undertaking on account of the fixed-duration nature of the employment.

(3) A less favourable treatment for reasons other than the part-time nature of the employment and/or the fixed-duration nature of the employment shall be permissible. Other reasons shall be in particular:
– the employee's qualification,
– the employee's work experience,
– the employee's performance,
– the employee's social situation,
– the distribution of the hours of work,
– the organisation of work in the undertaking.'

---

10 Article 8 of the working conditions proposed Directive and Article 5 of the proposed distortions of competition Directive.
11 Council Document 8094/93, SOC 226, dated 20 July 1993, 'Projet Directive du Conseil sur le travail atypique', Article 2.
12 Draft of 19 March 1994, Bonn, Ministry of Labour and Social Affairs; 'Draft Council Directive on the Promotion of Employment and the Protection of Part-time Employment Relationships and Fixed-duration Employment Relationships', Article 3.

In a later draft of 1994 proposing separate Directives for part-time workers and fixed-duration workers, the Council and the Commission made a Declaration in the Minutes relating to this principle, as regards comparable situations, by referring explicitly to ILO Convention No 175 on part-time work, adopted 25 June 1994. Article 1(c) of this Convention provides detailed indications of the general criteria allowing for a judgment of what constitutes a comparable situation.[13] Another reservation went on to declare a view of what constitutes 'objective reasons' in terms familiar from the case law of the European Court.[14]

The impact of the pre-existing law on equal treatment as between men and women is apparent in these proposals concerning specific forms of employment. The applicability of the equality principle to these new categories of workers is unquestioned. The critique of the equality principle developed in the context of sex discrimination, and the development of strategies of positive action did not impinge on the Commission's thinking. Nor is there in these provisions a recognition that the position of these categories of workers may require specific proposals reflecting changes in the labour market, and responding to social policies other than anti-discrimination.

Some recognition of *other* labour market policy implications of specific categories of work does emerge, albeit in contradictory fashion, from the proposals. The original Commission proposal of 13 August 1990 stated in the Preamble that 'recent recruitment patterns show a marked increase in part-time and/or temporary employment relationships'[15] and extolled this development in terms of flexibility in the economy, notably among firms in the context of job creation, and of the aspirations of certain workers. The proposed Directive on working conditions (Article 100) contained a number of provisions regarding not labour standards, but the operation of the labour market concerning the specific forms of employment: part-time and fixed-duration workers. Articles 2(3) and 2(4) provided:

> '3. Where the employer intends to have recourse to employees covered by this Directive he shall inform in good time the workers' representative bodies existing within the undertaking.
>   In undertakings with more than 1000 employees a regular report shall be drawn up on this type of employment with regard to the development of the workforce as a whole.
> 4. The employer shall state in the contract of temporary employment the grounds for recourse to this type of employment relationship.'

Article 5:

> 'Where the undertakings concerned recruit workers for full-time employment of an indefinite duration, they shall inform in good time the employees covered by this Directive so that consideration can be given to any applications they make.'

Article 6:

> 'Member States shall take the appropriate measures to ensure that clauses prohibiting or preventing the conclusion of a contract of employment between the user undertaking and the employee of a temporary employment business are null and void or capable of being declared so.'

13　Council Document SN 4683/94 (SOC) of 4 November 1994, 'Propositions de directives: Relations de travail à temps partiel et relations de travail à durée déterminée', Annex 1 bis, paragraph 3(2).
14　Ibid, paragraph 5.
15　Recital 1.

Similarly, the proposed Directive on distortions of competition (Article 100A) provided in Article 4:

'With regard to temporary employment Member States shall take the necessary measures to ensure that:
a) national laws provide for a limit on the renewal of temporary employment relationships of a duration of 12 months or less for a given job so that the total period of employment does not exceed 36 months . . .'

What is interesting about these provisions is that they appear *equivocal* concerning the use of these atypical forms.[16] Article 2(3) of the Article 100 proposed Directive, on the one hand, merely ensures that representatives of the existing workforce are informed of recourse to these forms of employment, which may secure for these employees some collective protection. However, it also allows for objections to be made to the employer's having recourse to these forms of employment at all, and consequently obstruct their use. Similarly, Article 2(4), while ensuring that the employer has grounds for recourse to these forms, does appear to presume the need for justification of such recourse.

Article 5, by providing for part-time and fixed-duration workers to be informed of full-time permanent vacancies, creates an incentive towards this latter type of employment. There is no countervailing incentive, for example, towards the offering of part-time employment to full-timers. Similarly, Article 6 explicitly prohibits any bar to alternatives to the part-time employment of workers hired on a part-time basis. And Article 6 of the Article 100A proposed Directive similarly puts a limit on the duration of temporary employment.

All these provisions are laudable and serve understandable social policy aims, but they also may be interpreted as ambivalent endorsements of the new types of employment. Their ambiguity has been demonstrated by their dilution in subsequent drafts. For example, the provision in Article 2(3) of the Article 100 proposed Directive requiring information in good time of workers' representatives of the employer's intention to have recourse to these forms of employment disappeared. It was replaced by a requirement that they merely be informed regularly concerning the numbers of such workers and made it optional to allow workers' representatives to participate before the recruitment.[17]

Even more significant, the apparent one-way incentive to part-timers and temporary workers to apply for full-time permanent vacancies was broadened to allow for an apparently more open-ended flexibilisation of forms of employment:[18]

'Member States shall take the measures required to ensure that the employer notifies an employee working for him and having informed him of his wish to change the

16 This is a point made by Professor Ulrich Mückenberger in a paper entitled 'New Forms of Employment, the EC Charter of Workers' Rights and Approaches to European Standard-Setting', updating a talk given to a conference at the European University Institute in December 1989.
17 Draft of 19 March 1994, Bonn, Ministry of Labour and Social Affairs; 'Draft Council Directive on the Promotion of Employment and the Protection of Part-time Employment Relationships and Fixed-duration Employment Relationships', Article 6.
18 Draft of 19 March 1994, Bonn, Ministry of Labour and Social Affairs; 'Draft Council Directive on the Promotion of Employment and the Protection of Part-time Employment Relationships and Fixed-duration Employment Relationships', Article 4; also Draft of 4 November 1994, Council Doc SN 4683/94 (SOC), Project: 'Directive du Conseil relative à la protection du travail a temps partiel et à la promotion de l'emploi', Article 4.

length or distribution of his working hours or the duration of his employment relationship of corresponding vacancies to be filled in the undertaking. Notification may take the form of a general notice displayed in an appropriate place in the undertaking.'

The recognition of the specific needs of certain forms of employment here has been combined with labour market policy and is already reflecting policy concerns which appeared also in the 1993 Working Time Directive and were later manifested in the Commission's Consultative Document on the Reconciliation of Work and Family Life in 1995.

TWO CATEGORIES OF REGULATED EMPLOYMENT: TEMPORARY OR FIXED-TERM WORKERS AND YOUNG WORKERS

To date, only two Directives have been approved by the Council of Ministers which attempt to address the needs of specific forms of employment. Council Directive 91/383 of 25 June 1991 supplementing the measures to encourage improvements in the safety and health of workers with a fixed-duration employment relationship or a temporary employment relationship,[19] and Council Directive 94/33/EC of 22 June 1994 on the protection of young people at work[20] may be seen as directly regulating certain specific categories of workers. Both are primarily concerned with health and safety in specific circumstances, due, not least, to the possibility of their legal basis, Article 118A, allowing for qualified majority voting. But their significance lies in a recognition in EU policy that special measures are necessary to accommodate the different qualities of different categories of workers.

Temporary workers

The specific character of the employment covered by Directive 91/383, the Temporary Workers Directive, is captured in the definition of its scope:[1]

'This Directive shall apply to:
1. employment relationships governed by a fixed-duration contract of employment concluded directly between the employer and the worker, where the end of the contract is established by objective conditions such as reaching a specific date, completing a specific task or the occurrence of a specific event;
2. temporary employment relationships between a temporary employment business which is the employer and the worker, where the latter is assigned to work for and under the control of an undertaking and/or establishment making use of his services.'

Ostensibly, the objective of the Directive is to do no more than treat temporary workers equally to those other workers not in a temporary employment relationship:[2]

'The purpose of this Directive is to ensure that workers with an employment relationship as referred to in Article 1 are afforded, as regards safety and health at work, the same level of protection as that of other workers in the user undertaking and/or establishment.'

19 OJ 1991 L206/19.
20 OJ L216/12 of 20.8.1994.
1   Article 1.
2   Article 2(1).

In some respects this does mean precisely the same treatment:[3]

'The existence of an employment relationship as referred to in Article 1 shall not justify different treatment with respect to working conditions inasmuch as the protection of safety and health at work are involved, especially as regards access to personal protective equipment.'

But in other respects, more is required, recognising the *specific* character of temporary employment.

Particularly interesting is the Directive's willingness to ignore the constraints imposed by any contract of employment. The temporary employment relationship is to be regulated to secure the objectives of the Directive, without regard to who are the parties to the contract of employment or to the duration of their contractual relationship. One specific quality of this type of employment is its *triangular* quality, involving not only the employer (a temporary employment business) and the worker, but also a user undertaking where the worker performs his services. Article 3 imposes obligations also on this third party to the employment relationship, the user undertaking:

'... before a worker with an employment relationship as referred to in Article 1 takes up any activity, he is informed by the undertaking and/or establishment making use of his services of the risks which he faces.'

In such cases, Member States must ensure that:[4]

'... each worker receives sufficient training appropriate to the particular characteristics of the job ...'

Article 5 allows for Member States to ban workers with temporary employment relationships from being used for certain dangerous work, and, if not so banned, to guarantee the necessary protection by way of appropriate special medical surveillance. Moreover, recognising the special quality of the relationship:[5]

'It shall be open to Member States to provide that the appropriate special medical surveillance referred to in paragraph 2 shall extend beyond the end of the employment relationship of the worker concerned.'

The obligations imposed by EU law extend *beyond* the parties to the contract of employment, and impose on the employer party to the employment contract obligations extending beyond the employee. Article 7 provides:

'1. ... a user undertaking and/or establishment shall specify to the temporary employment business, inter alia, the occupational qualifications required and the specific features of the job to be filled;
2. the temporary employment business shall bring all these facts to the attention of the workers concerned.'

Ignoring completely the confines of the contract of employment, Article 8 provides:

'1. ... without prejudice to the responsibility of the temporary employment business as laid down in national legislation, the user undertaking and/or establishment is/are responsible, for the duration of the assignment, for the conditions governing performance of the work;

---

3 Article 2(2).
4 Article 4.
5 Article 5(3).

2. for the application of point 1, the conditions governing the performance of the work shall be limited to those connected with safety, hygiene and health at work.'

Contractual constraints of typical employment relationships are not allowed to hinder the imposition of special requirements necessary to fulfil the objectives regarding this category of workers.

Young workers

The Commission declared that it 'wishes to create a basic set of minimum provisions in respect of health and safety at work for this category of workers'.[6] The special quality to be noted of this category of workers concerns their engagement in education or training. Their conditions of work must be accommodated to the exigencies of these other activities.

The Directive prohibits work by children (a young person under 15, or who is still subject to compulsory full-time schooling under national law). But Article 4(2)(b) allows for exemption of those in a combined work/training or work experience scheme, providing the work is performed in accordance with conditions laid down by the competent authority. Similarly, Article 5 allows for exemptions for various activities, providing a prior authorisation has been granted by the competent authority. But working conditions must be regulated and activities must not be harmful to their attendance at school, their participation in vocational guidance or training programmes approved by the competent authority, or their capacity to benefit from instruction received.

The restrictions on the working time of young workers also recognise the outside engagement of education and training. In so far as children are permitted to carry out light work or a combined work/training scheme under Article 4(2)(b) and (c), working time must be limited to eight hours a day and 40 hours a week for combined work/training or work experience schemes, two hours on a school day and 12 hours a week for work in term time outside of school hours, and seven hours a day and 35 hours a week outside term time. Night work between 8 pm and 6 am is prohibited. As far as possible, a period free of any work is to be included in the school holidays where children who are 14 or over carry out light work or a combined work/training scheme.

More conventionally, the Directive also requires Member States to assess the hazards to all young persons (a person under 18 years of age who has an employment contract or relationship defined or governed by law). Protective measures must be adopted, taking specific account of the risk to their health, safety and development, which are a consequence of their lack of experience, absence of awareness of existing or potential risks, or immaturity.

The significance of the Directive is that it is not difficult to draw parallels with *other* workers having outside engagements, domestic or public responsibilities, and so on. It becomes a question of policy whether work obligations in those other cases also must accommodate these particular engagements of special categories of workers. How far must work obligations be subject to the condition that it not be 'harmful to their attendance at (other activities), their participation in (other activities), or their capacity to benefit from (those other

6   Proposal for a Council Directive on the protection of young people at work, COM (91) 543 final – SYN 383, Brussels, 17 March 1992, Explanatory Memorandum, paragraph 17.

activities)'. Again, the constraints on working time evident in Article 13 of the Working Time Directive, requiring the employer to take account of the need to adapt the work to the worker, may derive benefit from the principles developed by the Young Workers Directive.

FRAGMENTATION AND ITS IMPLICATIONS FOR THE DEVELOPING EUROPEAN LABOUR LAW ON INDIVIDUAL EMPLOYMENT

As the account of the fragmentation of the workforce demonstrates, the employment relationship has been subject to great stresses. The legal concept of this relationship has for many years been the subject of criticism for its failure to accommodate the changes.

Contentions over the legal nature of the employment relationship are not new to European labour law. Frequently, it was the issue which, in some countries, enabled labour law to break free of civil law and become an autonomous discipline. The civil law rules of contract are perceived as inadequate to govern the contract of employment. Even in those countries which did not make such a break, it was widely acknowledged that the employment relationship could not be captured within the rules governing ordinary contracts, and that its nature required different regulation, usually by bringing in legislation, but also through collective agreements.

The dynamic of labour law development in the EU is inspired by and draws upon these preoccupations at national level, but, as always, filters them through a specific perspective, and produces a result which is still in the process of evolution. Again, this evolution has had a reciprocal effect on Member State labour laws. Examples include Member State recognition of the specific needs of certain categories of workers, which has produced EC law directed specifically at temporary workers' health and safety. Conversely, the dynamics of EU equality law have had a considerable impact on the law governing part-time workers in Member States.

These responses to the fragmentation of the workforce have produced in some Member States a fragmentation of labour law: as application with respect to new categories of workers of employment protection provisions previously available only to 'typical' workers. To some extent, this has produced a rather unreflective replication of employment protection provisions, merely extended to include categories previously excluded. But it has also occasionally meant that such extension has been accompanied by distinct provisions recognising the *specific* qualities of the new categories being protected. It is conceivable that a sufficiently widespread diversification of employment protection laws would lead to a *qualitative* change in labour law, by way of recognition that different categories of workers have different requirements for employment protection.

The concept of worker-citizen

But these profound changes in the workforce could also lead to an equally profound transformation in labour law's concept of the employment relationship. This would go beyond a recognition of the specificity of the employment 'contract', beyond supplementing contractual rules with legislative regulation or collective agreement, and even beyond the multiplication of employment protection laws for *specific* categories of workers.

To some extent, the signs of change are already evident in national labour laws. One striking manifestation is in the form of constitutional provisions of social and economic rights of workers.[7] The literature in many countries has increasingly come to speak of the worker as a *citizen* in the enterprise; for example, legislation on rights of expression in France; or protection of dignity and privacy in Germany. The enormous literature on worker participation is a reflection of this.

At EU level, the inspiration for change derived impetus from the happenstance that the concept of 'worker' first emerged in a 'non-contractual' context. For the first decades of its existence, the EC was concerned primarily with workers as a factor within the common market. It was their freedom of movement which was to be protected by EU law. Hence, it was not the relationship of the worker to the employer which was of initial concern, but the relationship of the worker to the State. As such, the preoccupation of EC law was to extend the concept of worker very widely to ensure that all those performing work were able to circulate freely among Member States.[8] It was the worker's rights against Member States' restrictions on free movement which were the prime subject of scrutiny by EC institutions in the formative years. The Court's willingness to adopt an autonomous and extensive legal definition of worker, however, was confined to the policy area of free movement. The Court deferred to national law definitions of 'worker' when applying EC Directives in other policy areas of labour law.[9]

It was perhaps this initial vision of the worker as a citizen entitled to free movement which contributed towards what is now emerging as a concept of the employment relationship at EU level. Again, the debate is not characterised by maximum clarity and linearity of development. But the signs are there to be read.

The concept of the employment relationship is being subsumed in the wider debate over EU citizenship. It is not surprising that this should occur, given the conjunctural evolution of a European polity at a time when there is a palpable political exigency for the support of the EU by labour movements, and, simultaneously, the legal conceptualisation of employment is under strain in the specific context of a common market. The first of these two factors produced the impulse towards creation of the 'social dimension' of the 1992 Single European Market programme in the general form of a Community Charter of Fundamental Social Rights approved by 11 Member States at Strasbourg in December 1989. The second contributed toward the specific form it took. The 1989 Charter was transformed late in the day from a Charter of the Rights of *Citizens* to a Charter for *Workers*.[10]

---

7   For details, B Bercusson 'Fundamental Social and Economic Rights in the European Community', in A Cassese et al (eds) *Human Rights in the European Community: Methods of Protection*, Nomos Verlag, Baden-Baden 1991, pp 195–294.

8   Case 66/85: *Lawrie-Blum v Land Baden-Württemberg* [1986] ECR 2121.

9   Case 105/84: *Mikkelsen* [1986] 1 CMLR 316.

10   This both broadens and narrows its scope: workers include non-citizens; citizens include non-workers. B Bercusson 'The European Community's Charter of Fundamental Social Rights for Workers', (1990) 53 *Modern Law Review* 624.

The worker-citizen's relationship to employer, State and trade union

The implications of the subsumption of worker into citizen are many. Specifically, its impact on the legal definition of the employment relationship is that it expands this to include the worker's relationship with the State and the trade union, as well as the employer.[11] The worker is no longer legally defined separately in terms of different legal concepts/ties: contractual with the employer, as citizen with the State, and as member (contract/status) of the union. Up to now, each of these relationships was separate and, to some extent, there was an hierarchical ordering. For example, employment was subject to statute, but only if parties opted for contractual employee status. Union membership was separate, but employment could be related by contractual terms to collective agreements.

What these examples, and many others show, is the pre-eminence of *contract* doctrines in determining the employment relationship. It was contract which determined the nature of the employment relationship, and hence whether statute applied (eg to whether there was a dismissal). It was contract which provided the rules determining whether a collective agreement applied. It was contract which usually determined the worker's entitlement to legislative benefits, and governed the worker's relationship to the union.

The question facing the EU law on individual employment is whether the elements of citizenship, union membership or affiliation and employer-worker relationship can be creatively combined into a new legal concept of 'worker-citizen'. This would involve the worker being defined as somebody who has relations with employer, State and union (fellow workers) – perhaps *without* a specific hierarchical ordering, and using (non-contractual) concepts to determine the rights and duties owed by each to the others. This could include rights not only as between employer–union–State and workers, but also as between employer and union and State, as well as with the worker.

What concepts operate in these different contexts, and can they be combined? In employment, as Alan Fox shows, free agreement through contract was subordinated to the almost inevitable mandatory implication of obedience.[12] State citizenship status was also hierarchical – but subject to, if not Rousseau's social contract, at least a formal tenet of democratic consent to be ruled. Unions came closer to democratic practice, though also hierarchical. Employment and union membership were both also conditioned by the possibility of resignation.[13] Unions also allowed for participation ('voice'), while employment demanded fidelity ('loyalty'), or, as Fox put it, 'trust.'

Can these concepts: agreement (market), democracy (polity), trust (family) (or exit, voice and loyalty, to use Hirschman's categories) provide an alternative to contract as the defining quality of the employment relationship? In the past, they combined in various ways: agreement (loyalty/exit – no voice) for the relationship to the employer; membership (voice/exit/loyalty) for the relationship to the union; citizenship (voice/loyalty – no exit) for relationship to the State. Can these elements be combined into a concept of worker-citizenship?

---

11   See R Benedictus and B Bercusson *Labour Law: Cases and Materials*, Sweet & Maxwell, London 1987, Chapter 1, pp 9–25.
12   Alan Fox *Beyond Contract: Work, Power and Trust Relations* (1974), pp 188–90.
13   The 'exit' option in Hirschman's categories: A O Hirschman *Exit, Voice and Loyalty*, Harvard University Press, 1970.

The concept of worker-citizen presupposes a fragmentation of the roles of worker and citizen, involving *shared responsibilities* of employer and State, and corresponding *shared loyalties* of the worker to employer and State. In the UK, the two are already frequently combined in the sphere of *responsibilities,* with the growth of the welfare state in the form of employer contributions to social security, statutory sick pay, statutory maternity pay, vocational training, and so on.

The sphere of shared *loyalties* is less developed. The concept that the worker has *social* duties (and rights) as a citizen to which employment duties can be subordinated is only partially recognised; examples include public duties, trade union duties, time off for family responsibilities. This involves developing a careful symmetry between social responsibilities and the allocation of costs of these between employer and State/society.

The position of the trade union in this context/complex of duties and responsibilities is difficult. Unions are perceived primarily as counter-parts to employers – though this is a conception of trade unionism to be found mainly in some western European States and in English-speaking countries. Elsewhere, they are seen mainly as political actors.[14] This may require a rethinking of trade unions' roles in the EU. Is it surprising that the transformation of employment relationships should now require transformation of unions – beyond merely increasing membership in previously unrecruited areas? This was already evident in neo-corporatist tendencies in Member States earlier in the post-war period.

If unions are to enter into the nexus of employment/citizenship, then they will have to assume a new role – perhaps as intermediary organisations; as coordinating mechanisms between workers and their other social roles; as mediators of the duties/responsibilities of State and employer. Already, trade unions in the UK are the most frequent representatives of claimants before social security tribunals. In other countries, unions occupy parts of the administration of the welfare state: pensions, vocational training, and so on. They have other capacities to be developed.

This may require a more diverse conception of trade unionism (already diverse), distinguishing the union at the workplace (relationships with other workers there) and the union outside (mediating relationships among workers in different workplaces).

Returning to the conceptual apparatus needed to define the worker-citizen, at present, the worker is in a contractual relation to the employer, in a status relation to the State, and in a contract/status relation to the trade union. The worker's relationship is with *all three* simultaneously. Each must interrelate rights and duties in a coherent package. This is not, cannot be, static (status); there must be flexibility; nor is it contractual (individualistic) – it must be social to incorporate the collective union/State dimension (democratic).[15]

Kahn-Freund's solution was 'regulated contract'.[16] Its merits were extolled: freedom of choice plus protection. Contract gave choice to enter; thereafter, terms were dictated by the State or collective agreements. This solution has its

14   See R Martin *Trade Unionism: Purposes and Forms,* Clarendon Press, Oxford 1989.
15   B Bercusson 'Law and the Socialist Enterprise', pp 90–112, in *Law, Democracy and Social Justice,* Special Issue of the *Journal of Law and Society,* edited by R Cotterrell and B Bercusson, Spring 1988, Blackwell, Oxford; see also (with R Cotterrell) 'Introduction', pp 1–4.
16   O Kahn-Freund 'A note on status and contract in British labour law', (1967) 30 *Modern Law Review* 635, at 640–2.

problems. First, it is premised on one type of employment contract. What if the State or collective agreements did not reach other types of employment relationships? One solution is to secure regulation by the State and collective agreements of other types of employment relationships. Secondly, it implied that choice of entry also meant choice of exit – certainly by the employee, but also by the employer (dismissal). The solution, again, is regulation by the State or collective agreements on dismissal.

Kahn-Freund's solution still sees the relationship with the *employer* as of primary importance, even where this relationship is *less* central to the worker than, for example, the relationship with the State (or even with the union), as it might be with 'atypical' workers, where family, training, social service etc activities might be paramount. Can European labour law take those on board? It depends on whether labour law is to remain confined to 'typical' workers, or altered to encompass other employment relationships.

The EU context, and a proposal: the worker-citizen

In the EU context, one serious candidate is the *citizenship* concept engaging the State at the centre instead of the employer. The question is whether, in the EU context, unions can play a more engaged role in relation to the State than they could in relation to the employer. Unions share with the State the *democracy* element. They share with the employer the *exit/market* factor. Which of these liaisons is the more promising?

The Maastricht Protocol on Social Policy shows already how unions could be integrated at macro-level. Bargaining in the shadow of the law, negotiated legislation, raises the prospects for an integration of unions, State and employers into a neo-corporatist model.[17] But there is a need for articulation of the macro-level with lower levels. This would at least require internal constitutional reforms of the ETUC and of national union structures. Legislation on worker participation is another reflection of these issues.

An alternative solution to Kahn-Freund's regulated contract is a mixture of citizen/worker roles. This would aim to achieve recognition of the social identities of workers' working lives, to include entitlements which protect and encourage their social roles. Examples include caring, public, community and social service. An example which shows the way is in the Working Time Directive, Article 13: the principle of adapting work to the worker.

Conceptually, this has to be more than additional legislative constraints on contract. It 'proceduralises' contract out of existence. It becomes 'relation(al)(ship) contract', evolving and permanently negotiable. Does it mean anything to continue to call this contract when, substantively, it is something else? It would be important to come up with new terminology to exclude (in UK common law) the old conceptual baggage. A number of questions need to be addressed.

17   P C Schmitter, 'Still the century of corporatism?', in P C Schmitter and G Lehmbruch (eds) *Trends Towards Corporatist Intermediation* (1979), Beverly Hills; for an application in the sphere of low pay and incomes policies, see B Bercusson *Wage Determination: Instrumentalist and Neo-Corporatist Approaches,* Paper presented at a Colloquium at the European University Institute, Florence, on 'Law and Economic Policy – Alternatives to De-Legalisation', 1985 (mimeo); for doubts in the EC context, see W Streeck and P C Schmitter 'From national corporatism to transnational pluralism: organised interests in the Single European Market', (1991) *Politics and Society* 2.

Is the concept of 'worker-citizen' feasible? It is not captured by the contract of employment, which fails to include the citizenship quality, that employment may be only one of many relationships of the worker, and not necessarily the most important. Is it necessary to have one overriding concept, or, as at present, to have a multiplicity: employment, citizen's rights, etc? The disadvantage is the growth of hierarchy among them, as relationships between their formal manifestations as legal instruments are needed. Is this worker-citizen a private or public law concept? This could matter in the UK, and certainly on the continent, given the highly developed system of administrative law.

What are the contours of the worker-citizen concept? The emerging EU labour law model incorporates a strong negotiable content of, and negotiable derogations from, labour standards. So there is a strong trade union role. This has implications for the law on the internal structures of unions: issues of democracy and members' rights, not yet broached, but are implicit in the emerging EU debate over representativeness (in the European social dialogue, European Works Councils, and for the purposes of negotiation and consultation as required by various Directives) and the role of the Commission in shaping it.

The element of choice remains in that the worker-citizen chooses roles and activities, one of which is employment in various forms. But employment becomes *relational* not *only* to the employer, but also to other roles and activities.

As in Article 13 of the Working Time Directive, the employer must take account of adapting work to the worker('s other roles). To do this, presumably, as in the Directive, he must consult the union. Perhaps the employer must also take account of/consult others: such as the family for family roles, training authorities, community, social services, etc.

What is the conceptual construct which emerges? Older models of contract are too bilateral. Concepts of multilateral contract involve too much formal negotiating among parties. Traditional concepts of citizenship are too unmediated by other relationships such as employment and union membership.

The Commission has recently proposed the concept of reconciliation (or combination) of working and family life.[18] The task is one of reconciling different social roles. Building on this proposal, one approach would be for a concept which left the choice to enter the relationship initially to the parties. Then, if there are disputes or complaints, these are to be resolved by Reconciliation Tribunals: judges who are experts in family, social and community affairs, etc. They are to resolve conflicts by determining rights and obligations (towards family, community, work, etc), just as, for example, family courts consider the interests of the children in divorce disputes. Industrial tribunals are replaced, or supplemented, by other tribunals when disputes occur over reconciliation of work and other roles and responsibilities.

The individual chooses, but *others* affected by the decision – employer, family, community, State, trade union – can complain to the Reconciliation Tribunal if they feel, for example, they are suffering a disproportionate burden; for example, too much work, too little family, too little work. It would, of course, be necessary also to promote the work identities of citizens. Those citizens whose attachment to working life is relatively marginal should be not only protected (by rights) but encouraged to develop this (by incentives). For the tribunals,

---

18 Commission Consultative Document, April 1995; see Chapter 15.

careful attention would have to be paid to problems of locus standi, procedures, remedies, (including incentives), and so on.

In what sense is this still labour law? Arguably, it is, in so far as labour itself has changed to encompass a wider spectrum of activities. The problem was the heretofore exclusive market orientation of labour law. Labour law has come back to being a socialised instrument.

In the EU context, the concept would have to be adapted to various national contexts. But the key shift would be that the employment relationship is opened out to embrace other relationships; and is both turned into a relationship which must take account of others (both employer and worker must do so), and also allows others legal standing to challenge it when it interferes with these other relationships.

The worker-citizen concept is no longer a contract in any recognisable (common law or other) sense. It is certainly not bilateral, as others can challenge it. But it is not a multilateral contract either, as others do not participate in its formation. As a legal instrument it is:

- *bilateral* (contractual) in formation (allowing for choice);
- *relational* in its implementation/application; other interests must be taken into account for its duration;
- *multilateral* in its enforcement (complaints can be made about its operation (and termination?) by others than the parties.

So far national labour law thinking has only some reflections of these orientations. An EU initiative would make it comprehensive and transform it into a new European law on individual employment.

Chapter 32

The Self-employed: Diversity and Solidarity in Social Protection and Labour Law

INTRODUCTION

Self-employed persons are a category of employment relationships hitherto generally ignored by national labour laws, more concerned to distinguish this category from that of employees, the proper subjects of labour law. The labour law of the EU, by virtue of principles of freedom of movement and freedom of establishment, has the advantage of beginning with a broad concept of work and economic activity which potentially embraces both these categories of worker. The application of EU social and labour law to self-employed persons was always on the agenda, as illustrated by the careful attention paid to this category of workers with respect to EU law on sex discrimination, where special Directives were approved concerning self-employed workers.

As with employees, however, the self-employed are often considered a generic category. Preceding chapters have conveyed how EU law is embarked on the path of *differentiation* among different categories of *employed* workers, motivated by various policies, ranging from health and safety to equal opportunities. Further differentiation of workers into specific categories arose following Council Recommendation 92/442/EEC of 27 July 1992 on the convergence of social protection objectives and policies,[1] in particular, the objective specified in Article I.A.1(e) of the Recommendation:

> 'to examine the possibility of introducing and/or developing appropriate social protection for self-employed persons.'

Examination of this question reveals the same process of *differentiation* among *self-employed* workers as has been evidenced above among employed workers.

Most of the attention in the EU has been focused not on the labour law affecting self-employed persons, but the issue of their social protection. This is a gap which will have to be filled eventually. One question will be whether, as has been argued to be the case with *employed* workers, regulation will follow the pattern of fragmentation into different categories of workers. This chapter aims to show that the pressures of social dumping and fragmentation will operate also on the emerging European labour law of self-employed workers.

Fragmentation of this category of workers, however, seems to follow *sectoral* lines, with further diversity *within* sectors. This will be illustrated through an analysis of the law on social protection of self-employed workers.

---

1   OJ L245/49 of 26 August 1992.

478

THE EC CONTEXT: CATEGORIES OF WORKERS, SOCIAL PROTECTION AND SOCIAL DUMPING

All *persons* face the risks of old age and invalidity, ill-health due to disease or accident. Most have at some time to support dependents – children, spouses, relatives and others. The ability of *workers* to sustain these risks and provide this support depends to a great extent on their work context: in particular, whether, and to what extent, individual capacity or collective solidarity at work can provide *social protection*. That social protection should be available to *all* is rarely questioned. What is at issue is what the scope and standards of this protection should be, and what form regulation should take. Here we are concerned only with the scope, standards and form of social protection available to *workers.*

Workers are not a uniform category from many different perspectives. In the different Member States there is great variation in the extent to which social protection is provided on the same or on a different basis to *employees* and *self-employed* workers, or not at all to the latter. The clarity of the provision to one or the other category is clouded by the differences in legal definitions of employees and self-employed persons for the purposes of social protection.

The availability of social protection for employees and for *atypical* workers is bedevilled by the same variety. This is owed to some extent to the lack of clarity in the definition of 'employee', which may serve to exclude some categories of 'atypical' workers. But it is more due to the various thresholds as to hours worked and qualifications as to continuous employment, both of which operate to exclude part-time and temporary employees from the social protection available to full-time permanent employees.[2]

It has been argued that there is a European social and labour law emerging, albeit slowly, with a distinctive approach to each category of worker, though not without some distortions. Social protection of these different categories is coming under increasing scrutiny due to the operation of the Single European Market. The costs of social protection are a factor to be taken into account: the debate is usually conducted under the rubric entitled 'social dumping'. In brief, the argument is that the creation of a single market leads to competition between different national regimes of social and labour law. Lower social and labour standards are alleged to give a competitive advantage to employers subject to that regime. The importance of this advantage is often overestimated, and may be compensated for by better infrastructures, higher skill levels and so on. Nonetheless, it is said to be one factor favouring national competitiveness.

Social security regulation of forms of work is an important factor in this competition. This is evident in the Commission's argumentation in support of the three proposed Council Directives on 'atypical work'.[3] In a section of the Explanatory Memorandum accompanying the proposed Directives entitled 'Part-time employment and temporary employment with regard to distortions of competition' the Commission highlights three categories of rules which may

2 A Lyon-Caen *Social Protection and the Atypical Worker*, Synthesis Report of national reports. Commission of the EC, DG-V, Doc V/0589/92, December 1991.
3 Proposal for a Council Directive supplementing the measures to encourage improvements in the safety and health at work of temporary workers. COM (90) 228 final – SYN 281, Brussels, 13 August 1990. Approved by the Council at Brussels, 21 June 1991; Proposals for Council Directives on certain employment relationships with regard to working conditions, and to distortions of competition. COM (90) 228 final – SYN 280, Brussels, 13 August 1990.

cause distortions in competition, one of which concerns the costs resulting from social protection. It argues that differences in these costs among the Member States of the Community are not justified by differences in the workers' productivity.[4]

With specific regard to distortions of competition involving part-time employment, the Commission produced a Table which shows that in some Member States costs resulting from statutory social protection schemes expressed as a percentage of gross wages vary according to whether certain part-time employment arrangements or a full-time employment relationship is considered. Four examples are given:

–   in the *Federal Republic of Germany* contributions amounting to 36% of gross wages are *not* paid if income is below DM 470 per month and unemployment contributions are waived for less than 19 hours per week; sickness insurance and pension contributions are waived for less than 15 hours per week. More than three million part-time contracts account for 12% of all employees. It is estimated that social security contributions are not paid in respect of 450,000 of these (some sources put the figure at one million); that is 16% or 34% of part-time employees and 2% or 4.4% of all employees.

–   in *Denmark* (where social protection is mainly financed through taxes or contributions at progressive, non-proportional rates), contributions are not paid to the complementary pension scheme in respect of less than ten hours per week, which amounts to about 2.5% of gross wages.

–   in *Ireland* the main social security contributions are waived in respect of employment for less than 18 hours per week; 15.95% of the gross wages of the workers concerned. This affects some 40% of part-time contracts.

–   in the *United Kingdom* contributions for part-time employment (some five million; 23% of all employees) are lower on account of the progressive contribution rates; the resulting difference ranges between 10% and 19.45% of the gross wages concerned. In addition, there is a lower income limit (£46 per week) below which no contributions are required. On the basis of the previous threshold of £43 it is estimated that no contributions are paid in respect of some 2,400,000 part-time jobs (11% of all employees), as the income concerned falls below the limit.

It is noted that in the other Member States, however, there is practically no such difference between part-time employment and full-time employment.[5]

The Explanatory Memorandum gives a detailed illustration of a form of distortion of competition caused by social security rules.[6] An employee in Germany who works less than 15 hours per week and does not pay social security contributions is compared with the statutory situation in the Netherlands. Since in 1984 the average hourly labour cost was around ECU 14.24 in Germany and ECU 13.68 in the Netherlands, use of a part-time worker *not* requiring employers' and workers' contributions would cost 36% less for one and the same job of work in Germany, presuming that the wages excluding contributions were paid at the same hourly rate. In this particular case (disregarding the negligible effect of

4   Ibid, paragraphs 28–29.
5   Ibid, paragraphs 32 and 38.
6   Ibid, paragraph 33.

including such workers in calculating average hourly labour costs) and taking into account the fact that in contrast to Germany there is no lower limit in the Netherlands, the hourly wage cost falls in Germany to about ECU 10.50, while in the Netherlands each hour worked costs ECU 13.68. In highly labour-intensive branches using a large proportion of part-time workers not covered by social security in a given country, competitive relationships in neighbouring regions may be affected.

It emerges that the differences are very marked and concern a great number of workers: in particular, a substantial proportion of new recruits engaged under this type of contract. This might cause a distortion of competition in certain cases. Therefore, the Commission's conclusion was that convergence of the coverage of various schemes applied throughout the Community is warranted.

The Commission also addressed the position with regard to distortions of competition involving temporary employment. Concerning fixed-duration employment relationships, it was noted that the indirect costs under statutory social protection schemes sometimes reflected differences in social cover for temporary employment and that for open-ended employment. In some countries, no cover is provided under social security schemes for very short-term employment relationships, so no contributions are due in such cases.[7]

A survey of management attitudes regarding whether employees with a fixed-duration contract cost less than employees with an open-ended employment relationship, found that in Spain management's view was that for 34% of their staff contributions were lower; the figures for other Member States were 11% in the UK, 6% in Italy, and 3% in Belgium and Germany. The conclusion was that, as in the case of part-time employment relationships, distortions of competition may be caused by the varying practices in different Member States.[8]

The overall conclusion was that, given the numbers of workers concerned, it would be advisable, in order to identify and preclude the risks of distortion of competition, to provide for the harmonisation of the rules governing the different types of employment relationships in the Community, and specifically as regards the very different practices noted as regards social protection and other social benefits, particularly in relation to part-time employment.[9]

Separate mention was made of social protection schemes which entail social benefits or assistance for persons who, for whatever reason, have not acquired sufficient rights to enable them to qualify for the contributory benefits normally reserved for workers and their beneficiaries. The Commission's conclusion was that the rules concerning procedures for access to and grant of social assistance and social welfare, and non-contributory social security benefits should be applied without discrimination to all employed persons, whatever the employment relationship applicable to them.[10]

Is social dumping relevant to social protection policy as regards self-employed workers? Competition between individual self-employed persons across national boundaries might seem unlikely. But if self-employed persons comprise a substantial proportion of workers in certain industries – construction, hotels (tourism), agriculture, professional services – lower social costs can

7 For example, in Germany for less than two months' employment per year and in the United Kingdom whenever weekly pay is below £43.
8 Ibid, paragraph 43.
9 Ibid, paragraph 47.
10 Ibid, paragraph 52.

provide competitive advantages. The argument for harmonisation of social protection for self-employed workers is equally strong.

However, this does not necessarily mean that social protection for self-employed persons, atypical workers and 'typical' employees should be identical. But at least each of these different categories should be treated the same across the EC. It may be argued that this harmonisation should also entail equal social protection – in the sense of covering the same risks and providing the same standard of protection – for all workers, whether typical employees, atypical workers or self-employed persons.

Whatever the scope and standards of social protection available for each category of workers, what regulatory form should this social protection take? One can learn here from emerging EC policy in social and labour law. But first a closer look at the category of self-employed workers is needed.

EMPLOYEES AND SELF-EMPLOYED WORKERS: SECTORAL DIVERSITY

The very concept of self-employment is translated often in terms of independence of the workers concerned. The notion of independence derives from the contrast with dependent workers – employees. Independent workers are not dependent on an employer –they are self-employed. The notion of dependence has taken on other dimensions in the context of employment law. It often incorporates not simply a notion of dependence in the sense of subordination to an employer, but also an element of economic dependence. Employees are dependent on their work for subsistence, paid for by the employer. In this sense of economic dependence it is not clear that self-employed workers are any less dependent economically on their work for subsistence, paid for by their clients or customers.

This dependence of employees has been mitigated by collective organisations of employee solidarity which operate in the field of labour law (employment conditions) and social protection (social security). Both industrial organisation, through trade unions engaged in collective bargaining or mutual aid, and political organisation, through the creation of welfare state mechanisms, have reduced the dependence of employed workers. The forms of collective solidarity adopted by independent workers, the self-employed, have also been been characterised by great diversity, both in the organisation of their working conditions (as in the case of professional regulations) and especially in the sphere of social protection. In the case of both dependent employees and independent self-employed workers the extent of collective organisation is often deficient. There are many gaps in coverage, inadequacies in standards and defects in organisation.

In the case of employees, there has been a traditional opposition to the principle of solidarity by the countervailing force of employers. Improvement of working conditions and social security usually entails costs for employers. In the case of self-employed workers, the independence which characterises this form of work has sometimes operated to isolate such workers and promote an anti-solidaristic mentality.

In the case of employees, legal recognition of the principle of solidarity is well established and highly sophisticated. There is a developed jurisprudence at Member State level, but also at European level in the Council of Europe, on freedom of association and collective bargaining, social security and social protection. In the case of self-employed workers, legal recognition of the principle of solidarity is less developed.[11]

The diversity and solidarity evinced among employees is also evident among the self-employed. Diversity is demonstrated by reference to the very divergent categories of self-employed workers and the variety of social protection regimes covering them. This diversity of organisational structures reflecting the diversity of categories of self-employed workers was a feature of an analysis of social protection of self-employed persons in the Member States of the European Community which argued that risks, standards and regulatory forms should normally follow the *dominant sectoral* pattern.[12]

Where the *self-employed* are the *majority* of workers in a sector (as in the *primary* sector), they should be recognised as a distinct category of workers whose social protection should correspond to the features and context specific to that sector. Where the *self-employed* are a *minority* in a sector, the implication is that the many other workers in the sector are not self-employed. The social protection exigencies of self-employed workers in that sector should adopt the model of social protection of these other workers. The assumption should not be that these others are 'employees' without more information. There are at least two alternatives.

First, these other workers may be '*typical*' employees. This is the case in the *secondary* sector. If there is a generally applicable system of social protection in the sector, there is a presumption that self-employed workers should be treated the same. Secondly, the other workers may not be 'typical' employees. Rather, as in the *tertiary* sector, a large proportion, if not the majority, are '*atypical*' workers. They have specific social protection needs. It is inappropriate to insist on the application of a social protection model devised for 'typical' employees in the secondary sector to the very different circumstances of 'atypical' workers and self-employed persons in a different sector.

Finally, there is the case where *self-employed* persons are *concentrated* in an industry or occupation within a sector. It may be arguable that a different model of social protection crafted to their needs is justified, even when they are outnumbered by other types of workers in the sector as a whole. Indeed, the solidarity or cohesion, not to mention the relative wealth and political power of certain occupations – liberal professionals in particular – may lead to autonomous social protection arrangements.

The conclusion is that European law should not assume that there is a single model of social protection to be applied to all workers, including the self-employed. Research on social protection of *atypical* workers shows how adaptation is necessary. Proposals on social protection for self-employed persons should learn from this. Both the substance (scope and standards) and the form of regulation of social protection of self-employed persons have to adapt to the exigencies of the sector in which they work.

11 However, support for this principle has come recently from the European Court of Justice. Case C-159/91: *Poucet v Assurances générales de France (AGF) et Caisse mutuelle régionale de Languedoc-Roussillon (Camulrac)*; Case C-160/91: *Pistre v Caisse autonome nationale de compensation de l'assurance vieillesse des artisans (Cancava)*, decided on 17 February 1993, [1993] CLY 4266; Conclusions of the Advocate-General M Giuseppe Tesauro presented on 29 September 1992.

12 B Bercusson 'Solidarity and Diversity: Social Protection for Self-employed Persons in the European Community', unpublished paper for a conference at the European University Institute and University of Siena, 14–16 October 1993.

THE SECTORAL DISTRIBUTION OF SELF-EMPLOYED PERSONS

The self-employed are generally recognised as being concentrated in a number of occupations: farmers, professionals, shopkeepers, helper-spouses, construction workers. This can be seen when the composition of the group is analysed in terms of sectors. The distribution across sectors is significant. One *sector may dominate* the category of self-employed persons: *most* are in this sector, though *they* do *not* constitute a majority of the workers in the sector. Again, the *self-employed may dominate* a sector: *most* workers in the sector *are* self-employed, but they may not constitute a majority of the self-employed in the economy as a whole. Either case will have implications for the regulation of social protection of self-employed persons.

There are two initial factual questions. First, how are the self-employed distributed among sectors, and how many are represented by a particular sector? In some cases this is tantamount to equivalence with an occupational group: being in the primary sector is likely to represent being a self-employed farmer. If it were to transpire that *most* self-employed in one country were in one particular sector, it would give some force to the argument that the social protection regime for the self-employed should reflect closely the general context and specific features of that sector. This would have implications for the nature of the risks deemed most important, the standard of protection required, the form of regulation best suited, the financial provision required, and so on.

Secondly, what is the proportion of self-employed persons in a sector? Again, if *most workers* in a sector are self-employed, sectoral features and context are determining as to which risks are most important, the standard of protection to be adopted, the form of regulation best suited, and so on.

The Table opposite indicates the sectoral distribution of self-employed persons in twelve Member States of the EC, as compiled from national reports.[13]

Primary sector

Taking the primary sector first, just over half of the self-employed are in this sector in Ireland (53%), Portugal (50.3%) and Greece (51.6%). In these three countries, the vast majority of workers in this sector are self-employed: Portugal, 80.5%, Ireland, 86.3% and Greece, 96.3%.

A substantial proportion of self-employed persons are in the primary sector in France (39%), Denmark (34.4%), Spain (30.6%), Germany (27.7%), the Netherlands (25%) and Italy (19%). In these countries, where figures are available from the national reports, they show that the majority of workers in the primary sector are self-employed: France, 90%, Denmark, 52.7%, Spain, 69% and Italy, 59.5%.

Only Belgium (10.7%) and the UK (8%) have relatively few self-employed persons in the primary sector. But even here, they constitute 46% of the workers in this sector in the UK.

---

13   These national reports for the then 12 Member States of the EU were prepared during 1993 for the conference in Florence on 14–16 October 1993.

	SECTORS					
	Primary		*Secondary*		*Tertiary*	
	%SE	%sec	%SE	%sec	%SE	%sec
Belgium[14]	10.7	–	23.0	–	66.0	–
Ireland	53.0	86.3	12.2	10.6	34.4	14.7
UK	8.0	46.0	34.0	11.2	58.0	11.0
Italy	19.0	59.5	19.0	17.0	61.5	30.5
France	39.0	90.0	16.4	24.0	44.2	–[15]
Netherlands	25.0	–	9.3	–	62.0	–
Portugal	50.3	80.5	16.7	12.5	32.9	19.0
Germany[16]	27.7	–	16.4	–	55.8	–
Spain[17]	30.6	69.0	18.3	14.2	51.0	23.9
Greece	51.6	96.3	16.2	29.6	32.1	34.4
Denmark	37.5	52.7	15.0	–	47.4	–

%SE = percentage of the total of self-employed workers.
%sec = percentage of all workers in the sector.

Secondary sector

In contrast to the lowest proportion of self-employed persons in the primary sector, the UK has highest proportion of self-employed persons in the secondary sector (34%), double the proportion in France and Germany (both 16.4%) and almost twice that of Italy (19%). Belgium is second highest (23%), as it was second lowest in the primary sector. But there is not much between Belgium and all the other countries, descending from 18.3% (Spain) down to 9.3% (Netherlands).

Generally speaking, except for Greece (29.6%), the self-employed constitute a small proportion of workers in the secondary sector, ranging from 24% in France to 10.6% in Ireland.

Tertiary sector

Almost two-thirds of the self-employed are in this sector in Belgium (66%), the Netherlands (62%) and Italy (61.5%), closely followed by the UK (58%), Germany (55.8%) and Spain (51%). Around one-third of the self-employed are in this sector in Ireland (34.4%), Portugal (32.9%) and Greece (32.1%). Between are France (44.2%) and Denmark (43.5%).

Despite the fact that most or many self-employed work in this sector, they form a *minority* of workers in the sector. A large proportion of workers in this sector are self-employed only in Greece (34.4%), Italy (30.5%), Spain (23.9%) and Portugal (19%). Only a small proportion of workers in this sector are self-employed in Ireland (14.7%) and the UK (11%).

14 This includes those in independent work both as a main and as a secondary activity.
15 Hotels and restaurants: 47%; repairs 47%; retailing 35%; financial services, health transport 18%; recreational and cultural services 21%; travel agencies 2%.
16 These figures are taken from Table 1 in the national report (other tables yield different figures).
17 These figures are from Table 2 (other tables would yield slightly different results).

Summary and analysis

In the *primary* sector, the self-employed are dominant as a proportion of total self-employed persons in Ireland, Greece and Portugal. They are insignificant as a proportion of the self-employed in the UK and Belgium. But in all countries they are dominant or important as a proportion of workers in the sector. Self-employment is dominant or important in agriculture everywhere. The self-employed are dispersed in more industrialised countries where large numbers of self-employed are also to be found in the secondary and tertiary sectors.

In the *secondary* sector, the self-employed are relatively insignificant as a proportion of total self-employment – except for the UK. They are relatively unimportant everywhere as a proportion of the workers in the secondary sector. In sum: the self-employed are not really important in the secondary sector, even where many of them, in one country (UK), may work in this sector.

The *tertiary* sector includes a substantial proportion of total self-employed persons in most countries, ranging from Belgium (66%) down to Greece (34.4%). Despite this important concentration of self-employed persons, they represent only a relatively small proportion of all workers in the tertiary sector. They are dispersed in a mass of employees.

Taking the spectrum of twelve countries in the EC, the picture that emerges is as follows. At one extreme there are countries where most self-employed persons are in the primary sector and most of the rest are in the tertiary sector.

Country	Primary	Tertiary	Total
Ireland	53	34.4	84.4%
Greece	51.6	32.1	83.7%
Portugal	50.2	32.9	83.1%

These are countries with few self-employed in the secondary sector. They are relatively unindustrialised countries.

At the other extreme are countries where most self-employed persons are in the tertiary sector and most of the rest are in the secondary sector:

Country	Tertiary	Secondary	Total
UK	58	34	92%
Belgium	66	23	89%

These are the oldest industrialised countries. They present the paradoxical feature that, in them, most self-employed persons are in the tertiary sector, but they nonetheless constitute a minority of workers in that sector. And although self-employed persons are least numerous in the primary sector (UK = 8%, Belgium = 10.7%), in the UK at least, only in that sector do they constitute a substantial proportion (46%) of workers in the sector as a whole.

In between is the range of countries where there is a high proportion of self-employed in the primary sector, but most are in the tertiary sector:

Country	Tertiary	Primary	Total
Italy	61.5	19	80.5
France	44.2	39	83.2
Netherlands	62	25	87.0
Germany	55.8	27.7	83.5
Spain	51	30.6	80.6
Denmark	43.5	34.4	77.9

The distribution of self-employed persons across sectors demonstrates that in all countries there is a general concentration in the primary sector and a further concentration in the tertiary sector. Self-employment is relatively scarce in the secondary sector, except for the UK and Belgium.

The primary sector is most striking. The sector dominates self-employment in the sense that the majority of workers in the sector are self-employed and these constitute a majority of self-employed persons in the economy generally. The secondary sector is least striking. The proportion of workers in the sector who are self employed is low, and they represent an insignificant proportion of self-employed persons. The dominant type of worker in this sector is the 'typical' employee. The tertiary sector is important. A significant proportion of self-employed persons work in the sector, even though they do not constitute a significant proportion of the workers in the sector. The dominant type of worker in this sector is the 'atypical' worker.

This distribution of self-employed persons among sectors would indicate that regulation of social protection for them should aim more at the primary and tertiary sectors where either most workers are self-employed, or, though a minority of workers in the sector, it includes a significant proportion of all self-employed persons.

The position in the *primary* sector is relatively clear: most are farmers and most are self-employed. The position in the other sectors merits further analysis.[18] Although the UK has the lowest proportion of self-employed persons in the primary sector, it has the highest proportion of self-employed in the *secondary* sector (34%), double the proportion in France and Germany (both 16.4%) and almost twice that of Italy (19%). Belgium is second highest (23%), as it was second lowest in primary sector. But there is not much between Belgium and all the other countries, descending from 18.3% (Spain) down to 9.3% (Netherlands). Generally speaking, the numbers of self-employed persons are even less significant taken as a proportion of workers in the secondary sector (with the exception of Greece). Further analysis of self-employment in the secondary sector yields the information shown in the table[19] overleaf (page 488).

Examined more closely, it appears that there is a disproportionate concentration of self-employed persons in the construction industry. In the UK, with 11.2% of self-employed workers in the secondary sector, only 4.4% of workers in the sector are in the energy, mineral and manufacturing industries. But 36% of self-employed workers in the secondary sector are in the construction industry – and these constitute 24% of all self-employed persons in the economy. Similarly, in Ireland, the self-employed are 10.6% in the secondary sector overall, but are 27% of all workers in the construction industry; in Italy they are 17% of workers in the sector overall, but 26.8% of construction workers; and in Spain, 14.2% overall, but 21% in construction.

The conclusion drawn is that self-employed persons in the secondary sector, though proportionately few in the overall context of secondary sector workers, are highly concentrated in the construction industry. It will be argued that this has important implications for social protection coverage as regards risks, standards and regulatory form.

---

18 Though the absence of data in the national reports is a constraint.
19 Compiled from the national reports.

SECONDARY SECTOR				
	Energy, Minerals, Manufacturing		*Construction*	
	%SE	%sec	%SE	%sec
Belgium	–	–	–	–
Ireland	5.0	5.8	7.0	27.0
UK	10.0	4.4	24.0	36.0
Italy	11.0	13.7	8.0	26.8
France	–	–	–	–
Netherlands	5.4	–	7.0	–
Portugal	10.5	–	6.3	–
Germany[20]	10.5	–	6.0	–
Spain[1]	11.2	11.3	8.0	21.0
Greece	–	–	–	–
Denmark	6.2	–	7.6	–

%SE = percentage of the total of self-employed workers.
%sec = percentage of all workers in the sector.

As regards the *tertiary* sector, the sparse data furnished by national reports makes further analysis of limited value:

TERTIARY SECTOR				
	Hotels, Restaurants, Commerce		*Liberal professions, Professionals, Services to Firms*	
	%SE	%sec	%SE	%sec
Belgium	–	–	–	–
Ireland	–	–	26.00[2]	16.90[3]
UK	25.00	15.60	28.00	8.50
Italy	24.00	–	9.40	–
France	16.40	–	27.80	18.00
Netherlands	26.80	–	11.00	–
Portugal	23.00	–	2.30	–
Germany	21.80	–	31.26	–
Spain	36.50	42.40	3.40	15.60
Greece	–	–	–	–
Denmark	19.10	–	16.20	–

%SE = percentage of the total of self-employed workers.
%sec = percentage of all workers in the sector.

20 These figures are taken from Table 1 in the national report (other tables yield different figures).
1   These figures are from Table 2 (other tables would yield slightly different results).
2   Professional services = 6%; Commerce etc = 20%.
3   Professional services = 8.1%; Commerce etc = 24%.

Some concentrations of self-employed in particular industries or occupations are evident in the tertiary sector. There are significant numbers of self-employed persons in the hotels/restaurant/commerce industries: they are over a third of all self-employed in Spain (36.5%), and comprise 42.4% of employment in these industries. The proportion in the hotels/restaurant/commerce industries in the other countries range from about one quarter of all self-employed in the Netherlands (26.8%), the UK (25%), Italy (24%) and Portugal (23%), and down to about one-fifth in Germany (21.8%) and Denmark (19.1%) and one-sixth in France (16.4%).

A second concentration of self-employed persons in the tertiary sector is to be found among the liberal professions and other professionals, including services to firms. The proportion of the total self-employed in these professions in some countries exceeds one quarter in Germany (31.26%), the UK (28%), France (27.8%) and Ireland (26%).

Conclusions

What are the implications of this sectoral distribution for the regulation of social protection of self-employed persons? The argument is that social protection of workers in a sector should follow from the regulatory framework governing workers in that sector.

At least three regulatory frameworks for social protection may be identified, each covering a different category of worker: that for 'typical' employees, that for 'atypical' workers, and that for self-employed workers. The regulatory framework of social protection was developed initially for typical employees. The application of that framework to atypical workers and the self-employed has produced unsatisfactory results.[4] It is usually presumed that the solution lies in the extension of the regulatory framework of social protection for employees to these *other* categories of workers. This approach ignores the significance of the sectoral distribution described above.

It would seem to be at least open to question whether the social protection regime of typical employees is appropriate for sectors where this category of worker is in a minority. This is clearly the case in most countries for the primary sector. It is also the case in the tertiary sector. Increasingly, if not already, the dominant category of worker in the tertiary sector is not the typical, but the atypical employee. The typical employee is dominant only in the secondary sector, where self-employed persons are least likely to be found and constitute the lowest proportion of those working in the sector.

The remainder of the argument derives from a traditional policy in European labour law: application of the same terms and conditions of employment across a sector. This is a long-standing policy aimed not only at fair treatment, but also to avoid unfair competition between enterprises in the same sector. The policy is reflected in the labour law policy of extension of collective agreements across sectors. This is a policy which is becoming increasingly a feature of EC policy in various instruments.

The argument that it is wrong for workers doing the same work in the same

---

4   As demonstrated by the series of national reports on these categories provided by the Commission.

sector to be treated differently as regards their terms and conditions of employment should also be applied to social protection. Allowing for different social
protection regimes is a consequence of the artificial division of labour law and
social security law. The same principles of fair treatment and elimination of
unfair competition apply.

The mechanism available in labour law for the application to all workers in a
sector of fair labour standards is often that of extension of collective agreements. Even in the absence of these, there are various legal mechanisms, some
of which have made a recent appearance in EC proposals. Collective agreements are not the normal mechanisms of social protection. But they still have a
role to play – at least in sectors where self-employed persons are a minority
working alongside employees who benefit from such social protection. The
construction industry can be put forward as an example. But in the absence of
collective agreements, other mechanisms are required.

Here one should be guided by mechanisms which may be found in the sector
concerned. In the case of the primary sector, agricultural workers have long-
established mechanisms.

The problem is peculiarly acute in the tertiary sector. In the tertiary sector
there are absent both extensive collective organisation, and, consequently, also
collectively agreed standards in the form of collective agreements. There is also
an uneven spread of the traditional cohesion/solidarity (economic and political)
present in the primary sector among farmers. Not for all in the tertiary sector:
professionals in particular do not suffer. But there are many others, and not least,
women workers: helper spouses and part-time self-employed workers.

The problem lies in the lack of collective organisation and consequent regulation of workers in the tertiary sector. This is a problem that afflicts labour law as
well as social security law. The problem is how to collectivise social protection of
workers in the tertiary sector; how to achieve the solidarity often painfully
acquired by workers in other sectors.

The two regulatory models offered by EC policy are, first, in social protection, equality: a principle of equivalence with the social security standards
available to permanent full-timers; and second, in labour law, solidarity: a principle of reference to collective agreements for employment standards.

Which of these is more appropriate for social protection of self-employed
workers? Both are consistent with the EC policy against social dumping. Equality
with permanent full-timers eliminates the attempt to undermine standards by
reducing protection for non-permanent employers or non-full-timers. Solidarity
through collective agreements secures general respect for specified standards
across the sector.

The equality principle embodies only an abstract principle, leaving to law
enforcement mechanisms the burden of securing respect for the principle. The
solidarity principle through collective agreements incorporates a self-policing
mechanism through the dynamics of the collective bargaining process.

However, self-employed workers are not always organised collectively. Where
they are, as in powerful agricultural lobbies, or professional associations, there is
scope for solidarity. Where they are not, equality may be the preferable principle. The conclusion to be drawn from the sectoral analysis of self-employed
persons is that different sectors have distinctive features and contexts which dictate a specific form of regulation for self-employed persons in the sector.
Recognition must be given to the *diversity* of self-employed persons.

However, the *solidarity* principle emerging in EC labour law may offer the better standard for social protection for self-employed persons. This can be clearly seen in all three sectors: in the primary sector with farmers, in the secondary sector with construction workers, and in the tertiary sector with professionals.

In general, European agricultural workers benefit from comprehensive social protection covering sickness, invalidity, old age, family, employment and (though with some exceptions) accidents. This reflects the solidarity principle to be found in the traditionally strongly cohesive agricultural sector. The very high concentration of self-employed workers in agriculture is indicative of the pattern. The solidarity among those who work in the same sector is a powerful force for organising social protection for these workers so as to reflect the features, context and exigencies of that sector.

The manifestation of the solidarity principle can be seen also by looking at the organisation of social protection for groups of self-employed workers in the liberal professions. Liberal professionals manifest qualities of cohesion and solidarity, albeit in another sector, similar to farmers in the primary sector.

What is the significance of this parallel form of regulation for two groups of workers who have little in common save for the fact that they are self-employed? The fact of their legal status is but one element in the broader profile of these workers. This profile reflects the solidarity which characterises a group with a tradition of cohesive organisation.

The interesting paradox is that the independence associated with self-employed workers is, with regard to social protection, capable of being overcome. Organisational solidarity assumes the role of protecting against the risks. The protection is social with a small 's': limited to the cohesive group.

In many, but not all cases, the standards of social protection available for these two groups are similar to those of employees. The principle of equality has been achieved, but the regulatory form is different.

However, this model of regulatory protection is unlikely to be appropriate for other groups of self-employed persons which do not possess the profile of group solidarity which characterises the tradition of cohesive organisation to be found in the cases of farmers and liberal professionals.

The tertiary sector presents the challenge of both diversity and solidarity. There is a wide range of categories of self-employed persons. The division between liberal professionals and workers in hotels, restaurants and commerce was remarked on earlier. The liberal professions offer certain parallels with self-employed workers in the primary sector. The solidarity principle manifested in traditional cohesive organisations has largely achieved wide scope and standards of social protection.

It is in the other groups of self-employed workers in the tertiary sector that the greatest need for social protection arises. Two groups in particular illustrate this relative lack of social protection: helper-spouses and part-time workers. Both are composed mainly of women. The two groups may overlap considerably: part-time self-employed women are often helper-spouses.

One estimate in 1986 gave the figures in the following table (page 492) for women assisting their husbands.[5]

---

5 *Non-Salaried Working Women in Europe*, Commission of the European Communities, September 1986, Doc V/1514/86, p IV.

Country	% of married women in husband's activity	Assisting wives (in thousands)
Greece	27.5	646
France	15.0	1,956
Ireland	14.1	106
Denmark	13.6	164
Italy	13.4	1,865
Germany	10.9	1,719
Britain	9.1	1,260
Netherlands	8.5	286
Belgium	7.7	180
Luxembourg	7.0	3
Europe 10	average: 12.2	Total: 8,185

The numbers of part-time self-employed women are given approximate indication for 1988 by the following Table. The first two columns include men and women:[6]

Country	% of part-time non-employees	% of part-time employees	% of part-time women
Belgium	4.3	11.0	87.1
Denmark	15.2	24.9	79.5
Germany	17.2	12.7	90.5
Greece	7.0	4.0	65.8
Spain	7.0	4.7	73.7
France	12.2	12.0	83.7
Ireland	7.6	8.2	68.4
Italy	7.3	5.0	62.2
Luxembourg	5.8	6.5	80.6
Netherlands	36.2	29.5	69.8
Portugal	0.6	4.5	67.1
Britain	16.2	22.8	85.7
Europe 12	11.3	13.6	81.8

These two groups, self-employed helper-spouses and self-employed part-timers, are employed mainly in the services sector. In every Member State in 1988, save Greece (48%) and Portugal (44.2%), the majority of total employment was in the services sector, ranging from 68.6% in the Netherlands to 53.1% in Spain.[7] Of workers in this sector in the EC, 16.7% were non-employees. In 1988, 73.1% of the female labour force in the EC was employed in the services sector.[8]

6   *A Social Portrait of Europe*, Luxembourg, Office for Official Publications of the EC (1991), p 49. Figures compiled from Tables 5.8 and 5.11, pp 62–3.
7   Ibid, Table 4.15 on p 48.
8   Ibid, p 49.

The organisation of social protection for these two groups of diverse workers presents a challenge for the application of the solidarity principle. The principle of solidarity which could be applied to helper-spouses is that outlined in the decision of the European Court in *Poucet v Assurances générales de France (AGF) et Caisse mutuelle régionale de Languedoc-Roussillon (Camulrac)* and *Pistre v Caisse autonome nationale de compensation de l'assurance vieillesse des artisans (Cancava)*.[9] The Court considered complaints by self-employed workers that compulsory contributions to the mutual funds established to provide social protection violated the principles of free competition in the common market as laid down in Articles 85–86 of the Treaty of Rome.[10] Rejecting the complaint, the Court characterised these regimes as having a social objective in accordance with the principle of solidarity, manifested in various ways.[11]

The principle of solidarity as outlined in this decision seems eminently suitable to be applied to the situation of helper-spouses. The decision to allow for such social protection is, as stated by the Advocate-General, a political choice relating to the financing of the regimes with implications for the redistribution of wealth; there is no direct link between contributions and payments.[12] As the Commission stated: the principle of 'generality' consisted in allowing all persons to benefit from social protection, including those at risk who are generally excluded from insurance schemes or subjected to heavy premium payments.[13]

The diversity of self-employed persons requires diverse forms of regulation with the common principle of solidarity requisite to social protection. One detailed example will illustrate this: construction workers in the secondary sector.

SOCIAL PROTECTION FOR SELF-EMPLOYED WORKERS IN THE SECONDARY SECTOR: THE CONSTRUCTION INDUSTRY

The regulation of working conditions for workers in the construction industry as a whole through collective bargaining offers a paradigm for the provision of social protection for self-employed workers in the secondary sector. This prospect is particularly significant because of the moves in the sector towards EC-level regulation of working conditions through the European social dialogue. EC-level regulation through social dialogue offers a different perspective on the possible mechanisms for the social protection of self-employed workers in other sectors.

Over the EC as a whole, self-employment in 1988 was lowest as a proportion of employment in the secondary sector: 11% in industry as contrasted with 16.7% in services and 74% in agriculture.[14] National reports indicated that in some Member States there was a concentration of self-employment in a particular sector of industry – construction. Self-employment now makes up a

---

9   Joined Cases C-159/91 and C-160/91, decided on 17 February 1993, [1993] CLY 4266.
10 Ibid; Conclusions of the Advocate-General M Giuseppe Tesauro presented on 29 September 1992. I have relied upon the text of the judgment and Conclusions in French.
11 See detailed discussion in Chapter 33.
12 Conclusions of Advocate-General Giuseppe Tesauro in Joined Cases C-159/91 and 160/91: *Poucet v AGF et Camulrac* and *Pistre v Cancava*, presented on 29 September 1992, paragraph 9.
13 Ibid, paragraph 5.
14 *A Social Portrait of Europe*, Table 4.17, p 49.

substantial proportion (more than 20%) of the construction workforce in five of the EC Member States:

SELF-EMPLOYMENT IN THE CONSTRUCTION INDUSTRY 1990 [15]			
Country	*Self-employed*	*Employees*	*% Self-employed*
Belgium	44,737	184,065	19.5%
Denmark	26,702	168,038	13.7%
France	316,600	1,264,500	20.0%
Germany	174,000	1,659,000	9.5%
Greece	80,499	174,735	31.5%
Ireland	20,100	51,700	28.0%
Italy	451,000	1,371,000	24.7%
Luxembourg	852	14,356	5–6%
Netherlands	32,000	381,000	7.7%
Portugal	76,000	305,100	19.9%
Spain	256,900	1,234,500	17.2%
UK	718,000	1,087,000	39.8%

Some sources suggest that the number of self-employed is even higher. One recent estimate was that there were 818,000 self-employed workers in construction in the UK in 1992 and that their numbers had increased by 89% between 1981 and 1990.[16]

One method by which self-employment has been introduced is by subcontracting. The European Federation of Building and Wood Workers (EFBWW) reports 'an observable increase in management contracting' a process whereby market leaders in Europe win the biggest construction orders and projects and execute them through a series of subcontractors and suppliers. 'This phenomenon' according to the EFBWW 'is creating major problems for the national and European trade union movement in their efforts to promote compliance with labour legislation and collective agreements'.[17]

Although the growth in self-employment within the last decade is not particular to construction, its increase is greater than in any other sector. The Table opposite (page 495) compares overall self-employment in the 12 Member States with that for construction and shows that the rate is about twice as high for Belgium, Denmark, France and Ireland and nearly four times higher in the UK. Moreover, with the exception of Spain and Luxembourg (where there was an overall fall in general self-employment during the decade) it is always higher in construction.

Unless unions can speak for the self-employed and negotiate on their behalf, the growth of this form of employment, at the expense of the employment of directly employed workers, will have a major impact on the unions' ability to conclude collective agreements, whether at national or at European level.

15   Source: ILO Yearbook of Labour Statistics (1992) calculated from statistics in Table 2A.
16   M Camphill and M Daly 'Self-Employment into the 1990s', (1992) *Employment Gazette* (UK) (June).
17   EFBWW *The General Policy Programme and Programme of Activities of the EFBWW for the period 1992–95* (1991), at page 5.

RATE OF SELF-EMPLOYMENT GENERALLY AND IN CONSTRUCTION[18]		
Country	*Overall self-employment* *% (1989)*	*In construction* *% (1990)*
Belgium	12.9	19.5
Denmark	6.9	13.7
France	10.5	20.0
Germany	8.4	9.5
Greece	26.9	31.5
Ireland	13.0	28.0
Italy	22.4	24.7
Luxembourg	7.4	5.6
Netherlands	7.8	7.7
Portugal	17.2	19.9
Spain	17.6	17.2
UK	11.5	39.8

To illustrate this, the following is an account of how the British trade unions in the construction industry have responded. The growth in self-employment has led the UK's major construction union, UCATT, to open up membership to the self-employed. According to UCATT 'self employment has now become the normal form of working in the construction industry'.[19] The union puts the overall number of those working as self-employed as higher than that estimated by the Department of Employment since the DE figures include all employed in the sector (professionals, clerical workers and so on). UCATT estimates that, taking operatives only, some 722,294 or 57% of the sector is self-employed.

Most work under what is known as the 714 system. Under this employees are directly assessed for income tax and have to keep their own records of income. Inland Revenue figures for 1990 obtained by UCATT give a total of 568,836. But UCATT believes that in recent years there has been an alarming growth in the number of uncertificated self-employed. Again, according to the Inland Revenue, these come to a further 125,000, but the figure is thought to be considerably higher.

UCATT's response to this growth has been to call for the registration of all self-employed workers. This proposal has the support of some large employers and the Construction Industry Training Board, but is opposed by the employers' organisations, BEC and FCEC, who fear that it might be too restrictive.

What has been achieved is an agreement with the employers' organisations that the self-employed would be employed under 'not less favourable terms'. However, union and employers interpret this clause differently. The employers argue that an arrangement to pay the self-employed a 30% addition in recognition of the fact that they have no entitlement to holidays, sickness benefits and other benefits ensures equality of treatment. UCATT disagrees and is trying to renegotiate the clause.

18 Source: Calculated from statistics in ILO Yearbook of Labour Statistics (1992) and DE Gazette (June 1992).
19 UCATT *Comments on TUC Employment Policy Paper* (1992).

UCATT is also pursuing a strategy of challenges to the definition of its members as self-employed. In a number of recent industrial tribunal cases it has argued for members' entitlement to redundancy pay and other benefits usually only available to those with employee status. In one recent case an industrial tribunal accepted that a self-employed person had an entitlement to redundancy pay because, on the facts, he had always worked for the same employer and was never truly in business on his own account.[20]

A further constraint on the ability of unions in Europe to bargain lies in the phenomenal growth in small firms, at the expense of large enterprises. The larger the workforce, the more favourable are the conditions for successful conclusion of collective agreements. The increasing fragmentation of the sector into smaller units, employing few workers, inevitably has an impact on bargaining strength.

In 1980, 43% of workers in construction were employed in small firms (defined as employing fewer than 50 workers). By 1990 this section of the workforce had grown to represent 54% of all construction workers. Over the same period the numbers employed in large firms (defined as those employing 500 or more) declined by 37%:

NUMBER OF EMPLOYEES BY SIZE OF FIRM: 1980/1990[1]					
	fewer than 50 employees			*500 or more employees*	
	1980	(000s)	1990	1980	(000s)	1990
Belgium	40		38	19		8
Denmark	101		92	7		8
France	450		855	291		203
Germany (W)	615		563	100		77
Netherlands	114		158	32		18
UK	418		349	258		203
Total	1,738		2,055	707		517

In 1980 there were 230,380 firms operating in seven Member States surveyed by the United Nations.[2] By 1990 the number had practicably trebled to 649,657. Almost all of this growth was in small firms employing fewer than 20 workers. Their number grew from 199,513 in 1980 to 597,967 in 1990, now representing 92% of all firms.

Thus whilst in 1980 each firm employed on average 17.25 employees, by 1990 this average had fallen to 5.85.

Already by 1989 an EFBWW conference was discussing the particular problems arising from the growth in small firms. There were problems over the observance of collective agreements and the need for the development of structures aimed at monitoring levels of compliance. The greater the number of

---

20 *Connelly v R O'Rourke & Son* (1992), unreported.
 1 Source: Calculated from statistics in the Annual Bulletin of Housing and Building Statistics for Europe, United Nations (1991).
 2 United Nations, Annual Bulletin of Housing and Building Statistics for Europe, 1991.

NUMBER OF FIRMS BY SIZE 1980/1990[3]				
	fewer than 50 employees		*500 or more employees*	
	1980	1990	1980	1990
Belgium	1,466	1,309	18	11
Denmark	25,586	25,956	15	12
France	19,472	306,898	193	149
Germany (W)	55,054	66,633	107	180
Netherlands	4,960	17,100	31	19
UK	110,088	207,711	209	116

firms operating, the more difficult it becomes both to recruit members and to build up bargaining structures to include them. The absence of national agreements covering the whole sector in some Member States contributes to this difficulty. Recent figures for trade union membership in the UK construction sector, for example, show that just 15% of those in small firms (employing fewer than 50) are in a union, compared to 43% where more than 50 are employed.[4] Small firms also have poorer safety records. Construction union UCATT points to a rise in fatal accidents in construction, currently averaging at more than 150 a year:[5]

'The proliferation of small sites and sub-contractors together with the de-regulation of the labour force has made it increasingly difficult for proper safety checks to be made.'

The lack of sectoral bargaining within a Member State is a constraint to the development of Europe-wide bargaining. In two Member States, Luxembourg and Spain, there is no national sectoral bargaining, although in Spain there may be large provincial construction agreements which are significant enough to set standards.

A multiplicity of representative bodies can also impede bargaining. Within the construction sector, in every Member State save Germany (for trade unions) and Belgium (for employers) there is more than one representative body. Where such organisations compete for membership there is greater difficulty in reaching accord.

However, outside of these two areas of difficulty, national bargaining systems in general tend to favour, rather than impede, the process of EC-level bargaining. In Germany, for example, although sectoral bargaining is almost always at the level of the Land (region), construction is an exception to the rule and a national sectoral agreement is in force. In the Netherlands, sectoral bargaining combined with extension mechanisms result in a mere 4% of the workforce being excluded. In Italy, the sectoral agreement for construction rates as one of the big four. The following Table shows how bargaining in construction occurs in Member States and what has been gained in recent bargaining rounds.

3 Source: Calculated from statistics in Annual Bulletin of Housing and Building Statistics for Europe, United Nations (1991).
4 (1993) *Employment Gazette*, 'Membership of Trade Unions' (May).
5 UCATT *Comments on TUC Employment Policy paper* (1992).

Bargaining outcomes in the construction industry

Belgium   New agreement on shorter working hours and an agreement on improved social security benefits concluded.

France   In 1990 the unions in construction renegotiated, after a 25-year lapse, a new agreement on job classification, leading to a call from the Ministry of Labour that all sectors overhaul their job classification procedures.

Germany   Construction is the sole sector over which bargaining takes place at national level. A Framework agreement for manual workers in 1990 allows for the making up of lost time as the result of bad weather. Agreements have also been reached on the working environment.[6]

Ireland   A Joint Industrial Council covers the sector.

Italy   Construction is one of the four most significant sectoral agreements. In the 1991 bargaining round a system of supplementary bargaining was introduced at territorial (rather than company) level to take account of the predominance of small firms.

Netherlands Sectoral bargaining is dominant in construction with 96% of the workforce covered either directly or by extension. The most recent bargaining round secured an agreement on early retirement.

Spain   Construction negotiations are at provincial level, but there are important agreements which help set norms.

UK   A Joint Industrial Council covers the sector.

Thus the combination of sectoral bargaining and extension procedures results in a situation that a single agreement in the construction sector already exists in eight Member States. The coordination of bargaining processes on the part of the social partners at Member State level to achieve this outcome lends itself strongly to a view that the sector would be amenable to a higher (EC) level of sectoral bargaining.

The existence of legislation guaranteeing extension/adoption of collective agreements could be a useful legal mechanism for the translation of a European framework agreement into Member State agreements. Procedures for extending collective agreements already exist in seven Member States. These would permit organisations affiliated to the EFBWW and the European employers' confederation, FIEC, in each Member State to themselves sign the agreement and then apply the extension/adoption procedures to cover those workers outside their collective responsibility.

How much are construction industry employers and trade unions committed to social dialogue? On the union side this desire for dialogue is articulated in its current constitution. However, in its recent action programme the EFBWW states that there is still 'a long way to go' to obtain European agreements on working conditions.[7] One particular obstacle is that 'the social partners lack the necessary mandates and legal basis'.

The employers' reasons for agreeing to enter into social dialogue are more complex. They stemmed from a view that the industry was no longer adequately

6 *European Industrial Relations Review*, No 210, July 1991.
7 EFBWW *The General Policy Programme and Programme of Activities of the EFBWW for the Period 1992–95* (1991), at page 7.

represented by the umbrella employers' organisation UNICE. Indeed it was originally in opposition to the position then argued by UNICE (which is that social
dialogue at European level is appropriate only between the three general players
– UNICE, CEEP and ETUC) that it agreed to respond to the EFBWW request
for dialogue. However, a willingness to enter into dialogue does not imply that
FIEC at present is committed to bargaining at European level.

Large-scale employers dominant within FIEC may well believe that it is in
their interests to reach accommodation with the unions at European level,
effectively to shake out some of the sector's smaller employers. Within individual Member States there have already been developments in this direction. In
Italy, for example, a new level of bargaining at territorial level has been agreed,
specifically to deal with the problem of the multiplicity of small firms.[8] The
growth in self-employment can also act as a block on developments within the
sector. UCATT's 1992 paper notes the concern of employers themselves:[9]

> 'There is a feeling amongst many of the large contractors that the industry is in dan-
> ger of spiralling out of control. Increasingly the complaint is being heard that even
> on the large well-organised sites the management contractors feel that they are not
> properly in control because the operatives on site work for a myriad of subcontrac-
> tors and labour agencies. There is also a growing concern about labour supply. The
> large contractors feel that they are at the mercy of labour agencies who often give
> them only sub-standard labour.'

Within the construction sector the work of the European Commission is and has
been central to the development of social dialogue. Without its practical assistance the social dialogue might never have commenced. It is the Commission
which funds the meetings, provides interpretation facilities, meets travel costs and
the cost of associated publications. A representative of the Commission is also in
attendance at all meetings of the social partners, although as an observer only.

The co-operation of the Commission within the process of social dialogue has
also brought its own rewards to the social partners. The Commission informed
the EFBWW and FIEC that it recognised them as representative and that it
would in future submit all components of its social action programme to the two
bodies for joint consultation. Although, according to the EFBWW this does not
always happen, it is something which both employers and trade unions desire.[10]
The Commission could therefore capitalise on this fact and encourage the social
partners to proceed towards collective bargaining in exchange for more in-
depth involvement in the consultative process. And of course the Commission is
uniquely placed to inform the parties that if they do not reach agreement then
the potential for a European Directive on the subject area always remains.

An illustration of the potential of the social dialogue in the construction industry
arises from the Commission's proposals for a Council Directive concerning the
posting of workers in the framework of the provision of services.[11] This proposed
Directive has particular relevance to the construction sector as developments
within the sector have resulted in the creation of companies with interests
throughout Europe. A look at two of the UK's major construction companies can
demonstrate this.

8   *European Industrial Relations Review*, No 227, December 1992.
9   Op cit.
10 EFBWW *Activity report by the EFBWW Secretariat* (1988–91).
11 COM (91) 230 final, SYN 346, Brussels, 1 August 1991.

P&O, better known for its shipping interests, nevertheless has a significant involvement in construction, with a quarter of its turnover in housebuilding, construction and development. Although its core area of operation remains the UK, it is its interests in the rest of Europe which have most recently shown growth. Thus, while UK turnover declined by 7.4% between 1991 and 1992, operations in the rest of continental Europe grew by 13.7%.[12] UK construction firm John Mowlem and Co too has experienced a decline in its UK operations but growth in the rest of Europe. UK turnover declined by 11.5% between 1991 and 1992 whilst that for other European states increased by 30.9%.[13]

The proposal that there should be a Directive specifically covering the rights of workers posted to another country reflects the deeply felt concerns of Member State unions in construction, but in particular those in Germany and the UK.

In Germany the collapse of the former Eastern Bloc countries has made available a market of low cost, but relatively highly skilled workers, uniquely well placed to compete with the indigenous workforce. IG Bau (the German construction union) has thus lobbied for a Directive to ensure that foreign workers entering Germany had to work on German terms and conditions. Their definition of foreign workers was not limited to the former Eastern Bloc states but included demands for the similar regulation of UK and Irish construction workers entering Germany.

At the same time, in the UK, the construction union UCATT was also lobbying for change, although in general its members were on the receiving end of inferior conditions as members of foreign labour forces. UK construction workers have been employed at Eurodisney near Paris, the Olympic Games stadium in Barcelona and for Expo 92 in Seville. The UK union had a number of objectives, including that all employees should have the right to benefit from a sectoral agreement in force in preference to any national legal minimum on wages, regardless of the status in law of that agreement, and that it should cover the self-employed.

Although the EFBWW has played a pivotal role in the consultation and drafting of the draft Directive, it has always recognised that there is a role for Member State unions. In a document to its Executive Committee in May 1993, it points to the work of the building sector unions and national confederations in some countries in lobbying for the Directive and calls on this work to be strengthened.

It is this interrelationship between national and European level organisations that is most of note when we look at the prospects for European collective bargaining. European level organisations must deliver the support of national unions in order to satisfy the requirements for representativity and accountability. To the extent that national unions can recruit and represent self-employed workers, these will be able to influence the formulation of EC-level regulation in the form of Directives, or even EC-level collective agreements. This influence could include provision for the social protection of self-employed building workers.

12   P&O Annual Accounts, 1992.
13   John Mowlem and Co, Annual Accounts, 1992. The UK's largest construction company is Alfred McAlpine. Unfortunately its annual accounts do not show a breakdown of European turnover, it being included under a general heading of 'rest of the world'. Nevertheless, it is only this entry that showed growth in the last year. Thus while turnover declined in the UK by 12% (and in the USA its second largest area of operation by 2.6%) it more than doubled in the 'rest of the world' category.

Part IX

The Collective Labour Law of the European Union

Chapter 33

A Framework of Principles for European Collective Labour Law

INTRODUCTION

Since the founding of the EC the development of social policy and labour legislation has been hampered by 'subservience to the process of market integration'.[1] The Protocol and Agreement on Social Policy of the Maastricht Treaty on European Union finally broke this stranglehold.[2] Still, the habits of thinking, and of action, of the preceding decades continue to influence perceptions of the future social policy and labour legislation of the European Union.[3]

Each Member State of the EU has a national system of labour law. There is also a body of international labour law. But there is also the law of the EU, as famously stated by the European Court of Justice in *Van Gend en Loos*: 'a new legal order of international law for the benefit of which the states have limited their sovereign rights, albeit within limited fields, and the subjects of which comprise not only Member States but also their nationals'.[4] This new legal order may also be said to have a labour law.

Not surprisingly, much of the attention devoted to the labour law of the EC has focused on those relatively highly developed areas pertinent to the functioning of the common market. Analysis of a number of recent textbooks on European labour law revealed an emphasis on free movement of labour, or Directives having the objective of harmonising labour standards throughout the Single European Market.[5] It has not been easy to perceive in the emerging law of a European common market a role for collective organisations of labour and capital. Freedom of association was not one of the founding principles and collective

---

1 '... subservience to the process of market integration fatally hinders the development of a rationale for Community action in the social policy field ... So long as a piece of Community labour legislation can be promoted only on the basis that it contributes to the integration of markets, Community law in this area will remain hobbled': P L Davies 'The Emergence of European Labour Law', in W McCarthy (ed) *Legal Intervention in Industrial Relations: Gains and Losses*, Blackwell, 1992, p 313 at pp 346–7.
2 B Bercusson 'Maastricht: a fundamental change in European labour law', (1992) 23 *Industrial Relations Journal* 177.
3 Expectations are modest, and cast in terms of 'values' and 'soft law'. S Sciarra 'Social values and the multiple sources of European social law', (1995) 1 *European Law Journal* 60.
4 Case 26/62: *Algemene Transport- en Expeditie Onderneming van Gend & Loos NV v Nederlandse administratie der belastingen (Netherlands Inland Revenue Administration)* [1963] ECR 1 at 12.
5 See Chapter 1. Also, B Bercusson 'The Conceptualisation of European Labour Law', (1995) 24 *Industrial Law Journal* 1.

bargaining was not one of the operating mechanisms of the common market. An interesting feature of the textbooks which have emerged has been the classification of those instruments of EC labour law which include mandatory information and consultation of workers' representatives under headings of individual rights and protection of individual interests.[6]

Accompanying this conceptual disarray about the nature of the law governing collective labour relations at EU level has been scepticism as to the feasibility of development of a system of industrial relations at the level of the EU.[7] The result has been a general pessimism about the prospects for collective labour law in the EU. Much of the confusion and some of the scepticism is due to the absence at EU level of legal measures and institutional and organisational structures recognisable in terms of traditional and familiar collective labour laws and national industrial relations systems. A similar situation has prevailed in much of the legal and political debate over the process of European integration and the development of the European polity in general.

This chapter argues that, up to now, the collective labour law of the EU is to be found embedded in a variety of legal measures which do *not* have the regulation of collective labour relations as their primary objective. These measures include those aimed at harmonising national labour laws, or regulating the implications for labour of transnational economic activities. However, more important than their regulation of discrete areas and issues is their *spill-over* effect.

The spill-over effect arises, in part, from the interpretation of these measures by the European Court, particularly in its review of national legislation implementing EU law.[8] But in addition, spill-over occurs because these EU measures incorporate in their substantive provisions *principles* of collective labour law reflecting *national* experience. *Both* their reflection and recognition in European Court judgments *and* their incorporation in EU legal measures transform these principles from having purely national effect into EU law. In this way, principles derived from *some* national experiences are imported into *other* Member States where their full implications can have unexpectedly spectacular effects, as has already been demonstrated in *EC Commission v UK.*[9]

The content of the collective labour law of the EU reflects the principles manifest in some of these EU law measures. The *dynamic* of its development has been the spill-over effect of these principles, through their translation into the status of EU law, and their development by decisions of the European

6   For example, in Roger Blanpain and Jean-Claude Javillier *Droit du Travail Communautaire*, Litec, Paris 1991, Part II, entitled 'Individual Labour Law', includes the Directives on collective dismissals and transfers of enterprises, which provide for information to and consultation of workers' representatives. Similarly, *Diritto del Lavoro della Comunità Europea*, Cedam, Padova 1992, by Massimo Roccella and Tiziano Treu, in Part III, entitled 'Individual Relations'; and *The Social Dimension of the European Community* (2nd ed) (1993) by Ruth Nielsen and Erika Szyszczak, Handelshojskolens Forlag, Copenhagen, Chapter 4 on 'The Protection of Employment Rights.'

7   W Streeck and P Schmitter 'From national corporatism to transnational pluralism: Organised interests in the Single European Market', (1991) 19 *Politics and Society* 133; W Streeck 'Neo-voluntarism: A new European social policy regime', (1995) 1 *European Law Journal* 31.

8   A role as engine of institutional change already played in the constitutional development of the EU. J H H Weiler 'The Transformation of Europe', (1991) 100 *Yale Law Journal* 2403.

9   Cases C-382/92 and C-383/92: [1994] ECR I-2435 and [1994] ECR I-2479.

Court.[10] It is even at this early stage arguable that these principles constitute a future framework of the collective labour law of the EU.

This chapter outlines a framework of principles which, it is argued, are currently embodied in the collective labour law of the EU, and which will be further developed in the future. They include collectively bargained labour standards, workers' collective representation, workers' participation and protection of strikers against dismissal. In addition, an example is provided of a parallel principle of collective solidarity which may also be emerging in the social security law of the EU.

The adoption of the Protocol and Agreement on Social Policy attached to the Maastricht Treaty on European Union has created the potential for autonomous development of EU collective labour law. The expansion of the substantive social competences of the EU by the Protocol and Agreement opens the way for development of the collective labour law of the EU without the considerable constraints of strict adherence to the objectives of market integration. Even more important to the development of such collective labour law is the principle of collective negotiation of labour policy embodied in the new institutional arrangements for the production of EU labour law introduced by the Protocol and Agreement on Social Policy. This may be seen as the founding constitutional basis for the collective labour law of the EU.[11]

COLLECTIVELY BARGAINED LABOUR STANDARDS

EU law has been inspired by recourse to collective agreements as labour standards in the labour laws of a number of Member States.

Collective agreements as 'essential' standards

First, the Commission's proposal for a Directive on proof of an employment relationship[12] was clearly inspired by the experience of the UK requirement that employers provide employees a written statement of particulars of terms and conditions of employment.[13] UK law reflected the role of collective bargaining in

---

10   The spill-over effect is not specific to collective labour law, but applies also to individual labour law. For example, the Working Time Directive 94/104/EC of 23 November 1993, Article 18(1)(b)(i), allows overtime working above the 48-hour weekly limit by individual agreement of the worker; but the worker is to be subject to no detriment for refusal to work more than 48 hours. Discipline or dismissal of a worker for refusing to work more than 48 hours is likely to be the starting point for the development of principles in this area of the individual labour law of the EU.

11   This is discussed in detail in Chapters 34 and 35. Also, B Bercusson 'The dynamic of European labour law after Maastricht', (1994) 23 *Industrial Law Journal* 1.

12   Commission Proposal for a Council Directive on a form of proof of an employment relationship, COM (90) 563 final, Brussels, 8 January 1991.

13   Employment Protection (Consolidation) Act 1978, sections 1–6, replaced by the provisions of the Trade Union Reform and Employment Rights Act 1993, Schedule 4. The Explanatory Memorandum accompanying the Commission's proposal included a Table (p 6) which indicated that only in the UK and Ireland was such a requirement imposed on employers. One explanation for the passage of this element of EC social legislation may be the less than principled willingness of the UK in the Council of Ministers to approve the extension at EC level of requirements already imposed on British employers, while vetoing similar such attempts by other Member States.

determining terms and conditions of employment by offering employers an *alternative* to individual detailed written statements specifying all or any of the prescribed terms and conditions. The alternative was to refer the employee to 'some document which the employee has reasonable opportunities of reading in the course of his employment or which is made reasonably accessible to him in some other way', which in practice usually meant reference to the collective agreement.

The EC Directive [14] modified the UK law slightly but significantly, by making such reference to collective agreements *explicit and direct.* Among the *'essential aspects* of the contract or employment relationship' to be included in the written document provided by the employer under the Directive are 'the *collective agreements* governing the employee's conditions of work'. [15] There is much that requires clarification in these provisions of the Directive and the UK law:

- Which collective agreements, and at which levels, must be covered?
- What information about the agreement needs be provided: parties, date, establishments and/or categories of employees covered, etc?
- Is coverage required of substantive terms of employment and/or also procedural provisions affecting the worker's representatives (eg representational rights, or others not so easily incorporated into individual contracts)?
- Does 'governing' mean :
    - legally binding on the employer as party to collective agreement (apparently not, since both the EC and UK provisions envisage the employer not being a party to the agreement);
    - legally binding in that they are incorporated into individual contracts of employment;
    - effectively governed, in that the employer observes in practice the same (or similar) terms?
- If a mere reference is made to an agreement in the employee's contract, does this imply that all provisions of the agreement apply, not only those specified in the Directive?

These issues await testing. For example, the Trade Union Reform and Employment Rights Act 1993, following the language of the Employment Protection (Consolidation) Act 1978, requires provision of 'particulars ... of ... any collective agreements which directly affect the terms and conditions of the employment including, where the employer is not a party, the persons by whom they were made'. [16] It is not clear what precisely is the information required to be conveyed in these particulars. Is the UK law's requirement that the agreement '*directly* affect the terms and conditions of the employment' an

---

14   Council Directive 91/533 of 14 October 1991 on an employer's obligation to inform employees of the conditions applicable to the contract or employment relationship, OJ 1991 L288/32.

15   Directive 91/533, Article 2(2)(j)(i). Collective agreements were *not* among the items of information required to be provided by the UK law. On the other hand, the Directive allowed for cross-reference to collective agreements, but only as regards a few key heads of the information required to be provided (Article 2(3): holidays, length of notice, remuneration, working hours). The transmutation of the UK law entailed by the passage of the Directive has meant that the UK law has had to be amended to bring it into line with the new requirements.

16   Schedule 4, paragraph 1(3)(j).

inaccurate transposition of the Directive?

There is scope for litigation where employers fail to include information on collective agreements; or include information contradicting collectively agreed provisions. If there is no reference to agreements which arguably govern conditions of work, this is a violation of the EU law which requires an adequate and effective remedy. Complaints to national tribunals could require a reference to the European Court to clarify these ambiguities.

EC law has clearly linked the determination of individual workers' terms of employment to the provisions of collective agreements; this will now be a requirement in the labour law of every Member State.

Collective agreements as universal standards

The Commission's Proposal for a Council Directive concerning the posting of workers in the framework of the provision of services[17] aimed to prescribe the 'working conditions applicable to workers from another State performing work in the host country in the framework of the freedom to provide services, especially on behalf of a subcontracting undertaking'.[18] The Commission relied upon the decision of the European Court in *Rush Portuguesa Lda v Office National d'Immigration.*[19]

In that case, the Court was confronted with a building and public works undertaking governed by Portuguese law, which had entered into a subcontract with a French company for works in France and, to carry out these works, brought its Portuguese workforce from Portugal. In response to the question put to the Court as to whether '... the right of a Portuguese company to provide services throughout the Community (could) be made subject ... to conditions ...',[20] the Court had made the following statement:[1]

'Finally, it should be stated, in response to the concern expressed in this connection by the French Government, that Community law does not preclude Member States from extending their legislation, or collective agreements entered into by both sides of industry, to any person who is employed, even temporarily, within their territory, no matter in which country the employer is established; nor does Community law prohibit Member States from enforcing those rules by appropriate means.'

The rule of EC law was that Member State regulation of terms and conditions of employment, by law or *collective agreement*, was permissible.

The Commission in its later proposal confirmed that 'Member States may decide to set and apply minimum pay levels applicable on their territory in order to ensure a minimum standard of living appropriate to the country concerned'.[2] The Commission was fully aware of the implications of competition in

---

17 COM (91) 230 final – SYN 346, Brussels, 1 August 1991. For detailed analysis of this proposal and its evolution, see Chapter 27.
18 Commission's Action Programme to implement the Community Charter of Fundamental Social Rights, 1989, Part II, Section 4B.
19 Case C-113/89: [1990] ECR I-417.
20 Ibid, at 1420.
1 Ibid, at 1445, paragraph 12.
2 Explanatory Memorandum, paragraph 9 bis.

labour standards for Community social policy:[3]

'National differences as to the material content of working conditions and the criteria inspiring the conflict of law rules may lead to situations where posted workers are applied lower wages and other working conditions than those in force in the place where the work is temporarily carried out. This situation would certainly affect fair competition between undertakings and equality of treatment between foreign and national undertakings; it would from the social point of view be completely unacceptable.'

In this context, the proposed Directive made a clear policy choice going beyond what had been stated by the Court to be the legal principle in EC law:[4]

'the need to eradicate discrimination between national and non-national undertakings and workers with respect to the application of certain working conditions, justifies a Community proposal which ... intends to create a hard core of mandatory rules laid down by statutes or by erga omnes collective agreements, without disrupting the labour law systems of the Member States and particularly their legislative or voluntaristic approach and their collective bargaining systems.'

Hence, Article 3(1) of the proposed Directive provided:

'Member States shall see to it that, whatever the law applicable to the employment relationship, the undertaking does not deprive the worker of the terms and conditions of employment which apply for work of the same character at the place where the work is temporarily carried out, provided that:
(a) they are laid down by laws, regulations and administrative provisions, *collective agreements* or arbitration awards, covering the whole of the occupation and industry concerned having an 'erga omnes' effect and/or being made legally binding in the occupation and industry concerned ...'

As with much of EC labour law, this relatively minor proposal creates potentially important consequences. The Directive, by providing an entitlement of posted workers to collectively agreed standards, raises a legitimate expectation that posted workers should not be better off in this respect than host country workers. To maintain the difference would be to discriminate against host country workers. Countries which extend generally applicable agreements to posted workers will be under pressure to extend them to all undertakings. Hence the Directive is a step towards the objective that *all* workers, whether posted or not, should not be deprived of the terms and conditions of employment laid down by law or collective agreements.

This would give a great new potential to collective agreements. Those countries where there are generally applicable agreements would have to extend them to cover first posted workers, and then all workers not so covered.

Collective agreements as EU standards: working time

The Commission's first proposal for a Directive on Working Time stated the intention 'to propose a groundwork of basic provisions on certain aspects of the

---

3   Ibid, paragraph 12.
4   Ibid, paragraph 18.

organisation of working time'.[5] However, 'other issues mentioned in the action programme in the field of the adaptation of working time should be left to both sides of industry and/or national legislation'.[6] The role of the social partners in negotiating flexibility of capacity utilisation through agreements on working time was acknowledged,[7] with reference to experience in Germany, the Netherlands, Belgium, Greece, France, Italy and Portugal.[8] The Explanatory Memorandum carefully outlined the division of competences between legislation and collective bargaining:[9]

> '... given the differences arising from national practices, the subject of working conditions in general falls to varying degrees under the autonomy of both sides of industry who often act in the public authorities' stead and/or complement their action. To take account of these differences and in accordance with the principle of subsidiarity the Commission takes the view that negotiation between the two sides of industry should play its full part within the framework of the proposed measures, provided that it is able to guarantee adherence to the principles set out in the Commission's proposals . . .'

The first two drafts of the Working Time Directive reflected this explicit recognition of the role of collective bargaining in the form of an important, if cautious, initiative by providing for the possibility of general derogation in Article 12(3), and also allowing for the possibility of implementation of the Directive through collective agreements.[10]

This traditional approach was transformed into a radical advance in the final draft, which gave collective bargaining a central role in the setting of some EC standards on working time.[11] This was a significant *qualitative* change from being confined to the role of derogating from established standards to itself independently prescribing standards. The present Directive allows for collective agreements to *fix* or *define* relevant standards. In one exceptional case, collective agreements are even given *priority* over Member State legislation. As regards *rest breaks* during working hours, the Directive gives *priority* to collective agreements over legislation in *determining* the EC standard:[12]

Breaks

'Member States shall take the measures necessary to ensure that, where the working day is longer than six hours, every worker is entitled to a rest break, the details of

5   COM (90) 317 final – SYN 295, Brussels, 20 September 1990; OJ C254 of 9.10.1990, p 4; Explanatory Memorandum, page 2, paragraph 2.
6   Ibid, p 3.
7   Ibid, p 4, paragraph 4.
8   Ibid, p 13, paragraph 25.
9   Ibid, p 4, paragraph 3 and again in paragraph 32 on pp 16–17.
10 Article 14.
11 Council Directive 93/104/EC of 23 November 1993 concerning certain aspects of the organisation of working time, OJ L307/18 of 13.12.93.
12 Article 4. This is a step further down the road taken by the European Court of Justice. In an early judgment concerning Denmark, the Court rejected the Commission's argument that collective bargaining was not an adequate means of implementing Community obligations under the Council Directive 75/117 on equal pay. The Court held: 'that Member States may leave the implementation of the principle of equal pay in the first instance to representatives of management and labour. That possibility does not, however, discharge them from the

which, including duration and the terms on which it is granted, shall be laid down in collective agreements or agreements between the two sides of industry or, *failing* that, by national legislation.'

Collective bargaining determines the EU standard.[13] Only in its absence is the standard to be prescribed by legislation.

In addition, according to the Directive's provisions, collective bargaining is engaged in *setting* substantive EU standards in relation to night work, daily rest breaks, maximum weekly working hours, including overtime and annual holidays. Member States are to consult the social partners before legislating standards on night work, and it is arguable that Article 13 requires employers to consult workers and their representatives when s/he 'intends to organise work according to a certain pattern'. Any derogations at enterprise level are explicitly subject to framework agreements negotiated at national or regional levels.

It becomes evident that the Directive is likely to engage national courts, and eventually the European Court, in questions of collective labour law not previously encountered. The Directive will bring before these courts issues of proper consultation of trade unions, by Member States or employers; the relations between collective agreements and law, different levels of collective agreements, and individual contracts and collective agreements. In this sense the Working Time Directive breaks new ground in the development of a European collective labour law.

WORKERS' COLLECTIVE REPRESENTATION

The collective representation of workers has been a principle manifested in numerous policy initiatives of the Commission. They owe their origin to national labour law provisions for representation of workers in enterprises, in the form of organs based on the workplace[14] or based on corporate structures.[15]

Although many of these proposals did not succeed in gaining the approval of the legislative organs of the Community, in two areas the EU has provided for workers' collective representation: regarding health and safety, and in the form of European works' councils. Further, on the basis of two other Directives, the European Court has declared that workers' collective representation is mandatory.

---

obligation of ensuring, by appropriate legislative and administrative provisions, that all workers in the Community are afforded the full protection provided for in the directive. That State guarantee must cover all cases where effective protection is not ensured by other means, for whatever reason, and in particular cases where the workers in question are not union members, where the sector in question is not covered by a collective agreement or where such an agreement does not fully guarantee the principle of equal pay'. Case 143/83: *EC Commission v Kingdom of Denmark* [1985] ECR 427, at 434–5, paragraph 8.

13   Though without specifying the appropriate level.
14   Draft Directive on procedures for informing and consulting employees, OJ C297 of 15.11.80 and OJ C217 of 12.08.83.
15   Draft Fifth Directive concerning the structure of public limited companies and the powers and obligations of their organs, OJ C240 of 19.08.83; draft Directive concerning the European Company Statute, OJ C263 of 16.10.89.

Mandatory representation

Mandatory recognition of employee representatives has been declared in Cases C-382/92 and C-383/92: *EC Commission v UK*, decided by the Court on 8 June 1994.[16] The cases concerned complaints by the Commission about defective implementation by the UK of the EC Directives on 'acquired rights'[17] and 'collective dismissals'[18] with respect to the duty to designate worker representatives.

Both Directives require workers' representatives to be informed and consulted. The UK legislation implementing the Directives provides for information and consultation only where there are 'recognised' trade unions.[19] The Commission complained that the UK had not provided rules for the designation of workers' representatives where this did not take place on a voluntary basis.

The Commission argued that the Directives impose an obligation on employers to inform and consult in every instance. The UK argued that the obligation arises only if national law and practice provide for representatives. In both cases the Court held that 'The United Kingdom's point of view cannot be accepted'. The Court took identical views with respect to both Directives:[20]

'26. ... as United Kingdom law now stands, workers affected by (collective redundancies/the transfer of an undertaking) do not enjoy protection under ... the directive(s) in cases where an employer objects to worker representation in his undertaking.

27. In those circumstances, United Kingdom law, which allows an employer to frustrate the protection provided for workers by ... the directive(s), must be regarded as contrary to those (directives) ...'

In this, the Court subscribed to the views of Advocate-General Van Gerven, in an opinion delivered on 2 March 1994:[1]

'... to make the activity of workers' representatives totally dependent on voluntary recognition by employers is incompatible with the protection of workers as apparent from the directives in the light of their objective, structure and wording.'

The nature of workers' collective representation is likely to become further regulated by EU law. Designation of worker representatives was made mandatory by the Court due to the consequences for the rights of workers under the Directive:[2]

'which require(s) Member States to take all measures necessary to ensure that workers are informed, consulted and in a position to intervene through their representatives in the event of collective redundancies (or the transfer of an undertaking).'

---

16 [1994] ECR I-2435.
17 Directive 77/187, OJ L61/26.
18 Directive 75/129, OJ L48/29.
19 Trade Union and Labour Relations (Consolidation) Act 1992, section 188(1); the Transfer of Undertakings (Protection of Employment) Regulations 1991, Regulation 10(2)).
20 Case C-383/92, paragraphs 26–27, in terms identical to those of Case C-382/92, paragraphs 29–30.
1 Paragraph 9.
2 Case C-383/92, paragraph 23; Case C-382/92, paragraph 26.

In order to effectively perform the tasks of information and consultation specified in the Directives, worker representatives must possess the experience, independence and resources required to protect the interests of the workers they represent. In order to achieve the objective of the EC Directive, Member State laws or practices for the designation of workers' representatives must ensure that the national law on workers' representation is adequate to attain this.

Health and safety representatives

The relevant law is the 'Framework' Directive 89/391/EEC of 12 June 1989.[3] The objective, structure and wording of the Framework Directive require that safety be the concern of *multiple* categories of workers and their representatives. Close analysis of the provisions reveals that the Directive appears to support a distinction between *representatives* (general representatives, who fulfil certain functions in health and safety, and specialist representatives in health and safety) and *workers* (some with specific responsibilities, and 'designated' workers). Different methods of *appointment* are indicated for each category of worker and workers' representative:

– general workers' representatives[4] – in accordance with the laws and/or practices of the Member States;
– workers' representatives with specific responsibility for the safety and health of workers – in accordance with national laws and/or practices;[5]
– designated workers – by the employer;[6]
– workers with specific responsibilities for safety and health[7] – no method of appointment indicated.

This may seem an excessive enumeration of different categories. However, the Directive was formulated in a *European* context, where there is a *variety* of experience. There is no need to emphasise the social and human aspects of safety and health, or its economic significance. Safety and health warrants more than the one set of representatives. Specialisation and diversification of responsibilities may be needed to secure the objective of safe and healthy workplaces. The Directive's multiple categories are an indication of this.

Specifically, the Directive prescribes a role in health and safety for *general* workers' representatives. They have rights to be consulted over the planning and introduction of new technologies;[8] to submit observations during inspection visits,[9] and generally to be consulted and take part in discussions on all questions relating to safety and health at work.[10]

---

3   Council Directive 89/391/EEC of 12 June 1989 on the introduction of measures to encourage improvements in the safety and health of workers at work, OJ L183/1.
4   Articles 6(3)(c), 11(1), 11(6).
5   Articles 3(c), 11(2), 11(3).
6   Articles 7(1), 8(2).
7   Articles 11(2), 11(4), 13(2)(d)–(f).
8   Article 6(3)(c).
9   Article 11(6).
10   Article 11(1). UK law, which fails to make any provision obliging employers to respect these rights of general workers' representatives, is not in compliance with EU law.

The Directive requires the appointment of workers' representatives. This requirement is *not* conditional on employer recognition of trade unions. Nor can it be substituted by information and consultation of *individual* employees.[11] EU law prescribes the system of appointing representatives as being in accordance with national laws and/or practices.[12] The Directive does not permit the functions of safety representatives appointed by trade unions to be limited to employees represented by those trade union representatives. The representatives act on behalf of all employees.[13]

European works councils

Directive 94/45/EC of 22 September 1994 requires the establishment of a European works council (EWC) or a procedure in Community-scale undertakings and Community-scale groups of undertakings for the purposes of informing and consulting employees.[14] The Directive is to be implemented by the Member States no later than 22 September 1996.[15] In the short term, the priority is the *establishment* of the Special Negotiating Bodies (SNBs) which negotiate the creation of the EWCs. Once the SNB is established, the next phase is the *negotiation* of an agreement creating a EWC and defining its composition, functions, and so on.

The method of election or appointment of SNB members appears to be by delegation to Member State rules:[16]

'. . . a SNB shall be established in accordance with the following guidelines:
(a) The Member States shall determine the method to be used for the election or appointment of the members of the SNB who are to be elected or appointed in their territories . . .'

The members of the SNB arguably must be employees' representatives. The SNB members-representatives from each Member State will reflect national criteria of election or appointment of employees' representatives.[17] A government, such as that of the UK, might try to legislate rules for the election or appointment of members of the SNB which ignore or exclude trade union representatives. This is challenged by various provisions of the Directive.

Subparagraph (2) of Article 5(2)(a) provides:

'Member States shall provide that employees in undertakings and/or establishments in which there are no employees' representatives *through no fault of their own*, have the right to elect or appoint members of the SNB.'

---

11 UK law, which restricts the appointment of safety representatives to where the employer voluntarily recognises a trade union, is not in compliance with EU law requirements. This is reinforced by the judgment of the European Court in Cases C-382/92 and C-383/92: *EC Commission v UK* [1994] ECR I-2435.
12 Article 3(c)). This means, in the light of UK practice, appointment by trade unions. It is arguable that EU law supports the appointment of safety representatives by trade unions even where they are not recognised. See *Griffin v South West Water Services Ltd* [1995] IRLR 15.
13 UK law which restricts their functions to the employees they represent is not in compliance with EU law.
14 OJ L254/64 of 30.9.94.
15 Article 14(1).
16 Article 5(2).
17 For example, in the UK context, this means trade union representatives.

It is arguable that this creates a presumption that employees *only* elect or appoint where 'there are *no* employees' representatives *through no fault of their own*...' Otherwise, it is employees' representatives who are, or elect or appoint, the SNB.[18]

The function of the SNB is to establish the EWC by agreement with the central management. The structure and objective of the Directive, and in particular the subsidiary requirements of the Annex, support the view that the SNB should reflect the eventual composition of the EWC. The Annex to the Directive prescribes:[19]

> 'The EWC shall be composed of employees ... elected or appointed from their number by the employees' representatives, or, in absence thereof, by the entire body of employees.
>
> The election or appointment of the EWC shall be carried out in accordance with national legislation and/or practice.'

The Annex envisages a EWC composed of, or elected or appointed by, the employees' representatives. An SNB which agrees to a EWC *not* so elected or appointed is arguably *not* achieving the objective of the Directive.

The Annex's subsidiary requirements apply where[20] the SNB and the central management so decide, central management refuses to commence negotiations within six months of a request or three years elapse after a request without an agreement. The negotiating strategy inherent in the structure of the Directive is based on an SNB composed of employees' representatives. The SNB is in a strong negotiating position. If central management refuses to negotiate within six months, or refuses to agree to employees' representatives nominated by the SNB within three years, the EWC will be set up comprising those elected or appointed by the employees' representatives alone.

WORKERS' PARTICIPATION

The Directives on Acquired Rights and Collective Dismissals have long provided for obligatory information and consultation of workers' representatives. To these have now been added further elaborations of collective participation by Directives on health and safety and on European works councils.

Participation in health and safety: beyond consultation?

The 1989 Framework Directive draws a distinction between consultation of workers' *general* representatives and consultation of workers' representatives *with specific responsibility for safety and health.*

---

18 The meaning of 'through no fault of their own' becomes clear in light of the following subparagraph 3 of Article 5(2)(a): 'This second subparagraph shall be without prejudice to national legislation and/or practice laying down thresholds for the establishment of employee representation bodies'. Such thresholds are *not* the fault of employees; hence, they then have the right to elect or appoint the SNB.
19 Paragraph 1(b).
20 Article 7(1).

With respect to workers' *general* representatives, Article 11(1) provides that employers:

'shall consult workers and/or their representatives *and* allow them to take part in discussions on all questions relating to safety and health at work.
This *presupposes*:
- the consultation of workers,
- the right of workers and/or their representatives to make proposals,
- balanced participation in accordance with national laws and/or practices.'

A statement was entered in the record by the Council and Commission at the conclusion of the Council discussions on the common position on the Directive. It sought to give a very broad 'formal' latitude to the meaning of 'balanced participation':[1]

'The notion of balanced participation embraces a range of multiple forms of worker participation which vary considerably between Member States. The present directive places no obligation on the Member States to provide a specific form of balanced participation.'

Whatever else it may mean, and however it may be formally defined, it seems clear that 'balanced participation' is *not* the same as consultation. Arguably, it must include some different and additional element of involvement of workers' representatives.

Similarly, with respect to workers' representatives *with specific responsibility for safety and health*, the Directive appears to highlight the difference in the two concepts by providing for alternatives:[2]

'... workers' representatives with specific responsibility for the safety and health of workers shall take part in a balanced way, *or* shall be consulted in advance and in good time by the employer, with regard to (the items listed).'

The scope of 'balanced participation' is thus beyond the concept of 'consultation' – perhaps even as defined in the European Works Council Directive 94/45/EC of 22 September 1994.

European works councils: the end of management prerogative?

The purpose of the Directive '... is to improve the right to information and to consultation of employees ...'[3] The consultation prescribed by the Directive is defined as:[4]

'... the exchange of views and establishment of dialogue between employees' representatives and central management or any more appropriate level of management.'

The *establishment of dialogue* required by the Directive implies an active and continuous process of communication and interaction between the European

---

1 Council Document 9869/88 RESTRICTED SOC 82 of 12 December 1988, p 22, quoted in Laurent Vogel *Prevention at the Workplace*: an initial review of how the 1989 Community Framework Directive is being implemented. European Trade Union Technical Bureau for Health and Safety (TUTB), Brussels 1994, p 83.
2 Article 11(2).
3 Article 1(1).
4 Article 2(1)(f).

works council and management.

The Directive requires the creation of a EWC for the purposes of information and consultation. Equipped with information, the EWC is, through consultation, to influence the decision-making of central management. Consultation takes time, and the EWC can use the threat of delay to influence management decisions.

In an apparently paradoxical provision, the Annex stipulates that a meeting 'shall not affect the prerogatives of the central management'.[5] But the whole purpose of the Directive is to subject management decision-making to a procedure of information and consultation. Breach of the procedure must lead to an EU law *remedy* capable of restraining unilateral management action – hence, the special Article on 'Compliance with this Directive'.[6] Management prerogatives are to be subject to procedures of information and consultation of the EWC, procedures which are to be enforced by effective EU law remedies.

PROTECTION OF STRIKERS AGAINST DISMISSAL

EU law provides no right to strike. But a right to strike is largely a right to protection against dismissal of strikers. Does EU law provide some legal support or protection for strikers?

In the UK, when workers strike, the employer may or may not terminate their contracts. If he does, there is little or no protection under UK law. This contrasts with many other Member States of the EU, where a constitutional right to strike does not allow the employer to dismiss. A strike means suspension of the contract of employment; strikers normally have a right to return to work.

EU law does have rules on collective dismissals. Council Directive 75/129 of 17 February 1975 on the approximation of the laws of the Member States relating to collective redundancies[7] contains the potential for legal tactics defending strikers against dismissal. Directive 75/129 requires the employer to inform and consult workers' representatives when he contemplates redundancy dismissals. The Directive defines 'collective redundancies' as meaning:[8]

'dismissals effected by an employer for one or more reasons not related to the individual workers concerned.'

The amendment of the Directive in 1992 reinforced this by adding a new paragraph that 'terminations of an employment contract which occur to the individual workers concerned shall be assimilated to redundancies'.

Where workers go on strike, the employer may contemplate dismissing strikers. These dismissals related to a strike would arguably be 'for one or more reasons not related to the individual workers concerned'. Hence, the Directive applies. If the employer tries to dismiss strikers before carrying out the procedures of information and consultation of the workers' representatives, a

---

5   Paragraph 3, subparagraph 4.
6   Article 11(1) and (3).
7   As amended; Council Directive 92/56/EEC of 24 June 1992 amending Directive 75/129/EEC on the approximation of the laws of the Member States relating to collective redundancies, OJ L245/3 of 26.8.92.
8   Article 1(1)(a).

litigation strategy would be to persuade a national tribunal to make a reference to the European Court for an interpretation of the Directive under Article 177 of the Treaty. An interim injunction to stop dismissals of strikers should be granted; alternatively, an undertaking in damages to compensate all workers affected if the claim is subsequently upheld.

The strategy may be particularly effective in the case of employers refusing to recognise, or withdrawing recognition from a trade union (derecognition). An employer refusing union recognition, or attempting derecognition may (and should) contemplate dismissals of employees (trade union members) refusing to accept this decision. Dismissals of trade union members for refusal to accept derecognition are dismissals by reason of 'one or more reasons not related to the individual workers concerned'. The Directive applies.

The employer who contemplates that dismissals may result from his decision to derecognise 'shall begin consultations with workers' representatives in good time with a view to reaching an agreement'.[9] The employer must examine 'ways and means of avoiding collective redundancies or reducing the number of workers involved'.[10] An employer genuinely concerned to avoid dismissals could easily continue recognition to avoid the dismissals. Continuing union recognition is even implicit in the provision that these consultations 'shall begin ... with a view to reaching an agreement'. They are premised on there being an agreement with (union) representatives.

It should, belatedly, be recognised that the Collective Dismissals Directive embodies an EU policy that striking workers may be defending *collective* interests. As such they are covered by EU law against dismissals effected for such collective 'reasons not related to the individual workers concerned.'

COLLECTIVE PRINCIPLES IN EU SOCIAL SECURITY LAW: SOLIDARITY

The collective principle in EU labour law has taken another form in the EU law on social protection. The Delors White Paper, Part A, 'The challenges and ways forward into the 21st century' included a section entitled 'An economy characterised by solidarity'.[11] In this section, reference was made to how the insufficiencies of the market led the Member States to develop collective solidarity mechanisms. The principle of *solidarity* has recently been upheld by the European Court in a case involving self-employed workers.

Joined cases C-159/91 and C-160/91, decided by the Court on 17 February 1993, concerned complaints by self-employed workers that compulsory contributions to the mutual funds established to provide social protection violated the principles of free competition in the common market as laid down in Articles 85–86 of the Treaty of Rome.[12]

---

9   1992 amending Directive, inserting new Article 2(1).
10   Article 2(2).
11   *Growth, Competitiveness, Employment* (1993), pp 15–16.
12   Case C-159/91: *Poucet v Assurances générales de France (AGF) et Caisse mutuelle régionale de Languedoc-Roussillon (Camulrac)*; Case C-160/91: *Pistre v Caisse autonome nationale de compensation de l'assurance vieillesse des artisans (Cancava)*, decided on 17 February 1993, Conclusions of the Advocate-General M Giuseppe Tesauro presented on 29 September 1992. I have relied upon the text of the judgment and Conclusions in French.

The complainants demanded the right to make contributions to any insurance company, without being subjected to the conditions unilaterally prescribed by the official organs which had the dominant position.[13] The first question before the Court was whether an organ responsible for the management of a special social security regime constituted an enterprise within the scope of Articles 85–86.

The representatives of the defendant social security organs argued that the system required solidarity among contributors, who pay regardless of their personal vulnerability to risks, in order to achieve the desired redistribution.[14] The French government cited Article L 111-1 of the Social Security Code which defines the principles of social protection in France: solidarity, compulsory affiliation. The profit-making orientation was absent, the activity being founded rather on the solidarity principle – hence outside Articles 85–86. The entire system of social security in France adheres to the solidarity principle – both within each regime and between them – in accordance with Article L 111-1.[15] Similar arguments were presented by the German government, without specific mention of the solidarity principle.[16]

The Commission explicitly characterised the activities of the social security organs in question as the application of the solidarity principle, which resided in the *absence* of the link between contributions and benefits, and the *presence* of a link between income and contributions – in contrast to private insurance. The principle was again illustrated with respect to sickness and old age, and also with respect to the supportive financial relationship between different regimes. The principle of 'generality' consisted in allowing all persons to benefit from social protection, including those at risk who are generally excluded from insurance schemes or subjected to heavy premium payments.[17]

Advocate-General Tesauro considered the economic character of the social security organs to be the key issue. He described the social security regimes as characterised by three fundamental elements: the absence of a profit motive, the pursuit of a social objective and the application of the solidarity principle – all of which are contrary to commercial insurance schemes.[18] The relevant organs exercise in the public interest a social objective, founded on the solidarity principle; hence his conclusion that they were not enterprises within the meaning of Articles 85–86.[19]

In its decision, the Court characterised the French social security regimes as

---

13   They did *not*, however, challenge the principle of compulsory affiliation to the social security system. To this extent, the solidarity principle did not come into question. Ibid, paragraph 3.

14   *Rapport d'audience*, Part I: *Observations écrites déposées devant la Cour*, paragraph 2. The plaintiffs belonged to the Confederation for the Defence of Traders and Artisans (CDCA). This organisation opposes obligatory contributions and rejects the principle of national solidarity underlying the functioning of social security in France. The claim was part of a litigation strategy aimed at paralysing the system.

15   This could be illustrated in various ways, which were later taken up by the Court; ibid, paragraph 3.

16   Ibid, paragraph 4.

17   Ibid, paragraph 5.

18   Conclusions of Advocate-General Giuseppe Tesauro in Joined Cases C-159/91 and C-160/91: *Poucet v AGF et Camulrac*; *Pistre v Cancava*, presented on 29 September 1992, paragraph 9.

19   Ibid, paragraphs 12–13.

having a social objective in accordance with the principle of solidarity.[20] The Court concluded that social security regimes rely on a system of compulsory affiliation, essential to the solidarity principle; their function is exclusively social and does not constitute economic activity necessary to constitute an enterprise within the meaning of Articles 85–86.[1]

In considering the principle of solidarity, the Court emphasised three features of the principle. First, regimes (as in the case of sickness and maternity) are financed by contributions proportional to income. Exemptions from contributions, however, are made for those below certain income levels. The principle of solidarity implies a redistribution of income among those with different income levels.[2]

Secondly, regimes (as in the case of old age pensions) are organised so that the contributions of those working finance the pensions of those in retirement. The principle of solidarity is also evident in that pension rights are not strictly related to contributions.[3]

Thirdly, there is solidarity among different social security regimes. Those with structural financial difficulties are supported by those with structural financial advantages.[4]

In his conclusions presented prior to the Court's judgment, Advocate-General Tesauro noted that the contributions were fixed by the public authorities, not by the social security organs. This was a political choice relating to the financing of the regimes with implications for the redistribution of wealth: there is no direct link between contributions and payments.[5]

The contributions in the case of sickness were not calculated on the basis of the risk but on the basis of the income of the person insured. In some cases of low income, no contributions are required.[6] He also referred to the pensions system providing for payments for pensioners to come directly from the contributions of those still economically active. He characterised this as a kind of 'solidarity over time between different generations of workers'. This solidarity was also evident in rights accruing for periods of economic inactivity (in the case in question, sickness, invalidity, unemployment, military service). In the case of helper spouses, the solidarity would be that recognised as the double burden of helper-spouses. He also noted the lack of a real relation between pensions rights and actual contributions.[7]

The principle of 'solidarity', derived originally from the French system, brought into Community law by the Court of Justice, modified through adaptation to other Member State systems, and diffused through the European Community, may become one of those principles which characterise the European law on social protection.

---

20   Ibid, paragraph 8.
1   Ibid, paragraphs 13, 17–18. The criterion of economic activity was laid down by the Court in the *Hofner* decision, C-41/90: [1991] ECR I-1979, paragraph 21.
2   Ibid, paragraph 10.
3   Ibid, paragraph 11.
4   Ibid, paragraph 12.
5   Conclusions of Advocate-General Giuseppe Tesauro in Joined Cases C-159/91 and C-160/91: *Poucet v AGF et Camulrac; Pistre v Cancava*, presented on 29 September 1992, paragraph 9.
6   Ibid, paragraph 10.
7   Ibid, paragraph 11.

THE NEXT STEP: THE SPILL-OVER EFFECT OF THE SOCIAL PROTOCOL

The spill-over effect of EU legislation to date, described in this chapter, is likely to be compounded by the operation of the new constitutional basis of collective labour law contained in the Protocol and Agreement on Social Policy of the TEU. The evolution of this new set of norms of collective negotiation of social policy and labour law may aspire, but cannot hope to achieve, *neutrality* of impact on national systems. Awareness of the role of judicial interpretation in the formation of national systems of collective labour law makes it evident that the existence of a new framework at EU level will produce judicial interpretations, by the European Court or national courts, which will be unlikely simply to replicate existing national norms.

The present congruence of different national systems with an emerging EU system of industrial relations and collective bargaining is variable. The compatibility of collective labour law at Member State level will be scrutinised to assess the extent to which it requires modification to accommodate the EU dimension. The formulation of a collective labour law at EU level is too obvious an opportunity to miss in at least beginning this process. At a minimum, certain Member State rules of collective labour law deemed essential to the desired development of EU-level industrial relations would have to be guaranteed in EU law, regardless of the position at Member State level.

This is not to underestimate the difficulty. For example, a precondition of national trade union participation in the EU social dialogue might be that the representativeness of the national trade union be somehow assessed. This might be contested either on the ground that national, not EU criteria, were appropriate, or, more fundamentally, on the basis of the principle of trade union autonomy.

Again, the equilibrium reached between trade unions and workers' representation at *enterprise* level is complex and variable among Member States. Collective labour law at EU level would be bound to impact upon this equilibrium. The question is how, and whether the impact should be oriented in a specific policy direction. For example, systems which were wholly oriented towards decentralisation of collective bargaining, and denied trade unions rights at any level above that of the enterprise, would be incompatible with the evolution of an EU system of industrial relations.

Given the *existing* links with Member State trade unions, it would strengthen the legitimacy of EU-level trade union organisations if collective labour law formulated at EU level reinforced *trade union* representation over enterprise- or workplace-based representation. The strengthening of *sector* or *multi-sector* trade union organisations in Member States is another choice to be made.

Moreover, a *new* factor has recently entered the equation: the creation of European works councils does, for the first time, promote a *transnational* system of worker representation *based on the enterprise.* It poses the possibility, for the first time, of a direct legitimising link being forged between enterprise representatives and EU level organisations. The emerging role of *sector* trade union representation on EWCs would indicate the reinforcement of EU-level sector trade union rights.

The formulation of a collective labour law of the EU will aim to *infuse* the national systems with the spirit of an emerging EU industrial relations system.

The content of the resulting legal framework is normatively driven by a vision of EU industrial relations. The development of a harmonious framework of collective labour law integrating Member State systems into an emerging EU system of industrial relations and social dialogue is a delicate task. It entails respect for the principles of national systems, while undertaking their adaptation to a transnational system, which as yet does not possess the accumulated legitimacy of traditional systems, and achieving this adaptation without disturbing national equilibria.

Differences in collective labour law among the 15 Member States are attributable to different national traditions and histories. Some basic trade union rights common to the Member States are found in ILO Conventions 87 of 1948 and 98 of 1949. Others are reflected in the EU legislation and decisions of the European Court of Justice analysed in this chapter.

There is wide variation among formal legislative provisions at Member State level. This is further highlighted by the *absence* of any formal provision in some Member States, for example, on trade union rights which, in others, are guaranteed constitutional status. The search for a group of *formal* legislative provisions on collective labour law common to the Member States is fruitless.

This *formal* diversity does *not* mean that there is *no* common recognition of collective labour law principles. In *substantive* terms, Member States *do* guarantee certain principles through a variety of formal provisions and effective practices.

For example, beyond the elementary, though fundamental, right of association, difficulties of formulation of common trade union rights emerge. Trade union rights in the Member States have developed a wide variety of rights to trade union recognition, worker representation, collective bargaining, and consultation and information. The search for categories of uniform regulation must begin with the reality of diversity.

To move from this reality to a formulation at EU level means addressing a deeper issue – how to act at EU level and, first, not unduly disturb national *equilibria*; secondly, *support* the emerging system of EU-level industrial relations and social dialogue.

National collective labour laws were *not* developed with *transnational* industrial relations or collective bargaining in mind. The law of the Member States needs to accommodate the European dimension, particularly in light of the Social Protocol and Agreement of the Treaty on European Union.

Questions arise as to how far transnational trade union rights are consistent with purely national-level trade union rights. And if, and how, they can be integrated into a harmonious whole. But, like it or not, a dynamic is at work whereby a framework of collective labour law at EU level is being formulated. EU legal interventions in areas of social policy and labour law lead inevitably to EU rules being established regarding collective labour relations – the 'spillover' effect.

The only question is what will be the relative contribution of the different actors involved – social partners, EU legislative institutions, or the European Court – to the process of formulation of this framework of collective labour law. The following chapters argue that there is a recognisable dynamic at work: 'bargaining in the shadow of the law'. But abstention is not an option.

Nor is this a mere desideratum of European integration. The Member State systems of industrial relations are threatened by decline unless there is an

EU-level framework of collective labour law. National systems are inadequate to protect against the operations of multinational enterprises. The development of an international European economy dictates an EU-level legal framework. Internationalisation of the economy beyond Europe, the global economy, may also challenge national systems. But the absence of machinery to create a global framework of rules does not mean action at EU level should be postponed. Ultimately, to defend Member State systems in the face of internationalisation of the economy, a framework of European collective labour law is needed.

Chapter 34

The Constitutional Basis for Autonomous Development of European Labour Law

INTRODUCTION

Developments in the European Community's labour and social policy since 1989 have been remarkable. Two events are outstanding: the approval by eleven Member States of the Community Charter of Fundamental Social Rights of Workers at the Strasbourg summit of December 1989, and the conclusion of a Protocol to the Treaty on European Union (TEU) and an Agreement on Social Policy at the Maastricht summit of December 1991. The United Kingdom was a party to neither the Community Charter nor the Agreement, but it accepted the Protocol.

Even after the Maastricht Treaty was ratified by national Parliaments, the United Kingdom looks likely, in the medium term, to remain outside the social policy process. But the instruments are now in place for a fundamental change in European labour and social law and policy, both in their substance and in the procedures for their formulation and implementation. The United Kingdom's absence may even assist their future success. The question remains whether the actors involved are capable of putting them into effect.

The substance of the Protocol and Agreement on Social Policy to the TEU is the focus of this and the next two chapters. But the procedure of their formulation and adoption is important. The key documents proposing the changes were drafted by the Member State holding the Presidency of the Council of Ministers – the Netherlands. But their final form, and most of the substance of the provisions which eventually became the Agreement between the eleven Member States were the result of negotiations between the peak organisations of employers (UNICE and CEEP) and of workers (ETUC) at European level.

These negotiations culminated in the Accord dated 31 October 1991 between the ETUC and UNICE/CEEP on a new draft of Articles 118(4), 118A and 118B of the Treaty of Rome.[1] With few modifications, this Accord was adopted by the

---

1 *Agence Europe*, No 5603, 6 November 1991, 12. This chapter focuses on five documentary sources:
   1. The first draft of the Dutch Presidency (*Europe Documents*, No 1733/1734, 3 October 1991).
   2. The accord between the ETUC/UNICE/CEEP concerning a new draft of Articles 118, 118A and 118B of the Rome Treaty (*Agence Europe*, No 5603, 6 November 1991, 12).
   3. The second draft of the Dutch Presidency (*Europe Documents*, No 1746/1747, 20 November 1991).
   4. The Protocol on Social Policy of the 12 Member States and the Agreement between the 11 Member States concluded at Maastricht on 9–10 December 1991 (*Europe Documents*, No 1750/1751, 13 December 1991).
   5. The Protocol on Social Policy of the 12 Member States and the Agreement between the 11 Member States signed at Maastricht on 7 February 1992 (*Europe Documents*, No 1759/1760, February 1992).

523

eleven Member States as the basis for the future labour and social law of the European Union. This remarkable success of the social dialogue at EC level provides a striking example of the fundamental change in European labour law and is the subject of this chapter.

EUROPE OF THE 14 AND EUROPE OF THE 15

The negotiations at Maastricht produced the Treaty on European Union signed by the Member States of the European Community on 7 February 1992, a Protocol on Social Policy and an Agreement, annexed to the Protocol, between eleven Member States, with the exception of the UK, also on Social Policy. The Protocol notes that eleven Member States 'wish to continue along the path laid down in the 1989 Social Charter [and] have adopted among themselves an Agreement to this end'; accordingly, all twelve Member States:

> '1. Agree to authorise those 11 Member States [excluding the UK] to have recourse to the institutions, procedures and mechanisms of the Treaty for the purposes of taking among themselves and applying as far as they are concerned the acts and decisions required for giving effect to the abovementioned Agreement.
> 2. The [UK] shall not take part in the deliberations and the adoption by the Council of Commission proposals made on the basis of this Protocol and the abovementioned Agreement . . .
>   Acts adopted by the Council . . . shall not be applicable to the [UK].'

The Agreement comprises a new formulation of some of the Articles on social policy of the Treaty of Rome. The question of whether the Agreement and its consequences are regarded as part of EC law is crucial, since the legal implications for the eleven Member States[2] are very different if the Agreement constitutes only an intergovernmental treaty, and is governed by public international law, not EC law.

The issue would have been resolved by the (perhaps expected) victory of the Labour Party in the British general election of April 1992, which presumably would have led to the UK becoming party to the Agreement. Its provisions would then have substituted for the provisions in the Treaty. As this did not happen, there continue in existence two parallel sets of provisions: one applicable to the 15 Member States in the Treaty, and one applicable to the 14 Member States in the Agreement. The outcome in practice is that the EC institutions and the 14 Member States are to undertake the operation of the new provisions in the expectation that, sooner or later, the UK will accede to the results. The desirability of this outcome depends on whether the UK's contribution to Community social policy is regarded as positive or negative.

This analysis of the implications of the Maastricht Treaty on European Union for the labour and social law and policy of the EC will provide a detailed interpretation of the texts. But it also addresses the dynamics of the Protocol and Agreement on Social Policy – how they may work in practice. This involves, first, an analysis of the legal nature of these instruments. The consequences of their legal status will powerfully influence the way in which the actors involved – EC institutions, Member States and the social partners – plan their strategies. The

2   Now 14, as the three new Member States adhered to the Agreement.

legal status of the instruments will also have a determining effect on a second issue to be analysed: the scope of potential social policy proposals emanating from the Commission.

It is the interaction between Commission proposals and the social dialogue which constitutes the defining quality of the emergent process of social policy formation in the EC: what I have called 'bargaining in the shadow of the law'.[3] The social dialogue takes place on many levels. Agreements at EC level, and the process of their articulation with Member State labour laws may encompass many different actors. This multiplicity of actors poses a complex problem of choice of levels for social policy formation and implementation. It can be summed up in the word 'subsidiarity'. This chapter seeks to provide some clarification of this principle as it may be applied in the area of EC labour and social law and policy.

THE LEGAL NATURE OF THE PROTOCOL AND THE AGREEMENT ON SOCIAL POLICY

The Protocol on Social Policy forms an integral part of the EC Treaty.[4] The Agreement is stated in the Protocol to be annexed to the Protocol. The presumption is that both Protocol and Agreement are, therefore, part of EC law. Similarly, any measures adopted using the institutions, procedures and mechanisms of the Treaty will have effects in EC law as far as the 14 Member States are concerned. Yet a number of arguments against the Agreement being part of EC law have been elaborated by Eliane Vogel-Polsky.[5]

Diplomatic practice or EC law?

A first argument characterised the Agreement as the result of a diplomatic conference of the Member States within the framework of the European Council. The results of such meetings are not EC law. Against this, it may be argued that, unlike such diplomatic practice, the Agreement on Social Policy is annexed to a Protocol which is part of the Maastricht Treaty, itself the product of the intergovernmental conference and undeniably EC law.

Opting out of EMU and opting out of social policy

A second argument compared Protocol No 14 on Social Policy with Protocol No 11 on Economic and Monetary Policy, which states that the voting rights of the UK in the Council shall be suspended,[6] but allows the UK later to choose to

---

3 B Bercusson 'Maastricht: A Fundamental Change in European Labour Law', (1992) *Industrial Relations Journal* 177.
4 Article 239: 'The Protocols annexed to this Treaty by common accord of the Member States shall form an integral part thereof'.
5 E Vogel-Polsky 'Evaluation of the social provisions of the Treaty on European Union agreed by the European Summit at Maastricht on 9 and 10 December 1991', Committee on Social Affairs , Employment and the Working Environment of the European Parliament, 7 February 1992, DOC EC/CM/202155, PE 155.405.I.
6 Article 7.

join the economic and monetary union.[7] Protocol No 14 on Social Policy authorises 14 Member States to 'have recourse to the institutions, procedures and mechanisms of the Treaty for the purpose of taking *among themselves* and applying *as far as they are concerned* the acts and decisions required for giving effect to the above-mentioned Agreement' (italics added). As it is relevant only to 14 Member States, it is said not to be EC law.

The claim is that the 14 Member States have made an international agreement regarding exclusively themselves. However, such an argument renders the Protocol meaningless. The UK's consent is not necessary for the 14 Member States to assume mutual obligations to which the UK is not a party. The Protocol only makes sense if EC law is engaged and the UK has to give its consent to such obligations. Without such consent, the agreement would fall foul of the European Court's Opinion 1/76 of 26 April 1977, which condemned international agreements engaging only some Member States in a field of EC competence as 'a change in the internal constitution of the Community ... not compatible with the requirements of unity and solidarity'.[8]

If it was merely an international agreement between the 14 Member States, under it the Commission might propose measures to be adopted by the 14 which would modify, by international agreement, existing EC law – a result contrary to the Commission's duty as 'guardian of the Treaties' for which the UK could even complain to the Court as a violation of the other Member States' Treaty obligations.

As EC law, the acts adopted by the EC institutions under the Protocol could come before the European Court under Article 177 without the problem canvassed in Opinion 1/91 of 14 December 1991 as to the incompatibility between interpretation of an international treaty and the EC Treaty in the context of the Community legal order.[9] The contrast may be made with Protocol 35 of the EEA Treaty, from which it appears that 'without recognising the principles of direct effect and primacy ... the Contracting Parties undertake merely to introduce into their respective legal orders a statutory provision to the effect that EEA rules are to prevail over contrary legislative provisions'.[10]

Further, it may be argued that both Protocols 11 and 14 have the consequence that the UK simply is excluded from one aspect of the European Union. Both Protocols have the same legal status. Both envisage the use by 14 Member States of institutions, procedures and mechanisms of the Community. In both cases, it would seem that the intention of the Member States was that the UK could rejoin economic and monetary union or the social policy of the other Member States. The problem is that in the case of the former, this was explicit: not so in the case of the latter.

To opt in or not to opt in; and if so, how?

Protocol 11 dealing with economic and monetary union provides:[11]

'Unless the United Kingdom notifies the Council that it intends to move to the third stage (of economic and monetary union) it shall be under no obligation to do so.'

---

7   Article 10.
8   *Re Draft Agreement establishing a European laying-up fund for inland waterway vessels* [1977] ECR 741, paragraph 12 at p 758.
9   *Re Draft Treaty on a European Economic Area* [1992] 1 CMLR 245.
10 Ibid, paragraph 27, p 269.
11 Article 1, paragraph 2.

However, Article 10 allows that the UK:

'may change its notification at any time after the beginning of (the third) stage.'

In other words, the procedure under Protocol 11 is that the UK is excluded unless it 'opts in' in one of two ways: either notification of UK intention to move to the third stage, for otherwise there is no obligation;[12] or change of its original notification, entailing obligations.[13]

Protocol 14 on Social Policy simply provides:[14]

'The United Kingdom of Great Britain and Northern Ireland shall not take part in the deliberations and the adoption by the Council of Commission proposals made on the basis of this Protocol and the abovementioned Agreement.'

Protocol 14 contains no explicit mechanism for 'opting in' by way of notification. Paragraph 2 of Article 2 merely goes on to outline the voting procedures in the absence of the UK, and paragraph 3 provides that the:

'Acts adopted by the Council and any financial consequences other than administrative costs entailed for the institutions shall not be applicable to the United Kingdom of Great Britain and Northern Ireland.'

At bottom, the issue is whether the Maastricht Treaty provisions on economic and monetary union were intended to allow eventual opting in by the UK, but those on social policy were intended *permanently* to exclude the UK. It is submitted that the latter cannot be seriously contended. Hence, the Protocol should be read not as an exclusion of the UK forever from the social policy of the EC. Rather, as with economic and monetary union, it is envisaged that the UK can (and will) eventually 'opt in'.[15]

Intergovernmental agreement or EC law?

A third argument advanced by Vogel-Polsky qualifies the Agreement as an intergovernmental agreement between 14 Member States and as such having effect in public international law, not EC law. Against this it may be argued that the 14 Member States appear to have intended the Protocol and Agreement to create EC law. Hence, the Agreement's effect in public international law would be to create the identical effects to those of EC law, using the institutions, procedures and mechanisms of the Community. This would include also the possibility of the European Court assuming jurisdiction over measures resulting from the Protocol (including the Agreement itself, proposed by the Commission and affirmed by the 14 Member States in the form of an EC measure!), since these, in terms of the Protocol, could be qualified as acts of the institutions of the Community under Article 177.[16] It seems absurd to create this 'shadow' EC law

12 Article 1.
13 Article 10.
14 Article 2, paragraph 1.
15 For a detailed analysis of the possible procedures for the UK opt-in, see Chapter 2.
16 The European Court, in considering its position on the Fund Tribunal provided for in the draft Agreement on the European laying-up fund for inland waterway vessels (Opinion 1/76, op cit), 'hoped that there is only the smallest possibility of conflicts of interpretations giving rise to conflicts of jurisdiction' between it and the Fund Tribunal. Nonetheless the Court felt 'obliged to express certain reservations' (p 761, paragraph 21). These risks, and therefore

to avoid the conclusion that it is EC law.[17]

To classify the Agreement as not part of EC law would be to render the Protocol effectively meaningless (by requiring, for example, subsequent repeated ratification by each of the 14 Member States of all measures adopted under it) and to contradict the express intention of the Member States. The argument that it is not EC law is based on the view that, a priori, there is absent an adequate legal basis for such an Agreement, and this frustrates the political will of the Member States. More accurate is the view that the legal power to create the Agreement as part of Community law exists.[18] In a choice between two interpretations, one of which gives rise to practical absurdity, the other should be preferred. This is particularly so where the authors of the document being interpreted strenuously support this other interpretation.

The issue of legal status is of fundamental importance. Its consequences will be apparent in the enforcement of the Agreement and measures (Directives, Decisions, EC level agreements between management and labour) which result from it.[19] Briefly, four methods are available to ensure that the labour law of the Member States reflects EC law: first, a Commission complaint to the Court under Article 169; secondly, references by national courts to the European Court under Article 177 and the requirement that national courts interpret national legislation in line with Community law;[20] thirdly, the possibility of 'direct effect';[1] and, finally, potential claims for compensation against Member States in the event of losses suffered due to non-implementation of EC law by those Member States.[2]

The question is whether some or all measures (Directives, Decisions, EC level agreements) which result from the Agreement can utilise these methods of enforcement. In the case of EC level agreements, this would possibly put the Court in the position of interpreting and enforcing such agreements.[3] Other consequences emerge as a result of the new competences attributed to the Community by the Agreement.

---

reservations, would be less in the case of the Court interpreting the EC Treaty and the same Court interpreting the Agreement on Social Policy.

On the other hand, in Opinion 1/91 (op cit), the differences between international law and EC law were such that the Court held 'that homogeneity of the rules of law throughout the EEA is not secured by the fact that the provisions of Community law and those of the corresponding provisions of the (EEA) agreement are identical in their content or wording' (p 269, paragraph 22); a fortiori in the case of the EC Treaty social provisions and those of the Maastricht Agreement on Social Policy. There would remain the problem of the effect of the Agreement and measures adopted under it in national courts in dualist systems, unless national legislation on EC law could be interpreted also to include this 'shadow EC law'.

17 I owe this point to an intervention by Professor Marie-Ange Moreau, in a session to which both Professor Vogel-Polsky and I contributed, at the 'conclave' organised by the Association Française de Droit du Travail at Saverne, 11–12 September 1992.

18 An analogy would be with the adoption of the Social Action Programme of 1974. As put by a former Commissioner for Social Affairs: it 'reflected a political judgment of what was thought to be both desirable and possible, rather than a juridical judgment of what were thought to be the social policy implications of the Rome Treaty'. M Shanks *European Social Policy, Today and Tomorrow* (1977), p 13. The results of that Programme are unquestionably part of EC law.

19 See Chapter 10.

20 Case C-106/89: *Marleasing SA v La Comercial Internacional de Alimentacion SA* [1990] ECR I-4135; B Fitzpatrick and C Docksey 'The duty of national courts to interpret provisions of national law in accordance with Community law', (1990) 20 *Industrial Law Journal* 113.

1 Case 43/75: *Defrenne v SABENA* [1976] ECR 455.

2 Cases C-6/90 and C-9/90: *Francovich and Bonifaci v Italian Republic* [1992] ECR I-5357.

3 Cases in which the European Court has had to come to terms with collective agreements within Member States include: Case 91/81: *EC Commission v Italian Republic* [1982] ECR

THE SCOPE OF COMMUNITY COMPETENCES AND MAJORITY VOTING PROCEDURES

Article 1 of the Agreement, the redrafted Article 117 of the Treaty of Rome, has greatly expanded the legal competences of the Community in the field of social policy:

'The Community and the Member States shall have as their objectives the promotion of employment, improved living and working conditions, proper social protection, dialogue between management and labour, the development of human resources with a view to lasting high employment and the combating of exclusion.'

Within this new sphere of Community social policy, the Council is authorised[4] to proceed by qualified majority voting to 'adopt, by means of directives, minimum requirements for gradual implementation' in the following five 'fields':[5]

'– improvement in particular of the working environment to protect workers' health and safety;
– working conditions;
– the information and consultation of workers;
– equality between men and women with regard to labour market opportunities and treatment at work;
– the integration of persons excluded from the labour market . . .'

This is an expansion of the capacity of the Community to act in the social policy area even where one or more Member States are opposed. Unanimity is required among the 14 (pending UK adhesion) in the following five 'areas':[6]

'– social security and social protection of workers;
– protection of workers where their employment is terminated;
– representation and collective defence of the interests of workers and employers, including co-determination, subject to paragraph 6;
– conditions of employment for third-country nationals legally residing in Community territory;
– financial contributions for promotion of employment and job-creation, without prejudice to the provisions relating to the Social Fund.'

Paragraph 6 of Article 2, however, provides that:

'The provisions of this Article shall not apply to pay, the right of association, the right to strike or the right to impose lock-outs.'[7]

These provisions expand both the legal scope and the ability of the EC to develop social policy and labour law at European level. In the past, there have

2133; Case 143/83: *EC Commission v Denmark* [1985] ECR 427; Case 235/84: *EC Commission v Italian Republic* [1986] ECR 2291 (possibility of implementation of Directives through collective agreements); Case 165/82: *EC Commission v UK* [1983] ECR 3431 (de facto effects of non-legally enforceable agreements); Case 312/86: *EC Commission v French Republic* [1988] ECR 6315 (discriminatory effect of agreements and tempo of reform).

4 By Article 2, paragraphs 1 and 2 of the Agreement, the redrafted Article 118 of the Treaty of Rome.
5 The Protocol, Article 2, deemed the new qualified majority in the Council, given the absence of the UK, to be 44 votes among the 11 Member States.
6 Article 2, paragraph 3.
7 This exclusion contradicts the expressed intention in the Protocol that 14 Member States 'wish to continue along the path laid down in the 1989 Social Charter; that they have adopted among themselves an Agreement to this end . . .' The Social Charter contained explicit guarantees

been many disputes over whether there was any legal basis for social policy measures, and, if so, whether the legal basis allowed for qualified majority voting or required unanimity in the Council. The new and more complex formulations of competence, and the apparent overlap between those fields allowing for qualified majority voting,[8] those areas subjected to unanimity,[9] and those excluded altogether[10] will doubtless give rise to much debate when measures are proposed by the Commission.[11]

What is the relation of the new competences in the Agreement to the old competences in Articles 117–118B of the Treaty?[12] The Protocol and Agreement aim, in the words of the latter's preamble: 'to implement the 1989 Social Charter on the basis of the *acquis communautaire*'. The 1989 Social Charter's objectives were ambiguous as regards consolidation or development of social rights. In particular, in the final draft of the Charter's Preamble a new clause was added: 'whereas the implementation of the Charter must not entail an extension of the Community's powers as defined by the Treaties'.[13] The Protocol and Agreement comprise a major extension of the Community's powers in the social field as regards the 14 Member States party to the Agreement. This implies the proposal of measures going *beyond* (hence 'without prejudice to') the present *acquis communautaire*, based on the powers in the EC Treaty to which that *acquis* was restricted, and henceforth engaging the new legal powers.[14]

Manfred Weiss has stated that the Agreement 'imposes an obligation upon the eleven signatory Member States to consider themselves bound by the Protocol, instead of Articles 117–121 of the Treaty'.[15] This can mean two things. First, that if the 14 Member States wish to adopt a social policy, they are now *obliged* to pursue the new Agreement *whenever* the old framework fails (either on grounds of alleged lack of competence or voting requirements (UK veto)). Secondly, if they wish to adopt a social policy, they are *precluded* from approving proposals narrowly conceived within the old framework, but *must* pursue

related to pay (Article 5), the right of association (Article 11) and the right to strike (Article 13). The implication must be that the exclusions in this paragraph are to be interpreted narrowly. In contrast, there is doubt as to whether paragraph 6 operates similarly to limit the scope of 'agreements concluded at Community level' under Article 4 of the Agreement.

8   Article 2(1).
9   Article 2(3).
10 Article 2(6).
11 A notorious example was the Commission's Social Charter Action Programme proposal on 'atypical workers', ultimately divided into three separate proposals, each with its own legal basis and voting procedure.
12 The recital to the Protocol stipulates: 'that this Protocol and the said Agreement are without prejudice to the provisions of this Treaty, particularly those relating to social policy which constitute an integral part of the *acquis communautaire*'. 'This Treaty' refers to the Treaty on European Union, which makes only one change to the relevant parts of the EC Treaty (Articles 117–121): Article G(33) replacing the first subparagraph of Article 118a(2).
13 B Bercusson 'The European Community's Charter of Fundamental Social Rights of Workers', (1990) 53 *Modern Law Review* 624 at 625.
14 As put in the Maastricht Treaty's Article B on the objectives of the Union: 'to maintain in full the *acquis communautaire* and build on it . . .' Article C again refers to 'respecting and building upon the *acquis communautaire*'. Fitzpatrick notes the potential problem of reconciling existing Directives with amendments to them approved under the Agreement. 'Community Social Law after Maastricht', (1992) 21 *Industrial Law Journal* 199, at p 204. The 1992 amendment of the Collective Dismissals Directive, the first such change to an EC labour law, is not a violation of the *acquis communautaire*.
15 M Weiss 'The significance of Maastricht for EC social policy', (1992) *International Journal of Comparative Labour Law and Industrial Relations* (Spring) 3 at p 6.

the new competences. If these are consistent with the old framework, the UK may participate. If not, the Agreement of the 14 applies.

Like the Community Charter of 1989, the Agreement should be regarded not only as a legal, but also as a political document.[16] It not only defines the new scope of Community social policy, *more important*, it directs the Commission to produce proposals to implement the new competences. It is not only a legal question of what the competences of the 14 v 15 Member States are in social policy. In practice, the crucial issue is the *Commission's* role. Social policy proposals can be conceived in either the old or the new framework of competences. The question is whether the Commission is *able* to continue in the old pattern, or is *obliged* to operate a new social policy within the framework of the new competences.

At least three options exist. First, the Commission could use the Agreement to promote previous proposals which failed to achieve requisite majority/unanimity. Secondly, it could redraft old proposals to fit in with the new parameters between majority/unanimity. For example, an old proposal vetoed by the UK, or confronted by a majority vote including the UK, could be redrafted to achieve requisite unanimity or a sufficient majority of the 14 Member States under the Agreement. Thirdly, it could draft new proposals in light of the new competences of the Agreement.

The key is the *scope* of proposals (their approval is secondary as the UK may or may not vote depending on the scope). Are they to be *formulated* in light of the Agreement or the old framework of competences? Is it satisfactory for the Agreement to constitute only the fall-back competences when the old framework fails because of the UK veto? A more positive vision would be for the Commission to work from the new conception of social policy. In this *political* rather than legal sense, it is not so much that the Agreement obliges the Member States, as that it obliges the *Commission* to operate within a new framework.

The position of the Commission probably depends, in part, on the status of the Agreement in EC law. If it is *not* EC law, the answer is simplest: the new competences are outside the Treaty. If it *is* EC law, the alternatives seem to be:

1. They *replace* the Treaty provisions – but, presumably, only so far as the 14 Member States are concerned.
2. They are *additional* to the Treaty – but, again, only so far as the 14 Member States are concerned. This has the disadvantage that it involves overlaps between new and old competences; also, perhaps, contradictions, in addition to those already inherent within Article 2, between paragraphs 2 (majority vote) and 3 (unanimity).
3. They *both* replace *and* are additional. For the 14, the Agreement *replaces* the old Treaty provisions as the basis for social policy. But where there are *overlaps*, they are (for the 14) *additional* to the old Treaty provisions. As far as the overlapping area is concerned, proposals may be made involving the UK. These proposals fit under *both* rubrics: the old Treaty provisions and the Agreement. Voting can take place with a number of consequences:
    (i)   unanimity – all 15 are bound;
    (ii) qualified majority – if available under the old provisions, it will bind all 15;
    (iii) if qualified majority is not available under the 15, then it may be upheld on unanimity or qualified majority voting among the 14.

16 B Bercusson, op cit.

This has the procedural consequence that *two* legal bases (the old Treaty provisions and the Agreement) will be invoked when voting on the same proposal. The ultimate legal basis will depend on the result of the voting.

A determining role may be played by the social partners. Under the Maastricht Agreement, they have the right to be consulted and, if they wish, to request that agreement be sought on the issue by way of social dialogue.[17] These rights only operate in the case of social policy proposals under the new competences. Since the Commission has the duty to promote social dialogue,[18] there is an implication that the new competences – allowing for social dialogue – should be used. Indeed, the question arises whether the social partners could challenge proposals under the old legal basis (the EC Treaty provisions) as excluding them unnecessarily.[19]

The substantive content of the policy, under whatever framework of competences, is only one issue. But at which level is the requisite action to be taken to achieve the policy? This is to be determined in accordance with the principle of subsidiarity.

SUBSIDIARITY

The subsidiarity principle was the subject of explicit elaboration in the Union Treaty agreed at Maastricht, though this does not mean it has necessarily been clarified:[20]

'The Community shall act within the limits of the powers conferred upon it by this Treaty and of the objectives assigned to it therein.

In the areas which do not fall within its exclusive jurisdiction, the Community shall take action, in accordance with the principle of subsidiarity, only if and insofar as the objectives of the proposed action cannot be sufficiently achieved by the Member States and can therefore, by reason of the scale or effects of the proposed action, be better achieved by the Community.

Any action by the Community shall not go beyond what is necessary to achieve the objectives of this Treaty.'

The choice among multiple levels of action

The issue has been made rather more complex by the injection of EC level action involving not EC institutions, but the social partners at EC level. The problem is that EC level action can now be undertaken *by the social partners* as well as by the Commission. Similarly action at national level can include that by the social partners as well as by Member States.

The question is: how does the principle of subsidiarity apply in the resulting complex of interactions? Formerly it could be said to apply to EC action v Member State action. But is the same standard applicable as between:

–   EC level action by the *social partners* v *Member State* action; or
–   EC action v action by the *social partners* within the Member State; or

---

17   Articles 3(4) and 4.
18   Article 3(1).
19   Could the UK similarly complain if the new competences were used, thereby excluding it? It is submitted that the answer is no: the UK always has the possibility of 'opting-in'.
20   Article 3B.

–   EC level action by the social partners v action by the social partners within
      the Member States?

Are any or all of these subject to the same principle of subsidiarity? Or are they
subject to a principle of subsidiarity formulated differently?

Finally, there is the question of whether EC action or action by the social
partners at EC level is preferable; similarly, at Member State level, whether
action by the State or the social partners is preferable. Neither of these choices
seems directly governed by the subsidiarity principle, but the choice between
them is subject to the same logic as the subsidiarity principle.

The result of the application of the subsidiarity principle to the classic choice
between Member State or EC action (but now also between EC social partner
action v Member State action/social partner action at Member State level) will
also be determined by the choices made as between Commission/EC-social
partner level action and Member State/social partner-within-Member-State
action.

Application of the subsidiarity principle in Community social policy

The principle of subsidiarity only applies when the EC and Member States *both*
have competence. The question is *which* of the two (EC or Member States) is to
exercise the competence. As defined in Article 3B of the Treaty on European
Union, there are *two* conditions for EC action: first, *insufficient* achievement by
Member States of the objectives of the proposed action; *and*, secondly, *better*
achievement by the Community by reason of the scale or effects of the proposed action.

The issue is to be posed in *relative* terms: which level is better (as in '. . . cannot be sufficiently achieved by the Member States and can . . . be better
achieved by the Community'). The EC could argue Member State insuffi-
ciency, and the Member States could argue that the EC is no better (or worse).
This raises the difficult question of which *criteria and standards* to adopt to assess
sufficiency. The allocation of competences depends on a reliable assessment of
relative sufficiency. The terms of the assessment are critical; in particular, what
is the role of economic or other criteria and standards?

The debate over subsidiarity may be influenced by the European Economic
Community logic of economic rather than political (let alone social) union.
Exclusivity/competences is the language of legal/political union. Efficiency
(sufficiently achieved) and 'scale or effects' are the language of economic union.
The ambiguity is apparent in the (slippery) terms in which the debate has been
conducted: (political-social) objections to centralisation are dressed up in (economic) terminology of efficiency. But economic theory includes political and
social considerations to varying extents. The neoclassical school of economics,
which underlies the old conception of the European Economic Community, is
unlikely to be sustainable in the context of the Treaty on European Union.

On the other hand, efficiency may have to be weighed against fundamental
constitutional principles of Member States which include other values. For
example, in the specific context of the application of the principle of subsidiarity to the question of whether the social partners at the EC or at Member
State level should take action, or whether it should be the EC or the Member

States themselves, the principle of the *autonomy of the social partners*, at EC level as well as at Member State level, should be brought into the equation. 'Efficiency' might dictate EC or Member State action, but long-standing hegemony of the social partners, at one or other levels of bargaining, over certain policy areas may dictate leaving it to management and labour to settle the substance of EC labour policy in that area.[1]

Subsidiarity being a relative test as between levels, if, for example, the social partners are unable to adopt measures as a result of the intransigence of one side, this will be a sign that the competence may be exercised at a different level. Similarly if the EC is unable to adopt measures due to majority or unanimous voting requirements, competence should be exercised by the social partners at the 'better' level.

There is a further point. The subsidiarity principle has been misconceived as implying an allocation of powers to *either* a higher or lower level. The test of relative sufficiency indicates that it is not a question of exclusive allocation. Instead, deciding which level is *better* implies that both have something to contribute. Though one may be better *overall*, the other may be more advantageous *in some respects*. The solution might be to use the subsidiarity principle to delineate the respective advantages of *each* level and promote *co-operation* between them, rather than assign exclusive jurisdiction to one or the other. *Within* the relevant field of competence, different levels can coordinate their action. This is a familiar problem in labour law and industrial relations: the relative roles of legislation and collective bargaining in regulating different policy areas.

This ties up with the problems of criteria and standards for efficiency. The allocation of competences, particularly if co-operation/interdependence rather than exclusivity is the objective, depends on a reliable assessment of relative sufficiency, a concept which should be expanded beyond its narrow economic confines. More than ever it becomes clear that a court of law is ill-equipped to deal with the issue.

The problem of subsidiarity becomes, therefore, one of practical application. What are the procedures and institutional structures appropriate for resolving conflicts over which level or levels take action? What may be required is a body which could adjudicate, mediate, arbitrate, report or whatever in an effort to unfreeze any stalemate, and, more importantly, give guidance aimed at coordination of co-operative action at different levels. Labour law and industrial relations dispute resolution machinery in Member States provides a reservoir of experience.

The Agreement invites the exploitation of this experience precisely because it makes explicit the use of collective bargaining/social dialogue – at EC level and within Member States – in the formulation and implementation of Community labour law.

---

1   A practical illustration of this principle may underlie the exclusion of competence on the right of association and the right to strike in Article 2(6) of the Agreement. However, there is an argument (see below) as to the social partners retaining competence on this issue to make 'agreements . . . at EC level (which) shall be implemented' (Article 4(2)). Article 2(3) of the Agreement still grants some competence for the EC institutions on matters of 'representation and collective defence of the interests of workers and employers'.

COLLECTIVE BARGAINING AND IMPLEMENTATION OF COMMUNITY LABOUR LAW – AFTER MAASTRICHT

The first Dutch Presidency draft proposed a new Article 118 which provided:[2]

'A Member State may entrust management and labour with the *implementation* of all or part of the measures which it has laid down in order to implement the directives adopted in accordance with paragraphs 2 and 3.'

It was not clear that the social partners were to be entrusted with implementation of Directives *directly*. Rather, the *Member State* lays down measures to implement Directives, and it is the implementation of *these* measures which may be entrusted to labour and management. This first draft was *not* an accurate rendering of the jurisprudence of the European Court.[3]

In *EC Commission v Kingdom of Denmark*, the Danish government's position was explicitly that *collective agreements* were, as allowed in Article 189 of the Treaty of Rome, its choice of form and method for implementation of the obligations of Council Directive 75/117 on equal pay.[4] It was argued that the Danish *legislation* was but a secondary guarantee of the equality principle in the event that this principle was not guaranteed by collective agreements. An agreement of 1971 made such provision and covered most employment relations in Denmark.[5] The Court held: 'that Member States may leave the implementation of the principle of equal pay in the first instance to representatives of management and labour'.[6] The Court reaffirmed this principle in a second case involving Italy, when implementation of Directive 77/187 was at issue.[7]

In light of this jurisprudence, and the Charter and subsequent Directives (proposed and approved)[8] it appeared that the proposed new Article 118(4) provided for *State measures* to *delegate* to the social partners the task of implementation, *not* of Directives, but of State measures implementing Directives. However, the jurisprudence authorises the social partners directly and independently of State measures to implement Directives through collective agreements. The State measures necessary only regard back-up provision where agreements are inadequate.

That this is so may be evidenced from the provision which replaced the Dutch Presidency's first draft. The sequence of events is important. This first draft was rejected by the Member States as a basis for negotiations at the

---

2   In paragraph 4. *Europe Documents* No 1734, 3 October 1991.
3   An interpretation of the draft as limiting the capacity of the social partners to implement directly EC Directives might have been challenged as an infringement of the *acquis communautaire*.
4   Case 143/83: [1985] ECR 427.
5   Ibid, p 434, paragraph 7.
6   Ibid, pp 434–5, paragraph 8.
7   Case 235/84: *EC Commission v Italian Republic* [1986] ECR 2291.
8   Community Charter, Article 27; Proposal for a Council Directive on certain employment relationships with regard to distortions of competition, Article 6; COM (90) 228 final – SYN 289, Brussels, 13 August 1990; Proposal for a Council Directive concerning certain aspects of the organisation of working time, Article 14; COM (90) 317 final – SYN 295, 20 September 1990; Council Directive 91/533 of 14 October 1991 on an employer's obligation to inform employees of the conditions applicable to the contract or employment relationship, Article 9(1), OJ 1991 L288/32. For further details on the evolution of this doctrine, see Chapter 9.

Maastricht Summit. In the interval between this and the second draft, presented by the Dutch Presidency on 8 November,[9] the ETUC, UNICE and CEEP[10] produced their Accord of 31 October 1991, including a redrafted Article 118(4):

> 'On a joint request by the social partners, a Member State may entrust them with the implementation of the directives prepared on the basis of paragraphs 2 and 3.
>
> In this case, it shall ensure that, by the date of entry into force of a directive at the latest, the social partners have set up the necessary provisions by agreement, the Member State concerned being required to take any necessary provisions enabling it to guarantee the results imposed by the directive.'

The substance of this provision became the text of the second Draft of the Dutch Presidency, which was rejected by the UK. It was adopted by the 11 Member States in their Agreement comprising Annex IV of the Treaty concluded at Maastricht and is now Article 2(4)[11] of the Agreement attached to the Protocol on Social Policy of the Treaty on European Union. It reads:

> 'A Member State may entrust management and labour, at their joint request, with the implementation of directives adopted pursuant to paragraphs 2 and 3.
>
> In that case, it shall ensure that, no later than the date on which a directive must be transposed in accordance with Article 189, management and labour have introduced the necessary measures by agreements, the Member State concerned being required to take any necessary measure enabling it at any time to be in a position to guarantee the results imposed by that directive.'

As always, it is optional for the Member State to entrust implementation to the social partners. It is not clear whether the Member State may prevent or obstruct the social partners from implementing Directives. There is no mention of *State* measures; *direct* implementation of directives by management and labour is the issue.

It should be noted that the ETUC/UNICE/CEEP Accord specified that 'the social partners' were to be entrusted with the implementation of Directives. It is not clear whether 'management and labour' signifies a wider choice of representatives of employers and workers, and also of levels of representation, than would be the case if 'social partners' had been the term used. This becomes particularly important since Member States cannot impose the burden upon social partners; it must be at their joint request. This can create problems where there are multiple parties: divided union movements or multiple employers' associations.

Delegation of implementation to management and labour presumes a level of collective bargaining (national, regional, enterprise) appropriate for this type of implementation. The result could range from peak organisations requesting block exemption for whole industries (or even multi-industry agreements), to enterprises and works councils requesting authority to implement the Directive in their workplaces. The Member State is not obliged to allow this. But one prospect is of legislation flexibly allowing the social partners[12] to opt out of State regulation by substituting a collective agreement, providing this guarantees the

---

9   *Europe Documents* No 1746/1747, 20 November 1991.
10 The European Trade Union Confederation, the Union des Industries de la Communauté Européen and the Centre Européen des Entreprises Publiques.
11 Proposed revision of Article 118(4).
12 But query: (i) what are appropriate levels; (ii) who are the eligible social partners?

results imposed by the Directive.[13] In its Medium Term Social Action Programme 1995–1997, the Commission announced that:[14]

> '11.1.9 ... in the light of the European Court of Justice case law and the Agreement on Social Policy, and taking into account diverse national practices, the Commission will present a Communication addressing the entire area of implementation of Community directives by collective agreements. The Communication will also consider and reflect on ways and procedures to involve the social partners in the process of control and transposition and enforcement of Community law (1996).
>
> 11.1.10 A clause concerning implementation by collective agreements will be inserted in all future directives, where the issues concerned may fall under the bargaining power of the social partners.'

This is the end result of the long process whereby first individual Member States, then the European Court, then the eleven Member States in Article 27 of the Community Charter, then the Commission in proposed, and the Council in approved Directives and now the Maastricht Agreement – all have formally recognised the role of collective bargaining in the implementation of EC labour law.

---

13 Such a provision was proposed in the Commission's initial proposal for a Council Directive concerning certain aspects of the organisation of working time, Article 12(3); COM (90) 317 final – SYN 295, Brussels, 20 September 1990; text in *European Industrial Relations Review* No 202, November 1990, p 27. It was retained in the second draft of the proposal (text in *European Industrial Relations Review* No 210, July 1991, p 27). The final text adopted by the Council is more complex, reflecting differences among the Member States; see *Agence Europe*, No 5991, 2 June 1993, pp 7–8.
14 Communication from the Commission, COM (95) 134 final, Brussels, 12 April 1995, paragraphs 11.1.9–11.1.10.

Chapter 35

The Role of European Social Dialogue in Formulating European Labour Law

INTRODUCTION

At EC level, collective bargaining derives two major impulses – linked to each other – from the Maastricht Agreement. The first is Article 3's alteration of Article 118B regarding the Commission's role in promoting the social dialogue at EC level. The second concerns the role of EC level collective bargaining in the formulation of Community labour law.

PROMOTION OF SOCIAL DIALOGUE

The first reinforcement of social partner action at EC level emerged, not from the Dutch Presidency's first draft, but from the ETUC/UNICE/CEEP Accord. This proposed to replace the existing Article 118B:

> 'The Commission shall endeavour to develop the dialogue between management and labour at European level . . .'

Instead, the new Article 118B proposed by the social partners at EC level was approved at the Maastricht Summit and is now Article 3(1) of the Agreement appended to the Union Treaty:

> 'The Commission shall have the task of promoting the consultation of management and labour at Community level and shall take any relevant measure to facilitate their dialogue by ensuring balanced support for the parties . . .'

This seems to reinforce the obligation of the Commission regarding the social dialogue at EC level beyond the former 'endeavour to develop'. But it also implicitly reflects on the subsidiarity principle. The most 'relevant measure' which the Commission can take 'to facilitate their dialogue' is to devolve to them the task of formulating and implementing agreements on EC labour law.

PARTICIPATION OF THE SOCIAL PARTNERS IN THE FORMULATION OF EC LABOUR LAW: 'BARGAINING IN THE SHADOW OF THE LAW'

Consultation

The second impulse to action by the social partners at EC level surfaced in the Dutch Presidency's first draft. This provided, first, formal recognition for what was already the practice at EC level. The proposed new Article 118A provided:

> 'Before submitting proposals in the social policy field, the Commission shall consult management and labour on the advisability of Community action.'

This also reflects on the subsidiarity principle, requiring consideration not only of the advisability of the *substance* of Community action, but also of the appropriate *level* of implementation.

More significant was the proposal which was in not the Dutch Presidency's first draft, but the second draft, which adopted an amended text of Article 118A agreed by the ETUC/UNICE/CEEP. The substance (and virtually the identical wording) of the text formulated by the social partners became Article 3, paragraphs 2–4 of the Agreement. The final text of the Agreement is as follows:

'2. To this end, before submitting proposals in the social policy field, the Commission shall consult management and labour on the possible direction of Community action.

3. If, after such consultation, the Commission considers Community action advisable, it shall consult management and labour on the content of the envisaged proposal. Management and labour shall forward to the Commission an opinion or, where appropriate, a recommendation.

4. On the occasion of such consultation, management and labour may inform the Commission of their wish to initiate the process provided for in Article 4. The duration of the procedure shall not exceed nine months, unless the management and labour concerned and the Commission decide jointly to extend it.'

One change appears in the Agreement from the text produced by the social partners. This was introduced by the Dutch Presidency and requires Commission consent to a prolongation beyond nine months of the independent procedure of the social partners.

However, it should be noted that a second change emerged in the Dutch Presidency's second draft, which does *not* appear in the text of the Union Treaty signed in Maastricht on 7 February 1992. The Treaty, following the wording in the social partners' Accord, provides that the second consultation of the Commission with the social partners is to be 'on the *content* of the envisaged proposal'. However, the Dutch Presidency's second draft *and*, astonishingly, the Agreement made at Maastricht in December 1991, both provided for this second consultation to be simply 'on the envisaged proposal'.

Comparison of the texts casts some light on their meaning. Consultations limited to 'the content of the envisaged proposal' might be interpreted as excluding, for example, issues to do with the appropriate legal basis, or even implementation procedures as opposed to 'substantive' content. Consultations 'on the envisaged proposal' might have been limited to whether a proposal should be made, and not its substantive content. The original wording of the social partners requiring consultation 'on the content of the envisaged proposal' was restored in the final Treaty. However, it is unlikely that this change will affect the practice of the Commission's consultation procedure.

The process of social dialogue at EC level: 'Bargaining in the shadow of the law'

The process referred to in Article 3(4) of the Agreement[1] is the subject of Article 4(1):[2]

'Should management and labour so desire, the dialogue between them at Community level may lead to contractual relations, including agreements.'

---

1   The redrafted Article 118A(4).
2   The redrafted Article 118B.

Since 1985, the Commission has stressed that negotiations between employers' and workers' organisations at EC level were a cornerstone of the European social area which goes hand in hand with the creation of the Single European Market.[3] These negotiations have come to be known as the 'European social dialogue.'

Collective bargaining/social dialogue *within* Member States is regarded as reflecting a balance of power between labour and capital, exercised traditionally through the weapons of industrial conflict. The Maastricht Agreement does not address even the possibility of industrial conflict at European level. Indeed, Article 2(6) seems explicitly to withhold regulatory competences which would be most relevant.

The logic to this auto-exclusion is, perhaps, that the current state of EC level social dialogue is qualitatively different in that the normal means of pressure – strikes – are not (yet) operational at Community level. The present prospect of the EC social dialogue implies rather a tripartite process – involving the social partners and the Commission/Community as a dynamic factor. This is the scenario I have elsewhere described as 'bargaining in the shadow of the law'.[4]

This prospect arises out of a major ambiguity as to the timing of the initiation of the process of social dialogue during the Commission's consultations. Article 3(4) simply states that the process may be initiated by the social partners 'on the occasion of such consultation'. The question is: *which* consultation of the two envisaged by Article 3 – before, and/or after the Commission produces its envisaged proposal?

Each possibility has implications for the bargaining tactics of the social partners at EC level. In both cases there occurs a familiar situation of 'bargaining in the shadow of the law'. If the procedure may be initiated at the stage of consultations when only 'the possible direction of Community action' is being considered, but *before* the Commission presents its envisaged proposal, the parties have to assess whether the result of their bargaining will be more advantageous than the unknown content of the EC action. There will be pressures on the social partners to negotiate and agree to avoid an imposed standard which preempts their autonomy, and which may be also a less desirable result.

This incentive is lost if the procedure may be initiated only at the stage of consultations *after* the Commission presents its envisaged proposal. The parties may be more or less content with the proposal. They may still judge that the result of further bargaining would be more advantageous than the known content of the proposed EC action, taking into account the possible amendment of the Commission proposal as it goes through the EC institutions. The side *less* satisfied with the envisaged proposal will have an incentive to negotiate and agree to a different standard. The side *more* contented may still see advantages in a different agreed standard. The social partners are often able and willing to negotiate derogations from specified standards which allow for flexibility and offer advantages to both sides.

---

3   It was thus stated by Jacques Delors in presenting the Commission's programme to Parliament in January 1985. Commission of the EC, *Joint Opinions,* European Social Dialogue Documentary Series, 'Introduction', p 19.
4   B Bercusson 'Maastricht: a fundamental change in European labour law', (1992) 23 *Industrial Relations Journal* 177, from which the next four paragraphs are taken.

Indeed, the negotiation of the Accord which led to the insertion of these provisions into the Maastricht Treaty Protocol can be invoked as a concrete example of the process in action. The combination of expansion of competences and extension of qualified majority voting proposed in the Dutch Presidency's first draft was sufficient to induce UNICE/CEEP to agree to a procedure allowing for preemption of what threatened to be Community regulatory standards in a wide range of social policy areas. This despite the potentially obligatory effects of agreements between the social partners proposed by the Dutch Presidency.

A hypothetical case of 'bargaining in the shadow of the law'

The possibility is not excluded that the procedure may be initiated at *either* occasion of consultation – before and/or after the proposal. This would allow for negotiations aimed at preempting a proposal; or, if these do not take place, or fail, negotiations allowing for agreed derogations and flexibility.

The tactics involved may be illustrated by a hypothetical case. The Commission, in accordance with Article 3(2) of the Agreement[5] consults the social partners on the possible direction of Community action regarding a specific aspect of working conditions. The assumption of the case is that such action is desired by the ETUC – which is willing to negotiate an agreement – and less so by UNICE.[6]

UNICE may judge that the Commission proposal is likely to set a standard too high and/or too rigid. In this case it will have an incentive to preempt this result by agreeing to initiate the procedure under Article 3(4).[7] Alternatively, UNICE may judge that the Commission proposal is likely to set a standard tolerably low and/or flexible. There will be less incentive to agree to initiate the procedure at this stage. But UNICE might still prefer to avoid any risk by initiating the procedure and trying to avoid the Commission proposing a standard.

If UNICE waits until the Commission produces its envisaged proposal, two scenarios emerge. First, the proposal is too high and/or too rigid. In this case UNICE will have an incentive to avoid this result by agreeing to initiate the procedure under Article 3(4). However, it does so from a weakened position, since the Commission proposal becomes a probable minimum standard. In the second scenario, the proposal is tolerably low and/or flexible. There will be less incentive for UNICE to agree to initiate the procedure, but negotiations may still be desirable to increase flexibility or allow for derogations.

Given the current positions of the social partners at Community level, the prospects of and incentives for negotiation and agreement are greater the *higher* the social policy standard espoused by the Commission. It is for the Commission to give a clear signal that the factor breaking any deadlock in bargaining will not be the classic weapons of class struggle as evident in national contexts, but the stimulus of Commission activity in the form of proposals for social legislation. This imposes a heavy burden of responsibility on the Commission. But this has been so ever since it launched the European social dialogue through the

---

5   Article 118A(2).
6   Though here, as elsewhere, the agglomeration of national interests in each of the social partners at Community level is assumed to be capable of generating a single view.
7   Article 118A(4).

Val Duchesse initiative in 1985. The Commission's initiative was crucial to the achievement of the Accord reached by the social partners on 31 October 1991 and incorporated into the Maastricht Agreement. It is by further such initiatives that the European social dialogue will continue to develop.

A 'twin-track' procedure?

The procedure of social dialogue has aspects which are clearly voluntary. First, it cannot be initiated without the consent of both the social partners.[8] Secondly, Article 4(1)[9] makes it clear that neither party is obliged to agree. Thirdly, the Commission seems free to produce proposals even when the social partners initiate the procedure, or during it. Finally, extension of the procedure beyond the nine-month period proposed is subject not only to the joint decision of the social partners, but also to the decision of the Commission.

The obligatory preemption, if any, by the social partners of EC labour law does not take effect at the point of initiation or for the duration of the procedure. It is not clear whether the Commission is precluded from pursuing its original social policy proposal even when informed by management and labour of their wish to initiate the process under Article 4 which may culminate in an agreement. The nine-month duration (which may be extended) does not explicitly preclude a parallel process of social policy formulation by the Commission. It might even be that such a 'twin-track' process would impart a certain dynamism to both Commission and social partners. However, while it is not clear that the Commission is thus preempted in the formulation of social policy, it is as regards the successful outcome of the procedure – 'agreements concluded at Community level' – that the potentially obligatory nature of the procedure emerges.

'AGREEMENTS CONCLUDED AT COMMUNITY LEVEL'

The debate over the potential of European social dialogue which has taken place since the first meetings between the social partners at Val Duchesse in 1985 has posited four types of 'European agreement':

(i) an inter-confederal/inter-sectoral agreement between the social partners organised at European level (ETUC/UNICE/CEEP);
(ii) a European industry/sectoral/branch agreement between social partners organised on an industry/ sectoral/branch basis at European level;
(iii) an agreement with a multinational enterprise having affiliates in more than one Member State;
(iv) an agreement covering more than one Member State.

To define the phrase 'agreements concluded at Community level' in Article 4(2) in restrictive terms of geography or of actors seems counterproductive. For example, if the UK does not adhere to the Agreement, 'Community level'

8 Article 3(4) (Article 118A(4)).
9 The redrafted Article 118B(1).

agreements may well engage the organisations of British employers and trade unions members of the ETUC and UNICE, but not the Member State in which these agreements are to be applied.

If the phrase 'agreements concluded at Community level' were taken to require that agreements must engage all and only Member State organisations of workers and employers, this could eliminate all the four types of agreements mentioned above as possibly emerging from the European social dialogue. The first two because the social partners at European level are not organised so as to include exclusively organisations of workers and employers of EC Member States. Non-Member State organisations are included, and some organisations within Member States are not included, the last two because the enterprises and regions concerned do not include all Member States.

The 'Community' dimension of 'agreements concluded at Community level' is considerably diluted by the potentially paradoxical fact that, in contrast to the limitations imposed by restricted competences and voting procedures on organs of the EC, such agreements are *not* subject to any explicit restriction either as to content or to majority or unanimous voting. Nor do the procedures of reaching agreements entail the direct involvement of EC institutions.[10] The European social dialogue is not formally dependent on EC law, whatever benefits it may derive from use of the Community legal framework.[11]

The conclusion proposed is that the phrase 'agreements concluded at Community level' can be understood in terms of the European social dialogue as carried on since 1985. Therefore, at the least, agreements emerging from the European social dialogue should be deemed to fall within the meaning of the phrase. But, in addition, other agreements with a European Community element (geographical, actors) may also be eligible for inclusion within the framework of Article 4(2).

IMPLEMENTATION OF 'AGREEMENTS CONCLUDED AT COMMUNITY LEVEL'

The *obligatory* implementation of agreements reached through the social dialogue at Community level was declared ('*shall* be implemented') in the first Draft presented by the Dutch Presidency. The ETUC/UNICE/CEEP Accord of 31 October 1991 (paragraph 1) repeated the Dutch first draft proposal regarding the voluntary nature of the dialogue which may lead to agreements. However, unlike the Dutch first draft, the second paragraph of the Accord's proposed Article 118B stated that: 'Agreements concluded at the Community level *may* be implemented . . .'[12]

---

10 At a time when the assertions are frequent as to the democratic deficit of measures adopted by Community institutions, this raises important questions of the legitimacy of such agreements. As to the democratic legitimacy of neo-corporatist outcomes, see P C Schmitter *Democratic Theory and Neo-Corporatist Practice*, EUI Working Paper No 74, 1983.

11 It may be argued that the Accord reached by ETUC/UNICE/CEEP and later incorporated more or less completely into the Maastricht Agreement could have survived any failure of the Member States to ratify the Treaty on European Union. However, the utility of the Accord after such a failure would have been much less of a practical prospect.

12 The French version is not so clearly permissive: 'La mise en oeuvre des accords conclus au niveau communautaire *interviendra . . .*'

The intention was clearly to make implementation of such agreements *voluntary also* as regards Member States or social partners within them, as well as in the case of action by the Community organs – which under the first Dutch draft was already voluntary in the sense that it was subject to the request of the social partners.

The second Dutch draft which followed the ETUC/UNICE/CEEP Accord raised problems because of the differences between the English and French versions. The *English* version *reinstated* the wording rendering implementation *obligatory*. The *French* version, however, *did not change* the wording relating to the obligatory or voluntary nature. The outcome is not helpful in understanding this key point.

The situation has been further confused by a change which occurred in the French version between the agreement in Maastricht in December and the signing of the Treaty in February. The English version remained the same: a high level of obligation: 'Agreements concluded at Community level *shall* be implemented...'[13] The French version changed one key word: instead of the December version: 'La mise en oeuvre des accords conclus au niveau communautaire *interviendra*...', there appears in the Union Treaty Agreement: 'La mise en oeuvre des accords conclus au niveau communautaire *intervient*...'

The key issue remains the degree of obligation regarding implementation of EC level agreements. Once an agreement has been concluded at Community level, there are two methods of implementing the agreement reached:[14]

'Agreements concluded at Community level shall be implemented either in accordance with the procedures and practices specific to management and labour and the Member States or, in matters covered by Article 2, at the joint request of the signatory parties, by a Council decision on a proposal from the Commission.

The Council shall act by qualified majority, except where the agreement in question contains one or more provisions relating to one of the areas referred to in Article 2(3), in which case it shall act unanimously.'

National practices and procedures

The first is that 'Agreements concluded at Community level shall be implemented ... in accordance with the procedures and practices specific to management and labour and the Member States...'[15] It should be noted that the reference to management and labour is supplemented by '*and* the Member States'. It seems from this formulation that some degree of obligation is imposed directly on Member States by the word 'shall'. One question is: if such implementation is obligatory, how does such an obligation operate? At least three possibilities exist.

One possibility is that the Member States are obliged to develop procedures and practices (which may be peculiar to themselves) to implement the agreements reached at EC level. This would seem to require some formal machinery of articulation of national standards with those laid down in the agreements. The experience of implementation of EC legal measures, such as Directives, through collective bargaining provides a basis for assessing whether Member States have complied with this obligation.

13 Article 4(2).
14 Article 4(2), the redrafted Article 118B.
15 Article 4(2).

A second possibility is that the Member States are not obliged to develop new procedures and practices to implement the agreements. But where there exists machinery of articulation of national standards with those laid down in the agreements, this is to be used.

A third possibility is that, given the nature of the authors of the standards (EC level organisations of employers and workers), the procedures and practices peculiar to each Member State may consist of mechanisms of articulation of Community agreements with collective bargaining in the Member State concerned. Member States are not obliged to create such mechanisms, but national law may not interfere with such mechanisms which already exist, or which may be created by the social partners within the Member State to deal with the new development at EC level.

This possibility of a process of articulation of 'agreements concluded at Community level' with 'procedures and practices specific to management and labour' does not detract from the significance of the following words: '*and* the Member States . . .' This may be a reflection of the jurisprudence of the European Court of Justice concerned with implementation of EC legal measures through collective bargaining, now encapsulated in Article 2(4) of the Agreement.

The extent of Member State obligations is the subject of a Declaration, on Article 4(2), attached to the Maastricht Treaty Agreement:

'The Conference declares that the first of the arrangements for application of the agreements between management and labour Community-wide – referred to in Article 118B(2) – will consist in developing by collective bargaining according to the rules of each Member State, the content of the agreements, and that consequently this arrangement implies no obligation on the member states to apply the agreements directly or to work out rules for their transposition, nor any obligation to amend national legislation in force to facilitate their implementation.'

This Declaration raises a series of difficulties. What is the legal effect of a declaration to an Agreement attached to a Treaty? Such declarations on Community legal instruments are not granted any status before the Court of Justice. If the Agreement's redrafted Articles of the Rome Treaty are subsequently incorporated into the Treaty, what will happen to this Declaration?

How, if at all, does it change and/or reduce the obligation of the Member States regarding implementation? The obligation is *transformed* from implementation to *developing* the content of the agreement by domestic bargaining. This is not necessarily implicit in the implementation process; indeed, it goes beyond it. Finally, if there is no obligation to apply agreements directly, or to transpose them, or even to facilitate implementation, what is left of the obligation to implement?

The fragile legal quality of such Declarations may be emphasised. The denial of obligations to take legislative action in support of implementation does not exclude the obligation to avoid legislation having a negative impact on the implementation of EC-level agreements. This is an unusual twist to the doctrine of 'inderogability' to be found in some Member States. That doctrine precludes individual employment contracts derogating from collective agreements, or, exceptionally, authorises collective agreements to derogate from legislative standards. Here, the doctrine would be invoked to preclude Member State legislation inhibiting articulation of agreements within Member States with EC-level agreements.[16]

16　For a discussion of the doctrine, see Lord Wedderburn 'Inderogability, Collective Agreements and Community Law' (1992) 24 *Industrial Law Journal* 245.

The scope of 'agreements concluded at Community level': different competences for the social dialogue and the EC institutions

Implementation is particularly affected by the possibility that agreements may be reached without the direct involvement of EC institutions, and are not subject to any explicit restriction either as to content or to majority or unanimous voting. One question is whether there is an obligation to implement agreements reached outside EC competence. The answer requires clarification of the meaning of Community competence.

For example, what is the position of agreements reached which are opposed by sufficient Member States to block approval had they been presented to the Council under either majority or unanimous voting requirements? It may be argued that voting requirements do not affect the agreement, as it has been reached in another forum authorised by the 14 Member States. If so, the Member States have authorised agreements outside the formal scope of EC competence in the sense that the agreement is at odds with the procedural requirements requiring unanimity or a specific majority for the exercise of the competence in question.

A double set of EC competences emerges: first, the new competences envisaged by the Agreement applicable to the measures adopted by EC institutions; but also, second, a different set of competences allotted to the social partners, and carrying with it the obligation to implement 'agreements concluded at Community level'. These latter would thus fall within the scope of EC law, with all the enforcement implications canvassed above.

This proposition is argued on the basis of the Agreement's adoption of extraordinary new procedures for the development of EC law, restricting the direct participation of Community institutions, and, in particular, rendering inapplicable the consequent restrictive voting requirements closely tied to specific areas of competence. This new approach to formulating EC labour law may imply that the detailed limits on competences carefully attached to the old institutions and procedures are not necessarily to be carried over to the new institutions and procedures.

For example, Article 2(2) of the Agreement provides that the Council may adopt Directives by qualified majority vote as regards the fields specified in Article 2(1), but must act unanimously as regards the areas specified in Article 2(3). But:[17]

'The provisions of *this Article* shall not apply to pay, the right of association, the right to strike or the right to impose lock-outs' (emphasis added).

The question is whether this exclusion of competences as regards the procedures in Article 2 applies to the radically different procedures laid down in Articles 3 and 4. If not, by implication, under Article 3, the Commission *may* make a proposal in a social policy field specified in Article 2(6) which, under Article 3(4), is then taken up by management and labour, with the possible result of an agreement on the subject at Community level,[18] which 'shall be implemented' in one of the ways specified in Article 4(2). This difference in potential competences may be understood because of the particular delicacy of

17   Article 2(6).
18   Article 4(1).

the matters listed in Article 2(6) touching, as they do, upon the area of the autonomy of the social partners (right of association, the rights to strike or impose lock-outs) and the most central of collective bargaining subjects (pay).

If it is possible to justify and understand this difference between Community competences for procedures involving the Commission, Council and Parliament on the one hand, and competences for procedures involving the Commission, management and labour on the other, then it may be that the competences listed generally in Article 2 are *not* to limit the potential of the social dialogue procedure prescribed in Articles 3 and 4.[19]

To summarise: the starting point is Article 1, which specifies the social policy objectives, and hence competences, of the Community and the Member States in very general terms. Article 2 then lays down certain processes for achieving such objectives by the usual procedure of Council Directives – specifying some of the competences for qualified majority voting, unanimity for others, and excluding still others.

Article 3(2) simply provides for Commission proposals 'in the social policy field' which may be taken up by management and labour in the new procedure of social dialogue. These proposals may go beyond those specified in Article 2, though still within the EC competences specified in Article 1.

Member State obligations to implement agreements at EC level within those competences flow from Article 4(2).[20] Finally, it is interesting to note that

19 It may be argued that the reference in Article 2(1) to 'the Community' implies that the competences referred to in Article 2 exhaust those which the EC can exercise in the field of social policy. The question remains whether the scope of EC competences can be separated from the mechanisms for the implementation of those competences, and whether Article 2(6) refers to the scope of the competences defined in Article 2, or only to the institutional mechanisms outlined in Article 2, paragraphs 2 and 3.

One indication is that Article 2(4) refers explicitly to paragraphs 2 and 3 (mechanisms only), whereas Article 2(6) refers to (the whole of) '(T)he provisions of this Article . . .'

Another is to compare Article 2(5) ('The provisions adopted pursuant to this Article . . .') and Article 2(6) ('The provisions of this Article . . .'). The additional words 'adopted pursuant to' indicate a distinction of mechanisms from competences, and limited to those adopted by the institutional mechanism described in Article 2, paragraphs 2 and 3. It could be argued that Article 2(6), while using slightly different language, implies the same.

A counter-argument is that Article 2(5) could be interpreted as meaning either (a) the provisions adopted *only* by the institutional legislative mechanism (with the Article 2(6) exclusion), or (b) *all* provisions adopted within the new competences, including those resulting from the social dialogue mechanism. It would seem that (b) is the more likely since it could hardly have been intended to allow Member States to adopt or introduce more stringent protective measures *only* when they take the form of Directives adopted under paragraphs 2 and 3 of Article 2.

If so, Article 2(6) which follows could be regarded either as also covering both mechanisms, or, by reason of the different language, differing in (impliedly) distinguishing the institutional from the social dialogue mechanism.

These arguments show how the language of the Article is not precise. Therefore, it is open to argument that Article 2(6) (which follows Article 2(5), but does not use the language 'adopted pursuant to') might nonetheless be read as referring only to the competences of the institutional mechanism. Hence, it does not exclude the competence of labour and management to negotiate agreements on pay etc within the framework of the Protocol/Agreement.

I am grateful to Marcus Geiss, an LL.M student at the University of Manchester, 1994–95, with whom I had fruitful discussions on this issue.

20 Also Article 5 of the Treaty: 'Member States shall take all appropriate measures, whether general or particular, to ensure fulfilment of the obligations arising out of this Treaty or resulting from action taken by the institutions of the Community.'

Article 4(2) provides for the second method of implementing agreements concluded at Community level – by a Council decision on a proposal from the Commission '*in matters covered by Article 2*', with a further paragraph specifying the voting requirements. This reinforces the argument that the range of competences in social policy reserved to the social partners is distinct from that of the EC institutions.

Council decision

A second method is envisaged to implement Community level agreements at Member State level. The second paragraph of a revised Article 118B proposed in the first Draft of the Dutch Presidency provided:

'In matters falling within Article 118, where management and labour so desire, the Commission may submit proposals to transpose the agreements referred to in paragraph 1 into Community legislation. The Council shall act under the conditions laid down in Article 118.'

Unlike paragraph 1, this makes implementation of agreements conditional on a Commission proposal. Moreover, unlike the obligation under the first paragraph to implement agreements, such a proposal of the Commission is made explicitly subject to the conditions of Article 118 as to competences and voting procedures.

The Commission's proposals are 'to transpose the agreements'. This seems expressly to limit the discretion of the Commission to change the content of the agreements reached. However, the nature of the Community legal instrument proposed is left to the Commission's discretion and the Council's action.

The ETUC/UNICE/CEEP Accord altered this provision to implementation of:[1]

'Agreements concluded at Community level ... in matters covered by Article 118 (Article 2), at the joint request of the signatory parties, by a Council decision on a proposal from the Commission concerning the agreements as they have been concluded.'

As with the Dutch Presidency's proposal, this makes implementation of agreements conditional on a Commission proposal. Again, such a proposal of the Commission is subject to conditions as to competences and voting procedures. Finally, while the word 'transpose' is deleted, its substance is retained by the requirement that agreements be implemented 'as they have been concluded.'

The final version adopted as Article 4(2) of the Agreement annexed to the Protocol on Social Policy incorporated the text agreed by the social partners with the exception of the provision agreed by the ETUC/UNICE/CEEP that the Commission proposal and Council decision must adopt the agreements reached by the social partners '... as they have been concluded'. This seems to open the way for the Commission possibly to change the content of the agreements. It is contested whether this is so. After all, the wording still is: 'Agreements ... shall be implemented ... on a proposal from the Commission'. The ambiguity remains a crucial one: how much are the Member States and the Commission entitled to vary the agreements reached at EC level?

Another critical issue is the nature of the instrument to be used to implement

1   Proposed revision of Article 118B(2).

the agreement. The first draft of the Dutch Presidency left it to the discretion of the Commission and Council to determine the appropriate instrument. The ETUC/UNICE/CEEP Accord and the final Agreement refer to a 'proposal from the Commission' and 'a Council decision'. A Council Decision is one of the specific instruments of Community legislation listed in Article 189. It is not clear whether the reference in Article 4(2) is to such an instrument, or rather reflects the Dutch Presidency's preference for the Commission and Council to have a choice of instruments.

In six of the then nine EC languages, the *same* word for 'decision' is used in Article 189 of the Treaty and Article 4(2) of the Agreement. The French and Italian versions, like the English, use the ambiguous term: 'prennent des décisions'; 'prendono decisioni';[2] 'une décision'; 'una decisione'.[3] In the German, Danish and Dutch versions of the Agreement, a different word is used in Article 4(2). Thus, in its Danish version, the Agreement uses the term for 'arriving at a decision' (*ved en afgørelse*), not the technical term to 'take decisions' (*ved besltninger*) used in Article 189.[4]

A possible choice of instruments to be decided upon by the Commission and Council is a much more flexible approach. It also avoids some of the technical problems of utilising a Decision which, under Articles 189–192 'shall be binding in its entirety upon those to whom it is addressed', 'shall state the reasons on which they are based and shall refer to the proposals or opinions which were required to be obtained pursuant to this Treaty' and 'shall be notified to those to whom they are addressed and shall take effect upon notification'. Further, on the terms of Article 2(4)[5] of the Agreement, implementation may be entrusted to management and labour only of *Directives*. Use of other instruments might preclude such articulation.

On the other hand, leaving it to Commission discretion and Council action to determine the instrument of implementation does leave open the possibility of their choosing non-legally binding instruments. This might be inconsistent with the intention of the social partners that their agreements should have legal effect. It would also contribute to an unequal application of agreements across Member States in some of which these agreements are or are not legally enforceable. Whatever the technical problems, a Decision would, given a sufficiently broad definition of a class of addressees, resolve some of the problems of general application and enforcement of agreements.

A further change occurred in the wording in the December agreement. As proposed by the Dutch Presidency, the Council decision was to be taken 'under the conditions laid down in Article 118'. The Maastricht Agreement changed this:[6]

'The Council shall act by qualified majority, except where the agreement in question contains one or more provisions relating to one of the areas referred to in Article 2(3), in which case it shall act unanimously.'

2 Article 189.
3 Agreement, Article 4(2).
4 I am grateful to Mr Tore Hakonsson, a researcher at the European University Institute, for providing this translation. The same point is made with reference to the German version by the European Trade Union Institute's Working Paper prepared for a conference in Luxembourg, 1–2 June 1992, *The European Dimensions of Collective Bargaining after Maastricht*, Working Documents, Brussels 1992, at p 104, paragraph 19.
5 Revised Article 118(4).
6 Article 4(2), paragraph 2.

Article 2(1) listed certain fields in which proposals were, by virtue of Article 2(2), subject to majority voting. The agreements might:

(i)   cover only such areas;
(ii)   cover areas neither within majority nor unanimous voting procedures, ie not within the competence of EC institutions;[7]
(iii) cover only areas within the unanimous voting procedure;
(iv)   cover areas which fell partly within more than one of the above ('one or more provisions . . .' (mixed agreements)).

Cases (i) and (iii) seem clear. Case (ii) is problematic as to whether a Council decision can be taken at all. Case (iv) seems, under the final version of the Maastricht Agreement, to subject 'mixed agreements' to unanimity.[8]

CONCLUSION

The outcome of the Maastricht summit is of outstanding importance for the future of Community labour law. The implementation of EC labour law through collective bargaining within Member States is explicitly recognised. A role for the social partners at EC level in formulating EC labour law is introduced. The procedure is that of 'bargaining in the shadow of the law'. The social dialogue is delicately timed to take place during the Commission's procedure of consulting the social partners about social policy proposals. This raises complex issues of subsidiarity. If the social partners at EC level reach agreements, it appears that Member States are obliged to implement these agreements within their national legal orders; it is not clear how this is to be accomplished.

This chapter, and the previous one, explored various issues which arise from the attempt to understand the problems of interpretation and implementation of the Maastricht Protocol and Agreement on Social Policy. As to the legal nature of the Agreement and its consequences, the conclusion was that the Agreement is probably part of Community law, as are the likely outcomes of the Agreement (Directives, Decisions, Community level agreements). The methods of enforcing EC law should be available for these instruments as well.

Regarding the scope of the new competences and majority voting, the conclusion was that the new competences probably replaced the Treaty of Rome for the 14 Member States, and that the Commission would play a key role depending on whether it accepted that it was now obliged to produce proposals based on these new competences.

Finally, as to the social dialogue and the role of subsidiarity, the conclusion was that social dialogue at EC level was characterised by its tripartite nature, and that the Commission would play a key role. The role of different levels in

---

7   Though within that of the social partners: see discussion above.
8   A similar argument arose concerning the interpretation of Article 100A(2) of the Treaty of Rome (as amended by the Single European Act 1986). This subjects to unanimity proposals relating to the rights and interests of employed persons. It was argued that if the proposal related solely to such rights and interests, it was subject to unanimity. If it related only marginally to such rights and interests, it was eligible for majority voting, even though it also related to them. The problems arose when the proposal related to such rights and interests, but also to other matters. B Bercusson 'The European Community's Charter of Fundamental Rights of Workers', (1990) 53 *Modern Law Review* 624 at pp 633–4.

developing social policy was likely to be influenced by the principle of subsidiarity – understood as a measure of the relative sufficiency of actions by the Community or the social partners. The decision as to relative sufficiency is a highly political one, and requires the development of appropriate procedures and institutional structures.

The future of European labour law lies with the instruments agreed by the Member States at Maastricht: Directives and Community level collective agreements, to be implemented within Member States, and enforced, inter alia, using the techniques developed to enforce EC law.

The European social dialogue thus emerges as a critical feature of EC labour and social law and policy.[9] It is important to appreciate the novel features of this process and avoid the temptation to chart the future path of European social dialogue following national models, either in detail or even in some of their basic principles. These are the product of much reflection and experience which must be respected. But at the same time their application in a transnational context is quite new, and hence requires new thinking.

For example, the fundamental principle of the autonomy of the social partners is granted almost, if not literally, constitutional status in the legal orders of Member States. This is reflected in the Maastricht Agreement's respect for the requirement that the social partners' consent be obtained before their agreements can be transmuted into EC legal measures. But once so transmuted, the need arises for enforcement of these measures, a process which national experience has shown to present dangers to the autonomy of the social partners which challenge even the most experienced labour tribunals. EC institutions will have to respond to these challenges.

Again, the legitimacy of the agreements adopted will raise questions of the legitimacy of the social partners who through them develop fundamental social and economic rights. Decline in membership and proliferation of organisational forms seem to be among the dominant characteristics of Western European labour at the present.[10] The implications for the role of the social partners in the European social dialogue are not hard to perceive. They can be summarised by asking two questions: first, what bodies or organisations claiming representativeness are to benefit from the rights granted by the Maastricht Agreement; and secondly, what legal obligations and liabilities are to be imposed upon them?

Traditionally, labour law has been much concerned with the external relations of the actors involved in industrial relations, specifically with their relations to each other through collective bargaining. Increasingly, however, labour law has been forced to grapple with the issue of internal constitutional structures, particularly of the new and changing actors emerging.[11] These questions become of the

---

9   My Report for the Community of October 1989 on Fundamental Social and Economic Rights in the European Community proposed that collective bargaining/the social dialogue in Member States and transnationally should be the primary instrument for developing and implementing fundamental social and economic rights in the EC. A Cassese et al *Human Rights in the European Community: Methods of Protection*, Nomos Verlag, Baden-Baden 1991, p 185 at pp 287–9.

10   B Bercusson 'Europäisches und nationales Artbeitsrecht – Die gegenwärtige Situation', (1991) 5 *Zeitschrift für ausländisches und internationales Arbeits- und Sozialrecht* 1, at pp 20–9.

11   It is worth recalling the prediction of Simitis that the 'third generation' of labour law would be concerned with this issue. S Simitis 'Juridification of Labor Relations' in G Teubner (ed) *Juridification of Social Spheres*, De Gruyter, Berlin and New York 1987, 113 at pp 142–3.

first importance if the process creating EC social policy and labour law bypasses existing institutions, such as the European Parliament and the Economic and Social Committee, and is based instead upon trade union and employer confederations organised at Community level. All the more so if the legal consequences of their activities extend beyond the existing membership of trade unions and employers' associations.

Chapter 36

The Application of the Protocol and Agreement on Social Policy of the TEU

THE COMMISSION'S COMMUNICATION

Soon after the ratification of the Maastricht Treaty the Commission presented to the Council and the European Parliament a *Communication concerning the application of the Agreement on Social Policy.*[1] The Commission acknowledged that, at least until the Intergovernmental Conference (IGC) scheduled for December 1996, the social policy of the European Union would be governed both by the EC Treaty and by the Agreement annexed to the Protocol, what it called 'two free standing but complementary legal frames of reference'.[2] It observed that: 'This situation has never occurred in the Community before'.[3]

Unlike the EC Treaty, there are no decisions of the European Court of Justice which could provide reasonably definitive interpretations of the meaning of the provisions of the Agreement. Such decisions will be critical, for example, to understanding the scope of the new competences in the social policy field provided by Article 2 of the Agreement, particularly in determining which competences require unanimity in the Council of Ministers and which allow for approval of measures by qualified majority voting.

The provisions of the Agreement concerned with the involvement of the social partners in the formulation of the social policy of the Union are contained in Articles 3 and 4 of the Agreement. These provisions are, in large part, concerned with the procedures to be followed by the Commission and the social partners in creating and implementing the future social policy of the Union.

Since much of these procedures is to be initiated and carried through by the Commission, its interpretation of these provisions is authoritative, though not definitive.[4] It is above all of great importance to the practical operation of the procedures in the period up to the 1996 IGC. Given the procedural nature of the provisions, this practice is likely to be influential if and when the European Court is called upon to provide the definitive legal interpretation of their meaning.

---

1 COM (93) 600 final, Brussels, 14 December 1993.
2 Ibid, paragraph 8.
3 Ibid, Summary, paragraph 3.
4 For example, the Communication, in paragraph 6(b), appears to state that there are excluded from the Agreement 'any matters relating to pay, the right of association, the right to strike and the right to impose lock-outs'. This quotation seems to reflect Article 2(6) of the Agreement, which, however, only excludes these matters from: 'the provisions of this Article (2)' – impliedly allowing for such matters to be dealt with under Articles 3 and 4 of the Agreement. The problems of interpreting Article 2(6) are compounded by Article 6 of the Agreement, which is explicitly concerned with EC competence on pay equality between men and women.

THE PROCEDURE OF SOCIAL POLICY FORMATION AS SEEN BY THE COMMISSION

In the Communication, the Commission gave its point of view on the application of the provisions laying down these procedures, and hence it limited itself to Articles 3 and 4, in which the involvement of the social partners is laid down. The procedure which the Commission proposes to follow falls into *two distinct phases*, indicated from headings in the Communication to be, first, 'Consultation of the Social Partners', and, secondly, 'From Consultation to Negotiation'.

The *first phase* incorporates *two separate stages*, reflecting in the Commission's view, the two separate consultations envisaged by Article 3(2) and (3). The first consultation begins on receipt of a letter sent by the Commission to the social partners. This consultation is required by Article 3(2) before the Commission submits proposals in the social policy field. Its purpose is to ascertain the possible direction of Community action. At this stage, the Commission will be explaining the problem in social policy for which it may seek to find a solution in the form of measures taken at European level. This consultation period, as specified by the Commission, 'should not exceed six weeks', and it 'may be by letter or, if the social partners so desire, by the convening of an ad hoc meeting'.[5]

The first stage completed, the Commission, 'in the light of comments received ... will decide whether to proceed to the second phase'. The Commission thus maintains its discretion to proceed or not, whatever the view of the social partners consulted. If so, the second consultation stage too 'will be initiated with the receipt of the second letter sent by the Commission, setting out the content of the planned proposal together with indication of the possible legal basis'.[6] The Commission proposes that the social partners should deliver a written opinion, where they wish through an ad hoc meeting, and: 'Where appropriate, they should deliver a recommendation setting out their joint positions on the draft text'.[7] Again, the duration of this second phase is restricted by the Commission to a period not exceeding six weeks.

In the course of these stages of consultation, the social partners do not only consider the substantive questions prefigured in the provisions of Article 3(2) and (3): whether the Community should act; if so, the possible direction of Community action; and the content of the Commission's envisaged proposal. They must also address the question posed by Article 3(4): whether they wish to initiate the process provided for in Article 4 – the social dialogue which may lead to contractual relations, including agreements. The possibilities open to the social partners in expressing the opinion or recommendation include:

1. The Commission should not undertake any form of EC action.
2. The Commission should undertake one or other forms of EC action, possibly including various legal measures.
3. The Commission's envisaged proposal is acceptable, and should take the form of various EC actions, possibly including legal measures.
4. The Commission's envisaged proposal is not acceptable, but, if persisted with, should take the form of various Community actions, possibly including legal measures.

---

5 Ibid, paragraph 19.
6 Ibid.
7 Ibid.

5.   The social partners wish to initiate the social dialogue process provided for in Article 4.

The forms and contents of the responses of the social partners in this consultation phase may be very different. The Commission suggests that, even before the social partners undertake to initiate the social dialogue process provided for in Article 4:[8]

'The formal consultation of the social partners provided for in Article 3 of the Agreement may lead to the adoption of opinions, recommendations or agreement-based relations (including agreements) within the social partners' sphere of competence.'

The second phase described by the Commission is initiated when the social partners opt for the social dialogue process under Article 4: 'From Consultation to Negotiation'. Article 3(4) provides that: 'The duration of the procedure shall not exceed nine months, unless the management and labour concerned and the Commission decide jointly to extend it'. As envisaged by Article 4(1), this dialogue 'may lead to contractual relations, including agreements', and these 'shall be implemented' according to procedures laid down in Article 4(2).

THE OPINION OF ECOSOC

The Economic and Social Committee of the EC (ECOSOC) decided to prepare an Opinion on the Commission's Communication and in March 1994 began its deliberations with a view to drafting an Opinion.[9] The ECOSOC Study Group on the Commission's Communication met four times, after which the draft Opinion was submitted to the Social Policy Section in November 1994. The Plenary Session of ECOSOC approved the draft Opinion by a large majority on 24 November 1994.[10] What follows are a number of issues concerning the application of the Protocol and Agreement raised by the Commission's Communication and taken up in the ECOSOC Opinion.

Subsidiarity

The Agreement's confirmation of the fundamental role of the social partners in the implementation of the social dimension at EC level is seen by the

8   Ibid, paragraph 28.
9   Opinion 94/C 397/17, OJ 397/40 of 31.12.94. The procedures of ECOSOC provide for the establishment of a Study Group for any Commission document which is relevant for ECOSOC. One of the members of the Study Group is designated the Rapporteur of the Opinion. Together with a designated Expert to the Rapporteur, a draft Opinion is prepared which reflects the deliberations of the Study Group. If the majority of the Study Group is in favour of the text of the draft Opinion, it will be submitted to the relevant Section of ECOSOC. ECOSOC consists of nine Sections, organised around certain subjects, such as industry, economic and financial matters, agriculture, external relations and social policy. At the end of deliberations in the Section, there is a vote. If all the members of the Section are in favour of the draft Opinion, it will be treated in the Plenary Session of ECOSOC as an item without discussion, on which there is simply a vote. If one or more members of the Section opposes the draft Opinion, a discussion is required in the Plenary Session. Amendments can be submitted by members. At the end of the discussion in the Plenary Session, the final vote on the draft Opinion is taken. If favourable, it becomes the Opinion of ECOSOC.
10   The Rapporteur of the ECOSOC Opinion was J J van Dijk; the Expert to the Rapporteur was B Bercusson. This chapter is based on our joint article which appeared in the *International Journal of Comparative Labour Law and Industrial Relations* in 1995, vol 11, pp 3–30.

Commission's Communication as:[11]

> 'recognition of a *dual form of subsidiarity* in the social field: on the one hand, subsidiarity regarding regulation at national and Community level; on the other, subsidiarity as regards the choice, at Community level, between the legislative approach and the agreement-based approach.'

This is said to be 'in conformity with the fundamental principle of subsidiarity enshrined in Article 3B of the Treaty on European Union'.

The concept of subsidiarity was originally invoked in the context of the difficult issue of allocation and exercise of competences as between Member States and the Community. If this concept is also to be invoked in the context of allocation and exercise of competences as between the EC and the social partners, it has to be carefully scrutinised.

The European Parliament has emphasised the distinction between horizontal and vertical subsidiarity. *Vertical* subsidiarity refers to the division of competences between *different levels*: European and national. *Horizontal* subsidiarity refers to the division of responsibilities between public authorities and, for example, the social partners *at the same level*.

The ECOSOC Opinion was alert to the implied subsumption of both horizontal and vertical subsidiarity under Article 3B. The Opinion emphasised that the criteria specified in Article 3B of the TEU refer only to vertical, not horizontal subsidiarity. In its Opinion, ECOSOC tried to operationalise the two concepts. As regards *vertical* subsidiarity, the Opinion indicated a choice of action at European level in a number of situations.

There is a risk of downward pressure on social standards arising from competition between Member States on the basis of their social or labour costs. Member States seek to attract inward investment from foreign capital sources, as a way of increasing employment for their nationals. In so far as high social and labour costs are a factor in investment decisions, there is pressure on Member States to reduce social and labour standards to increase their attraction. Vertical subsidiarity supports action at European level. European level measures establishing minimum social and labour standards for all Member States can resist such negative competitive pressures.

Different national labour and social standards can lead to enterprises in some Member States deriving competitive advantages from standards set below those required of enterprises in other Member States with higher labour and social standards. Again, European-level measures can eliminate this competitive advantage by providing for harmonised standards of social and labour protection applicable to all employers. It was on this basis that Article 100 justified the approval of Directives on collective dismissals[12] and transfers of undertakings.[13]

Some problems have a distinctive European dimension. The environment is not divided by national political demarcations. Pollution does not halt at the frontiers of Member States. To establish an effective environmental policy will require a European approach, with implications for regulation of the standards of enterprises. An example in the social field is the Directive on European

---

11 Communication of the Commission, op cit, paragraph 6(c).
12 Directive 75/129, OJ L48/29.
13 Directive 77/187, OJ L61/26.

Works Councils.[14]

Finally, European Community legislation may have negative consequences for some groups, which make compensatory measures at EC level necessary, For example, as a result of the completion of the internal market, the amount of work of customs officials was reduced. The MATTHEUS programme was set up to give these customs officers the opportunities of retraining.

There is no indication that Article 3B has any relevance to the application of the principle of *horizontal* subsidiarity – the choice between action by the social partners or public authorities, at EC level (ETUC/UNICE/CEEP or EC institutions) or at Member State level (social partners or the Member State). The criteria for choosing which set of actors at the same level is appropriate are not necessarily those of Article 3B. This has important implications for applying the principle of horizontal subsidiarity evident in Articles 3 and 4 of the Agreement: in deciding whether the EC or the social partners should act.

Careful reading of the Protocol and Agreement on Social Policy and the attached Declarations enabled the ECOSOC to provide examples of *horizontal* subsidiarity.

The Declaration on Article 4(2) of the Agreement provides an indication of the application of horizontal subsidiarity at national (Member State) level. The Member States expressly delegate to collective bargaining the development of the content of EC-level agreements and acknowledge no obligation to undertake legislation.

Article 2(4) of the Agreement provides another example of the application of horizontal subsidiarity at national (Member State) level. The implementation of Directives at Member State level may be entrusted to management and labour, subject to a guarantee by the Member State of the results imposed by the Directive.

Similarly, support for different criteria for the application of the principle of horizontal subsidiarity follows from decisions of the European Court.[15] This jurisprudence emphasised that the competence of the social partners, as opposed to the public authorities, to implement EC measures through collective agreements must satisfy certain conditions. The agreements concerned must cover all employees, and must include all the Directive's requirements.

The possibility of implementing Directives through the actions of the social partners at national level was confirmed by the Commission in an exchange of letters with the Danish social partners. The Commission recognised the principle that Directives relating to labour market matters may be implemented in Denmark through collective agreements without the need for legislation.[16] This

---

14   Council Directive 94/45/EC of 22 September 1994 on the establishment of a European Works Council or a procedure in Community-scale undertakings and Community-scale groups of undertakings for the purposes of informing and consulting employees, OJ L254/64 of 30.9.94.

15   In Case 143/83: *EC Commission v Kingdom of Denmark* [1985] ECR 427, the European Court of Justice held: 'that Member States may leave the implementation of the principle of equal pay in the first instance to representatives of management and labour' (paragraph 8). The Court reaffirmed this principle in a second case involving Italy, Case 235/84: *EC Commission v Italian Republic* [1986] ECR 2291, when implementation of Council Directive 77/187 was at issue.

16   This exchange of letters took place on 11 May 1993. A similar exchange of letters took place between the Commission and the Swedish Government on 29 May 1993.

principle had been introduced earlier by the Danish Commissioner Henning Christophersen.[17]

The ECOSOC referred to the generally recognised constitutional principle of the autonomy of the social partners.[18] This should influence any choice as to the responsibilities of the social partners and of the authorities.

The conclusion to be drawn from these examples might be that the principle of horizontal subsidiarity is confirmed by a wide range of institutions at European level: the Council, the Court of Justice and the Commission. However, the criteria set out in Article 3B do not apply to the concept of horizontal subsidiarity, only vertical subsidiarity. The criteria for the application of horizontal subsidiarity remain to be elaborated.

Representativeness

The Commission must promote the consultation of management and labour[19] and shall consult management and labour.[20] Management and labour may initiate the social dialogue[1] which may lead to contractual relations including agreements between them.[2] Such agreements shall be implemented in accordance with practices specific to management and labour, or at their joint request, by a Council decision.[3]

Who are 'management and labour'? Which organisations can claim the rights to consultation, to initiate social dialogue and reach and implement agreements? The identification of organisations claiming to fall within the meaning of the 'management and labour' given entitlements under the Agreement raises numerous potential difficulties. Organisations making claims are very different. Some organisations present themselves as European when they have affiliates in only some Member States. Different organisations claim to comprise the same categories of labour or management. The claims of some organisations are disputed by other organisations. An example would be employers in small and medium enterprises. Both UNICE and UEAPME claim to represent such employers, but UEAPME claims to be more representative.

The Agreement never uses the word 'representativeness'. But the Commission was clearly drawn to this criterion for identifying the relevant organisations of management and labour. The Commission's Communication refers to the fact that:[4]

> 'Since the adoption of the Maastricht Treaty, the Protocol on Social Policy and the Agreement, a number of the organisations which do not participate in the existing social dialogue have submitted formal requests to the Commission to take part directly in the social dialogue. To take a position on this question in full knowledge of the facts, the Commission carried out a study of European employers' and workers' organisations so as to enable the Commission to understand more clearly the

---

17 H van Zonneveld 'De Europese sociale dialoog', in Jan Jacob van Dijk and Eric Heres (eds) *Werken aan Europa* (1994), Kampen, p 120.
18 As in ILO Convention No 98.
19 Article 3(1) of the Agreement on Social Policy.
20 Article 3(2) and 3(3).
1   Article 3(4).
2   Article 4(1).
3   Article 4(2).
4   Communication, paragraph 23.

different mechanisms by which representative social dialogues are established at national level, and to assist in assessing how this process might best operate at Community level.'

Annex 3 to the Communication is entitled: 'Main Findings of the "Social Partners Study (Representativeness)"'. The concept of representativeness plays a key role in the Communication's discussion of the application of the Agreement. But its role is not that of selecting organisations eligible for consultation under the Agreement.

On the one hand, the Commission's study was undertaken to assist in identifying 'labour and management'. This study, as its title indicates, used 'representativeness' as a key criterion. The conclusions of the study are summarised in Annex 3 in the form of answers to specific questions. As regards systems of recognition of social partners, the conclusion is:

'For collective bargaining, in most countries mutual recognition is the basic mechanism, but additional formal or legal requirements may have to be fulfilled.'

As regards criteria for representativeness, the conclusion is that the systems for recognition:

'make use (sometimes implicitly) of quantitative criteria of various types in about half of the Member States. Generally speaking, qualitative criteria appear to be at least as important. The study confirms the great diversity in approaches used.'

From these conclusions, the Commission drew two main messages:[5]

'(a) the diversity of practice in the different Member States is such that there is no single model which could be replicated at European level, and
(b) the different Member States' systems having all taken many years to grow and develop, it is difficult to see how a European system can be created by administrative decision in the short term.'

Despite these negative messages regarding the feasibility of developing criteria for identifying labour and management at European level, the Commission's Communication without more ado immediately sets out the criteria it proposes for organisations to be consulted. They should:[6]

'– be cross industry or relate to specific sectors or categories and be organised at European level;
– consist of organisations which are themselves an integral and recognised part of Member State social partner structures and with the capacity to negotiate agreements, and which are representative of all Member States, as far as possible;
– have adequate structures to ensure their effective participation in the consultation process.'

Annex 2 to the Communication gives an overview of the organisations which, in the Commission's view, 'currently comply broadly with these criteria'. In addition, the Commission inevitably acknowledged the special status of certain organisations:[7]

'... the Commission recognises that there is a substantial body of experience behind the social dialogue established between the UNICE, CEEP and ETUC.'

---

5 Ibid, paragraph 23.
6 Ibid, paragraph 24.
7 Ibid, paragraph 25.

Other organisations are more problematic. The Commission rejected the option of creating itself 'some form of consultation body or umbrella liaison committee'.[8] At most it expressed the desire 'to promote the development of new linking structures between all the social partners so as to help rationalise and improve the process'.[9]

The Commission's criteria ignore the problems that bedevil the use of 'representativeness' as a criterion. The conclusions of the study highlighted these problems. Representativeness as a criterion is not necessarily the most straightforward method of identifying labour and management entitled under the Agreement. Rather than facing the difficult option of explicitly renouncing the criterion of representativeness, the Commission put forward criteria which refer only to representativeness of Member States, and then only as far as possible. The Commission has effectively opted for administrative decision as the short term solution to the problem of selecting which organisations fall within the scope of labour and management in the Agreement.

The question is whether the Commission's use of the study on representativeness demonstrates its implicit commitment to this criterion in the long term, or, on the contrary, confirms its belief that it is impracticable. The Commission's final word, that its selection:

'will be reviewed in the light of experience acquired in applying the new procedures instituted by the Agreement, and of the way the social dialogue develops'

contains no commitment to representativeness as a criterion to be used in the future. However, the issue is unlikely to disappear. Disappointed candidates for inclusion in the procedures may seek to claim directly effective rights based on the provisions of the Agreement, as part of the Treaty.[10] The issue may yet end up before the European Court.

The ECOSOC Opinion stated bluntly the tautology that 'To render the EC social dialogue representative, it is essential that the management and labour be represented'.[11] However, it followed this up with two problematic questions:

'(a) what criteria are to be used to identify these representatives, and
(b) how crucial is "representativeness" as one of the criteria?'

The Opinion stated that the criteria selected as indicating the representativeness of an organisation should reflect the specific context of the EC-level social dialogue, a conclusion consistent with the variety of practices at Member State level which themselves reflected the specificity of national circumstances. It concluded that the definition of 'representativeness' could be shaped in two ways:[12]

'(a) designate as representative EC level social partners those organisations recognised by **national** social partners **deemed** representative by **national** law and practice;
(b) the social partners at EC level are to be selected having regard to the nature of the **process** and of the **outcome** of EC social dialogue. These would indicate transnational criteria linked to national social partners, and organisational capacity.'

---

8 Ibid, paragraph 27.
9 Ibid, paragraph 26.
10 The Confédération Européenne des Syndicats Indépendants (CESI), for example, is not given the same recognition in Annex 2 as the ETUC. CESI is trying to obtain such recognition from the Council and the European Parliament.
11 Opinion, paragraph 2.1.7.
12 Opinion, paragraph 2.1.9.

The ECOSOC Opinion's second criterion is also indicated in the Commission's Communication.[13] Whether it was merely formally indicated, or carried much weight in the Commission's selection depends on the assessment of the organisations designated by the Commission in Annex 2.

The Commission's summary of its 'new approach to consultation' reflected a subtle and studied ambiguity.[14] It began with a generous invitation in the form of a 'policy of wide-ranging consultation (covering) all European, or, where appropriate, national, organisations which might be affected by the Community's social policy'. This was rapidly tempered by the following paragraph's restriction that:

> 'Within the framework of Article 3 of the Agreement it will undertake formal consultations with the European social partners' organisations which are listed in Annex 2 and which meet the criteria set out in para 24.'

Implicit here is a criterion of selection which distinguishes the processes of informal consultation of everybody from formal consultation of a more select group. The qualities of the latter group are also indirectly indicated by the acknowledgment that:

> 'The formal consultation of the social partners ... may lead to the adoption of opinions, recommendations or agreement-based relations (including agreements) within the social partners' sphere of competence.'

The ECOSOC Opinion focused on this issue:[15]

> '2.1.12. The criteria proposed by the Commission in paragraph 24 are ambiguous as to the need for a **negotiating** capacity of the EC social partners. Article 3(4) of the Agreement links consultation with **dialogue** and agreements (Article 4). Criteria should also include capacity to **negotiate** for and bind national structures.
>   Agreements negotiated by the social partners at EC level should be capable of binding national social partners concerned, and affect directly, or by extension, all workers and employers in the Member States.
> 2.1.13. The Commission's view is that (paragraph 26): "Only the organisations themselves are in a position to develop their own dialogue and negotiating structures". A criterion requiring negotiating competence and ability to make agreements could assist EC level partners to achieve this.
> 2.1.14. Member State social partners comprising the EC level organisations should be encouraged to grant bargaining mandates to the EC level social partner organisations. Member States should be encouraged to provide the procedures and guarantees securing the general effect of EC level agreements reached. Both these are implicit in the means of implementing agreements provided in Article 4(2).'

In ECOSOC's more explicit view, criteria of selection were linked to the functions of the organisations concerned as envisaged by the Agreement. Article 3(4) of the Agreement links consultation with dialogue and agreements. During the consultation phase envisaged by Article 3, the participating organisations have to be potentially capable of negotiating agreements which can bind national structures. Only European organisations which can meet the criterion of capacity to negotiate for and bind national structures can satisfy the requirements for participation

---

13 Communication, paragraph 24, quoted above.
14 Communication, paragraph 28.
15 Opinion, paragraph 2.1.12–2.1.14.

in the consultation phase. This clearly has implications for limiting the number of organisations which may be involved.

The debates within ECOSOC were perhaps most intense on this point, which reflects its composition. ECOSOC consists of representatives of a wide range of different groups. The members of the Workers Group are mainly representatives from the ETUC. The ETUC was concerned to maintain its monopolistic position in the social dialogue process. At the same time, other European organisations, such as the Confédération Européenne des Syndicats Indépendants (CESI) and the Confédération Européenne des Cadres (CEC) also wish to be involved. In addition, some national trade union confederations, which are not affiliated to European organisations, want to have the possibility of taking part in negotiations. In particular, the CGT in France, which is not in the ETUC, wished to be able to state their position at the bargaining table.

The difficulties are not only on the trade union side. On the employers' side the situation was even more complicated. Although there are already two European employers' organisations participating in the social dialogue (UNICE and CEEP), a large number of employers are not represented. UNICE claims to represent small and medium enterprises, but this is denied by UEAPME, which claims to be the most representative organisation for small and medium enterprises, or at least more representative of this group of employers than UNICE. The debates which led to the final Opinion adopted by ECOSOC fully explored these controversies, and reflect a reality of European industrial relations.

The consultation process

Article 3(2) and 3(3) of the Agreement set out the two stages of the process of consultation of labour and management. First, consultation 'on the possible direction of Community action', and, secondly, 'on the content of the envisaged proposal'. The Communication specified with precision how the Commission proposed to implement this process:[16]

'– the first consultation of the social partners should take place on receipt of the letter from the Commission. The requested consultation may be by letter or, if the social partners so desire, by the convening of an ad hoc meeting. The consultation should not exceed six weeks ...

– the second consultation phase will be initiated with the receipt of the second letter sent by the Commission, setting out the content of the planned proposal together with indication of the possible legal basis;

On the occasion of this second consultation, the social partners should deliver to the Commission in writing and, where the social partners so wish through an ad hoc meeting, an opinion setting out the points of agreement and disagreement in their respective positions on the draft text. Where appropriate, they should deliver a recommendation setting out their joint positions on the draft text. The duration of this second phase shall also not exceed six weeks.'

Article 3(4) of the Agreement provides an alternative outcome of the consultation process – the social dialogue process. This was acknowledged by the Communication, but it seemed that the Commission took a strict and rigid view of when this development could arise out the consultation process. The

---

16   Communication, paragraph 19.

Communication saw it following on the *second* phase of consultation: [17]

> 'The social partners consulted by the Commission on the content of a proposal for Community action may deliver an opinion or, where appropriate, a recommendation to the Commission. Alternatively, they may also, as stated in Article 3(4), "inform the Commission of their wish to initiate the process provided for in Article 4".'

This vision of the social dialogue as arising only after both stages of consultation is evident in the Operational Chart showing the implementation of the Agreement on Social Policy in Annex 4 to the Communication.

The Commission's Communication presents a particular view of the consultation process which can be questioned. The specific nature of the Commission's view can be demonstrated by comparing it with the Commission's consultation practice on social policy proposals arising *before* the Maastricht Agreement. This earlier practice was outlined by the Commission itself in the Communication: [18]

> 'The social partners are consulted jointly on each proposal in two stages – a first consultation taking place on the basis of a Commission discussion paper, followed by a second one held within the following three months on the basis of a fresh Commission working paper, more detailed and closer to the preliminary draft which the responsible departments envisage presenting to the Commission. After these consultations, the departments of the Commission draw up an inventory of the points of agreement and disagreement, as expressed by the social partners, and pass it on to the Commission for its final deliberations on the proposal.'

Compared with this earlier practice, the Commission's proposed implementation of the Agreement's consultation process seems less elaborate.

Under the first stage of the *previous* procedure, the Commission's discussion paper, containing its initial ideas, allowed for the social partners to exert their influence. The Commission would organise a meeting of the social partners, which gave them the opportunity to reach a compromise joint response to the Commission's proposal. This first stage would be undertaken over a period of three months, during which the social partners at EC level had to coordinate the internal consultation procedures with their national affiliates, as well as their bilateral dealings. In contrast, the first stage of the *new* procedure begins with a letter; it may be that the social partners never meet and only respond separately, which makes the possible coordination of a joint response less likely; and the duration of the first stage is not to exceed six weeks.

The second stage of the *previous* procedure would follow up with a fresh and detailed Commission working paper, not yet, though close to, a preliminary draft, as the basis for further joint consultations. The effort to achieve consensus during these joint consultations was evident in the practice of drawing up an inventory of the points of agreement and disagreement before the Commission begins its final deliberations on the proposal. In contrast, the second stage of the *new* procedure is again initiated on the basis of a letter setting out the content of the planned proposal; the social partners may meet, but may confine themselves to a written response in the form of an opinion or recommendation – the whole second stage also not to exceed six weeks.

The ECOSOC Opinion was critical of the new procedure envisaged by the Commission on three points in particular. First, during the initial stage, the social partners are supposed to be consulted over 'the possible direction of Community

17   Ibid, paragraph 29.
18   Ibid, paragraph 16.

action'. This implies a consideration of various alternative directions, which have to be proposed, researched and analysed before a final selection is made. The short time period of six weeks for this stage makes it unlikely that the social partners could effectively determine a new possible direction during the first consultation round. It is a golden rule that the earlier there is involvement, the greater the possibility of exercising influence. A period of only six weeks from start to finish implies that the social partners would be involved relatively late in the policy formulation process, when much of the reflection had already been undertaken, and decisions made, by the Commission on the possible direction of Community action.

Secondly, the new procedure appears to entail less dynamic involvement by the Commission. There is less pressure on the social partners to hold meetings even with the Commission, or joint meetings. Communications between the Commission and the social partners may only be in writing. The Commission does not operate to promote compromises, indicated by the last stage of consultations being the relevant departments undertaking the drafting of points of agreement and disagreement.

Finally, the social partners at EC level are complex organisations comprising a multitude of very different national organisations, often confederations of national trade unions or employers' organisations. Proper consultation of these national organisations, which in turn have complex internal procedures requiring consultation of their affiliates, can be time-consuming. It is necessary, however, if the EC-level social partners are to be able to undertake to engage themselves and their affiliates to support a social policy initiative at European level. A period of six weeks seems unlikely to suffice.

In addition to these three points, the ECOSOC challenged directly the Commission's view that the initiation of the social dialogue could only commence at the end of the second stage of consultations. ECOSOC's view was that Article 3(4) does not clearly require this, and that:[19]

'There are advantages in allowing the social partners to initiate the Article 4 procedure also after the first consultation, before the Commission proposal is tendered.'

The advantages listed were clearly linked to the ECOSOC's criticisms of the Commission's new procedure as far as the social partners involvement was concerned:[20]

'– it allows for initiation more quickly;
– it leaves more space for negotiation, rather than being bound by a proposal which becomes the basis for negotiation;
– it does not preempt the Commission continuing work on its proposal, perhaps in dynamic interaction with negotiations.'

To remedy the defects it perceived in the Commission's proposed implementation of the new consultation process, ECOSOC made two proposals to improve the involvement of the social partners. First, it proposed to incorporate the best of the old procedures of consultation. This would mean discussion and working papers instead of letters, meetings instead of written consultation, and a longer period for each stage of the consultation: eight weeks instead of six weeks.[1]

Secondly, to enable the social partners to participate fully in social policy at

19 Opinion, paragraph 4.1.2.
20 Ibid.
1 Specifying a time period for the two phases also helps to push the Commission to take action.

European level, they should be given adequate resources to enable them to respond properly to the challenges in this field. To that end, it was proposed to create an Independent Secretariat.

The Commission's influence on the social dialogue process is conditioned by a number of factors. On the one hand, there is the new status of the social dialogue following the Protocol and Agreement on Social Policy. The European Union has provided for the mandatory participation of the social partners in the formulation of policy in the social policy field, and even delegated to them some of these competences for independent action. On the other hand, the Commission is the initiator of the legislative process of social policy. But it has been heavily involved in the social dialogue process. The current position is, therefore, that the Commission is involved in *both* processes of creating the social policy of the European Union arising out of the Maastricht Protocol and Agreement.

As a result of the Social Protocol, the role of the Commission in the social dialogue process will differ from that in the past. It does not appear to envisage the pro-active stance of the past: automatically stimulating the process by arranging, preparing and often chairing meetings of social partners. All these have involved considerable outlay of resources by the Commission in support of the social dialogue – as provided by Article 118B of the Treaty, introduced by the Single European Act.

The changes foreseen in implementing the new process of the Agreement include a more independent role for the social partners, acting autonomously of the Commission through the social dialogue to formulate social policy. There is an inherent element of competition between the Commission, as the initiator of legislation, and the Commission as an intervenor in the social dialogue process.

The law-making process in which the Commission is a key player enjoys one major advantage. The Commission has at its disposal considerable financial resources and an extensive organisation. With these, it can do research, organise meetings and conferences, draft proposals, and undertake the many tasks necessary to prepare and formulate social policy. The social partners at European level do not have at their disposal such resources.

Given that the law-making role of the Commission to initiate legislation on social policy is now paralleled by the new competences of the social dialogue, the independent action of the latter, already reflected in the Commission's Communication, needs to be accompanied by the means to undertake such independent action.

To support the commitment of the social partners to social dialogue, they require a Secretariat in which they have confidence, and which is completely independent of the Commission. The proposal of ECOSOC was that the social partners should receive adequate resources to establish such an Independent Secretariat. The Commission was not eager to establish such an Independent Secretariat. The Commission preferred to build up its own experience and know-how, through a special department for the social dialogue within the Commission.

The social dialogue process

During the consultation process:[2]

> 'management and labour may inform the Commission of their wish to initiate the process provided for in Article 4. The duration of the procedure shall not exceed

2 Article 3(4) of the Agreement on Social Policy.

nine months, unless the management and labour concerned and the Commission decide jointly to extend it.'

This process is a:[3]

'dialogue between them at Community level (which) may lead to contractual relations, including agreements ... (which) shall be implemented either in accordance with the procedures and practices specific to management and labour and the Member States or, in matters covered by Article 2, at the joint request of the signatory parties, by a Council decision on a proposal from the Commission.'

The nine months duration of the social dialogue process contrasts with the 2 × six weeks allowed for the consultation process. The duration may even exceed nine months. The Commission stipulates that the social partners then 'request the Commission to decide with them upon a new deadline'.[4]

The ECOSOC discussions paid close attention to the question of the autonomy of the social partners in the social dialogue process envisaged by the Agreement and, in particular, what was the role of the Commission. A number of critical questions were raised concerning the autonomy of the social dialogue and the autonomy of the agreement reached.

First, did the social dialogue process depend on an initiative from the Commission, or could the social partners undertake the process of social dialogue without any initiative or involvement of the Commission? It was acknowledged that the social partners had been, prior to the Agreement, and were afterwards always perfectly free to independently engage in negotiations and reach agreements. Such independent action was not conditional on any Commission social policy initiative. Otherwise, the autonomy of the social partners would be compromised.

Connected with this was the question whether, once the social partners had negotiated an agreement, the Commission was obliged to submit the agreement to the Council 'at the joint request of the signatory parties', or whether the Commission had discretion and could refuse to propose the agreement to the Council.

ECOSOC had already taken the view that, once the Commission had begun the consultation process, the social partners were free to engage in social dialogue at any point, and were not bound to await the second stage of consultation under Article 3(3). An agreement negotiated by the social partners, having begun the social dialogue at any point during the consultation process, fell to be implemented under Article 4.

The further argument that followed was that if the social partners reached an agreement *entirely* independently of the consultation process, that too fell to be implemented under Article 4. The autonomy of the social partners meant that agreements reached through the social dialogue, undertaken completely independently of any Commission involvement, fell within Article 4.

These propositions appear to be consistent with the view of the Commission, which emphasised in the Communication 'the principle of the autonomy of the social partners ... which underlies Articles 3 and 4 of the Agreement'.[5] The Commission seemed happy to confirm the autonomy of the social dialogue process.

A sharp division emerged between ECOSOC and the Commission, however,

---

3   Article 4.
4   Communication, paragraph 33(c).
5   Communication, paragraph 35.

over what happened to agreements reached as a result of the social dialogue. The Commission's view was that:[6]

'By virtue of its role as guardian of the Treaties, the Commission will prepare proposals for decisions to the Council following consideration of the representative status of the contracting parties, their mandate and the "legality" of each clause in the collective agreement in relation to Community law, and the provisions regarding small and medium-sized undertakings set out in Article 2(2) ...

Where it considers that it should not present a proposal for a decision to implement an agreement to the Council, the Commission will immediately inform the signatory parties of the reasons for its decision.'

ECOSOC took the view that it is up to the social partners to decide whether their collective agreement should be put to the Council. The Commission has no discretion; if there is a joint request by the signatory parties, the Commission must propose it. Of course, the *Council* may reject the proposal. But the right to reject it is *not* given to the Commission. There is nothing in the Agreement which hints that the Commission can assess the agreement in terms of the criteria listed in the Communication: representativeness and mandate. These go to the heart of the autonomy of the social partners.

The only restriction in the Agreement is that the proposal be concerned with matters covered by Article 2. There is no indication that only agreements which *began* with the Commission's consultation process are eligible for implementation under Article 4. Every agreement reached under the social dialogue process should be put to the Council if the parties so request. Both process and outcome are autonomous of the Commission.

An interesting contrast with the Commission's claim that it could sit in judgment on the agreement before proposing it to the Council is its position on whether the Council can alter the agreement. In the paragraph preceding its claim, the Commission sternly warns that its proposal:[7]

'would give the Council no opportunity to amend the agreement ... the Commission will merely propose ... the adoption of a decision on the agreement as concluded.'[8]

Presumably, this is in line with the principle of autonomy of the social partners and their agreements.

The obligation to present the agreement to the Council does not prevent the Commission from having an important role. The Commission is very sensitive to the Council's decision-making process, and could exercise influence over the final content of any agreement. For example, on the basis of its understanding of the Council's views, the Commission could explain to the social partners how the agreement might be shaped to achieve a positive Council decision.

Alternatively, if the proposal of the agreement to the Council was rejected, the Commission might on its own initiative present a proposal for a legislative measure embodying elements of the agreement. It was clear that:[9]

'without prejudicing the principle of the autonomy of the social partners ... the Commission feels that the European Parliament must be fully informed at all stages of any consultation or negotiation procedure involving the social partners.'

6   Ibid, paragraph 39.
7   Ibid, paragraph 38.
8   Again, ibid, in paragraph 41: 'The Council decision must be limited to making binding the provisions of the agreement concluded between the social partners, so the text of the agreement would not form part of the decision, but would be annexed thereto.'
9   Ibid, paragraph 35.

According to ECOSOC, it too should be informed. It would avoid wasting time and energy if the members of ECOSOC and the Parliament were aware of the circumstances of any failures. Such failure might lead to legislative measures being undertaken in the event of negotiations not producing an agreement on a social policy regarded as necessary or desirable.

Implementation of agreements: procedures and practices

If the outcome of the social dialogue process is successful in producing an agreement between the social partners, Article 4(2) provides that:

> 'Agreements concluded at Community level shall be implemented . . . in accordance with the procedures and practices specific to management and labour and the Member States . . .'

The Commission's Communication characterises this method as 'the voluntary route'.[10] The Commission has little to say about this method, and what it does say appears to be very negative.

It starts by quoting the Declaration on Article 4(2) attached to the Agreement by the eleven Member States:

> 'The 11 High Contracting Parties declare that the first of the arrangements for application of the agreements between management and labour at Community level – referred to in Article 4(2) – will consist in developing, by collective bargaining according to the rules of each Member State, the content of the agreements, and that consequently this arrangement implies no obligation on the Member States to apply the agreements directly or to work out rules for their transposition, nor any obligation to amend national legislation in force to facilitate their implementation.'

The peremptory tone of the Declaration may explain why the Commission simply states that Article 4(2) 'is subject to' this Declaration. However, the Declaration does raise considerable difficulty hinted at in the ECOSOC Opinion.

The Declaration, unlike Article 4(2) which refers to straightforward implementation of EC level agreements, characterises this implementation as consisting in the *development of the content* of the EC level agreements. This is a much more dynamic articulation of the two levels of collective bargaining. It may explain why the Member States 'consequently' hastened to renounce any obligation. But such a renunciation cannot override the clear wording of Article 4(2) which provides that agreements '*shall* be implemented'.[11]

Avoiding confrontation with the Member States, the Commission appears to regard the obligatory implementation of agreements required by Article 4(2) as consisting of the fact only that:[12]

> '. . . the terms of this agreement will bind their members and will affect only them and only in accordance with the practices and procedures specific to them in their respective Member States.'

This recognition by the Commission of the legally binding articulation of 'agreements concluded at Community level' with 'procedures and practices specific to management and labour' is important. But it is not clear why the same legally

---

10 Communication, paragraph 37.
11 The ETUC/UNICE/CEEP agreement of 31 October 1991 had provided that the agreements '*may* be implemented.'
12 Communication, paragraph 37.

binding quality does not extend to the following words: '*and* the Member States...' A similar legally binding quality of EC-level instruments is to be found in the jurisprudence of the European Court of Justice concerned with implementation of Community Directives through collective agreements, now encapsulated in Article 2(4) of the Agreement. The Commission's Communication is quite explicit in the case of implementing Directives by articulation with collective bargaining that:[13]

> 'the Member State concerned must provide for procedures to deal, where appropriate, with any shortcomings in the agreement implementing the directive, the purpose being to ensure that the workers concerned are in practice afforded their rights...'

The jurisprudence on which this statement is based emphasised that the collective agreements must cover all employees, and must include all the Directive's requirements. Otherwise, there must be a back-up in the form of a State guarantee (usually legislation). In line with this principle, and contrary to the Commission's view, implementation of sectoral or multi-sectoral agreements may imply extension of their coverage to all employees.

The Communication states categorically that the first mode of implementation of agreements in Article 4(2) 'is subject to the ... declaration'. But normally a Declaration is not a part of the Treaty, and the Declaration does appear to contradict the clear meaning of Article 4(2), that 'Agreements ... shall be implemented'.[14] It is hard to escape the conclusion that the Member States are under some obligation to implement the agreements concluded by the social partners.

CONCLUSION

The implementation of the Protocol and Agreement on Social Policy is of fundamental importance to the future social policy of the European Union. In its Resolution of 6 December 1994 on certain aspects for a European Union social policy: a contribution to economic and social convergence in the Union, the Council:[15]

> 'NOTES that, as a means of further defining and following up its communication on implementation of the Agreement on social policy, the Commission intends to submit a working paper on the development of social dialogue.'

The dynamic of the social dialogue may progress faster than expected. The social partners are gearing up to assume their responsibilities. One indication is the new

13 Ibid, paragraph 47.
14 E A Whiteford argues that the Agreement annexed to the Protocol is part of EC law, but also that the Declarations to the Agreement are of a different nature to normal Declarations. Unlike normal Declarations, as analysed in academic doctrine, the Agreement's Declarations may be part of EC law. If so, she concedes, they strip Article 4(2) of much of its potential. However, if the legal effect of these declarations is unclear, and previous doctrine on the legal status of declarations would deny them the status of EC law, then an interpretation which (i) conflicts with earlier doctrine; and (ii) empties of all content a provision of EC law (Article 4(2) of the Agreement), should be avoided. 'Social Policy after Maastricht', (1993) 18 *European Law Review* 202–22.
15 OJ C368/6 of 23.12.1994, paragraph 23.

Article 11b of the Constitution of the ETUC, adopted at its 8th Statutory Congress in May 1995: (my italics)

'The Executive Committee shall determine the composition and mandate of the delegation for negotiations with European employers' organisations in each individual case, in accordance with the voting procedures set out in Article 16. The decision shall have the support of at least two thirds of the member organisations directly concerned by the negotiations.

In case of urgency, decisions concerning the mandate for composition of the delegation may be made in writing.

The Executive Committee shall establish the internal rules of procedure to be followed in the event of negotiations. The Secretariat shall supervise the bargaining delegation.

The Executive Committee shall be given regular progress reports on bargaining in process.

Decisions on the outcomes of negotiations shall be taken by the Executive Committee in accordance with the voting procedures set out in Article 16. The decision shall have the support of at least two thirds of the *organisations directly concerned* by the negotiations, which shall have had the opportunity to hold internal consultations.

Regular reports on European sectoral bargaining, carried out by European industry committees, shall be made to the Executive Committee. Its consistency with ETUC policy shall thus be ensured.'

At its meeting at the end of June 1995, the ETUC Executive Committee adopted Rules of Procedure for implementing Article 11b of the Constitution. These included the following:

'3. The "organisations concerned" shall be confederations from EU Member States, including the TUC, regardless of the UK opt-out, confederations from EEA countries, European industry committees and the Women's Committee ...

. . .

6. ... Once the agreement has been transmitted to the Council by the Commission, the latter may adopt a Decision on the agreement which makes it legally applicable by the 14 Member States under the scope of the Protocol.

In the UK and EEA countries, however, the union and employers' organisations may decide to implement the agreement on a voluntary basis.

. . .

14. If the negotiations do not achieve a result before the 9-month deadline, the Secretariat shall inform the Executive Committee to that effect and make a recommendation either to prolong the deadline provided by the Social Agreement or else to stop the negotiations and ask the Commission to restart the legislative process.'

Other developments are slowly taking place. A European Centre for Industrial Relations was inaugurated in October 1995 in Florence under the auspices of the social partners, ETUC, UNICE AND CEEP, with the mission of training the personnel from these organisations and their affiliates in the development of the European social dialogue. The second initiative to invoke the social dialogue procedure under the Agreement, on parental leave, advanced well and produced a result in the form of the first European Framework Agreement on 7 November 1995. These are crucial signals being sent to the Member States in the preparations for the 1996 Intergovernmental Conference on the possible revision of the Maastricht Treaty on European Union, including the Social Protocol and Agreement.

Title IV

The Future of European Labour Law

Part X

Fundamental Social Rights and Future Strategy

Chapter 37

The Charter of the Fundamental Social Rights of Workers

INTRODUCTION

On 9 December 1989, the Member States of the European Community, gathered together in the European Council at Strasbourg, solemnly declared, with the sole dissent of the United Kingdom, a Charter of the Fundamental Social Rights of Workers.[1] The development of the 1992 programme carried with it increasing concern about the social consequences of the creation of the Single European Market. The social policy of the EC, as developed over its first 30 years, did not seem adequate to the task.[2] An attempt to overcome the stalemate preventing the Council approving many Commission proposals on social policy was made by the launching in 1985 of the Val Duchesse 'social dialogue' between the European level trade union and employers' organisations (ETUC, UNICE and CEEP), reinforced by the provision in Article 118B of the Treaty inserted by the Single European Act.[3] But this effort did not fulfil the perceived need for the formulation and implementation of a comprehensive social dimension for the 1992 programme.

Building upon the Belgian Presidency (the Labour and Social Affairs Council of May 1987) and an opinion of the Economic and Social Committee (the Beretta report of November 1987),[4] a working party of the Commission in 1988 proposed a body of minimum social provisions.[5] Thereafter, the development was very rapid: following an Opinion of the Economic and Social Committee in February 1989[6] and a Resolution on Fundamental Rights of the European Parliament in March 1989,[7] a first draft of a Community Charter of Fundamental Social Rights was published by the Commission in May 1989, a second draft was produced in

1 Commission of the European Communities, *Charter of the Fundamental Social Rights of Workers*, Luxembourg, Office of Official Publications of the European Communities, 1990. The Text of the Charter and of the two earlier drafts of the Charter are reproduced in a special issue of *Social Europe* (1990).
2 For a summary of the social policy of the Community during this period, see *Social Europe*, 1/87, pp 51–62; 1/88, pp 19–20.
3 For an outline of the development of the social dialogue in the Community, see Annex 10 to *The Social Dimension of the Internal Market*, Interim Report of the Interdepartmental Working Party of the Commission, *Social Europe*, Special Edition, Brussels 1988.
4 *Opinion of the Economic and Social Committee on the social aspects of the internal market (European social area)*, Brussels, 19 November 1987, CES(87) 1069.
5 See Report of the Interdepartmental Working Party, op cit.
6 *Opinion of the Economic and Social Committee on Basic Community Social Rights*, Brussels, 22 February 1989; CES 270/89 F/OUP/CH/ht.
7 Resolution of 15 March 1989, OJ C96, 17 April 1989, p 61.

October 1989 and the December summit approved the final Charter. Shortly before, the Commission had produced a Communication concerning its Action Programme relating to the implementation of the Community Charter.[8]

The precise nature of the political commitment of 11 Member States which approved the Charter took concrete shape over the following months and years in the actions of the Commission, which elaborated various Community instruments, drawing upon the Community Charter as an indication of the direction of developments in this area. In this sense the Charter was similar in intent, though much more precise in form, to the 1972 declaration of the Council in Paris which launched a dynamic phase of social policy in the Community. The results of the impetus given to social policy by that declaration were manifest in the many instruments adopted during the 1970s.

The Commission has now replaced the 1989 Social Action Programme with a new Medium-Term Social Action Programme for 1995–1997. It states in the introduction to the new programme:[9]

> 'The new social action programme seeks to (build) on and (take) forward the achievements of the past – and particularly the 1989 Social Action Programme, which this replaces – while at the same time articulating a strategy to meet new needs and new challenges.'

However, even the most sympathetic observer would admit that the achievements under the 1989 Programme were not up to the expectations expressed by the Community Charter. The commitments undertaken by 11 Member States in 1989 remain unfulfilled.

The future of social policy in the EU, however, remains tied to these commitments. For this reason, a detailed analysis is necessary of exactly what it was the 14 Member States have undertaken to achieve by way of social policy. Moreover, the Charter itself is under intense debate in the preparations for the 1996 Intergovernmental Conference, which will consider the aftermath of the Maastricht Treaty on European Union. The possible integration of the Charter, and the Protocol and Agreement on Social Policy of the TEU, is one strategy being considered.

This concluding Part of the book is divided into three chapters reflecting this debate over the future of European labour law and social policy. First, in this chapter, what was the vision adopted by the Member States (with the exception of the United Kingdom) in December 1989? A detailed scrutiny of the Charter allows for a review of the multitude of issues which can comprise the substance of Community social policy and labour law. Secondly, in Chapter 38, how does this vision accommodate developments since then, and in particular, the European Union which emerged from the Maastricht Treaty? Finally, in Chapter 39, a strategy for the future of European labour law and social policy in the form of integrating the Charter with the Maastricht Protocol and Agreement is outlined.

Due to the opposition of the UK government, the Charter could not be integrated into the Treaty of Rome in 1989. Its legal status remains that of a political declaration. As such it has had important legal consequences through its inspiration of the Social Action Programme which resulted in various legally binding measures. In the longer term, the Court of Justice may be called upon to adjudicate upon the meaning, and perhaps challenges to the validity, of these measures

8   COM (89) 568 final, Brussels, 19 November 1989.
9   Medium Term Social Action programme 1995–1997, COM (95) 134 final, Brussels, 12 April 1995, p 1b.

proposed by the Commission and adopted by the Council (some by qualified majority). It may be expected that the decision of the Court will be influenced by the wording of the Charter.

Examination of the content of the Charter in this chapter, therefore, attempts to clarify the meaning of the Charter approved by the Member States. This analysis will identify the possible scope of the initiatives which could be taken by the Commission in fulfilment of the desire of these Member States to develop Community policy in the form of fundamental social rights, and will elaborate the background against which decisions of the Court of Justice on these initiatives may be taken. The detailed analysis which follows will focus upon some (though not all) important elements of social policy manifest in the Charter, particularly in light of changes which occurred in arriving at the final draft approved in December 1989.

THE PREAMBLE

Social policy and the internal market

The Preamble highlighted hesitancy and ambivalence about the relative independence of Community social policy from the general objective of a European internal market in 1992. The first Draft referred to 'the implementation of a social policy at Community level, particularly in view of the impending completion of the internal market'.[10] This was altered in the second and final Drafts to 'the same importance must be attached to the social aspects as to the economic aspects and, whereas, therefore, they must be developed in a balanced manner'. The first Draft's formulation is in terms of a social policy in general, with particular reference to the internal market. This implies a greater degree of independence of this policy compared to the final formulation's insistence on linking the two – so that Community action is seen as limited to the social aspects of the internal market.

However, a reinforcement of the emphasis on the independence of social policy from the internal market emerges from the first Draft's provision that 'the implementation of the Single European Act must be accompanied ... by a development of the social rights of citizens'.[11] This phrase is preceded in the second and final drafts by the requirement that this implementation 'must take full account of the social dimension of the Community' – *not* of the internal market only. This is a fundamental guideline for both Commission and Court in interpreting the Charter.

Citizens v workers

The title of the final Draft of the Charter specifies that it is 'of workers'. This was not so clear in the earlier drafts. Thus the first Draft stipulated that 'the completion of the internal market must *also* offer improvements in the social field for *citizens* of the European Community ...' (my italics).[12] The second Draft deleted

10 Recital 2.
11 Recital 12.
12 Recital 6.

the word 'also', but kept the reference to 'citizens' – thus reinforcing their status. However, the final Draft replaced the word 'citizens' with 'workers'. Similarly, a subsequent Recital of the first and second Drafts promises 'development of the social rights of *citizens* of the European Community', but the final Draft confines this to 'development of the social rights of *workers* of the European Community'.

The category 'workers of the European Community' is both narrower and wider than that of 'citizens'. 'Workers' is *narrower* in so far as persons *not* working may not be covered, though they may be citizens. The precise coverage of 'worker' could raise problems as regards persons who have never worked (eg school-leavers), but may work in the future (eg mothers), who are not currently working (unemployed), or who no longer work (retired).

'Workers' is *wider* if it is deemed to include workers who are not citizens, but are nonetheless working in the Community. Questions then arise as to whether workers who are not Community nationals must be lawfully resident. Earlier drafts which referred to 'citizens' went on to guarantee comparable treatment only to 'workers from third countries' (first Draft) or 'workers from non-member countries' (second Draft) '*who are legally resident in a member state of the Community*'. The final Draft also contains such a formulation in a subsequent Recital concerning the Member States' obligation to guarantee comparable treatment. It is not clear whether this condition of legal residence also applies to the final Draft's paragraph promising improvements to 'workers of the European Community'.[13]

The consequences of the shift from 'citizens' to 'workers' in the final Draft of the Preamble are partially mitigated by a later Recital in the Preamble which specifies that 'it is for Member States to guarantee that workers from non-member countries and *members of their families* who are able to enjoy, as regard their living and working conditions, treatment comparable to that enjoyed by workers who are nationals of the Member State concerned'. However, the change from 'citizens' to 'workers' remains an important restriction on the scope of the Preamble to the Charter.

Conclusion

The Preamble makes clear that fundamental social rights are to become an integrated part of Community social policy. Social *rights* develop in the context of the social dimension, not of the internal market, but of the Community. The social dimension includes rights, but implies more – Commission initiatives, freedoms as well as rights. The reference to 'context' implies links between social rights and these other aspects of the social dimension. Efforts should be made to ensure they complement each other. The Preamble's emphasis that implementation of the Single European Act must take account of the social dimension, but that development of social rights must be ensured, indicates the new role for fundamental social rights in the Community.

---

13 The category 'workers' also raises the question of whether there are included only employees, or also the self-employed. A subsequent paragraph in the final Draft of the Preamble
states that 'it is necessary . . . to ensure . . . the development of the social rights of *workers* of
the European Community, *especially workers and self-employed persons* . . .' The final Draft is
ambiguous as to whether self-employed persons (in earlier drafts a separate category of citizens from workers) are now part of the category of workers, which includes both employed
and self-employed workers (persons).

FREEDOM OF MOVEMENT (ARTICLES 1-3)

The section of the Charter on Freedom of Movement suffered a considerable reduction during the course of reaching its final version. The first Draft contained eight articles, the second Draft six, and the final Draft only three articles. It also underwent a change of title: the first two Drafts were headed 'Rights to freedom of movement'; in the final Draft, the title is simply 'Freedom of Movement'.

Restriction on freedom of movement: public security and public policy

The 'right to freedom of movement throughout the territory of the Community', declared in Article 1 of all three Drafts, is stated in the first Draft, to be 'subject to restriction justified on 'public *policy*, public *security* or public health'. In the second and final Drafts, the first two restrictions become 'public *order*' and 'public *safety*' (in the French version: '*d'ordre public*' and '*de sécurité publique*'). '*Ordre public*' has general implications of public 'policy' in a much wider sense than the English phrase 'public order'. The English version seems to imply justifications relating more to internal public order. The significance of this ambiguity is emphasised by the change from the first two Drafts' granting these rights to 'every *citizen* of the European Community', whereas the final Draft substitutes 'every *worker* of the European Community'. In the context of the Preamble, it was noted earlier that this could imply exclusion of non-workers, and also conditions of legal residence in the Community (though in Article 2, the qualification 'of the European Community' is absent; 'any worker' is protected). In the context of this section, however, if the Charter's right to freedom of movement covers non-citizens of Member States who are workers of the Community, the possible exclusion of justifications based on external security and general public policy becomes more significant.

Equal treatment in any occupation or profession

Article 2 of the Charter states that 'the right to freedom of movement' has consequences for the ability of 'any worker to engage in any occupation or profession in the Community'. The significance of the guarantee to any worker in Article 2 is highlighted by the deletion in the final Draft of the earlier phrase qualifying the ability to engage in any occupation or profession as being 'on the same *terms* as those applied to nationals'. Instead, the ability to engage in any occupation or profession is specified in the final Draft as operating 'in accordance with the principles of equal treatment *as regards access to employment, working conditions and social protection*'. The bare word 'terms' could be construed as limited to terms *during* employment, thereby excluding circumstances prior or subsequent to employment. It is now clear that the ability guaranteed by Article 2 must equal the protection available to nationals against discrimination in hiring and social protection, as well as in their terms of employment ('working conditions'). The 'right of freedom of movement' is said *also* to imply 'harmonisation of conditions of residence in all Member States'.[14]

14   Article 3.

Special categories of workers: subcontractors, public contracts

The first two drafts[15] provided for guarantees of identical terms/equal treatment in particular to those performing work on a *subcontracting* basis in other Member States,[16] and those employed on *public contracts*.[17] These provisions lay special emphasis on certain categories of workers, deemed either especially vulnerable (subcontracting), or previously often subject to special national regulations governing working conditions (public works).

The final Draft deleted all these provisions. As a result, the opportunity was lost to assert that these workers have special fundamental social rights deserving protection. Despite the failure of the Charter to refer to subcontracting or public contracts, the Commission's Action Programme made proposals for concrete actions. Regarding *subcontractors*, the Commission proposed an:[18]

'instrument on working conditions applicable to workers from another State performing work in the host country in the framework of the freedom to provide services, especially on behalf of a *sub-contracting* undertaking.'

In the absence of a specific mandate in the Charter, the grounds for this initiative are stated in the Action Programme to be only incidentally those of avoiding prejudicial working conditions. Rather, the Commission justifies this instrument by referring to possible distortions of competition arising where workers employed by the subcontractor are subject to working conditions regulated by the country where the subcontractor has his registered office which may be more disadvantageous than those of the country where the work is undertaken – thus prejudicing contractors from that country.

Specifically on public contracts, the Commission proposes an instrument on the introduction of a labour clause. Reference is made to Directive 89/440/EEC amending the Works Directive to introduce a 'transparency clause' whereby the contracting authority may provide tenderers with the necessary information concerning working conditions applicable to the work envisaged. Further:[19]

'On the basis of an analysis regarding the effective use by enterprises of the opening of public contracts and in the light of the current work in the domain of "excluded" sectors, the Commission could formulate a proposal aiming at the introduction of a "social clause" into public contracts.'

Experience in a number of Member States demonstrated the close ties of such 'social clauses' with objectives of extending *ordre public* and collectively agreed standards. The use by public authorities of their contracting power to promote the application of labour law and the improvement of labour standards is a method of labour administration with a long history in Britain.[20] It received a setback at *national* level in 1983, when the Conservative government limited the use by government departments of their contracting power by repealing the Fair Wages Resolution of 1946. A Commission proposal to implement social policy

---

15   Draft 1, Articles 6 and 8 and Draft 2, Articles 5–6.
16   Draft 1, Article 6; Draft 2, Article 6 (limited to 'non-temporary work').
17   Draft 1, Article 8; Draft 2, Article 5.
18   Commission Action Programme, p 23.
19   Action Programme, ibid, p 24.
20   B Bercusson *Fair Wages Resolutions*, Mansell, London 1978.

through the technique of contract compliance is one point of potential conflict with the present UK government.

EMPLOYMENT AND REMUNERATION (ARTICLES 4–6)

Freedom to choose an occupation

The first Draft[1] specified a freedom 'to choose and engage in an occupation' without qualification. The second Draft added, and the final Draft[2] retains the qualification: '*according to the regulations governing each occupation*'. This qualification renders ambiguous whether the Charter guarantees a fundamental freedom, or merely seeks to reflect existing EC law on freedom of movement. For example, if national regulations prohibited certain occupations, or restricted entry to them (perhaps thereby also violating *other* fundamental rights), but did not discriminate among Community nationals, would there be a violation of this Article?

Remuneration

The formulation of Article 5 remained stable as regards its first line in all three Drafts: 'All employment shall be fairly remunerated'. But thereafter, the Article underwent substantial changes before the final Draft.

Method of formulating the wage standard: law, collective agreements, practice

Draft 1[3] and Draft 2[4] provided for *decent* wages to be '*established*' and '*an equitable reference wage*' to be '*laid down*' by '*law or by collective agreement at national, regional, interoccupational, sectoral or company level*' (Draft 1), or even, as added by Draft 2 '*in accordance with national practices*'. The final draft does not clearly refer to a method of establishing or laying down a wage standard: rather, '*in accordance with arrangements applying in each country*', an 'equitable wage' is to '*be assured*'; and workers '*shall receive*' an equitable reference wage.

The provision seems to be concerned as much with effective implementation as with formulation of the standard. The latter is implicit – but the final Draft does not make clear where the standard to 'be assured' is to be found: in law, collective agreements at various levels, national practices, or any of these.

The failure to explicitly specify the source of the standard is highlighted by the last paragraph of the Article which (in all Drafts) prescribes that wages can be 'withheld, seized or transferred' – only in accordance with national *law*.

If, as earlier Drafts indicate, the wage standard is impliedly to be formulated through collective bargaining at various levels, there arise problems of assessing whether and which *collective agreements* are sufficiently comprehensive in scope and coverage to provide an adequate standard. Even this is relatively easy compared with the problem of assessing the scope and coverage of '*national practices*'. In this context 'national' presumably refers to their quality as

1 Article 10.
2 Draft 2, Article 7; final Draft, Article 4.
3 Article 9.
4 Article 8.

pertaining to one of the Member States, not their scope. Otherwise wage setting practices which were not national in scope, but only regional would not be eligible.

Method of enforcing the wage standard: law, collective agreements, practice

Whatever source is resorted to as setting the wage standard, Article 5 provides that the resulting equitable wage '*shall be assured*', or, in the case of the equitable reference wage, shall be received. This emphasises enforcement of the standard, without specifying the method. It gives maximum flexibility to Member States to choose their preferred method of wage *setting* and to provide for *enforcement* of the standard set. The separation of the two activities implies that the same instrument or institution that fixes the wage may not be responsible for assuring it. Problems arise when the mechanism of enforcement is not law, or when legal mechanisms are separate from industrial relations standard-setting machinery.

Normally legal mechanisms of enforcement will be integrated with the legal rules setting the wage standard. But resort to legal enforcement mechanisms may not be the normal practice. This will be so particularly where collective bargaining, not law, is the effective wage-setting mechanism. In these cases, questions may arise as to whether the Charter rights are being adequately implemented.

The definition of the decent/equitable wage

The entitlement in both earlier drafts was simply to a '*decent wage*'. The second Draft added to the first Draft's right to a decent wage: 'particularly at the level of the *basic* wage'. This refinement disappeared in the final Draft. But the final Draft substituted for the bare 'decent' wage entitlement of workers the standard of an '*equitable* wage . . . *sufficient to enable them to have a decent standard of living*'. It is not clear whether the decent standard of living for the *worker* includes also the worker's family, as is explicit in the clause concerned with withholding wages in the same article, which seems to postulate a lower standard: 'the *necessary means of subsistence* for himself and his family'. The 'equitable reference wage' is not defined. It is not clear whether the word 'reference' implies a qualitative change.

The coverage of the decent/equitable wage

In the first Draft, the equitable reference wage standard is assured only to workers *not* on contracts 'of unfixed duration'; ie workers covered are those on fixed term or temporary contracts. The second and final Drafts exclude 'open-ended full-time' contracts. The difference is that under the final Draft *part-timers* – even those on open-ended/unfixed duration contracts – may also benefit from the guarantee of an equitable reference wage.

It is not clear in any Draft whether the *equitable reference wage* standard is *additional* or *alternative* to the *decent/equitable* wage standard. If they are *alternatives*, then the guarantee of an equitable reference wage *excludes* assurance of a decent/equitable wage. In this case, a qualitative difference between the standards becomes significant.

The first Draft refers to both 'workers' and '*employed persons*'. Only 'workers' appear in the second and final Drafts. This avoids the possible need for clarification as to the difference, but leaves open the precise extent of coverage. For example: do 'self-employed' workers receive wages? If so, how are they to be assured an 'equitable wage'?

IMPROVEMENT OF LIVING AND WORKING CONDITIONS (ARTICLES 7–9)

Fundamental social rights regarding working time

Article 8 refers to 'a weekly rest period' and 'annual paid leave'. A 'weekly rest period' could imply some restriction of the maximum duration of work, night work, week-end work and systematic overtime.

Constitutions providing that the maximum length of the working day shall be regulated by law are those of Italy,[5] Portugal[6] and Spain.[7] A constitutional right to 'rest and leisure' is guaranteed by France 'to all' and particularly to the child, mother and aged worker.[8] In Luxembourg the law organises 'rest for workers'.[9] The Netherlands 'shall promote ... leisure activities'.[10] Portugal proclaims the right to rest and leisure,[11] and the 'systematic development of a network of leisure and vacation centres in co-operation with social organisations'.[12] Spain guarantees 'necessary rest ... and the promotion of suitable centres';[13] and it 'shall facilitate adequate utilisation of leisure'[14] and a system of special services which shall take care of leisure.[15]

As to timing and compensation, Italy's constitution makes provision for a paid annual holiday, and the worker cannot renounce the rest and paid holidays given.[16] Portugal calls for a 'weekly rest' and the worker is guaranteed 'paid periodic vacations';[17] also Spain.[18] Sundays and holidays recognised by the State are given special mention in the German Federal Republic as 'days of rest from work and of spiritual education'.[19]

According to a Commission Study,[20] legislation provides for periods of weekly rest in all countries, save the UK. Public holidays are recognised by law in all Member States save Denmark and the UK. Paid annual leave is provided by legislation in all Member States save the UK.

This background of domestic law on working time indicates that formulation and definition of fundamental rights in this field at EC level is not a new departure.

---

5   Article 37.
6   Article 60(1d)(2b).
7   Article 40(2). This information is to be found in D Ziskind 'Labor Provisions in the Constitutions of Europe', (1984) 6 *Comparative Labor Law* 311; quoted in Bercusson, Report for the Community on Fundamental Social and Economic Rights (1989), op cit.
8   Preamble, paragraph 3.
9   Article 11(5).
10 Article 22(3).
11 Article 60(1d).
12 Article 60(2d).
13 Article 40(2).
14 Article 43.
15 Article 50.
16 Article 37.
17 Article 60(1d).
18 Article 40(2).
19 Article 139.
20 *Comparative Study on Rules Governing Working Conditions in the Member States: A Synopsis*, SEC (89) 1137.

SOCIAL PROTECTION (ARTICLE 10)

Article 10 prescribes standards of social protection, social security and social assistance for different categories of workers and persons. These standards and their extent of coverage are to be applied in all Member States 'according to the arrangements applying in each country'. These arrangements may not detract from the standards or narrow the categories of those eligible.

The two paragraphs of the Article prescribe two types of provision: (1) social protection and social security benefits, and (2) 'sufficient resources and social assistance'. Each type of provision covers a different group. The final Draft, however, changed the coverage of each type of provision as prescribed by the earlier drafts. In its final form, the Charter reserves 'social protection' and social security for *workers*; '*persons*' receive social assistance.

In contrast, the first two Drafts prescribed 'a right to adequate social protection' for 'Every *citizen* of the European Community'.[1] In addition, 'all *workers*, whatever their status' were to enjoy 'social security' benefits or cover. Conversely, the final Draft provides 'a right to adequate social protection' *only* to 'Every *worker* of the European Community'. Every *worker* 'whatever his status', as in earlier drafts, is *also* to 'enjoy an adequate level of social security benefits'. The second paragraph of this Article provides for '*persons*' to receive 'sufficient resources and social assistance'.

Standards of social security

In the first Draft, the right to 'adequate social protection' is distinguished from 'social security cover proportional, where appropriate to length of service and pay and to their financial contribution to the appropriate social protection system'. The second Draft refers to 'adequate social protection' and 'adequate levels of social security benefits', but it maintains the requirement that the latter be 'proportional, where appropriate to length of service and pay and to their financial contribution to the appropriate social protection system'.

The final Draft *deletes* qualification of the level of social security by reference to a criterion of proportionality. It simply specifies, without further definition, 'an adequate level of social security protection'. This deletion in the final Draft implies that the standard need *not* be proportionally related to employment history (eligibility for unemployment benefit). The final Draft distinguishes social security for the unemployed from social assistance. The level of social security benefits for the unemployed is to be 'adequate', regardless of their employment history.

Social assistance: unemployed and others

The first Draft[2] and the second Draft[3] specified *two categories* entitled to social assistance: first, workers/persons *out of the labour market and not entitled to unemployment*

---

1 First Draft, Article 14; second Draft, Article 13.
2 Article 15.
3 Article 13.

benefit;[4] secondly, persons '*regardless of labour market*'[5] who lack '*adequate means of subsistence*'. In the final Draft there is only *one category* of 'persons' entitled, and they must satisfy two eligibility conditions. First, they must be out of the labour market ('have been unable either to enter or re-enter the labour market'). This may imply that they must be seeking work, but does not explicitly refer to eligibility for unemployment benefit. Secondly, they 'have *no* (as contrasted with "inadequate") means of subsistence'.

Standard of social assistance

The first Draft specified a *single* standard of social assistance to be received, regardless of employment history: 'a minimum income and appropriate social assistance'. The second Draft specified *two* standards. That specified by the first Draft was given only to those out of the labour market and no longer eligible for unemployment benefit. A slightly different standard was specified for 'persons, especially the elderly, who do not have adequate means of subsistence': 'a minimum income modulated or complemented by appropriate social assistance'.

The final Draft's standard is described as 'sufficient resources and social assistance in keeping with their particular situation'. Three points of difference are evident. First, resources are substituted for income. Second, the resources are to be sufficient, not minimum. Third, the standard is to be in keeping with their particular situation, though no criteria are given. This absence of criteria can be compared with the emphasis in earlier Drafts on the standard of social security being proportional to employment history. The final Draft makes no mention of unemployment benefit: those entitled to this standard are out of the labour market and 'have no means of subsistence'.

FREEDOM OF ASSOCIATION (ARTICLES 11-14)

Right/freedom to belong/join

The first Draft of Article 11 of the Charter[6] provided for a right to *belong* to an organisation; in the second Draft,[7] this became a right to *join* an association. However, the *following* article in both Drafts[8] specified that 'This right shall entail recognition of the right to *belong*...'

In the first Draft, this simply duplicates the preceding Article. But the addition of a right to 'belong' to the second Draft's right to 'join' requires that the scope of each be distinguished. One possibility is that the right to 'join' refers to active *adhesion*, whereas 'belong' only protects passive *existing* membership. A provision allowing only for a right to 'belong' could, perhaps, be interpreted as permitting

---

4 First Draft: 'Workers who are excluded from the labour market without being able to continue claiming unemployment benefit'; second Draft: 'persons who have been unable either to enter or reenter the labour market and who are no longer eligible for unemployment benefit'.
5 The second Draft specifies the elderly.
6 Article 16.
7 Article 14.
8 First Draft, Article 17; second Draft, Article 15.

restrictions on active adhesion. The potential significance of a difference in scope between *joining* and *belonging* emerges in the final Draft's provisions.

The second paragraph of Article 11 of the final Draft, like the first Draft,[9] provides *not* for a 'right' but for a '*freedom*' to *join*. The difference between a 'freedom' and a 'right' requires definition. A 'freedom' may be said not to give rise to a positive legal action – a claim – but renders unlawful restraints upon it. A freedom granted also has to compete against other freedoms (an example would be the freedom to picket competing with the freedom of passage along the public highway). However, the relative weakness of *freedoms* granted becomes evident when *rights* are concerned. Rights granted may be limited by competing rights: for example, the workers' right to strike by the employer's right to fulfilment of contractual employment obligations. But rights granted will usually overcome competing freedoms.

Experience of similar provisions in national constitutional orders indicates that this distinction could have implications for the substance of a Community legal instrument. In the first two Drafts, the right to join might overcome a freedom implicit in the existence of a labour market. A mere freedom to join (as in the second paragraph of Article 11 of the final Draft) has to compete with other freedoms, and is subordinate to other rights.

Right of association

The distinctions between freedom and right, between joining and belonging, are made more complex by the provision in the first paragraph of Article 11 of the final Draft, which refers to a '*right of association*'. The precise content of this right is clarified by analysis of provisions in earlier Drafts.

The first Draft's[10] right to *belong* to a '*trade union organisation*' became the second Draft's[11] right to *join* 'any *profession,* or *any association . . .*' Article 15 of the second Draft, however, does specify that this entails the right to '*belong* to a *union*'. As noted earlier, a right to 'belong to' may be different from a right to 'join', and this possible difference may be important in the final Draft. Article 17 of the first Draft did not help clarify these differences by providing for a 'freedom to join any association of a democratic nature or to denounce [sic] this right'.

The final Draft (Article 11, first paragraph), provides a more generic '*right*[12] *of association* in order to constitute *professional organisations or trade unions*'. The second paragraph of Article 11 specifies a *freedom* to *join* 'such organisation'. Two questions arise: first, does '*association*' subsume *both* 'belong' and 'join'; or *only* 'belong'; second, does this right refer to organisations or unions, or both?

There appears to be only one interpretation of this 'right of association' which does not lead to duplication. According to this interpretation, the right to associate in the first paragraph of Article 11 means a *right to belong* to both organisations and unions. To this is added by the second paragraph a *freedom to join* 'such' organisations (including, perhaps, also unions).

---

9   Article 17.
10   Article 16.
11   Article 14.
12   Contrast the more familiar 'freedom'.

The only alternative interpretations require some duplication. Thus, if the right to associate means the right to join, or to both belong to and to join organisations and unions, the second paragraph's freedom to join 'such organisations' leads to Article 11 guaranteeing both a right *and* a freedom to join.

Of course, duplication may be the lesser evil in this case, if the alternative is to reduce the right to join to a mere freedom. Formulation and implementation of other fundamental rights may depend on successful protection of rights of association (including both the right and freedom to join organisations and unions) guaranteed by Article 11.

The inclusion of a 'right to join' in Article 11's 'right of association' is supported by a phrase which did not appear in earlier drafts. The final Draft specifies that the right of association is '*in order to constitute* professional organisations or trade unions of their choice'. To *constitute* – ie to bring into being – is more like active joining than passive belonging.

The formulations in the three drafts of the Charter may be summarised as follows:

First Draft: –   right to belong to union (twice);
                    –   freedom to join any association.[13]
Second Draft: –   right to belong to union;
                    –   right to join any association.
Final Draft: –   right of association[14] of professional organisations or trade unions;
                    –   freedom to join 'such organisations'.

Nature of organisations protected by the right

The final Draft restricts employers' and workers' right of association 'to constitute professional organisations or trade unions of their choice for the defence of their economic and social interests'. It should be noted that this phrase could be read as limiting the nature of the organisations protected: those concerned with the *defence*, as contrasted with the advancement of interests; only those concerned with *economic and social*, not political interests. Indeed, the concept of *interests* itself could produce different definitions of interests so as to distinguish among organisations eligible for protection. These distinctions are almost impossible to maintain in practice, so that decisions overruling the choice of those involved would be controversial. The whole tenor of the provisions is that those involved should determine ('their choice') these questions.

Constitutive activities

There is considerable debate over whether and how far a fundamental 'freedom of association' protects the *activities* of the trade union established by workers. The upgrading by Article 11 of this freedom into a 'right of association' could be interpreted in light of this debate. Thus, the additional phrase '*in order to constitute* professional organisations or trade unions of their choice' may enhance the

---

13   Cf subsequent 'denounce this right'.
14   Query: only belong to or also join?

substance of Article 11's 'right of association' by implying a right to engage in activities necessary to constitute such organisations. Examples would be meetings of workers (at the workplace, or during working time) to discuss constituting trade unions; or strikes in pursuit of claims for union recognition pure and simple. A right of association should protect such activities aiming to constitute trade unions.

The additional phrase '*for the defence of their economic and social interests*' indicates the potential scope of such constituting activities (which would be additional to the activities specified in Articles 12–14). For example, a strike to obtain recognition for negotiations over a specific economic or social issue might be protected by a right of association to constitute trade unions to defend those specific economic and social interests.

On the other hand, as mentioned above discussing the nature of the organisations protected by the right, this phrase may contain an implicit limitation on the activities connected with *economic and social*, not political interests. There are controversial precedents on whether certain activities are objectively or subjectively in the interests of workers. As was concluded earlier: the whole tenor of the provision is that those involved should determine ('their choice') these questions.

'Negative' freedom of association

The second paragraph of Article 11 links the 'freedom to join *or not to join* such organisations'. The significance of this, as regards the well-known issue of the (negative) freedom not to be in a union, may be appreciated by examining the wording from earlier drafts.

The first Draft[15] provided for 'freedom to join any association of a democratic nature or to renounce this right [sic] without any personal or occupational damage being thereby suffered by the individual concerned'. This was slightly shortened by the second Draft[16] to 'freedom to exercise this right (to join) or to renounce it without any personal or occupational damage being thereby suffered by the individual concerned'. In the second Draft, the ambiguous *freedom/right* to renounce joining becomes more clearly only a *freedom* to renounce it. There is perhaps a reversal of emphasis: a right to renounce joining becomes only a freedom.

The right/freedom to *renounce a right* or its exercise is not clearly the same as a right *not to join.* This ambiguity was clarified by the final Draft[17] which provides for 'freedom to join or not to join . . . without any personal or occupational damage being thereby suffered by him'.

The earlier distinctions between right and freedom, and between joining and belonging to unions should now be recalled. First, Article 11 provides only a *freedom* not to join, as contrasted with the *right* of association. Secondly, this is limited to a freedom not to *join.* There is no mention of a right or freedom not to *belong.*

The specific implications of this could include that once a worker has joined, there is no right or freedom not to belong. Resignation, for example, could therefore be subjected to conditions.

---

15   Article 17.
16   Article 14, second paragraph.
17   Article 11.

The general implications might become clearer by addressing the question against whom these freedoms are to be exercised. Two potential issues emerge: anti-union employers on the one hand, and trade unions excluding non-members, or requiring compulsory membership, on the other.

The first paragraph of Article 11 ('right of association' as right to belong) emphasises the protection of *existing* union members (right to belong) from *employers*. Even the mere freedom to join is sufficient as against employers, since no countervailing employer freedom can be asserted which would not immediately conflict with the right of association of existing union members.

The protection of non-members (right of association/freedom to join) from exclusionary practices of *unions* is less easily accommodated. Similarly, the practices of some unions (for example, the British closed shop) which require compulsory union membership will encounter the provision in the second paragraph of Article 11 of a freedom *not to join*. The solution to both conflicts lies in the right of association itself, which may be read as placing collective *rights* of existing union members on a higher plane than individual freedoms of non-members to join or not to join. The two individual *freedoms* to join or not to join are each to be weighed against the collective *right* of association – which may include rights to constitutive activities.

The context is of existing practices of *encouraging or requiring* union membership on the one hand, and, in some cases, *excluding* non-members (as in the British closed shop) on the other. It is *not* a case of balancing the freedom to join with the freedom not to join – for they are not in direct conflict. The balance is between the *right of association* and the *freedom not to join*; or, in some cases of exclusionary union practices, the *freedom/right to join* and the *constitutive right of association* of existing members.

The provision of freedom/right to join and mere freedom not to join allows for balancing of these individual freedoms against, on the one hand, employer freedoms to be anti-union, and, on the other, existing members' collective rights of association to *either* exclude non-members or to require membership.

Nonetheless, the individual 'freedom to join or not to join' is reinforced by a stipulation in all three drafts that this be 'without any personal or occupational damage being thereby suffered by the individual concerned'.[18] This is a measure of the weight of this freedom. Thus, for example, others might have to demonstrate that their freedoms will not cause this damage. Or that these others will suffer equivalent damage also.

An EC measure which respected these balances of principle would require exceedingly delicate draughtsmanship. The Commission's Action Programme states that the 'responsibility for the implementation . . . rests with the Member States in accordance with their national traditions and policies'.[19]

Collective rights to negotiate and conclude collective agreements

According to the first two drafts of Article 12, the right of every employer and every worker to belong to organisations,[20] or the right to join associations[1] 'shall

---

18 Final Draft: 'him'.
19 Action Programme, p 29. The Maastricht Agreement on Social Policy was equally cautious: Article 2(6).
20 First Draft, Article 16.
1 Second Draft, Article 14.

entail recognition of . . . the *freedom* to negotiate and conclude collective agreements',[2] to which the second Draft added: 'which should be promoted'. In this formulation, the status of this entitlement was that of a freedom, linked to an *individual* right.

The final Draft changed this formulation to declare that the entitlement was to a '*right* to negotiate and conclude collective agreements', which was conferred on *collective* '[e]mployers or employers' organisations, on the one hand, and workers' organisations, on the other'.

Subject to conditions laid down by national legislation and practice – not jurisprudence

However, the final Draft subjected this right to: '*the conditions laid down by national legislation and practice*'. Observations already made in connection with a similar formulation in Article 14 of the second Draft apply here. There is little sense in formulating a transnational standard only to subordinate it to national standards.

Such formulations are sometimes used when *specific exceptions* are made to a general transnational standard; for example, the reference to the internal legal order qualifying these, and other rights, as regards certain categories of workers: the armed forces, the police and the civil service.[3] The formulation in this Article might be construed as such an exception by holding that *other* provisions were *not* subject to national law or practice. The only candidate for this would be the rights connected with European-level social dialogue or agreements.[4] On this view, the European social dialogue prescribed there ('must be developed'), and the possibility of resulting contractual relations *could not be subjected to* 'conditions laid down by national legislation and practice'.

One possible consequence of subjecting the rights to negotiate and conclude agreements to national legislation and practice could be to raise a *presumption* of interpretation *favouring* such rights when there is *ambiguity* in national legislation and practice. For example, as to whether legislation restricts the content of collective agreements, or restrains negotiating tactics (refusal to reveal, or demand for disclosure of, specific types of information). Or as to whether practice excludes a certain workers' organisation from being a party to an agreement. An EC measure could achieve this result by reiterating the supremacy of conditions laid down by national legislation and practice, but prescribing this presumption in favour of the rights in Article 12. This could become one of the grounds for challenging a national court's interpretation in an action before the European Court of Justice.

This result is facilitated by the fact that the subordination of the Charter's provision of rights to negotiate and conclude agreements is limited to conditions laid down by national legislation and practice – *but not those laid down by other legal norms – in particular, jurisprudence.* In those jurisdictions where the courts have been an important, sometimes the most important, source of rules governing collective bargaining, the implications of this omission are potentially enormous. Jurisprudence prescribing conditions governing these rights

2   First Draft, Article 17; second Draft, Article 15.
3   Article 14.
4   Second paragraph of Article 12.

cannot infringe the rights declared by the Charter. When court judgments become the authority for interpretations of legislation or practice which contradict the Charter rights, they can be impugned.

The right to strike at European level

The first Draft of the Charter listed in the *same* Article 17 the rights to negotiate and conclude agreements and *also* 'the right to resort to collective action . . . including the right to strike'. The *following* Article 18 began: 'this right shall imply that relations based on agreements may be established . . . at European level'. The implication may be made that the Draft intended that *all* the rights in Article 17 – including the right to strike – applied at European level.

In contrast, the second draft[5] and final Draft[6] specify *only* the rights to negotiate and conclude agreements – and continue in the *same* Article with a reference to European-level dialogue and possible outcomes. The reference to the right to strike only comes in the following and separate Article.[7]

The question is whether this separation of the Charter's encouragement of dialogue at European level from the Charter's right to strike is intended to exclude a right to strike at European level? There appears to be no reason for such an exclusion: if rights to negotiate and agree are generally guaranteed, with special mention of European level, the same could be said for the right to strike.

Right to resort to collective action

Article 13 provides that 'The right to resort to collective action in the event of a conflict of interests shall include the right to strike'. The first Draft[8] had a similar provision as part of the Article concerning also other collective action (negotiate and conclude collective agreements). But already in the second Draft[9] and then in the final Draft, the right to strike was prescribed in a separate article.

The implication of the phrase that the right to resort to collective action '*shall include*' the right to strike is that the right includes also *other* forms of collective action. Industrial action may take various forms protected by the Charter: picketing, secondary boycotts and working-to-rule, to name but a few of the many forms of workers' collective action potentially protected by this provision.

'Subject to the obligations arising under national regulations and collective agreements'

In the first Draft of the Charter, there was no qualification of the right to resort to collective action by reference to national law. The second Draft, however, qualified this right by the clause: 'save in exceptions specified in existing legislation'.[10] This could have meant simply that the right is limited as regards

5   Article 15.
6   Article 12.
7   Article 16 of the second Draft; Article 13 of the final Draft.
8   Article 17.
9   Article 16.
10   Article 16.

certain exceptional *categories of workers.* This meaning was made explicit in the final Draft,[11] which refers to the armed forces, the police and the civil service.

The 'exceptions' referred to in the second Draft, however, could also be interpreted as meaning that the right to resort to collective action in general, as regards all workers, was to be limited in certain exceptional *circumstances,* determined by national legislation. This introduced potential restrictions on the Charter right, though still maintaining that such restrictions be 'exceptional'. The wording finally adopted in the final Draft: 'subject to the *obligations* arising under national regulations and collective agreements' seems to further undermine the transnational standard by giving free rein to national standards.

It may be noted, however, that the scope of '*obligations arising under national regulations and collective agreements*' is presumably different from the restrictions imposed by the Charter's Article 12 on the rights to negotiate and conclude collective agreements, which refers to '*conditions*' laid down by *national legislation and practice*'.[12] It was noted that Article 12's formulation did *not* include conditions laid down in jurisprudence. It is unclear whether 'national regulations' includes jurisprudence. If not, many obligations subjecting the right to resort to collective action, which have emerged through judicial elaboration in some Member States of the law on industrial conflict, may not be acceptable under the Charter.

Rights of the armed forces, the police and the civil service

There are difficulties in defining the scope of the armed forces and the police. But there will be even greater inconsistencies among Member States regarding the extent of persons falling within 'the civil service'. The conditions and extent of application of the rights are left to 'the internal legal order of the Member States', but the definition of the categories covered is not and remains to be determined.

This Article does not *exclude* the rights prescribed by Articles 11–13. It indicates 'under which conditions and to what extent' they apply. It is, in theory, possible under this Article for the 'internal legal order of the Member States' to provide *no* extent for some or all of the rights. But such a general proscription of the content of the Charter's section on Freedom of Association arguably contradicts the implicit logic of the transnational standard, which envisages the existence of these rights to some extent.

Even proscription of only some of the rights in Articles 11–13 would present difficulties. It is arguable that some rights *imply* others. Association is only meaningful if collective negotiation is allowed. Negotiation implies that it is possible to conclude collective agreements and to resort to collective action – without which negotiation is futile.

Alternatively, proscribing, or imposing conditions on one of the rights may imply fewer or different conditions for others. For example, if the right to resort to collective action is banned or limited, a right to negotiate and conclude agreements may be effectively nullified. To compensate for this there may have to be

---

11   Article 14.
12   Both these seem narrower than the formulation in Article 14, which refers to the 'internal legal order of the Member States'.

provided conditions which legitimise other effective means of exercising bargaining power. Or if the right to negotiate and conclude agreements is banned or limited, the right of association should carry with it conditions which allow for other activities to promote participation in determining conditions of work.

VOCATIONAL TRAINING (ARTICLE 15)

Training and retraining: individual right and/or State obligation

The final Draft contains one Article (15), whereas the first two Drafts each had two articles identical in all respects.[13] The first Article of the first two drafts provided that 'Every European Community worker *shall have the opportunity* to *continue* his vocational training *during* his working life'. The final Draft amended this to '*must be able* to have access to vocational training *and* to receive such training throughout his working life'. Neither of these formulations ('shall have the opportunity' nor 'must be able') makes it clear whether, if this is an individual *right*, it imposes a *positive obligation* to provide opportunities or access to training.

All three drafts go on to require or encourage[14] the setting up of 'continuing and permanent training systems'. But these systems are said to be the responsibility of: 'The public authorities, enterprise or, where appropriate, the two sides of industry, each within their own sphere of competence';[15] or: 'The competent public authorities, undertakings or the two sides of industry, each within their own sphere of competence'.[16] The obligation on public authorities goes beyond setting up the requisite systems. There is also the task of coordinating private and public action.

One requirement links public and private action with individual rights: all three drafts specify that systems provide for training 'especially through *leave for training purposes*'.

EQUAL TREATMENT FOR MEN AND WOMEN (ARTICLE 16)

Reconciling occupational and family obligations

The second Draft of Article 16 introduced a new paragraph which encouraged equal treatment enabling men and women to '*reconcile their occupational and family obligations*'. This was retained, with some changes, in the final Draft.

The second Draft was less direct: it stated that equality action 'shall imply the development of *amenities* enabling' such reconciliation '*more easily*'. Amenities or facilities allow for easier reconciliation. In the final Draft this becomes '*Measures* should also be developed', and the reference to 'more easily' is deleted. The use of 'measures' implies more far-reaching action. The deletion of 'more easily' implies a stricter standard of reconciliation. Reconciliation is not just to be made

13 First Draft, Articles 19–20; second Draft, Articles 17–18.
14 '. . . shall set up' – first two Drafts; 'should set up' – final Draft.
15 First two Drafts.
16 Final Draft.

more easy. Reconciliation of these obligations *tout court* is the goal.

The singling out by the final Draft of 'working conditions' for particularly intensive equality action is one indication of the Charter's objectives in this sphere. The Commission's Action Programme emphasised that 'The work place must therefore be adapted to ... allow women to carry out both their work and maternal responsibilities ... in particular, improving the protection of pregnancy and maternity'. It proposed a Recommendation prescribing minimum rules 'which would however have to be implemented [by Member States] within a certain time limit'.[17]

The Article assumes that the 'equal treatment' guaranteed in the first paragraph of Article 16 is consistent with reconciliation of occupational and family obligations. Yet it is likely that the achievement of this reconciliation will necessitate, at least in some cases, *positive action measures* favouring women more than men. In the introduction to its Action Programme, the Commission emphasised that 'it sees its own task as ensuring that formal equality can become genuine equality', and that it would 'give consideration to the legislative and positive measures needed ... In particular ... what legal and positive action is necessary to ensure that the rights enshrined in Community law on the principle of equality are fully available in practice at national level'.[18]

One question is whether this paragraph may be taken as a Community-level legitimation of such positive action measures in national legal systems where they may confront constitutional or other legal obstacles. Another question is whether it requires measures to be developed enabling *men* to undertake (non-traditional) family obligations. In this context, the Commission's Action Programme recalled the failure of the Council to approve the proposal for a Directive on parental leave and referred to its recommendations for action on child care in its Second Action Programme on Equal Opportunities (1986–90). For the future, however, it could only conclude:[19]

> 'Child care methods, parental leave and maternity leave form part of a whole which enables people to combine their family responsibilities and occupational ambitions. A Community response alone will not suffice if this objective is to be attained.'

INFORMATION, CONSULTATION AND PARTICIPATION FOR WORKERS (ARTICLES 17–18)

Practices v norms

The relevant Articles in the first[20] and second[1] Drafts began by referring to forms of activity or practices – 'information, consultation and participation' – which 'must be developed' *taking account of present norms* – 'the laws, collective (or contractual) agreements and practices in force in the member states'. The objective of the Article was a practice to be achieved.

The final Draft removes all reference to laws and collective agreements. The

---

17   Action Programme, p 38. The (then) unforeseen outcome is the first European Framework Collective Agreement on Parental Leave of 7 November 1995.
18   Ibid, p 35.
19   Ibid, p 37.
20   Article 22.
1   Article 20.

only thing to be taken account of is '*practices* in force in the *various* Member States'. This deletion of the requirement to take account of formal norms appears to emphasise Article 17's requirement of *functional* development. The objective is to achieve information, consultation and participation, whatever the norms in force.

One question is whether the final Draft's reference to 'practices in force in the *various* Member States' implies less respect for each State's autonomy. The preceding formulation referred to 'practices in force in the member states' – a requirement on each Member State to take account of *its* norms. The final Draft requires attention to be paid to practices in *more* than one Member State. It may thus posit a *standard* of information, consultation and participation to be derived *not* from the practice of *each* Member State, but from the composite practices of *several* of them.

The requirement ('must') in Article 18 of implementation of information, consultation and participation is a general one. The Article applies 'particularly in the following cases', but these are only examples. It may be that the development of information, consultation and participation is not identical in all cases. For example, in the second paragraph of Article 19 of the final Draft there was inserted a provision referring to the need, in the case of health and safety at the workplace, to take account of 'information, consultation and *balanced* participation of workers'.[2]

HEALTH PROTECTION AND SAFETY AT THE WORKPLACE (ARTICLE 19)

Balanced participation of workers

Article 19 introduces a requirement in a second paragraph regarding the content of the measures implementing the Charter's provision on health and safety. These, inter alia, 'shall take account, in particular, of the need for the training, information, consultation and balanced participation of workers'.

The concept of '*balanced* participation' in the sphere of health and safety contrasts with the Charter's general requirement to develop 'participation'.[3] The second paragraph of Article 19 continues the reference to balanced participation with the phrase 'as regards the risks incurred and the steps taken to eliminate or reduce them'.

This phrase might be taken to imply that the balance must weigh the risks incurred against the steps to be taken. This balancing act is often found in the jurisprudence of Member States assessing the liability of employers for their actions or omissions concerning risks resulting in injury. The implication of this new paragraph could be that such a balancing act is now relevant to the acts or omissions of Member States in adopting measures promoting 'participation' of workers with respect to safeguarding them from risks. Failure of a Member State to adopt measures promoting the requisite participation in steps taken to eliminate or reduce risks will be a violation of the Charter.

Alternatively, the reference to balance may apply to weighing training, information and consultation, on one hand, against participation on the other. The

2 Discussed in Chapter 24 on health and safety representatives.
3 Articles 17–18.

former are to be taken into account as regards risks; the latter as regards steps taken. In the case of employers taking steps to eliminate or reduce risks, worker participation is required, not merely training, information and consultation. These latter are suitable more for the identification of risks.

Positive and negative provisions regarding implementation of the internal market

Apart from the 'measures' referred to in the preceding paragraphs, the third paragraph of Article 19 requires that 'The provisions regarding implementation of the internal market shall *help to ensure* such protection'. Earlier drafts only provided that such protection '*not be jeopardised*' by these provisions.

The first Draft went on to instance the need for this negative injunction 'especially where public contracts are concerned'.[4] The second Draft moved from the purely negative injunction by using the case of public works to illustrate a positive provision: 'especially as regards the *awarding* of public works *contracts*'.

The final draft extended this approach into a general positive injunction, though the specific reference to public works contracts is dropped. *All* provisions appear to be covered – ie *all* instruments of policy implementing the internal market are engaged.

The public contracts example, however, may be a pointer to the type of provisions affected by this paragraph of Article 19. Protection is to be ensured not be retroactive correction of negative effects of various provisions on health and safety, but by *positive* provision. Taking the cue from public works contracts, this could be done by express provisions imposing obligations regarding health and safety of workers on activities regulated by single market provisions.

PROTECTION OF CHILDREN AND ADOLESCENTS (ARTICLES 20–23)

Some of the promised protection has been implemented through Council Directive 94/33/EC of 22 June 1994 on the protection of young people at work.[5] Adopted under Article 118A of the EC Treaty, the Directive sets limits on the work of children: minimum age of employment, maximum daily and weekly hours of work, minimum rest periods and prohibition of certain activities, as well as risk evaluation and health assessments.

Nature and duration of vocational training entitlement

The first Draft[6] provided for '*at least two years . . . complementary* vocational training in order to adapt to the requirements of their working life'. The second Draft[7] changed this to '*two years* of *initial* vocational training . . .' In Article 23 of the final Draft, this became '*initial* vocational training *of a sufficient duration* to

---

4   Article 24.
5   OJ L216/12 of 20.8.1994.
6   Article 26.
7   Article 25.

enable them to adapt to the requirements of their future working life'.

As regards the nature of the training, the first emphasis on 'complementary' training implied that young people *already in work* were the targets. The change in later Drafts to '*initial*' expands the entitlement to young people who have not yet obtained employment.

As to duration, the initial promise of *at least* two years became strictly two years, and then 'of a sufficient duration'. The two-year minimum has disappeared. It is not clear, though certainly arguable, that a higher standard replaces it.

Eligibility for entitlement to vocational training

In the first Draft,[8] the entitlement was available to '*Young people of more than 16 years of age who are in gainful employment*'. This was changed in the second Draft[9] so as to make it available *only* to young people '*for a period of at least two years, following the end of compulsory education*'. It was ambiguous as to whether this meant the entitlement was available only during the two years after the end of compulsory education. Two years could have referred to the duration of the training. But since a two-year duration was specified in the phrase immediately following, such repetition seemed otiose. On the other hand, there was an inexplicable comma between the phrases.

The time limits in the final Draft are more open-ended. The two-year period is eliminated both from the eligibility requirement and from the duration requirement. In the case of duration: it must be sufficient. In the case of eligibility: it must follow the end of compulsory education – without specifying how long after it may follow.

ELDERLY PERSONS (ARTICLES 24–25)

An unfortunate lapse: exclusion of non-workers enjoying inadequate pensions from guarantee of adequate standard

The first and second Drafts, having provided income or resources in the previous Article for '*citizens*' or '*persons*' in retirement or early retirement, in the following Article[10] provided for 'citizens' or 'persons' in retirement 'but who [are] not entitled to a pension'. The final Draft first provides[11] for every *worker* at the time of retirement, and in Article 25 provides for 'Every *person* who has reached retirement age but who is not entitled to a pension'.

The assumption appears to be that *workers* enjoying pensions should be entitled to a level of resources affording a decent standard of living. Those persons *not* enjoying pensions fall under Article 25. However, *non-workers enjoying* pensions are covered by neither provision, being neither workers, nor without pensions. Thus, they are left without a guarantee as to a decent standard of living[12] or sufficient resources.[13]

8   Article 26.
9   Article 25.
10 First Draft, Articles 29–30; second Draft, Article 28.
11 Article 24.
12 Article 24.
13 Article 25.

In the first two Drafts this category *was* covered by the subsequent provision which added to the protected category of those 'not entitled to a pension', also those without 'other adequate means of subsistence'. This could cover non-workers enjoying pensions which were, however, inadequate. The final Draft, however, extends this second category of protected persons only to a person 'who does not have other means of subsistence'. The deletion of the word 'adequate' seems to exclude those non-workers enjoying any pensions, however inadequate.

DISABLED PERSONS (ARTICLE 26)

Positive action measures

The first Draft stipulated 'Measures shall be taken to ensure the fullest possible integration of the disabled into working life'. The second and final Drafts are formulated in a way which may be given effect in a significantly different way: 'All disabled persons ... [shall/must] be entitled to *additional* concrete measures aimed at improving their social and professional integration'. The insertion of the word 'additional' is a clear signal that it is *positive action measures*, over and above those available generally for integration into working life, which are envisaged.

IMPLEMENTATION OF THE CHARTER (ARTICLES 27–30)

Instruments of Member State action

The first two Drafts[14] provided that the *instruments* of Member State action were to be: 'either through *legislative measures* or by encouraging both sides of industry to conclude *collective agreements at national, regional, sectoral or company level*'.

In contrast, the final Draft[15] provides: 'in accordance with national practices, notably through *legislative measures* or *collective agreements*'. The lack of specification of which types of agreements should not preclude different levels of agreements. The deletion of the injunction 'encouraging' the conclusion of agreements is perhaps compensated by the emphatic 'notably', which places collective agreements on the same level as legislative measures.

---

14   First Draft, Article 32; second Draft, Article 30.
15   Article 27.

Chapter 38

The Future of the Community Charter

INTRODUCTION

The Community Charter of Fundamental Social Rights of Workers of 1989 represents a commitment by the Member States of the European Union to a set of social policy and labour law objectives. But it is not a *final* document embodying the ultimate aspirations of social and economic rights or the definitively highest ideals regarding social and economic rights. It has to be put in its historical context. The 1989 Charter was a phase in the evolution of the European Community in the context of the completion of the 1992 Single European Market programme.

The *changing* nature of economic and social rights was noted in the debates over whether the European Convention on Human Rights should be extended to include such rights, in light of the Council of Europe's European Social Charter. The need to take account of this changing nature was emphasised in the formulation of such rights:[1]

> 'there are no "ideal" standards, as standards may be, and are, adjusted by law to take account of a variety of factors such as social changes, higher productivity, health and hygiene requirements resulting from advancing industrialisation, etc. It is therefore impossible, in a text designed to be permanently valid, to lay down precise rules applicable to all European countries for a long period, if not for ever.'

A Report prepared for the European Parliament and the Commission during 1989, prior to the approval of the Community Charter, stated:[2]

> 'The challenge for the EC is to formulate and define social and economic rights in such a way and in such an instrument as will allow for their flexible and dynamic character.'

THE NATURE AND FUNCTION OF THE CHARTER

In practice, the 1989 Charter served as the political legitimation for the Commission in formulating its legislative programme. It is cited in the Preambles to measures proposed by the Commission and approved by the Council since

---

1 A Berenstein 'Economic and Social Rights: Their Inclusion in the European Convention on Human Rights, Problems of Formulation and Interpretation', 2 *Human Rights Law Journal* (1981) (n 3–4) 257, at 272–3.
2 B Bercusson *Fundamental Social and Economic Rights in the European Community*, July and October 1989; published in A Cassese et al (eds) *Human Rights in the European Community: Methods of Protection*, Nomos Verlag, Baden-Baden 1991, pp 195–294, at 201.

then, as well as in the Preamble to the Maastricht Protocol and Agreement on Social Policy.[3] This demonstrates the Charter's function as the inspiration for an as yet unrealised social programme.

An alternative view of the function of the Charter could be as the fall-back safeguard against which alleged infringements of fundamental social rights may be tested and disallowed. The contrast is between a *passive* safeguard document, which allows for review of EU and national measures by mechanisms to be created; and a *dynamic* document serving to inspire action at EU and national level.

A *passive* safeguard document would require control procedures, with, for example, reporting and expert review of EU and national measures, as well as complaints and adjudication procedures, and appropriate remedies and sanctions. It is not necessarily the case that the European Court of Justice is the best qualified for a role in such procedures. One risk is that, as it is to test not only EU legislation but also Member State legislation, conflicts may arise with national constitutional courts, as has already happened with national constitutionally protected human rights.

The alternative, a *dynamic* document serving to inspire action at EU and national level, was the role of the 1989 Charter. The function of the Charter is to assist in the social evolution of the EU. This may not be the traditional role for a 'constitution', but economic and social rights in the new and revised national constitutions of Member States during the 1970s and 1980s have an essentially programmatic nature.[4] The challenge of European integration calls for new developments in the role of Charters of Fundamental Rights.

Implicit in such a role for the Charter would be the need for periodic review, a reflection of the changing nature of social and economic ideals and conjunctures. This might be done at regular intervals, or by various mechanisms; for example, procedures for convocation or revision if called for by specified majorities in the EU institutions, a special constituent assembly with tripartite representation, and so on.

What is called for is something *between*, at one extreme, a once and for all time Charter – immutable – and a conjunctural legislative programme specific to the immediate short- and medium-term objectives of a government. The Charter should take a long-term view. But it should also acknowledge the mutability of social and economic conditions by allowing for periodic revision.

A new role for the Charter will require new mechanisms of formulation, implementation and enforcement, involving the EU institutions and the social dialogue. Specifically, it has implications for deciding *which* EU institutions are to have a primary role. For example, is the Charter to be Commission (executive) oriented – a programmatic statement for future action – or European Court (judicial) oriented – a summation of values against which action, future and past, may be tested? Much depends on the vision and expectations one has of these bodies and their capabilities. Is the Court too politically delicate? Is the Commission dynamic enough to exploit effectively such a Charter?

---

3 The Protocol begins by 'Noting that 11 Member States . . . wish to continue along the path laid down in the 1989 Social Charter . . .' The Agreement begins: 'The undersigned 11 High Contracting Parties . . . Wishing to implement the 1989 Social Charter on the basis of the *acquis communautaire* . . .' The Declaration by the Governments of the EFTA States on the Charter provides that they 'endorse the principles and basic rights laid down in the Charter'.
4 B Bercusson *Fundamental Social and Economic Rights in the European Community* (1989), op cit.

If the Charter was oriented towards the European Court, as a test for EU and Member State level action, are there fundamental social rights specific to the EU system, which do not simply repeat national constitutional protections? Can such rights be formulated to add to national safeguards something worth protecting; for example, a transnational dimension of protection required to overcome the threat to such rights of developments in the international economy; or to defend Member State social action programmes promoting such rights against the spread of detrimental competitive practices; or to promote action against common national developments threatening such rights?

In a Commission-oriented document, similar questions arise as to what could be the programmatic content. It would have to take the measured long-term view so as to inspire concrete measures without being too transitory in nature. It would have a renewable quality to reflect changing programmatic requirements.

There are two corresponding types of formulation possible in such international instruments. They may give rise to a judicial investigation at the instigation of persons who could be described as victims of the violation of the right. Or they may be framed in terms of the obligations and undertakings of States rather than in terms of the rights of individuals, and make provision for progressive implementation rather than for immediate guarantees.[5]

THE SPECIFICITY OF THE EU: ECONOMIC AND SOCIAL CITIZENSHIP

The 1989 Charter was transformed late in the day from a Charter of the Rights of *Citizens* to a Charter for *Workers*. This both broadens and narrows its scope: 'workers' includes non-citizens; 'citizens' includes non-workers.[6] Whatever the conjunctural reasons for the change at that time, one should consider carefully before giving way to the easy temptation to simply recast the Charter's personal scope in terms of citizens. The concept of EU citizenship is the subject of much debate.

While the original Charter conceptualisation of rights in terms of citizenship was seemingly distorted towards workers' rights, this may have been an inspired intuition. Given the overriding antecedent connotations of *civil* and *political* citizenship in Member States, EU citizens should benefit from EU rights of a qualitatively different kind. These should focus on *economic* and *social* citizenship, an area of complex overlap between citizens' rights and workers' rights.

The separation of citizen and worker is founded on the narrow concept of worker – the Standard Employment Relationship (SER): full-time, permanent, male employment. This concept conflicts with the growth of new forms of employment which diverge from this model. The implications of this fragmentation of the workforce have been at the centre of debates within the fields of labour economics, labour law and industrial relations for the last two decades. They constitute what has been described in this book as one of the pillars of the emerging European labour law.

---

5   Berenstein, op cit; also F Jacobs 'The Extension of the European Convention on Human Rights to include Economic, Social and Cultural Rights', (1978) 3 *Human Rights Law Review* 166.
6   B Bercusson 'The European Community's Charter of Fundamental Social Rights for Workers', (1990) 53 *Modern Law Review* 624.

The implications of fragmentation of the workforce are reflected in the recent Commission Green and White Papers on the future of European Social Policy. They seek to break away from the narrow SER concept of the worker and to develop policies appropriate for multiple forms of work. The White Paper on 'European Social Policy: A Way Forward for the Union' refers to the Delors 'White Paper on Growth, Competitiveness and Employment':[7]

> 'The (Delors) White Paper stresses the need to widen considerably access to work, to widen the concept of work, and to build a new solidarity ... particularly in view of the increasing participation rates of women, changing family structures and roles, and the need to maximise the potential of all the Union's human resources...'

The White Paper on the future European social policy emphasises:[8]

> '... a new approach to the organisation of working life, with a higher degree of alteration between work, training and leave ... (and) the internal flexibility of firms being promoted through new training efforts enabling employees to reorganise their work and their working time on a more flexible basis.'

It refers to the proposals outstanding before the Council on non-standard employment, as regards working conditions and distortion of competition and insists that 'In the next phase of social policy, the Commission believes that the highest possible priority must be given to bringing these proposals to a successful conclusion'.[9] Referring specifically to new forms of employment, the White Paper stipulates that:[10]

> 'there is general concern to make a breakthrough at Union level in this area ...
> _   ... the possibility of a first step through a new directive on part time work ...
> _   ... a framework directive covering the issues of reconciling professional and family life ... Such a proposal would seek gradually to encourage the development of new models better suited to the changing needs of European society, and be specifically designed to facilitate the full integration of women into the labour market ...'

In general the White Paper emphasises that:[11]

> '6.   ... It will be necessary to reassess the value given to jobs traditionally performed by women, jobs like childcare, care of elderly people, work in family enterprises and care in the home local services. In addition, new forms of work organisation will tend to create more flexible jobs not only for women but also for men. Policies are necessary which will lead to both sexes taking advantage of the potential benefits of flexibility ...
> ...
> 10.   ... there is now an urgent need, in the interests of society as a whole, for working life and family life to be more mutually reinforcing ... major issues such as the relationship between working time and care time. Changing demographic trends mean that the responsibility for elderly dependants is moving up the social agenda, although childcare is still the major problem for working parents in many Member States. New social infrastructures are needed to support the household and the family, and the question of how families can be helped to carry the costs remains to be addressed.'

7   Section I, paragraph 9.
8   Section II, paragraphs 8–9.
9   Section III, paragraph 4.
10   Paragraph 8.
11   Section V, paragraphs 6, 10.

Finally, the White Paper concludes:[12]

'1.   ... the traditional social protection systems of Europe – based on the concept of the welfare state – are an important achievement that needs to be maintained. But ... (t)his means giving a top priority to employment, securing new links between employment and social policies by developing a "trampoline" safety net, and recognising that those who are not in the labour market also have a useful role to play in society. While the European social model provides a good foundation, it needs to be developed to provide a new synergy between the welfare and wealth-creating functions of society.

2.   This is all the more important because the EU will experience significant changes in its demographic structure within the next 20 years ...'

The future of European social policy and labour law requires a vision of social roles involving not only paid work, but also other activities constituting the social identity of citizens. As put in the Commission's Consultation Document, 'Reconciliation of Professional and Family Life': 'a policy rooted in equal opportunities has developed into one focused on quality. Quality of family life, quality of working life and quality of human resources'.[13]

The essence of EU social and economic rights is the support and reinforcement of the changing social identity of workers as citizens and citizens as workers. This was the inspiration of the Commission's initial Green Paper:[14]

'The industrial revolution and the technology of the production line not only separated the work and welfare functions but also rigidified the separation of work from other activities. Yet work has other functions in addition to providing income: purposeful activity and personal fulfilment, dignity, social contacts, recognition and a basis for organising daily or weekly time ... changes could mean that the division between "working time" and "other time" will again fade, so that work is reintegrated into a wider pattern of activities. They present the challenge of realigning work and welfare in ways that help as many as possible to participate actively in their societies, while taking advantage of the greater flexibility that new modes of production allow.'

This requires a reconsideration of both the personal and material (and perhaps also the territorial) scope of fundamental social rights and their implementation through social policy and labour law in Europe.

Personal scope

The Charter should define 'worker' in terms of the *worker-citizen*. There are different approaches, including:

(a)   entitlements to all those with an employment 'relationship', as well as those with an employment 'contract';

(b)   entitlements specific to certain categories of workers; codes of rights for temporary, part-time, casual, disabled workers and so on;

(c)   different rights to different groups of workers depending on policy;[15] this

12   Section VI, paragraphs 1–2.
13   Op cit, paragraph 10.
14   Section II.C.3.
15   An example in the present Charter is Article 5, 2nd indent: workers with other than an openended full-time contract.

could mean a varying personal scope so that, for example:
- health and safety and discrimination rights apply to all workers;
- security of employment applies to varying groups to different extents (eg less so to temporary workers);
- equitable wages or maximum hours varying according to different categories.

The essential principle is that the personal scope of the Charter is defined in terms of the *work* roles of *citizens*, with the concept of *work* greatly extended to include a variety of social roles – caring (for children, families, aged, disabled), community and social service activities.

The change would be from the *passive* vision of *protective* standards for old people, children, and women to a Charter embodying *positive* recognition, through the conferral of rights, of the social citizenship roles of carers, volunteer social and community workers, children and old people.

Material scope

Certain Articles of the Charter have been implemented through legal measures which develop them in much more detail. For example, Article 8 through the Working Time Directive;[16] Article 9 through the Directive requiring information on conditions of employment;[17] Article 16 through the amended Article 119 of the EC Treaty in the Maastricht Agreement; Article 17 in part by the European Works Councils Directive;[18] Article 19 through the 'Framework' health and safety Directive;[19] Article 22 through the Young Workers Directive;[20] and Article 27 through Article 2(4) of the Maastricht Agreement on Social Policy.

However, almost all the Articles in the 1989 Charter are framed in the perspective of the Standard Employment Relationship. If the personal scope of the Charter is to be transformed to encompass 'worker-citizens', the material scope of the Charter should reflect the exigencies of, first, the *social identities of workers*, and, secondly, the *work identities of citizens*.

To achieve recognition of the *social identities of workers'* working life, the Charter must include entitlements which protect and encourage their *social* roles. Examples include caring, public, community and social service. An example which shows the way is in the Working Time Directive, Article 13: the principle of adapting work to the worker.

To promote the *work identities of citizens*, those citizens whose attachment to working life is relatively marginal should be not only protected (by rights) but encouraged to develop this (by incentives).

16 Council Directive 93/104/EC of 23 November 1993 concerning certain aspects of the organisation of working time, OJ L307/18 of 13.12.1993.
17 Council Directive 91/533 of 14 October 1991 on an employer's obligation to inform employees of the conditions applicable to the contract or employment relationship, OJ 1991 L288/32.
18 Directive 94/45/EC of 22 September 1994 on the establishment of a European Works Council or a procedure in Community-scale undertakings and Community-scale groups of undertakings for the purposes of informing and consulting employees, OJ L254/64 of 30.9.94.
19 Council Directive 89/391/EEC of 12 June 1989 on the introduction of measures to encourage improvements in the safety and health of workers at work, OJ L183/1.
20 Council Directive 94/33/EC of 22 June 1994 on the protection of young people at work, OJ L216/12 of 20.8.1994.

The Commission's Consultation Document, 'Reconciliation of Professional and Family Life' shows the way. Its inspiration was the long-standing equal opportunities policy for men and women.[1] But, as has been described in detail in an earlier chapter, the Document makes a quick shift to the theme of reconciliation. In Section II, The General Socio-Economic Context embeds equal opportunities policy in many contexts.

First, equal opportunities means reconciliation for *all* workers.[2] Secondly, it means new employment opportunities for men and women. Thirdly, it has implications for improving the functioning of the European labour market by encouraging women's labour market participation.[3] There is specific reference to the organisation of working time. Fourthly, the policy aims at the family, to support family relationships (specifically, through public recognition of the value of personal relationships) and family responsibilities, with specific reference to men's role in the raising of children and care of family members. Finally, there is the training and education dimension: reconciliation as allowing for the improvement of human capital. Training and education may be accommodated with family responsibilities, or could be used as an incentive to undertake family responsibilities.

Enlarging the material scope of the Charter means recognising that *multiple social roles* may entail *entitlements* going beyond what is conceived of for *workers* in standard employment relationships as regards education and training, health, housing and income security. This is now within the competences of the EU in accordance with the Maastricht Protocol and Agreement on Social Policy. The White Paper on the future of Social Policy twice emphasises in Section VI (Social Policy and Social Protection):[4]

'13. Article 2(2) of the Agreement on Social Policy gives the Union a role in supporting and complementing the activities of the Member States . . .

. . .

17. The Union must demonstrate that it is not silent or inactive on this issue, and that it is able to act not only in the interests of the employed but also of the unemployed and socially excluded. Moreover, Article 2(2) of the Agreement on Social Policy gives the Union a specific role in supporting and complementing the activities of the Member States as regards the integration of persons excluded from the labour market. The Commission therefore believes that there is a good case for examining the possibility of:
   – further Union action on the integration of those excluded from the labour market, covering both the economic and social dimensions of this integration, providing a legal framework for supporting and stimulating the efforts in the Member States.'

Territorial scope

Citizens of the EU and enterprises based in the EU may be found outside the territory of the EU. It is an open question whether the Charter should be applied to either. As regards enterprises, this is an issue linked to social dumping. Should

1 Paragraph 2.
2 Paragraph 6.
3 Paragraph 7.
4 Paragraphs 13 and 17.

they be bound to observe the standards prescribed by the Charter: in particular, where these firms export jobs through the undercutting of the Charter's labour standards? As regards workers-citizens: should they be entitled to the protection of the Charter, whether they work for EU firms or not? There are, of course, problems of extra-territorial enforcement.

IMPLEMENTATION

The subsidiarity principle defined in Article 3B of the Treaty on European Union is concerned with the competences shared by the EU and the Member States. Recognition of social dialogue in both the 1989 Charter[5] and the Maastricht Agreement means not only vertical but also horizontal subsidiarity: there is a role for both Member State/EU mechanisms and social partner mechanisms – at EU and national levels.

There may also be a role for other enforcement agencies, such as inspectorates. There can be a varying equilibrium between different mechanisms: inspectorates, courts, social partners. Other enforcement mechanisms, such as contract compliance in the realm of public procurement, may be available.[6]

CONCLUSION

Labour and workers' rights were given special relevance in the 1989 Charter. The Charter should continue this focus. But the concept of labour and the worker needs to expand to include multiple life-activities, including those of caring, social and community activities, which reach out to concepts of citizenship.

The rights of the citizens of Europe should be constructed on the basis of this new concept of work and worker. Fundamental rights should be constructed around the concept of work as expanded. Hence the emphasis on *social* and economic rights.

The evolution of European society in the present conjuncture justifies this focus on workers' rights and social dialogue. This is elaborated in the White Paper on the Future of European Social Policy with its emphasis on the fragmentation of the workforce into new forms of work and the need for a new concept of work. In the absence of new social formations capable of safeguarding these new developments in the world of work, much depends on the ability of the traditional collectivities, trade unions, to change and adapt.

Formulation, implementation and enforcement of individual worker-citizen rights requires collective organisation. This means also collective rights. A start has been made with the Maastricht Protocol/Agreement. The task of recasting the present Charter's formulations to reflect these requirements will be a heavy one. It needs to be undertaken.

5   Article 27.
6   As explored in Chapter 8.

Chapter 39

A Strategy for the 1996 Intergovernmental Conference

The 1989 Charter emphasised labour and workers' rights. Labour and workers' rights were also reflected in the role given to the social dialogue in the Maastricht Protocol and Agreement. The Charter and the Protocol and Agreement have an obvious synergy.

A strategy towards the 1996 Intergovernmental Conference would be to integrate the Charter and the Maastricht Protocol and Agreement into one constitutional document for incorporation into the Treaty.

The logic of this strategy is that the two documents complement each other. The Charter is a set of substantive provisions which, by virtue of their nature as fundamental social rights, possess a high degree of political legitimacy; but the Charter lacks legal status and an implementing mechanism. The Maastricht Protocol and Agreement are a dynamic mechanism for formulating, implementing and enforcing social rights, but only potentially: they provide a set of competences, but no driving substantive content which will set it in motion.

A new role for the Charter requires new mechanisms, currently absent, of formulation, implementation and enforcement of fundamental social rights. The obvious step is to link the Charter with the Maastricht Protocol and Agreement on Social Policy.

The Protocol and Agreement, at the moment, only provide for passive competences. The Charter will provide the social policy objectives to be achieved through the mechanisms of the Protocol and Agreement. These fundamental social objectives will confer a further legitimacy on the mechanisms of the Protocol and Agreement.

In exchange, the legal status of the Protocol and Agreement, as part of the Treaty on European Union, will provide the engine for the implementation of the Charter. This could be furthered in various ways; for example:

(a) qualified majority voting would suffice for measures implementing fundamental social rights;

(b) periodic revision would mean a time limit on implementation of fundamental social rights;

(c) failure to implement the fundamental social rights specified could allow for them to become directly effective; or for the European Parliament to complain to the European Court about the failure to act.

Combining the Charter and the Protocol and Agreement would provide the Charter with a mechanism for implementation, and incorporate into the Protocol and Agreement a set of fundamental social rights granting them greater legitimacy.

607

The objective is a social constitution for the EU which mandates the implementation of specified fundamental social objectives, and provides an instrument, a timetable and a set of fall-back mechanisms to stimulate their achievement.

The task of recasting the present Charter's formulations to reflect these requirements will be a heavy one. However, the current cautious stance of the Commission, the trend towards conservatism in social policy on the part of some Member States, and the fragility of the Charter and Protocol and Agreement, if taken separately into the Intergovernmental Conference of 1996, makes such a strategy worth considering.

The 1996 Intergovernmental Conference presents an opportunity for the strategic integration of the Charter and the Protocol and Agreement into a social constitution for the European Union.

Index